The Invention of Paris

The Invention of Paris

A History in Footsteps

◆

Eric Hazan

Translated by David Fernbach

VERSO
London • New York

Ouvrage publié avec le concours du Ministère français chargé de la culture—
Centre national du livre

This work was published with the help of the French Ministry of Culture—
Centre national du livre

This paperback edition first published by Verso 2011
First published in English by Verso 2010
© Verso 2010
Translation © David Fernbach 2010
First published as *L'Invention de Paris. Il n'y a pas de pas perdus*
© Éditions du Seuil 2002

1 3 5 7 9 10 8 6 4 2

Verso
UK: 6 Meard Street, London W1F 0EG
US: 20 Jay Street, Suite 1010, Brooklyn, NY 11201
www.versobooks.com

Verso is the imprint of New Left Books

ISBN-13: 978-1-84467-705-4

British Library Cataloguing in Publication Data
A catalogue record for this book is available from the British Library

Library of Congress Cataloging-in-Publication Data
A catalog record for this book is available from the Library of Congress

Typeset by Hewer Text UK Ltd, Edinburgh
Printed in Sweden by ScandBook AB

'Lost steps? But there aren't any.'
– André Breton, *Nadja*

Contents

A Few More Wrinkles: Preface to the English-Language Edition   ix

Acknowledgements   xv

Part One: Walkways

1. Psychogeography of the Boundary   3

2. Old Paris: The Quarters   17
   THE RIGHT BANK QUARTERS: Palais-Royal, 19 –
   Carrousel, 26 – Tuileries-Saint-Honoré, 31 – Bourse, 33 – The
   Arcades, 38 – Les Halles, 40 – Sentier, 48 – Marais, 55 – The
   Grands Boulevards, 71
   THE LEFT BANK QUARTERS: The Left Bank Boulevards,
   87 – The Latin Quarter, 91 – Odéon, 98 – Saint-Sulpice, 99 –
   Saint-Germain-des-Prés, 100 – Faubourg Saint-Germain, 102
   –Haussmann's Cuttings, 105

3. New Paris: The Faubourgs   109
   THE RIGHT BANK FAUBOURGS: Champs-Élysées, 116
   – Faubourg Saint-Honoré, 120 – Faubourg Saint-Antoine, 121
   – Popincourt and Faubourg du Temple, 125 – Faubourg Saint-
   Martin and Faubourg Saint-Denis, 133 – Faubourg Poissonnière
   and Faubourg Montmartre, 139 – Saint-Georges and Nouvelles-
   Athènes, 144 –Quartier de l'Europe, 146 – Plaine Monceau 149
   THE LEFT BANK FAUBOURGS: Faubourg Saint-Marcel,
   151 –Faubourg Saint-Jacques, 160 – Montparnasse, 163

4. New Paris: The Villages   174
    THE LEFT BANK VILLAGES: Vaugirard and Grenelle,
    182 –Plaisance, 185 – Denfert-Rochereau and the 14th
    Arrondissement, 187 – The 13th Arrondissement, Butte-aux-
    Cailles, the Italie Quarter, 188
    THE RIGHT BANK VILLAGES: Passy and Auteuil, 190 –
    Batignolles and Clichy, 194 – Montmartre, 196 – Clignancourt,
    199 – Goutte d'Or, 200 – La Chapelle and La Villette, 202
    – Buttes-Chaumont, 205 – Belleville and Ménilmontant, 210 –
    Père-Lachaise and Charonne, 217 – Bercy, 220 – The Zone, 222

Part Two: Red Paris

5. Red Paris   227
    The Birth of the Barricade, 242 – Victor Hugo's Redemption, 299

Part Three: 'Crossing the swarming scene ...'

6. Flâneurs   315

7. The Visual Image   340

Preface to the English-Language Edition: A Few More Wrinkles

To spot what has changed in Paris since the time this book was written, one should really have returned after a long absence. Instead of this, I have left the city for only short periods in the last ten years, and so I see it changing like the wrinkles on a beloved face that one observes every day. The city within the walls, the subject of *The Invention of Paris*, is now changing only slowly. Time is needed for a district of Kabyl cafés to be transformed into fashionable bars, for the Chinese rag trade to advance a street or two, or for what is called renovation to press the poor a notch more towards the Périphérique.

The physical transformations of Paris can be read as a ceaseless struggle between the spirit of place and the spirit of time. Take for example the nameless spot formed by the widening of Rue Mouffetard below the church of Saint-Médard. The ancient food shops, the market stalls, the immense trees that cast their shade onto the porch of the church, the remains of the little cemetery where the 'convulsionaries' danced on the tomb of Deacon Pâris in the reign of Louis XV (see p. 158), the two large cafés facing each other across the road – this whole panoply of eras, styles and events gives this place a spirit that cannot be compared with any other. Old Parisians are aware that under their feet flows the River Bièvre in its descent towards the Jardin des Plantes, and that this district was crossed by the main road towards Italy. As well as a spirit of place, therefore, the spirit of the time has also succeeded in making itself felt: the middle of Rue Mouffetard is occupied by an enormous floral parterre with a fountain at the centre. The combined action of the Voirie and Espaces Verts departments has attempted the impossible, to transform this area into one of those thousands of roundabouts that punctuate the roads right across France. For me, respect for the spirit of place has nothing to do with the sad idea of 'heritage', any more than distrust of the spirit of time means rejecting the contemporary. Over the last twenty or thirty years, some innovations have indeed managed to create a new spirit of place. I. M. Pei's pyramid, for example, gave life to Napoleon III's Louvre courtyard, formerly a dusty parking area for the museum staff, and not far away is a whole new quarter, with its good points and bad, organized around the Beaubourg centre. (I never say 'Centre Pompidou', as the late president had deplorable artistic taste – his office decorated by Agam – and besides he was opposed to the Piano-Rogers project, which was only adopted thanks to the stubbornness of the jury chair, the great Jean Prouvé.)

Conversely, I may say, the charm of certain places has evaporated in the last ten years without the historical décor having changed. On the Place Saint-Sulpice, the Café de la Mairie used to be an establishment where it was pleasant to drink coffee in the first rays of sunshine – this was indeed where I wrote those pages in my book that discuss this spot, as a homage to Georges Perec who wrote his *Tentative d'épuisement d'un lieu parisien* [*Attempt to Exhaust a Parisian Space*] there (p. 99). The setting is the same, but I avoid it now because of its clientele, made up of smart tourists and elegant ladies taking a rest there after doing their shopping in the haute-couture boutiques nearby. Easy to avoid, but then where to go? The answer is difficult, given how rare now are terraces on the historic Left Bank that are worth a visit.

Among the active agents of urban deterioration in these last ten years, I would give top marks to the Service des Espaces Verts. What they call '*végétalisation*' runs rampant in every quarter, striking places that ask only to be left in peace. Along the line of the former wall of the Farmers-General (p.109 ff.), the Boulevards de Rochechouart and de Clichy (from Barbès to Place Clichy via Place Pigalle and the Moulin Rouge on Place Blanche) used to be divided by a central reservation that was used partly for parking, partly by the local kids as a football pitch, partly as somewhere you could drink a can of beer on a bench, but above all by Eastern European tourists emerging from the neighbouring sex shops and kebab joints. In sum, an undefined space, just what is needed to give the city some air. But the *mairie* is not fond of such spaces. Right along the length of these old boulevards, the Service des Espaces Verts has established plantations hemmed in by metal grilles, with plants of a particular ugliness that are found now throughout Paris, selected so that they never flower and get rapidly covered with an unpleasant dust.

Sometimes this *végétalisation* is effected by shrubs in tubs or enormous pots, as for example in the Rue des Rosiers in the old Jewish quarter of the Marais: in combination with the newly laid paving and its central gutter, these sickly stems have given the coup de grâce to this street, which ten years ago still kept something of its Ashkenazi–proletarian past.

But I shouldn't exaggerate. These last few years have not known any disaster comparable with the destruction of upper Belleville in the 1960s, or the ravaging of the Bastille by the installation of Carlos Ott's opera house twenty years later. They have even seen a number of successes, like the walkway on the old viaduct leading to the Bastille station, or Marc Mimram's footbridge which cleverly links the Orsay museum with the Tuileries gardens. In point of fact, the very widespread impression that Paris has changed a great deal in recent years is quite correct, but what has changed is not so much the mineral and vegetable setting as the way in which the city is inhabited.

This development can be precisely located. On the Left Bank there has been scarcely any change. Apart from the great Chinatown of the 13th arrondissement, the population has remained almost uniformly white and bourgeois. The Blacks are street sweepers, the Arabs are grocers, the police are rarely seen and the historic streets are as clean as in the pedestrianized zones of the provinces. Everything is just a little older than when I started to write *The Invention of Paris*: the friendly beggar whose pitch had always been the five metres between the La Hune bookshop in St-Germain-des-Prés and the newspaper kiosk nearby now has grey hair and wears glasses to read the books that the bookshops pass on to him. Nothing happens anymore on the Left Bank, whereas in my youth we hardly needed to cross the Seine: the Right Bank was like a faraway desert.

Today the Right Bank is no more homogeneous than it was back in the insurrectional days of June 1848 or during the Commune. In what are rather ironically called the '*beaux quartiers*' – let's say west of a line that runs from Les Halles to the flea market via Rue Poissonière, Rue du Faubourg-Poissonière and Boulevard Barbès – almost nothing has changed in ten years. The Batignolles, Plaine Monceau, the Faubourg Saint-Honoré, Auteuil and Passy slumber peacefully. The Avenue des Champs-Élysées has gone downhill – I wrote in the closing years of the last century how it evoked 'the duty-free mall of an international airport, decorated in a style that is a mixture of pseudo-Haussmann and pseudo-Bauhaus' (p. 121); this is still the case, but the airport is now more down at heel, and you can scarcely find a table to have a drink except in the chains of faux pizzerias, genuine fast-food outlets, or pseudo-1900 cafés.

Working-class Paris occupies the east of the city – the northeast to be precise. People often say that this is also getting gentrified, that the marginal, the poor, the immigrants are steadily being driven out by the irresistible advance of the '*bobos*' ('bohemian bourgeois' – intellectuals, artists, designers, journalists, etc.) who cultivate their superficial nonconformism and benign antiracism in these quarters, while driving up the rents with the help of property speculators. This opinion needs some shading. It is true that certain places which formerly were little visited at night have become meeting points for a more or less gilded youth: the banks of the Canal Saint-Martin, the surrounds of the Place Gambetta, Rue Oberkampf at its intersection with Rue Saint-Maur. At that very point, some fifteen years ago, I witnessed the start of this phenomenon: in this hidden corner, an old-established *bougnat* – the name once given to alcohol outlets kept by Auvergnats who also supplied wood and coal to the storeys above – had been transformed into a smart café, the Café Charbon, and in the wake of its success bars mushroomed to the point of invading the Rue Oberkampf and the Rue Saint-Maur a hundred metres in each direction. It is also true that streets that were very poor and dilapidated some ten years ago, like Rue Myrha or Rue Doudeauville to the north of the Goutte d'Or, have been gradually renovated, which leads to the expulsion of their vulnerable African population, often without documents or work.

But working-class Paris is resisting rather better than people say. The Chinese at Belleville, the Arabs at the Goutte d'Or, backed by well-estab-lished Algerian traders who own their freeholds, the Turks at the market of the Porte Saint-Denis, the Africans of the Dejean market (recently threat-ened, it's true), the Sri Lankans and Pakistanis on the Faubourg Saint-Denis near La Chapelle – all these welcoming enclaves are holding their own, and even gaining some ground here and there. Besides, the presence in the same streets of Blacks, Arabs, and a precarious and proletarianized white youth, tends to create ties, particularly to face up to a police pressure that is much stronger than ten years ago. The expulsion by the police of the undocu-mented African hunger strikers who were occupying the Saint Bernard church at La Goutte d'Or aroused great indignation in 1996. Today it is lost in the flood of arrests, raids and expulsions that are the common lot of the working-class quarters of Paris. I am not claiming that these districts are in an effervescence like that of certain periods described in Part Two of this book. But solidarity and common action have gradually created a new situ-ation, especially since the revolts of suburban youth in October–November 2005 forced the government to proclaim a state of emergency, for the first time since the Algerian war in the early 1960s.

These revolts had the effect, among other things, of raising once again the old question of how to put an end to the divide between Paris and its suburbs. This question will certainly seem very odd to English readers, long familiar with a Greater London that stretches almost to the sea. But Paris has always grown in a very different fashion from London: you will read how, from the wall of Philippe Augustus (1165–1223) to the Périphérique of Georges Pompidou (1911–1974), the city developed in concentric rings, like an onion, to the rhythm of its successive defences. It is a city materially and administratively closed in on itself that has now to be opened up, as has always happened in its history when the latest of its walls became too tight a constriction.

In the last few years, this opening of Paris towards the *banlieue* has been broadly achieved to the west, on a wide arc that runs from Levallois – formerly the domain of secondhand car dealers, and rich today in the headquarters of showbiz and arms multinationals – through to Vanves and Malakoff. Along this arc, both geographical and social conditions were favourable. The transition zone (between the 'boulevard of the marshals' and the Périphérique – see p. 223) is not disrupted, you can cross it on foot without risking your life. And the population on either side is homogeneous, white, and fairly well-off.

It is a different matter to the east of the city. Around 2000, I wrote: 'It would need a Hugo to make the comparison between the Porte de la Muette with its pink chestnut trees, a sumptuous embarkation for Cythera, and the Porte de Pantin, an unbridgeable barrage of concrete and noise, where the Périphérique passes at eye level, with the Boulevard Sérurier beneath it engulfed in a hideous cutting in which the scrawny grass of the central reservation is littered with greasy wrappers and beer cans, and where the only human beings on foot are natives of L'viv or Tiraspol trying to survive by begging at the traffic lights' (p. 224). The situation has hardly changed since then. The gulf between Paris and the *banlieue* remains a yawning one in this sector, for reasons that are political in the strong sense of the word. The present population of the former Paris 'red belt' (from Ivry and Vitry in the south to Saint-Denis and Aubervilliers in the north) is now for the greater part 'of immigrant origin', i.e., made up of Blacks and Arabs, the very people (or their relatives) who had been driven out of the city by renovation and rising rents. This process, moreover, is very much in line with the history of Paris, in which, ever since the great confinement of 1657 that locked up the poor, the deviant and the mad in the buildings of the Hôpital Général (p. 155), the combined action of town planners, property speculators and police has never stopped pressing the poor, the 'dangerous classes', further from the centre of the city. In these conditions, what is the point of making a Greater Paris here, why risk retrieving on the periphery those whom it took so much trouble to evacuate from the centre? At the request of the president of the Republic, the *fine fleur* of official architecture recently presented their projects for a Greater Paris, rather along the lines of gyroscopes or centrifuges: the question was to make the poor revolve around the city at a distance, preventing them from returning for any longer than their work as cashiers or night watchmen required.

Fortunately, thanks to the economic crisis, none of these plans will be realized. Greater Paris will be limited to a reorganization of police forces: last week, it was decided that the Paris prefect of police will have his authority extended to all the surrounding departments. But administrative decisions are one thing in the history of Paris, and what actually happens is something else, possibly very different. Already some years ago a new osmosis began to operate between the working-class quarters of the city – from Montmartre to Charonne via Belleville and Ménilmontant – and the old proletarian bastions of the adjacent *banlieue* – Gennevilliers, Saint-Denis, Aubervilliers, Les Lilas, Montreuil. On both sides of the line, for many young people, the way of life, the music and the struggles are the same. It is true that you have to take the Métro to get from one side to the other. But as Hugo wrote in *Notre-Dame de Paris*, 'a city such as Paris is constantly growing', and the bureaucrats in power will be unable to stop this growth.

Eric Hazan
June 2009

Acknowledgements

Jean-Christophe Bailly, Dominique Eddé and Stéphane Grégoire had the patience to immerse themselves in the manuscript of this book at various stages. Their encouragement and suggestions contributed greatly to its final form. Sophie Wahnich and Jean-Christophe Bailly found in three minutes the title and subtitle ('Il n'y pas de pas perdus', in the original French edition) I had spent months searching for. The authors of the books on Paris I have published in Éditions Hazan – Jean-Pierre Babelon, Laure Beaumont, Maurice Culot, François Loyer, Pierre Pinon, Marie de Thézy – will be able to recognize here and there all the borrowings I have made from them. Finally, Denis Roche of Éditions du Seuil showed confidence in me from the start, and welcomed this book into his own series – a surprise that I have still to get over.

PART ONE

Walkways

I

Psychogeography of the Boundary

The city is only apparently homogeneous. Even its name takes on a different sound from one district to the next. Nowhere, unless perhaps in dreams, can the phenomenon of the boundary be experienced in a more originary way than in cities. To know them means to understand those lines that, running alongside railroad crossings and across privately owned lots, within the park and along the riverbank, function as limits; it means to know these confines, together with the enclaves of the various districts. As threshold, the boundary stretches across streets; a new precinct begins like a step into the void – as though one had unexpectedly cleared a low step on a flight of stairs.
– Walter Benjamin, The Arcades Project[1]

If you cross Boulevard Beaumarchais and turn down towards Rue Amelot, you are conscious of leaving the Marais for the Bastille *quartier*. If you pass the statue of Danton and follow the high back wall of the École de Médecine, you know you are leaving Saint-Germain-des-Près and entering the Latin Quarter. The boundaries between the districts of Paris are often drawn with this surgical precision. Sometimes the reference points are monuments – the rotunda of La Villette, the Lion of Denfert-Rochereau, the Porte Saint-Denis; sometimes the contours of the ground – the fold of the Chaillot hill on the plain of Auteuil, the gap between the Goutte d'Or and Buttes-Chaumont that marks the roads to Germany and Flanders; sometimes again major arteries, of which the Boulevards Rochechouart and Clichy are an extreme example, forming such a firm demarcation between Montmartre and Nouvelle-Athènes that it is not so much two districts that face each other here, but more like two worlds.

Not all of Paris's inner boundaries are lines with no thickness. To pass from one quarter to another, you sometimes have to cross neutral zones,

---

1   Walter Benjamin, *The Arcades Project* (Cambridge, MA: Harvard Univ. Press, 1999), p. 88.

transitional micro-quarters. These often take the form of embedded pockets: the Arsenal triangle between the Boulevards Henri-IV and Bourdon
– the starting point of Flaubert's *Bouvard and Pécuchet*, on a bench with
the thermometer at 33 degrees C – with its acute angle at the Bastille,
and dividing the Saint-Paul quarter from the approaches to the Gare de
Lyon; Épinettes, in the space between the Avenue de Saint-Ouen and the
Avenue de Clichy, which ensures smooth passage from the Batignolles to
Montmartre; or again, wedged between the Sentier and the Marais, the
right-angled triangle of Arts-et-Métiers, whose apex is the Porte Saint-
Martin and its hypotenuse the Rue de Turbigo, marked in the direction of
the city centre by the bell tower of Saint-Nicholas-des-Champs.

These boundaries may be more vague, like the region of missions and
convents centred on the Rue de Sèvres, which you have to cross in order
to pass from Faubourg Saint-Martin to Montparnasse, and which old taxi-
drivers call the Vatican. Or those streets beyond the Luxembourg that fill
the space between the Latin Quarter and Montparnasse, between Val-de-
Grâce and the Grande-Chaumière, between the allegory of quinine on
Rue de l'Abbé-de-l'Épée and the heroic figure of Marshal Ney in front of
the Closerie des Lilas. Already at the end of *Ferragus*, when the former head
of the Devorants spends his days silently watching the *boules* players and
sometimes lending them his cane to measure their shots, Balzac noted this

> space which lies between the south entrance of the Luxembourg and the
> north entrance of the Observatoire – a space without a name, the neutral
> space of Paris. There, Paris is no longer; and there, Paris still lingers.
> The spot is a mingling of street, square, boulevard, fortification, garden,
> avenue, high-road, province, and metropolis; certainly, all of that is to
> be found there, and yet the place is nothing of all that, – it is a desert.[2]

Like the background of certain Dadaist photomontages, composed out of
jostling fragments of city photographs, the most commonplace transitions
sometimes have the most surprising shocks in store. Leaving the greyness

---

2 Honoré de Balzac, *Ferragus* (trans. Wormeley). Perhaps Victor Hugo had this
passage in mind when he described the surroundings of the Salpêtrière in *Les
Misérables*: 'It was no longer solitude, for there were passers-by; it was not the
country, for there were houses and streets; it was not the city, for the streets had
ruts like highways, and the grass grew in them; it was not a village, the houses were
too lofty. What was it, then? It was an inhabited spot where there was no one; it
was a desert place where there was someone; it was a boulevard of the great city,
a street of Paris; more wild at night than the forest, more gloomy by day than a
cemetery' (trans. Wilbour).

of the Gare de l'Est along the former convent wall of the Récollets, what could be more surprising than to suddenly stumble on the sparkling water of the Canal Saint-Martin, the lock of La Grange-aux-Belles with its swing bridge and walkway hidden among the chestnut trees, and behind it the pointed slate roofs of the Hôpital Saint-Louis? And at the other end of Paris, the contrast between the bustle of the Avenue d'Italie and − just behind the Gobelins factory − the shady square marking the beginning of the Glacière quarter, with the stream of the Bièvre at its far end.

Certain quarters, even some of the oldest and most clearly defined, may contain an undefined part within them. For many Parisians, the Latin Quarter ends at the top of the Montagne Sainte-Geneviève, just as in Abélard's day. Balzac located the Pension Vauquer in Rue Neuve-Sainte-Geneviève (now Tournefort), between the Latin Quarter and the Faubourg Saint-Marceau, 'in the streets shut in between the dome of the Panthéon and the dome of the Val-de-Grâce, two conspicuous public buildings which give a yellowish tone to the landscape and darken the whole district that lies beneath the shadow of their leaden-hued cupolas'.[3] Today, however, on the southern slope of the Montagne, the École Normale Supérieure, research institutes and student residences, the historic laboratories of Pasteur and the Curies, along with the Censier university, may well justify extending the Latin Quarter as far as the Gobelins.

Differences over boundaries can be far more serious, putting in question the very identity of the district in question. Where does Montmartre begin, when you leave the city centre heading north? History − the boundaries of the village before its annexation to Paris − agrees with common sentiment that Montmartre starts when you cross the route of the no. 2 Métro line, whose stations Barbès-Rochechouart, Anvers, Pigalle, Blanche and Clichy precisely mark the curve of the former wall of the Farmers-General. But Louis Chevalier, in his masterpiece *Montmartre du plaisir et du crime*, places the Montmartre boundary much lower, on the Grands Boulevards, including in his book both the Chaussée d'Antin, the Saint-Georges quarter, the Casino de Paris and the Faubourg Poissonnière.[4] And quite apart from *plaisir* and *crime*, physical geography would support this dividing line, as the slopes of Montmartre begin well below the Boulevards Rochechouart and Clichy. The land starts to rise once you cross the ancient course of the Seine, a few dozen metres beyond the Grands Boulevards. Walter Benjamin, a peerless Paris pedestrian, noted how, when the flâneur has reached Notre-Dame-de-Lorette, 'his soles remember: here is the spot where in former

---

3   Honoré de Balzac, *Old Goriot* (trans. Marriage).
4   Louis Chevalier, *Montmartre du plaisir et du crime* (Paris: Robert Laffont, 1980).

times the *cheval de renfort* – the spare horse – was harnessed to the omnibus that climbed the Rue des Martyrs towards Montmartre'.[5]

It might be objected that Montmartre is a special case, not just a quarter like any other, being both a district on the map of Paris and a historical–cultural myth, with a different boundary in each of these senses. But isn't this ambiguity the very mark of quarters with a strong identity? And if such an identity is lacking, can one even talk of a quarter? Such questions lead, as we shall see, to a more general one: what, fundamentally, is a Paris quarter?

The administrative divisions – twenty *arrondissements*, with four *quartiers* in each – give the beginnings of a reply *a contrario*: a list of this kind, quite abstract and without any ranking, is only useful for the tax office and the police. But it is by no means certain that more subtle procedures would be able to define a basic urban unit for Paris, where the term 'quarter', despite its ancient roots in the language and its apparent simplicity, is far from denoting anything homogeneous and comparable. Saint-Germain-des-Prés, the Plaine Monceau and the Évangile, for example, are all three of them Paris quarters – each has its history, its boundaries, its map, its architecture, its population and its activities. The first, developing over the centuries on the territory of the great abbey and grouping very ancient streets around the 'modern' intersection of the Boulevard Saint-Germain and the Rue de Rennes, has kept nothing of the postwar years in which it was so celebrated, and has fallen into the sterility of a museum. The second, planted out by the Pereire brothers in the mid nineteenth century – a 'luxury quarter sprouting amid the wastelands of the old Plaine Monceau' – is that of Nana, in her 'Renaissance-style hôtel, with the air of a palace'. Marked by the memory of the academic '*artistes pompiers*' who were among its original inhabitants – Meissonier, Rochegrosse, Boldini, Carrier-Belleuse – this is a typical residential quarter, and the successors of the business bourgeoisie of the Second Empire still occupy its neo-Gothic and neo-Palladian *hôtels particuliers* today. The Évangile, at the end of the world between the railway tracks of the Nord and the Est, is built on a bit of the former village of La Chapelle, where the contractors who carted out the Paris refuse came to dump their load. ('Tumbrils carry off muck and filth, which is spilled into the nearby countryside: woe to any who find themselves neighbour to these infected mounds', wrote Sébastien Mercier.[6]) The monstrous gasometers that lined the Rue de l'Évangile are no longer to be seen, but the Calvary photographed by Atget is still in place, and the covered market of La Chapelle is one of the most colourful in Paris.

---

5   Benjamin, *The Arcades Project*, p. 416.
6   Louis Sébastien Mercier, *Tableau de Paris* (1781).

The customary oppositions of east/west, Left Bank/Right Bank, or centre/periphery are too simplistic to account for this diversity, and sometimes out of date. We have to look elsewhere, especially in the city's particular mode of growth. Nowhere else in Europe has a great capital developed in the same way as Paris, with such discontinuity and in so irregular a rhythm. And what gave the city this rhythm was the centrifugal succession of its walled precincts. Cities without walls – apart from those strictly organized on a rectangular grid, like Turin, Manhattan, or Lisbon as laid out by the Marquis de Pombal – grew up any which way, like the tentacles of an octopus, or a bacterial plaque multiplying in its culture. In London, Berlin or Los Angeles, the city limits and the shapes of districts are vague and variable: 'The rampant proliferation of the immense megalopolis that is Tokyo gives the impression of a silkworm eating a mulberry leaf ... The form of such a city is unstable, its border an ambiguous zone in constant movement ... It is an incoherent space spreading without order or markers, its limits only poorly defined.'[7]

Paris, on the other hand, so often threatened, besieged, or invaded, has from the dawn of time been constrained by its city walls. This has always given it a more or less regular circular form, and it has only been able to extend in a succession of dense and concentric rings. From the wall of Philippe Auguste to the modern Périphérique, six different walls followed one another in the course of eight centuries – without counting reinforcement, retouching or partial correction. The scenario has always been the same. A new wall is constructed, with broad dimensions that afford free space around the area already built up. But this space is rapidly covered over. Available land within the walls becomes increasingly scarce, buildings are pressed together, plots filled up, and the growing density makes life difficult. Meanwhile, outside the walls, and despite the laws against it – a constant over many centuries and political regimes, but never respected (this is the zone *non aedificandi*, which Parisians little familiar with Latin quickly came to call simply the *zone*, a word still in use today[8]) – houses

---

7 Yoshinobu Ashihara, *L'Ordre caché. Tokyo, la ville du XXIe siècle* (Paris: Hazan, 1994).
8 An ordinance of 1548, for example, cited in Pierre Lavedan, *Histoire de l'urbanisme à Paris* (Paris: Association pour la publication d'une histoire de Paris, 1975), stated: 'From now on there shall be no more construction or building in the faubourgs, by persons of any station or condition whatsoever, under penalty of confiscation of funds and building, which shall be entirely demolished.' At the end of the eighteenth century, Mercier wrote: 'The circumference of Paris is ten thousand yards. Several attempts have been made to define its boundaries; buildings have crossed these limits, marshes have disappeared and the countryside has retreated daily before the hammer and the set square.'

A historical map showing the successive Paris enceintes and fortifications.

with pleasant gardens are constructed in the faubourgs. When the *intra-muros* concentration becomes intolerable, these faubourgs are absorbed into the city and the cycle begins again:

> Philippe Auguste ... imprisons Paris in a circular chain of great towers, both lofty and solid. For a period of more than a century, the houses press upon each other, accumulate, and raise their level in this basin, like water in a reservoir. They begin to deepen; they pile storey upon storey; they mount up on each other; they gush forth at the top, like all laterally compressed growth, and there is a rivalry as to which shall thrust its head above its neighbours, for the sake of getting a little air. The street grows narrower and deeper, every space is overwhelmed and disappears. The houses finally leap the wall of Philippe Auguste and scatter joyfully over the plain, without order and all askew, like runaways. There they plant themselves squarely, cut themselves gardens from the fields, and take their ease. Beginning with 1367, the city spreads to such an extent into the suburbs that a new wall becomes necessary, particularly on the Right Bank; Charles V builds it. But a city like Paris is perpetually growing ... So Charles V's wall suffers the fate of that of Philippe Auguste. At the end of the fifteenth century, the faubourg strides across it, passes beyond it, and extends further.[9]

Like the growth rings of a tree, quarters between any two walls are contemporary, even if space was not filled at the same pace at all points on the circumference – the west side and the Left Bank always lagging behind. The same era and the same conception of the city explains why Belleville and Passy have many things in common, both finding themselves in the same stratum, only belatedly annexed to Paris and both maintaining certain features of Île-de-France villages – the high street, church and cemetery, the theatre (now 'municipal'), the lively central square where cakes are bought for Sunday. Analogies of this kind can be found not just in the faubourgs but at the very heart of the city, yet since the movement of Paris more often follows a radius than a circular arc, the diachronic diversity is more visible than the affinity between contemporary quarters.

Of Paris's two medieval fortifications,[10] the older, built under Philippe Auguste around 1200, has left its clearest traces on the Left Bank, where it circumscribed the 'Université' on the north slope of the Montagne Saint-Geneviève (these 'traces' are not old stones and archaeological remnants,

---

9 Victor Hugo, *Notre-Dame de Paris* (trans. Hapgood), chapter 2, 'A Bird's-Eye View of Paris' (1832).
10 There were two walls before the thirteenth century, but they have been lost in the depths of time.

which can be found on both banks, but rather the still apparent urban consequences, as can be read on a map or noted on foot). This wall started from
the Seine at the Tour Nesle, where the Institut de France now stands. Its
counterscarp followed the line of what is now Rue Mazarine (formerly
Fossés-Saint-Germain) as far as the Porte de Buci, the direction in which Paris
faced the abbey of Saint-Germain-des-Prés. The wall then continued along
Rue Monsieur-le-Prince (formerly 'Fossés-Monsieur-le-Prince'), which still
marks, and not by chance, the boundary between the Latin and the Odéon
quarters. It reached the top of the Montagne Saint-Geneviève, where the
names of streets and squares still perpetuate its memory: Fossés-Saint-Jacques,
Estrapade, Contrescarpe. It then descended towards the Seine in a straight line,
following Rue des Fossés-Saint-Victor (now Cardinal-Lemoine) and Rue des
Fossés-Saint-Bernard, reaching the river at the tower of La Tournelle.[11]

Despite breaches and destruction, eight centuries later the ghost of this
wall still defines the Latin Quarter. It is in this semi-ellipse – the neighbourhood of the Cordeliers refectory, the ossuary of Saint-Séverin, the robinia
tree of Saint-Julien-le-Pauvre, around the Rue de la Harpe, Place Maubert,
and behind the Collège de France – that a medieval layout still survives
on the Left Bank: one of narrow plots in a dense and unbroken tissue, a
whirl of streets going in all directions. To experience this, you need only
leave the Sorbonne and cross the precinct, climb Rue Saint-Jacques as far
as Rue des Ursulines, Rue des Feuillantines beloved by Victor Hugo, Rue
Lhomond and Rue de l'Abbé-de-l'Épée. Here, the high walls, trees and
gardens glimpsed behind fences, the calm and regular pattern of the plan,
show that you are *extra muros*, in a relaxed space, on the lands of former
convents, along the roads leading to Orléans and Italy.

Since July 1789, when the Bastille was destroyed and its stones made into
souvenirs – just as fragments of the Berlin wall would be sold exactly two
centuries later – there is nothing left of the wall of Charles V: its curtain, its
rampart walk, its fortress gates, its bastions used for evening strolls, its moats
where people fished with rods. Nothing physical, at least.[12] But its route

---

11 On the Right Bank, the wall of Phillipe Auguste began at the Louvre (its
keep forming part of the wall), and followed a route corresponding to Rues Jean-
Jacques-Rousseau, Montmartre, and Réamur. It then turned southeast, as far as
Rue de Sévigné, and reached the Seine in the middle of the Quai des Célestins,
close to Rue de l'Ave-Maria.
12 Except what was discovered when work was under way for the Grand Louvre,
and incorporated into the décor of the underground shopping centre, as well as a
small pile of stones from the Bastille that decorates the square at the corner of the
Boulevard Henri-IV and the Quai des Célestins.

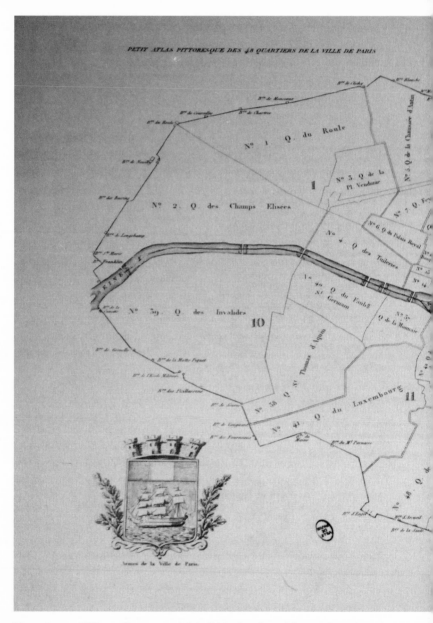

The twelve pre-1860 arrondissements, and their division into forty-eight named quarters.

la feuille coloriée, chez E. GARNOT rue Poupée St André des Arts N.º 7

TABLEAU
des Arrondissemens
ET DES QUARTIERS
de la Ville de
PARIS

along the ancient course of the Seine is still one of the fundamental lines of the city structure, completing in a wide circular arc the rectilinear plan inherited from the Romans. Between the Bastille and the Porte Saint-Denis, the noble curve of the boulevards that today bear the names of Beaumarchais, Filles-du-Calvaire, Temple and Saint-Martin precisely matches the line of the old wall. The design of the Grands Boulevards was already prefigured.[13]

This wall would last a good while. Reinforced by great bastions under Henri II, doubled here and there to face up to the Spanish artillery, it defended a Paris ruled by the Ligue against the forces of Henri III and Henri IV. Half a century later it would challenge royal power for a final time, in the magnificent episode of the Fronde, when La Grande Mademoiselle – Anne-Marie-Louise d'Orléans – had the guns of the Bastille fired against Turenne's army, to cover the retreat of Condé's forces through the Porte Saint-Antoine.

Louis XIV, as a child, had to flee from Paris under the Fronde. In the 1670s, he ordered the old wall to be razed and an avenue of trees planted in its place, making a walkway more than thirty metres wide right round the city. Those in charge of this unprecedented project, François Blondel and Pierre Bullet, drew a line that followed the old wall from the Arsenal and the Bastille to the Porte Saint-Denis, continuing in a line that is now that of the Grands Boulevards up to the site of the Madeleine. The route then reached the Seine via the Rue des Fossés-des-Tuileries, passing the far end of the gardens and the present Rue Royale.[14] This was 'an avenue planted in three lines, the one in the middle being sixteen yards wide ... bordered by walls of dressed stone, thanks to the gentlemen provosts of merchants, who were also responsible for the conduct of all these ramparts and avenues that serve the public as a promenade. It has been ordered that ditches twelve yards wide will be left, as a course for the city sewer ... and within the rampart a paved street four yards wide.'[15]

Established on the former fortifications, Louis XIV's avenue received the

13   After the Porte Saint-Denis, the wall of Charles V turned straight towards the Louvre, following a line that today runs through the Rue d'Aboukir and the Place des Victoires. It reached the Seine close to what is now the Pont du Carrousel. On the Left Bank, which had scarcely developed in the meantime, this wall followed the earlier one of Philippe Auguste.

14   On the Left Bank, the route more or less followed the Boulevards des Invalides, Montparnasse, Port-Royal, Saint-Marcel and de l'Hôpital, but building on this side, along what are known as the 'boulevards du Midi', would get under way later, and on maps from the late eighteenth century you can still see the boulevard proceeding through open fields, well beyond the most outlying buildings of the city.

15   Henri Sauval (1620–70), *Histoire et recherches des antiquités de la ville de Paris*, posthumous edition (Paris, 1724).

name *boulevard*, which entered current usage and was used for a number of Paris boundaries, with slippages that can cause confusion today. In the nineteenth century, the boulevard that took the place of the wall of the Farmers-General was called the 'external' boulevard (Goncourt brothers' *Journal*, just after the destruction of the wall: 'I walked along the external boulevards widened by the suppression of the rampart walk. The aspect is completely changed. The *guinguettes* have disappeared'). 'External' is used here as opposed to the 'internal' boulevard, that of Louis XIV, which, in its segment running from the Château-d'Eau to the Madeleine, had become permanently known as the Grands Boulevards, or simply the Boulevards ('The Boulevards may be compared to two hemispheres. Their antipodes are the Madeleine and the Bastille. The equator is the Boulevard Montmartre, where warmth and life flourish.'[16]). Later, in the 1920s, when Thiers's fortifications had been demolished, the label 'external' came to be applied to the boulevard constructed in their place (Francis Carco: 'In the scattered bars of the external boulevards, and the sloping streets that join them, he would enter with the air of waiting for someone unknown'[17]). The boulevard of the Farmers-General suddenly lost this name and never found a new one in the Paris vocabulary. In the 1960s, with the building of the Périphérique – and no doubt to avoid confusion between the 'external boulevards' and this 'external' Périphérique, dear to ladies who listen to the radio for news of Paris traffic jams – a new expression appeared to denote the boulevards that had taken the place of the *'fortifs'*: the 'boulevards of the marshals'.

It will be helpful if I use the term 'Old Paris' for the part within the boulevard of Louis XIV, and 'New Paris' for the part outside. This New Paris is itself divided into two concentric rings. Between the boulevard of Louis XIV and the wall of the Farmers-General is the ring of the faubourgs; between the wall of the Farmers-General and the 'boulevards of the marshals' is the ring of the villages of the crown. But this is not just a matter of names. Whenever Paris advanced from one boundary to the next, this signaled a time of changes in technology, society and politics. The shift in stones and ditches was not the cause; it was rather as if the emergence of a new epoch led both to the obsolescence of the old walls and to transformations in the city's life.

We can take the example of street lighting and the maintenance of order, important both in terms of entertainment and in order to 'discipline and punish'. In the Middle Ages, only three places in Paris were permanently illuminated at night: the gate of the Châtelet tribunal, where Philippe le Bel had

16   Émile de La Bédollière, in *Paris Guide, par les principaux écrivains et artistes de la France* (1867). This guide, written for the benefit of visitors to the Éxposition Universelle, had a preface by Victor Hugo.
17   Francis Carco, *L'Équipe, roman des fortifs* (Paris: Albin Michel, 1925).

placed a wood-framed lantern filled with pig bladders to deter the criminal enterprises that were hatched right outside; the Tour Nesle, where a beacon marked the entry to Paris for boatmen coming up the Seine; and the lantern of the dead in the Innocents cemetery. Those heading into the dark of the city were advised to make use of an escort of armed torchmen, as one could hardly trust the protection of the watch, whether civic or royal.

At the same time as Louis XIV made Paris an open city, and launched the construction of his new avenue, he took two measures that marked the beginning of the modern age: he had nearly three thousand lanterns installed in the streets – glass cages protecting candles, hung from ropes at first-floor level – and he established the post of lieutenant-general of police, in command of a significant armed force. (It was the first of these officers, La Reynie, who emptied out the courts of miracles and embarked on the 'great confinement', shutting up beggars and deviants in the new prison hospitals of the Salpêtrière and Bicêtre.)

A century later, in parallel with the building of the wall of the Farmers-General, the technical headway made in the Age of Enlightenment had its effects on street lighting: the old lanterns with their candles were replaced by oil lamps equipped with metal reflectors, with a longer range. Sartine, the lieutenant-general of the time, held that 'the very great amount of light these give makes it impossible to believe that anything better could ever be found'. Sébastien Mercier was of a different opinion: 'The lampposts are badly placed ... From a distance, this reddish flame hurts the eyes; close up, it gives only little light, and below, you are in darkness.'

It was the 1840s, the time when Thiers's fortifications enclosed the city once again, that saw the general spread of gas lighting and the uniformed *sergents de ville*. Electric light replaced gas after the First World War, when the '*fortifs*' were demolished. In the 1960s, the construction of the Boulevard Périphérique – the latest of Paris's fortifications and not the least formidable – was accompanied by the replacement of incandescent lamps by neon lighting, the disappearance of bicycle police with their capes, known as *hirondelles* (swallows), and the proliferation of motorized patrols; the blessings of community policing were still to come.

It would be possible, therefore, to write a history of Paris in politics and architecture, art and technology, literature and society, the chapters of which would not be centuries – a particularly inappropriate division in this case – nor again reigns and republics, but rather the expanding city precincts, which mark a discontinuous and subterranean time. In the fifteenth of his 'Theses on the Concept of History', Walter Benjamin remarked that 'calendars do not measure time as clocks do'. The time of city walls resembles the time of calendars.

2

Old Paris: The Quarters

Whilst the triumphal arch of the Porte Saint-Denis and the equestrian statue of Henri IV, the two bridges,[1] *the Louvre, the Tuileries and the Champs-Élysées all equal or surpass the beauties of ancient Rome, the city centre — dark, enclosed and hideous — stands for an age of most shameful barbarism.*

— Voltaire, *The Embellishments of Paris* (1739)

Alas, Old Paris is disappearing at terrifying speed.

— Balzac, *The Lesser Bourgeoisie* (1855)

After many detours, I first reached Rue Montmartre and the Pointe Saint-Eustache; I passed the square of the Halles, then open to the sky, through the great red umbrellas of the fishmongers; then Rues des Lavandières, Saint-Honoré and Saint-Denis. The Place du Châtelet was quite wretched at this time, the fame of the Veau Qui Tette restaurant overshadowing its historical memories. I crossed the old Pont-au-Change, which later I had to have rebuilt, lowered and widened, then followed the line of the former Palace of Justice, on my left the sorry huddle of low dives that then dishonoured the Île de la Cité, which I would have the joy of razing completely — a haunt of thieves and murderers, who seemed able there to brave the correctional police and the court of assizes. Continuing my route by the Pont Saint-Michel, I had to cross the poor little square that the waters of Rues de la Harpe, de la Huchette, Saint-André-des-Arts and de l'Hirondelle all spilled into, like a drain ... Finally, I sunk into the meander-ings of Rue de la Harpe before climbing the Montagne Sainte-Geneviève and arriving — via the Hôtel d'Harcourt, Rue des Maçons-Sorbonne, Place Richelieu, Rue de Cluny and Rue des Grès — on the Place du Panthéon, at the corner of the École de Droit.[2]

---

1   These two bridges were the Pont-Neuf and the Pont-Royal.
2   E. G. Haussmann, *Mémoires* (1890–3).

Such was Haussmann's itinerary as a law student living on the Chausée-d'Antin in the early years of the July monarchy. At this time, the city centre had changed little in the past three hundred years. Paris as circumscribed by the boulevard of Louis XIV, a square with slightly softened angles that could be seen as a figure of density and constraint, was still a medieval city. Like the famous knife of Jeannot, which sometimes had a new handle and sometimes a new blade, but always remained Jeannot's knife, the streets of Paris, though their buildings were replaced over the years, remained medieval streets, crooked and dark. 'Victor Hugo, summoning up the Paris of Louis XI, only needed to look around him; the streets bathed in shadow into which Gringoire and Claude Frollo disappeared were not so different from the streets of the Marais, the Cité, even the boulevards that he wandered in the 1830s and later described to us, in sentences similarly weighted with darkness and danger – in a word, of night – in *Things Seen*.'[3]

In the 1850s, Privat d'Anglemont described 'behind the Collège de France, between the Sainte-Geneviève library, the buildings of the old École Normale, the Saint-Barbe college and Rue Saint-Jean-de-Latran, a large block of houses known by the name of Mont-Saint-Hilaire ... a whole quarter made up of narrow and dirty streets ... old, dark and crooked'.[4] And the trades practised there – worm sellers, vegetable steamers, meat lenders, cheap illustrators, pipe seasoners – also went back to the depths of the Middle Ages.

Twenty years later, under the Second Empire, gas lighting, the great cuttings of the new boulevards, plentiful water and new sewers transformed the city's physiognomy more than the three previous centuries had done. ('Take any good Frenchman, who reads *his* newspaper each day in *his* taproom, and ask him what he understands by "progress". He will answer that it is steam, electricity and gas – miracles unknown to the Romans – whose discovery bears full witness to our superiority over the ancients', Baudelaire wrote in 1855 in *L'Exposition universelle*). Yet Paris did not completely leave the Middle Ages behind in the nineteenth century. Just before the Great War, Carco could still describe a Latin Quarter where Villon would not have felt so out of place: 'The Rue de l'Hirondelle, a couple of steps from the Seine, which you reach via the narrow and stinking corridor of Rue Gît-le-Coeur, its clientele made up of anarchists, prowlers, students, oddballs, tarts, down-and-outs, regaling themselves on the cheap ... If there are places in the world, quarters reserved for human perversity, that surpass in ignominy these bordering on the Seine and stretching around the Rue Mazarine, where are they?'[5] And until the late

---

3   Chevalier, *Montmartre du plaisir et du crime*.
4   Alexandre Privat d'Anglemont, *Paris anecdote* (Paris, 1854; republished by Les Éditions de Paris, 1984).
5   Francis Carco, *De Montmartre au Quartier Latin* (Paris: Albin Michel, 1927).

1950s, the alleys between the Place Maubert and the river – Rue de Bièvre, Rue Maître-Albert, Rue Frédéric-Sauton – the Saint-Séverin quarter and Rue Mouffetard, were still filthy and wretched. In his itinerary among the Paris poor, Jean-Paul Clébert described in Rue Maître-Albert, 'this dog's leg of an alley that outsiders avoid, kitchens invisible from the main road, and which you enter from the side, taking the corridor that leads to the upper floors; you push open a door chosen at random and step down into a room as big as a chicken coop, in the midst of a family.'[6] The Place de la Contrescarpe had more tramps than Situationists, and there were some cafés that were hard to enter if you were not a ragged alcoholic. There were no tourists, restaurants or shops to be seen. Hotels rented rooms by the day to immigrant workers, without asking to see their papers. The offices of Messali Hadj's Movement for the Triumph of Democratic Liberties were on Rue Xavier-Privas, a couple of steps from Notre-Dame. Contrary to a widespread idea, the final eradication of the Middle Ages in Paris was not the work of Haussmann and Napoleon III, but rather of Malraux and Pompidou, and the emblematic literary signal of this disappearance was not Baudelaire's 'The Swan' but rather Perec's *Les Choses*.

THE RIGHT BANK QUARTERS

Palais-Royal

The character of Paris as a town formed in the Middle Ages is still visible in the way that its quarters are assembled. The Right Bank has four large and compact nuclei, that of Palais-Royal being the most recent, with satellites in the Tuileries-Saint-Honoré and Bourse quarters; Les Halles is the oldest of the four, and has been treated worst; the Sentier is changing now before our eyes; and the Marais is not so much a single quarter as several. Between these main regions there are transition zones that fill the gaps. This is the most densely built region of Paris.[7]

---

6 Jean-Paul Clébert, *Paris insolite* (Paris: Denoël, 1952).
7 A decree of Louis XIV dated December 1702 defined twenty quarters, fifteen of these being on the Right Bank. These were the Cité, Louvre, Palais-Royal, Montmartre (around the Place des Victoires), Saint-Eustache, Halles, Sainte-Opportune (around Saint-Germain-l'Auxerrois), Saint-Jacques-de-la-Boucherie (Châtelet), Saint-Denis, Saint-Martin, Saint-Avoye (Rue de la Verrerie, Rue Vieille-du-Temple, Rue Sainte-Croix-de-la-Bretonnerie …), Marais, Grève (Hôtel de Ville, Saint-Gervais), Saint-Antoine and Saint-Paul. The five quarters on the Left Bank were Maubert, Saint-Benoît (the Écoles quarter – there is still an Impasse du Cimetière-Saint-Benoît behind the Collège de France), Saint-André-des-Arts, Luxembourg and Saint-Germain-des-Prés, which had only recently become part of Paris.

It is easy to imagine that the centre of the world was once where the ruined columns of Athens and Rome now lie, precisely because these are ruins. At the Palais-Royal, on the other hand, in the avenues of its gardens or under the colonnades where stalls selling tin soldiers with their crosses and ribbons, pipes, soft toys and needlepoint form an old-fashioned back-drop, nothing allows you to imagine that for fifty years this place was the agora or forum of Paris, its fame spreading right across Europe. When the Allied forces entered the city after the battle of Waterloo, 'What was the first thing they asked for in Paris? The Palais-Royal! A Russian officer entered the building on horseback. What was the first thing in the Palais-Royal that they wanted? To sit down in one of the restaurants, whose glorious names had reached even their ears.'[8]

'No matter what the weather, rain or shine', Diderot's narrator explains at the beginning of *Rameau's Nephew*, 'it's my habit every evening at about five o'clock to take a walk around the Palais-Royal. I'm the one you see dreaming on the bench in the Argenson avenue, all alone.' This was written in the 1760s, so it is still the old Palais-Royal that is referred to here. Cardinal Richelieu had bought a series of buildings and plots at the end of Rue Saint-Honoré, grouping them into a single quadrilat-eral that is today bordered by Rues Saint-Honoré, des Petits-Champs, de Richelieu and des Bons-Enfants.[9] The Palais-Cardinal constructed by Lemercier stood close to where the Conseil d'État is today. The rest of the land formed a garden: the Argenson avenue that Diderot mentions was to the right, alongside what would become the Galerie de Valois; the avenue opposite took its name from the Café de Foy, the first of those establishments that would be the glory of the Palais-Royal. (The Caveau was founded a little later. Diderot in his old age wrote to his daughter on 28 June 1781: 'I get bored at home. I go out and get bored even more. The sole and supreme happiness I can enjoy is to go regularly each day at five o'clock to have an ice at the Petit-Caveau.') In the same year, the Duc de Chartres, future Philippe-Égalité, commissioned Victor Louis to construct the buildings that today surround the garden on three sides.[10]

---

8   Eugène Briffault, *Paris à table* (1846).
9   So that his new quarter would be within the Paris walls, Richelieu had the fortification slightly moved (as mentioned above, this ran in a straight line from the Porte Saint-Denis to the Place des Victoires and the Louvre), more or less along the line of the boulevards from the Porte Saint-Denis to the Madeleine. This was the precinct 'des Fossés jaunes', from the name of the colour of the shifted earth. Its existence was brief, as the contractor went bankrupt and the walls were soon knocked down.
10   Richelieu's palace was then demolished. All that remained were the Galleries des Proues, between Rue de Valois and the Cour d'Honneur, with columns

Endowed with its hundred and eighty arcades, the Palais-Royal enjoyed an immediate success:

> A unique point on the globe. Visit London, Amsterdam, Madrid or Vienna, you will see nothing like it: a prisoner could live there without getting bored, and it would be years before he even dreamed of freedom ... It is called the capital of Paris. Everything is to be found there: and for a young man of twenty, with fifty thousand livres invested in government stock, there could be nothing else wanting in life, and he would never even emerge from this fairyland ... This enchanted abode is a small town of luxury enclosed in a greater one; it is the temple of pleasure, from where scintillating vices have banished even the phantom of shame; no tavern in the world is more graciously depraved.[11]

Towards the end of Louis XVI's reign, the Palais-Royal saw a proliferation of clubs. By July 1789 the agitation was constant, and the Palais became what Hugo called 'the nucleus of the comet Revolution'. Camille Desmoulins relates the date of 13 July as follows:

> It was half past two, and I had gauged the mood of the people. My anger against the despots had turned to despair. I could not see any groups ready for an uprising, however strongly affected they were. Three young men, standing hand in hand, struck me as inspired by a more resolute courage. I could see that they had come to the Palais-Royal with the same intention as myself. A number of passive citizens followed them. 'Messieurs,' I said, 'here is the beginning of a civic force: one of us must take the initiative and stand on a table to harangue the people.' 'Get up, then.' I agreed. Rather than climbing, I was immediately hoisted up on the table [in the Café de Foy]. Right away I found myself surrounded by an immense crowd. Here is my speech, which I shall never forget: 'Citizens, there is not a moment to lose. I have come from Versailles. Necker has been dismissed; his dismissal is the signal for a St Bartholemew's Night of patriots. This evening, the Swiss and German battalions will come out of the Champ-du-Mars to

---

installed by Buren. The nautical trimmings recall that Richelieu was also superintendent-general of shipping. The buildings on the fourth side, towards Rue Saint-Honoré, were a later addition. Richelieu made a gift of the Palais-Cardinal to Louis XIII, and Louis XIV then gave it to his brother, Monsieur, the Duc d'Orléans. Renamed the Palais-Royal, it remained in the Orléans family until 1848, except for the interruption of 1789 to 1815.

11   Mercier, *Tableau de Paris*.

massacre us. Just one single recourse remains, to seize arms and choose a rosette by which to recognize one another.'[12]

In the course of the Revolution, however, the Palais-Royal, rechristened Palais-Égalité, rapidly became a rallying place for royalists, moderates, Feuillants, all those whom Robespierre called *fripons* (rogues). At the Mafs restaurant, the contributors to the royalist newspaper *Les Actes des apôtres* – Abbé Maury, Montlausier, Rivarol – held their 'evangelical dinner' each week. They wrote up their discussions at a corner of the table, and 'the issue composed in this way was left on the Mafs menu, and from Mafs went to Gattey, the famous shop in the Palais' Galeries de Bois'.[13] On 20 January 1793, the day that the Convention voted to send Louis Capet to the guillotine, it was in a modest restaurant – chez Février – in the Galerie de Valois that the bodyguard Pâris assassinated Le Peletier de Saint-Fargeau. At the Convention, on 19 Nivôse of year II, 'the revolutionary committee of the Montagne denounced the restaurant owners and caterers of the Palais de l'Égalité, which had merely changed its name and could still bear that of Palais-Royal from the insolent luxury displayed there'.[14] Barras – who lived in the Palais-Royal, above Véfour's – and his friends prepared the coup of 9 Thermidor at a table in the Corazza's ice-cream parlour, and under the Directory the *incroyables* pursued republicans in the gardens, white cockade in hat and bludgeon in hand.

The apogee of the Palais-Royal, the time when it became a myth with no counterpart anywhere in modern Europe, was the twenty years following the entry of the Allies into Paris in 1815. The arrival of Russian, Austrian, Prussian and English soldiers and officers gave a new impulse to the two most profitable activities of the site, prostitution and gambling. This was when the Galeries de Bois, wooden buildings lined up transversally where the double colonnade of the Galerie d'Orléans now stands, had their moment of glory:[15]

The Wooden Galleries of the Palais-Royal used to be one of the most famous sights of Paris. Some description of the squalid bazaar will not be

---

12   Cited from Victor Champier and G.-Roger Sandoz, *Le Palais-Royal d'après des documents inédits* (Paris: Société de propagation des livres d'art, 1900).
13   Edmond and Jules de Goncourt, *La Société française pendant la Révolution* (1880). Gattey was a royalist bookstore.
14   Champier and Sandoz, *Le Palais-Royal*.
15   The Galerie d'Orléans was constructed by Fontaine, official architect of the Palais-Royal under the Restoration, after the Galeries de Bois were demolished in 1828.

out of place; for there are few men of forty who will not take an interest
in recollections of a state of things which will seem incredible to a younger
generation. The great dreary, spacious Galerie d'Orléans, that flowerless
hothouse, as yet was not; the space upon which it now stands was covered
with booths; or, to be more precise, with small, wooden dens, pervious to
the weather, and dimly illuminated on the side of the court and the garden
by borrowed lights – styled windows by courtesy but more like the filthi-
est arrangements for obscuring daylight to be found in little wineshops in
the suburbs. The Galleries, parallel passages about twelve feet in height,
were formed by a triple row of shops. The centre row, giving back and
front upon the Galleries, was filled with the fetid atmosphere of the place,
and derived a dubious daylight through the invariably dirty windows of
the roof ... The treacherous mud-heaps ... were in keeping with the
seething traffic of various kinds carried on within it; for here in this shame-
less, unblushing haunt, amid wild mirth and a babel of talk, an immense
amount of business was transacted between the Revolution of 1789 and
the Revolution of 1830. For twenty years the Bourse stood just opposite,
on the ground floor of the Palais ... People made appointments to meet
in the Galleries before or after 'Change; on showery days the Palais-Royal
was often crowded with weather-bound capitalists and men of business ...
Here dwelt poetry, politics, and prose, new books and classics, the glories
of ancient and modern literature side by side with political intrigue and the
tricks of the bookseller's trade.[16]

In this blessed age, when the trades of bookseller and publisher were still
combined (sometimes indeed with that of printer as well), the Galeries de
Bois saw the beginnings of certain publishing houses that were marked
out for a fine future: Stock, Garnier, Le Dentu – supposedly the model
for Dauriat in *Lost Illusions*, to whom Lucien de Rubempré tries to sell his
sonnets on 'Easter Daisies' ('For me the question is not whether you are a
great poet, I know that you have a great deal, a very great deal of merit; if I
were only just starting in business, I should make the mistake of publishing
your book. But in the first place, my sleeping partners and those at the back
of me are cutting off my supplies').

---

16   Honoré de Balzac, *Lost Illusions* (trans. Marriage). Jules Janin reviewed Balzac's
book in 1839, in the *Revue de Paris*: 'We know how M. de Balzac excels in this
kind of muddy description: the rotten wood, the stagnant water, the washed linen
in basins hanging from ropes – a worthy treatment for vicious places. Nothing
escapes him, not a wrinkle, not a sticky crust of this filthy plague. Despite the
power that a writer must have to reach this point, we may wonder what pleasure
the readers of M. de Balzac can derive from these horrific details.'

The colonnades were not a place for reading but rather for gambling, at *creps, passe-dix, trente-et-un* and *biribi*. Stall number 9 (which occupied spaces 9 to 12 of the colonnade) offered two tables of *trente-et-quarante*, a table for *creps*, and the gamblers could drink punch flambé. At the beginning of Balzac's *The Magic Skin*, the unfortunate Raphael climbs the staircase of number 36 ('As you enter a gaming-house the law despoils you of your hat at the outset. Is it by way of a parable, a divine revelation?'). But the most famous establishment was undoubtedly number 113: eight saloons, with six roulette tables. Marshal Blücher, the victor of Waterloo, hardly left this gambling den. He ran through six million livres during his stay in Paris, and left the city with his estates all mortgaged. Mortgage agents actually stationed themselves close at hand, and in the evening, readily available girls mingled with the gamblers. Those who strolled beneath the Wooden Galleries and in the little avenues of the gardens were known as 'semi-beavers', those in the Galleries themselves as 'beavers', and those on the Caveau terrace as 'complete beavers'.

You could also eat and drink in the galleries of the Palais-Royal. The Café de Foy was the only one that served in a garden pavilion. On the first floor, its chess club, whose members included Talleyrand and David, competed with that in the Café de la Régence, the setting of *Rameau's Nephew*. The Café des Mille Colonnes, run by a famous beauty, was Balzac's particular preference. The Café de la Rotonde, close to the Passage du Perron, had been during the Revolution the headquarters of the Brissotins (who were not known in their time as Girondins), after being the site under Louis XVI of the quarrels between the champions of Gluck and those of Piccini. Café Lemblin was frequented by those nostalgic for the Empire. Philippe Brideau 'was one of the faithful Bonapartes of the Café Lemblin, that constitutional Boeotia; he acquired the habits, manners, style, and life of a half-pay officer.'[17] Behind the counter, the waiters had swords wrapped in green serge, ready to hand to their customers for duels. Some evenings there was such a demand that they had to excuse themselves: 'Messieurs, they're in use.' Among the establishments specializing in prostitution, the most famous was the Café des Aveugles, which took its name from the composition of its orchestra. ('Why blind men, you will say, just in this café, which is scarcely more than a cupboard under the stairs? It's because in its early days, which went back to the time of the Revolution, things happened that would have shocked the decency of an orchestra.'[18])

Of the three great restaurants featured in *La Comédie humaine*, two were in the Palais-Royal, the third being Le Rocher de Cancale, on Rue

17   Honoré de Balzac, *The Two Brothers* (trans. Wormeley).
18   Gérard de Nerval, *Les Nuits d'octobre* (1852).

Montorgeuil. 'Is it a dinner for foreigners or provincials whom you want to give an exalted idea of the capital? Then you must take them to Véry's ...This is the most expensive caterer, which allows us to conclude that he must be number one in the hierarchy of worth of his profession, one of the most enlightened artists among those who see to the preservation of good taste, and opposed to the invasions of middle-class cuisine.'[19] When Lucien de Rubempré arrived from Angoulême, unhappy and humiliated, he made his way towards the Palais-Royal:

> He did not know the topography of his quarter yet, and was obliged to ask his way. Then he went to Véry's and ordered dinner by way of an initiation into the pleasures of Paris, and a solace for his discouragement. A bottle of Bordeaux, oysters from Ostend, a dish of fish, a partridge, a dish of macaroni and dessert – this was the *ne plus ultra* of his desire. He enjoyed this little debauch, studying the while how to give the Marquise d'Espard proof of his wit, and redeem the shabbiness of his grotesque accoutrements by the display of intellectual riches. The total of the bill drew him down from these dreams, and left him the poorer by fifty of the francs which were to have gone such a long way in Paris. He could have lived in Angoulême for a month on the price of that dinner.[20]

Véry's was eventually taken over by its neighbour Véfour, the former Café de Chartres where Alexander von Humboldt, on return from Central America, very often dined under the Empire. In 1815, Rostopchin, the man who had given the order to burn Moscow, frequently caroused there with his French teacher Flore, a lovely actress from the Théâtre des Variétés: 'There was not a foreigner, an elegant lady, or even a bourgeois from the Place Royale who did not know these three young people from the Durance, who had arrived in Paris with nothing to support themselves except the secret of *brandades de morue* [cod pounded with garlic, oil and cream], which eventually led to their receiving tribute from the whole of civilized Europe, from the mouth of the Tagus to the shores of the Neva.'[21]

---

19 Honoré Blanc, *Le Guide des dîneurs, ou statistique des principaux restaurants de Paris* (1814).
20 Balzac, *Lost Illusions.*
21 Blanc, *Le Guide des dîneurs.* In Balzac's *Lily of the Valley*, when Félix de Vandenesse as a boy dreams of Paris, he imagines that 'the first day we were to dine in the Palais-Royal, so as to be near the Théâtre-Français', but, after being forced to admit a debt, 'I was sent back to school in charge of my brother. I lost the dinner at the Frères Provençaux, and was deprived of seeing Talma in *Britannicus*' (trans. Wormeley).

The heyday of the Palais-Royal ended on a precise date: at midnight on 31 December 1836, when games of chance were banned in Paris. The decline was rapid. The dandies, gawpers, bon viveurs and call girls migrated a few hundred metres, and the Boulevards became the new *promenade enchantée.*

In those days, when quarters went out of style, they fell into a kind of lethargy that could last a very long while. They had not suffered in their heyday the accelerated commercial metabolism that since the 1960s has ravaged quarters such as Saint-Séverin, Mouffetard, the Bastille and the Marais, and is now at work on the Butte-aux-Cailles, or the Saint-Blaise quarter around the Place Charonne, Rue Montorgeuil and Rue Oberkampf. The Palais-Royal, for its part, has remained as it was when the crowds left and moved further north. Its essential charms, however, did not withstand Victor Louis's bays, the monotony of which is reinforced by the impeccable alignment of the four avenues of lime trees. What still does have its surprises is the way in which the Palais-Royal, an enclosed space, communicates with the surrounding streets. Certain passages have a monumental beauty, with statues, candelabras and gilded railings – such as that which leads via the Place de Valois towards the entrance of the Galerie Véro-Dodat; or the two covered colonnades by which you leave the bottom of the gardens for Rue de Beaujolais, the one on the left passing Véfour's restaurant, the one on the right towards the Passage des Deux-Pavillons, Passage Colbert and the Bibliothèque Nationale. Others, on the contrary, slip along in an almost clandestine fashion, like the Passage du Perron with its outlet opening on Rue Vivienne between antique dolls and musical boxes, or the three graceful stairways that lead from Rue de Montpensier towards Rue de Richelieu.

Carrousel

For Diderot or Camille Desmoulins, it was quite easy to pass from the Palais-Royal to the Tuileries. Thirty years later, however, Géricault, Henri de Marsay or Stendhal would have had to cross the new main road through the quarter, Rue de Rivoli, though not yet confront the Avenue de l'Opéra or bypass the enormous mass of Napoleon III's extensions to the Louvre. The Palais-Royal was not hemmed in as it is today, but connected with the Tuileries-Saint-Honoré quarter. A direct connection, or almost direct, as it was still necessary to cross obliquely a quarter that – unlike any other in the centre of Paris – has disappeared without leaving the slightest trace, even in memory: the Carrousel. The verse from Baudelaire's 'The

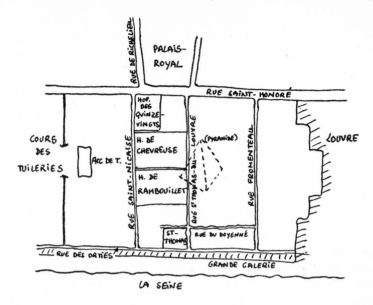

Swan': 'Once a menagerie was set up there;/There, one morning, at the hour when Labour awakens,/Beneath the clear, cold sky when the dismal hubbub/Of street cleaners and scavengers breaks the silence,/I saw a swan that had escaped from his cage ...' is not a purely poetic vision like his 'Albatross'. Alfred Delvau, rambler and chronicler of street life under the Second Empire, recalled:

> It used to be charming, the Place du Carrousel – today populated with great men in stone from Saint-Leu. Charming like disorder, and pictur-esque like ruins! It was a forest, with its inextricable tangle of wooden stalls and mud-walled shacks, occupied by a crowd of petty trades. I often strolled among this caravanserai of bric-a-brac, amid this laby-rinth of planks and zigzags of tiny shops, and I knew its denizens almost intimately – men and animals, rabbits and parrots, pictures and cheap ornaments.[22]

The Joanne guidebook of 1870 also uses Baudelaire's magic word *baraque* ('I see only in memory that camp of stalls'), and laments the disappearance of 'this plethora of little stalls, like a perpetual fair of curiosities, old iron and live birds, that used to stretch from the Musée to Rue de Chartres'.

---

22 Alfred Delvau, *Les Dessous de Paris* (Paris: Poulet-Malassis, 1862).

The extraordinary quarter of the Carrousel lay between the Horloge pavilion of the Louvre and the avenues of the Tuileries. It was bordered on the south, along the Seine, by the Grande Galerie that had linked the two palaces from the time of Henri IV. The inner side of this gallery was adjacent to a street with the name Rue des Orties [Nettles]. To the north, the boundary of the Carrousel was Rue Saint-Honoré. Three streets perpendicular to the river connected Rue des Orties with Rue Saint-Honoré: Saint-Nicaise, Saint-Thomas-du-Louvre and Fromenteau.

The Rue Saint-Nicaise, continuing the line of Rue de Richelieu, would today coincide with the Louvre's ticket offices. On the side of Rue Saint-Honoré it bordered onto a large hospital, the Quinze-Vingts, founded by Louis IX to care – so legend goes – for three hundred knights who had returned blind from the Crusades, the Saracens having put out their eyes. (Curiously, most historians of old Paris relate this story as if it were an established fact, just as they do that of the Jew Jonathan who, around the same time, supposedly boiled a host from the church of the Billettes, which emitted blood – for which crime he was burned alive, as can be seen on Paolo Uccello's predella in Urbino.[23]) The hospital precinct sheltered a whole population of craftsmen, exempt from taxation as they also were at the Temple. In 1780, the Quinze-Vingts was transferred to the former barracks of the Black Musketeers in Rue de Charenton, where it remains today.

The Rue Saint-Thomas-du-Louvre would today pass through Ieoh Ming Pei's pyramid. As well as the Hôtel de Chevreuse, it served a building of unparalleled importance in French literature, the Hôtel de Rambouillet. 'I need not say that it is the most famous in the kingdom,' wrote Sauval, who was a regular there,

> as no one has any doubt on this score. The entire *beau monde* has read its praise and description in *Le Grand Cyrus*, and in the works of the most refined minds of the century. Perhaps there is not even any need to recall that in *Cyrus* it is known as the palace of Cléomire, and elsewhere it is always called the palace of Arthénice, an anagram of Catherine, the baptismal name of Catherine de Vivonne, Marquise de Rambouillet, the mansion having been devised by Malherbe. Illustrious figures have all published the name of this heroine to their heart's content, leaving me

---

23   Jean-Marc Léri, for example, relates it in the following terms: 'It seems that this sacrilege was committed on Easter Day, 2 April 1290, in the house of the Jew Jonathan, which was then given the name of the House of the Miracle' (in *Le Marais, mythe et réalité*, exhibition catalogue [Paris 1987]). In this text, 'it seems' introduces doubt as to the date, but in no way as to the reality of the fact.

almost nothing to say about her hôtel ... And as well as this, they have also told us that she devised it and gave it its design, that she alone undertook, conducted and completed it. Her fine and elegant taste revealed to our architects conveniences and perfections unknown even to the Ancients, and which they have since extended to all proud and prestigious dwellings.[24] By the discoveries that Arthénice made in architecture, by way of a pleasant diversion, it is possible to judge those that she made in literature, where she occupied a pinnacle. The virtue and merit of Catherine de Vivonne attracted to her house, for many years, all fine minds of the court and the century. In her blue chamber a circle of illustrious figures gathered each day, indeed we should say the Academy; for this is where the Académie Française had its origin; and it is from the great minds who attended here that the most noble section of this very considerable body was composed. This is the reason why the Hôtel de Rambouillet was long known as the French Parnassus ... Those who were not known there were seen simply as ordinary persons, and it was enough to have entered there to be ranked among the illustrious figures of the century.[25]

Rue Fromenteau followed the moat of the Louvre along the Horloge pavilion, ending up at Rue Saint-Honoré close to Rue de Valois. It always had a bad reputation: 'Is not Rue Fromenteau both murderous and profligate?', Balzac asks at the start of *Ferragus*. Connecting Rue Fromenteau with Rue Saint-Thomas-du-Louvre, the little Rue du Doyenné hosted a street market where, in the Romantic epoch, eighteenth-century French canvases could be bought at a low price. This is where Cousine Bette lived at the beginning of the eponymous novel: 'As we drive in a hackney cab past this dead-alive spot, and chance to look down the little Rue du Doyenné, a shudder freezes the soul, and we wonder who can lie there,

---

24 The marquise had the idea of placing the staircase on the side of the building, thus freeing the central space and permitting a continuous succession of rooms.

25 The familiars of the famous *chambre bleu* included Malherbe, La Rochefoucauld, Descartes, Saint-Amand, Mme de Lafayette, Mme de Sévigné, Scarron, Vaugelas, Corneille, Rotrou, Ménage, Racan, Voiture ... For fifteen years, Catherine's daughter, Julie d'Angennes, was courted by Montausier, supposedly Molière's model for Alceste in *The Misanthropist*. Montausier had the idea of offering his beloved an album in which each page was devoted to a flower and each flower compared with Julie: sixty-one madrigals written by Montausier himself and seventeen other poets who were habitués of the hôtel, inscribed on vellum by Nicolas Jarry, the greatest calligrapher of his day, and illustrated by Nicolas Robert. This was the celebrated *Guirlande de Julie*, which she found one day deposited on her bed. It was still another four years before she agreed to marry Montausier.

and what things may be done there at night, at an hour when the alley is
a cut-throat pit, and the vices of Paris run riot there under the cloak of
night.' In the 1830s, a group of young writers still little known established
themselves in Rue du Doyenné in a kind of squat, their number including
Gérard de Nerval:

> It was in our common lodgings in Rue du Doyenné that we came to
> recognize one another as brothers ... in a corner of the old Louvre des
> Médicis, very close to the spot where the former Hôtel de Rambouillet
> stood ... Good old Rogier would smile into his beard, from the top
> of a ladder, where he was painting on one of the three mirror frames a
> Neptune – who looked like himself! Then the two swing doors opened
> abruptly: it was Théophile [Gautier]. We hurried to offer him a Louis
> XIII armchair, and he read in his turn his first verses, while Cydalise I,
> or Lorry, or Victorine, swung nonchalantly in blonde Sarah's hammock,
> stretched across the enormous salon ... What happy days! We gave
> balls, suppers, costumed parties ... We were young, always gay, and
> often rich ... But now I come to the sad note: our palace was demol-
> ished. I rummaged through its debris last autumn. Even the ruins of the
> chapel [of the Doyennés, which was part of Saint-Thomas-du-Louvre],
> which so gracefully stood out against the green of the trees ... were not
> respected. Around that time, I found myself, one day, rich enough to
> buy back from the demolishers two lots of woodwork from the salon,
> painted by our friends. I have the two Nanteuil architraves; Vattier's
> signed *Watteau*, Corot's two long panels representing Provençal land-
> scapes; Châtillon's *Red Monk*, reading the Bible on the curved haunches
> of a naked sleeping woman; Chassériau's *Bacchantes*, who have tigers on
> a leash like dogs ... As for the Renaissance bed, the Médicis dresser, the
> two sideboards, the Ribera, the tapestries of the *Four Elements*, all that
> was scattered a long time ago. 'Where did you lose so many fine things?'
> Balzac asked me one day. – 'In misfortune,' I replied, citing one of his
> favourite phrases.[26]

Rue Saint-Nicaise was where royalist plotters exploded a bomb on 24
December 1800, while the First Consul was proceeding from the Tuileries
to the opera in Rue de Richelieu. The attack killed eight people, and
marked the beginning of the end for the Carrousel quarter. Bonaparte realized the danger of having cutthroats like these so close to his residence, and
had the damaged houses pulled down as well as a number of others. He

---

26   Gérard de Nerval, *Petits Châteaux de Bohême* (1852).

later demolished the stalls and wooden barriers that closed off the Tuileries avenues,[27] and had the triumphal arch of the Carrousel constructed as a gateway of honour to the palace. Demolition continued slowly until 1848, when the pace accelerated in order to make work for the National Workshops. 'Three-quarters of the square was cleared in 1850. There only remained [on Rue Saint-Nicaise] the former building of the royal stables ... and right in the middle of the new esplanade, the Hôtel de Nantes, which had resisted until the end all the offers of the expropriation assessors. The hôtel has since been demolished, and the royal stables as well.'[28]

The Carrousel today is a dusty steppe between the Louvre pyramid and the railings of the Tuileries gardens, crossed by a stream of cars – required by some odd notion to navigate a one-way roundabout – and by an underground tunnel whose concrete entrances give a final touch to the whole ensemble. As the triumphal arch makes no sense in the middle of this desert, the idea was conceived of linking it to the Tuileries gardens and the Napoleon III wings of the Louvre by little fan-shaped plantations over which the heads or thighs of Maillol's fat ladies emerge: there are academic gardens just as there are academic painters. Happily, some very fine chestnut trees have been saved, which in summertime provide shade for the ice-cream and postcard sellers around Percier and Fontaine's monument.

Tuileries-Saint-Honoré

In 1946, the Place du Marché-Saint-Honoré was renamed Place Robespierre, a decision reversed in 1950 when the French bourgeoisie raised its head again. Their hatred towards Robespierre had never diminished since Thermidor. Beside the Incorruptible himself – who lodged with his sister Charlotte and brother Augustin in carpenter Duplay's house

---

27 It was between these barriers and Rue Saint-Nicaise that the little Place du Carrousel was located, 'which still keeps this name' – wrote Germain Brice in the 1720s – 'because this is where the superb tournament was held in 1662, to mark the birth of Monseigneur le Dauphin'. Under the Empire, the destruction had advanced to the point that at the start of Balzac's *A Woman of Thirty*, set just before the Russian campaign, 'The magnificent review commanded for that day by the Emperor was to be the last of so many which had long drawn forth the admiration of Paris and of foreign visitors'.

28 Adolphe Joanne, *Paris illustré en 1870. Guide de l'étranger et du Parisien*. An anonymous daguerreotype from 1850 shows the Hôtel de Nantes, a building of six storeys in the middle of the empty esplanade, surrounded by cabs and carriages. The caption notes that it was demolished on 1 October 1850 'in order to clear the approaches to the Louvre and the Tuileries'. Reproduced in *Paris et le daguerréotype*, Musée Carnavelet exhibition catalogue (Paris-Musées, 1989).

at the end of Rue Saint-Honoré – other actors in the Revolution also lived in the Tuileries-Saint-Honoré quarter: Sièyes, Olympe de Gouges, Héron, and Barère whom Robespierre praised in the ambiguous words: 'He knows everything and everyone, he is ready for anything.' Not that this was a particularly revolutionary quarter, but Rue Saint-Honoré was the geographical axis of political life. Between 1789 and 1791, the club of La Fayette and the Moderates held its sessions in the former convent of the Feuillants, where Rue de Castiglione now runs. The Society of the Friends of Liberty and Equality was remembered in history under the name of the Jacobins club, the buildings of the Dominican order (known as Jacobins in France) having occupied what is now the Place du Marché-Saint-Honoré as far as Rue Gomboust. The Constituent Assembly, the Legislative Assembly, and initially also the Convention, sat in the Salle du Manège in the Tuileries gardens, close to where Rue Saint-Roch comes out into Rue de Rivoli. After 10 August 1792, the Convention moved to the Salle des Machines, which Soufflot had transformed and where Sophie Arnould had previously triumphed in Rameau's *Castor et Pollux*. The Convention tribune, which according to the specifications was a low construction painted in antique green, decorated with yellow pillars with bronzed capitals and three crowns in faux porphyry, was situated close to the present Marsan pavilion. The Committee of Public Safety met in the opposite wing, the south end of the palace.

After Thermidor, the Convention had the Jacobins' premises demolished – Merlin de Thionville having denounced it as a 'bandits' lair' – and the gap this created was known for a while as the Place du Neuf-Thermidor. But when royalist pressure became worrying, Barras secured the services of a young officer who was seen as a Robespierrist, Napoleon Bonaparte, and made arrangements to protect the Assembly during the royalist uprising of 13 Vendémaire in year IV (5 October 1795); the insurgents were crushed on the steps of the church of Saint-Roch, by grapeshot from an eight-pounder set up at the end of the Cul-de-sac Dauphin, today the part of Rue Saint-Roch between Rue Saint-Honoré and the Tuileries.

The two main squares in the Saint-Honoré quarter are the Place du Marché-Saint-Honoré and the Place Vendôme, and though quite different from one another, they have both experienced similar disfigurement in recent times. The former already suffered a town-planning assault in the late 1950s, when the market that Molinos had built under the Empire was demolished – four halls, and in the middle a fountain supplied by Chaillot's steam pump – and in its place a concrete block constructed that doubles as a fire station and police precinct. More recently, the Paribas bank commissioned Bofill to construct a new building there. Aware that his hollow columns and pseudoclassical fronts were beginning to look tired, the architect conceived a pseudo high-tech building, badly proportioned and completely foreign to the spirit of the place, with a chilling effect that the proliferation of restaurants fails to conceal.

The Place Vendôme, for its part, has been endowed by the architects in charge of public buildings and national palaces with an indescribable paving scattered with sheets of brushed steel, and bunker entrances to its underground car park. The chauffeurs dusting their limousines outside Cartier, the Ritz, or Crédit Foncier wear dark suits and dark glasses, and have the appearance of bodyguards. Whenever I pass that way, I think fondly of the National Guards, canteen-women, Gavroches, armed civilians and gunners at their posts, posing in groups for the photographer in front of the debris of the column in May 1871.

Bourse

Between the gardens of the Palais-Royal and the Boulevards, the district often known as the Bourse quarter is one of the most homogeneous and harmonious in old Paris. In these blocks that are called neoclassical for want of a better word, many buildings date from the reign of Louis XVI, others from the Revolutionary years – Rue des Colonnes, whose miniature neo-Grecian vocabulary, Doric columns without pediment, palm-leaf mouldings and strange windowed balustrades form such an original ensemble that great architects from all over Europe – Gilly, Soane, Schinkel – came to admire and draw it. Others in this style were constructed under the Empire, like Brongniart's Bourse. The paradox of so grandiose a building devoted to so mundane an activity did not escape his contemporaries:

> I vex myself every time I enter the Bourse, the beautiful edifice of marble, built in the noblest Greek style, and consecrated to the most contemptible business – to swindling in the public funds ... Here, in the vast space of the high-arched hall, here it is that the swindlers, with all their repulsive faces and disagreeable screams, sweep here and there, like the tossing of a sea of egotistic greed, and where, amid the wild billows of human beings, the great bankers dart up, snapping and devouring like sharks – one monster preying on another ...[29]

29   Heinrich Heine, *French Affairs: Letters from Paris* (trans. Leland), 27 May 1832. And almost the same year, Victor Hugo wrote in *Notre-Dame de Paris*: 'If it is according to rule that the architecture of a building should be adapted to its purpose in such a manner that this purpose shall be immediately apparent from the mere aspect of the building, one cannot be too much amazed at a structure which

The Bourse quarter is crossed by three parallel streets with a more or less north-south orientation – Rue Vivienne, Rue de Richelieu and Rue Sainte-Anne – and two transversals. One of these is very ancient, Rue des Petits-Champs, which links the two royal sites of Place des Victoires and Place Vendôme.[30] The other is Rue du Quatre-Septembre, one of the least successful of Haussmann's cuttings. Under the Second Empire it went by the name of Rue du Dix-Décembre, commemorating the election of Louis Bonaparte as president of the Republic in 1848. The Society of 10 December, founded by the prince-president, recruited among the Paris lumpenproletariat caricatured by Daumier's character Ratapoil, playing a role comparable with that of the Gaullist Service d'Action Civique in the 1960s.

For a very long time this quarter has been devoted to three activities that have resisted pretty well the changes in fashion and luxury goods: books, finance, and music. 'Since the reign of Henri IV,' Germain Brice tells us, the Bibliothèque Royale

> had been maintained very negligently on a private house in Rue de la Harpe. In 1666 it was moved to another house on Rue Vivienne, on the orders of Jean-Baptiste Colbert ... In 1722 it was decided to install it in the Hôtel de Nevers, or rather in the apartments that had been used for some time for the Bank, to which others had been added, built on neglected gardens that were close by, in such a way that the public would have the satisfaction of seeing it to better advantage than before, when it was scattered in a number of rooms in that shabby building on Rue Vivienne.[31]

From the Regency to the 1990s, the Bibliothèque – royal, imperial, or national – remained in this quadrilateral between Rue Vivienne and Rue de Richelieu. To sum up the spirit of this archaic institution, exasperating and blessed, I would choose Gisèle Freund's photograph of Walter Benjamin at work, with his glasses and his dishevelled hair, bent over a book that he holds open with his left elbow, and taking notes with a large black pen. And as caption I would cite a connoisseur of libraries:

---

might be indifferently – the palace of a king, a house of commons, a town hall, a college, a riding school, an academy, a warehouse, a courthouse, a museum, a barracks, a sepulchre, a temple, or a theatre. However, it is an Exchange.'

30   After the Liberation, the name of a proletarian heroine, Danielle Casanova, was given to the section of Rue des Petits-Champs above Avenue de l'Opéra.

31   Germain Brice, *Nouvelle Description de la ville de Paris et de tout ce qu'elle contient de plus remarquable* (Paris, 1725).

It may well be that in having branches of trees painted high up on the very lofty walls of the Bibliothèque Nationale in Rue de Richelieu, Henri Labrouste, an architect with a literary bent, had an intuition of this connection between reading and nature. That is in any case what one may believe in reading the remark that Benjamin wrote about this room which he knew so well, and which was basically the only true 'apartment' that he had in Paris: 'When you leaf through pages below, you can hear a murmur above.'[32]

The quarter's links with finance also date from the eighteenth century. For Sébastien Mercier, 'there is more money in this single street' – Rue Vivienne – 'than in all the rest of the city; it is the capital's purse':

> The major counting-houses have their offices there, in particular the Caisse d'Escompte. This is the stamping ground of the bankers, the money changers, the brokers, all who make a trade out of money ... The whores are more financial here than in any other quarter, and never mistaken in marking out a henchman of the Bourse. These moneymen might have a greater need for reading than any others, so as not to completely lose the faculty of thought; but they don't read at all; they provide material for those who write ... All the inhabitants of this street are men who literally work against their fellow citizens, without feeling any sense of remorse.

The banks have now left Rue Vivienne for the Boulevards, but there are still several shops that sell coins, where gold is changed just as in Balzac's time.

Rue de la Banque leads from the Bourse to the quarter's other financial institution, the Banque de France. The Hôtel de La Vrillière, designed by François Mansart, was confiscated during the Revolution and the Imprimerie Nationale established there. Robespierre's speeches were printed in runs of 400,000, and Marat needed three presses in the courtyard to print *L'Ami du peuple*. The famous Galerie Dorée – whose paintings by Pietro da Cortona, Tintoretto and Veronese had been transferred to the Louvre to make them accessible to the people – was used as a paper warehouse. The Banque de France took over the building from the Imprimerie in 1808,[33] and like all banks, it destroyed the marvel that had been entrusted

---

32 Jean-Christophe Bailly, *Panoramiques. La tâche du lecteur* (Paris: Christian Bourgois, 2000).
33 The Imprimerie then left for an outbuilding of the Hôtel de Rohan, in Rue Vieille-du-Temple, where it remained until it was moved to Rue de la Convention in 1925.

to it. Mansart's doorway disappeared, which, according to Germain Brice, 'was seen as his masterpiece because he had been able to preserve the regularity of the Ionic order despite the pairing of columns, which had previously been viewed as very difficult'. The gardens likewise disappeared, on which Sauval had written that they 'offered two admirable vistas: on the one hand a large parterre surrounded by mock privets, and accompanied by a great number of statues and busts, both ancient and modern, of bronze and marble; on the other, the length of Rue des Fossés-Montmartre [now d'Aboukir], receding towards Rue Montmartre … Of all the palaces that Paris contains, only the Palais d'Orléans [Palais-Royal] and this possess such a long avenue, and enjoy such a rare perspective.' In 1870 the Galerie Dorée was likewise demolished, 'the most perfect in Paris and perhaps in the whole of France', according to Sauval; its fifty metres ended in an overhang supported by a pendentive above Rue Radziwill.

This quarter, with only a single church (Notre-Dame-des-Victoires, where the moneymen met while the new Bourse was being constructed), has had three opera houses – without counting the Opéra Garnier, which is no distance at all as the crow flies. On the square facing the main entrance to the Bibliothèque Nationale, the site of the former Hôtel Louvois, where three streets dedicated to great ministers of the ancien régime – Richelieu, Colbert and Louvois – converge, Victor Louis built a theatre for the great actress Mme Montansier. Its entrance was a peristyle with thirteen arches and a balcony onto the street. The vestibule was supported by two ranks of Doric columns; four monumental staircases painted in white and gold served the five levels. Under a quite fallacious pretext – Chaumette to the Commune, 14 November 1793: 'I denounce Citoyenne Montansier for having had her theatre built on Rue de la Loi [now Richelieu] in order to set fire to the Bibliothèque Nationale; English money made a large contribution to the construction of this building, and the *ci-devant* queen provided 50,000 écus' – the Convention confiscated the hall and decided to move the Opéra National there, which was done on 20 Thermidor, eleven days after the fall of Robespierre. It was after attending the French premiere of Haydn's *Creation* here that Bonaparte nearly met his end in Rue Saint-Nicaise, and on 13 February 1820, the Duc de Berry was struck by a dagger while coming out of a show. Just as the Château des Tournelles had been razed after Montgomery killed Henri II there with an unfortunate blow of his lance, so Mme Montansier's hall was demolished after the death of the heir to the throne. There was a plan to erect an expiatory monument on the site, but Louis-Philippe preferred to have Visconti construct the graceful Fontaine des Fleuves. All that remains of the opera here are the names of the streets bordering the square – Cherubini, Rameau, and Lully, whose house is not far off, at the corner of Rue Sainte-Anne and Rue des Petits-Champs, 'decorated outside with tall pilasters of a mixed order, and a few sculptures that are not badly conceived'.[34]

After this catastrophe, the Opéra shifted for a few months to the Salle Favart, built in the 1780s on the lands of the Duc de Choiseul, which had up to then been devoted to Italian comedy. Its odd position, with its back turned to Boulevard des Italiens and opening into the little Place Boieldieu, is explained by the desire of the actors not to be mistaken for the mountebanks of Boulevard du Temple.[35] In 1821, the Opéra was moved a few metres, crossing Boulevard des Italiens to settle at the corner of Rue Le Peletier. This was the grand Opéra of the nineteenth century, the mythical hall of Rossini, Boieldieu, Meyerbeer, Donizetti and Berlioz, as well as of Balzac and Manet. It also burned down in 1873, and the Opéra spent a few months in the Bourse quarter, at the Salle Ventadour,[36] before it moved into the new hall built by Garnier, inaugurated in 1875 with *La Juive* by Scribe and Halévy.

Finance and opera were not mutually exclusive activities. West of Rue de Richelieu ('street of business and pleasure' in the words of Alfred Delvau), and overspilling the line of what would later be Avenue de l'Opéra, was a mound of rubble, the result among other things of the demolition of the old wall of Charles V and the Porte Saint-Honoré. This Butte des Moulins was one of the high places of Parisian prostitution. At the start of *Scenes from a Courtesan's Life*, the touching character of Esther lives in Rue Langlade, a tiny alley between Rue de Richelieu and Rue Traversière-Saint-Honoré (now Molière):

> These narrow streets, dark and muddy, where such industries are carried on as care little for appearances, wear at night an aspect of mystery full of contrasts. On coming from the well-lighted regions of Rue Saint-Honoré, Rue Neuve-des-Petits-Champs, and Rue de Richelieu, where the crowd is constantly pushing, where glitter the masterpieces of industry, fashion, and art, every man to whom Paris by night is unknown would feel a sense of dread and melancholy, on finding himself in the labyrinth of little streets which lie round that blaze of light reflected even from the sky ... Passing through them by day, it is impossible to imagine what they become by night; they are pervaded by strange creatures of no

---

34 Brice, *Nouvelle Description de la ville de Paris*.
35 Since the nineteenth century this building, redesigned in the wake of two fires, has been the venue of the Opéra-Comique.
36 This building is today occupied by the Banque de France's welfare services, but here again the adjoining streets – Monsigny, Méhul – recall its musical past.

known world; white, half-naked forms cling to the walls – the darkness
is alive. Between the passenger and the wall a dress steals by – a dress that
moves and speaks. Half-open doors suddenly shout with laughter ...
Snatches of songs come up from the pavement ... This medley of things
makes you giddy.

The Butte des Moulins was cleared to allow Avenue de l'Opéra to connect
with Rue Saint-Honoré. A photograph by Marville shows the gigantic
work this involved, with the new Opéra glimpsed in the background
through the dust. But the tradition of love for sale long survived in Rue
des Moulins, depicted in Toulouse-Lautrec's famous *Salon*, as well as Rue
Chabanais, which before the Second World War still contained one of
the most select brothels in Paris – hence the expression that was once very
common in *Le Canard enchaîné*: 'a fine *chabanais*'.

The Arcades

The majority of the great Paris arcades are found between Avenue de
l'Opéra, the Place des Victoires, Rue des Petits-Champs and the Grands
Boulevards. Some have been renovated, or frozen into museums, like
the Passage Colbert. Others have become commercial galleries of semi-
luxury, like the Galerie Vivienne. But certain of them, however changed
from their day of splendour, still keep a particular charm: the Galerie
Véro-Dodat – where Mlle Rachel lived, and which housed the offices
of Philipon's *La Caricature* – with its dark woodwork and checkerboard
paving;[37] the Passage Choiseul, where Lemerre published the Parnassians
and whose bustle still offers unexpected surprises; and especially the ances-
tor of them all, the Passage des Panoramas. This took its name from the two
wooden turrets framing its sentry on Boulevard Montmartre. A group of
painters, including Daguerre, executed panoramic views of Toulon, Tilsit,
Napoleon's camp at Boulogne, and the battle of Navarino, on immense
canvases close to a hundred metres in circumference and twenty metres tall.
At the centre of the rotunda, spectators were immersed in a spectacle lit
up from above. Chateaubriand, in his *Itinerary from Paris to Jersualem*, wrote:
'The illusion was complete, I recognized at first glance the monuments
that I had indicated. No traveller was ever confronted with so rude a test; I
could not wait for Jerusalem and Athens to be transported to Paris in order

---

37   Its name derives from two rich sausage makers, Messrs Véro and Dodat, who
undertook the work in 1823, giving rise to the adage that this arcade was 'a fine
piece of art between two quarters'.

to convince myself of the truth or otherwise.' The rotundas have disappeared, but the Théâtre des Variétés remains, where Offenbach had his triumphs, succeeded by Meilhac and Halévy, Lavedan, Capus, de Flers and Caillavet. It was in front of the entrance that poor Count Muffat waited for Nana, where

> a perfect stream of brilliancy emanated from white globes, red lanterns, blue transparencies, lines of gas jets, gigantic watches and fans, outlined in flame and burning in the open. And the motley displays in the shops, the gold ornaments of the jeweller's, the glass ornaments of the confectioner's, the light-coloured silks of the modiste's, seemed to shine again in the crude light of the reflectors behind the clear plate-glass windows, while among the bright-coloured, disorderly array of shop signs a huge purple glove loomed in the distance like a bleeding hand which had been severed from an arm and fastened to a yellow cuff.

The melancholy beauty of the Passage des Panoramas extends across Boulevard Montparnasse, through Passage Jouffroy and Passage Verdeau, as far as Rue de Provence, a long walk completely out of the rain. This was indeed the main reason behind the fashion for these arcades, from the Directory to the end of the Second Empire: you could stroll there without stepping into the famous Parisian mud, or the risk of being run down by carriages. (At the start of the twentieth century: 'Gourmont explained to me that when he was at the Bibliothèque Nationale, he lived on Rue Richer and in bad weather could walk to the Bibliothèque, almost without experiencing it, via the Passages Verdeau, Jouffroy and des Panoramas, Rue des Colonnes, etc.'[38]) In 1800, Paris only had three streets provided with sidewalks: Rues de l'Odéon, Louvois, and de la Chaussée-d'Antin. Elsewhere, the gutter was most commonly in the centre of the road, as in the Middle Ages. 'With the least shower', wrote Sébastien Mercier, 'rickety bridges have to be put down', in other words, boards on which street children helped pedestrians to cross in return for payment. Frochot, prefect of the Seine department under the Empire, could still lament: 'The capital of France, adorned with admirable monuments and possessing so many useful establishments, offers those who cross it on foot only an excessively difficult and even dangerous way, which seems to have been exclusively designed for the movement of carriages.'[39] Fifty years later, the picture had scarcely changed. Baudelaire wrote in his little prose poem 'Loss of a Halo':

---

38 Paul Léautaud, *Journal*, 23 January 1906.
39 Cited by Henry Bidou, *Paris* (Paris: Gallimard, 1937).

'My dear, you know my terror of horses and carriages. Just a little while ago, as I was crossing the boulevard very hastily and jumping about in the mud, through that moving chaos in which death comes galloping towards you from all sides at once ...' The decline in these arcades coincided with the completion of Haussmann's first great cuttings: 'Our wider streets and more spacious pavements have made easy the sweet flânerie impossible for our fathers except in the arcades.'[40] By the end of the century the arcades were already being spoken of in the past tense: 'The arcade, which for Parisians was a kind of walking saloon where you could smoke or chat, is now no more than a kind of shelter which you suddenly remember when it rains. Certain arcades keep a certain attraction because of this or that famous shop that is still to be found there. But it is the renown of the tenant that keeps the fashion going, or rather the death agony.'[41]

Though abandoned and down-at-heel, the Paris arcades are still present in twentieth-century literature – the Passage de l'Opéra in Aragon's *Paris Peasant*, which gave Walter Benjamin the idea for his *Passagenwerk*, the extraordinary Passage des Bérésinas – actually Choiseul – described in Céline's *Death on the Installment Plan* as 'a kind of sewer'. What is stranger is that scarcely a trace of them can be found in books written in the age of their glory. To my knowledge, there is no mention of the arcades either in *La Comédie humaine* or in such other texts of Balzac's as 'Histoire et physiologie des boulevards de Paris', nor in Nerval, nor in Baudelaire's *Tableaux parisiens* or his prose poems, even though Poulet-Malassis, the publisher of *Les Fleurs du mal*, had his offices in the Passage Mirès (later Passage des Princes, before its recent demolition), nor in *Les Misérables* or Eugène Sue's *Mysteries of Paris*. Perhaps the arcade, such a poetic place today, was for its contemporaries simply an urban detail that, however convenient, had little intrinsic interest, any more than shopping centres, multiplex cinemas or underground car parks have for us today.

Les Halles

To pass from the Palais-Royal to Les Halles is to pass from the newest quarter of old Paris, as well as the most elegant and best preserved, to a quarter that is quite the opposite. The most visible border between them is Rue du Louvre, a widened version of the very ancient Rue des Poulies. Another frontier, perhaps more precise as it follows the trace of the walls of Philippe Auguste, is Rue Jean-Jacques-Rousseau, which went under the

---

40   Edmond Beaurepaire, *Paris d'hier et d'aujourd'hui* (Paris: Sevin & Rey, 1900).
41   Jules Clarette, *La Vie à Paris* (Paris, 1895).

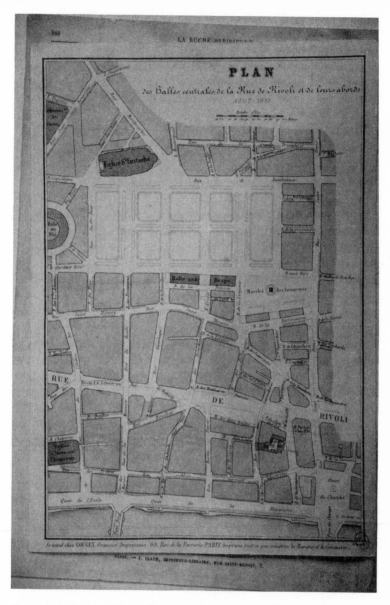

The market and quarter of Les Halles in 1850, before Haussmann's 'improvements'.

name of Rue Plâtrière when Jean-Jacques lived here, earning his living as a music copyist. 'His imagination', wrote Sébastien Mercier, 'dwelt only in the meadows, waters and woods, with their animated solitude. Yet as he approached the age of sixty, he came to live in Paris, in Rue Plâtrière, in other words the most noisy, uncomfortable, crowded and diseased of bad places.'

The destruction of the market halls in the 1970s was such a trauma that the demolitions of Baltard at the start of the Second Empire were almost forgotten.[42] Yet close to four hundred buildings had been razed to make way for the new market: the central street which became Rue Baltard continued Rue du Pont-Neuf towards the Pointe Saint-Eustache; Rue des Halles, which came obliquely from the Châtelet, and Rue Rambuteau, already opened up under Louis-Philippe, but which had to be widened. The land was cleared to construct the ten metal pavilions designed by Baltard, six to the east and four to the west of the central axis.[43] This was a brutal intervention right at the heart of the city, but – unlike the disaster of 1970 – it did no more than perpetuate an old tradition, by which this quarter was periodically transformed without ever losing its role or its spirit.

The first halls dated from Philippe Auguste, who had two great buildings constructed to cover a market that was already held there, in the open air, on a little hillock called Les Champeaux. These halls were surrounded by walls, and the gates closed at night; it was like entering a town. The surrounding buildings had a recessed ground floor and upper storeys supported by pillars, forming a gallery that housed shops. The *grands piliers* of Rue de la Tonnellerie [barrel-making] – in the line of the future Pont-Neuf – were differentiated from the *petits piliers*, those of the pewterers, which faced a small triangular place in front of the original small church of Saint-Eustache. This open-air market where three streets converged – Coquillière, Montmartre and Montorgeuil – was known as the Carreau des Halles, and wheat and fresh fish arrived here from the west and north. At the centre stood a fountain and a pillory that was like an inverted Bentham panopticon, 'an old octagonal stone tower with large windows at all sides of its upper level. In the middle of this tower was a rotating wooden device pierced with holes, for placing the head and arms of fraudulent bankrupts,

---

42   See Jean-Pierre Babelon, 'Les revelés d'architecture du quartier des Halles avant les destructions de 1852–1854', *Gazette des Beaux-Arts*, July–August 1967. This article reproduces the drawings commissioned by Davioud, with the object of keeping a record of the buildings that would be destroyed.
43   Baltard had begun by constructing a heavy stone pavilion, which Parisians soon came to call the 'fortress' of the Halles, and which was rejected and demolished.

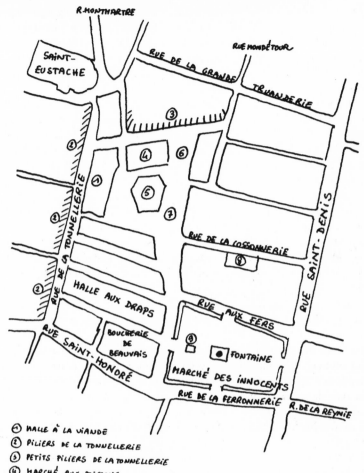

1. HALLE À LA VIANDE
2. PILIERS DE LA TONNELLERIE
3. PETITS PILIERS DE LA TONNELLERIE
4. MARCHÉ AUX POISSONS
5. MARCHÉ AUX ŒUFS
6. CARREAU DES HALLES
7. MARCHÉ AUX POIRÉES
8. HALLE AUX POISSONS D'EAU DOUCE
9. TOMBE DES MORTS DE JUILLET

extortionists and other condemned criminals of this kind. They were exposed there for three market days, two hours each day; and each half hour they were made to turn round in the pillory, exposed to the insults of the people.'[44]

The Innocents cemetery, the largest in Paris for a number of centuries, occupied the corner between Rue Saint-Denis and Rue de la Ferronnerie.[45] Philippe Auguste also had this surrounded by a wall with four gates. The dead were cast into common graves several metres deep, which could accommodate up to a thousand bodies. When one grave was full, it was closed and a new one dug. In the fifteenth century, the interior of the surrounding wall was supplemented by arched galleries with spaces above, a charnel house where bones from earlier graves were piled up to make room. On the side of Rue de la Ferronnerie, the walls of the gallery were decorated with a *danse macabre*, a motive found throughout France in these years. In an age when people were only too familiar with death, the cemetery was one of the most frequented places in Paris, just as the Galerie Mercière of the Palace of Justice and the gardens of the Palais-Royal were later on. It was a place to find linen-maids, public scribes, clothes merchants, sellers of books and pictures, and various kinds of charlatans.

The market had been somewhat disorderly ever since the time of Louis IX, who had authorized 'poor women' to retail sea fish close to the main fish market, a privilege retained until its final destruction: these are the women with their large red umbrellas that the young Haussmann encountered on his way to the Faculty of Law. Along the cemetery wall, linen-maids and old-clothes dealers were also able to present their wares free of charge. To the north of the Innocents, near the church of Saint-Leu-Saint-Gilles, Rue de la Grande-Truanderie well justified its name for a number of centuries: Sauval wrote that 'it took its name from the rogues who formerly lived here, and was not just a court of miracles, but perhaps the earliest and largest one in Paris'.

The first great 'reformation' of the Halles was conducted under Henri II in the early 1550s, at the same time as construction started on the church of Saint-Eustache. 'In 1551', wrote Gilles Corozet, 'the Halles of Paris were entirely knocked down and rebuilt, equipped with finely worked buildings, hotels and sumptuous houses for those townspeople who took

---

44   Jean-Aymar Piganiol de la Force, *Description historique de la ville de Paris et de ses environs* (Paris, 1765).
45   This section of Rue de la Ferronnerie is now known as Rue de La Reynie, after the first official to hold the post of lieutenant-general of police, in the latter years of the seventeenth century.

the old sites.'[46] The old wall of the Halles was then demolished, and future access was through regular streets. The allocation of space was more clearly defined. On the south side, where Rues des Bourdonnais, Sainte-Opportune, des Deux-Boules and des Lavandières now run, was the hall for linen and cloth. Butchers were also to be found there, though the greater part of their activity was in the quarter of Saint-Jacques-de-la-Boucherie – the Saint-Jacques tower is a vestige of this large church – where flocks were brought to the slaughterhouses on the hoof.

To the northwest, close to where the Bourse du Commerce now stands, was the Halle aux Blés, close to the hotel that Catherine de Médicis had built by Philibert de l'Orme ('A modern writer', stated Germain Brice two centuries later, 'whom one can follow on this occasion, says that, after the Louvre, there is no more noble building in the kingdom than this hotel.') On the northeast side, towards the Pointe Saint-Eustache, was the Carreau des Halles, extending to the market for *poirées*: 'Throughout the year, and every day, all kinds of vegetables and herbs are sold here, including medicinal ones, and all kinds of fruit and flowers, so that this place is a real garden, where the flowers and fruits of all seasons can be seen.'[47] This arrangement – textiles and meat to the south, grain, fish and vegetables to the north – would last until Baltard's time.

At the end of the ancien régime, the Halles were once again transformed from top to bottom. The hotel of Catherine de Médicis – Hôtel de Soissons – was demolished, and in its place Le Camus des Mézières built a new Halle aux Blés, a large circular building that Molinos covered in the 1780s with an immense wooden dome, an innovation new to Paris. The halls dating from the Renaissance were replaced by new buildings. And above all, the buildings surrounding the Innocents cemetery were pulled down, on Rues aux Fers[48] (now Berger), de la Lingerie and Saint-Denis.

This destruction did away with the church of Les Saints-Innocents, but spared the adjacent fountain, a monument much admired: 'Signor G. L. Bernini, one of the most renowned architects of the last several centuries, always very sparing with his praise, and who affected to think nothing of all the beautiful things that he saw in this city, could not prevent himself from exclaiming when he inspected this incomparable work, and declar-

---

46   Cited in Jean-Pierre Babelon, 'Le XVIe siècle', *Nouvelle Histoire de Paris* (Paris: Association pour la publication d'une histoire de Paris, 1986).

47   Piganiol de La Force, *Description historique de la ville de Paris*.

48   'Rue aux Fers, running like a river that carries fruit, flowers and vegetables, between the hundred booths on its right and the thousand little shops on its left . . .' Alexandre Dumas, *The Mohicans of Paris* (1854).

ing that he had not noticed anything like it in France.'[49] The fountain of
the Innocents was then given a fourth arch, completing those that Jean
Goujon had already sculpted, so that it no longer had to stand against a
wall, but could be placed at the centre of the new Marché des Innocents.
The cemetery, in fact, was closed. In an ecological vein, Mercier wrote
that 'in this narrowly enclosed space, infections attacked the life and health
of the inhabitants. The knowledge newly acquired about the nature of air
[Lavoisier!] had cast light on the danger of this mephitism ... The danger
was imminent; soup and milk spoiled in a few hours in the houses close to
the cemetery; wine turned acid when it was poured; and the miasmas from
the corpses threatened to poison the atmosphere.' The skeletons were then
removed to the quarries to the south of Paris that became the Catacombes:
'We can only imagine the lit torches, this immense grave opened for the
first time, the many beds of corpses suddenly stirred, the debris of skeletons,
the sparse lights fuelled by the planks of coffins, the moving shadows of
funeral crosses, this fearsome precinct suddenly lit up in the silence of the
night.'[50]

The Paris landscape can be understood from observing the development of
the Halles site over the centuries. It is impossible to avoid a sense of regret
for the ridiculous fate of this place, which, as Sauval wrote centuries ago,
'is full of everything: vegetables, the fruit of gardens and fields, fish from
river and sea, things that can assist the convenience and delights of life, and
indeed all that is most excellent, exquisite and rare in land and air, arriving in Paris and taken there'. But despite such regret, we should not forget
the circumstances that led to this end. Louis Chevalier observed it from
the inside, hearing all the arguments brought up in bad faith in favour of
destruction:

> The economic argument, the most mysterious and obscure ... was the
> one most often cited. And then public health. The legendary dirtiness
> of the Halles ... I cite the words that I found in these speeches as they
> come, without trying to put them in order – as one might arrange goods
> for sale, vegetables for example, in harmonious constructions that, under
> the striking light of lamps, exude order, beauty, taste, and indeed, to
> be sure, cleanliness ... To dramatize things still more, rats ... And to
> complete this spectacle à la Gustave Doré, Villon's fat prostitutes, who

49   Brice, *Nouvelle Description de la ville de Paris*. One of the fountain's great champions was Quatremère de Quincy.
50   Mercier, *Tableau de Paris*.

were certainly not very discreet, and some of whom even displayed their charms on the steps of Saint-Eustache.[51]

Chevalier went to see his old fellow student from the École Normale Supérieure, Georges Pompidou, whom he had dinner with from time to time: 'It seemed to me – pure illusion, perhaps – that Pompidou, knowing how my ideas on the matter were quite the opposite of his own, cast me an inflexible and facetious glance that undoubtedly meant that with people of my sort, Parisians would still be stuck in the huts where Caesar found them.'

Once the decision was made to transfer the market to Rungis, disaster was certain. The 1960s and '70s were an all-time low for French architecture. Major commissions went to members of the Institut de France, to whom we owe – among other things – the administrative building on Boulevard Morland with its pergola, the Palais des Congrès at Porte Maillot, the Tour Montparnasse, the Radio building, and the Faculty of Sciences at Jussieu. And in a detrimental scissors effect, corruption and collusion within semipublic companies, between the promoters and scoundrels of Parisian Gaullism, was at its height. It was not enough, therefore, to pull down Baltard's pavilions: to make the operation profitable, the destruction had to spread far wider. The space between Rue de Turbigo and what remained of Rue Rambuteau, and the whole region between what was Rue Berger and Rue de la Ferronnerie, were replaced by office blocks and flats so aggressive in their ugliness that you have to go a long way – the far end of the Italie quarter or the Front de Seine – to find their match. On top of all this, the 'gardens' on the site of Les Halles also show what decrepitude French landscapists had reached in their art. Hemmed in by mutilated streets, decked out in the worst panoply of postmodernism, these 'spaces' transform the old itineraries of Paris into assault courses, by their complex arrangement of metal barriers, ventilation columns, walkways overlooking ditches of wretched plantations, the orifices of underground roads, and fountains clogged up with empty drink cans. As for the underground shopping mall that goes by the noble name of Forum, the most surprising thing is that its author is still classed as an architect. But the whole ensemble is so badly constructed, with such poor materials, that its ruin in the near future is inevitable. One might even say it has already begun.

The Beaubourg plateau, between Rue Beaubourg and Rue Saint-Martin, bounded to the north by Rue du Grenier-Saint-Lazare and to the south by the church of Saint-Merri, is an outcrop of Les Halles, linked to

---

51   Louis Chevalier, *L'Assassinat de Paris* (Paris: Calmann-Lévy, 1977).

them – across Boulevard Sébastopol – by the very old streets of Rue de Leynie and Rue Aubry-le-Boucher. In the 1950s Doisneau photographed this 'old rubbish-tip of the Halles where lorries park, where an entire nighttime population comes out to work – and sometimes to play – in the shadows, far from the pavilions dazzling with light, like actors warming up in the corridor before going on stage'.[52] This immense paved promenade, this strange emptiness in such a dense region, was the work of Haussmann, though not finished until the 1930s. He assiduously destroyed the network of little streets – Rues Maubuée, de la Corroierie, des Vieilles-Étuves, du Poirier, du Maure – that had served as a tragic setting for almost all the insurrections of the first half of the nineteenth century. The minuscule Rue de Venise, opposite the Centre Beaubourg, is the sole remaining vestige of this group, which used to be known as the Cloître Saint-Merri, and which the *journées* of June 1832 made famous throughout Europe. Around the Centre itself, which is now part of the Parisian landscape – good architecture always ends up triumphing over whinging critics – , semipublic companies have wrought their ravages: the 'Horloge quarter' with its gloomy passages, bankrupt shops, wretched gadgets and suspect smells, has the same relationship to a genuine quarter as a works canteen has to a traditional Paris bistro.

Sentier

The district marked out between Les Halles and the Grands Boulevards is underpinned and organized by Rue Montmartre, which plays the role of guardian to two successive enclaves, one on each side of Rue Réaumur. Previously, it was the Montorgueil quarter that approached Rue Montmartre via Rue Tiquetonne, Rue Bachaumont built on the site of the Passage du Saumon, and Rue Léopold-Bellan, which in the eighteenth century had the lovely name of Rue du Bout-du-Monde. Despite its new guise as a pedestrian zone, Rue Montorgueil remains lively by virtue of its market, which, even if not completely genuine, plays the same protective role as Rue Mouffetard or – increasingly less so – Rue de Buci. Further afield, between Rue Réuamur and Boulevard Montmartre, is the old press quarter, which long predates rotary printing. Lucien de Rubempré, when he 'went out one morning with the triumphant idea of finding some colonel of such light skirmishers of the press . . . arrived in the Rue Saint-Fiacre off the Boulevard Montmartre. Before a house, occupied by the offices of a small newspaper, he stopped,

---

52   Ibid.

and at the sight of it his heart began to throb as heavily as the pulses of a youth upon the threshold of some evil haunt.'[53]

In the heyday of the daily press, between the end of the Second Empire and the First World War, all the major newspapers, even the less major ones, had their editorial office and printing press one above the other in the same building. *Le Petit Journal* was on the corner of Rue de Richelieu and Boulevard Montmartre, which had been the site of the famous Frascati's. The ground floor was occupied by a bookshop and an immense bazaar, where an aquarium of exotic fish jostled with the works of Corot and Meissonier. In the Rue Montmartre, at the end of the century, you had *La Presse, La France, La Liberté, Le Journal des voyages*, and the Paul Dupont printworks, whose building housed *L'Univers, Le Jockey, Le Radical* and *L'Aurore*. Rue de Croissant was the site of *La Patrie, Le Hanneton, Le Père Duchesne, Le Siècle, La République, L'Écho de l'armée* and *L'Intransigeant*. *Le Soleil* was in Rue Saint-Joseph, *L'Illustration* in Rue de Richelieu, *La Rue* and *Le Cri du peuple* in Rue d'Aboukir. Some newspapers had crossed Boulevard Montmartre: *Le Temps* was in Rue du Faubourg-Montmartre, *La Marseillaise* in Rue Bergère, and *Le Figaro* at 26 Rue Drouot, in a fine neo-Gothic building. Léon Daudet recalled:

> This is where I made a start in 1892 under Magnard. I signed short pointed moral tales and rather acerbic snippets as 'a modern young man'. At the same time, Barrès, a young man himself, and as lively and fond of a joke as I was, was a contributor to this illustrious house. We were Magnard's darlings, and he kept us in his private office while more important figures kicked their heels on the floor below, decorated with a bust of Villemessant. One day we noticed Verlaine in the cashier's office, with his face of a retired satyr. He'd come for his money, not very much – a group of us had given him a little pension. Naturally he was drunk, and raising a fat and dirty finger in the air, he laughed and repeated with a malicious and indescribable air: 'notwithstanding ... however'.[54]

It is not so far back that you could not even imagine driving by car along Rue du Croissant, where lorries were constantly discharging spools of paper for the Imprimerie de la Presse. The crisis of the written press, the merger of titles, and the migration of printing works to the suburbs, have left behind only pale vestiges of this glorious age: the *Figaro* building on the corner of Rue du Mail, the *Tribune* building, the fine caryatids of the building of

53   Balzac, *Lost Illusions.*
54   Léon Daudet, *Paris vécu* (Paris, 1929).

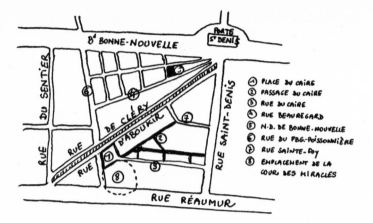

La France, journal du soir, and the plaque on the Café du Croissant recalling that 'Jaurès was assassinated here on 31 July 1914'. Along Rues du Croissant, des Jeûneurs and Saint-Joseph, the neighbouring Sentier quarter has infiltrated into the gaps left by the press.

The Sentier is today the only Parisian quarter whose name denotes both a territory, an economic activity that was exclusive to it until recent times – the garment trade – and a social type. The recent establishment here of 'new technologies' has increased property prices, but has not yet shattered the Sephardic monopoly or reduced the bottlenecks, which are the worst in Paris. Other names of quarters also used to have this ability to characterize their inhabitants. From the ancien régime to the era of Les Misérables, coming from the Faubourg Saint-Marcel meant, for Sébastien Mercier, belonging to 'the poorest section of the Paris population, the most rebellious and refractory'. Through to the 1950s, coming from Belleville and even Montmartre was almost equivalent to stating one's skin colour. These particularisms have disappeared, except for the Sentier, which remains a quarter difficult to enter, physically isolated, socially removed, little studied or visited, famous but poorly known.[55]

---

55 The very origin of the name is unclear: whether a *sentier* or path leading to the rampart, or a corruption of *chantier* (works), building here having started on the site of a large woodyard. Two books recently published are Werner Szambien and Simona Talenti (eds), *Le-Sentier-Bonne-Nouvelle, de l'architecture à la mode* (Paris: Action artistique de la Ville de Paris, 1999), and Nancy Green, *Du Sentier à la 7e avenue, la confection et les immigrés, Paris-New York 1880–1980* (Paris: Le Seuil, 1998). Nadine Vasseur, *Il était une fois le Sentier* (Paris: Liana Levi, 2000), has some interesting material on the economic activity of the quarter today.

It is often believed that Jews who arrived in France at the end of the Algerian war took over the rag trade from East European Jews, who had arrived in successive waves between the great pogroms of the early twentieth century and the 1930s. In reality, the Sentier's textile tradition goes back much further. In the eighteenth century, the Compagnie des Indes, which imported cotton among other things, had its premises near Rue du Sentier. Local manufacturers and dyers were unhappy with this competition, and waged a veritable 'battle of cottons' against it. The Marquise de Pompadour, who had been born in the quarter on Rue de Cléry, and lived at 33 Rue du Sentier when she married the farmer-general Le Normant d'Étioles, backed the promotion of local cloth by using it for her interior decoration. The development of the textile industry then led to the construction of a particular kind of building, many examples of which are still to be seen. In the details, their vocabulary is that of neoclassicism, but what is unusual, and gives Rue de Cléry, Rue d'Aboukir and Rue d'Alexandre their particular physiognomy, is the density of buildings and their great height: the same building had to house the shop, the warehouse on the courtyard, the production workshops on the upper floors, as well as family accommodation. This combination of density and height is a characteristic of immigrant quarters in big cities everywhere: the Sentier's buildings recall those of the Venice Ghetto, as well as those of another historical textile district, La Croix-Rousse in Lyon.

In the twentieth century, each historical period saw the arrival of new immigrants here. In the last twenty years, it has been Turks (often Kurds), Serbs, Southeast Asians and Chinese, Pakistanis, Sri Lankans, Bangladeshis, Senegalese and Malians who have come to offer their labour-power as packers or finishers, when they are not simply employed by the hour or the day to unload a lorry or clear a warehouse.

The Sentier is shaped like a square, its boundaries being Rues Réaumur and Saint-Denis, Boulevard de Bonne-Nouvelle and Rue du Sentier. It is divided in two by the diagonal of Rue de Cléry and Rue d'Aboukir, stretching between the Porte Saint-Denis and the Place des Victoires along a segment of the walls of Charles V whose traces are still very clear: Rue de Cléry is built on the counterscarp of the wall, and Rue d'Aboukir, very clearly lower, takes the line of the moat (it was formerly known as Rue du Milieu-du-Fossé, before being changed to Rue de Bourbon-Villeneuve, then to Aboukir in 1848).

Of the two triangles divided by this diagonal, the more frenetic is on the side of Rue Réaumur and Rue Saint-Denis. This is Paris's 'return from Egypt' quarter.[56] The street names (Rue du Nil, Rue d'Alexandrie, Rue

---

56   Apart from the modest Palmier fountain on Rue de Sèvres, however, close to Métro Vaneau, I can see no other architectural evidence of the Egyptomania of that time.

de Damiette, Rue du Caire), and above all the extraordinary façade that frames the entrance to the arcade from the Place du Caire – columns with lotus capitals, incised frieze in the Egyptian style, the three heads of the goddess Hathor – are evidence of the enthusiasm of Parisians for Egypt at the time of Bonaparte's expedition, an enthusiasm that remains today.

The Place du Caire, where Pakistanis and Malians wait with their trolleys throughout the day, occupies the former site of the city's largest court of miracles.[57] As Sauval put it:

> A place of very considerable size, and a very large cul-de-sac – stinking, muddy, irregular and devoid of any paving. Previously confined to the outer limits of Paris, it is now located in one of the most badly built, dirty and out-of-the-way quarters of the city ... like another world ... When the ditches and ramparts of the Porte Saint-Denis were removed to the place where we see them now,[58] the commissioners conducting this undertaking resolved to cut through this court of miracles with a street that would ascend from Rue Saint-Sauveur to Rue Neuve-Saint-Sauveur; but whatever they might do, they found it impossible to bring this to completion: the builders who started work on the street were beaten by the ruffians there, and these rogues threatened those in charge with an even worse fate.

What a time!

At the heart of the quarter, in the Passage du Caire which is the oldest of Paris arcades (1798), several shops, including the finest of their number, exhibit material for shop windows – mannequins, busts, gilded price-tags, plastic trees and paper fur. This activity continues the oldest tradition of this arcade, specialized from its origins in lithography for *calicots*, which were the streamers with which shops announced their wares.[59]

The opposite triangle – opposite in every sense of the word – is the section of the Sentier bordering on Boulevard de Bonne-Nouvelle, built on an artificial hillock made up of rubble, mud and filth of all kinds that

---

57   There were a number of these, particularly on the Rue de la Truanderie, as already mentioned, Rue des Tournelles, Rue Saint-Denis, Rue de la Jussienne, and on the Butte Saint-Roche, which specialized in prostitution.

58   This is the wall 'des Fossés jaunes'; see above, p 20, n.9.

59   By extension, the word came to denote shop workers: 'I do not at all hesitate to write – monstrous as this may seem to serious writers on art – that it was the sales clerk [*calicot*] who launched lithography', Henri Bouchot, *La Lithographie* (Paris, 1895), cited by Benjamin, *The Arcades Project*, p. 57.

accumulated over the centuries and was called the Butte-aux-Gravois.[60] Under the League, the windmills and the small church that crowned this hill were razed in order to fortify the rampart. And it is still with the air of a wall that buildings overlook the boulevard on the side of Rue de la Lune or Rue Notre-Dame-de-Bonne-Nouvelle, while Rue Beauregard recalls the view it once offered over the country to the north, with the windmills of Montmartre in the distance.

You climb from the Porte Saint-Denis to the Butte-aux-Gravois past the strangely sharp edges of the buildings at the end of Rues de la Lune, Beauregard, and de Cléry. Further up the quarter, Rues Notre-Dame-de-Recouvrance, de la Ville-Neuve and Thorel are old streets where certain walls have low openings that are neither doors nor windows, but the displays of former shops. In Egypt, bakeries still open onto the street through small basement windows with grills that are opened when the bread is cooked.

Of the church of Notre-Dame-de-Bonne-Nouvelle, built in the seventeenth century, there only remains the bell tower, whose inclination towards Rue Beauregard denotes an unstable subsoil.[61] The rest of the present building dates from the 1820s, so that it was in a nearly new church that the funeral of gentle Coralie took place in *Lost Illusions*, after she had been forced by Lucien de Rubempré's escapades to leave her dwelling on Rue de Vendôme (now Béranger) for a fourth-floor apartment on Rue de la Lune.

The border between Les Halles and the Sentier on one side, and the Marais on the other, is formed by three north-south axes in close parallel: Rue Saint-Denis and Rue Saint-Martin, which are old Roman roads, and, in the middle, Haussmann's cutting par excellence, the Boulevard de Sébastopol. The contrast between Rue Saint-Denis with its metered sex, bloody memories, and nighttime brawls, and the chaste and peaceful Rue Saint-Martin, can already be read from the boulevard, on the two gates that the Paris burgesses dedicated to 'Ludovico Magno' (Louis XIV). The

---

60   There existed – and still do – several mounds of the same kind in Paris: the labyrinth in the Jardin des Plantes on which Verniquet constructed his belvedere, La Butte des Moulins whose terrible nighttime fauna has already been noted, and the promontory above Rue Meslay and the pavements of Boulevard Saint-Martin, close to the Place de la République.

61   Hillairet notes that 'the excavations carried out in 1824 for the foundations of the new church showed successive stratifications over the original ground to a height of nearly 16 metres. The site had been a vineyard, and still intact stocks were recovered from it' (*Connaissance du Vieux Paris* [Paris: Éditions Princesse, 1956]).

Porte Saint-Martin with its vermicular embossage and calm bas-reliefs is as modest as a triumphal arch can be. The 'very fine and very useless Porte Saint-Denis,' as André Breton calls it in *Nadja*, presents on the contrary the political-decorative programme of absolute monarchy at its apogee:

> Its main gate stands between two pyramids set into the body of the arch and decorated with falling weapons as trophies, ending with two globes with the arms of France ... At the base of these pyramids are two colossal statues, one of which represents Holland in the figure of a woman in dismay seated on a crouched and dying lion, which holds in its paws seven arrows denoting the United Provinces. The other symmetrical statue is that of a river, holding a cornucopia and representing the Rhine. In the tympani are two Fames, one of which, by the sound of its trumpet, announces to the whole earth that the king's army has just crossed the Rhine in the presence of his enemies ... The bas-relief on the face of the gate facing the faubourg represents the taking of Maastricht.[62]

There is an interesting parallel with the ceiling of the Painted Hall at the Royal Naval College in Greenwich, where the defeated Louis XIV drags himself wretchedly at the feet of William III.

Though Rue Saint-Denis is pretty down-at-heel, and not all its shops brilliant, it keeps the unity and noble vestiges of a royal road. To cite Sauval again:

> In olden times Rue Saint-Denis was known for a long while simply as the Grand'Rue, as if for its excellence. In 1273, it was still referred to as *magnus vicus* ... This was very fitting, for not only was it for many centuries the only main road in the quarter that we call the Ville, but also the only road leading to the Cité, which made up the whole of Paris at this time. Subsequently, it served as another triumphal way by which our kings generally made their magnificent entrances when they came to the throne, after their coronation, on their marriages, or on their victorious return from defeating their enemies; and finally, for more than three hundred years, it was the route they were carried after their death to Saint-Denis, where their mausoleums are.

The buildings bordering the street are very old, rickety and irregular towards Les Halles, with a proliferation of sex shops and peep shows, shading to fine neoclassical residences as you approach the Porte Saint-Denis.

---

62 Piganiol de La Force, *Description historique de la ville de Paris*.

Rue Saint-Martin, by comparison, is almost village-like. This is not just a matter of toponymy, running as it does past Saint-Martin-des-Champs and Saint-Nicolas-des-Champs. It is wide and airy, with a fine place to pause under the chestnut trees of the square facing the high wall of the Conservatoire des Arts et Métiers. Towards the centre, you still have the narrowness of a medieval street, but greatly deteriorated. It is better to take Rue Quincampoix, which has hardly changed since John Law established his central bank there, and 'crowds rushed into this narrow street to convert coin into paper'.[63]

Marais

Once you cross Rue Saint-Martin – some would rather say Rue Beaubourg – you enter the Marais.[64] The appearance of this word to denote a region of Paris is relatively recent: it was not until the seventeenth century that only the zone of the Marais that was still really marshy was called by that name, around the present convergence of Rues de Turenne, Vieille-du-Temple, de Bretagne and des Filles-du-Calvaire, not far from the Cirque d'Hiver.[65] In referring to the Paris quarter, *marais* means a region of watered gardens (*maraîchers*) rather than an actual marsh. If there was such a marsh, if the battle of Lutetia between Camulogène and Caesar took place around here, the fortifications of Charles V subsequently served as a dyke, and its moats as a drainage canal. This arrangement is still very visible: Boulevard Beaumarchais, built on the line of the walls, is in such a raised position that Rue des Tournelles and Rue Saint-Gilles, coming from the Marais, have to rise quite steeply in their final stretch in order to meet it. And on the other side, to descend to Rue Amelot – formerly Rue des Fossés-du-Temple – it was necessary to install a stairway.

---

63 'In the evening, people carrying bags and demanding paper notes had to be driven away. There were those with millions in their pocket; some believed they had twelve, twenty, or thirty million. There was the hunchback who lent his hump to speculators as a kind of platform, making himself rich in a matter of days; the lackey who bought his master's carriage. The demon of greed brought the philosopher out of his study, and you could see him mingle in the crowd of gamblers and purchase the paper he wanted' (Mercier, *Tableau de Paris*).

64 Except to the north, near the Boulevards, where the triangle of Arts-et-Métiers and the magnificent parallels of Rues Meslay, Notre-Dame-de-Nazareth and du Vertbois intersect between Rue Saint-Martin and Rue de Turbigo, forming a transition between the Sentier and the Marais.

65 This marsh was the remains of the ancient course of the Seine, which then followed the line of Rues du Château-d'Eau, de Provence, Saint-Lazare and La Boétie, rejoining the present river at the Pont de l'Alma. It thus described a wide meander at the foot of the hills of Belleville, Montmartre and Chaillot.

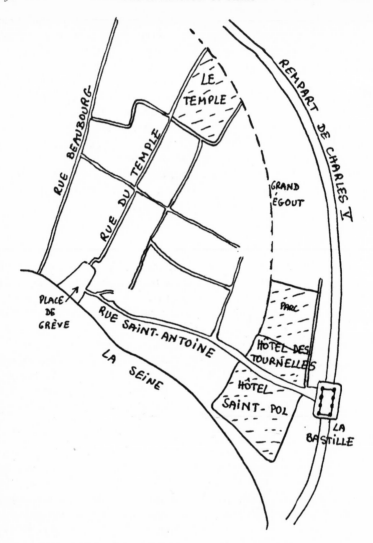

It is strange, and has no other equivalent in Paris, how the physiognomy of the Marais today is haunted by the phantoms of three great domains, which have left their names and yet not a single stone: the Temple, the Hôtel Saint-Pol and the Hôtel des Tournelles.

The mother house of the order of Knights Templar, founded in Jerusalem in the twelfth century, was located at the far end of the region's major north-south axis, on Rue du Temple.[66] Its lands fell into two distinct sections. The heart was the *enclos*, a fortified quadrilateral whose boundaries would now be Rues du Temple, de Bretagne, Charlot and Béranger. At the centre of this enclosure was the keep, used as a prison for Louis XVI and his family after 10 August 1792, and later for Babeuf and Cadoudal. A large part of the enclosure was rented out to artisans, exempt here from tax as in all the religious precincts of the city.

To the south and east of the enclosure, the Templars possessed large tracts of agricultural land: this was the *censive*, whose limits defined a further quadrilateral, extending to Rue du Roi-de-Sicile and thus corresponding to a large section of the Marais today. The wall of Philippe Auguste cut through this *censive*, along the line of Rue des Francs-Bourgeois.[67] On the side facing the city, these lands were gradually populated along the axes, particularly along Rue Vieille-du-Temple, which was then called Rue de la Couture-du-Temple [*couture* = cultivation], but on the outward side there was nothing but market gardens until the sixteenth century.

The other major axis of the Marais, its east-west orientation, was Rue Saint-Antoine, as it still is today. At the end of this, the outer limit of Paris, two royal dwellings stood face to face, the Hôtel Saint-Pol and the Hôtel des Tournelles. Saint-Pol was the creation of the Dauphin, the future Charles V. Tired of the old Palais de la Cité, where he had been forced to confront popular insurrection and Étienne Marcel, he decided to establish himself somewhere more calm. He bought buildings and gardens from the Comte d'Étampes, the archbishop of Sens, and the abbés of Saint-Maur, ending up with all of the land between Rue Saint-Antoine and the Seine, and from Rue Saint-Paul right through to Rue du Petit-Musc. Saint-Pol was not a single building, an *hôtel* in the usual sense, but rather a group of buildings surrounded by gardens, and linked by covered galleries that framed a succession of courtyards, a cherry orchard, a vineyard, a *sauvoir* for raising salmon, aviaries, and a menagerie where lions were kept, pensioners of the hotel down to its final days. (In his *Vies des dames galantes*, Brantôme recalled how 'one day when François I was amusing himself by watching his lions fighting, a lady who had let her glove fall said to de Lorges: if you

---

66 Until the twentieth century, the present Rue du Temple, heading north, went successively under the names of Rue Barre-du-Bec and Rue Saint-Avoye, becoming Rue du Temple at the junction with Rue Michel-le-Comte.

67 On the present site of the Hôtel d'Almeyras, there was in the fifteenth century a 'house of alms'. 'It was this asylum that gave the street the name Francs-Bourgeois, since those who stayed in this hospital were "*francs*", i.e., exempt from all taxes and charges' (Jaillot, *Recherches critiques, historiques et topographique sur la ville de Paris* [Paris, 1782; reissued Paris: Berger-Levrault, 1977]).

want me to believe that you love me as much as you swear every day, go
and pick up my glove. De Lorges went down into the lions' den, picked
up the glove from among these fearsome animals, came up, threw it in the
lady's face, and since then, despite all the troubles and pains that she took
towards him, never wanted to see her again.')

From the main gate of the Hôtel Saint-Pol you could see on the other
side of Rue Saint-Antoine the gateway of the Hôtel des Tournelles, which,
according to Piganiol de La Force, 'took its name from the number of
towers by which it was surrounded'. In the 1420s, under the English occupation, the Duke of Bedford, acting as regent, made his residence in a
small hotel that was situated between Rue de Birague and the Impasse
Guéménée. 'John, Duke of Bedford, stayed there during the disturbances
of the Bourguignons and the Armagnacs', wrote Sauval. 'He extended it
and had it magnificently built, so that it has since been a royal residence,
which our kings have preferred to Saint-Pol, and where Charles VII, Louis
XI, Charles VIII, Louis XII and François I all stayed for long periods.'
Piganiol de La Force relates that 'this palace counted several courtyards,
a number of chapels, twelve galleries, two parks and six large gardens, as
well as a labyrinth known as the Daedalus, and a further garden or park
of nine acres, which the Duke of Bedford had his gardener plough up'.[68]
After its return to the French crown, the hotel was surrounded by a large
park, where François I raised camels and ostriches, and which gave its name
to Rue du Parc-Royal. The park was also used for equestrian sports, but
tournaments as such were held on Rue Saint-Antoine, which was widened
between the two hôtels, a layout that still exists alongside the statue of
Beaumarchais.

The way in which these three groups of buildings disappeared goes a
long way to explain the contemporary Marais. The Hôtel Saint-Pol was the
first to go: François I, always short of money and wanting to renovate the
Louvre and make his residence there, decided to sell it off as building plots.
'There is no longer anything remaining of these buildings, which included
a large number of hôtels, such as the Hôtel de La Pissotte, the Hôtel de
Beautreillis, the Hôtel-de-la-Reine, the Hôtel Neuf (known as the Hôtel
d'Étampes), etc. And it is on their ruins that the streets were laid out that
are now those of the Saint-Paul quarter as far as the ditches of the Arsenal,
and preserve the names of the buildings that were there at the time of the
Hôtel Saint-Pol, such as Rues de Beautreillis, des Lions, du Petit-Musc and

68 Piganiol was writing after the destruction, but he had access to archives that
have since disappeared. Bedford had acquired lands to the west, as far as what is
now Rue de Turenne (at that time still an open sewer). Rue des Tournelles ran
between Bedford's lands and the wall.

de la Cerisaie.'[69] Like all of the Marais that was built in the Renaissance, this part of the Saint-Paul quarter, despite the street names that seem taken from an illuminated manuscript, was designed in a modern fashion: the plots are regular, and the streets laid out in a grid, in contrast with the medieval lattice beside the Hôtel de Sens, Rue des Nonnains-d'Hyères and Rue de l'Ave-Maria.

The destruction of the Hôtel des Tournelles was not provoked by financial difficulties but by an accident: in 1559, while a tournament was being held in Rue Saint-Antoine to celebrate the marriage of the princesses, Henri II was mortally wounded in front of the palace by the blow of a lance wielded by Gabriel de Montgomery, 'the fairest man and the best man-at-arms of that time', according to Sauval. Catherine de Médicis, his widow, decided to raze the hotel to the ground, and moved into her new hotel close to the Halles. The abandoned park was for many years the site of a horse market.

During this time, however, in the more central part of the Marais, a new quarter was constructed between the two fortifications – the wall of Philippe Auguste around the central and denser part of the city, and the wall of Charles V, which ran through open fields. Once the 'false gates' of the old fortifications were crossed, you entered a region where gardeners peacefully cultivated their cabbages and leeks. This was a paradise for property developers, as demand was strong in the first half of the sixteenth century, before the Wars of Religion. François I set the example by dividing up the Hôtel de Tancarville, whose lands were located on each side of the wall of Phillipe Auguste, at the corner of Rue Vieille-du-Temple and Rue des Rosiers. The religious communities – in particular Saint-Catherine-du-Val-des-Écoliers, which owned the wide fields of Sainte-Catherine, towards Rue Payenne – likewise sold off their lands for building.[70] The movement extended along Rue Barbette and Rue Elzévir. A modern quarter was built there, much influenced by the new taste that came in from Italy, the Hôtel Carnavalet being a sumptuous example among the buildings that remain.

This surge, held back for a long while by the Wars of Religion, the League, and the terrible siege, got under way again when Henri IV entered Paris in 1594. Through the voice of the provost marshal, he proclaimed that 'his intention is to spend years in this city, and live there like a true

---

69 Hurtaut and Magny, *Dictionnaire historique de la ville de Paris et de ses environs* (Paris: Moutard, 1779; reissued Geneva: Reprint Minkoff, 1973).
70 Many religious communities have left their names to Marais streets: the Blancs-Manteaux, the Guillemites, the Hospitalière de Saint-Gervais, the Minimes, the Haudriettes, the Célestins …

patriot, to make this city beautiful, tranquil, and full of all the conveniences and ornaments that will be possible, desiring the completion of the Pont-Neuf and the restoration of fountains ... even desiring to make a whole world of this city and a wonder of the world, in which respect he displays towards us a love that is more than fatherly'.[71]

What was then lacking in the Marais – and in Paris more generally – was a large square 'for the inhabitants of our city, who are most tightly pressed in their houses owing to the multitude of people who arrive from all directions'.[72] Henri IV and Sully had the idea of constructing this Place Royale (now the Place des Vosges) on the Parc des Tournelles, which had been neglected, being far from the centre. And to kill two birds with one stone, the king decided to establish on the north side of the square a manufactory for silk sheets embroidered with gold and silver thread, a luxury product that had up till then been imported from Milan:

> And indeed in 1605 those who were to undertake these manufactories had put up a large building that occupied all of one side. The king for his part marked out there a large place some seventy-two yards square which he desired to be known as the Place Royale, and he gave sites on the three other sides for one gold écu in tax (*cens*), in return for covering them with pavilions according to the elevations to be supplied to them. As well as this, he had the streets leading to them widened and began at his own expense both the royal pavilion, placed at the end of Rue Royale [now de Birague], and the pavilion of the queen, placed at the end of Rue du Parc-Royal ... Each pavilion consisted of three storeys, all built in brick, with stone arches, piers, embrasures, entablatures and pillars, all covered with a slate roof in two sections, ending in a ridge garnished with lead. The red of the brick, the white of the stone and the black of the slate and the lead made such an agreeable mixture or shading of colours ... that it has since been used even for the houses of the bourgeois.[73]

Elegant shops were established under the arches, but there were also bawdy houses (*tripots*), as later at the Palais-Royal, and it became a favourite place

71   Cited in Jean-Pierre Babelon, 'Henri IV urbaniste de Paris', in *Festival du Marais*, exhibition catalogue (Paris, 1966).
72   'Lettres patentes pour la place Royale' (1605), reproduced in Babelon, 'Henri IV urbaniste'.
73   Sauval, *Histoires et recherches des antiquités de la ville de Paris*. The manufactory soon went into decline, and the fourth side of the square was then built up to match the other three.

for prostitutes.[74] The centre of the square, inaugurated by Louis XIII at the great festival of 1612, was flat, sandy, and clear; it was used as a ground for equestrian events, tournaments, tilting, and sometimes also for duels, some of which have remained famous.[75]

Not far from here, Henri IV and Sully had conceived another great site, a kind of administrative complex that would house the Grand Conseil as well as other bodies. There was an opportunity to be had, as the grand prior of the Temple was dividing up his *censive*. The projected 'Place de France' was a semicircle whose diameter – close to two hundred metres – would coincide with the fortifications. A new royal gate, between Rue du Pont-aux-Choux and Rue des Filles-du-Calvaire, opened towards the road to Meaux and Germany. Six streets radiated from the place in the direction of the city, bearing the names of those provinces that were seats of sovereign courts – the first example, Sauval says, of streets named geographically. The design of diverging roads from a city gate was fashionable at the time, after the trident from the Porta del Popolo in Rome.[76] The project came to an end with the death of Henri IV, but it persists in the name of certain streets (Poitou, Picardie, Saintonge, Perche, Normandie ...), which, even if they do not correspond to the original plan, perpetuate its toponomy. The initial design is also recalled by the radial course of Rue de Bretagne, and espe-cially the semicircle formed by Rue Debelleyme. There also remains the market of Les Enfants-Rouges,[77] intended to supply these large establish-ments. Ravaillac had a greater influence than is generally imagined on the

---

74 As Babelon notes, the word *tripot* originally denoted a tennis court. But it soon came to have its later sense.

75 Somewhat later, in 1639, Richelieu had the equestrian statue of Louis XIII erected in the centre of the square, hoping that it would intimidate duellists. The railings were installed towards the end of that century.

76 The details of this project have been preserved thanks to an engraving after Claude Chastillon, the engineer in charge, already at work on the alignments of the Place Royale. In the foreground of this bird's-eye view, on a wide canal parallel to the lower edge of the image (the ditch of the fortification), are barges carrying barrels. Right at the bottom, across the canal on the far side (this is the land of the convent of the Filles du Calvaire), are carriages, horsemen and walkers. There is a bridge over the canal, with a triumphal arch in the Italian style with embossments, niches and statues. On the bank facing the city, a long building parallel to the canal is breached at the centre by an imposing gate that gives access to the Place. Bordered by seven identical pavilions, this is a kind of archaic version of the Place Royale, with corner turrets and high pointed roofs with skylights. Between the pavilions, six diverging streets point towards the Louvre, Notre-Dame, Saint-Paul, and the distant hills, crowned with churches and windmills.

77 Les Enfants-Rouge was an orphanage founded by François I, whose young wards were dressed in red.

Paris cityscape, for if this great project had been concluded, the centre of gravity would have been permanently shifted eastward.

Since the timescale of places is neither continuous nor homogeneous, a quarter can suddenly gather speed, so that events that previously took two centuries now happen in twenty years. With the Place Royale and its surroundings, this was the first time that a Paris quarter was specifically designed for what was not yet called *flânerie*, a 'promenade' for a society that was reviving after the nightmare of the Wars of Religion. There was no peace as yet: in 1636, the very time when the fashion for Spain was at its height and *Le Cid* was having its premiere in Paris, the Spanish army had reached Corbie, three days' march from the city; it was a good while yet until the danger was allayed, after the battle of Rocroi. Nor was there religious tolerance: in 1614, in a memorandum from the Ville de Paris to the États Généraux, the desire was expressed that Jews, Anabaptists and others not professing the Catholic faith, or the reformed religion 'tolerated by the edicts', should be put to death.[78] All the same, a kind of love affair developed between the new quarter and a certain cultivated aristocracy, an open-minded haute bourgeoisie, and an intellectual and artistic milieu that was rapidly expanding. One of Corneille's first plays was *La Place Royale* (1635); it did not actually deal with the place itself, but it is revealing that he chose this title for a play about fashionable youth.[79] Ten years later, when the valet of Dorante, Corneille's eponymous *Liar*, is charged with inquiring about a pleasant encounter in the street: 'The coachman's tongue has done its duty well/The fairest of the two, he says, is my mistress,/She lives on the place, and her name is Lucrèce.'/ 'What place?' 'Royale, and the other lives there too.' Paul Scarron, leaving the quarter, said his *Adieux aux Marets et à la place Royale*: 'Farewell then until after the fair/When you shall see me return/For who can stand living for long /So far from the Place Royale?/ Farewell fine place where only live/Persons of true elite,/And farewell such illustrious place/The lustre of an illustrious city.'

It was in the Marais that the intelligentsia of baroque Paris held their gatherings. In Rue de Béarn, behind the Place Royale, the new convent of the Minimes had just been completed, with a chapel decorated by Vouet, La Hyre and Champaigne, and a doorway that was seen as François Mansart's masterpiece. Père Mersenne – 'a savant in whom there was more than in all the universities together', as Hobbes said of him in his own Paris exile

---

78   Marcel Poëte, *Une vie de cité, Paris de sa naissance à nos jours*, vol. 3 (Paris: Auguste Picard, 1931).

79   Alidor, the 'extravagant lover' of the play's subtitle, when he meets his friend Cléandre, expresses his surprise: 'To meet you in the Place Royale/Alone and so close to your sweet cell/Well shows that Philis is not at home.'

– gave hospitality to Descartes for a number of months, before his move to Holland. Mersenne also received Gérard Desargues, a geometer who specialized in the design of staircases, along with his young student, Blaise Pascal, who lived not far away on Rue de Touraine. This was a curious establishment, in the lead not just in the struggle against misguided thinkers – the '*confrérie des bouteilles*', Théophile de Viau, Saint-Amant, Guez de Balzac – but also in scientific research, with a library of 25,000 volumes. At the Hôtel de Montmort, on Rue du Temple, you could meet Huygens, Gassendi (who bequeathed Galileo's personal telescope to Hubert de Montmort, counsellor to the Parlement), or Claude Tardy, the doctor who introduced into France William Harvey's new ideas on the circulation of the blood and the role of the heart: there was a passionate controversy in the salons between the 'circulationists' and the 'anti-circulationists' who defended Galien's system. Every Monday, Lamoignon de Malesherbes would invite writers to his hôtel on Rue Pavée[80] – Racine, Bouleau, La Rochefoucauld, Bourdaloue – often also joined by Guy Patin, doctor to the king and professor at the Collège de France.

Women held salons as well. Some of them were what would later be called *demi-mondaines*: Marion Delorme, whose salon was on the Place Royale, and Ninon de Lenclos, whose residence on Rue des Tournelles was the rendezvous of the 'libertines', i.e., freethinkers, though this did not prevent her from having among her regulars La Rochefoucauld and Mme de Lafayette, Boileau, Mignard, and Lully. Legend has it that Molière read his *Tartuffe* here for the first time, before La Fontaine and Racine, who had come with the actress La Champmeslé. Mme de Sévigné wrote to her daughter on 1 April 1671, concerned about her son: 'This Ninon is a real danger! If you knew how dogmatic she was about religion, it would horrify you … we are making every effort, Mme de la Fayette and I, to extricate him from such a dangerous commitment.' Virtuous intellectuals could also be found: Mlle de Scudéry, a *précieuse* if ever there was one, was at home every Saturday in her small hôtel on Rue de Beauce, its courtyard adorned with an acacia – still rare – and an aviary. This was where she wrote, along with her brother, *Le Grand Cyrus* and *Clélie*, illustrated with the famous Carte du Tendre. Mme de Sévigné spent her entire Parisian life in the Marais. She was born in the house of her grandfather, on the corner of the Place Royale and Rue de Birague. As an orphan, she lived at her uncle's, first on Rue Barbette and then on Rue des Francs-Bourgeois. After her marriage to Saint-Gervais, she established herself on Rue des Lions. Soon widowed, she moved with her two children to Rue de Thorigny, opposite

---

80 Now the Bibliothèque Historique de la Ville de Paris.

the Venetian embassy, then to Rue des Trois-Pavillons (now Elzévir), and finally to the Hôtel Carnavalet: 'It is an admirable affair, we shall all stay here and enjoy the fine air. Since it is impossible to have everything, we shall have to dispense with parquet floors and fashionable little stoves; but at least we have a fine courtyard, a beautiful garden, and nice little blue girls who are most convenient.'[81]

Each major residence on the Place Royale, wrote Scarron, hid 'its sumptuous interior, its wondrous panelling, its rich ornaments and priceless paintings, its rare cabinets, canopies and balustrades'. The Duc de Richelieu, great-nephew of the cardinal, built up in his hôtel (now no. 21) a collection with more than ten paintings by Poussin, including *Eliezer and Rebecca* – subject of a famous lecture that Philippe de Champaigne gave to the Académie – and *Moses Rescued from the Waters*, which was later bought by Louis XIV and is now in the Louvre. Bernini, a great admirer of Poussin, visited the duke during his stay in Paris, as he would visit Chantelou to see the *Seven Sacraments*. After selling the Poussins, the duke bought several works by Rubens, including *The Massacre of the Innocents* and *The Lion Hunt* which is now in Munich. President Amelot de Gournay lived at no. 10. His son's tutor was Roger de Piles, whose theoretical writings lay at the origin of a famous controversy between the supporters of Poussin – the majority of the Académie – and those of Rubens, defenders of colouring who were denounced as corruptors of the visual arts, as they had 'introduced by their plotting all kinds of libertine painting that were quite released from all the constraints that formerly rendered this art so admirable and difficult'.[82]

Many artists chose to live in the Marais, close to their secular or religious patrons. There were painters such as Quentin Varin, whose workshop was on Rue Saint-Antoine at the corner with Rue de Birague; Claude Vignon, on the same street near the Visitation; La Hyre, who lived on Rue d'Angoumois (now Charlot) and painted a *Nativity* for the church of his neighbours, the Marais Capuchins, at the corner of his street and Rue du Perche. A little later, all the great names of French architecture were concentrated in the Marais: François Mansart, who had a very simple house built on Rue Payenne (now no. 5); his nephew by marriage, Jules Hardouin-Mansart, who lived on Rue des Tournelles in an hôtel decorated

---

81   These nuns, whose convent was situated between the Hôtel Carnavalet and the Hôtel Le Peletier on Rue Sainte-Catherine (now de Sévigné), where the Lycée Victor-Hugo now stands, 'wear a blue habit, a blue cloak and scapular, which has led to their being known as Heavenly Annonciades or Blue Girls' (Jaillot, *Recherches critiques, historiques et topographiques*).
82   Roland Fréart de Chambray, *Idée de la perfection de la peinture démontrée par les principes de l'art* (Le Mans, 1662).

by Mignard, Le Brun et La Fosse; Libéral Bruant, on Rue Saint-Louis (now de Turenne);[83] Le Vau in the same street, and Jacques II Gabriel on Rue Saint-Antoine.

The Marais quarter had its theatre, the most popular in Paris, challenging the Comédiens du Roi of the Hôtel de Bourgogne. It was inaugurated in 1629 in a tennis court on the Impasse Berthaud – behind the Centre Beaubourg – with *Mélite ou les Fausses Lettres*, the work of a young and unknown provincial, Pierre Corneille. The success was immediate, thanks to the talent of the troupe's leading actor, Montdory. When the theatre moved to another tennis court, the Maretz on Rue Vieille-du-Temple,[84] Montdory would interpret the title role of *Le Cid*. After the first few performances, he wrote to Guez de Balzac: 'Le Cid has charmed the whole city. He is so good-looking that the most well-mannered ladies have fallen in love with him, their passion breaking out several times in the public theatre . . . The crowd at our doors was so large that the nooks and crannies of the theatre that usually served as places for pages became favoured spots for blue-ribbonned guests, and the stage has regularly been bedecked with knights of the Order.'[85]

In the second half of the seventeenth century, the momentum of baroque Paris quietened down, and the great hôtels in cut stone that were subsequently constructed in the Marais, with courtyard in front and garden behind, no longer followed Italian fantasies. The Hôtel d'Aumont on Rue de Jouy (architect: Le Vau), the Hôtel Guénégaud de Brosses on Rue des Archives (François Mansart), the Hôtel de Beauvais on Rue Saint-Antoine (Le Pautre), the Hôtel Amelot de Bisseuil on Rue Vieille-du-Temple (Cottard), the Hôtel d'Avaux on Rue du Temple (Le Muet), the Hôtel Salé on Rue de Thorigny (de Bourges): everything here now represented the classical French hôtel.

Towards the end of Louis XIV's reign, however, Farmers-General and councillors of the Parlement, marshals, dukes and peers of France, felt hemmed in by the dense construction of the Marais and began to spread out into the Faubourg Saint-Honoré and especially the Faubourg

---

83 At what is now no. 34 – and not in the splendid small hôtel that he built on the corner of Rue de la Perle and Rue des Trois-Pavillons (now Elzévir), where Peronnet would establish the École des Ponts et Chaussées in the 1770s.

84 The site of what is now no. 90. In the meantime, the troupe had occupied two other tennis courts, one of these also being on Rue Vieille-du-Temple, and the other on Rue Michel-le-Comte. For more on matters theatrical, see Babelon, 'Henri IV urbaniste de Paris'.

85 Cited in Jacques Wilhelm, *La Vie quotidienne au Marais au XVIIe siècle* (Paris: Hachette, 1966).

Saint-Germain, where there was still a great deal of land to build on. This migration had definite consequences on the city's physiognomy, with the elegant residential sector shifting in the space of a few years from east to west, where it would remain. Balzac was aware of this change many years later: 'The noblesse began to find themselves out of their element among shopkeepers, left the Place Royale and the centre of Paris for good, and crossed the river to breathe freely in the Faubourg Saint-Germain, where palaces arose already around the great hôtel built by Louis XIV for the Duc de Maine – the Benjamin among his legitimate offspring.'[86] The decline of the Marais was completed by the end of the ancien régime, by which time Mercier could write in *Le Tableau de Paris*:

> Here at least you rediscover the century of Louis XIII, both in its manners and in its outdated opinions. The Marais is to the brilliant quarter of the Palais-Royal what Vienna is to London. It is not poverty that holds sway there, but the full complement of old prejudices: those with a modest fortune take refuge there. That is where you find grumbling old men, gloomy enemies of all new ideas, and highly imperious ladies who denounce without having read them those authors whose names they have heard of: the *philosophes* are referred to here as 'people to be burned'.

During the Revolution, emigration emptied this quarter of such aristocracy as still remained. In *La Comédie humaine* this is where Balzac situates the déclassés, the worthy, isolated and humble misfits. As early as the 'Prolegomena' to his *Treatise on Elegant Life*, he explains how 'the petty retailer, the second lieutenant, the sub-editor … if they do not save like casual workers in order to ensure their board and lodging in old age, the hope of their bee-like life scarcely goes beyond this: possession of a very cold room on the fourth floor, in Rue Boucherat' (now de Turenne). Comte Octave, in *Honorine*, who 'occupied one of the highest legal appointments', led a life of 'hermit-like simplicity', as 'his house was in the Marais, on Rue Payenne, and he hardly entertained'. Cousin Pons, Balzac's most important Marais figure, whose character and condition were identified with the quarter, lived on Rue de Normandie, 'one of the old-fashioned streets that slope towards the middle; the municipal authorities of Paris as yet have laid on no water supply to flush the central channel which drains the houses on either side, and as a result a stream of filthy ooze meanders among the cobblestones, filters into the soil, and produces the mud peculiar to the city'.[87]

---

86   Honoré de Balzac, *The Duchesse de Langeais* (1833–4), trans. Wormeley.
87   Honoré de Balzac, *Cousin Pons* (trans. Marriage).

Fortunate to escape Haussmann's demolitions – by a hair: the baron planned to extend Rue Étienne-Marcel as far as Boulevard Beaumarchais – the Marais remained out of fashion until the mid twentieth century. In the immediate postwar years it was still a poor quarter, the courtyards of its great hôtels clogged up with vans, lean-tos with galvanized metal roofs, piles of pallets, and carts with iron-trimmed wooden wheels. The years of de Gaulle, Malraux and Pompidou soon put paid to this anachronism. Property developers realized the profit they could make on these edifices – so historical, so down-at-heel, and inhabited by a population so little able to defend itself. In the space of twenty years the Marais became unrecognizable, and the old hôtels – façades scrubbed down, outlines tidied up, door frames plasticized, security and parking assured – are now in the hands of a well-off bourgeoisie, an opposite change to that which saw their forerunners emigrate west en masse some two centuries earlier.

The boundaries assigned to the Marais have fluctuated over the years. In the eighteenth century, it stretched as far as the city limits of the time. For Piganiol de la Force, it was 'bordered on the east by the ramparts and Rue du Mesnil-Montant [now Oberkampf], to the north by the further reaches of the Temple quarter and the Courtille [Boulevard de Belleville], to the west by the main street of the same faubourgs [Rue du Faubourg-du-Temple]', and thus included a large part of what is now the 11th arrondissement. Today, what is known as the Marais denotes everything between the Boulevards, Rue Beaubourg and the Seine, with a little inset along Rue de la Verrerie for what remains of the Hôtel de Ville quarter. But the dual origin of the Marais – the artisanal north around the Temple enclosure, the aristocratic south around the royal hôtels – has left such deep traces that it is almost an abuse of language to call both by the same name. Though the quarter dates almost entirely from the same short epoch, it includes so many local particularities that it can only be read as an archipelago.

Artisanal Marais begins to the north of the axis formed by the sequence of Rues Saint-Gilles, du Parc-Royal, de la Perle, des Quatre-Fils, des Haudriettes and Michel-le-Comte. It is divided in three by the 'T' formed by Rue de Bretagne and Rue du Temple. First, between Rue de Bretagne and the Place de la République, on the site of the Temple enclosure, there is the typical municipal equipment of the Third Republic: *mairie*, police station, square and market, represented here both by the Enfants-Rouges and the Carreau du Temple, with a very old tradition as an old-clothes market.[88] Second, set amidst Rue de Bretagne, Rue du Temple and the boulevard is a labyrinth of short and narrow streets, running in all directions as if the abandonment of the projected Place de France had left chaos behind. Rue Charlot and Rue de Saintonge, parallel straight lines, are superimposed on this anarchic lattice. 'Rue Charlot and all the surrounding streets,' wrote Sauval, 'were bordered with houses by Claude Charlot, a poor peasant from the Languedoc whom fortune nourished, fattened and stuffed until, as adjudicator-general of the *gabelles* and the five great tax-farms, and lord of the duchy of Fronta, he fell down and died in the mud out of which fortune had pulled him.' The old metal trade, surviving alongside pleasant galleries of contemporary art, occupies these calm streets in which signs in gilded type proclaim the activities of another age – etching and embossing, hallmarking and stamping, plating, electrolysis, low-fusion porcelain, lost wax and polishing. Third, in one of those contrasts that make for the quarter's charm, on the other side of Rue du Temple and through to Rue Beaubourg is the busy district of clocks and watches, jewellery, and leatherwork. Jews and Asians coexist peacefully on the territory of the Revolutionary section of the Gravilliers, fiefdom of the Enragés, 'hot and vehement souls, men who enlighten, lead and subjugate', as Jacques Roux wrote to Marat.[89] The courtyards of Rues Volta, au Maire, des Gravilliers and Chapon are still those of the old Marais: gates wide open, vans and trolleys, piles of boxes, bottlenecks and car horns, all the clinical signs of life.

The southern part of the quarter, the Marais of kings, business leaders, historians and tourists, is divided and organized by Rue Saint-Antoine, one of the finest in Paris – a genuine city of streets, which cannot be said of New York, Tokyo, or even Rome, which is rather made up of alleys and squares. Rue Saint-Antoine stands at the balancing point between regularity, in the alignment of its buildings, its width and its harmony of colours, and tension, in its double curve and the way it widens out at the end. (For streets, there is no beauty without regularity: Rue des Archives, broken up by constant variations in width, missing teeth and heteroclite

---

88   'In this bazaar, any kind of new merchandise is generally forbidden; but the tiniest scrap of any kind of old material ... finds a seller and a buyer. There are dealers in bits of cloth of all colours and patterns, all qualities and all ages, destined for the patches that are applied to torn or worn-out garments ... Further along, at the sign of *Le Goût du jour* you can see hanging like ex-voto offerings myriads of clothes of all colours and shapes, in still more extravagant styles' (Eugène Sue, *The Mysteries of Paris*, 1842–3).

89   Roland Gotlib, 'Les Gravilliers, plate-forme des Enragés', in Michel Vovelle (ed.), *Paris et la Révolution* (Paris: Publications de la Sorbonne, 1989).

additions, does not stand comparison with its contemporary neighbour, the very regular Rue du Temple. Conversely, regularity without tension can become boring if overly long, like the arcades on Rue de Rivoli or Boulevard Magenta. Beauty in strict modular repetition is a particular feature of short streets, such as – however different in style – Rues du Cirque, des Colonnes and de Marseilles, or Rue des Immeubles-Industriels which so intrigued Walter Benjamin.)

The curves of Rue Saint-Antoine (there is more than one curve, as Rue François-Miron is historically its initial segment) are punctuated by two domes that for me – and certainly many others – are not just mere silhouettes but old friends. That of Saint-Paul-Saint-Louis, the church of the Jesuits, is the oldest large dome in Paris, still a little clumsy, too small on a too large base, giving the church the charm of an adolescent run to seed, particularly its back view from Rue des Jardins-Saint-Paul.[90] The Visitation, designed by François Mansart, a remnant of the convent of the Visitandines that stretched right to the gate of the Bastille, is on the contrary the most perfect cupola on a centred plan that can be found in Paris, along with Libéral Bruant's chapel of the Salpêtrière.

The Marais archipelago extends on either side of Rue Saint-Antoine. On the river side are the silent streets of the Saint-Paul quarter. The other side has, from east to west, the Place des Vosges, the great museum island[91] and the Jewish island. 'The Rue de la Juiverie [since 1900 Rue Ferdinand-Duval] is thus called because in former times the Jews lived here, before they were expelled from France by Philippe Auguste for their excessive usury, and the execrable impieties and crimes they committed against Christians', wrote Abbé Du Breuil.[92] Sauval was of a different opinion, noting that 'as regards the streets of this Jewish quarter, some are very narrow, crooked and dark ... All the houses bordering on them are tiny, tall, poorly built, and similar to the Jewish quarters in Rome, Metz or Avignon.' The Jewish quarter today is prosperous and lively, despite the pressure of fashionable boutiques on the one hand and gay bars on the other. And the inevitable disappearance of the old Bundists with their caps has not prevented the

---

90   There used to be the dome of the Petits-Augustins (now the École des Beaux-Arts), 'the first church', wrote Félibien, 'that Paris had seen built in this form', also that of Saint-Joseph-des-Carmes (now the Institut Catholique), but both of these were small and rudimentary.

91   Within a few dozen metres from each other are the Musées Carnavalet, de l'Histoire de France, Victor-Hugo, Picasso, de la Chasse et de la Nature, de la Serrurerie, Cognacq-Jay and du Judaïsme.

92   R. P. Jacques Du Breuil, *Le Théâtre des Antiquités de Paris* (1639).

civilization of *pickelfleish* and *gefiltefish* from resisting as best it can that of the falafel.[93]

On the Right Bank, Old Paris forms an approximate semicircle. Its circumference is defined by the arc of the Boulevards, and its diameter by a narrow band along the Seine, between Rue de Rivoli and the *quais*, from the colonnade of the Louvre to the Hôtel de Ville – or, if you like, from the flamboyant Gothic of Saint-Germain-l'Auxerrois to the classical façade of Saint-Gervais. This band is a special case, where the successive layers, instead of resonating together like harmonics, as they do elsewhere, form a discordant and confused ensemble. This is not for want of fine buildings, picturesque details, or historic memories, but these are lost in such a heteroclite patchwork that the general sense is no longer legible. You have a hotchpotch of Haussmannian cuttings that are unfinished (Avenue Victoria) or ravaged by the feeders and entries of underground roads (Rue du Pont-Neuf, Rue des Halles), squares that have been gutted (the Place du Châtelet, still ravishing in 1860 on a Marville photograph – quite small, and almost closed around its fountain) or 'improved' in a ridiculous fashion (the Place de l'Hôtel-de-Ville, the Square de la Tour Saint-Jacques), old streets massacred by renovation (Rue Bertin-Poirée) or by car traffic (Rue des Lavandières-Sainte-Opportune, where a roundabout disguised as a Zen garden draws in all the traffic from Rue Saint-Honoré). Even Haussmann, generally rather content with himself, confusedly felt there was something wrong, which he attributed to the difficulties of the terrain: 'The difference in level across the whole quarter around the Place du Châtelet, caused by the slope to the east of the hill crowned by the Tour Saint-Jacques, and by the rise to the west of the Quai de la Mégisserie and its surroundings, required the demolition of all the houses from Rue des Lavandières to Rue des Arcis [now Saint-Martin], between the line of the *quais* and Rue de Rivoli', a manner of justification that is unusual in the *Mémoires* of a man who called himself an 'artist of demolition'.

Yet the worst was avoided: there was a real threat that the extension to Rue de Rivoli would start from the middle of the Louvre colonnade. 'War on the demolishers!' cried Hugo in *La Revue des Deux Mondes* on 1 March 1832: 'The vandals have their own characteristic idea. They want to run a great, great, great road right across Paris. A road of a whole league! What magnificent devastation they could wreak! Saint-Germain-l'Auxerrois would be in the way, the admirable tower of Saint-Jacques-de-la-Boucherie

---

93   The Bund was the revolutionary-syndicalist movement of Jewish workers in Yiddishland. See Henri Minczeles, *Histoire générale du Bund* (Paris: Austral, 1995), and visit the fine Medem library at 52 Rue René-Boulanger.

perhaps too. But no matter! A road of a league! ... a straight line from the Louvre to the Barrière du Trône!' Haussmann, being a Protestant, rejected the project, fearing that the destruction of Saint-Germain-l'Auxerrois would be interpreted as a revenge for Saint Bartholemew's Night, the signal for which, it is said, was given by the bells of that church.

The Grands Boulevards

'The life of Paris, its physiognomy, was in 1500 on Rue Saint-Antoine; in 1600 on the Place Royale; in 1700 on the Pont-Neuf; in 1800 in the Palais-Royal. All these places were the Boulevards of their day! The earth was impassioned there, as the asphalt is today under the feet of the stock-brokers on the steps of Café Tortoni.' When Balzac wrote his 'Histoire et physiologie des boulevards de Paris' in 1844, it was nearly ten years since the Palais-Royal had gone out of fashion, ten years since the Paris of Manon Lescaut, Adolphe, and Henri de Marsay had disappeared, along with its Argand lamps, half-pay officers, the vogue for Cherubini and the successes of Byron, Walter Scott and Fenimore Cooper. In a movement of taste that accompanied dandies, whores, journalists and gourmets in their migration to the Boulevards, a new romanticism made its appearance, that of Berlioz, Frédérick Lemaître and La Fanfarlo. But in one of the thousand and one ways that facts have of messing up the categories of art history, it so happens that the Boulevards, the great stage of Parisian Romanticism, are a long procession of neoclassical architecture – a paradox to match that which the clever Lousteau explained to Lucien de Rubempré around 1830:

> [O]ur great men are ranged in two hostile camps. The Royalists are 'romantics', the Liberals are 'classics'. The divergence of taste in matters literary and divergence of political opinion coincide; and the result is a war with weapons of every sort, double-edged witticisms, subtle calumnies and nicknames à outrance, between the rising and the waning glory, and ink is shed in torrents. The odd part of it is that the Royalist-romantics are all for liberty in literature, and for repealing laws and conventions; while the Liberal-classics are for maintaining the unities, the Alexandrine, and the classical theme.[94]

From the Madeleine to the Bastille, there remain none of the legendary dwellings built on the ramparts at the end of the ancien régime, with their view over the city on one side and across market gardens on the other:

---

94   Balzac, Lost Illusions.

nothing of Beaumarchais' house and its garden designed by Belanger, where Mme de Genlis came to witness the demolition of the Bastille along with the children of the Duc d'Orléans, nothing of the Pavillon de Hanovre built for the fine suppers of the Maréchal de Richelieu – 'the fairy pavilion', Voltaire called it – nothing of the hôtel built by Ledoux for the Prince de Montmorency on the corner of the Chaussée-d'Antin, whose entablature bore, as a homage to Palladio, the statues of eight high officials of the Montmorency family, 'heroic virtues that vandalism has destroyed, a deep impression that time does not wipe out'.[95] On Boulevard de la Madeleine it was still possible until recently to admire the two rotundas framing the beginning of Rue Caumartin, one of the hôtel of the Duc d'Aumont, and the other of the hôtel of the Farmer-General Marin de la Haye – its roof formerly boasting a hanging garden in which, according to Hillairet, two small Chinese bridges crossed a stream that, after forming an island, supplied water to the dining rooms and baths of the building. They have just been newly '*façadisés*', which is perhaps worse than being demolished.[96]

But despite the destruction, the length of the Boulevards remains a great walking catalogue of Parisian neoclassical architecture from Louis XVI to Louis-Philippe, especially on the inner side, that of the odd numbers (the southern side, if you prefer), whose owners had front seats on the promenade. Many even had terraces built that overlooked the Boulevards' animation.[97] By turns you have pure Louis XVI (Hôtel Montholon on

---

95   Claude-Nicolas Ledoux, *L'Architecture considérée sous le rapport de l'art, des moeurs et de la législation* (Paris, 1804). The gardens of the Beaumarchais residence – which gave its name to the former Boulevard Saint-Antoine – stretched widely over the Saint-Antoine bastion, i.e., a triangle now bounded by Boulevard Richard-Lenoir, Boulevard Beaumarchais, and Rue du Pasteur-Wagner. The house was demolished to make way for the Saint-Martin canal. In the 1930s the Pavillon de Hanovre was removed to the Parc de Sceaux, and the Palais Berlitz was constructed in its place.

96   '*Façadisation*' consists in preserving (more or less) the façade of a building whilst gutting it like a fowl to install office floors. A façadized building is to the original building what a stuffed animal is to its living form. See on this subject F. Laisney, 'Crimes et façadisme', in *Les Grands Boulevards, un parcours d'innovation et de modernité*, exhibition catalogue (Paris: Action artistique de la Ville de Paris, 2000).

97   Opposite, on the outer side, urbanization was later, as the line of the Boulevards was disrupted by the triangles of the old bastions – see the angular course of Rue de Bondy (now René-Boulanger). Besides, the Boulevard was often doubled at a lower level by outside streets along the former ditches. Rue Amelot – formerly Rue des Fossés-du-Temple – is one of these 'low roads', the most famous being Rue Basse-du-Rempart where, as we shall see, the decisive shot in the revolution of February 1848 was fired.

Boulevard Poissonière, with its six colossal Ionic columns supporting the third-storey balcony), the style of the Empire and Restoration, more severe and archaeological, and that of the July monarchy, decorated and smiling, with its great apartment blocks built for investment, looking like Italian palaces, where you can smell the eclecticism that lurked behind the taste for antiquity.[98]

If it is hard to imagine the seductive power of the Boulevards in the time of their splendour, this is because their sequence was then one of unbroken rhythmic scansion. Despite their length, they had a continuity, something of an enclosed space, that had made for the success of the Place Royale and the Palais-Royal. They were like the succession of rooms in an immense palace, each with its décor, timetable, and habits. But from Haussmann through to Poincaré this urban intimacy was hollowed out. The Opéra Garnier and its roundabout, the junction of Boulevards Haussmann and Montmartre creating the shapeless 'Richelieu-Drouot' intersection, and the brutal implantation of the Place de la République where the Faubourg du Temple and the Boulevard du Crime meet, replaced these subtle caesuras with gaping empty spaces. When the father of Lucien Leuwen, that exquisite patron of the Opéra dancers, 'strolled on the boulevard, his lackey gave him a cloak to pass in front of Rue de la Chaussée-d'Antin'. What precautions would he have had to take to cross the Place de la République!

The segmentation of the Boulevards has become very sharp. Between the Madeleine and the Opéra you have the big hotels and travel agencies; from the Opéra to Richelieu-Drouot the banks. Then, until the République, a portion that, whilst rather the worse for wear, is certainly the closest in spirit to the original Boulevards. Finally, the stretch between République and Bastille is the domain of motor scooters, photography and music, which may well have its charm and its special places, but is no longer really part of the Boulevards.

As a point of inflection in time, the beginning of the Boulevards' long downward descent, the image that comes to me is that of the death of Nana in a room of the Grand-Hôtel, on Boulevard des Capucines:

> 'Come, it's time we were off,' said Clarisse. 'We shan't bring her to life again. Are you coming, Simonne?' They all looked at the bed out of the corners of their eyes, but they did not budge an inch. Nevertheless, they began getting ready and gave their skirts various little pats. Lucy was again

---

98 For the ancien régime, as well as the Hôtel Montholon, see also 41 Boulevard Saint-Martin; 39 Boulevard de Bonne-Nouvelle; and the Hôtel Cousin de Méricourt at 19 Boulevard Poissonière.

leaning out of the window. She was alone now, and a sorrowful feeling began little by little to overpower her, as though an intense wave of melancholy had mounted up from the howling mob. Torches still kept passing, shaking out clouds of sparks, and far away in the distance the various bands stretched into the shadows, surging unquietly to and fro like flocks being driven to the slaughterhouse at night. A dizzy feeling emanated from these confused masses as the human flood rolled them along – a dizzy feeling, a sense of terror and all the pity of the massacres to come. The people were going wild; their voices broke; they were drunk with a fever of excitement which sent them rushing toward the unknown 'out there' beyond the dark wall of the horizon. 'À Berlin! à Berlin! à Berlin!'

The Boulevards was where the novelties of the modern city appeared one by one: the first Paris public transport line – the famous Madeleine-Bastille – the urinals, the cab ranks, the newspaper kiosks, the Morris columns. But the great transformation that had its birth in the Passage des Panoramas in 1817 and spread out along the Boulevards in the 1840s was gas lighting. We can grasp in Baudelaire the change from *Les Fleurs du mal*, lit by unsteady oil lamps ('By the light of lamps flickering in the wind/ Prostitution lights up in the streets') to *Paris Spleen*, illuminated by gas ('The café was sparkling. The gaslight itself sent forth all the ardour of a debut and lit with all its force walls blinding in their whiteness ...').[99] It was gas that made it possible to live the darkest hours of the night. 'Cross the line that marks the axis of Rue de la Chaussée-d'Antin and Rue Louis-le-Grand, and you've entered the domain of the crowd. Along this Boulevard, on the right side especially, it's all sparkling shops, impressive displays, gilded cafés, permanent illumination. From Rue Louis-le-Grand to Rue de Richelieu the flood of light that shines from the shops enables you to read a newspaper while walking along', wrote Julien Lemer in *Paris au gaz*, published by Le Dentu in 1861.[100] At closing time, 'on the Boulevards, inside the cafés, the

---

99   Charles Baudelaire, 'Evening Twilight' and 'The Eyes of the Poor', *Les Fleurs du mal*. [I have used throughout the translation of *Les Fleurs du mal* made by William Aggeler (published as *The Flowers of Evil*, Fresno, CA: Academic Literary Guild, 1954) – Tr.]

100   See the excellent book by Simone Delattre, *Les Douze heures noires, la nuit à Paris au XIXe siècle* (Paris: Albin Michel, 2000). Lemer was himself a publisher, of Baudelaire in particular. 'You often pass along Boulevard des Italiens. If you meet Julien Lemer, let him know my state of mind; tell him that I have worked out – that I will never again be able to have anything printed, – that I will never be able to earn a sou – that I will never again see my mother or my friends, – and that finally if he has disastrous news to tell me, he should let me know rather than leaving me in uncertainty' (letter to Champfleury, Brussels, 13 November 1865).

gas mantles of the chandeliers very quickly blow out into darkness. Outside you hear the brouhaha of chairs being stacked in fours on the marble tables.'[101] But thanks to gas, nocturnal life carried on uninterrupted. Alfred Delvau, a professional noctambulist, offered a guide for the late bedder to the Boulevards of the Second Empire:

> After midnight one may withdraw to the Café Leblond; its entrance on Boulevard des Italiens closes at midnight, but the exit on the Passage de l'Opéra remains open until two in the morning. The Café des Variétés [in the Passage des Panoramas], which has a licence until half past one, receives a large number for supper after the theatres close. At the Café Wolf, 10 Rue du Faubourg-Montmartre, the noctambulists of the Breda quarter congregate around midnight ... to drink beer and eat onion sausages, until it's time to close. At two o'clock the Brabant, at the corner of the Boulevard and Faubourg Montmartre, is still open, as well as Bignon, on the corner of the Chaussée-d'Antin, and especially Hill's Tavern, on Boulevard des Capucines, where the fashionable crowd mingles with the carefree bohème.

It was on the Boulevards in the 1850s that a custom spread, so rooted now in Paris life that it is hard to imagine the city without it: cafés set tables out on a terrace. 'All the cafés have provided seating on the pavement outside their premises: there is a notable group of these between Rue Laffitte and Rue La Peletier, and it is not uncommon to see, in the heat of summer, wilting promenaders linger until one in the morning outside the café doors, sipping ices, beer, lemonade and soda water.'[102] When Georges Duroy, the eponymous *Bel-Ami* – 'empty pockets and boiling blood' – cruised Boulevard des Italiens on a stifling evening, 'the big cafés, full of people, spilled out onto the pavement, displaying their clientele of drinkers under the sharp and rough light of the illuminated windows. In front of them, on little tables square or round, glasses contained red, yellow, green and brown liquids of all shades; and within the carafes you could see the big transparent cylinders of ice that chilled the fine clear water.'

'Nothing is easier or more agreeable than a promenade of this kind. The ways reserved for pedestrians are tiled or asphalted, shaded with trees and furnished with seats. The cafés are at frequent intervals. Every now and

---

101   Villiers de L'Isle-Adam, *Contes cruels*, 'Le désir d'être un homme', published in *L'Étoile de France* (1882).
102   Lemer, *Paris au gaz*.

then cabs are stationed on the roadway. Finally, omnibuses constantly run from the Bastille to the Madeleine.' In the opposite direction from that proposed by the Joanne guide of 1870, the promenade began with Boulevard de la Madeleine and Boulevard des Capucines. For a long time the whole of this segment, as far as the break at Rue de la Chaussée-d'Antin, remained outside the life of the Boulevards. 'From the Madeleine to Rue Caumartin,' wrote Balzac, 'there is no flânerie. This is a stretch dominated by our imitation of the Parthenon, a large and fine thing, whatever may be said of it, but spoiled by the hideous café sculptures that dishonour its lateral friezes ... This whole zone is sacrificed. You cross it, but do not stroll on it.'[103]

A decade and half later, a sense of greater liveliness can be felt: 'Coming from the Madeleine, there is still only one pavement that is really alive, the right-hand side; the other is occupied by a street, Rue Basse-du-Rempart, currently being ravaged by demolition to make way for the future opera house.'[104] And by 1867, the year of the Exposition Universelle, everything seems to have changed, to judge from the *Paris Guide*:

> In our day, the most monumental section of the Boulevards is that stretching from Rue de la Chaussée-d'Antin to the Madeleine. The new Opéra is surrounded by palaces. The richness and comfort of the interior fittings of the Grand Hôtel, the hotel that the Jockey Club has moved into, match the magnificence of the outside. There remain only remnants of the damp Rue Basse that was filled with the dead and wounded of the shooting of 23 February [1848]. The buildings and shops rival each other in their sumptuousness.

But the picture ends in a singular conclusion in which La Bédollière repeats words straight from Balzac: 'And yet, on Boulevard des Capucines and Boulevard de la Madeleine, it seems that an arctic cold can be felt. People cross them without lingering; they live there but don't stop there. The lines of carriages returning from Vincennes, in the afternoons of racing days, turn off and leave the Boulevards at Rue de la Paix. When all is said and done, to use a typically Parisian expression: *ça n'est plus ça!*'[105]

Known in 1815 as the Petit-Coblenz, after the town that had symbolized the emigration, Boulevard de Gand (Ghent where Louis XVIII found

---

103   'Histoire et physiologie des Boulevards de Paris', in *Le Diable à Paris* (1844); reissued in Honoré de Balzac, *À Paris!* (Brussels: Complexe, 1993).
104   Lemer, *Paris au gaz*.
105   La Bédollière, 'Les Boulevards de la porte Saint-Martin à la Madeleine', in *Paris Guide*.

refuge during the Hundred Days) only later acquired its definitive name, Boulevard des Italiens, from the former theatre of the Comédiens-Italiens in the Salle Favart – though, as we have seen, this turned its back on the Boulevard. Between Rue de la Chaussée-d'Antin and Rue de Richelieu was the Boulevard par excellence for 'those who have been called in turn refined, fine, marvellous, *incroyables*, dandies, fashionable, lions, *gandins*, mashers, fops'.[106] Here, writes Balzac, 'begin those strange and marvellous buildings that seem to be drawn from a fairy tale or the pages of *The Thousand and One Nights* ... Once you have set foot here, your day is lost if you are a man of thought. It is a gilded dream and an unbeatable distraction. The engravings of the print sellers, the daily entertainments, the tidbits of the cafés, the gems in the jewellers' shops, all is set to intoxicate and overexcite you.'[107] When Bixiou and Léon de Lora want to show Paris to their provincial cousin, this is where they take him, 'from one end to the other of that sheet of asphalt on which, between the hours of one and three, it is difficult to avoid seeing some of the personages in honour of whom Fame puts one or the other of her trumpets to her lips'.[108]

Elegant cafés and restaurants were more numerous on Boulevard des Italiens than anywhere else ('Are there still *gandins*, those men of severe dress, at table in the Café du Helder? Do you not notice on the forehead of most of them traces of the sun of Algeria, Cochin-China or Mexico?'[109]): the Café de Foy at the corner of the Chaussée-d'Antin, the Café Anglais with its twenty-two private rooms, including the famous Grand-Seize, the Grand-Balcon between Rue Favart and Rue Marivaux, the Café Riche, Café Hardy, Frascati's patisserie on the site of the celebrated gambling house closed in 1837, the Bains-Chinois on the corner of Rue de La Michodière, the Maison Dorée restaurant at the corner of Rue Laffitte, etc. The epicentre was located precisely between Rue Le Peletier and Rue Taitbout, framed at one end by two mythical establishments: on the left, the Café de Paris, and on the right, Tortoni, whose terrace, with three steps leading up to it, was one of the most famous places in the world for all of half a century. Tortoni was frequented by dandies and artists – Manet spent every evening there – as well as financiers: 'You leave the battlefield of the Bourse to go to the restaurants, passing from one digestion to another. Is Tortoni not both the preface and the dénouement of the Bourse?' And two of the finest villains in *La Comédie humaine* naturally meet here: 'About one o'clock, Maxime [de Trailles] was chewing a toothpick and talking with

106   Joanne, *Paris illustré en 1870*.
107   Balzac, 'Histoire et physiologie des Boulevards de Paris'.
108   Honoré de Balzac, *The Unconscious Comedians* (trans. Wormeley).
109   É. de La Bédollière, 'Les Boulevards', in *Paris Guide*.

Du Tiller on Tortoni's portico, where speculation held a little Bourse, a sort of prelude to the great one.'[110] The main entrance to the Opéra was two steps away, on Rue Le Peletier, and the Passage de l'Opéra with its two galleries – du Thermomètre and du Baromètre – afforded direct access from the Boulevard.

In the sections of Rue Laffitte and Rue Le Peletier adjacent to the Boulevards, there formed in the 1870s something that had never been seen before in Paris, a gathering of art dealers on the same pavement. In 1867, Paul Durand-Ruel moved his gallery from Rue de la Paix to 16 Rue Laffitte, with a branch on Rue Le Peletier.[111] At no. 8 on the same street there was already the gallery of Alexandre Bernheim, son of a paint-seller from Besançon, who sold the canvases of his friend Courbet, as well as Corot, d'Harpignies and Rousseau. Despite well-known sarcasms (Albert Wolff in Le Figaro, 1876: 'Rue Le Peletier is having a bad time. After the fire at the Opéra, here is a new disaster that has struck the quarter. Durand-Ruel has just opened an exhibition of what is said to be painting . . .') others followed, and in a short while these few metres had become the key territory of art in Paris. Baudelaire wrote to Nadar: 'If you were an angel, you'd go and pay homage to a certain Moreau, a picture-seller, Rue Laffitte . . . And you'd get from him permission to make a beautiful double photographic copy of The Duchess of Alba, by Goya (vintage Goya, utterly authentic).' Manet often said that 'it's good to go to Rue Laffitte'. Degas, who came down from Pigalle by bus, often visited there as a client. 'He contemplated Bernheim's Corots,' said Romi, 'criticized the Fantin-Latours at Tempelaere's, and presented himself with a Delacroix that he had delivered to his house, like a great lord.' Gauguin, who worked at a broker's on the same Rue Laffitte, stopped in front of these magic windows for twelve years until the day when, unable to stand it any more, he abandoned the Bourse for painting. Certain galleries were devoted to Boudin, to Corot, to Daumier; others showed the expensive paintings of Henner, Bouguereau and Meissonier. Close to Durand-Ruel's revolutionary showroom was the respectable gallery of M. Beugnet, who permanently displayed Madeleine Lemaire's bouquets of polished flowers. Every month, an admirer of this society artist came to spray on her violets, carnations and roses a light

---

110   Balzac, 'Histoire et physiologie des boulevards de Paris', and Beatrix (trans. Wormeley).
111   His father, a stationer on Rue Saint-Jacques under the Empire, had the idea of supplementing his section of artists' materials with a few paintings. He moved to Rue des Petits-Champs, where he showed paintings by Delacroix, Decamps and Diaz. Paul subsequently transferred the gallery to 1 Rue de la Paix, then to Rue Laffitte.

cloud of the corresponding perfume. 'A poetic advertisement!' said M. Beugnet. In 1895, Ambroise Vollard triggered a scandal when he showed fifty canvases by Cézanne in his new gallery at 39 Rue Laffitte (he had previously been at no. 8). Vollard invited guests for dinner in his cellar. As Apollinaire relates in *Le Flâneur des deux rives*, 'Everyone had heard speak of this famous hypogeum ... Bonnard did a painting of the cellar, and as far as I recall, Odilon Redon appears in it.' In the same street could be found the offices of 'the friendly, open-to-all' *Revue blanche*, where diarists, illustrators and friends spent their days – Mallarmé and Jarry, Blum and Gide, Lautrec, Vallotton and Bonnard.

Two reasons explain the catastrophe that struck Boulevard des Italiens and its artistic life, turning the one into a centre of fast food and the other into a gloomy desert. The first was the proliferation of banks and insurance companies, which invaded the quarter at the turn of the century. From the construction of the ponderous building of the Crédit Lyonnais in the 1890s – which caught fire at a most timely moment, when scandal had thrust the bank into public obloquy – to the denaturing of the Maison Dorée in the 1970s by one of the first and worst examples of *façadisation*, each of the pavements on which these 'strange and wonderful' buildings were located was ravaged. The Banque Nationale de Paris, which owned the whole of the north of the Boulevard from Rue Laffitte to the Richelieu-Drouot intersection, was not content to disfigure the Maison Dorée; it offered there a concentrate of what has since spread to hundreds of Parisian streets and crossroads. Insurance companies divided up the streets of modern art and transformed them into grey canyons peopled by security guards and swept by torrents of cars. They were assisted – and this is the second reason – by the extension of Boulevard Haussmann in the 1920s, the only cutting in the centre of Paris carried out in the twentieth century, which led to demolition on a gigantic scale, in particular that of the famous Passage de l'Opéra:

'Today, Boulevard Haussmann has reached Rue Laffitte', remarked *L'Intransigeant* the other day. A few more paces by this giant rodent and, after it has devoured the block of houses separating it from Rue Le Peletier, it will inexorably gash open the thicket whose twin arcades run through the Passage de l'Opéra, before emerging diagonally on to Boulevard des Italiens. It will unite itself to that broad avenue some-where near where the Café Louis XVI now stands, with a singular kind of kiss whose cumulative effect on the vast body of Paris is quite unpredictable.[112]

112   Louis Aragon, *The Paris Peasant* (London: J. Cape, 1971), p. 29.

Boulevard des Italiens ends at Rue de Richelieu, that's a fact. But didn't
elegant life continue beyond this, on Boulevard Montmartre? Did it not
stretch to the crossroads formed by the intersection of Rue Montmartre,
Boulevard Montmartre and Rue du Faubourg-Montmartre, such a
dreadful crossing that it was known as the 'crossroads of accidents'? Some
people replied in the negative: 'What was then called "the Boulevard"
extended only from the Chaussée-d'Antin to the Passage de l'Opéra,
perhaps up to Faubourg-Montmartre because of the Variétés, but it was
very bad form to be seen any further up. It was rare for dandies to parade
beyond the Café Anglais; the Variétés marked their outer limit.'[113]
For most people, however, it was Rue du Faubourg-Montmartre that
formed the border between the elegant and the plebeian boulevards.
For Balzac, 'the heart of present-day Paris ... beats between Rue de la
Chaussée-d'Antin and Rue du Faubourg-Montmartre ... From Rue
Montmartre to Rue Saint-Denis, the physiognomy of the Boulevard
changes completely.'[114] If Boulevard Montmartre belonged more to
artists and shopkeepers than to literary folk and dandies, it still remained
for Julien Lemer a recommended promenade, and even the favourite of
La Bédollière:

> The raging stream we have just crossed [Rue du Faubourg-
> Montmartre] is a kind of Bidassoa separating two countries, and
> we are now in the realm of literature. Here are journalists, novel-
> ists, diarists, satirists, dramatists, even lecturers ... It is not without
> reason that great literary salons and an international bookshop have
> established themselves on Boulevard Montmartre ... And all of
> them, like bees, buzz around the Théâtre des Variétés and the doors
> of cafés, especially at the absinthe hour ... The arcades – Jouffroy,
> Verdeau, the Passage des Panoramas – are what the Palais-Royal
> used to be. They are silent in the mornings, only disturbed by the
> steps of apprentices, clerks and shopgirls on their way to work ...
> Around eleven o'clock the habitués of the Dîner de Paris, the Dîner
> du Rocher, and the Dîner du Passage Jouffroy make their appearance
> ... At five p.m. sharp, the evening papers are sold from the boule-
> vard kiosks ... At six o'clock, a great hustle and bustle, the faubourg
> is on its way down! The inhabitants of the Bréda and Notre-Dame-
> de-Lorette quarters advance to conquer the Boulevards. The region

113   Paul d'Ariste, *La Vie et le monde du Boulevard (1830–1870)* (Paris: Tallandier,
1930). Cited by Jean-Claude Yon, 'Le théâtre aux boulevards', in Laisney, *Les
Grands Boulevards*.
114   Balzac, 'Histoire et physiologie des boulevards de Paris'.

is signalled from a distance by the clicking of jade, the scent of musk, the rustling of silk.[115]

To cross the Montmartre intersection, and proceed along Boulevard Poissonière and Boulevard de Bonne-Nouvelle, meant passing from elegance to commerce, from literature to cottons, from the avant-garde of art to the most traditional crafts:

Le Gymnase vainly displays its charming little façade there; further on, the Bonne-Nouvelle bazaar, as fine as a Venetian palace, has arisen from the earth as if at the stroke of a fairy wand:[116] but the effort is completely wasted! The passersby here are no longer elegant, fine dresses would be out of place, the artist and the literary lion no longer venture into these parts ... One single boulevard in between produces this total change.[117]

During the daytime, however, Boulevard Poissonière was lively enough:

Enter Baurain's restaurant and you will find a good many representatives of commerce, here to buy and sell velvet, linen, raw or printed cloth, spun or twisted cotton. Enter the Théâtre du Gymnase and you will recognize in the audience leading lights of novelty and calico, applauding Sardou or Alexandre Dumas *fils* as they used to applaud Scribe and Mélesville. Take a turn on the little overlapping promenade, shaded by thin sycamores, on the corner of Rue d'Hauteville. The boys and girls playing there and eating their biscuits were born in the midst of tulle, barege, blond-lace, woollens and silks. They've known since an early age the meaning of Tarare, Saint-Quentin, and A.G. goods.[118]

The building of Le Pont-de-Fer was located on Boulevard Poissonière, a kind of commercial centre under an immense double metal arcade; also the Dock du Campement that specialized in travel goods, and the house

---

115 La Bédollière, 'Les Boulevards de la porte Saint-Martin à la Madeleine', in *Paris Guide*.
116 It was in this Bazar, normally occupied by the shops of La Ménagère, that an exhibition was held in 1846 which Baudelaire reported in a short masterpiece: 'The Museum of Classics at Bazar Bonne-Nouvelle', in which he particularly describes David's *Marat* – 'There is something at once both tender and poignant about this work; in the icy air of that room, on those chilly walls, about that cold and funereal bath, hovers a soul' (Charles Baudelaire, *Art in Paris, 1845–1862* [London: Phaidon 1965]), p. 35.
117 Balzac, 'Histoire et Physiologie des Boulevards de Paris'.
118 La Bédollière, 'Les Boulevards de la porte Saint-Martin à la Madeleine'.

of Barbedienne, 'which sells antique models in bronze, reproduced by the
Colas process, and medals of David [d'Angers] ... A little further on are the
rooms of the Brébant restaurant ... the carpet shops of M. Roncier, and,
two houses further, the Industrie Française store, with two floors displaying
the most varied riches.'[119]

The section of the Boulevards between Rue du Faubourg-Montmartre
and the Porte Saint-Denis is that which has changed least since the nineteenth century, despite the Grand Rex and the rather unfortunate post
office on Rue de Mazagran. This is perhaps the reason why the Surrealists
made this segment their particular boulevard, even if they also frequented
the Passage de l'Opéra and in particular Café Certa – 'the place where,
one afternoon towards the end of 1919, André Breton and I decided to
start meeting our friends there, detesting as we did Montparnasse and
Montmartre, as well as from a taste for the ambiguity of the arcades' – and
the Théâtre-Moderne – 'that hall with great worn-out mirrors, decorated
at the bottom with grey swans slipping through yellow reeds, with enclosed
stalls quite deprived of air and light, not at all reassuring'.[120] These few
metres, which for want of a better name were known as Strasbourg-Saint-
Denis, exercised on Breton an attraction that he explained by 'the isolation
of the two gates you see there, which owe their touching aspect to the fact
that they used to be part of the Paris city wall, giving these two vessels, as
if they were carried along by the centrifugal force of the town, a totally
lost look'.[121] For him, however, the centre of the world in those years was
Boulevard de Bonne-Nouvelle: 'Meanwhile, you can be sure of meeting
me in Paris, of not spending more than three days without seeing me pass,
toward the end of the afternoon, along the Boulevard Bonne-Nouvelle
between the *Le Matin* building and the Boulevard de Strasbourg. I don't
know why it should be precisely here that my feet take me, here that I
almost invariably go without specific purpose, without anything to induce
me but this obscure clue: namely that it (?) will happen here.'[122]

Beyond the Porte, Boulevard Saint-Martin played a transition role
between the boulevard that was still a little bit bourgeois and the genuinely plebeian boulevard, 'as the jacket is a transition between the suit and

---

119   Joanne, *Paris illustré en 1870.* Le Brébant still exists today, on the corner of
Rue du Faubourg-Montmartre and Boulevard Poissonière.
120   Aragon, *The Paris Peasant*, p. 87, and André Breton, *Nadja* (New York:
Grove, 1960), p. 38.
121   André Breton, *Communicating Vessels* (Lincoln, NE: University of Nebraska
Press, 1990), p. 98.
122   Breton, *Nadja*, p. 32; the question mark is Breton's own. The building of *Le
Matin* was on the corner of Boulevard Poissonière and Rue du Faubourg-Poissonière.

the overall'.[123] What was most striking here in the nineteenth century was its canyon-like aspect: Rambuteau's levelling work had only affected the carriageway, which was subsequently 'lowered, and so much so, that from the Porte Saint-Martin to the Théâtre de l'Ambigu-Comique it was necessary to install a railing on each side, with steps every now and then. In this place, therefore, the carriageway was set down like a railway ... When the return of the troops under Marshal Canrobert from the Italian war of 1859 was announced, on the previous evening this part of the boulevard was invaded, the places against the railing were taken, and people spent the whole night there.'

This was the site of some of the great romantic theatres: the Théâtre de la Porte-Saint-Martin, built by Lenoir in forty days on the orders of Marie-Antoinette, where Frédérick Lemaître and Marie Dorval were hailed in *Marion Delorme*, and Mlle George in *Lucrèce Borgia*; the Ambigu, devoted to serious drama ('this is where you must go, lovers of great plays, dark and mysterious, but in which innocence always triumphs in the end, between eleven o'clock and midnight'[124]); the Folies-Dramatiques in Rue de Bondy (now René-Boulanger), 'where vaudeville is generally played, drama mixed with song, and finally the *Fantaisie*'. For Heine, this is where theatre was at its best, and it steadily declined as one went further east, towards the 'Boulevard du Crime', finally reaching 'Franconi's, where the stage scarcely counts as such, as the plays performed there are more fit for horses than for men'.[125]

With Franconi, we cross from Boulevard Saint-Martin to Boulevard du Temple. At no. 52 – a plaque notes that Gustave Flaubert lived here from 1856 to 1869 – the line of buildings curves northward, to the right if you face the nearby Place de la République. The last of these out-of-phase buildings abuts an immense blind wall, perpendicular to the boulevard and replacing in the general alignment the few metres that precede the Place. This arrangement has a simple explanation: the curve of the staggered buildings indicates the course of the 'original' Boulevard du Temple, before the cutting of Boulevard du Prince-Eugène (now Boulevard Voltaire) and the Place du Château-d'Eau (now Place de la République).

---

123 Lemer, *Paris au gaz*.
124 Paul de Kock, 'Les Boulevards de la porte Saint-Martin à la Bastille', in La Bédollière et al, *Paris Guide*. The Ambigu, at the acute angle formed by Rue de Bondy and the boulevard, was one of the finest halls in the city, built by Hittorff. It was destroyed in the 1960s by an insurance company, with the blessing of André Malraux, and replaced by a particularly frightful block of flats that breaks the alignment, the scale, and the harmony of tones of the boulevard.
125 Heine, *French Affairs*, letter 8, 1837.

This first Boulevard du Temple reached Boulevard Saint-Martin close to the present site of the Garde Républicaine barracks. Rue du Temple and Rue du Faubourg-du-Temple were then continuous, on either side of the Boulevards. This slightly dilated crossroads formed a small square, with a fountain in the middle where a flower market was held on Tuesdays and Thursdays.[126]

This is the most famous part of Boulevard du Temple, destroyed by the works of 1862: the Boulevard du Crime, thus named 'not by the Imperial prosecutors, but by vaudeville artists jealous of their fame for melodrama'.[127] Its popular favour began under the last years of the ancien régime. In its heyday, under the Restoration and the July monarchy, 'it was a Paris festival, a perpetual fair, an all-year carnival ... You could see birds doing tricks, hares bowing, fleas pulling carts; Mlle Rose with her head down and feet in the air: the spatchcocked Mlle Malaga, jugglers, conjurors, dwarves, giants, skeleton-men, ugly customers, boiling oil. Finally, Munito, the savant dog, a great calculator who did not disdain to give performances and lessons to the domino players at the Café de la Régence.'[128] In 1844, Balzac could still write that 'this is the only place in Paris where you hear the cries of Paris, you see the people thronging, rags to astonish a painter and looks

---

126   The succession of waterworks on this site is quite complicated. In the early nineteenth century the original 'Château d'Eau' was located on the open space that still separates Rue de Bondy (now René-Boulanger) from Boulevard Saint-Martin. 'Leaving the Ambigu,' La Bédollière wrote in *Le Nouveau Paris* (1860), 'we pass in front of the Château d'Eau, erected in 1811 after the design of M. Girard.' This was 'a superb fountain, whose waters came from the basin of La Villette, composed of three circular plinths in the middle of which is a double bowl in bronze, surrounded by four figures of lions that spout water from their jaws. It is distressing that such a fine monument is not surrounded by a square worthy of it.' In the 1860s one could read in various texts that this fountain was out of proportion with the immense Place de la République. On many maps of the time it is shown in the square, in front of the Prince-Eugène barracks. It was then removed to La Villette, where it can still be seen in front of the Great Hall. In 1867, Davioud installed a more impressive fountain in the middle of the new square. In 1883, the République monument replaced this second fountain, which today stands, also decorated with lions, in the middle of Place Daumesnil. 'The new Château d'Eau, which recalls the old one, had been placed right opposite the barracks and in the line of Boulevard du Prince-Eugène, at the point where one now sees this enormous statue of the République, a bit too massive. Leaving aside any political purpose, it produced there a happier effect, and a freshness that was much appreciated in summer' (Haussmann, *Mémoires*).
127   Joanne, *Paris illustré en 1870*. These are the few metres referred to in the famous song by Désaugiers: 'The only worthwhile promenade/The only one that holds me/The only one I take with a laugh/Is the Boulevard du Temple in Paris.'
128   Félix and Louis Lazare, *Dictionnaire des rues et monuments de Paris* (Paris, 1855).

to frighten a man of property. The late Bobèche was there, one of the local glories ... His accomplice was called Galimafrée. Martainville wrote sketches for these two illustrious acrobats who made children, soldiers and maids laugh enormously, their costumes always dotting the crowd on this famous boulevard.'[129] Haussmann, as we saw, was set on removing as soon as possible 'these unhealthy distractions that increasingly degrade and brutalize the popular masses'.

As reinscribed in collective memory by the joyful papier-mâché of *Les Enfants du Paradis*, seven theatres stood side by side on the left side of the boulevard, looking towards the Bastille. All these establishments had their stage door on Rue des Fossés-du-Temple (now Amelot), which formed a kind of common corridor. There was the Théâtre-Lyrique, which had 'mistakenly strayed into these parts', according to Haussmann. Massenet, when a student at the Conservatoire, played the kettledrum there in the evening to earn his living. 'I have to confess that I sometimes came in at the wrong place, but one day Berlioz complemented me for this, and said: "You're actually right, which is unusual!"'[130] At the Cirque-Olympique, run by the Franconis, the alternating attractions were Indian jugglers, Chinese and Italian acrobats, and savant animals – as well as military parades that revived the epic of the Empire. Then there were the Folies-Dramatiques, the Gaîté, devoted despite its name to the gloomiest melodramas, and the Funambules, whose star was the mime Debureau, as played by Jean-Louis Barrault in *Les Enfants du Paradis*. The diarist for *Le Globe*, the Saint-Simonian newspaper, wrote on 28 October 1831:

There is in this man's comedy something intangibly bitter and sad: the laughter he provokes, this laughter that comes so freely from his breast, is painful at the end, when we see, after having been so well entertained in all these ways, poor Debureau – or rather poor people! – fall totally back into the state of subjection, abasement and servitude in which we found them at the start of the play, and from which they escaped only for a moment to delight us so much. Adieu Pierrot! Adieu Gilles! Adieu Debureau! Adieu people, till tomorrow![131]

The line of theatres ended with the Délassements-Comiques and the Petit-Lazzari – which owed its name to an Italian mime of the eighteenth century – very close to the house where Fieschi exploded his bomb when

129 Balzac, 'Histoire et physiologie des Boulevards de Paris'.
130 Georges Cain, *Promenades dans Paris* (Paris: Flammarion, 1907).
131 Cited by Jacques Rancière, *The Nights of Labor* (Philadelphia: Temple University Press, 1989).

Louis-Philippe was approaching in 1835. After that, writes Haussmann, there were 'other well-forgotten dives'.[132]

These theatres were the stimulus for a proliferation of small trades, 'from the opener of carriage doors to the collector of cigar butts, and especially the seller of pass-out tickets, of whom there were few at the doors of other theatres'.[133] If there were cigar butts to collect and doors to open, this betokens a fashionable clientele who came slumming on the Boulevard du Crime: 'These ladies come into the little halls that in theatrical slang are called dives [bouis-bouis], in the same fashion that under the Regency the "impure" entertained themselves from time to time at the Théâtre de la Foire.'[134]

Haussmann's great works led to the disappearance of almost all these marvels. There remained the Théâtre Déjazet ('The name alone brings a smile, reminding you of a charming actress whom you must have applauded a hundred times, and will applaud again. Déjazet is an eighth wonder of the world, and for my part, I prefer her by far to the colossus of Rhodes'[135]), which owed its salvation to the fact that it was the only one on the opposite pavement from where demolition was taking place. There was also the Cirque d'Hiver, the former Cirque Napoléon built by Hittorff, where on Sunday afternoons the lions and clowns were replaced by concerts organized by Pasdeloup. 'Works by Haydn, Beethoven, Mozart, Weber, etc. were played here. This was not the place for quadrilles or polkas, but rather for strict and serious music, great music indeed.'[136]

'The rest of the Boulevard, from Rue d'Angoulême [now Jean-Pierre-Timbaud] through to the Bastille, has – we must confess – a sad scent of the Marais, which after nine in the evening is a kind of cemetery.'[137] Balzac

---

132   On the site of a wretched café, *L'Épi-Scié*, Alexandre Dumas established the Théâtre-Historique to produce his own works, and legend has it that on the theatre's opening the public queued for three days and nights at the box office for the premier of *La Reine Margot*. Haussmann, in his *Mémoires*, explains that 'the city did not have to concern itself with the more or less desirable position of these latter establishments' (the 'dives'). The Théâtre-Lyrique and the Cirque-Olympique were reconstructed opposite one another on the Place du Châtelet. The Gaîté was moved to the Square des Arts-et-Métiers, until it was destroyed while Chirac was mayor to make way for a mechanical billiards hall. The Folies was situated on Rue de Bondy, and the Funambules on Boulevard de Strasbourg.

133   Lemer, *Paris au gaz*. These 'pass-out tickets' were pieces of card given to the audience when they went out at the interval.

134   Ibid.

135   De Kock, 'Les Boulevards de la porte Saint-Martin à la Bastille'.

136   Ibid.

137   Lemer, *Paris au gaz*.

shows scarcely any greater esteem for the two major establishments to be found there: 'The famous Cadran Bleu has not a single window or floor which is evenly balanced. As for the Café Turc, it is to Fashion what the ruins of Thebes are to Civilization ... Soon the deserted boulevards begin, those without walkers. The pensioner strolls in his dressing gown if he feels like it; and on fine days, you see blind people playing card games. *In piscem desinit elegantia.*'

THE LEFT BANK QUARTERS

The Left Bank Boulevards

In general, towns built on a river grow on one of the two banks, and the other forms a surburb – often plebeian, often picturesque, but a suburb all the same: Trastevere, Oltranto, Lambeth, Brooklyn. The Danube does not run through Vienna, and in Budapest it divides two cities that back away from one another. In Paris, on the contrary, the Right and Left Banks have been in symbiosis since the dawn of time, and despite the spreading concrete, the river itself – its quays, bridges, islands, branches – is at once origin, frontier, tie, scenery and structure. But this 'great mirror of Paris, always alive', as Benjamin called it, is often veiled by a paraphernalia, a body of clichés that are among the most conventional of all that the city has given birth to. Songs, postcards, poems (even 'Pont Mirabeau'), technicolor and fashion photos have ended up giving the Seine a washed-out and commercial image, when it has not been prettified in literature (a frequent case, which provoked a furious outburst from André Breton on the death of Anatole France: 'To wrap up his corpse, we could empty out from the quays a box of those books *that he loved so much*, and throw the whole thing in the Seine. This man must not be allowed to go on making dust even when he's dead'[138]). Sentimental drivel should not lead us to forget that the role of the Seine has not always been for the best; from the days when it was 'covered with wounded and half-drowned people', as d'Aubigné put it, those massacred on St Bartholemew's Night, through to the Algerians murdered and thrown into the water in October 1961 by the police of Maurice Papon and Charles de Gaulle.

The asymmetry of the two banks – in both Old and New Paris – is not simply due to the shape of the meander that encircled the Left Bank and restricted its expansion. The difference today – six arrondissements on the Left Bank against fourteen on the Right – is essentially due to the

---

138   André Breton, 'Refus d'inhumer', October 1924.

differing pace of development, the delayed urbanization on the left side. In the heyday of the ancien régime, while the Right Bank broke its official bounds, all empty spaces were filled, houses rose in height, and construction spilled over its authorized limits, the Left Bank seemed asleep in its colleges, convents and gardens, and did not even manage to fill up the space that regulation attributed to it. This uneven development can be seen on the very banks of the Seine: 'What an eloquent contrast', wrote Sébastien Mercier, 'between the magnificent Right Bank of the river, and the Left Bank which is not even paved, and still full of mud and filth! It is only covered by workshops and shacks inhabited by the dregs of the population.' Delagrive's map, dating from 1728, shows a zone of dense urbanization on the Left Bank in a semicircle centred on the Place Maubert. Its outer limits today would be the Pont-Neuf in one direction and the Jussieu University at the other, with its circumference passing through the Odéon intersection, the Luxembourg Métro station and the Place de l'Estrapade, or more or less the walls of Philippe Auguste. On this map, the Faubourg Saint-Germain appears as a quarter of gardens, which it indeed remained. Rue Saint-Jacques, the main route towards Orléans, very soon becomes a country road between the orchards and vegetable gardens of the Ursulines, the Feuillantines, the Carmelites, the Visitandines, the Chartreux, Port-Royal and the Capucines. The other arteries of the Left Bank – Rue de la Harpe, or the sequence of streets Rue Galande/Rue Saint-Geneviève/Rue Mouffetard leading to the road to Italy – appear in Regency-era Paris as local paths, once the inner zone of greater density has been left behind.

The Left Bank did not really wake up until the late eighteenth century. On the site of the Hôtel de Condé, acquired by Louis XVI to house the Comédiens-Français, Peyre and Wailly designed the Théâtre de l'Odéon – inaugurated in 1782 with Racine's *Iphigénie* – the semicircular space facing it, and the diverging streets Rue de l'Odéon, Rue Crébillon and Rue Voltaire (now Casimir-Delavigne). This was one of the first modern residential developments in Paris, with pavements like those in London.[139] The two buildings that still frame the end of Rue de l'Odéon opposite the theatre, with a certain nobility, served as a shopwindow for this operation.

Around the same time, the Comte de Provence, the king's brother and future Louis XVIII, sold off a section of the Luxembourg, where Chalgrin designed the development of Rue de Fleurus, Rue Jean-Bart, and

---

139   'We are finally beginning to build one [a pavement] on both sides of the new road of the Théâtre-Français; but the fault committed is to have badly positioned posts that prevent coachmen from bringing the wheels of their carriages on to the sidewalk' (Mercier, *Tableau de Paris*). For the residential developments, see Pierre Pinon, *Paris, biographie d'une capitale* (Paris: Hazan, 1988).

Rue Duguay-Trouin, though these were not built until later, under the Restoration and the July monarchy. During the Revolution, one of the proposals of the Commission des Artistes was to open up the Chartreux enclosure.[140] ('The Charterhouse garden has a deserted character; the soil of the avenues is unturned; the trees do not bear signs of the sickle, they are puny and bent like the monks who greet you without looking at you', wrote Sébastien Mercier.) This is the origin of the crow's foot whose middle branch is Avenue de l'Observatoire, locating the Paris meridian between Rue de l'Est (now Boulevard Saint-Michel) and Rue de l'Ouest (now Rue d'Assas).

Despite these beginnings, the Left Bank was still very empty in the early nineteenth century. At the time in which *Les Misérables* was set, Montparnasse was counted as one 'those singular places' with which 'almost no one is familiar', in the company of La Glacière, Mont-Souris and La Tombe-Issoire. In *The Mysteries of Paris*, when the Chourineur follows the diabolical Tom and Sarah, their cab stops in a night so black that, in order to get his bearings, 'he drew his knife, and made a gash in one of the trees near which the carriage had stopped': this sinister place was Avenue de l'Observatoire. In 1836, at the corner of Rue Notre-Dame-des-Champs and Rue de l'Ouest, 'neither of which was paved at this point in time … it was only possible to walk beside the wooden fences that enclosed the market gardens, or alongside the houses, on narrow paths that were soon flooded by stagnant water that converted them into streams'.[141] At the beginning of *The Mohicans of Paris*, Alexandre Dumas remarks that 'Paris's Left Bank is naturally stationary, and tends rather to lose people than to gain them', and, as the only new constructions on the Left Bank between 1827 and 1854, he cites 'the Cuvier place and fountain, Rue Guy-Labrosse, Rue de Jussieu, Rue de l'École-Polytechnique, Rue de l'Ouest, Rue Bonaparte, the Orléans embankment [Gare d'Austerlitz] and the barrier of the Maine [Gare Montparnasse]'.

This gap of nearly a century is explained by the fact that there was nothing on the Left Bank that was in any way equivalent to the Grands Boulevards. Bullet and Blondel did indeed intend the new route to surround the whole city. But on the Right Bank it had the whole of the past to support it, the

---

140   A report to the Convention on 14 Thermidor of year II declared that the sale of national goods was suspended because 'a commission of artists is occupied at this time with a plan for the embellishment of Paris' (Lavedan, *Histoire de l'urbanisme à Paris*). The Commission's role tends to be underestimated, in the general movement of devaluing the Revolution, at least from 1793. Do people realize that such efforts were made to beautify Paris during the Terror?

141   Honoré de Balzac, *The Wrong Side of Paris* (1848).

ancient course of the Seine, the stones of medieval walls, monuments as solid as the Bastille and the Temple, whereas the 'boulevards du Midi' were traced amid quarries, fields and windmills, leaving outside them the most important contemporary buildings such as the Invalides, the Observatoire, and the Hôpital Général or Salpêtrière. It was not until much later that the belt of the southern boulevards was completed, in the second half of the nineteenth century, with two consequences that are still evident today: on the one hand, they do not coincide with the actual limit of Old Paris, which did not extend this far, and remains separated from them by a strip of 'modern' building; on the other hand they were – and remain – above all a route for traffic. The only sector suited for promenading, Boulevard Montparnasse between Avenue de l'Observatoire and Boulevard d'Enfer (now Raspail), was a world away from Boulevard des Italiens: 'This pavement is not asphalted, but planted with century-old lime trees, full of shade and joie de vivre in the spring . . . In the morning it is invaded by gardeners from the cemetery; in the evening, the silence is broken from time to time by the songs of drunkards coming back from the *barrière* or by the kisses of lovers returning from the radiant country of love.'[142]

Among those places that express in a clear and subtle fashion the swing of fashion from one bank to the other, there are the gardens that Paris owes to the two Florentine queens, Catherine and Marie de Médicis. During the greater part of the nineteenth century, the favoured shady haunt of dandies, lovers and writers was the Tuileries. In the flamboyant opening pages of Balzac's *The Girl With the Golden Eyes* (dedicated, we recall, to 'Eugène Delacroix, painter'), it is quite naturally on the Terrasse des Feuillants that Henri de Marsay meets Paquita Valdès. But starting with Verlaine and symbolism, and continuing right through the twentieth century (even if the Tuileries fountain still plays a role in *Nadja*), youth and poetry migrate towards the Luxembourg. The *Journal* of Paul Léautaud, 4 May 1901: 'Dusk gave the whole garden an endless depth, and a light mist was floating. I was on the terrace not far from the door to the greenhouses. In the lower part of the garden, the fountain rose and fell almost noiselessly. Soon the drum began to beat. They were about to close. I dreamed that I was facing a beautiful landscape of Baudelaire's . . .' Whether Jules Vallès, Léon Daudet, André Gide, Jules Romain, Jean-Paul Sartre, Michel Leiris or Jacques Roubaud, there is scarcely a Parisian novel or diary that does not feature the Luxembourg, central and symbolic site of a Left Bank that is seen as maternally welcoming students, writers, publishers and book-shops, art and experimental cinemas, avant-garde galleries and artists, not

---

142   Delvau, *Les Dessous de Paris*.

to mention the foreigners who arrived in the wake of Oscar Wilde, James Joyce, Joseph Roth and Henry Miller. The fragility of this construction, in large part mythological, has been rather sadly demonstrated in recent years.

As a hall or a landing opens onto the successive rooms to which it gives access, so the Luxembourg opens onto all the central quarters of the Left Bank. Near the school of apiculture it touches Montparnasse; its main entrance is towards the Observatoire; on the side of the Orangerie and the monument to Delacroix it borders on Saint-Sulpice, and in this way communicates with Saint-Germain; only Rue de Vaugirard separates it from the Odéon. And it is above all else, as Léon Daudet says, 'the respiratory centre, the vegetable lung, of the hard-working Latin Quarter'.

The Latin Quarter

Along with Les Halles, the Latin Quarter is the region of Old Paris that has been most transformed from the time of Baudelaire's childhood and Rastignac's youth. Perrot's atlas, dating from 1834, shows the quarter as it was for Balzac, organized around the two main north-south arteries of Rue de la Harpe and Rue Saint-Jacques. The first of these starts – as it still does – from Rue Saint-Séverin, climbs alongside Cluny to reach the Place Saint-Michel (now Place Edmond-Rostand), then continues along Rue d'Enfer: this is almost the route of Boulevard Saint-Michel today. The parallels of Rue de la Harpe and Rue Saint-Jacques are linked by a number of transverse streets: Rue de la Parcheminerie, whose name comes from the illustrators and bookbinders who worked there since the twelfth century; Rue du Foin; Rue des Mathurins (now replaced by Rue du Sommerard); Rue des Grès, near the law faculty on the present course of Rue Cujas; Rue Saint-Hyacinth, which obliquely connects the Place Saint-Michel with Rue des Fossés-Saint-Jacques, crossing the route of the future Rue Soufflot. Between Rue de la Harpe and Rue Monsieur-le-Prince – another main artery of the quarter – the street layout on the 1834 map is not very different from today's, except for Boulevard Saint-Germain. On the other side of the hill, however, east of the Place Maubert, no one could recognize where they were, at least without a few landmarks that remain: the École Polytechnique, the church of Saint-Nicolas-du-Chardonnet, Rue d'Arras, Rue de Pontoise and Rue de Poissy.

The Luxembourg opens onto the Latin Quarter through Rue Soufflot. This is a 'recent' street; when Père Goriot lived in Mme Vauquer's pension, it had been built only between the Panthéon and Rue Saint-Jacques, which caused problems for the gunners trying to dislodge the insurgents who had barricaded themselves in the monument in June 1848 – I shall return to this later. On what for a long time was known as the Place Saint-Michel – changed to Place du Luxembourg when the present Place Saint-Michel was built by the bridge on the small arm of the Seine, then to Place Edmond-Rostand in the 1950s – the start of Rue Soufflot was formerly framed by two old cafés, the Capoulade on the left and the Mahieu on the right. Léautaud's *Journal*, 19 January 1933:

> There was a whole period in my youth, reading the poets, reading Verlaine and often encountering him on his evening wanderings on Boulevard Saint-Michel, once also on Rue Monsieur-le-Prince at the junction with the little Rue de Vaugirard, badly dressed, limping, an infernal noise as he struck the pavement with his cane, another evening at the cellar of Le Soleil d'Or where I ventured (the café at the corner of Boulevard Saint-Michel and the quay, was that the Soleil d'Or?), one afternoon I saw him sitting, accompanied by Eugénie Krantz, on the terrace of the café on the corner of Rue Soufflot and Boulevard Saint-Michel (Café Mayeux, I believe), the side facing the boulevard, very close to the building that separates the café from the tobacconist's, and I got a child to take him a bunch of violets.

Rue Soufflot climbs towards Rue Saint-Jacques, which is the real highway of the Latin Quarter – more than Boulevard Saint-Michel, conceived in order to neutralize the old streets with their riots and barricades, and which I have always experienced as a corridor of noise and ugliness. Between the river and Rue des Écoles, a number of old bookshops-cum-publishers remain to remind you that until the end of the ancien régime, Rue Saint-Jacques had a virtual monopoly of printing – from the time that the three Gering brothers, who came from Konstanz, established their presses at the sign of the Soleil d'Or in 1473 – as well as of publishing and bookselling, activities that were then combined. The establishments listed in the *Catalogue chronologique des librairies et librairies-imprimeurs de Paris depuis l'an 1470, époque de l'établissement de l'Imprimerie dans cette capitale jusqu'à présent* (1789)[143] are almost all grouped on Rue Saint-Jacques and its immediate neighbours – Rue des Poitevins, Rue des Anglais, Rue Galande, Rue Serpente and Place de la Sorbonne. The Estiennes, printers from father to son, starting with the great Robert Estienne whose workshop was visited by François I in person, were on Rue Saint-Jacques, and the Didots on Rue Saint-André-des-Arts. 'There is nothing more comic than the timid and conceited beginnings of a poet who, burning

---

143 'Chez Jean-Roch Lottin de Saint-Germain, Imprimeur-libraire ordinaire de la ville, Rue Saint-André-des-Arts, no. 27, 1789.'

with impatience to appear before the public, approaches for the first time a typographer in Rue Saint-Jacques, who in turn gives himself airs and comes to appreciate literary merit', writes Sébastien Mercier. In the early nineteenth century, before the book world crossed the Seine to lay siege to the Palais-Royal, it spilled over onto the Quai des Grands-Augustins, where there was to be found, among others, 'the firm of Fendant and Cavalier [which] had started in business without any capital whatsoever. A great many publishing houses were established at that time in the same way, and are likely to be established so long as papermakers and printers will give credit for the time required to play some seven or eight of the games of chance called "new publications".'[144] On such matters as games of chance, credit and bankruptcy, Balzac was of course in his element.

Between Rue des Écoles and Rue Soufflot, Rue Saint-Jacques was completely rebuilt in the 1860s, but it is still possible to admire the setting formed by the little sloping garden in front of the Collège de France, where chestnut and plane trees, limes and acacias (no doubt planted when Claude Bernard held the chair of medicine) have reached gigantic size, the Lycée Louis-le-Grand (my own *lycée*), and the Sorbonne crowned by its observatory tower with the silhouette of a minaret – and in the background, at the top of the hill, the Jansenist bell tower of Saint-Jacques-du-Haut-Pas.

To the left of Rue Saint-Jacques, or the east if you prefer, Rue des Écoles separates two different regions. The lower one, modern and active, stretches towards the Jussieu University and the Jardin des Plantes. Its centre is the Place Maubert. In 1862, Delvau could still write that this was

perhaps the only part of Paris that has kept its former physiognomy. Ten steps away, Paris has dressed itself from head to foot in fresh stone and plaster: only the Place Maubert cynically vaunts its old rags! It is not a square, but a vast puddle of mud ... It is like a living tradition of medieval Paris. If you blink your eyes, you might believe you were still seeing and hearing its population from the time of Isabel of Bavaria and Louis XI! A prolific and tenacious breed, which resisted all efforts to destroy or even civilize it – as M. Joseph Prudhomme said. Nothing did the trick, not guns, or plague, or famine, or starvation, or debauchery – not even mutual education![145]

The property speculation of the 1960s succeeded where guns and plague had failed.

144   Balzac, *Lost Illusions*.
145   Delvau, *Les Dessous de Paris*.

The top of the Montagne, a very ancient region that stretches across the Place du Panthéon towards the Mouffetard quarter, has been partly disfigured by the proliferation of restaurants and crêperies. The Place de la Contrescarpe and Rue Mouffetard, 'a localized swarm, a kind of Villonesque survival' from the time of Léon Daudet, which the Situationists of the 1950s made into the '*continent Contrescarpe*', are now no more than shadows of their former selves. And yet, on the irregular territory bordered by Rues Tournefort, Lhomond, de l'Arbalète, Claude-Bernard, d'Ulm and de l'Estrapade, in a modest and almost village-like architectural setting, memories of Diderot and the four sergeants of La Rochelle (in 1970 there was still a café bearing their names on the corner of Rue Descartes and Rue Clovis, and it is right, I believe, that the memory of their republican martyrdom should have been cherished so long on this counter[146]) merge with memories of Eugène Rastignac, still the naïve boarder at Mme Vauquer's, as well as those of another student – young Vingtras, alias Vallès.

'No one knows why certain quarters become degraded and vulgarized, morally as well as materially; why, for instance, the ancient residence of the court and the church, the Luxembourg and the Latin Quarter, have become what they are today . . . why the elegance of life has left that region . . . why such mud and dirty trades and poverty should have fastened on a hilly piece of ground, instead of spreading out upon the flat land beyond the confines of the ancient city.' Such is Balzac's musing in *The Lesser Bourgeoisie*. Twenty years later, Théodore de Banville asked in similar vein:

> How could the student of today insist on being what the student of an earlier age was, when the inevitable Duval restaurants, with their mouldings, gilt decoration and exotic wooden ceilings, have established themselves in a palace, on the very spot where modest eateries were formerly sited, and when you can see, right on Rue des Grès, where the Middle Ages left such a strong imprint, an English tavern offering its roast beef, York ham, pickles and sauces of ground-up cockchafer (see Balzac), washed down with pale ale, as in Rue Royale?[147]

---

146   Jean-François Bories and the three other sergeants, who were members of a republican secret society, were executed on the Place de Grève on 21 September 1822 (some say they were shot, which would have been 'normal' for soldiers, but the Place de Grève was the site of the guillotine . . .). 'The quays were thick with people. Despite a formidable military and police presence, the condemned received the sympathy of an immense number.' Those are the words of a seventeen-year-old witness, Auguste Blanqui, who was marked forever by this execution (Jeanne Gilmore, *La République clandestine, 1818–1848* [Paris: Aubier, 1997]).
147   'Le quartier Latin', in La Bédollière et al, *Paris Guide*.

And in 1964, Yvan Christ would not have believed he had hit the nail on the head quite so accurately in predicting that 'in twenty years, new and tender greybeards will shed melancholy tears over the old Latin Quarter of the 1960s, the best years there ever were'.[148]

Ever since the time of Villon, the Latin Quarter, as the quarter of youth, was prey more than any other to nostalgia for the good old days. But however much one might distrust such feelings, it is impossible not to regret the profusion, variety and liveliness of the cafés of the quarter between 1850 and 1914 – not their physical setting, which was in no way comparable with the fairyland establishments on the Boulevards, but their atmosphere. Some of them were political first and foremost. Vallès relates that in 1850, in the Café du Vote Universel, 'there were people said to have been leaders on the barricades of Saint-Merri, prisoners at Dullens, insurgents of June 1848'. Close by, in the Café de la Renaissance, opposite the Saint-Michel fountain, the public 'had a particular physiognomy at the absinthe hour and in the evenings. Untidy students with their hair in disorder, *women students* ... The masters of Paris under the Commune held their sessions there, preparing their sinister plan of campaign that would end up in fire and murder.'[149] In Rue Saint-Séverin, where François Maspero's La Joie de Lire served as a political university for a whole generation, the Brasserie Saint-Séverin was one of the canteens for the leaders of the Commune. According to Lepage, who can hardly be suspected of objectivity, 'Above them ruled Raoul Rigault ... arriving on horseback, turning his mount on Boulevard Saint-Michel, and gazing arrogantly at the women from behind a double lorgnette.'

Other places were more prosaic. The immense d'Harcourt, on the corner of the Place de la Sorbonne and Boulevard Saint-Michel (the side opposite the present PUF bookstore[150]) was a *café à femmes*. For poor students, the most welcoming restaurants were Flicoteaux and Pension Laveur. 'In exceptional cases, you have Flicoteaux', Dumas explains in *The Mohicans of Paris*. You ate there on long tables, in two rooms at right angles, one of which overlooked the Place de la Sorbonne and the other Rue Neuve-de-Richelieu (now Champollion). When Lucien de Rubempré no longer had a sou, he dined at Flicoteaux, which is where he made the decisive acquaintance of Lousteau:

148   Article 'Quartier Latin', in *Dictionnaire de Paris* (Paris: Hazan 1964).
149   A. Lepage, *Cafés littéraires et politiques de Paris* (Paris: Dentu, 1874).
150   [Editorial note: now replaced by a men's casual clothing store.]

Few indeed were the students who lived in the Latin Quarter during the last twelve years of the Restoration and did not frequent that temple sacred to hunger and impecuniosity ... Verily, the heart of more than one great man ought to wax warm with innumerable recollections of inexpressible enjoyment at the sight of the small, square window-panes that look upon the Place de la Sorbonne, and Rue Neuve-de-Richelieu. Flicoteaux II and Flicoteaux III respected the old exterior, maintaining the dingy hue and general air of a respectable, old-established house, showing thereby the depth of their contempt for the charlatanism of the shop-front, the kind of advertisement which feasts the eyes at the expense of the stomach, to which your modern restaurant almost always has recourse.[151]

As for Pension Laveur, this was, in Léon Daudet's words, 'a real historic institution which had seen three generations pass, situated on Rue des Poitevins opposite the École de Médecine, in a dilapidated old hôtel ... You reached the dining rooms and tables by a stone stairway with worn and polished steps, like the border of a Breton well. Aunt Rose, affectionate and venerable, presided over the cash desk, assisted by the brunette Mathilde and Baptiste, who took orders with a smile and brought the dishes grumbling.'[152] And Francis Carco, around the same time: 'I had credit at the Pension Laveur and ate twice a day. Ah, that pension! Despite the smell of cats in the stairway and its lack of pretensions, Baptiste did us well ...'[153] Thirty years earlier you could sometimes meet Courbet there – not yet the 'famous demolisher' as Lepage called him – but his usual establishment was rather Brasserie Andler on Rue Hautefeuille, where he had his studio. Courbet's arrival at Andler's did not pass unheeded: 'He advanced, holding his head high – like Saint-Just – and was surrounded! He sat down – and people made a circle around him! He spoke – and people listened to him! When he left, they were still listening.'[154] On the list of regular customers, mostly now forgotten ('Simbermann, experimental chemist and member of the meteorological society, Dupré, professor of anatomy, Furne, publisher'), there appears, as if in an obscure corner, 'Charles Baudelaire, author of *Les Fleurs du mal*, which was still unpublished, and who tried out his Edgar Allan Poe effects on the heads of his companions'.

---

151   Balzac, *Lost Illusions*.
152   Daudet, *Paris vécu*.
153   Carco, *De Montmartre au Quartier Latin*.
154   Alfred Delvau, *Histoire anecdotique des cafés et cabarets de Paris* (Paris: Dentu, 1862).

The literary cafés included some very modest ones, such as Le Soleil d'Or, on the corner of the Place Saint-Michel and the *quai*, where the symbolists held their La Plume evenings, or the Paradox dairy on Rue Saint-André-des-Arts, where you could meet

> Auguste Poulet-Malassis, student at the École de Chartes, today a book-seller; a tall chap, very pale, with a certain resemblance to Henri III ... a charming conversationalist, very intelligent and learned, whom every-one would have loved had he not bent all his efforts to being hated ... Nadar, a novelist who was not yet a photographer, Asselineau, a young bibliophile who was not yet a critic, Charles Baudelaire, a poet who was not yet a candidate for the Academy, Privat d'Anglemont, a young explorer of the underside of Paris who was not yet in the Montmartre cemetery.[155]

But the most famous of these cafés was the Vachette, on the corner of Rue des Écoles and Boulevard Saint-Michel, frequented by Maurras, Catulle Mendès, Heredia, Huysmans, sometimes Mallarmé, Barrès ('It is here,' he said, 'that young people acquire the dyspepsia that gives them a distin-guishable physiognomy around the age of forty'), and above all Moréas. 'I arrived at the Vachette,' Carco recalled, 'just in time to know Moréas. To the young people who surrounded him, he declared: "Base your-selves firmly on principles." Then stroking his moustache and adjusting his monocle with an air of authority, he added: "They will certainly end up giving way!"'

At the western edge of the quarter, the symbolists of *Le Mercure de France* and the theatre people had their haunts around the Odéon. In the Café Tabourey, at the corner of Rue Molière (now Rotrou) and Rue de Vaugirard, in the age of *réalisme*, you could often see 'Champfleury, Pierre Dupont the rustic poet, Charles Baudelaire the materialist poet, Leconte de Lisle the pantheist poet, Hippolyte Babou, Auguste Préault the sculp-tor, Théodore de Banville ... I had the honour of seeing there – my little one, my obscure adolescent! – the great and glorious M. de Balzac on the morning of the first performance of his *Les Ressources de Quinola*.'[156] Much later, in the Café Voltaire on the Place de l'Odéon, where Pierre Louÿs and Henri de Régnier often came, Paul Fort celebrated the marriage of his daughter to Severini: 'The Prince of Poets, standing on the piano, sang.

---

155 Ibid. Poulet-Malassis, whom Baudelaire called Coco-Malperché, was the publisher of *Les Fleurs du mal*.
156 Ibid. Hippolyte Babou was the friend of Baudelaire who suggested to him the title for *Les Fleurs du mal*.

Marinetti, whose proud white automobile stood on the grey paving of the Place de l'Odéon, abandoned himself to the joys of Futurism. He broke the glassware. It was splendid.'[157]

Odéon

As for the Odéon quarter – an isosceles triangle with its apex at the Odéon intersection, its sides formed by Rue Monsieur-le-Prince and Rue de Condé – is it part of the Latin Quarter? Léautaud was categorical, and he knew what he was talking about, as he lived at various times on Rue Monsieur-le-Prince, Rue de l'Odéon and Rue de Condé, working at *Le Mercure de France* on the same street. In his *Journal*, on 6 October 1903, he wrote: 'Move from Rue de Condé to Rue de l'Odéon, 6 October. Hatred of this whole Latin Quarter. When will I be able to live somewhere else?' For him, it was crossing Rue Tournon that brought you into Saint-Germain-des-Près. In the early twentieth century, and in the years between the wars, this point of view was certainly justified. If the Odéon quarter was not really a student district, the booksellers under the theatre colonnade played a role in literary life. For the *bachelier* Vingtras–Vallès, 'the Odéon is our club and our asylum. Rummaging on the bookstalls there gives you the air of a man of letters, and at the same time you're sheltered from the rain. We come there when we get tired of the silence and smell of our hovels.' Many years later, Léon Daudet – a student in medicine, which did not work out for him – was also attracted by 'the famous galleries of the Flammarion bookshop around the Odéon, bristling with books. These are connected for me with meeting rather wild young people, and also with my first success, *Les Morticoles*. I did not dare inquire about it in the two weeks after the volume appeared. The booksellers, who knew me, signalled to me from a distance, and one of them cried out: "Great success!" '[158]

And around the same time, Léon-Paul Fargue: 'We read under the galleries of the Odéon, standing up, our noses as far forward as possible in pages that were not cut, seeking our food.'[159] Behind the theatre, on the corner of Rue de Tournon and Rue de Vaugirard, Foyot's restaurant was frequented by intellectuals – senators too – until an anarchist bomb blew them up.[160] The *Mercure*, and the bookshops of Adrienne Monnier and

---

157   Carco, *De Montparnasse au Quartier Latin.*
158   Daudet, *Paris vécu.*
159   Paul Fargue, 'La Classe de Mallarmé', in *Refuges* (Paris: Émile-Paul Frères, 1942; republished Paris: Gallimard, 1998).
160   According to Joan Halperin, the impeccable biographer of Fénéon, it was he who placed the bomb, in a flower pot – *Félix Fénéon, Aesthete and Anarchist in Fin-de-Siècle Paris* (New Haven: Yale University Press, 1988). Laurent Tailhade lost an eye in the explosion.

Sylvia Beach on Rue de l'Odéon, gave the triangle a literary coloration that succeeded in attaching it to the Latin Quarter, but has since almost entirely disappeared.

Saint-Sulpice

To pass from the Luxembourg to Saint-Germain-des-Près you have to cross the little quarter of Saint-Sulpice, and to reach its central square you must choose between three streets which, although all parallel, sloping, short and of the same era, have each to my eyes a different charm. Rue Férou has perhaps the most perfect architecture. Rue Servandoni is the setting for an important episode in *The Three Musketeers*, on which Umberto Eco writes: 'Alas, our empirical reader will certainly be moved at the mention of the Rue Servandoni, because Roland Barthes lived there, but Aramis couldn't have, because the action takes place in 1625 whereas the Florentine architect Giovanni Niccolo Servandoni was born in 1695, designed the façade of Saint-Sulpice church in 1733, and had the street dedicated to him only in 1806.'[161] For my part, I always choose the third, Rue Garancière, not for the little fountain of the Princess Palatine, nor for the rams of the Hôtel de Sourdéac and the memory of the Plon-Nourrit publishing house, but to greet once again, at the foot of Saint-Sulpice, the lead pelican on top of the large bulbous roof of the chapel of the Assumption, and above all the pendentive supporting the overhang of the axial chapel above the street, a masterpiece of Paris stereotomy, perhaps even finer than the one on the Hôtel Portalis, at the corner of Rue Croix-des-Petits-Champs and Rue de La Vrillière.

> There are many things on the Place Saint-Sulpice. For example: a *mairie*, a tax office, a police station, three cafés – one selling tobacco –, a cinema, a church on which Le Vau, Gittard, Oppenordt, Servandoni and Chalgrin worked, and which is dedicated to an almoner of Clotaire II who was bishop of Bourges from 624 to 644, with his feast day on 17 January, a publisher, an undertaker, a travel agent, a bus stop, a tailor's, a hotel, a fountain decorated with the statues of four great Christian orators (Bossuet, Fénelon, Fléchier and Massillon), a newspaper kiosk, a shop selling pious objects, a car park, a beauty parlour and many more.[162]

---

161 Umberto Eco, *Six Walks in the Fictional Woods* (Cambridge, MA: Harvard University Press, 1994), p. 104.
162 Georges Perec, *Tentative d'épuisement d'un lieu parisien* (Paris: Christian Bourgois, 1975).

By contamination from the style of plaster saints known as *saint-sulpicien*, this square and its church have often been badly thought of ('Herrera lived on Rue Cassette, near Saint-Sulpice, the church to which he was attached. This building, hard and stern in style, suited this Spaniard, whose discipline was that of the Dominicans.'[163]). But there are now many who admire the double portico of Servandoni's façade, and regret that his death prevented him from finishing the square and realizing the grand arch he had designed along the axis of the church, under which Rue Neuve-Saint-Sulpice would have opened.[164]

Saint-Germain-des-Prés

Of the quarters defined by the *ordonnance* of 1702, Saint-Germain-des-Près was the twentieth and last, a sufficient sign that it was not similar in kind to the others. The old abbey, which had remained outside Charles V's walls but was fortified at the same epoch, kept its defences until the 1670s and was never part of Paris. When all the fortifications were pulled down, the abbey also demolished its crenellated precinct and filled up the ditches over which the major streets of the present-day quarter were built.

Around the monastery – of which the bell tower of Saint-Germain-des-Près indicates the centre – a whole community of merchants and artisans developed, living peacefully there just as in other Parisian enclosures. It was known indifferently as the *bourg* or *faubourg* Saint-Germain. In the eighteenth century it was a quadrilateral, with three of its sides corresponding to modern streets: Rue Saint-Benoît, Rue Jacob, Rue de l'Échaudé (the name does not refer to a 'scalded' person, but to a triangular cake – and by extension to a block of houses of this shape bounded by this street, along with Rue de la Seine and Rue Jacob). The fourth side was formed by a sequence of three streets, more or less along the line of Boulevard Saint-Germain: from west to east, these were Rue Taranne – where Diderot lived for a long time, commemorated by a statue there – Rue Sainte-Marguerite and Rue des Boucheries.[165] Other streets were laid down within the abbey grounds, of which Rue Abbatiale (now Passage de la

---

163   Honoré de Balzac, *Scenes from a Courtesan's Life* (1838), trans. Waring.
164   Only one building was finished after his plans, no. 6, on the northeast corner of the square close to Rue des Canettes. This was the office of the publisher to which Perec alludes: Robert Laffont, bought up long ago now by the Presses de la Cité group, alias CEP, alias Havas, alias Vivendi.
165   Remnants of this are the old houses on the odd-numbered side of Boulevard Saint-Germain, between Rue des Saints-Pères and Rue de Rennes. Rue Gozlin is a fragment of Rue des Boucheries.

Petite-Boucherie), Rue Cardinale and Rue de Furstemberg remain (Place de Furstemberg was the stable yard of the abbey). Despite the cutting of Rue de l'Abbaye and Rue Bonaparte in the early nineteenth century, as proposed by the Commission des Artistes, and the incomparably more brutal cutting of Boulevard Saint-Germain and Rue de Rennes, the centre of Saint-Germain-des-Prés is still today the Abbaye quarter.

Between the *bourg* of Saint-Germain and the city, the centre of activity was focused on two crossroads that have preserved despite everything their life and energy. The first was the confluence of Rue de Buci with Rue du Four and Rue des Boucheries – now the Mabillon intersection. From here, Rue de Montfaucon led to the Saint-Germain fairground, one of the great attractions of Paris since the twelfth century. This was held each year on Palm Sunday, a week before Easter, on the site of the present market, surrounded by four streets with the names Clément, Mabillon, Lobineau and Félibien, all eminences of the Benedictine order.[166] It was initially a luxury market selling rare objects, 'sweet nothings' from Flanders and Germany, Venetian mirrors, Indian cloth, and wonders from other far-off countries brought in by the Portuguese merchants that Scarron conjures up: 'Take me to the Portuguese/We shall find at low price/Goods from China./We shall find ambergris/And varnished woods/From that divine country/Or rather from that paradise.' But the fair was also a place of entertainment for a very mixed population, prefiguring the Wooden Galleries of the Palais-Royal or the slopes of La Courtille. The aristocracy visited there after supper. People played skittles, *tourniquet* (a kind of roulette), dice or cards. Women of the highest rank, with black velvet masks, watched the games or played themselves, their eyes reflecting the light of the torches. Mixed in with this elegant crowd were quarrelsome 'schoolboys', lackeys, bourgeois, and thieves who picked pockets and cut purses. 'There, men six feet tall, with high boots and hair styled like sultans, passed for giants. A shaved and depilated female bear, clothed in jacket and trousers, was taken for a unique and extraordinary animal. A wooden colossus spoke, having hidden within it a four-year-old boy.'[167]

The other lively crossroads was at the Porte de Buci, where Rue Saint-André-des-Arts crossed the Paris fortifications (level with Rue Mazet). This gate controlled an old road which, until the building of the Pont-Neuf, was the obligatory itinerary for the inhabitants of Saint-Germain, if they wanted to

---

166 The modern market is a reconstruction, supposedly identical, of the neoclassical market designed by Blondel. It is the work of Olivier Cacoub, the favourite architect of Jacques Chirac, responsible for many other Parisian disasters, including the 'Le Ponant' building overlooking the Parc André-Citroën.

167 Mercier, *Tableau de Paris*.

cross to the Cité by the Petit-Pont: the artery of Rue du Four–Rue de Buci–Rue Saint-André-des-Arts. Rue Dauphine, a major route in the first operation of concerted town planning in Paris – along with the Place Dauphine and the Pont-Neuf – reached this crossroads obliquely. Nine metres across, this was the widest street in Paris. Henri IV wanted it to have a regular architecture. On 2 May 1607 he wrote to Sully: 'My friend, following what I have told you that work is beginning on the buildings that are in the new road going from the end of the Pont-Neuf to the Porte de Bussy, I wanted to send you this word to tell you that I would be very happy if you would explain to those who start building in this road that they should make the front of their houses entirely in the same order, for it would be a fine ornament to see from the end of the bridge this road with one and the same façade.'[168]

When the fortifications were demolished, the Porte de Buci was taken down and the ditches filled in to make what are now Rue Mazarine and Rue de l'Ancienne-Comédie, adding to a liveliness that remains after three centuries. Thus, on the site of 4 Rue de Buci, opposite Rue Grégoire-de-Tours, gastronomic and literary events were held at a restaurant named Landelle, attended by Piron, Crébillon (father and son), Duclos and Helvétius. This is also where the first Masonic lodge in Paris met, founded by the English. During the Revolution, the building housed the printing press of *Le Courrier français*, Brissot's newspaper. In 1860, its tenants were the painter Giacomelli and the publisher Poulet-Malassis, who had just had serious problems with the law after publishing *Les Fleurs du mal*.[169]

The streets surrounding the École des Beaux-Arts, the Institut, and the Monnaie, are different from the rest of Saint-Germain. The shadows of these great buildings, a certain detachment, and the proximity of the river, lend them a silent dignity to which poets and visitors were always sensitive. Plaques that their habitués know by heart indicate that Saint-Amant, Racine, Balzac, Heine, Mickiewicz, Wagner and Oscar Wilde lived and worked here – as well as Picasso, if you press on to the hotel on Rue des Grands-Augustins where he painted *Guernica*, in the same building where Balzac wrote *An Unknown Masterpiece*.

Faubourg Saint-Germain

By an aberration of toponymy, the section of the 7th arrondissement between Rue des Saint-Pères and Boulevard des Invalides is known as the

---

168 *Lettres missives d'Henri IV*, vol. 7 (Paris, 1858); cited by Pinon, *Paris, biographie d'une capitale*.
169 G. Lenôtre, *Secrets du vieux Paris* (Paris: Grasset, 1954).

Faubourg Saint-Germain. A curious faubourg, given that it lies inside Old Paris, lacks a dominating thoroughfare – Boulevard Saint-Germain is of course much more recent – and is also quite different from the other great aristocratic faubourg of Saint-Honoré. This anomaly is explained by the delay in urbanization: the quarter was built in an empty space, inside the old city but at the same time as the 'real' faubourgs, which were already outside, and thereby acquired the same designation.

The Faubourg Saint-Germain, moreover, belongs to the realm of myth as well as that of geography, given how it recalls for many people the two great scenes for which it served as both backdrop and cast, *La Comédie humaine* and *À la Recherche du temps perdu*. Balzac:

> The thing known in France as the Faubourg Saint-Germain is neither a quarter, nor a sect, nor an institution, nor anything else that admits of a precise definition. There are great houses on the Place Royale, the Faubourg Saint-Honoré, and the Chaussée d'Antin, in any one of which you may breathe the same atmosphere of Faubourg Saint-Germain. So, to begin with, the whole faubourg is not within the faubourg. There are men and women born far enough away from its influences who respond to them and take their place in the circle; and again there are others, born within its limits, who may yet be driven forth forever.[170]

And Proust, apropos the Hôtel de Guermantes: 'The presence of the body of Jesus Christ in the host seemed to me no more obscure a mystery than this leading house in the Faubourg being situated on the Right Bank of the river and so near that from my bedroom I could hear its carpets being beaten.'[171]

The construction of this faubourg proceeded in two stages, with an interval of close to a century. In the early 1600s, '*la reine Margot*' – Marguerite de Valois, the first wife of Henri IV – bought an immense piece of land parallel to the river, opposite the Louvre. She had an hôtel built with gardens extending to Rue des Saints-Pères, and continuing from there, through a park that was not closed by walls, to occupy the entire space between Rue de l'Université and Rue de la Seine, with only countryside beyond.[172] On Marguerite's death, Louis XIII sold off this land in plots to pay his debts. The long parallels of Rue de Lille, Rue de Verneuil and Rue de l'Université have marked for close to four centuries now the course of the avenues in the park of *la reine Margot*.

---

170   Balzac, *The Duchess of Langeais*.
171   Marcel Proust, *The Guermantes Way, Remembrance of Things Past* (Penguin: Harmondsworth, 1983), vol. 2, p. 25.
172   The main entrance to this hôtel was close to 6 Rue de Seine.

Towards the end of Louis XIV's reign, construction began on a new Faubourg Saint-Germain, beyond Rue des Saints-Pères, for the aristocracy who were leaving the Marais. Rue Saint-Dominique, Rue de Grenelle with Bouchardon's splendid fountain of the Quatre-Saisons, and Rue de Varenne, were then drawn parallel to the streets of Margot's domain. The grid was completed by streets perpendicular to the river: Rue de Bellechasse and Rue de Bourgogne, and above all the commercial Rue du Bac, a major route connecting the faubourg with the Right Bank following the construction of the Pont-Royal. This was the route that duchesses took to pay court at the Tuileries. This very loosely patterned urban grid still marks out today the large blocks; their hôtels placed between a front courtyard and a back garden have passed from the hands of the aristocracy to those of the ministerial technocracy, but this has not made them more accessible than they were before, when it was possible to enter many noble dwellings without a badge or identity papers.[173]

The 'existentialist' Saint-Germain-des-Près also has its legend, fuelled largely by hate-filled articles in the 'right-wing' press – the apostrophes are needed, as in the great years of the Tabou, the Rose-Rouge, the Bar-Vert and the Montana, between the Liberation and 1950, no one would say they were on the right, given that the term was at this time equivalent to 'collaborator', and right-wing figures were often in prison or prudently living abroad. But what is certain is that Saint-Germain-des-Près was until the late 1980s the centre of French publishing. This certainly had its extensions elsewhere, in the Latin Quarter (Maspero-La Découverte by the Sorbonne, Hachette in its historic building on the corner of Boulevard Saint-Germain and Boulevard Saint-Michel), in Montparnasse (Albin Michel, Larousse), and even on the Right Bank (Calmann-Lévy). But the bulk of publishers were grouped in the 6th arrondissement, until concentration, the search for economies of scale, and a contempt for history dispersed the large conglomerates and their controlling directors into air-condi-

---

173 'At that time' (in the 1780s), 'there was not a door that would not open at the slightest request of an unknown tourist; no reference was demanded, no recommendation ... Anyone who possessed paintings, a collection of prints, a library, or simply fine furniture, freely offered their treasures to the admiration of all comers. It was in no way difficult to enter the home of the Duc d'Orléans at the Palais-Royal, the Prince de Condé, M. Beaujon whose apartments were famous, the Prince de Salm whose hôtel was scarcely finished, or the Duc de Praslin where one could inspect his sumptuous furniture ... You could likewise go from door to door, visiting the picture galleries of the hôtels of Chabot, Luynes, Briassac and Vaudreuil, the natural-history collections of Chaulnes and La Rochefoucauld, or the gardens of M. de Biron or M. de Saint-James' (Lenôtre, *Secrets du vieux Paris*).

tioned towers, sheltered from any contagion with actual books, readers or bookshops.[174]

Haussmann's cuttings

Within the limits of Old Paris, the cuttings of the nineteenth century were fairly reasonable, though less from any archaeological scruple than due to a lack of time. It was thanks to the disasters of Metz and Sedan, thanks to the military talent of Mac-Mahon and Bazaine, that the complete gutting of Saint-Germain-des-Près was avoided, Rue de Rennes not pushed through to the Pont des Arts and the Marais ravaged by the extension of Rue Étienne-Marcel to the Bastille. The routes that were completed had clear town-planning reasons. Two east-west carriageways were connected perpendicularly to the great north-south axis Sébastopol–Saint-Michel, one on each bank: the extension of Rue de Rivoli, and Boulevard Saint-Germain (with Rue des Écoles an aborted first attempt). This orthogonal system was completed by transversals such as Rue Réaumur, and obliques like Rue de Turbigo and the Avenue de l'Opéra.

These cuttings certainly left their scars on the old quarters. On either side of the Place Saint-Michel, that paradigm of Haussmannism, Place Saint-André-des-Arts and the Saint-Séverin quarter form an intact frame, architecturally at least.[175] 'Sue, Hugo, and of course Balzac, would recognize around them, unchanged, Paris of the Middle Ages, the same as we could find still alive, despite Haussmann, until not so long ago, in the bits of those streets that used to connect Rue Saint-Denis and Rue Saint-Martin, but which, pierced in the middle by Boulevard Sébastopol, had found a way to reconstitute at their two extremities their old and still unchanged glory.'[176] What contributed to the peaceful character of this coexistence was the care taken by the nineteenth-century architects in connecting their cuttings with the old roads, as for example at the junction between Rue de Rennes and Rue du Vieux-Colombier, where Second Empire architecture repeats in a more modern vein the orders of the eighteenth century.[177] The

174 There are still some independent houses in the quarter – Gallimard, Le Seuil, Minuit and Christian Bourgois, among others.

175 Those who deplore the invasion of this quarter by doner kebab can at least refer to Mercier's *Tableau de Paris*: 'The Turks who arrived in the train of the last Ottoman ambassador found nothing more agreeable in the whole of Paris than Rue de la Huchette, on account of the rotisseries there and the succulent smoke they exhaled ... Cooked fowl could be obtained there at any hour of the day; the spits were constantly on an ever-burning fire.'

176 Chevalier, *Montmartre du plaisir et du crime*.

177 François Loyer, *Paris XIXe siècle, l'immeuble et la rue* (Paris: Hazan, 1987).

two buildings on the Place des Victoires that frame the beginning of Rue Étienne-Marcel are also extraordinary adaptations of rhythms and proportions from the age of Louis XIV. This concern for integration sometimes even led to the reuse of a whole side of a street in the new openings – Rue Taranne partly integrated, as we saw, into Boulevard Saint-Germain, or entire sections of the old Rue Pélipeaux and Rue Thévenot absorbed into Rue Réaumur, near the Temple.

The Île de la Cité was an exception, as here Haussmann caused complete disaster. For him it was 'a place obstructed by a crowd of shacks, inhabited by bad characters, and crossed by damp, twisted and dirty streets', a description that is repeated in a different form in certain of Meryon's engravings, such as *L'Hôtellerie de la Mort* or *La Rue des Chantres*, in which 'the depth of perspective is augmented by the thought of all the dramas they contain'.[178] Undoubtedly it was necessary to clean up this 'labyrinth of obscure, crooked, and narrow streets, which extend from the Palais de Justice to Notre-Dame', as Sue describes it at the start of *The Mysteries of Paris*. But it was only a step from this to emptying out the quarter altogether, so that 'the cradle of the capital, entirely demolished, now contains simply a barracks, a church, a hospital and a palace'.[179] If this step was taken, it was for political and military reasons above all. During the June days of 1848, which so strongly marked the epoch, there was much fighting in the Cité and the adjacent part of the Latin Quarter (I shall return to this later), and this centre of insurrection had to be eradicated.

I am aware that this last sentence goes counter to contemporary historiography. By an amalgam that is characteristic of the spirit of our time, the (useful) reappreciation of nineteenth-century architecture has led to a positive revaluation of Haussmann, to the point of a ridiculous minimization of his anti-insurrectionary concerns, just as it is good form to present Napoleon III as a philanthropic Saint-Simonian.[180] But Haussmann was explicit: at the time when the opening of Rue de Turbigo and the widening of Rue Beaubourg led to the disappearance of Rue Transnonain,

178   Charles Baudelaire, 'Salon de 1859', on Meryon.
179   Victor Fournel, *Paris nouveau et Paris future* (Paris, 1868).
180   The two most recent books on Haussmann are quite instructive in this respect. *Haussmann le Grand*, by Georges Valance (Paris: Flammarion, 2000): 'Why Haussmann? Because he has left us Paris, one of the finest, most liveable, most visited and most envied cities in the world.' In some 350 pages, this book devotes just ten lines to the baron's anti-revolutionary worries. And Michel Carmona, in his *Haussmann* (Paris: Fayard, 2000), describes the clearing of the Place de la République in these terms: 'The little crooked square with its modest water tower (opposite the present Rue Léon-Jouhaux) was expanded into the fine quadrilateral that we know today.'

The Île de la Cité and the historic centre of Paris before the Revolution.

he exulted: 'I read, in a book which enjoyed great success last year, that the streets of Paris had been enlarged to permit ideas to circulate, and, above all, regiments to pass. This malicious statement (which comes in the wake of others) is the equivalent of saying that Paris has been strategically embellished. Well, so be it ... I do not hesitate to proclaim that strategic embellishments are the most admirable of embellishments.'[181]

Leaving the Cité by the Pont Saint-Michel, you find yourself face to face with a depiction of the strategic triumph of order:

> For how many people crossing the Place Saint-Michel today do the figures on the fountain, surrounded by beer and Coca-Cola cans, still have something to say? Who is able to decipher historically this allegory for tourists, to recognize that the archangel with his spear stuck into the back of Satan was supposed at the time to represent the triumph of Good over the Evil people of June 1848? But in the era of insurrections, on the threshold of the rebel arrondissement, this statue had a meaning that was in no way ambiguous. Everyone knew that this Saint Michael symbolized the Second Empire crushing the demon of revolution, and that Rue Saint-Jacques and the Latin Quarter could recognize their own image in the infernal beast hurled to the ground.[182]

181   *Paris nouveau jugé par un flâneur* (Paris: Dentu, 1868), cited by Benjamin in *The Arcades Project*, pp. 129–30.
182   Dolf Oehler, *1848. Le Spleen contre l'oubli* (Paris: Payot, 1996).

3

New Paris: The Faubourgs

The word faubourg means the section of a town that is outside its gates and its precinct. But this definition has for a long time ceased to be appropriate for the faubourgs of Paris, which, being forced to expand, has ended up enclosing them all within its walls. This name, however, given the weight of long usage, has been preserved for them, and helps a topographical understanding of the capital.

– A. Béraud and P. Dufay,
Dictionnaire historique de Paris (1832)

The Wall of the Farmers-General

This inconceivable wall, fifteen feet high and nearly seven leagues round, which will soon surround the whole of Paris, is supposed to cost 12 million; but as it should bring in 2 million each year, it is clearly good business. Make the people pay for something that will only make them pay more, what could be better? . . . Battalions of workers will circulate in the shelter of this rampart. The Farmers-General would have liked to enclose the whole Île de France. Just imagine good king Henri IV seeing this wall! But what is revolting from every aspect is to see the lairs of the tax office transformed into colonnaded palaces that are genuine fortresses. These monuments are supported by colossal statues. There is one on the Passy side that holds chains in its hands, presenting them to those who arrive: it is the spirit of taxation in person under these genuine attributes. Oh, Monsieur Ledoux, you are a dreadful architect![1]

Sébastien Mercier was not alone in this opinion: the condemnation of the wall was so general that its contractors were forced to begin their work at the most deserted point, alongside the Salpêtrière hospital. Through an

---

1   Mercier, *Tableau de Paris*.

irony of fate, Lavoisier, a conspicuous Farmer-General, was held responsible for a project that the Parisians charged would prevent pure air from
entering the city, and his discoveries – on the very subject of the composition of air – did not save his head from the Revolutionary tribunal.[2]

The *octroi* system, however, predated the wall. Many years before, the
Ferme-Générale had already established offices around Paris to collect
entry charges on certain goods and commodities, including foodstuffs,
wine, and firewood.[3] But the vagueness of the boundaries – certain streets
were subject to *octroi* on one side only – permitted all kinds of fraud.
Sébastien Mercier noted that 'every day a countless number of lies are
uttered by the most honest of people. It is a pleasure to deceive the tax
office, and the conspiracy is general; people are proud of it and celebrate
it.' In the 1780s, as the public finances went increasingly into deficit,
Breteuil and Calonne decided to improve receipts by means of a wall. But
what aroused public anger at this time was not just the greater difficulty
of fraud. A bookseller wrote in his diary that 'the Parisians had all the
more reason to murmur and show their discontent in this circumstance,
since all the enjoyment of an outdoor walk was removed and they were
deprived of the sweet pleasure of being able to contemplate the green
countryside, of breathing purer air on Sundays and holidays after having
worked the whole week in dwellings that were often both gloomy and
unhealthy'.[4]

The wall was purely an instrument of taxation, without any military purpose. Its dimensions already demonstrate this: three metres
high and less than one metre deep. Historians have given it the name
of the 'wall of the Farmers-General', but during the eighty years of
its existence, Parisians called it the '*octroi* wall'. Thus the Clos Saint-
Lazare, where the last insurgents of June 1848 held out on the building
site of the Lariboisière hospital, was described by Marouk as 'waste
ground that stretched from the Poissonière barrier [now the Barbès-

---

2   'It is Lavoisier, of the Academy of Sciences, to whom we owe these heavy
and useless barriers, a new oppression exercised by the contractors over their fellow
citizens. But alas, this great physicist Lavoisier was a Farmer-General' (Sébastien
Mercier, *Le Nouveau Paris*, 10 Frimaire, year VII/1798). The Ferme-Générale was
a private tax administration. Its offices were venal, and the receipts divided between
the city of Paris, the royal Treasury, and the Farmers themselves. The Constituent
Assembly suppressed the *octroi* in 1790, but it was re-established by the Directory.
3   On the other hand, those who lived inside the zone subject to *octroi* were
exempt from one of the other major taxes of the ancien régime, the *taille*.
4   The diary of Hardy, Paris bookseller (BN, ms. Fr. 6685), Thursday, 21
October 1784. Cited by B. Rouleau, *Villages et faubourgs de l'ancien Paris. Histoire
d'un espace urbain* (Paris: Le Seuil, 1985).

Rouchechouart crossroads] to the Nord railway, from the church of
Saint-Vincent-de-Paul to the *octroi* wall'.[5] Gervaise, from the window
of the Hôtel Boncoeur, on Boulevard de la Chapelle, looked

> to the right, towards Boulevard de Rochechouart, where groups of
> butchers, in aprons smeared with blood, were hanging about in front of
> the slaughterhouses; and the fresh breeze wafted occasionally a stench of
> slaughtered beasts. Looking to the left, she scanned a long avenue that
> ended nearly in front of her, where the white mass of the Lariboisière
> hospital was then in course of construction. Slowly, from one end of
> the horizon to the other, she followed the *octroi* wall, behind which
> she sometimes heard, during nighttime, the shrieks of persons being
> murdered; and she searchingly looked into the remote angles, the dark
> corners, black with humidity and filth, fearing to discern there Lantier's
> body, stabbed to death.[6]

With the notable exception of the Montagne Saint-Geneviève, Old Paris is
low-lying and flat. The course of the new wall, on the other hand, followed a
hillside route, taking its bearings from the heights above the valley hollowed
out by the Seine. In today's Paris, it corresponds to the two lines of the
overhead Métro – Nation-Étoile via Barbès, and Nation-Étoile via Denfert-
Rochereau.[7] There was a raised covered walkway on the inside of the wall,
and a wide boulevard on the outside. Ledoux, architect for the Ferme-
Générale, conceived the fifty-five barriers. Whether modest or imposing,
they seem to have been taken from a construction set based on models from
antiquity or the Renaissance – the Roman Pantheon, Bramante's Tempietto,
Palladio's Villa Rotonda – combined with a vivid imagination. In his *Essai sur
l'architecture* (1753), Abbé Laugier regretted that the entry into Paris amounted
to 'a few wretched palisades erected on wooden foundations, rolling on two

5   Victor Marouk, *Juin 1848* (Paris, 1880; republished Paris: Spartacus, 1998).
6   Émile Zola, *L'Assommoir*. The Rochechouart slaughterhouse was situated
where the Lycée Jacques-Decour and the Square d'Anvers now stand. It was
one of a series of slaughterhouses built under the First Empire: those of Grenelle,
between Avenues de Saxe and de Breteuil, Popincourt (Square Maurice-
Gardette, on Avenue Parmentier), Roule, on Avenue de Messine, and l'Hôpital,
between Boulevards de l'Hôpital and de la Gare (Pinon, *Paris, biographie d'une
capitale*).
7   On the Left Bank it follows Boulevards Vincent-Auriol, Blanqui, Saint-Jacques,
Raspail, Edgar-Quinet, Vaugirard, Pasteur, Garibaldi and Grenelle. On the Right
Bank, from the Trocadéro it follows Avenue Kléber, Avenue de Wagram, and
the Boulevards Courcelles, Batignolles, Clichy, Rochechouart, La Chapelle, La
Villette, Belleville, Ménilmontant, Charonne, Picpus, Reuilly and Bercy.

old jambs, and flanked by two or three dunghills', to the point that foreigners found it hard to believe they were not still in some adjacent country town. Ledoux had promised something quite different: 'I shall *de-village* a population of eight hundred thousand and give them the independence that a city draws from its insulation; I shall place trophies of victory at the closed exits of its tendential lines.' He justified his propensity to architectural hyperbole in these terms: 'The artist has chosen to give these offices a public character, and so that the architecture was not dissolved by immense spaces, he deemed it necessary to employ the most severe and decisive style.'[8]

To the west of Paris, the wall passed outside the built-up area, almost into the countryside. It enclosed the Champ-de-Mars and the École Militaire, the few houses of Chaillot village, and a broad zone, not yet constructed, which fifty years later would become the Europe quarter. To the north and east, however, where urbanization was already far more dense, the course of the wall had to take into account what was already there, both inside and out. Hence certain irregularities that may seem curious, salients to enclose the Faubourgs Saint-Martin and Saint-Antoine, and reentrants to exclude large estates such as Montlouis, the summer domain of the Jesuits, which would later become Père-Lachaise. There was even a case in which the resistance of the inhabitants forced the contractors to depart from the line that had been drawn for them, and make a reentrant between Boulevards de Clichy and de Rochechouart.[9]

Contrary to the walls that preceded and followed it, the wall of the Farmers-General gave concrete form to recent extensions of the city rather than triggering new ones.[10] During the twenty years or so between the end of the military disasters of Louis XV's reign and the beginning of the pre-revolutionary crisis in 1785, the economy boomed and with it speculation in property. Moreover, the city centre was increasingly difficult to live in, with its overly tall buildings, crowded plots, and courtyards crowded with hovels. There is a noticeable difference in tone between Boileau's pleasant *Embarras de Paris* and Mercier's *Tableau*. For the latter:

The lack of pavements makes almost all the streets dangerous: when a man with a bit of credit is sick, dung is spread outside his door to dull

---

8   Ledoux, *L'Architecture considérée sous le rapport de l'art*.
9   Béraud and Dufay, *Dictionnaire historique de Paris* (Paris, 1832). This reentrant angle is still very clear, at the end of Rue des Martyrs.
10   Pinon noted that 'the moment of its completion corresponded with the sale of national properties [confiscated by the Revolution], which saturated the market for land and buildings within the city for many years, or even decades' (*Paris, biographie d'une capitale*).

the noise of carts; that is particularly when you need to take care … Slaughterhouses are not outside the city or at its limits, they are right in the middle. Blood flows in the streets, congealing under your feet and reddening your shoes … The fumes given off by the tallow boilers are thick and diseased. Nothing spoils the air more than these crude vapours … Narrow and badly built streets, houses that are too tall and interrupt the circulation of air, slaughterhouses, fish markets, sewers, cemeteries, all corrupt the atmosphere, fill it with unclean particles, and this enclosed air becomes heavy and malign in its influence.

We have seen how the aristocracy deserted the Marais in the late seventeenth century for the Faubourgs Saint-Germain and Saint-Honoré. A century later, all those with the means to do so tried to leave the old centre. The pattern that was then sketched out was one of segregation between residential and plebeian quarters, and the formation of a Paris-West for the rich. Until this time, noble hôtels and hovels could be found side by side on the same streets. Even the royal palaces were surrounded by wretched dwellings:

> Opposite the proud colonnade of the Louvre, which every foreigner admires, bundles of old rags can be seen, suspended from ropes to make a hideous display … Chinese umbrellas made from waxed cloth, ten feet tall, serve as shelter to a multitude of old-clothes dealers displaying their wares, or rather their rags. When these umbrellas are lowered at night, they give the appearance of two lines of immobile giants, looking as if they guard the Louvre.

And on the other side of the palace, in the Carrousel quarter, 'a maze of houses is surrounded by a marsh on the side of Rue de Richelieu, an ocean of rolling cobbles on the side of the Tuileries, sinister booths on the side of the Galleries, and wastes of cut stone and demolitions on the side of the old Louvre'.[11] Paris mingled rich and poor in close proximity, but also in a vertical order. The same building would house shops on the ground floor – the shopkeeper living on the mezzanine – apartments for the aristocracy on the second storey (the 'noble' floor before the invention of the lift), and workers in the attics. This mix had not yet completely disappeared even in the early 1960s, when for example on the Montagne Saint-Geneviève, or on Rues Laplace, Lanneau, and Valette, lodgings under the roofs were still occupied by workers – even if now with water on the landings.

---

11   Mercier, *Tableau de Paris*; cf. also Honoré de Balzac, *Cousine Bette* (1846).

American-style zoning by income was never really established until the era of de Gaulle, Malraux and Pompidou, at the time when the old quarters, massively renovated, were reoccupied by the bourgeoisie.

At the start of the eighteenth century, the belt between the Grands Boulevards and the region where the wall of the Farmers-General would be built saw a new style of construction: instead of taking place in dense and close-packed nuclei, urbanization advanced in a centrifugal fashion through the faubourgs, which radiated out in an extension of the major arteries of the old city. The major barriers of the *octroi* wall were constructed at the edge of these faubourgs. (This was when the word *barrière* acquired its metaphorical sense: 'Hardly has the last vibration of the last carriage coming from a ball ceased at its heart before its arms are moving at the barriers and Paris shakes itself slowly into motion.' And as if an echo of this: 'The dawn, shivering in her green and rose garment,/Was moving slowly along the deserted Seine,/And sombre Paris, the industrious old man,/Was rubbing his eyes and gathering up his tools.')[12]

And yet this first stratum of New Paris should not be conceived along the lines of a wheel with spokes regularly spaced around its whole circumference. To the north and east of the city, the old faubourgs of working people had long formed a tight band. The land surrounding them, which was still agricultural, was rapidly built up, from the centre to the periphery. To the west, on the other hand, as we have noted, the wall passed at a certain distance from the city, the only road bearing the name of a faubourg being Rue du Faubourg-Saint-Honoré. In the whole of this immense sector urbanization advanced only slowly, in wide developments, and it was only in the late nineteenth century that these came together to create a continuous fabric. As for the Left Bank, New Paris developed there with scarcely any resort to the radial system of faubourgs.

The growth of the capital, in both surface and population, made a new division necessary. To replace the districts of Louis XIV, the Constituent Assembly established in 1790 twelve municipalities, each including four

---

12   Balzac, *Ferragus*; Baudelaire, 'Dawn', *Les Fleurs du mal*. Baudelaire had an admiration for Balzac that he did not genuinely feel for any other contemporary French writer. 'Balzac, the prodigious meteor that will cover our country with a cloud of glory, like a bizarre and exceptional sunrise, an aurora borealis flooding the icy desert with its fairy light' ('*Madame Bovary* par Gustave Flaubert', published in *L'Artiste*, 18 October 1857). And again: 'Honoré de Balzac, you the most heroic, the most extraordinary, the most romantic and the most poetic of all the characters that you have produced from your womb' ('The Salon of 1846. Heroism of Modern Life', in Charles Baudelaire, *The Mirror of Art* [London: Phaidon, 1955], p. 130).

sections. This organization would last until the demolition of the *octroi* wall: simply that in 1805 the municipalities became arrondissements and the sections – a term charged with too many Revolutionary memories – became *quartiers*.[13] But it became hard now to find one's way in this greater Paris. Choderlos de Laclos, who invented the system of street numbering, presented this in June 1787 in *Le Journal de Paris*:

> It seems to me that it would not be useless to provide all the inhabitants of this immense city with a means of crossing it and knowing where they are; with the result that each person could be sure of arriving where he intended to go. I also believe that there could be no more favourable moment for this operation than the one at which the limits of Paris seem to have been fixed for a long time by the new wall that has just been constructed.

In 1779 a German by the name of Marin Kreefelt undertook a systematic numbering at his own expense. 'I placed the first number on Rue de Gramont,' he wrote, 'on the small door of the police station, now the wet-nurses' office' – the corner with Rue Saint-Augustin.[14] The Parisians gave a cold welcome to this initiative. On 15 Frimaire of year IX (6 December 1800), the prefect of police reminded the minister of the interior: 'The disquiet aroused by this operation, which was seen as the precursor to new taxation, placed such obstacles on it that it had to be carried out at night; these hindrances gave rise to a number of mistakes.' The aristocrats and haute bourgeoisie had other reasons for their hostility. As Sébastien Mercier asked:

> How can the hôtel of M. le Conseiller, M. le Fermier-Général, or Monseigneur the bishop be given a common number, and what is the object of this proud marble tablet? Everyone was like Caesar, not wanting

---

13 The 1st arrondissement corresponded to the Champs-Élysées and the Faubourg Saint-Honoré; the 2nd to the Palais-Royal and the Chaussée-d'Antin; the 3rd to the Faubourgs Poissonière and Montmartre; the 4th to the Louvre and Les Halles; the 5th to the Faubourg Saint-Denis and the Sentier; the 6th to the Arts et Métiers and the Temple; the 7th to the Marais; the 8th to the Faubourg Saint-Antoine and the Quartier Popincourt; the 9th to the two Îles; the 10th to the Faubourg Saint-Germain; the 11th to the Latin Quarter; the 12th to the Faubourgs Saint-Jacques and Saint-Marceau. Out of these twelve arrondissements, only three were on the Left Bank.
14 Cited by Jeanne Pronteau, *Les Numérotages des rues de Paris du XVe siècle à nos jours* (Paris: Commission des travaux historiques, 1966), an impressive work which I have borrowed from in the following pages.

to be second in Rome: but a noble carriage gate would be found after a mere shopkeeper's premises. That would stamp an air of equality, which was to be carefully guarded against.

Kreefelt had envisaged numbering the entire left side of a street in one direction, then the right side in the opposite sense, so that the first and last numbers would be face to face – as can still be seen in certain London streets. The Constituent Assembly abolished this marking and set up a system designed purely for taxation, with continuous numbering of all streets in a section, one after the other. The beginning of each street thus received its number by chance, which no doubt made the search for any particular address as difficult as it is today in Tokyo. The present system was then inaugurated in 1805, with numbers painted in black (odd) or red (even) on an ochre ground. The porcelain plaques with figures that stood out 'in white on a dark blue base' date from 1847, and are still to be seen on many Parisian buildings.

THE RIGHT BANK FAUBOURGS

Champs-Élysées

It is clearly not by chance that the two faubourgs whose names are most weighed down with opposite connotations, the Faubourg Saint-Antoine and the Faubourg Saint-Honoré, are situated at opposite extremes of this New Paris. And yet the major east-west axis today, leading from the Château de Vincennes to the towers of La Défense by way of the Bastille, the Louvre, and the Étoile, and served by Métro line no. 1, the axis on which one can see the sun set beneath the Arc de Triomphe, does not pass through the Faubourg Saint-Honoré but along the Champs-Élysées, and this is such a well-established Paris topos that it is quite hard to remember how recent it is. Until the 1860s, when Haussmann improved Avenue de l'Impératrice (Avenue du Bois in Proust's time, then Avenue Foch), the road out to Neuilly and Normandy passed through the Faubourg Saint-Honoré.[15] This was the itinerary on which Des Grieux set out to attack the escort leading Manon Lescaut into exile ('I learned, by the soldier's report, that they would go out towards Rouen, and that it was from Le Havre-du-Grâce that they were to sail for America. We at once went to the gate

---

15   Only the part of the present faubourg between the Porte Saint-Honoré – at the level with Rue Royale – and the site of Saint-Philippe-du-Roule was actually known as the Faubourg Saint-Honoré. Beyond this, and up to the Roule barrier – the site today of the Place des Ternes – was the Faubourg du Roule.

of Saint-Honoré ... We assembled at the end of the faubourg. Our horses were fresh.').

The wide hilly stretch between the Faubourg Saint-Honoré and the Seine has undergone extraordinary transformations from the time when the young Louis XIII hunted fox there. At that time, he would have already left Paris on crossing the stone bridge built across the moat of the Tuileries. What would later become the Cours-la-Reine, the elegant promenade of the age of *Le Cid*, was thus outside the city when it was improved in the 1620s:

> A new word and a new thing, the invention of Marie de Médicis. Until her regency, no other way of promenading was known in France except on foot and in gardens, but she brought from Florence to Paris the fashion of promenading by carriage at the coolest hours after dinner ... With this object, she had avenues of trees planted along the Seine, to the west of the Tuileries gardens. The queen then gave her name to this way, which she modelled after the *corsi* of Florence and Rome.[16]

Following the old Chaillot road, the Cours-la-Reine was divided from the river by the Versailles road that followed the Seine. It was planted with four ranks of elms, with ditches on either side and closed off with fences at each end. At the midpoint, a roundabout (now the Place du Canada) enabled carriages to turn. In *Le Grand Cyrus*, where Paris is called Suze and Princesse Mandane has the golden hair of the Duchesse de Longueville, one of the beauties of the Fronde, it is said that

> Along this fine river [the Choaspe, as the Seine is called here], four avenues are to be found, that are so wide, so straight, and so shaded by the height of their trees that it is impossible to imagine a more pleasant promenade. This is also the place where the ladies all come in the evening, in little open-top cars, the men following behind on horseback; with the result that, free to go either in one direction or the other, the promenade serves for both promenade and conversation, and is without a doubt most entertaining.

At this time, the Champs-Élysées was still a marshy field, which had yet to be given a name:

> This was formerly a plain to be seen on the right-hand side of the Cours-la-Reine, to which one crossed by a small stone bridge. In 1670 it was

---

16   Sauval, *Histoire et recherches*.

planted with elms, which formed fine avenues up to the Roule, ending in the form of a star, at a height from which a part of the city and the countryside around could be seen; this was then named the Champs-Élysées. The central avenue was more spacious than the others, and led at one end to the large esplanade facing the swing-bridge of the Tuileries, which has since been made into the Place de Louis XV [now Place de la Concorde], and at the other end to the Étoile.[17]

Under Louis XV, the Marquis de Marigny, brother of La Pompadour and superintendent of the king's buildings (he and his sister made a fine minister of culture), 'had all the trees planted in 1670 uprooted, and, in order to make the viewpoint more spacious ... had the high ground that was close to the part known as the Étoile levelled, and the lower ground raised, so that the road was made gentler and more uniform, and in 1765 began to replant with trees this whole section of the Champs-Élysées, so that these trees today have the finest effect possible.'[18]

It was said at the time that Marigny had undertaken this work to give his sister, who had just bought the Hôtel d'Évreux (now the Élysée palace), a clearer view of the promenade and the Invalides. That is possible, but at all events the beginning of the Champs-Élysées' fashionability dates from these improvements. As Mercier wrote:

> The magnificent garden of the Tuileries is abandoned today for the avenues of the Champs-Élysées. One admires the fine proportions and design of the Tuileries; but the Champs-Élysées is where all ages and classes of people gather: the pastoral character of the place, the buildings decked out with terraces, the cafés, a wider and less symmetrical ground, all this acts as an invitation.

In the 1770s, when dance halls – known as *vaux-halls* – proliferated in Paris, Le Camus de Mézières, whom we saw at work on the Halle aux

---

17   Hurtaut and Magny, *Dictionnaire historique*. In texts of this time, the term 'Étoile' denoted either the present Étoile (as it was from the late eighteenth century), or else the Rond-Point des Champs-Élysées, sometimes called the 'Étoile des Champs-Élysées'. In the present text, I believe it is the Rond-Point. In actual fact, the avenues of the Champs-Élysées gardens did not extend above the Allée des Veuves (now Avenue Montaigne), so that it was impossible that they 'ended up in the form of a star' at the present Place de l'Étoile. In the same way, the 'height' that was razed by the Marquis de Marigny was more likely a small hill on the side of the Rond-Point rather than the large prominence on which the Arc de Triomphe was later constructed.
18   Ibid.

Blés, built the Colisée – likewise a rotunda – between the Allée des Veuves (Avenue Matignon[19]), Rue du Colisée and the Champs-Élysées. This establishment, which included five rooms for dancing, fashionable shops for clothing and jewellery, a naumachia, cafés, and entertainments, was famed for its fireworks and masked balls, attended by no less than Marie-Antoinette herself. The best society frequented the Ledoyen restaurant, where in summer you could dine outdoors; the Café des Ambassadeurs; and the Restaurant de la Bonne-Morue in the street of the same name (now Rue Boissy-d'Anglas), where Grimod de La Reynière, Farmer-General and celebrated gastronomist, had a hotel built that was decorated by Clérisseau in the Pompeian style.[20] On the wide expanse of waste ground in front of the Tuileries, which had long served as a storage site for marble, Gabriel finished the Place Louis XV, which must have been very pretty with its oval of floral ditches, sentry boxes, balustrades, and in the centre the equestrian statue of the king by Bouchardon, which would soon be replaced by the guillotine.

The gardens of the Champs-Élysées, before the ageing Blanqui came, unknown to anyone, to review his secret army,[21] or the young narrator of *À la Recherche du temps perdu* felt the first torments of love, were for the whole of the nineteenth century one of the great sites of Parisian pleasure. In 1800 already, Chateaubriand, arriving through the Étoile barrier and rediscovering the city he had left nine years previously, recalled in his *Memoirs*: 'On entering the Champs-Élysées I was amazed to hear the sound of violins, horns, clarinets and drums. I saw halls where men and women were dancing; further on, the Tuileries palace appeared at the far end of its two great stands of chestnut trees.'

Later on in the century, the Champs-Élysées was, for Victor Fournel, 'the centre of that flood of harmony which descends on Paris in the summer months. It is impossible to take a step, from the Rond-Point and as far as the Place de la Concorde, without receiving the full impact, like artillery fire, of a romance, a little song, and further on a great aria or an opera

---

19 The Allée des Veuves, perpendicular to the Champs-Élysées, is now on one side Avenue Matignon and on the other Avenue Montaigne.

20 This was demolished in 1935 and replaced by the US embassy, supposedly symmetrical to La Vrillière's hôtel built by Chalgrin on the corner of Rue Saint-Florentin.

21 In the first few days of January 1870, 'Blanqui conducted his review, without anyone suspecting the strange spectacle. Leaning against a tree, upright in the crowd among those who watched as he did, the attentive old man saw his friends arrive, soldiers among the throng of people, silent amid murmurs that from one moment to the next rose into shouts' (Gustave Geffroy, *L'Enfermé* [Paris, 1926]).

overture.'[22] In 1844, at the height of the polka mania, the Mabille brothers opened a ballroom in the Allée des Veuves, 'which presented a charming aspect in the evenings, when its trees, flower baskets and ponds were lit up by gas lamps. The orchestra enjoyed a deserved reputation. It was here that successive choreographic celebrities shone who were more or less suspect, known to the public by such names as Reine Pomaré, Céleste Mogador, Rigolboche, etc.'[23] Then, during the great vogue of cafés-concerts, it was in the Champs-Élysées gardens that the most luxurious of these were to be found, such as the Alcazar in summer, whose star was the famous Thérésa, and the Café des Ambassadeurs, immortalized by Degas and Lautrec.

Faubourg Saint-Honoré

The Faubourg Saint-Honoré was 'formerly relatively uninhabited and insignificant', wrote Piganiol de La Force in 1765, 'but fifty or sixty years ago people began to build the most magnificent hôtels there, so that it is now one of the finest faubourgs of Paris'. The elegant hotels were on the odd-numbered side of the street, with gardens opening onto the Champs-Élysées: the Hôtel d'Évreux or Élysée, the Hôtel de Charost that belonged to Pauline Bonaparte before becoming the British embassy, the Hôtel d'Aguesseau which Visconti transformed into a neo-Renaissance palazzo and would be one of Rothschild's hôtels. But at the same time, higher up, between the Rond-Point and the present Place de l'Étoile, both sides of what was still called Avenue de Neuilly remained almost deserted. In 1800, there were no more than six buildings on this stretch.[24] Further up again, the land along Rue de Chaillot (now de Berri) belonged to the Oratory fathers, and the land on the left to the Sainte-Geneviève abbey, which ran the Sainte-Périne retirement home. Still further, the left side was occupied by the Marbeuf gardens, an ancient folly that the Convention had turned into a public garden. On the right, an immense estate was named after Beaujon, receiver-general of finances under Louis XVI, who had built there a kind of 'charterhouse' for his intimate gatherings, along with a dairy and a home for eighty orphans, including six for children 'who showed an early talent for drawing'.[25] Under Louis-Philippe, new streets were built across these well-endowed lands, including Rue Fortunée, where Balzac

---

22   Victor Fournel, *Ce qu' on voit dans les rues de Paris* (Paris, 1858).
23   Joanne, *Paris illustré en 1870*. See also François Gasnault, *Guinguettes et lorettes, bals public à Paris au XIXe siècle* (Paris: Aubier, 1986).
24   D'Ariste and Arrivetz, *Les Champs-Élysées* (Paris, 1913).
25   The Convention turned this into a hospital, and in 1936 it was transferred to Clichy.

moved, after great labours, to receive Mme Hanska in a setting worthy of her.[26]

The Champs-Élysées in the present sense is thus a 'recent' quarter, which has only really existed since the 1830s or '40s. Its development accelerated when Haussmann improved the Place de l'Étoile and Avenue de l'Impératrice (now Foch), thus opening the road to the Bois de Boulogne and the west. 'It is frightening,' Delvau wrote in 1865, 'the number of promenaders and carriages of all kinds – broughams and britzskas, flies and tandems, barouches and four-wheelers, cabs and wagonettes – that cross this square each day on their way either to the Bois de Boulogne or to Neuilly, which are both in this direction.'[27] But despite this animation, Avenue des Champs-Élysées essentially dates only from the twentieth century. That is exceptional for a major Paris artery, and we should perhaps see it as one of the reasons that make it seem like a stranger in the city, even if in certain faraway countries it is seen as one of the main symbols of Paris.

In the 1950s there were still good reasons for visiting the Champs-Élysées: a certain flashiness, an entertaining kitsch, Claridge's, Fouquet's, the chrome displays of De Soto and Packard – and above all the cinemas. To see the latest Hitchcock in its original version, there was no other choice than the magnificent theatres of the Marignan, the Normandie, or the Colisée (in the boulevard cinemas these films were only shown dubbed in French, and on the Left Bank the art and specialist cinemas only projected classics or avant-garde films). But today, especially after the recent 'improvements', the Champs-Élysées is more like the duty-free mall of an international airport, decorated in a style that is a mixture of pseudo-Haussmann and pseudo-Bauhaus, as revisited by Jean-Claude Decaux.

Faubourg Saint-Antoine

At the time when the surroundings of the Champs-Élysées were still unpopulated and sometimes dangerous – in *Les Mystères de Paris*, the Coeur

---

26   25 September 1846: 'I have corrected the whole of *Cousine Bette*, and am working on the end of the manuscript; in six days from now, on 3rd October, it will be finished, and *Cousin Pons* will be finished on the 12th ... Santi, the architect, is working like a slave, and on Sunday I shall know the sum of his quotation for the repairs and constructions, as the front wall has to be taken back, this being obligatory in the Beaujon quarter ... I have reason to believe that the repairs will come to 15,000 francs. Thus the property would cost a total of 67,000 francs, made up of 50,000 the purchase price, 2,000 expenses, and 15,000 on repairs and embellishments. That is nothing in the present conditions of Paris, and we would not have had for 12,000 francs this home that I shall have the pleasure of presenting to you.'

27   A. Delvau, *Histoire anecdotique des barrières de Paris* (Paris: Dentu, 1865).

Sanglant, an underground dive where the Schoolmaster tries to drown Rodolphe, is at the end of the Allée des Veuves, i.e., on the Place d'Alma – the Faubourg Saint-Antoine was in its heyday. Its turbulence was proverbial. When Madame Madou, a dealer in dried fruit in the Halles, broke in on poor César Birotteau to demand her money, Balzac wrote that she 'bore down like an insurrectionary wave from the Faubourg Saint-Antoine'. The faubourg had gained this reputation during the Revolution, right from the fall of the Bastille. The sections of Quinze-Vingts and Montreuil had then played leading roles on 10 August – led by Santerre, the brewer from Rue de Reuilly, whom the insurrectionary Commune appointed commander of the National Guard – and on the *journées* of 31 May and 2 June 1793, which saw the fall of the Girondins. After Thermidor, it was still this faubourg that launched the hunger riots of Prairial in year III and suffered their terrible repression. As Delvau wrote, 'the history of this faubourg is the history of Paris – written in musket fire'.[28]

The lines of the Faubourg Saint-Antoine and its neighbouring streets have not changed since the Middle Ages, when the Porte Saint-Antoine was the starting point for a number of different roads.[29] The Faubourg in the strict sense led in the direction of the abbey of Saint-Antoine-des-Champs, devoted to 'mad women desirous of getting well again', and then on to the Château de Vincennes. The roads to Charenton, Charonne, Reuilly and Montreuil led to ancient villages that supplied a good part of the capital's wine, fruit and vegetables. 'Montreuil is the finest garden that Pomona could glorify', wrote Mercier. 'Nowhere has industry taken the cultivation of fruit trees further, and especially that of peaches. A Montreuil gardener is highly sought after throughout the Île de France.'

The rise of the faubourg began in the seventeenth century. 'The Faubourg Saint-Antoine increased prodigiously', wrote Piganiol de La Force, 'from the large number of houses that were built there, both because of the good air and because of the king's letters patent of 1657, which exempted from the qualification of mastership all artisans and tradespeople who lived there.' This favour of Louis XIV was not the only reason for the development of handicrafts in the faubourg. Wood that was brought downstream by barge was unloaded close by, at the Quai de la Rapée on the Louviers island, so that both firewood and timber for construction were stored in the faubourg. It was only a small step from this to carpentry, also

---

28   Ibid.
29   Under Henri II, the Porte Saint-Antoine was embellished with a triumphal arch designed by Jean Goujon. Located alongside the Bastille, this was demolished in 1777 to ease the flow of traffic. The Saint-Antoine-des-Champs abbey was situated where the Saint-Antoine hospital now stands.

spurred on by the construction of the wall, as there was no longer any advantage in building up supplies of raw materials within the zone subject to *octroi*. Storehouses and barns were therefore turned into workshops, all the more so as a new and highly skilled labour force was available in the form of Flemish and German artisans who had arrived to profit from the Parisian economic boom (many of them were Protestants, hence the rise of the Charenton chapel in the eighteenth century). But perhaps 'profit' is too strong a word. 'I do not know how this faubourg survives', wrote Mercier. 'Furniture is sold from one end to the other; and the poor population that live here have no furniture at all.'

The wood industry, which had begun with timber for housing, steadily developed into more delicate activities. The faubourg had cabinetmakers, carvers, gilders, polishers and turners. And wood was not the only material now worked: in Rue de Reuilly (not far from Santerre's brewery), where the barracks now stands, was the royal manufactory of mirrors, which Colbert had set up to compete with Venetian imports. In Rue de Montreuil, on a section of the demolished Folie-Titon, the Réveillon factory became under Louis XVI the royal manufactory of wallpaper – when this contractor decided to reduce the wages of his workers, the faubourg devastated the plant in April 1789, troops intervened, and this episode, in which several dozen people died, is often seen as a prelude to the Revolution. In 1808, the spinning works of François Richard and Lenoir-Dufresne employed 750 workers in a former convent on Rue de Charonne. The power for its machines was supplied by horses, and most of the workers employed were children.[30]

Like Belleville, another indomitable bastion that Haussman divided between two arrondissements in the interest of controlling it, the Faubourg Saint-Antoine was partitioned between the 11th and 12th arrondissements. But to better mark its difference, it kept the old names for its cul-de-sacs, courtyards and passages: le Cheval-Blanc, la Main-d'Or, la Bonne-Graine, la Boule-Blanche, la Forge-Royale, la Maison-Brûlée. 'The municipality has numbered the streets here, as in all other parts of Paris; but if you ask one of the inhabitants of this suburb for his address, he will always give you the name his house bears and not the cold, official number.'[31]

After the night of the Second Empire, and after the Commune – whose final act, as we shall see, took place around the *mairie* of the 11th arrondis-

---

30 *Le Faubourg Saint-Antoine, architecture et métiers d'art* (Paris: Action artistique de la Ville de Paris, 1998). Boulevard Richard-Lenoir is named after this factory.

31 Sigmund Engländer, *Geschichte der französischer Arbeiterassociationen* (Hamburg, 1864), vol. 3, p. 126; cited by Walter Benjamin in *The Arcades Project*, p. 521.

sement – the Faubourg Saint-Antoine remained a red focus. 'As long as the Dreyfus crisis lasted', Daniel Halévy related,

> the Faubourg Saint-Antoine was our fortress ... in this little room on Rue Paul-Bert, where we huddled together, workers and bourgeois, where we squeezed our chairs one against the other ... One day in autumn 1899, we watched for hours the return of the crowd of workers who had been parading on the Place du Trône, before the *Triomphe de la République*, Dalou's bronze statue that had been unveiled that day. I doubt that 1848, with its famous festivals, or 1790, on the day of the Federations, saw a greater movement of the masses, or one so powerfully possessed by the spirit of the Revolution.[32]

This was the first time in the history of Paris that a crowd paraded with red flags at its head without being gunned down.

The present Faubourg retains few material traces of this glorious past, and only the friends of Red Paris mentally raise their hats when they cross Rue Charles-Delescluze and remember that at the crossroads of Rue du Faubourg Saint-Antoine and Rue de Cotte they are on the site of the barricade where the representative of the people Alphonse Baudin was killed for twenty-five francs.[33] But even if the proximity of the Bastille Opera now disagreeably contaminates the first few metres of the Faubourg, even if Rue de Lappe, long since deserted by the Auvergnats, is no longer the haven that it once was for modern art,[34] still the Aligre market, the fountains on the corner of Rue de Charonne and in the square in front of the Saint-Antoine hospital, the courtyards where illustrators and computer buffs, Chinese artisans and photographers, work cheek by jowl – this unique mixture maintains the quarter's identity as plebeian and industrious. If, taking up Marcel Duchamp's idea, we should manufacture cans of Air de Paris, it is certainly that of the Faubourg Saint-Antoine with which I would fill mine.

---

32 Daniel Halévy, *Pays parisiens* (Paris: Grasset, 1932; republished in Les Cahiers rouges, 2000).

33 The name of Baudin has been given to a graceless little street giving on to Rue Saint-Sébastien. There is also a Hôtel Baudin on Avenue Ledru-Rollin. This is not very much for a man to whom republicans wanted to erect a monument at the end of the Second Empire; the collection gave rise to incidents throughout the country and a trial with strong political echoes.

34 Fortunately there remains the magnificent Durand-Dessert gallery.

Popincourt and Faubourg du Temple

To the south, Rue de Charenton separates the Faubourg Saint-Antoine from the quarter of the Gare de Lyon – one of ill repute since the late 1970s, specially the Chalon block famous for its squats, dope dealers, and Vietnamese restaurants where you could get a meal for 10 francs, now eradicated and replaced by an ensemble of underground streets, expressways, and office towers with reflective curtain walls. The northern limit of the faubourg is rather more vague: we could choose either Rue de Charonne, which led to the *octroi* wall at the Fontarabie barrier (now Métro Alexandre-Dumas), or Rue de la Roquette, another old street with Auvergnat connections (the present Bastille theatre was still in 1965 a dance hall that preserved the culture of the *bourrée*, 'Le Massif-Central'), ending up on the boulevard at the Aunay barrier, opposite the main entrance to Père-Lachaise.

Between the Faubourg Saint-Antoine and its northern neighbour, the Faubourg du Temple, is the Popincourt quarter.[35] This old centre of Protestantism was – and still is – organized around two major transversals. One of these, leading from Temple to the Saint-Antoine abbey, is now Rues de la Folie-Méricourt, Popincourt, and Basfroi (the two latter, devoted to the wholesale fashion trade – now run by Asians – are like a second Sentier). The other, the road from Saint-Denis to Saint-Maur, now corresponds to the sequence of Rue Saint-Maur, Rue Léon-Frot and Rue des Boulets, extended eastward by Rue de Picpus. The grid was completed by three radials, more or less parallel to Rue du Faubourg-du-Temple: Rue du Chemin-Vert, Rue de Ménilmontant (now Oberkampf), and Rue d'Angoulême (now Jean-Pierre-Timbaud), which continued through Rue des Trois-Bornes and Rue des Trois-Couronnes until the barrier of that name (now Métro Couronnes). This was the site of the Delta gardens, whose great attraction was the Montagnes Françaises, 'where so many fragile bonneted virtues came a cropper, alongside bold sellers of novelties commonly known as "*calicots*" [counter-jumpers]'.[36]

Industry in the Popincourt quarter only dates from the nineteenth century. More recent than that of the Faubourg Saint-Antoine, it is also less specialized. On Rue Popincourt or Rue Saint-Maur alongside the Saint-Louis hospital, successive working-class courtyards, remarkably deep, are more reminiscent of the Berlin *Mietskasernen* of the late nineteenth

---

35   Named after a president of the Paris parlement under Charles VI, who had his country house there.
36   Delvau, *Histoire anecdotique des barrières de Paris*. On *calicots*, see above, p. 52, note 59.

century than the passages of Rue du Cheval-Blanc or Rue de la Main-d'Or: 'These courtyards shelter an entire population ... The proprietor, a large manufacturer, installed a steam engine there for his factory; but, wishing to attract small workshops, he had all of his ground floors, i.e., a length of over a hundred metres, transversed by the axle of his machine, so that he could rent out to each of his tenants, along with accommodation, a belt to which they could fit a machine.'[37]

Where Rue du Faubourg-du-Temple crosses the Canal Saint-Martin there are two facing statues, each going back to the years of Parisian Romanticism. On the right as you come down is the bust of the greatest actor of the day, Frédérick Lemaître, famous for the role of Robert Macaire in *L'Auberge des Adrets*, illustrious as Vautrin and Don César de Bazan, as much at home on the Boulevard du Crime as at the Ambigu or the Gymnase ('Sublime gestures, in short', wrote Baudelaire. 'Delacroix is only rivalled outside of his own art. I scarcely know any others except Frédérick Lemaître and Macready.'[38]) On the other side of the street is the standing figure of a young woman with uncertain features, who offers the passerby the flowers that she holds in her turned-up apron. She is *La Grisette de 1830*, the term being defined by the Robert dictionary as 'a girl of petty condition (generally a factory worker or employed in tailoring, fashion, lingerie ...) with bold and easy manners'. In *La Caricature* for 6 January 1831, Balzac evoked 'these little creatures nice enough to eat, with their mischievous air, turned-up nose, short dress and well-turned legs, who are known as *grisettes*'.

The date of 1830 is not a reference to the Trois Glorieuses, but rather to a regular event that took place on that site in these years: the *descente de la Courtille*.[39] In the early morning of Ash Wednesday, from the 1820s until after June 1848, this parade marked the end of Carnival. It was a ritual whose apparent gaiety did not manage to conceal its latent violence. Privat d'Anglemont, a prince of the bohemian world, gave a nostalgic description of it:

Ah, the descent from the Courtille, that was a real bacchanalia of the French people! What a crowd, what confusion! What cries, what noise!

---

37   Privat d'Anglemont, *Paris anecdote*. This arrangement was not invented here, there were pictures of it in the technical magazines of the time. Certain of these driving belts even cut through the ceilings to reach the upper floors.

38   Baudelaire, 'Salon de 1846'. Macready was an English actor, contemporary with Lemaître, famous in particular for his interpretation of *Richard III*.

39   I.e., the procession down from the hillside taverns of what is now known as Belleville. [Tr.]

Pyramids of men and women clinging to carriages, hurling abuse at each other across the street, a whole city in the street ... we might say, with no exaggeration, that *tout Paris* was there. Everyone said: 'It's monstrous, depraved', but the most refined society, duchesses in domino masks and short-skirted women of easy virtue in their dishevelled finery, courtesans dressed up as bold fishwives, bourgeois as peasants or Swiss milkmaids, hastened at four in the morning to leave the salons of the Opera, the subscription balls, the theatres, and even, we have to say, official balls, to make their way there ... There was no good Carnival without a noisy descent from the Courtille; every window was rented a month in advance, with crazy prices paid ... People spilled out of the cheap dance halls, and were everywhere, even on the rooftops; all you could see were heads, all shouting, crying out, splashing each other with wine. Carriages arrived filled with masked figures, and took three hours to get from the boulevard to the *barrière* ... People bawled at each other from carriage to carriage, from house windows to carriages, from the street to the windows; each group had its especially loudmouthed character, a kind of rasping corncrake with lungs of steel, whose job was to respond to everyone else.[40]

The voice of working-class consciousness was quite different. Benjamin Gastineau, a typographer and former colleague of Proudhon's, hated the Carnival and had a particular horror of the descent from the Courtille, in which he saw the brutalization of his brothers and the degradation of his sisters:

People expelled from the taverns who make their way there drunk and staggering, trampling over those who fall, women wearing policemen's caps over their ears and a broken pipe between their teeth, disguised as clowns, pierrettes, fishwives or urchins ... women dishevelled, filthy, with disordered hair, the stupefied look of those exhausted by vice, green lips, crumpled breasts, stained clothes ...[41]

In terms curiously close to this proletarian moralism, Alfred de Musset expresses his hatred of the people through the character Octave in *The Confession of a Child of the Century*:

---

40 Privat d'Anglemont, *Paris anecdote*.
41 Benjamin Gastineau, *Le Carnaval* (Paris, 1854). Cited from Jacques Rancière, 'Le bon temps ou la barrière des plaisirs', in *Les Révoltes Logiques*, 7, spring–summer 1978.

The first time I saw the people – it was a frightful morning of Ash Wednesday, near La Courtille ... Masked carriages filed hither and thither, crowding between hedges of hideous men and women standing on the sidewalks. That sinister wall of spectators had tiger eyes, red with wine, gleaming with hatred ... from time to time a man in rags would step out from the wall, hurl a torrent of abuse at us, then cover us with a cloud of flour ... I began to understand the time and comprehend the spirit of the age.[42]

The construction of the wall of the Farmers-General turned the geography of the Courtille taverns upside down. Previously, from the Regency to the beginning of Louis XVI's reign, the quarter had been dominated by the Ramponeau phenomenon. This establishment, with the sign of the Tambour-Royal, occupied the corner of Rue Saint-Maur and Rue de l'Orillon.[43] Its sign showed the landlord astride a barrel, and below this the lines: 'See France run to the barrel [*tonneau*]/that serves as throne to Monsieur Ramponeau.' 'The name Ramponeau,' wrote Mercier, 'was a thousand times better known to the multitude than those of Voltaire or Buffon.' Almost a century later, Delvau still offered an amazed image:

Ramponeau! What a character! He created almost as much noise as a battle in his journey through this world. The people had adopted him, and wanted no one else ... He was spoken of everywhere, from alleys to high circles, from the breakfasts of duchesses to the suppers of actresses, to the point that the entire world of fashion, so frivolous and idle, forgot the disgrace of M. de Choiseul [1770] and his exile, in their concern for

---

42   Baudelaire wrote about Musset: 'I've never been able to bear *this master of foppery* with his spoiled-child impudence, calling on heaven and hell for matters concerning his bed and board, his muddy torrent of grammatical and prosodic errors, finally his complete inability to understand the work that transforms reverie into art' (letter to Armand Fraisse, 18 February 1860, *Selected Letters of Charles Baudelaire* [London: Weidenfeld & Nicholson, 1986], p. 117; translation modified). Rimbaud wrote: 'Musset is fourteen times loathsome to us, suffering generations obsessed by visions – insulted by his angelic sloth! ... It is all French, namely detestable to the highest degree' (letter to Paul Demeny, 15 May 1871, Arthur Rimbaud, *Complete Works and Selected Letters* [Chicago: University of Chicago Press, 2005], p. 379).
43   The *barrière* at the end of Rue de l'Orillon was eventually known as the *barrière Ramponeau*. The present Rue Ramponeau continues Rue de l'Orillon on the other side of Boulevard de Belleville. The Tambour-Royal disappeared under the Consulate.

the Courtille that made such a row, and the rabble that flaunted themselves there in such good spirits.

But when the Farmers-General's wall increased the duties on wine in Paris, the taverns migrated to the other side of the *barrière*, at the foot of Belleville. On the night of Mardi Gras, before the descent from Courtille, revellers would get drunk at Favié's or Desnoyers', the fashionable establishment of those years:

> The great *guinguette* of the immortal Desnoyers, and a number of others whose gigantic saloons filled up in winter with thousands of families, and their gardens in summer, with dancing men and women who had not received their lessons from conservatory professors. No one gave any heed to the Greeks, or the 3 per cent stocks, or the Jesuits, or the Holy Alliance, or the republic of Haiti. All they had in mind was having a good drink, a good feed, and a good dance.[44]

Even those most strapped for cash could try their luck at Guillotin's. As Vidocq wrote:

> The Guillotin I refer to here was simply a modest adulterator of wine, whose establishment, well known to thieves of the lowest level, was situated opposite Desnoyers' filthy dive, which the tipplers of the *barrière* called the 'Grand salon de La Courtille'. Even the scum of the earth thought twice about crossing the threshold of Guillotin's tavern, with the result that the only people you saw in this receptacle were prostitutes and their pimps, hoodlums of all kinds, a few low-class swindlers, and a good number of disturbers of the night, intrepid denizens of the faubourgs, who divided their existence into two parts, one devoted to rioting, the other to theft.[45]

These famous establishments disappeared without leaving any other trace than some street names, but as if to prove that there is indeed some such thing as the spirit of a place, Rue Oberkampf, Rue Jean-Pierre-Timbaud and Rue Saint-Maur have seen in recent years the birth of a new generation of cafés, restaurants and bars that are often characterized as *branchés* [cool], a vague term that also says something of the character of the times. Fortunately,

---

44 Legrand d'Aussy, *Vie publique et privée des Français* (Paris, 1826). Desnoyers was on the corner of Rue de Belleville and the street that today bears his modernized name, Desnoyez.
45 E. Vidocq, *Mémoires* (1828).

the working-class population of the quarter ('working-class' today meaning 'immigrant') contains and waters down this phenomenon. Rue du Faubourg-du-Temple remains one of the most 'amalgamated' in Paris, just as in Privat's time. You can eat Turkish and Chinese food – 'Planète Istanbul' standing cheek-by-jowl with 'Les Folies de Sin-Wang' – as well as Pakistani, Malian, Tunisian, Greek or Cambodian. You can buy halal meat, all the spices of the East, every kind of rice, mysterious African vegetables and Chinese wedding cakes a metre and a half tall, topped by dancing couples in a tender embrace, their various tiers each bearing a gaggle of children. The garment factories are at work in every courtyard by eight in the morning. In the Pakistani shops you can find Korean toasters and paper flowers, plastic stools, bundles of mats, and imitation Italian *cafetières*. Above Rue Saint-Maur, 'Mabel' offers a choice of holy statuettes from all religions, along with bath oils, love potions, hairpieces, incense, and a liquid that protects against magic spells. The very narrow shop fronts have multicoloured signs that offer cut-price phone calls to the Comoros, Ethiopia, Paraguay or Togo. Not to mention the countless shops for mobile phones and trainers, suitcases with wheels and socks at ten francs for three pairs. Rue Faubourg-du-Temple, often dirty, always noisy and busy, boasts two theatres, the Palais des Glaces with its gigantic wooden elephant, and a tiny stage on the corner of the Passage Piver that has taken the name of Tambour-Royal in homage to Ramponeau, as well as a hammam, two dance halls, and five tobacconists. 'It's a whole little world in itself,' as Privat d'Anglemont already said a hundred and fifty years ago, 'this great rise that starts at one boulevard and ends on another. It is a kind of free zone, the Latin Quarter of the Right Bank. Everyone there lives just as they please, without being bothered by their neighbours.'

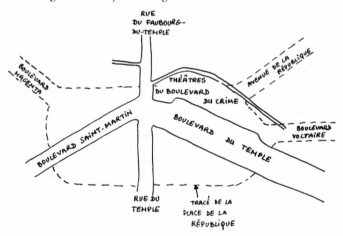

In the mid nineteenth century the Faubourg Saint-Antoine, the Popincourt quarter and the Faubourg du Temple formed a region where the working and 'dangerous' classes were concentrated to an alarming degree. This is why the region was the object of Haussmann's full attention. On any map of Paris you can see how brutally the immense Place de la République was implanted on an old and delicate urban fabric. And this brutality is equally manifest in the square itself, which was flanked by two monumental buildings: the Magasins-Réunis (still today a consumerist temple, combining Habitat, Go Sport, Gymnase Club and Holiday Inn), and the Prince-Eugène barracks built on the site of Daguerre's Diorama. The strategic importance of this barracks, with wide avenues converging on the square in a star, was clear enough at the time, even for a polemicist of the Catholic right such as Louis Veuillot:

> There is also the Prince-Eugène barracks, which is a fine building, and the boulevard brings the barracks into communication with the Château de Vincennes, which is not a small castle. Vincennes is at one end, the barracks at the other, and alongside it the boulevard leading to the square of the former Bastille.[46] This is a rectangular barracks able to house a few thousand men, who could fire in all four directions: a double crossfire. It would be a dangerous spot for any subversive ideas that might take their chance here.[47]

In the same way, the Reuilly barracks controlled the Faubourg Saint-Antoine, crosshatched by Avenue Daumesnil, Boulevards Mazas (now Diderot), du Prince-Eugène (Voltaire) and de la Reine-Hortense (Richard-Lenoir). Haussmann was quite explicit. When he explained to Napoleon III that it was possible to lower the water level of the Canal Saint-Martin, and cover it over so that Boulevard de la Reine-Hortense could cross it, he exulted: 'I have rarely seen my august sovereign enthusiastic. This time he was so without reserve, so great an importance did he place ... on the work by means of which I proposed to remove the permanent obstacle

---

46   At the time of the 1851 coup d'état: 'The corner where we were standing was lonely. On the left there was the Place de la Bastille, dark and gloomy; you could see nothing there, but you could sense a crowd; regiments were out in battle array; they were not bivouacking, they were ready to march; the muffled sound of breathing could be heard; the square was full of that glistening shower of pale sparks which bayonets give forth at night time. Above this abyss of shadows rose up black and stark the Column of July' (Victor Hugo, *History of a Crime* [trans. Joyce and Locker], 1877).
47   Louis Veuillot, *Odeurs de Paris* (Paris, 1867).

... to the line of control from which one could, in case of need, take the Faubourg Saint-Antoine from the rear.'

Whilst the Faubourg Saint-Antoine stretched broadly across the plateau of eastern Paris, the Faubourg du Temple abutted the hill of Belleville, making this quarter a narrower one. The road to Meaux and Germany avoided the high ground, taking Rue du Buisson-Saint-Louis and exiting Paris through the Barrière de la Chopinette ('where Parisians would go to celebrate St Monday, and drink like canons', says Delvau). You could also take Rue de la Grange-aux-Belles, which led to the Pantin *barrière*, later commonly known as the Barrière du Combat:[48]

> Since 1781 a circus like the one in Madrid has been held outside the Barrière de Pantin, on the corner of the present Rue de Meaux and opposite Rue de la Grange-aux-Belles ... Its bulls were most commonly wolves, bears, deer, donkeys and bulldogs, which you could watch tear each other's guts out for the petty sum of 65 centimes for a third-class seat ... At the beginning, people of fashion patronized this parody of the bloody games of the Madrid circus. Fine gentlemen and beautiful ladies were not afraid to brave the exhalations of this municipal Lake Stymphalos and would arrive to attend the authorized butchery.[49]

We may wonder which was the greater transgression, that of the elegant lady spectators at the Combat in the final years of the ancien régime, or that of the voters for Balladur who recently betook themselves just opposite, to the premises of the 'Communist' party, to attend the Prada fashion parade in the famous Oscar Niemeyer building.

Between the Faubourg du Temple and the Faubourg Saint-Martin there is a border zone on either side of the canal, 'the Versailles and the Marseille of this proud and strong district'.[50] On the further bank of the canal, most of this space is taken up by the Saint-Louis hospital, one of the oldest in the city – it was on his way to inaugurate the chapel there that Henri IV was assassinated – as well as the finest, along with the Salpêtrière. Between the hospital and the Boulevard de la Villette a few little old streets, such as Rue Saint-Marthe and Rue Jean-Moinon, have strongly resisted destruction in an overall context of poverty and dilapidation. On the near side, there was the idea under the Restoration of building along the canal a 'Place

48   Since 1945, the Place du Colonel-Fabien.
49   Delvau, *Histoire anecdotique des barrières de Paris*. The Combat was finally closed in 1833.
50   Léon-Paul Fargue, *Le Piéton de Paris* (Paris: Gallimard, 1932).

du Marais', the site of which is today marked by Rue de Marseille, Rue Léon-Jouhaux (formerly Rue Samson and later Rue de la Douane[51]) and Rue Yves-Toudic (formerly Rue des Marais-du-Temple). All that remains of this abortive project is the Douanes customs warehouse – rebuilt in the 1930s on the site of the old one, which stretched to the water's edge – and some very regular streets where the wholesale carpet trade recalls the customs activity of the previous century.

If you turn your back on the canal and set out towards the Grands Boulevards, neoclassical elegance soon replaces business wealth. Rue de Lancry, Rue des Vinaigriers, Rue de Bondy (now René-Boulanger) and the Cité Riverin offer a thousand and one variations on decorative themes that were fashionable when David was working on *The Oath of the Horatii*. Between Boulevard Magenta and the Passage des Marais, the Cité du Wauxhall, reached through a neo-Palladian portico, reminds us that

on the corner of Rue de Bondy and Rue de Lancry an Italian firework-maker called Torré opened a large theatre in 1764, where he put on pantomimes in which fireworks played a great role. In 1769 this theatre was rebuilt and given the name of the Wauxhall d'Été. In 1782 this Wauxhall, known now as the Fêtes de Tempé, enjoyed a tremendous vogue. It was a kind of love exchange, in which deals of *galanterie* were made, and marketable assets of this kind were cashed. This was where the Prince de Soubise made the acquisition of a very pretty girl, the niece of Mlle Lamy, who remained his mistress for many years.[52]

Faubourg Saint-Martin and Faubourg Saint-Denis

The two faubourgs of Saint-Martin and Saint-Denis, false twins separated by Boulevard de Strasbourg, are each themselves divided in two – by the Gare de l'Est in the first case, and the Gare du Nord in the second. One

---

51 I long believed that the name of Samson here, often spelled as Sanson, was because the great public executioner of this name lived close by, in Rue des Marais-du-Temple, in a building 'protected by an iron railing, which was entered through a small gate; in the middle was a metal slot like a letterbox, in which were posted the missives from the Procureur-Général to alert the executioner that his services would be required' (Eusèbe Girault de Saint-Fargeau, *Les 48 Quartiers de Paris* [Paris: Blanchard, 1850]). Gavroche wrote to the two children he had taken under his protection: 'And then we'll go to see the guillotine work. I'll show you the executioner. He lives in Rue des Marais. Monsieur Sanson. He has a letterbox at the gate' (*Les Misérables*, Volume IV, book 6, chapter 2). But the etymology is wrong; this Samson was a local property owner.

52 Girault de Saint-Fargeau, *Les 48 Quartiers de Paris*.

might believe it was the enormous footprint of the stations that broke their continuity, but in actual fact this break long predates the railway. It was made by two religious establishments whose remaining vestiges do not give any idea of their great size – Saint-Laurent and Saint-Lazare. The faubourg that today bears the name of Saint-Martin was for many years known as Saint-Laurent in its upper part, as far as the Barrière de La Villette (now Place de la Bataille de Stalingrad). In the same way, the present Faubourg Saint-Denis was formerly known as Faubourg Saint-Lazare, between the convent-hospital-prison and the Barrière de La Chapelle. And there is no doubt that it was precisely this old discontinuity that guided the siting of the stations.

In their oldest sections, between the triumphal gates and glass roofs of the stations, there is the same difference between the two streets as between the well-mannered Rue Saint-Martin and the violent Rue Saint-Denis. The Faubourg Saint-Martin is broad, flat, and rectilinear, only enlivened by the silhouette of the *mairie* of the 10th arrondissement. It spills out in front of the station in a triangular place, where the 'Armurerie Gare de l'Est', the brasserie 'Au Triomphe de l'Est', shops selling work clothes, the apse of the Saint-Laurent church and the wall of the former monastery of the Récollets form a landscape that could be in Metz or Mulhouse – such mimetism often makes the surroundings of Parisian stations similar to those of the destinations of the trains that leave from them.

Rue du Faubourg Saint-Denis begins, in the shadow of the Porte Saint-Denis, with a noisy and busy large market, Turkish for the most part, as is the gloomy Passage du Prado, an 'L' shape between the Faubourg and Boulevard Saint-Denis, the domain of the sewing machine, including secondhand ones and repair shops. The Faubourg then climbs in a curve up to Boulevard Magenta. The square on the corner there marks the site of the Mission Saint-Lazare, a former leper colony transformed by Vincent de Paul, to become in the eighteenth century a prison for young offenders, then a Revolutionary prison, and eventually a hospital specializing in venereal diseases.[53]

The two faubourgs, nearly parallel before the stations, are linked by a series of arcades that are so lively and varied, so full of urban invention, that on some days you might prefer them to the historic arcades of Old Paris. There is first of all the Passage de l'Industrie, which on the other side of Boulevard de Strasbourg is known as Rue Gustave-Goublier, with the

---

53   In his *Madness and Civilisation* (London: Routledge, 2001), Michel Foucault shows the role of former leper colonies – become useless, like TB sanatoriums in the 1960s – in the organization of repression in the seventeenth century.

same neo-Palladian motif at each end as you find at the Wauxhall – a porch
with three openings, the central one of which is vaulted in an arch with
caissons and columns, higher and wider than the two lateral lights. The
next one is the Passage Brady, devoted to Indian and especially Pakistani
cuisine between Rue du Faubourg-Saint-Denis and the Boulevard, though
on the other side, towards Rue du Faubourg-Saint-Martin, it maintains the
old tradition of theatre costumiers. Further up still, opposite the Cour des
Petites-Écuries, which was until the 1960s where leather traders gathered,
is the magnificent Passage Reilhac, also the least frequented. As for the final
one, the Passage du Désir, despite its name it is reminiscent of the calmness
of a Flemish convent.

After Rue de Metz, Boulevard de Strasbourg itself, along with the
adjacent section of Rue du Château-d'Eau, is the domain of African hair-
dressing. All the equipment for this can be found here – hairpieces, dyes,
tresses, and wigs in many colours. On weekend evenings, the salons are so
lively, so full of pretty women, children, husbands and lovers, that hair-
dressing is transformed into a festival largely open to the street – one of the
most charming spectacles to be seen today in Paris.

Between the Mission Saint-Lazare and the Récollets monastery – today,
in other words, between one station and the other – there was held in
the eighteenth century the Saint-Laurent fair, which lasted from the end
of June to the end of September. This was a site for games of all kinds, a
dance hall, cafés and restaurants. Lécluse, a former actor with the Opéra-
Comique, had a theatre built where the most lively plays of the time were
performed. Lesage, Piron, Sedaine, Favart and many others worked for
the Théâtre de la Foire. All the boulevard theatres, and even the Opéra-
Comique before it was merged with the Comédie-Italienne, were obliged
to give performances there. In the last years of Louis XVI's reign, a 'Chinese
Bastion' was constructed in competition with the Wauxhall d'Été. But the
Revolution would soon bring an end to the Saint-Laurent fair. The land
there remained unused until the building of the stations of the Strasbourg
and Nord railways in the 1830s.

Beyond the stations the two faubourgs diverge, their roads respectively
fanning out to the north and east. The Rue du Faubourg-Saint-Martin
is relatively straight until it reaches the site of the former Barrière de La
Villete, which has now taken – permanently, without a doubt – the name
of Stalingrad. (Though Parisians adopt or reject the new names for old
places: no one refers to the Étoile as the Place Charles-de-Gaulle, or says
Place André-Malraux to mean Place du Théâtre-Français.) It was from this
immense intersection of cobbles, water and steel that the Citroën coaches

used to leave, their terminus being below the overhead Métro. Some lines served the factories to the east of Paris. Others, which left in the evenings, carried cargoes of immigrant workers back to Spain, Portugal, or North Africa. In the 1980s the space around Ledoux's Rotonde was cleared, and the Métro line carefully shifted so that passengers can now see at the same time the Saint-Martin canal, the pool of La Villette, and the Sacré-Coeur.

Until the 1960s, Rue du Faubourg-Saint-Denis came into the Gare du Nord, and the Boulevard de la Chapelle was black with the coal of the trains. This was one of the toughest quarters in Paris. At the casualty ward of the Maison Dubois, each night brought its share of knife injuries, stomach shots and 'criminal' abortions. Beneath the elegant galleries with their Doric colonnades, and in the avenues planted with lime trees, there were not many who remembered how this Maison, 'very useful for those who cannot have themselves treated at home, and yet fear the forced promiscuity of the big hospitals',[54] had in its day treated Nerval as well as Baudelaire's mistress Jeanne, or that two figures of the Romantic bohème, Murget and Privat d'Anglemont, had ended their days here. Today, the top of Rue du Faubourg-Saint-Denis is the main South Asian colony in Paris, something of an overseas agency for India. Here you can buy saris, jewellery, spices, cloth, videocassettes, tin-plate cutlery and luminous sandals. You can sample the cuisines of Kashmir, Pakistan, Tamil Nadu, Bangladesh, Sri Lanka and Singapore. The smell of incense and spices wafts out as far as the former Barrière de La Chapelle, where the magnificent overhead Métro station overlooks two little squares, the Théâtre des Bouffes du Nord, and Rue de Jessaint with its bridge over the railway to connect with Rue de la Goutte-d'Or.

Bordering the wall of the Farmers-General, between Rue du Faubourg-Saint-Denis and Rue du Faubourg-Poissonière, descending southward towards Rue de Paradis, the quadrilateral of the Saint-Lazare enclosure belonged to the priests of the Mission throughout the ancien régime. This was the largest enclosure in Paris, even more extensive than that of the Temple. After being nationalized by the Revolution, it was ceded in 1821 to a group of financiers led by the banker Lafitte, and its land used to construct the finest monumental ensemble of the 1830s and '40s. This is where Hittorff built his two masterpieces: the façade of the Gare du Nord, with 'its central pavilion with wide and luminous bays, its bold columns,

---

54 Alexis Martin, *Promenades dans les vingt arrondissements de Paris* (Paris: Hennuyer, 1890). The Maison Dubois, which bore the name of the surgeon who founded it, is today the Fernand-Widal hospital.

its statues proudly displaying themselves nude, and the two surrounding pavilions',[55] and the church of Saint-Vincent-de-Paul, whose stairways and curved ramps form an ideal theatrical backdrop along with the fine buildings of the Place Franz-Liszt. This is also the site of the most harmonious of the Paris hospitals from the nineteenth century, the Lariboisière, adjacent to the Gare du Nord:

> In 1846, when construction was begun under the direction of the architect Gauthier, the building was going to bear the name of King Louis-Philippe. The square where it was built was wasteland, bumpy and stony, known as the Clos Saint-Lazare. A few elderly Parisians still remember the lively aspect it had by day, thanks to the crowds of children who met there to play with kites, though in the deep solitude of the night.[56]

I will describe later on the terrible battles that took place on the hospital building site during the June days of 1848. The establishment was then called the Hôpital de la République, later Hôpital du Nord after the coup d'état of 1851, and took its present name when Countess Lariboisière, who died childless, gave her whole fortune to the city of Paris, which used it to complete the work in 1854.

Along the plebeian faubourgs to the north and east, the wall of the Farmers-General, over the eighty years of its existence, stimulated a very particular kind of urban development, which still leaves its traces in stones as well as minds. This was not the case on the inside of the wall; the raised walkway between the last houses and the wall was a gloomy one. That is where Nerval collapsed on the edge of madness at the end of *Aurélia* ('I wander, prey to despair, over the abandoned ground that divides the faubourg from the barrier'), also where the Goncourts' Germinie Lacerteux, another poor wanderer, 'covered the whole space where the mob gets drunk and satisfies its lust on Mondays, between a hospital, a butchery, and a cemetery – Lariboisière, the Abattoir, and Montmartre'.

It was rather outside the wall, on the wide boulevard surrounding it, that a new kind of activity developed:

> Once you crossed the wall erected by the Farmers-General, you reached a kind of relative paradise, where barriers and customs posts were

55 Ibid.
56 Ibid.

unknown, where the unchallengeable advantages of an independent and unrestrained life were combined with the benefits of civilization. Many emigrants upped sticks and set out for this zone free from duties on meat, wine, cider, beer, vinegar, coal, firewood, gypsum, etc. This is how those villages were formed; their real founder was the Paris *octroi*.[57]

This zone, with aspect of both a court of miracles and an oriental bazaar,

> was in former times still occupied exclusively by outlets for *vin bleu* with burlesque shop signs, with dealers in bric-a-brac, old shoes, old linen, rags and scrap metal; then there were shady hotels, a good number of anonymous business houses, shacks that exhibited sequined phenomena and savant dogs, impossible fish and sword-swallowers; and then again dealers in patched-up suits, who, mounted on trestles, would display their wares in the evenings by the light of smoky torches, thrashing about as if possessed.

The demolition of the wall led to the disappearance of this picturesque fauna, but the present flea markets along the 'boulevards of the marshals' (Saint-Ouen, Montreuil, Vanves ...) can be seen as the direct heirs of the stalls of the Romantic era.

It was not just taverns and old-clothes dealers that nestled against the wall, but theatres as well. To reward the Seveste brothers, who had found for him the remains of his brother and Marie-Antoinette, Louis XVIII granted them a monopoly over theatres in this 'zone'.[58] They began with the construction of the Belleville theatre – now a Chinese supermarket, after having first been converted into a cinema in the 1950s. Other stages followed, at Montmartre, Grenelle, and Montparnasse. These theatres enjoyed an exceptionally advantageous position, in terms of repertory, cast, and public. Situated outside the wall, they were treated as provincial theatres, which gave them the freedom to perform plays from other theatres forty days after their premiere. The proximity of the capital brought them a guaranteed audience, delighted at being able on the same evening to see plays from the Odéon, the Gymnase and the Palais-Royal. Finally, they could choose from the best provincial actors, for whom the suburban theatre was the final step before reaching Paris itself.

---

57   Émile de La Bédollière, *Le Nouveau Paris. Histoire de ses vingt arrondissements* (Paris: Barba, 1860).
58   Pierre Seveste was the grandson of the gravedigger at the Madeleine cemetery, where Louis XVI and Marie-Antoinette were buried along with many others. Louis XVIII had the Chapelle Expiatoire built on the site, designed by Percier and Fontaine.

This arrangement explains the geography of Paris theatres today, most of which are still located on two concentric circles. The inner circle is on the Grands Boulevards, as we have seen (the association of 'theatre' and 'boulevard' has not always had the connotation of bourgeois vulgarity). The outer one is the circle of theatres along the wall of the Farmers-General: the Bouffes du Nord, Dullin's Atelier which is the former Montmartre theatre, the Européen behind the Place de Clichy, the Hébertot which was formerly the Batignolles, the Ranelagh, the Grenelle at the corner of Rue du Théâtre and Rue de la Croix-Nivert, the Gaîté-Montparnasse, the Saint-Marcel on Rue Pascal. You can make a circuit of Paris in this way, including all the old cinemas that were onetime theatres.

Because of this zone beyond the wall of the Farmers-General, the north-eastern boulevards, from Clichy to Ménilmontant, have been forever marked with the sign of entertainment and pleasure. Sex shops, porno theatres, shops selling X-rated videos, down-at-heel nightclubs, the whole 'diamantiferous mud' of our time is the lineal descendant of the circuses, music halls, balls, taverns and *maisons de passe* of the Paris of Vidocq and Eugène Sue, and later of Maupassant, Lautrec and Atget.[59]

Faubourg Poissonière and Faubourg Montmartre

If the frontier between the plebeian and the patrician sections of Paris were to be traced through the ring of Right Bank faubourgs, one might hesitate between Rue du Faubourg-Saint-Denis and Rue du Faubourg-Poisssonière, and not without reason: south of the Saint-Lazare enclosure, the region between Rue du Faubourg-Saint-Denis and Rue de Clichy – i.e., the major part of the 9th arrondissement – cannot be read as clearly as the old parts of the eastern and northern faubourgs. This broad zone is indeed crossed by two streets that have the name of faubourgs – Poissonière and Montmartre – but these did not act as the structuring matrix that this status would imply, in the time when thousands of carts rolled over beaten earth and later on cobbles, when the market gardens on either side were slowly transformed into courtyards, barns for animal feed, stables and workshops, when the lands of religious houses and aristocratic parks were sold off or confiscated, divided up and built on. It is only over a timescale of centuries that a faubourg can stimulate and govern the growth of a quarter. Now, if Rue du Faubourg-Saint-Martin was already a major route

---

59 'And no one would make you turn your eyes away from the diamantiferous mud of the Place de Clichy' (André Breton, *Ode to Charles Fourier* [London: Cape Goliard, 1969]). The plinth of the statue of Fourier is still there, in the middle of the boulevard in front of the Lycée Jules-Ferry.

in the time of Emperor Julian, and the road that was to become Rue du Faubourg-Saint-Antoine played a major role in Paris at the time of the Crusades, Rues du Faubourg-Montmartre and du Faubourg-Poissonière were not really developed until the late eighteenth century. Moreover, this whole region underwent transformations that were both radical and compact in time. Rue de la Chaussée-d'Antin for example:

> In the past [seventeenth] century this was simply a road that began at the Porte de Gaillon and led to the Porcherons, with an open sewer running along it. It was known as the Chemin des Porcherons, the Rue de l'Égout de Gaillon, the Chaussée d'Antin, and finally the Chemin de la Grande Pinte, on account of the tavern that is now run by the famous Ramponeau.[60]

In the 1770s, when, according to Mercier, the three classes that made money were bankers, notaries and builders, Rue de la Chaussée-d'Antin and those adjacent to it were taken over by financiers. These were Swiss such as Necker, or Mme Thélusson who commissioned from Ledoux the most remarkable hotel of the day – on Rue de Provence, 'composed of an immense hemispherical arcade, across which could be seen the colonnade of a rotunda, raised on bosses of jagged rock, mingled with bushes'[61] – or indeed Farmers-General such as Grimod de La Reynière or Jean-Jacques de Laborde, banker to Louis XVI, who divided up his fief of La Grange-Batelière and had the great sewer covered up at his own expense in order to add value to this land.[62] The best architects of the day, Ledoux, Brongniart, Boullée, Célérier and

---

60 Hurteau and Magny, *Dictionnaire historique de la ville de Paris*. In 1760, Ramponeau left the Tambour-Royal on Rue du Faubourg du Temple to his son, and established himself at the Grande Pinte – the church of La Trinité would later be built on this site. The saloon there could accommodate six hundred people at table.

61 *Mémoires* of the Marquise de Créquy. Sébastien Mercier, unable to pardon Ledoux for the wall of the Farmers-General, notes that 'Mme Thélusson's house is a spiral shell; you need to be a snail to live there: circular lines predominate, to the point that the head turns ... The most dangerous creature for the government is the architect, if he ever has a fit of delirium.'

62 On these divisions, and this quarter in particular, see Pinon, *Paris, biographie d'une capital*. This great sewer continued that of Rue de Turenne, passed beneath the theatres on the Boulevard du Temple and then followed the route of a number of present streets, some of which were built at the same time as it was covered, in the 1760s: Rue du Château-d'Eau, Rue des Petites-Écuries, Rue Richer, Rue de Provence, then Rue de la Pépinière, Rue La Boétie, Rue du Colisée and Rue Marbeuf. Its outlet to the Seine was near the present Place de l'Alma. This was the prehistoric course of the Seine.

Vestier, all built houses there for the bankers' lady friends. For Mlle Guimard, the prima ballerina of the Opéra, protégée of the bishop of Orléans, the Farmer-General Laborde, and the Maréchal de Soubise, Ledoux conceived an hôtel with a theatre for private performances and an oval surrounded by a colonnade, after the model of Palladio's Olympic theatre. Decorated by Fragonard and David, this was 'the happiest and most brilliant assemblage of all the arts ... The apartments suggested the interior of the palace of Eros embellished by the Graces ... A warm conservatory within the apartment took the place of a garden in winter. The landscape there is tender without damaging the effect, the trellises are subject to the rules of fine architecture, the arabesques are in no way fanciful ... You will see a small and delightful bathroom, perhaps unique in the style of its ornaments.'[63]

The Guimard hotel was presented by Napoleon to the tsar as an embassy, which did not prevent it from being demolished in 1826 in order 'to build plastered houses there, which made all Parisians of heart and soul tremble'. In this quarter of the Chaussée-d'Antin, whose splendour it is hard to recapture today, as soon as financial speculation was again at its peak in the mid 1820s (viz. the vexations of César Birotteau), a start was made on demolishing wonderful buildings that were not yet fifty years old. Very soon the big cuttings began: Rue La Fayette was started under Charles X, whose name it bore until 1830. The construction of the Opéra Garnier, the department stores, and eventually Boulevard Haussmann, brought the coup de grâce to this quarter of actresses and dancers, so that today only a few scholars are aware of its remnants, scattered among the traffic jams and perfumeries, shop-windows with Christmas toys and post-Christmas sales.

Between Rue de Trévise, which climbs towards Rue de Montholon, and Rue d'Hauteville, which climbs to Rue Saint-Vincent-de-Paul, this section of the faubourg that was at one time very elegant still keeps its noble aspect, even if it is now basically devoted to the wholesale fur trade. Where Rue du Conservatoire now runs, there was in the eighteenth century the Hôtel des Menus-Plaisirs, a kind of ministry of the arts – people said 'les Menus' as they say today 'le Quai d'Orsay' or 'la Place Beauvau' – where the organization of big public festivals was conceived, as well as the design of the royal furniture.[64] The music Conservatoire was founded in these

63 Jacques-François Blondel, *L'Homme du monde éclairé par les arts*, vol. 2. Reproduced in J. Adamson, *Correspondance secrète*, vol. 8 (London, 1787).
64 Pascal Étienne, *La Faubourg Poissonière, architecture, élégance et décor* (Paris: Action artistique de la ville de Paris, 1986). The first two directors of the Menus were Michel-Ange Slodtz and Michel-Ange Challe, this succession marking the transition from rococo to neoclassical taste.

buildings by a decision of the Committee of Public Safety on 7 Floréal of year II (26 April 1794). Gossec, Méhul and Cherubini were among its first professors. For Sarrette, the director, 'the gap left by the suppression of the rituals of fanaticism must be filled by the songs of Liberty, and the people must augment with its voice the solemnity of the festivals consecrated to the virtues that the Republic honours'. The stage sets for the festival of the Supreme Being were produced in the workshops of the Menus-Plaisirs from the drawings of David.

In the nineteenth century, other music could be heard in this quarter: at the Alcazar d'Hiver on Rue du Faubourg-Poissonière, the Concert-Parisien on Rue de l'Échiquier, whose star was Yvette Guilbert, and above all at the Folies-Bergère. Young Léautaud, who may have met Manet there, visited the Folies for the first time with his mother:

> I had already been to the Boule-Noire, the Élysée-Montmartre and the Comédie-Française; the lighting and costumes were nothing new for me. But what I saw now seemed incomparably more brilliant and coloured, more elaborate and rhythmical, and the women also struck me as more beautiful, compared with those of the Boule-Noire and the Élysée-Montmartre, often rather familiar, and those of the Comédie, always so stiff.[65]

And Huysmans, before being touched by divine grace:

> They are outrageous and they are magnificent as they march two by two round the semicircular floor of the auditorium, powdered and painted, eyes drowned in a smudge of pale blue, lips ringed in startling red, their breasts thrust out over laced corsets ... You watched, entranced, as this gaggle of whores passes rhythmically by, against a dull red backdrop broken only by windows, like wooden merry-go-round horses that twirl in slow motion to the sound of an organ around a bit of scarlet curtain embellished with mirrors and lamps.[66]

Between the end of the ancien régime and the fall of the Second Empire, the continual great transformations in what is today the bottom of the 9th arrondissement have wiped three small quarters off the map: Porcherons, Nouvelle-France, and Breda. Very much present in accounts, novels, and

---

65 Paul Léautaud, *Le Petit Ami* (Paris: Mercure de France, 1903). Léautaud's father was a prompter at the Comédie-Française.

66 J.-K. Huysmans, *Parisian Sketches* [1880] (Sawtry: Daedalus, 2004), p. 34.

songs of the period, they have disappeared without leaving a trace, not even a street name. 'The Porcherons', Hurtaut and Magny wrote in their dictionary of 1779, is 'a particular quarter within that of Montmartre, filled only with taverns in which people consume large quantities of wine, the same as at the Grande Pinte, because it is cheaper here'.[67] A rhyme from 1750 says that 'To see Rome without seeing the Courtille/Where rejoicing crowds swarm/Without visiting the Porcherons/The gathering place of lively lads/Is like seeing Rome without the pope'. In the early nineteenth century, the Porcherons gave way to the housing development of La Tour-des-Dames, and the 'gathering place of lively lads' became one of the most fashionable quarters of Paris.

Nouvelle-France was close to the Poissonière *barrière* (now the Barbès-Rochechouart intersection). This part of the Faubourg Poissonière was for a long time called the Chemin de la Nouvelle-France, the name relating to the young offenders who were parked in a nearby barracks after their arrest, before being deported to Canada. In the eighteenth century, a number of great lords had follies built in the midst of the fields, country taverns and windmills of Nouvelle-France:

> The Comte de Charolais, a peer of France, governor of Touraine and prince of the blood: to all appearances, he lived in the Hôtel de Condé, but for the girls of the Opéra and a few fellow debauchees he had his real home in a little house with courtyard and garden towards the top of the Chemin de la Nouvelle-France. It was only in the Hôtel de Condé that he was called the Comte de Charolais; in the faubourg he was familiarly called 'prince Charles', and addressed as '*tu*'.[68]

As for the Breda quarter, this was the upper end of the Faubourg-Montmartre around the then new church of Notre-Dame-de-Lorette, thus a more recent quarter, contemporary with the Boulevards coming into vogue:[69]

---

67   The invasion of the Chaussée-d'Antin by noble hotels pushed the market gardeners and taverners to the north, and they now established themselves in a part of the domain of the abbey of Montmartre, bordered by Rues des Porcherons (now Saint-Lazare), Blanche, La Bruyère and Notre-Dame-de-Lorette.

68   Delvau, *Histoire anecdotique des barrières de Paris*. The Nouvelle-France barracks, opposite the ends of Rue de Montholon and Rue de Bellefond, had been built at the turn of the century by the Maréchal de Biron. Legend has it that Hoche and Bernadotte had been sergeants there. No. 82 on Rue du Faubourg-Poissonière is still occupied by a barracks of the *garde républicaine*, the present buildings dating from the 1930s.

69   Rue Breda is today divided between Rue Henri-Monnier and Rue Clauzel.

So many kept women, those of the demimonde and its still lower depths, lived in the Breda quarter around Notre-Dame-de-Lorette, that they acquired the popular name of *lorettes*; the term *biche* [literally 'doe'] was hardly in use until 1852 … The property-owners of the Breda quarter, gallant despite themselves, gave hospitality to these outcast women, who, braving rheumatism, were keen to become the first tenants of the new houses. Once they were in possession of the new quarter, from which their turbulence repelled the peaceable and well-behaved bourgeois, they never abandoned it. A joyous, careless, disorderly colony perpetuated itself in this fashion, paying its rent with the most regular irregularity.[70]

Saint-Georges and Nouvelle-Athènes

Around 1825, between *The Raft of the Medusa* and *Liberty Guiding the People*, New Paris, which had previously remained in the river basin, crossed Rue Saint-Lazare, surrounded the Porcherons, and climbed the lower slopes of Montmartre, following 'this steady movement by which the Paris population has abandoned the Left Bank and made its way up the heights of the Right Bank'.[71] Historians make careful distinctions between the Saint-Georges development, that of the Tour-des-Dames, and Nouvelle-Athènes, and it is true that as you climb from Notre-Dame-de-Lorette to the former Barrière Montmartre (now Place Pigalle), the architecture changes from a polite neoclassicism to the beginnings of Art Nouveau. But the dominant style on these slopes, what created the dazzling city of Balzac, Chopin and Delacroix, was the architecture of the late Restoration and the July monarchy, tastefully picturesque, homogeneous but not to the point of boredom, ornate without being finicky, noble without ostentation, sometimes melancholy like the end of an era, sometimes joyous like a new adventure. And against this calm and regular backdrop, certain masterpieces stand out, whether monumental like the Hôtel de la Païva on Place Saint-Georges, or modest, like the building on Rue Henri-Monnier opposite the Villa Frochot where Lautrec had his studio.

In this new quarter – the taste for living in old buildings scarcely goes back a century – there formed a kind of colony of writers and artists. It all began with theatre folk, already celebrated under the Empire. On Rue de la Tour-des-Dames, Mlle Mars established herself at no. 1, Mlle

---

70   La Bédollière, *Le Nouveau Paris*. '*Lorette,*' Balzac explains, 'is a decent word to express the condition of a girl in a condition hard to name, and which, out of modesty, the Académie Française had neglected to define, given the age of its forty members' ('Histoire et physiologie des Boulevards de Paris').
71   Balzac, *The Lesser Bourgeoisie*.

Duchesnois at no. 3, and the great Talma at no. 9. Then Chopin and George Sand came to live on the Square d'Orléans,[72] and, to be closer to them, Delacroix moved to Rue Notre-Dame-de-Lorette. It was at this time that he painted his double portrait of the pair. On Rue Saint-Georges, where Balzac's Nucingen installed poor Esther in a 'leetle balace', the aging tenor Manuel Garcia gave singing lessons. His two daughters, Pauline Viardot and Malibran, would soon reach a fame that is perhaps only comparable with that of Maria Callas in recent times.[73] The magic of this quarter attracted Victor Hugo (on Rue de La Rochefoucauld), as well as Henri Monnier, Gavarni (who would later have his monument on the Place Saint-Georges), Alexandre Dumas, Auber, Boieldieu, and Émile de Girardin – whose salon, hosted by Delphine Gay, had Hugo, Musset, Balzac and Lamartine among its regulars. Later on, Barrès, Wagner and Gounod settled there, as well as the Goncourt brothers before they moved to Auteuil; Murger, whose father was a concierge in Montmartre; Millet; Lautrec; Gustave Moreau; and Villiers de L'Isle-Adam, who died at 45 Rue Fontaine, almost opposite the building where André Breton lived.

In *Le Petit Ami*, a marvellous little book, Paul Léautaud recalled his childhood in this quarter at the turn of the century:

> The region that was most familiar to me, where my eyes filled with images that I would always keep, was that between Rue Notre-Dame-de-Lorette and Rue Fontaine, Boulevard de Clichy and Boulevard de Rochechouart, and between Rue Rochechouart and Rue Lamartine ... I spent whole afternoons playing with a flock of charming little girls at the top of Rue Milton, which was then bordered on either side by waste ground surrounded by wooden fences. Each morning, for several years, I accompanied my father to his barber on Rue Lamartine, at the corner with Rue Rochechouart ... On Rue des Martyrs was the paint dealer with his multicoloured shop front; the *lavoir* with its metal flag; the little bazaar on the corner of Rue Hippolyte-Lebas (Rue Haute-Lebas, as women new to the quarter said, because of the abbreviation on the nameplate) ... On Rue Clauzel was the girls' school, as well as the house of an artist with its elaborate façade ... and on Rue Rodier, opposite our own, a house where women with thick face powder sang the whole day long.

---

72   Miraculously intact, its entrance is at 80 Rue Taitbout.
73   Pauline Viardot lived on the Square d'Orléans, and la Malibran had her hôtel – still standing – not far away, on Rue de l'Élysée-des-Beaux-Arts (now André-Antoine).

Quartier de l'Europe

When you cross the 9th arrondissement from east to west, you eventually come to Rue de Clichy, across which begins a region as different from La Nouvelle-Athènes as Nana was from Coralie, Manet from Géricault, or Gounod from Cherubini: this is the Quartier de l'Europe. The faded elegance of Rue de Clichy is unmistakable, and yet the Maréchal de Richelieu, before having the Pavillon de Hanovre built, owned a folly there which extended as far as Rue Blanche, and which Louis XV often visited with Mme de Pompadour. A little further up was the debtors' prison, which replaced Sainte-Pélagie (Rue de la Clef, on the Left Bank) in 1826. Creditors who requested the incarceration of a debtor were required to pay thirty francs a month for the prisoner's maintenance. Close to the Barrière (now Place) de Clichy, the Folie-Bouxière – from the name of a Farmer-General – became a celebrated pleasure-ground in the mid 1820s, the Tivoli gardens, where pigeon-shooting first took off in France. Later, it was across these gardens that Rue Ventimille and Rue de Bruxelles were built, as well as the peaceful Square Berlioz where Vuillard had his studio, and which he depicted in his series of *Jardins publiques*.

The plan of the Quartier de l'Europe is a simple one, like that of the Plaine Monceau that followed it. These were the last additions to the quarters in the old ring of faubourgs, and they have been very little altered since their construction – the former under the Restoration and the July monarchy, the latter under Napoleon III.

When the Gare Saint-Lazare and the Quartier de l'Europe arose between 1825 and 1840, this was still almost in the countryside. Up till then, the present site of Rue du Rocher and Rue de la Bienfaisance was known above all for its windmills. Where the Square Henri-Bergson is now, close to the Saint-Augustin church, the land was used for a *voirie*, in other words a refuse dump, and known as Les Grésillons, meaning 'bad flour'. Between Rue du Rocher and Rue de Clichy there were still fields, some growing potatoes or cereals, others fallow.

Lower down Rue du Rocher was Petite-Pologne.[74] 'Porte Saint-Jacques, Porte Paris, the Barrière des Sergents, the Porcherons, the Galiote, the Célestins, the Capucins, the Mail, the Bourge, the Arbre-de-Cracovie, the Petite-Pologne, the Petit-Picpus, these are names of old Paris that float into the new. The memory of the people floats on these wrecks of the past', wrote Hugo in

---

74 Called after the shop sign 'Au Roi de Pologne', a reference to the Duc d'Anjou, king of Poland and the future Henri III, who had a country house where the Gare Saint-Lazare now stands.

the fifth book of Part Two of *Les Misérables*. At the end of *Cousine Bette*, when the Baroness Hulot joins Mme de la Chanterie in her pious works,

> One of the Baroness's first efforts in this cause was made in the ominous-looking district, formerly known as la Petite-Pologne – Little Poland – bounded by Rue du Rocher, Rue de la Pépinière, and Rue de Miromesnil. There exists there a sort of offshoot of the Faubourg Saint-Marceau. To give an idea of this part of the town, it is enough to say that the landlords of some of the houses tenanted by working men without work, by dangerous characters, and by the very poor employed in unhealthy toil, dare not demand their rents, and can find no bailiffs bold enough to evict insolvent lodgers. At the present time speculating builders, who are fast changing the aspect of this corner of Paris, and covering the waste ground lying between Rue d'Amsterdam and Rue Faubourg-du-Roule, will no doubt alter the character of the inhabitants; for the trowel is a more civilizing agent than is generally supposed.

As far as the change in the population goes, we can say that Balzac's prediction was justified. The cutting of Boulevard Malesherbes led to the disappearance of Petite-Pologne in the 1860s (there was a scent in this region of the expiation of regicide: Malesherbes, Tronche and de Sèze, the three defenders of Louis XVI, each have their street here, and Louis XVIII had the Chapelle Expiatoire constructed by Percier and Fontaine). But the development of the quarter had already begun earlier: in 1826 a finance company had traced the plan of a quarter whose largest square would be known as the Place de l'Europe, with the streets having the names of various capitals. This development took off once Émile Pereire obtained the concession for the railway from Paris to Saint-Germain. Its station was built on Rue de Stockholm with an exit on Rue de Londres, thus right against the Place de l'Europe, under which a tunnel had to be dug.[75]

---

75   This was the first Gare Saint-Lazare. The station was moved to its present site in 1860, and entirely rebuilt in the 1880s. The original tunnel should not be confused with the Batignolles tunnel, which was much further north. Other sites had been envisaged for the station: 'When the question of its building arose, the site that had been intended for it, on the Place de l'Europe, turned out to be so far from the business centre, and built-up Paris, that the option was seriously considered of locating the station at the southeastern corner of the Place de la Madeleine and Rue Tronchet. The rails, supported on "elegant cast-iron arches raised twenty feet above the ground, with a length of 615 metres", according to the report, would have crossed Rue Saint-Lazare, Rue Saint-Nicolas, Rue des Mathurins and Rue de Castellane, each one of which would have had its particular station' (Maxime Du Camp, *Paris, ses organes, ses fonctions et sa vie dans la seconde moitié du XIXe siècle* [Paris: Hachette, 1869]).

And yet in the 1840s success was not guaranteed. Balzac could still evoke in his *Beatrix* 'those solitudes of carved free-stone, the like of which adorns the European streets of Amsterdam, Milan, Stockholm, London, and Moscow, architectural steppes where the wind rustles innumerable papers on which a void is divulged by the words, "Apartments to let"... When Monsieur de Rochefide first encountered Madame Schontz, she lived on the third floor of the only house that remained in Rue de Berlin.' It was only under the Second Empire that the Lycée Bonaparte (now Condorcet) became the lycée of the Parisian 'elite', and the quarter that of the haute bourgeoisie. Many lamented the invasion of metal and coal. As La Bédollière wrote in 1860, 'the proposal is to throw metal bridges across the Place de l'Europe, and so destroy the garden at its centre. What is constant nowadays?' What distressed him then was precisely what enchants us today, the encounter between the railway and the city, so well seen by Proust: '... those vast, glass-roofed sheds, like that of Saint-Lazare into which I went to find the train for Balbec, and which extended over the eviscerated city one of those bleak and boundless skies, heavy with an accumulation of dramatic menace, like certain skies painted with an almost Parisian modernity by Mantegna or Veronese, beneath which only some terrible and solemn act could be in process, such as a departure by train or the erection of the Cross.'[76]

This quarter is still centred on the hexagonal Place de l'Europe, whose particular beauty derives from the contrast between the decreed heaviness of the buildings – colossal pilasters, triangular façades, raised lofts – and the aerial situation, suspended above the rails, open to the winds, bordered by lattices, posts, fences, trees of exotic species in little gardens that are always empty. The cast-iron balustrades and large riveted struts, essential motifs in master-pieces by Monet and Caillebotte, disappeared in 1930. In order to see them, you have to climb Rue de Rome and observe, opposite the Lycée Chaptal, the premises of the former Messageries depot now converted into a garage, whose metal and brick architecture, overlooking the railway, stretches from the Place de l'Europe through to the Boulevard des Batignolles.

If the heavy cast iron has disappeared from the square, the railings are still there, the same as can be seen in the background of two famous pictures – Manet's *Le Chemin de fer* in which Victorine Meurent, wearing round her neck the same black ribbon that was her only garment in *Olympia*, casts her unfathomable gaze against the smoke, and *Derrière la gare Saint-Lazare*, a photograph by Cartier-Bresson that dates from 1932, in which a shadow,

---

76 Marcel Proust, *Within a Budding Grove, Remembrance of Things Past*, vol. 1, p. 694.

wearing a soft hat, crosses an immense puddle with an improbable leap, while a poster stuck to the railings announces a forthcoming concert by Brailowsky. The streets of the Quartier de l'Europe are full of such ghosts, but for me they rather conjure up the Princesse de Parme as evoked by Proust, 'as little Stendhalian as is, for example, the Rue de Parme, which bears far less resemblance to the name of Parma than to any or all of the other neighbouring streets, and reminds one not nearly so much of the Charterhouse in which Fabrice ends his days as of the waiting room in the Gare Saint-Lazare'.[77]

Plaine Monceau

The Plaine Monceau, if we remain strictly within the 'ring of faubourgs', is bordered by Rue du Faubourg-Saint-Honoré and Boulevard de Courcelles – the frontier with the Quartier de l'Europe being Boulevard Malesherbes. But here the wall of the Farmers-General was very far from the area then built up, and does not play its bordering role as clearly as it does elsewhere, all the less so as it was lowered in a ditch so as not to spoil the view of the rich property owners of the district, just as the Boulevard Périphérique is today where it crosses the Bois de Boulogne. So it is quite legitimate to see the Plaine Monceau as extending across Boulevard de Courcelles through to Boulevard Pereire.

Its geographical and historical centre is the Parc Monceau. In 1778, Grimod de La Reynière sold this land to the future Philippe-Égalité. Carmontelle, a writer and amateur architect, advised the duke to create an extraordinary English garden, which was known as the Folies de Chartres (Philippe being Duc de Chartres at that time):

> You could see there every kind of wonder that the imagination might create: Greek and Gothic ruins, tombs, an old crenellated fortress, obelisks, pagodas, kiosks, warm greenhouses forming a pleasant winter garden, lit up in the evenings by crystal lamps hung from the branches of trees; grottos, rocks, a stream with an island, a mill with the miller's rustic dwelling, waterfalls, a dairy, swings, a game of Chinese quoits, etc.[78]

Nationalized by the Revolution, and presented by Napoleon to Cambacérès, the park was restored to the Orléans family – i.e., to Louis-Philippe – by the Restoration:

---

77 Marcel Proust, *The Guermantes Way*, *Remembrance of Things Past*, vol. 2, p. 443.
78 Girault de Saint-Fargeau, *Les 48 quartiers de Paris*.

The park is the property of His Majesty King Louis-Philippe I, who allows entrance every Thursday in the summer months on presentation of a ticket, which is rarely refused for societies that make such a request to the superintendent of the king's domains at the Palais-Royal.[79]

Whether there was a charge for the ticket is not stated, but what is clear is that this land was a speculation for the 'king of the French'. Balzac, always on the hunt for a 'good deal', thought of buying a plot in the park. On 6 March 1845 he wrote to Mme Hanska: 'Finally, I've not said anything more about Monceaux because it is an excellent deal, and concluded I hope. Plon [who was acting for Balzac here] can only settle it by a payment to L-Philippe.' Of course the deal did not come off.

Under the Second Empire, what remained of the park, now much reduced in size, was improved by Alphand, and the surrounding land developed by the Pereire brothers. Without intending to do so, they continued the operation that Philippe d'Orléans had already begun with the Palais-Royal, constructing houses that faced the park and were served by new peripheral roads.[80] The quarter was now on the up, and the time was long past when Delacroix could lose his way there (*Journal*, 26 November 1852: 'Long walk with Jenny along the outer boulevards, Monceau, the Barrière de Courcelles and the Place de l'Europe, where we almost lost ourselves'). Spectacular hotels arose on all sides, like the neo-Gothic extravaganza that Février built on the Place Malesherbes (now Place du Général-Catroux), or that of Saccard in Zola's *The Kill*, who 'had taken advantage of his good understanding with the Hôtel de Ville to have a key given him of a little gate in the gardens ... It was a display, a profusion, a crush of riches. The mansion disappeared under sculptures. Around the windows, along the sills, were branches and flowers; there were balconies parallel to baskets of greenery, which supported large naked women with twisted hips, their breasts pointing forward.'

The population of the Plaine Monceau was not entirely made up of scum like Saccard. For many years Manet had his studio on Rue Guyot (now Médéric). Other serious and respected artists and writers also lived there – Gervex, Puvis de Chavannes, Gounod, Debussy, Reynaldo Hahn, Fauré, Messager, Chausson, Dumas *fils*, Edmond Rostand, Henry Bernstein – and it was clearly the focal quarter for Marcel Proust and Oriane de Guermantes.

---

79   Ibid.
80   Pinon, *Paris, biographie d'une capitale*.

THE LEFT BANK FAUBOURGS

Faubourg Saint-Marcel

It is by its faubourgs that the Left Bank as it is today differs most from the Right Bank. Between Rue du Cherche-Midi, the Daguerre market, the Observatoire and the Salpêtrière, apartment prices are sky-high, private educational establishments are most expensive as well as mainly secular, the grocers are Arab and the street sweepers Black. Everything has the good order of a prosperous provincial town, and a certain attention is needed – to texts, to certain streets, to a few high walls – to perceive that these were once the most wretched and dangerous faubourgs, haunted by the sinister couples of crime and punishment, suffering and imprisonment, sickness and death.

This can be shown by citing three texts. The first is from the end of the ancien régime, and depicts the Faubourg Saint-Marceau (also known as Saint-Marcel at this time) as seen by Sébastien Mercier:

> This is the quarter where the poorest part of the Paris population live, the most shifty and most refractory to discipline. There is more money in a single house in the Faubourg Saint-Honoré than in the entire Faubourg Saint-Marcel taken together. It is in these dwellings, far from the motion of the centre, that ruined men, misanthropists, alchemists, maniacs and pensioners of limited means hide away, as well as a few studious sages who genuinely do seek solitude, and wish to live completely ignored and cut off from the spectacles of the noisy quarters. No one will ever come to seek them out in this extremity of the city ... this is a people who lack any relationship with Parisians, the polite dwellers on the banks of the Seine ... There is in this faubourg more mischief, more inflammable and quarrelsome material, more readiness for mutiny, than in the other quarters. The police fear to press them too hard; they are handled with kid gloves, as they are capable of breaking out in the greatest excesses.

The second text is from Balzac, familiar with this area as in 1829 he lived at 1 Rue Cassini, i.e., at the corner of Rue du Faubourg-Saint-Jacques, which he evoked as follows in *Ferragus*:

> Around this spot without a name stand the Foundling hospital, the Bourbe, the Cochin hospital, the Capucines, the La Rochefoucauld hospital, the Deaf and Dumb Asylum, the hospital of the Val-de-Grâce; in short, all the vices and all the misfortunes of Paris find their asylum

there. And (that nothing may lack in this philanthropic centre) Science there studies the tides and longitudes, Monsieur de Chateaubriand has erected the Marie-Therese infirmary, and the Carmelites have founded a convent. The great events of life are represented by bells which ring incessantly through this desert – for the mother giving birth, for the babe that is born, for the vice that succumbs, for the toiler who dies, for the virgin who prays, for the old man shaking with cold, for genius self-deluded. And a few steps off is the cemetery of Mont-Parnasse, where, hour after hour, the sorry funerals of the Faubourg Saint-Marceau wend their way.[81]

The third quotation is from Maxime Du Camp's great work on Paris, written just after the demolition of the *octroi* wall:

The world of thieves ... has shifted en masse towards the former *barrières*, in these quarters that have been newly annexed to the city, and whose attachment to Old Paris still seems to be no more than purely administrative. Here they get together in taverns where they are certain of not being arrested, but are able to meet up and make arrangements for the dirty tricks they have in mind. It is around the Barrières d'Italie, des Deux-Moulins, de Fontainebleau, du Mont-Parnasse, du Maine, and de l'École-Militaire that these dives open their hospitable doors to all bandits.[82]

The common stigmata of the three southern faubourgs did not prevent there from being major differences between them – between Saint-Marceau with

---

81　La Bourbe was the popular name for the maternity hospital of Port-Royal, which, before the opening of the boulevard of that name, opened onto the little Rue de la Bourbe. The Enfants-Trouvés (Foundlings) was on Rue d'Enfer (originally *via infera*, now Denfert-Rochereau, having added the name of the colonel in command of the Belfort garrison in 1870–1, through a kind of municipal pun), where the hospital of Saint-Vincent-de-Paul now stands. This was in fact one of three Enfants-Trouvés in Paris, along with that on Rue du Faubourg-Saint-Antoine, now the site of Square Trousseau, and that on the Île de la Cité, opposite the Hôtel-Dieu. The Marie-Thérèse infirmary had been founded by Chateaubriand and his wife for aged and needy priests.

82　Du Camp, *Paris, ses organs*. The Barrière d'Italie (or de Fontainebleau, they were one and the same) was at what is now the Place d'Italie. The Barrière des Deux-Moulins was behind the Salpêtrière, on what is now Boulevard Vincent-Auriol (the *octroi* wall originally left the Salpêtrière outside of the city, but its course was altered later on to include it). The Barrière de Mont-Parnasse was at the end of Rue du Montparnasse, on what is now Boulevard Edgar-Quinet; and the Barrière du Maine was at the end of the Chausée de Maine, very close to where Avenue du Maine passes under the esplanade of the Gare Montparnasse.

its ragpickers, Saint-Jacques with its sisters of mercy, and Montparnasse with its ruffians. (In *Les Misérables*, you may recall, one of the members of the terrible quartet who 'governed the lowest depths of Paris between 1830 and 1835' is called Montparnasse: 'They generally met at nightfall, the hour when they awoke, on the plains that border the Salpêtrière. There they conferred, and, as they had the twelve dark hours before them, they settled their employment accordingly.')

The Faubourg Saint-Marceau has at least one point in common with the Faubourg Saint-Germain: it is a faubourg without a central street. If there is no longer a Rue du Faubourg-Saint-Marceau, any more than there is a Rue du Faubourg-Saint-Germain, it is for precisely the same reason: neither of the two was formed by a radial and centrifugal expansion of Old Paris. These were both very old towns on the periphery, with an independent life outside the city. The Faubourg Saint-Marceau, to be sure, was crossed through its entire length by Rue Mouffetard, which extended to the Barrière (now Place) d'Italie. But it was not this that gave birth to it, or around which it was structured. In *Une vie de cité*, Marcel Poëte explains that the traveller arriving from Lyon or Italy via Villejuif found himself faced with a choice, just outside the Barrière d'Italie. The main branch led towards Place Maubert, through Rue Mouffetard, Rue Bordelle (now Descartes) and Rue de la Montagne-Saint-Geneviève. The other had the same final destination, but by way of Rue du Marché-aux-Chevaux (now Geoffroy-Saint-Hilaire), Rue du Jardin-du-Roi (now Linné) and Rue Saint-Victor. At the point where the two branches forked, the traveller coming into Paris crossed what was known as the town of Saint-Marcel, which in 1612 Du Breuil could still describe as enclosed 'by high walls that distinguish and divide it from the faubourg of Paris that is also named after the same Saint Marcel'.

From Louis XIV to Louis-Philippe, or more accurately perhaps from La Reynie to Vidocq, the boundaries and topography of the Faubourg Saint-Marceau scarcely changed. It formed the south of what was then the 12th and last arrondissement of Paris, described by Balzac as the poorest quarter of Paris, 'that in which two-thirds of the population lack firing in winter, which leaves most brats at the gate of the Foundling hospital, which sends most beggars to the poorhouse, most ragpickers to the street corners, most decrepit old folks to bask against the walls on which the sun shines, most delinquents to the police courts'.[83] (This passage, like a

---

83   Honoré de Balzac, *The Commision in Lunacy* (1836). The gate or 'tower' of the Enfants-Trouvés was a mechanism of the kind used to deposit parcels in post offices: it enabled a mother to abandon her baby without giving her name.

number of others, shows the degree to which Balzac, despite his defence of throne and altar, differed from Tocqueville, Du Camp or Flaubert: you never find in him the least expression of contempt for ordinary people.) Starting from the Barrière de la Gare on the Quai d'Austerlitz (this *gare* being for river traffic), the boundary of the faubourg followed the wall of the Farmers-General (now Boulevards Vincent-Auriol, Blanqui, Saint-Jacques) as far as the Barrière de la Santé (now the corner of Rue de la Santé and Boulevard Saint-Jacques). It then turned towards the city centre, up to what is now the Gobelins intersection, included Sainte-Pélagie and the La Pitié hospital, and came down alongside the Jardin des Plantes to reach the Seine again by Rue Buffon. The Faubourg Saint-Marceau was thus located on the southern slope of the Montagne Sainte-Geneviève, on either side of Louis XIV's wall, represented here by Boulevard de l'Hôpital.

It was in these unwelcoming parts that the royal power decided to construct the Salpêtrière, on the site of a former arsenal. Entrusted to Le Vau, with Libéral Bruant responsible for the chapel, this was the central element in an ensemble known as the Hôpital Général. Hurtaut and Magny list the buildings involved in this: 'Saint-Jean de Bicêtre, Saint-Louis de la Salpêtrière, Notre-Dame de la Pitié, Sainte-Pélagie, Sainte-Marthe de Scipion, the Enfants-Trouvés and Saint-Nicolas-de-la-Savonnerie'.[84] Contrary to what the name may suggest, this Hôpital Général, entirely located in the Faubourg Saint-Marceau apart from the Savonnerie and Bicêtre,[85] had nothing to do with medicine. It was rather an instrument for achieving the dream of all who have governed Paris, past and present, to rid the city of scum: 'The large number of poor and beggars that flood Paris and inconvenience its inhabitants suggested the project of this hospital, for

---

84   La Pitié was not as it is today an extension of the Salpêtrière, but more or less where the mosque now stands; Sainte-Pélagie was on Rue de la Clef; Sainte-Marthe-de-Scipion was the hôtel of Scipion Sardini, on Rue Scipion, which served as the hospitals' central bakery right up to the 1980s; the Savonnerie was, according to Hurtaut and Magny, 'a large old building constructed close to Chaillot, after the railings that enclose the Cours de la Reine'. It had previously been converted from a soap factory into the 'Royal manufacture of works *à la turque*', in other words carpets. Around the chapel, built by Marie de Médicis in 1615, there was a place of charity 'for the reception, feeding, maintenance and instruction of children taken from the hospitals for the sick poor'.

85   'Bicêtre, a dreadful ulcer on the body politic, wide, deep, and pus-filled, which you can only imagine by turning your gaze away. Even the air of the place can be smelled four hundred yards off, everything about it says that you are approaching a place where force is exercised, an asylum of misery, degradation and misfortune' (Mercier, *Tableau de Paris*).

which the king offered the Château de Bicêtre, several other plots of land, and the building of La Pitié.'[86]

The 'great confinement' took place in the year of Pascal's *Provincial Letters* and Poussin's *Blind Orion*:

> It was then announced in sermons and in all the Parishes of Paris that the Hôpital Général would open on 7 May 1657 for all the poor who wished to enter of their own accord, and the magistrates ordered the town criers to announce that it was henceforth illegal to beg for alms in Paris; and rarely was an order so well executed. On the 13th, the high mass of the Holy Spirit was sung in the church of the Pitié, and on the 14th the Confinement of the Poor was carried out without any emotion. On that day, Paris underwent a change of face; the vast majority of beggars returned to the Provinces, and the wisest of them thought of leaving of their own accord. Doubtless the protection of God smiled on these great works, for few would have believed that the operation would be executed with such ease, and that success would be so complete.[87]

Michel Foucault has described at length the population imprisoned in this 'homeland and place of redemption for both sins against the flesh and offences to reason'. It mingled together 'venereals', 'sodomites', prostitutes, blasphemers and attempted suicides, as well as the actually mad, who were never more than a tenth of the total number: 'It was between the walls of internment that Pinel and nineteenth-century psychiatry discovered the mad; it is here, we should not forget, that they left them, not without having claimed the glory of redeeming them.'

In 1818, the wall of the Farmers-General, which had until then passed in front of the Salpêtrière, was pushed back to its periphery on Boulevard de la Gare (now Vincent-Auriol). The buildings of the Salpêtrière were far less extensive than they are today, and the new course of the wall enclosed a large tract of open land that was for a long time the most obscure and sinister region of Paris. It was 'in the deserted places beyond the Salpêtrière' that

---

86   Hurtaut and Magny, *Dictionnaire historique de la ville de Paris*.
87   'L'Hôpital général', an anonymous pamphlet of 1676, published as Annex 1 to Michel Foucault's *Madness and Civilisation*. Almost a century later, 'it is impossible to admire too highly the strict order that reigns in this establishment, and that keep in subordination several thousands of poor of both sexes and every age, the majority of whom are impossible to discipline, either because of the wantonness that led to their enclosure, or for lack of education'.

Montparnasse tried to rob Jean Valjean.[88] 'These few streets leading from Boulevard de l'Hôpital and ending at the Barrière des Deux-Moulins', writes Delvau, 'are bordered by squat houses built with a little plaster and much mud. They resemble rabbit holes or the huts of the Lapps more than the houses of civilized people.'[89] Just opposite, on Boulevard de l'Hôpital, was where Hugo located the Gorbeau house in *Les Misérables*:

> Facing no. 50–52 there stood amid the trees on the boulevard a large elm that was three parts dead; almost opposite began Rue de la Barrière des Gobelins, a street that was then without houses and unpaved, planted with unsuitable trees, green or muddy according to the season, which ended up right at the surrounding wall of Paris ... This barrier itself cast evil shadows in the mind. It was the road to Bicêtre. This was the way that, under the Empire and the Restoration, men condemned to death would return to Paris on the day of their execution.

It is in this disturbing setting, now covered by the railway tracks from the Gare d'Austerlitz, that one could see in the 1850s 'something unbelievable, incomparable, curious, frightful, charming, desolate and admirable', a community of ragpickers known as the Cité Doré:

> Not ironically [i.e., from *doré* meaning 'golden'], but because M. Doré, a distinguished chemist, was the owner of this land ... In 1848 he had the idea of dividing his property with the object of renting plots to the bourgeois of Paris, who, as is well known, have a particular passion for gardening. He expected to see at least some Némorin from Rue Saint-Denis or a Chloë from the Quartier du Temple, but who actually did appear was a ragpicker of the first water, a hood on his back and a hook in his hand ... At dawn the next morning he was already at work, surrounded by a large family. They dug the foundations of their country villa, bought rubble from demolitions at 50 cents the barrow, and a few days later they bravely started to build ... At the end of three months their house was finished, and its roof in place. They had made this roof out of

---

88   You may recall that the 'old man' got the better of the hoodlum, and gave him a long lecture, which concluded: 'Now go, and think over what I have said to you. By the bye, what did you want of me? My purse? Here it is' (Hugo, *Les Misérables*, Volume IV, book 4, chapter 2).

89   Delvau, *Les Dessous de Paris*. The streets referred to here are Rue des Deux-Moulins, the main Rue d'Austerlitz, and Rue de la Barrière-des-Gobelins, which were absorbed by the new hospital of La Pitié, adjacent to the Salpêtrière.

old tarpaulin, with beaten earth placed on top ... This wonder was visited by fellow ragpickers, who all envied the good fortune of the owners, and each wished to have their own place here. A new town came into being.

When winter came, however, the experiment with earth and tarpaulin proved unsuccessful. The water soaked the earth, and the ensuing weight burst the cloth:

> At this point one of the ragpickers had a sublime idea! Everything in Paris is sold except old tin ... They set out to collect what others disdained, so that today the greater part of houses in this colony are covered in tin ... The inhabitants are better off, they get on much better together, and scenes of savagery are no longer to be seen in the area, nor drunks falling into the streams, as happens so often in other parts of this unfortunate 12th arrondissement.[90]

Opposite the gateway of the Salpêtrière, the horse market, another attraction of the faubourg, occupied a long rectangle between Boulevard de l'Hôpital and Rue du Marché-aux-Chevaux (there still exists, off Rue Geoffroy-Saint-Hilaire, an Impasse du Marché-aux-Chevaux, almost on the corner with Boulevard Saint-Marcel). This was specially devoted to carthorses, and to former luxury horses reduced to lower tasks. A semicircle made up of two tracks elevated in the middle, forming a rise and fall, was used to try out the horses – hence the name of Rue de l'Essai between the market and Rue Poliveau.

On the other side of Rue du Marché-aux-Chevaux, Rue Poliveau continued – and still continues – through Rue du Fer-à-Moulin, which was long known as Rue aux Morts. This was the way to the Clamart cemetery, the last resting place of executed criminals and those who died in hospital:

> Those bodies that the Hôtel-Dieu vomits out each day are brought to Clamart: this is a large cemetery, whose mouth is always open. The corpses are not on biers, but simply covered with a cloth. They are hastily taken from their bed, and more than one sick person, supposedly dead, wakes up in the very cart that is taking him to the grave. This cart is pulled by twelve men; a dirty and encrusted priest, a bell, a cross, that is all the equipment that the poor can expect ... This lugubrious carriage leaves the Hôtel-Dieu every day at four in the morning; it rolls in the

---

90 Privat d'Anglemont, *Paris anecdote*. This is rather like old Mabeuf in *Les Misérables*, growing indigo in the same part of the faubourg.

silence of the night …This soil, rich in burials, is the field where young surgeons come by night, climbing the wall, to take corpses to subject to their inexperienced scalpels: and so even after the poor person has passed away, his body can still be stolen.[91]

Surprising as it may seem, this illegal practice ended up by giving its popular name to the place that, after the cemetery was closed in the early nineteenth century, became the anatomy theatre for the hospitals. I myself worked in the library there for many years, in the low buildings that had seen the passage of Larrey, Broussais, and Dupuytren. You would say 'I'm going to Clamart', without anyone realizing where this strange expression came from. The entrance was under marvellous arbours of flowers, and in summer, with the windows open, a scent wafted into the lecture hall that I can still remember, the odour of roses mingling with that of formaldehyde.

The riotous tradition of the Faubourg Saint-Marceau goes back very far into the past. In the sixteenth century it was the main popular bastion of Protestantism in Paris, along with the Popincourt quarter on the Right Bank. On 27 December 1561, following an obscure business about bells spoiling a meeting held by the Calvinists on Rue Patriarche (now Rue Daubenton, opposite Saint-Médard), the latter sacked the Saint-Médard church. This affair, known as the 'Saint-Médard disturbance', led to a number of deaths, and is often seen as a prelude to the wars of religion. It was also at Saint-Médard, in the little cemetery alongside, today a square, that one of the most celebrated disorders in the history of the faubourg took place, that of the 'convulsionaries', in which 'people danced on the grave of Deacon Pâris, and ate earth from his tomb, until the cemetery was closed: *De par le roi, défense à Dieu / De faire miracle en ce lieu*'.[92]

Later on, the Faubourg Saint-Marceau was involved in all the great Revolutionary *journées*. During the 'subsistence troubles' of 1792, the people of Faubourgs Saint-Marceau and Saint-Denis went en masse to the wholesalers, knocking down their doors and forcing them to sell their goods at their previous price. In 1793, the Faubourgs Saint-Marceau and Saint-Antoine delivered a joint address to the Commune:

Legislators, it is the brave sans-culottes of 14 July and 10 August, whose blood marked the fall of a despicable throne, whose faubourgs

---

91   Mercier, *Tableau de Paris*. The cemetery was situated where the gardens of the former Hôtel de Clamart stood.
92   Ibid. ['By order of the king, God is forbidden to perform miracles on this site' – one of the most celebrated graffiti in history, which appeared on the wall of the cemetery soon after it was closed' – Tr.]

Saint-Antoine and Saint-Marceau are proud to address you today. In their breast they have been nourished in a hatred of tyranny and in the republican spirit. They ask you to let them form up in their companies to fly to the defence of the Fatherland ... The children of the faubourgs Saint-Antoine and Saint-Marceau will carry these names to the banks of the Rhine. They will make Frédéric [Friedrich Wilhelm II of Prussia] and François [Franz II, the Holy Roman Emperor] see so closely the scars of 10 August that they tremble at being kings.[93]

Saint-Marceau had a far older industrial tradition than did Saint-Antoine. As far back as the 1440s, a Flemish manufacturer by the name of Gobelin established his business in a house on Rue Moffetard (now Avenue des Gobelins), backing onto the River Bièvre.

This became known as the River Gobelins after Jean Gobelin, an excellent dyer of wool and silk, in all kinds of colours, especially scarlet, came to live in a big house that he had built close to Saint-Hippolyte, the church of the Faubourg Saint-Marceau. This illustrious man did not just build up a great property there, but also ... made such a name for himself in his art, that his house, his scarlet, his dye, and the river he used, were all given his name.[94]

The Gobelins thus started out as dyers, as Jean de Julienne, the friend of Watteau, still was in the eighteenth century, himself in the little Rue des Gobelins. Tapestry came long after carpets, when Colbert established the royal manufactory of furnishings and tapestries of the crown, its first director being Le Brun. Curriers and tanners could also be found on the Bièvre. An 1890 guide explains:

We are now in some quite outlying quarters; the penetrating smell of tannin rises to the nose; a fine red dust floats in the air, sometimes leaving a light deposit in which the feet of the rare passersby leave their traces ... The tannery drying-rooms set up their great partitioned bays where the wind can blow through, and nearby are workshops making mats, their courtyards cluttered with immense heaps of screenings.[95]

A land of tumult and revolt, the Faubourg Saint-Marceau was destroyed like

---

93 *Adresse des habitants des faubourgs Saint-Antoine et Saint-Marceau à la Convention nationale*, printed by order of the National Convention.
94 Sauval, *Histoire et recherches*.
95 Martin, *Promenades dans les vingt arrondissements de Paris*.

Carthage, except that its eradication took place in two stages. The cuttings of the nineteenth century did the bulk of it. The Boulevard de Port-Royal, which followed the route of the former Rue de la Bourbe and Rue des Bourguignons, absorbed the fields of the Capucins, destroyed the old Saint-Marcel theatre, and transformed Rue Broca and Rue Pascal into canyons. Boulevard Saint-Marcel swallowed up the Place de la Collégiate, the horse market, and the little streets of Rue des Francs-Bourgeois and Rue du Cendrier that led there. Boulevard Arago was built where the Saint-Hippolyte church and street had stood. The narrow Rue Mouffetard, well suited for barricades, was hemmed in between the new Gobelins intersection and the Place d'Italie, and replaced by Avenue des Gobelins, more than forty metres wide. Rue Monge with its barracks, and the artery of Rue Claude-Bernard and Rue Gay-Lussac, made it possible to attack the quarter from the rear.

Yet despite this network of trenches, some parts of the ancient fabric remained until the 1950s. I remember making '*Les Misérables* walks' with my father, who led us on Sunday mornings to Rue du Banquier or Rue du Champ-de-l'Alouette, where Marius had gone to dream of Cosette. The destruction of the plebeian quarters after the war began here, in this Faubourg Saint-Marceau that never understood the new situation and continued to be *red*. In the 1950s and '60s, the cul-de-sacs, alleys, court-yards and workshops of the old 'faubourg of suffering' were systematically destroyed, and no one today would conceive the idea of taking a walk through what has replaced them.

Faubourg Saint-Jacques

The Rue du Faubourg-Saint-Jacques, an extension of Rue Saint-Martin and Rue Saint-Jacques, formed for many years the southern segment of the ancient north-south route across Paris. But starting in the seventeenth century it was replaced in this role by Rue d'Enfer (now Boulevard Saint-Michel, Rue Henri-Barbusse, Avenue Denfert-Rochereau). 'The Faubourg Saint-Jacques', Dumas wrote in *The Mohicans of Paris*, 'is one of the most primitive in Paris. What is the reason for this? Is it because, surrounded by four hospitals like a citadel is by four bastions, these hospitals warn the tourist away from the quarter? Is it because, not leading to any major road, not ending up in any centre, in complete contrast to the larger Paris faubourgs, the passage of carriages there is very rare?'[96]

---

96 These four hospitals would presumably have been the Val-de-Grâce, the Cochin hospital, the Port-Royal maternity hospital, and the hospital of Saint-Vincent-de-Paul. But Broca, Tarnier, Sainte-Anne and others could also have been added.

Thanks to owners who could not be dislodged – hospitals, ecclesiastical communities, the Observatory, the Société des Gens de Lettres – this faubourg escaped serious destruction. From Rue du Val-de-Grâce to Boulevard Saint-Jacques, between Rue de la Santé and Avenue Denfert-Rochereau, is today a calm quarter, airy and much visited. And yet in the 1930s, when Walter Benjamin lived for years at the edge of it, on Place Denfert-Rochereau and Rue Boulard, he could still describe it in terms close to those of Balzac:

> For in [the 14ᵗʰ arrondissment] are found, one after another, all the buildings of public misery, or proletarian indigence, in unbroken succession: the birthing clinic, the orphanage, the hospital (the famous Santé), and finally the great Paris jail with its scaffold. At night, one sees on the narrow unobtrusive benches – not, of course, the comfortable ones found in the squares – men stretched out asleep as if in the waiting room of a way station in the course of this terrible journey.[97]

The scaffold was the great spectre of the faubourg. Hugo wrote of the Place Saint-Jacques in *Les Misérables* that it was 'almost predestined and has always been horrible'. Previously, apart from the Revolutionary years, executions had always been carried out on the Place de Grève, in full daylight. The windows of buildings on the route taken by condemned prisoners from the Conciergerie or Bicêtre were hired long in advance.[98] But after the revolution of 1830 the Place de Grève was no longer appropriate. 'The Place de Grève', wrote the prefect of the Seine department on 16 November 1831, 'can no longer serve as a site for executions, after generous citizens so gloriously spilled their blood there for the national cause. Besides, the difficulty of traffic circulation in the tightly packed quarter around the Place de Grève has for a long time imposed the need to find a different place for capital executions.'[99] This 'different place' would now be the Place Saint-Jacques, at the corner of Rue du Faubourg-Saint-Jacques and Boulevard Saint-Jacques.

In 1832, in his preface to *The Last Day of a Condemned*, Victor Hugo wrote:

97   Benjamin, *The Arcades Project*, p. 86.
98   Balzac noted in 'Le Dictionnaire des enseignes': '*Aux bons enfants*. Louvet, wine-merchant, no. 9, Place de Grève. Lovers of tragedy, hasten to M. Louvet's, ask him for a litre and place yourself at one of the tables in his saloon; four o'clock strikes, the crowd gets agitated; the climax is approaching; you see the patient mount the fatal steps … There are so many sensitive people nowadays, that on days of executions on the Place de Grève, the rooms of wineshops, even if they were as big as the Louvre galleries, would be unable to contain them all.'
99   105 AN, BB18 1123. Cited by Louis Chevalier, *Classes laborieuses et classes dangereuses à Paris pendant la première moitié du XIXe siècle* (Paris: Plon, 1958).

At Paris, we have come back to the time of secret executions; since July they no longer dare to decapitate in the Grève; as they are afraid, as they are cowardly, here is what they do. They took lately from the Bicêtre prison a man, under sentence of death, named Désandrieux, I think; they put him in a sort of basket on two wheels, closed on each side, bolted and padlocked: then, with a gendarme in front, and another at the back, without noise or crowd, they proceeded to the deserted Barrière Saint-Jacques. It was eight in the morning when they arrived, with but little light. There was a newly erected guillotine, and, for spectators, some dozens of little boys, grouped on the heaps of stones around the unexpected machine. Quickly they withdrew the man from the basket; and, without giving him time to breathe, they furtively, secretly, shamefully, deprived him of life! And that is called a public and solemn act of high justice! Infamous derision![100]

In 1851, the guillotine was removed for a while from the Faubourg Saint-Jacques. Executions were then performed in front of the La Roquette prison. The condemned man only had to walk from his cell to the scaffold. Maxime Du Camp asked:

> What makes up this throng that Paris flings towards the Place de la Roquette during the night that precedes an execution? People of the quarter excited by the spectacle, and who are there, as they themselves put it, as neighbours, prowlers of all kinds, vagabonds, ruffians and beggars who, not knowing where to find shelter, come and spend there the hours of a night that they would otherwise no doubt have spent under a bridge or in the cage of a police station.[101]

In April 1870, when Paris was at boiling point after the murder of Victor Noir by Pierre Bonaparte, it was here that the execution of Troppmann was carried out, as described by Turgenev, ending in a manner that might be surprising for a man who was friendly with Du Camp, Flaubert, and the Goncourts: 'I will be content and excuse my own misplaced curiosity if my story supplies a few arguments to those who are in favour of the abolition of capital punishment, or, at least, the abolition of public executions.'[102]

In April 1899, when the men's prison of La Roquette was demolished, the guillotine returned to the Faubourg Saint-Jacques, on the corner of

---

100   Victor Hugo, *The Last Day of a Condemned* (trans. Eugenia de B.).
101   Maxime Du Camp, *Les Convulsions de Paris* (Paris, 1878–80). For Du Camp, who received the cross of the Légion d'Honneur for his role in the repression of the June days of 1848, this crowd was a prefiguration of the Commune.
102   Ivan Turgenev, 'The Execution of Troppmann'.

Boulevard Arago and Rue de la Santé. It remained there right to the end, even if after 1939 executions were no longer public but carried out within the prison. Under the Occupation, French hostages were shot in the courtyard, but during the Algerian war, the FLN militants condemned for murder were guillotined. On 28 November 1972 the series was closed with Claude Buffet and Roger Bontemps, whom Georges Pompidou refused a presidential pardon.

Montparnasse

Montparnasse, the third of the southern faubourgs, is a case apart. On the one hand, it is a Parisian name famous across the world, matched only by Montmartre and Saint-Germain-des-Près. On the other, it is a quarter with a weak identity, whether in terms of geographical limits, history – aside from the 'crazy years' that have so often been recounted – architecture or population. Montparnasse is proof *a contrario* of the importance of walls in the definition of Paris quarters: it was built so late in the nineteenth century that Louis XIV's boulevard, today represented by Boulevard Montparnasse, was never its actual border. As for the wall of the Farmers-General (now the route of Boulevards Raspail and Edgar-Quinet), it had already been demolished. Thus the borders of Montparnasse were always vague. If they may be fixed on one side by Rue du Faubourg-Saint-Jacques, and on another by Avenue Denfert-Rochereau and the Observatoire intersection, and if, in the direction of Faubourg Saint-Germain, Montparnasse scarcely goes beyond Rue du Cherche-Midi, on the outer side no one knows where it comes to an end, so that estate agents do not flinch at extending its glorious name as far as the Porte de Vanves, or even the Porte d'Orléans.

It is not entirely correct to deny Boulevard Montparnasse any border role, as in its route across the quarter it divides two arrondissements between which there is a certain difference, Montparnasse being rather more bourgeois in the 6th arrondissement, and rather more plebeian in the 14th. This uneven development between the two sides of the boulevard goes back to the origins of the quarter. In the 1830s, urbanization began on the side of Rue Notre-Dame-des-Champs and Rue du Montparnasse – of which Hurtaut and Magny had already written, fifty years earlier, that 'newly opened, it is beginning to be equipped with some very fine houses'. But these roads were still semirural in character. Balzac's Godefroid, for example, in 'The Initiate', was 'surprised to find such puddles of mud in so magnificent a district',[103] at the end of Rue Notre-Dame-du-Champs on

103   Balzac, *The Wrong Side of Paris*.

the Observatory side. At the same time – that of his *Cromwell* and *Hernani* –
Victor Hugo lived with Adèle in a small house at the other end of the road.
He was only a few steps away from Boulevard Montparnasse, and among
the many promenaders attracted by the taverns of the *barrières*, the open-air
shops, the sideshows and the cemetery. Facing the cemetery was an acrobats' booth. This opposition of parade and burial confirmed him, Hugo
said, in his idea of a theatre in which extremes met, and it was this that gave
him the idea for the third act of *Marion Delorme*, in which the Marquis de
Nangis's mourning is contrasted with the grimaces of Le Gracieux. Sainte-
Beuve was a neighbour of the Hugos, which led to complications that are
well known. Later on, established artists, those exhibited at the Salon, came
to live in the '6th arrondissement part' of Montparnasse. Gérôme had his
studio on Rue Notre-Dame-des-Champs, known as the Tea Chest because
its entrance was decorated with two Chinese figures. Opposite, at no. 70
bis, there was the house of Bouguereau, the idol of Douanier Rousseau.[104]
Henner, who had his museum close by on Rue Jean-Berrandi; Baudry,
who decorated the foyer of the Garnier opera; Jules Thomas, sculptor of
the gilded bust of Charles Garnier that can be seen on Rue Auber by
the monument; Jean-Paul Laurens; Ramey; Moreau-Vauthier – all these
famous artists lived on Rue Notre-Dame-des-Champs. Carolus-Duran was
on Rue Jules-Chaplain, Rochegrosse on Rue de l'Ouest (now d'Assas), and
Falguière on Rue Vavin. Thus Montparnasse, famous for having been the
cradle of modern art, was earlier on the favoured quarter of academic painters, along with Rue Monceau. How strange it is to think that, in these same
years, Gauguin lived – between his voyages – with 'Anna the Javanese' on
the other side of the boulevard, on Rue Doulart, Rue Delambre that was a
haunt of ragpickers and prostitutes, and Rue Vercingétorix.

In the romantic period these streets did not yet exist. Beyond the cemetery
was no longer Paris. There were fields and windmills, some of which have left
their names to streets in this quarter, such as Rue du Moulin-de-la-Vierge and
Rue du Moulin-du-Beurre (now du Texel), which housed one of the most
famous *guinguettes* of the age, that of Mother Saguet. For twenty sous you
got two boiled eggs, a sauté chicken, cheese, and as much white wine as you
liked. Over the years there, you could have met Scribe, Béranger, Devéria,
Dumas, Hugo, Baudelaire or Murger, who used the setting for one of his
Scènes de la vie de bohème. After 1840, the countryside slowly began to retreat
with the building of the railway, which you took from the Chartres station.

---

104   The Douanier himself lived at various times on the Chaussée du Maine,
Rue Vercingétorix, Rue Gassendi and Rue Daguerre, before settling at Plaisance
on Rue Perrel.

But this did not prevent the *guinguettes* from spreading. Around the Barrière du Maine, you had the choice of the Californie, 'the great popular eatery' as Delvau describes it, or the restaurant of the Cuisiniers Associés, operated as a cooperative, and where the socialists held their banquets in 1848. Or you could opt for one of the tramps' dens on the Impasse d'Odessa, which did not yet reach through to Boulevard Montparnasse. Rue Campagne-Première was the domain of the horse, around the stables of the Société Générale de Voitures à Paris. Farriers, carriage makers and saddlers frequented the coachmen's restaurants, where 'you ate large portions quite decently cooked, with a certain overdose of veal Marengo. Algerian wine jostled with that of Narbonne; the cheeses did not lack character'.[105]

But the main road of the *guinguettes* was Rue de la Gaîté. Wine cost less outside the *octroi* wall – the Barrière Montparnasse was on Boulevard Edgar-Quinet. This *barrière* played the same role for the south of Paris as Rue de Paris (now de Belleville) did for the east, or Rue de la Chapelle for the north. This was the site of the Îles-Marquises – which still exists – close to a police station run by the symbolist novelist Ernest Raynaud, a friend of Moréas; the Belle-Polonaise, where you could eat in the garden against the cemetery wall; the tavern of Les Vrais-Amis; the Mille-Colonnes, popular with the *bohème* of the Latin Quarter under the Second Empire, headed by Courbet and Vallès. It was a magnificent street. In Huysmans's words:

I soon reached Rue de la Gaîté. The strains of quadrilles escaped from open windows; large posters, outside the doors of a café-concert, announced the opening of Mme Adèle, a popular singer, and the return of M. Adolphe, an eccentric comedian; further along, under the sign of a wine merchant, there were piles of snails, their blond flesh sprinkled with parsley; and here and there, pastry cooks displayed great quantities of cakes in their windows, some dome shaped, others flat and topped with a pink and trembling jelly, some with brown stripes, others hollowed out and showing succulent flesh of a sulphurous yellow. This street well justified its joyful name.[106]

But nighttime was not completely safe in this popular and joyous Montparnasse:

There was still waste ground, even right on the boulevard ... badly enclosed by shaky fences which fell down under the weight of the posters

105   André Salmon, *Montparnasse* (Paris: André Bonne, 1950).
106   J.-K. Huysmans, *Le Drageoir aux épices* (1874).

stuck to their boards, from the contradictory announcements of the radical distiller Jacques and General Boulanger, to the first images devoted to the novel triumph of the bicycle. It was deplorable but a well-known fact that when night fell and children were in bed, this wasteland was a place for the plots of evil ruffians ... Nighttime attacks were not a daily occurrence at the heart of Montparnasse, but they were common enough on its borders, in the outer reaches of the station and especially under the railway bridge. Murders conveniently took place along the Boulevard Edgar-Quinet, under the cemetery walls. Woe to those going out at night![107]

As late as 1911, the second volume of J.-H. Rosny the elder's trilogy *Les Rafales*, whose action takes place in Montparnasse, was titled *Dans les rues, roman de moeurs apaches et bourgeoises*. Maurice and Jacques, the two 'apache' brothers, are pursued by policemen on bicycles. They flee through Rue Gassendi and Passage Tenaille, and reach Avenue du Maine where they separate:

> The cyclists sped like lightning towards the *mairie*: on the other side, the sergeants barred the road in the direction of the Gaîté ... 'I'm done for,' the boy thought. His best chance of escape seemed to be through the Passage de la Tour-de-Vanves [now Rue Olivier-Noyer] ... He reached Rue Didot and cut diagonally across into Rue de l'Eure ... On Rue Maindron, the narrow Passage des Thermopyles was tempting, and he ran into it as fast as he could ... His urgency prevented him from taking a decision: the little steel and rubber machines were on his heels at top speed, so that he found himself in Rue des Plantes without having made any firm decision.[108]

The Montparnasse balls in the nineteenth century also offered material for tales. The oldest and most famous was the Grande-Chaumière, founded in 1788 by one of those Englishmen who played such an important role in the spread of 'country dancing' in Paris, where it was naturalized as *danse champêtre*. This was a very large garden on the corner of Boulevard Montparnasse and Boulevard d'Enfer (now Boulevard Raspail), where the block of houses now stands that is isolated by the little Rue Léopold-Robert. It was immensely fashionable in the 1830s, and gave the whole life

107   Salmon, *Montparnasse*.
108   In 1933 a film was made of this book, with Jean-Pierre Aumont and Madeleine Ozeray.

of this quarter its rhythm. When Godefroid asked whether the house on Rue Notre-Dame-des-Champs was inhabited by quiet people, the porter 'made a graceful gesture and said: "Monsieur has done well for himself in coming here; for except on the days of Chaumière, the boulevard is as deserted as the Pontine marshes." '

The majority of customers at the Grande-Chaumière were students from the Latin Quarter. 'They heroically quaffed a horrible spirit disguised under the fallacious name of old cognac. This general system of refreshment beloved by the Chaumière led to a rowdiness, craziness, and disorder that it is hard indeed to imagine.'[109] The quadrille was the popular dance, often degenerating into the forbidden dances of the *chahut* and the *cancan*, at which Lola Montès excelled. The 1831 edition of the *Manuel des sergents de ville* noted: 'Police constables charged with supervision of dance halls must ensure that no indecent dance such as the *chahut* or *cancan* is performed.'[110] The vigilance of the police was not limited to proper morals. They also had to keep their eye on a crowd of students who were always ready to shout seditious slogans – 'Down with Louis-Philippe!' or 'Vive la République!' Enjolras and his lieutenants would certainly have visited the Chaumière from time to time; it remained closed for a year after the insurrection of June 1831. There were rivals to the Chaumière quite close at hand: a few steps away was the Jardin des Montagnes Suisses; on the opposite corner of the same crossroads the Arc-en-Ciel dance hall, which specialized in waltzes; the Ermitage, favoured by legal clerks; and the Élysée-Montparnasse, frequented by *barrière* prowlers.

The preeminence of the Chaumière lasted until 1847, when a certain Bullier, the proprietor of the Prado – the only large dance hall on the Île de la Cité – bought an old garden on Avenue de l'Observatoire and established there a dance hall that he christened La Closerie des Lilas.[111] With its brilliant gas lighting, this was admired for 'an Oriental decoration, and gaudy murals that a joker called "Alhambra style"'.[112] The success of the establishment that would become famous under the name of the Bal

---

109   Edmond Texier, *Tableau de Paris* (Paris, 1850).
110   Cited in François Gasnault, *Guinguettes et lorettes.*
111   The name seems to have been taken from that of an inn on the Orléans road, where Chateaubriand sometimes stopped for refreshment. The Bullier dance hall was where the Centre des Oeuvres Universitaires now stands.
112   Alexandre Privat d'Anglemont, *La Closerie des Lilas, quadrille en prose* (Paris, 1848), cited in Gasnault, *Guinguettes et lorettes.* The name Closerie des Lilas later passed to the establishment on the other side of Avenue de l'Observatoire, which still remains. The statue of Marshal Ney, which was next to the Bullier dance hall, was moved to make way for the railway station of the RER line to Sceaux.

Bullier lasted until the outbreak of the First World War, on the eve of which Sonia Delaunay came to dance there in her *robe simultanée*, along with Mayakovsky in his famous cadmium-yellow shirt.

Who was responsible for transforming a Montparnasse of rustic dance halls into a place that would shake up the old world, between the years of symbolism and August 1914? For André Salmon:

> Paul Fort, the master of the Closeries and sustainer of its memorable games ... was the real creator of modern Montparnasse ... He listed to me, in a rush of names I could hardly keep up with, all the poets whose work had held the stage at the Gaîté-Montparnasse, and those whose enthusiasm led to heated brawls: Henri de Régnier, Jean Moréas, Émile Verhaeren, Vielé-Griffin, Stuart Merrill, Paul Claudel, Maurice Barrès, Saint-Pol-Roux-le-Magnifique, André Gide, Pierre Louÿs, just to stick with those who became contributors to the literary review *Vers et Prose*, founded by Paul Fort in 1905 at the heart of Montparnasse: 18 Rue Boissonard.

This street was more recent than its parallel, Rue Campagne-Première. To quote Ramuz:

> Rue Boissonnade, however, had a great intimacy. It was largely inhabited by painters, gentlemen and ladies who came from all parts of the world, but especially from Russia, and there is still a certain cosmopolitan Paris of which Montparnasse is one of the centres. This cul-de-sac also housed a working-class population employed in a large printing house, and a number of quiet households of retired people or pensioners.[113]

For Carco:

> Apollinaire gave birth to Montparnasse; he was the first to take us to Baty's and was fêted everywhere. As soon as he spoke, Guillaume gave a voice to the crowd of poets and painters who, when they listened to him, believed that they heard themselves, and read his words as addressed to them. Before you could notice, adjacent to his cousin Paul Fort whose domain included the long *boul' Mich'*, Bullier, the Luxembourg and the Closerie des Lilas, he traced the boundaries of his own fiefdom, and, from the café of Les Deux-Magots where Jarry had once decorated

---

113 Charles-Ferdinand Ramuz, *Notes d'un Vaudois* (Paris: Gallimard, 1938). Ramuz lived in a passage between Rues Boissonnade and Campagne-Première.

him with the order of the Grande Gidouille, extended this via Rue de Rennes and Boulevard Raspail through to the point where this boulevard crosses with that of Montparnasse. Had he not already sent his scouts out towards Plaisance, where Douanier Rousseau lived, and made his headquarters for a while in the friendly Rue de la Gaîté?[114]

In 1913, Apollinaire described Montparnasse in the following prophetic fashion:

Montparnasse has replaced Montmartre, the Montmartre of another age, that of artists, singers, windmills and taverns ... All those expelled for riotous living from the old Montmartre, destroyed by property owners and architects ... have emigrated in the guise of Cubists, Peaux-Rouges, or Orphic poets. Their loud voices have disturbed the echoes of the crossroads of the Grande-Chaumière. Outside a café established in a house of licentious memory, they set up a redoubtable competitor, the Café de la Rotonde. The Germans were just opposite. The Slavs were keener to come in. The Jews went indifferently from one to the other ... Let us start by sketching the physiognomy of the crossroads. It will in all likelihood change very soon. At one of the corners of Boulevard Montparnasse a large grocer displays to the eyes of a whole crowd of international artists his enigmatic name 'Hazard' ... Here on the other corner is the Rotonde ... André Salmon sometimes stops on this terrace, distant like a spectator at the back of a theatre box; Max Jacob is often there, selling his Côte and his drawings, sometimes even the long and serene figure of Charles Morice can be seen against the wall inside. At one corner of Boulevard Montparnasse and Rue Delambre is the Dôme: a clientele of regulars, rich people, aesthetes from Massachussets or the banks of the Spree ... On another corner is Baty or the last wineshop. When he retires, this profession will have all but disappeared in Paris ... Soon, I would wager, without wishing it, Montparnasse will have its nightclubs and its songsters, as it has its painters and its poets. The day when the songs of someone like Bruant celebrate the different corners of this quarter full of imagination, its creameries, the workshop-barracks of Rue Campagne-Première, the extraordinary dairy-cum-grillroom on Boulevard du Montparnasse, the Chinese restaurant, Tuesdays at the Closerie des Lilas – that day Montparnasse will have given up the ghost.[115]

114 Carco, *De Montparnasse au Quartier Latin*.
115 Cited by Salmon, *Montparnasse*.

It is true that after 1914 Montparnasse never regained this grace and innocence, despite Modigliani, despite Pascin's bowler hat, despite Kiki, Picasso
and Joyce, Brassaï and Man Ray – everything has been said, after all, on
the 1920s. But anyone who has experienced the destruction of a quarter
as a result of its success can understand why, in 1924, Breton and Aragon,
'out of hatred of Montparnasse and Montmartre', decided, as we have seen,
to establish their headquarters in a district long out of fashion, at the Café
Certa in the Passage de l'Opéra.

Yet Montparnasse had its final moment in the 1950s, when it was no
longer fashionable and not yet ravaged. The cafés there were quite gloomy,
and their floors strewn with cigarette butts even in the mornings. The only
two cinemas were the Studio Raspail in its magnificent modernistic building, and the Studio Parnasse on Rue Jules-Chaplain, where on Tuesday
evenings after the last showing the owners asked impossible questions and
cineastes could win free tickets. Writers and artists still lived in the quarter
and quietly got on with their work. Once on the same morning I happened
to pass Sartre in Rue d'Odessa and Giacometti who was coming out of the
Raspail-Vert. Each of them was alone, small, badly dressed; they walked
just like anyone else – or almost so, since Giacometti limped a bit, as is
well-known.

Even today, if you avoid the Dôme, which should never have been
allowed to call itself the café of Trotsky and Kertész, the Coupole that
is now part of a chain of eateries, and the Closerie with its ex-Maoist
balladuriens, Montparnasse has preserved its attractions (writing this word,
I suddenly remember *Andromaque*: '. . . and the fate of Orestes/Is to never
cease loving your attractions/And to always swear that this will never end',
a verse that matches very well my feeling for the quarter of my childhood).
Everyone is free to trace their own itinerary there, in architecture, art, or
love, as they pass the Art Déco buildings on Rue Campagne-Première;
the little workshop-houses with pointed roofs on Rue Boissonnade; the
Cartier foundation with its 'Look at me!' spirit that is not out of place in the
quarter, and at least has the merit of having preserved Chateaubriand's cedar
tree; the pretty rationalist building of the École Spéciale d'Architecture on
the opposite side; the little gardens and studios at the top of Rue Notre-
Dame-des-Champs; the shaded courtyard of Reid Hall with its library, on
Rue de Chevreuse; and the Tschann bookshop, ending up on the little
triangular place formed between Rues Vavin and Bréa, overlooked by the
hanging garden that belonged to Matisse's paint supplier, and by the white-
and-blue-porcelain steps of the Sauvage building.

Among the countless anonymous triangles that are formed in this way by
the convergence of two streets, this is one of my favourites, along with one

at the other end of Paris, which the junction of Rue Jean-Pierre-Timbaud and Rue des Trois-Couronnes makes with Rue Morand, the site of the Maison des Métallos and a mosque, where children play under the catalpa trees around a curious variant of Rodin's *Thinker*. It is undoubtedly such places that Walter Benjamin had in mind in *The Arcades Project* when he evoked

> the little timeless squares that suddenly are there, and to which no name attaches. They have not been the object of careful planning, like the Place Vendôme or the Place de Grève, and do not enjoy the patronage of world history, but owe their existence to houses that have slowly, sleepily, belatedly assembled in response to the summons of the century. In such squares, the trees hold sway; even the smallest afford thick shade. Later, however, in the gaslight, their leaves have the appearance of dark-green frosted glass near the street lamps, and their earliest green glow at dusk is the automatic signal for the start of spring in the big city.[116]

---

116   Benjamin, *The Arcades Project*, p. 516.

The modern division of twenty arrondissements introduced in 1860.

4

New Paris: The Villages

I go astray and lose myself in this immense city, even I no longer recognize the new quarters. Now we have Chaillot, Passy and Auteuil quite linked to the capital; a bit more of this, and Sèvres will touch it as well; and in a hundred years' time it will extend to Versailles on the one hand, Saint-Denis on the other, and from the Picpus side to Vincennes will all be a maze of confusion.

— Sébastien Mercier

On 15 July 1840, twenty-five years after Waterloo, Britain, Prussia and Russia signed a treaty of alliance in London. They committed themselves to supporting the Ottoman Empire against the ambitions of the Egyptian khedive, Muhammad Ali, who was supported by France. There was talk of war. Thiers, as prime minister, was inclined to a show of strength, and the fortification plans for Paris that had been under discussion for over ten years rose suddenly to the top of the agenda. Champions of a continuous wall came to agreement with those who preferred detached fortresses: a continuous rampart would be constructed, reinforced by seventeen separate fortresses outside of the wall. The spokesmen of the liberal opposition, François Arago and Lamartine, denounced this operation as one that could be turned against the people of Paris, evoking the recent examples of the Russians in Warsaw and the Bourbons in Barcelona. Even Chateaubriand emerged from his silence to write a 'Lettre sur les fortifications': 'Internally, the peace of the barracks; outside these ravelins the silence of the desert ... What a result of our Revolution!' Not to worry, the 'monstrous gnome', as Marx would call him, replied from the tribune of the Chamber of Deputies: 'What! To fancy that any works of fortification could ever endanger liberty! And first of all you calumniate any possible government in supposing that it could some day attempt to maintain itself by bombarding the capital ... but that government would be a hundred times more impossible after its victory than before.'[1] The army, the department of bridges and roads, and private contractors mobilized twenty-five thousand workers on this construction more than thirty kilometres long, and by 1843 the new Paris fortifications were completed.[2]

The route of the new wall corresponded to what are now known as the 'boulevards of the marshals', their names actually being taken from those of the military road that ran on the inner side of the fortifications. It was dictated by strategic considerations, in other words by the contours of the land. To the north of the city, on the Saint-Denis plain, the wall ran in a straight line from the Porte de La Villette to the Porte de Clichy, beyond the line of the heights between Charonne and Montmartre. It then turned to run parallel to the bend of the Seine, to take in Monceau, Passy and Auteuil. Crossing the river at the Point du Jour, it circled Vaugirard and Grenelle, then cut across the communes of Issy, Montrouge, Gentilly and Ivry in a wide curve.[3] Back on the other bank it ran due north, from the Porte de Charenton to the Porte des Lilas and across the communes of Bercy and Saint-Mandé. Finally, it swung between the final heights of Belleville and the Pré-Saint-Gervais. This was its most hilly section, and today the most picturesque part of the 'boulevards of the marshals', its hair-pin bends overlooking the broad plain of the northern suburbs.

Among the villages surrounding Paris, some were thus entirely included within the wall, and others cut in two with one section remaining outside the fortifications.[4] The communes that were totally or partially included were thus within the fortifications but outside Paris itself, its official limit remaining the wall of the Farmers-General. The *octroi* was now levied at the new gates, the wall of the Farmers-General was demolished, the number of arrondissements increased from twelve to twenty, with boundaries that remain today.

---

1 Louis-Adolphe Thiers, cited by Karl Marx in 'The Civil War in France', *The First International and After* (Penguin: Harmondsworth, 1974), pp. 191–2.
2 Jean-Louis Cohen and André Lortie, *Des fortifs au périf* (Paris: Picard, 1991). 'The fortifications ... comprised, from the inside looking out, a rampart road with a carriageway of six metres (the "military boulevard"), a continuous wall doubled by a ditch forty metres wide, a counterscarp and a glacis.'
3 The fortresses that would play a large role at the time of the Commune, as we shall see, were built on the southern heights.
4 The main communes totally absorbed were on the Right Bank, Auteuil, Passy, Les Batignolles, Montmartre, La Chapelle, La Villette, Belleville and Charonne; on the Left Bank, Grenelle and Vaugirard. The larger communes that remained partly outside the wall were Neuilly, Bercy, Saint-Mandé, Gentilly and Montrouge.

The 'villages' that Paris swallowed at this time were no longer hamlets reached by long roads across fields, as when Rousseau went to botanize at Gentilly on the banks of the Bièvre or by Ménilmontant.[5] At the time of their annexation, the *banlieue* – this was when the word entered general usage – was already populated, urbanized, and partly even industrialized, to the point that Haussmann and Louis-Napoleon were concerned at the concentration of factories and workers to the north and east of Paris.

Nostalgia for the happy time when the countryside began at the city gates and filtered in through all interstices, the sense of a lost paradise and the deploring of nature destroyed – all these themes that emerged in the late eighteenth century spread greatly when Paris was expanded. You can find them in Privat d'Anglemont:

> The Romaineville woods with their donkey rides, the park of Saint-Fargeau so popular with the *grisettes*, the Saint-Gervais meadows that delight the petty bourgeois, have all been turned into streets, squares and crossroads; houses have sprung up in the place of green swards, hundred-year-old trees and flowering lilac. The Île d'Amour, that enchanted spot where so many ephemeral ties were made, has in a singular irony become a *mairie*; you get married there for real, no laughing matter. The Sauvage, that dance hall that defined a whole era in the memory of Parisians, has become a good, worthy and honest bourgeois house.[6]

La Bédollière, writing the history of the twenty new arrondissements of Paris, urged his readers to go and contemplate the last vestiges of the countryside while there was still time. At Ménilmontant, between Père-Lachaise and the new fortifications,

> On the graceful slopes facing the sun and richly cultivated by our rural Parisians of the 20th arrondissement, you find the Ratrait, an earthly paradise, an oasis where the workers of the neighbouring faubourgs used to regularly come and spend their Sundays and Mondays, a place of country delights of which soon only the memory will remain.[7]

---

5 'For some days the vintage had been harvested; the walkers from the city had already gone home, the peasants also were quitting the fields for the labour of the winter. The country, still green and smiling, but unleafed in part, and already almost desert, offered everywhere the image of solitude and of the approach of winter' (J.-J. Rousseau, *The Reveries of a Solitary Walker*, trans. Fletcher).
6 Privat d'Anglemont, *Paris anecdote*.
7 La Bédollière, *Le Nouveau Paris*. The Ratrait (not 'Retrait' as the street there is wrongly spelled) was the name of a vineyard.

Chimney sweeps walking by the Île de la Cité, photographed by Charles Nègre, the earliest of the street photographers.

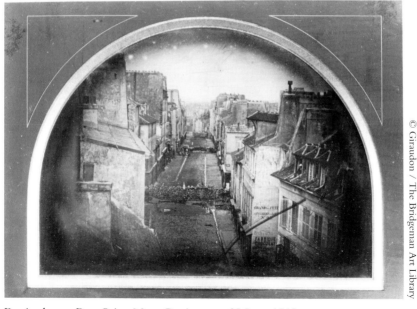

Barricades on Rue Saint-Maur-Popincourt, 25 June 1848.

The cannons of Montmartre during the Paris Commune, 1871.

Banks of the Bievre, at the bottome of Rue des Gobelins, taken sometime between 1858 and '78, by Charles Marville.

Street paver, 1910, by Eugène Atget

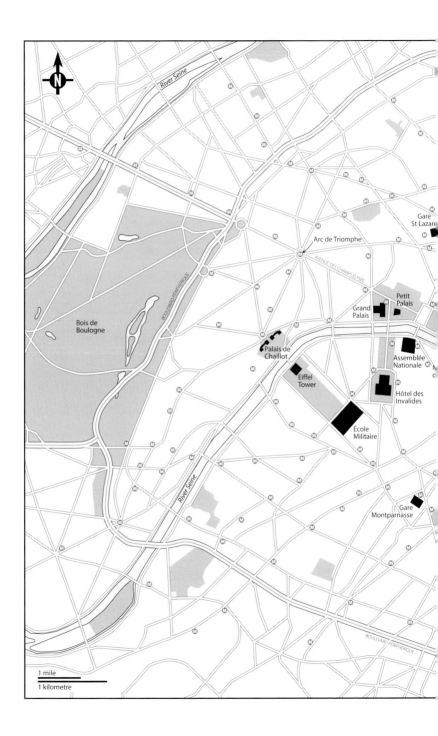

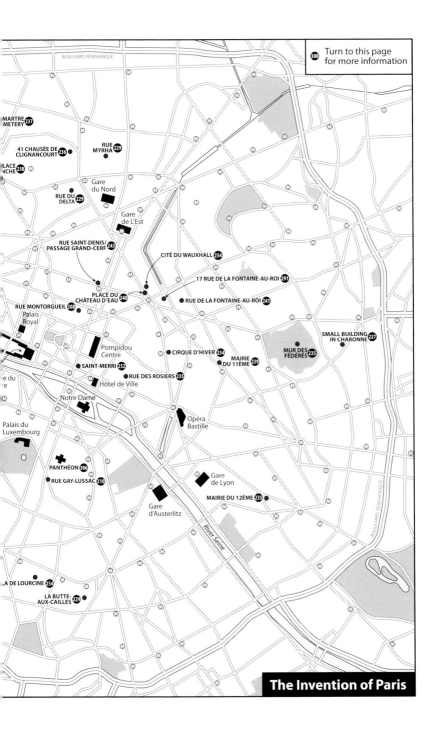

Turn to this page
for more information

BOULEVARD PÉRIPHÉRIQUE

MARTRE
METERY 337

41 CHAUSÉE DE
CLIGNANCOURT 236

RUE
MYRHA 229

LACE
NCHE 238

Gare
du Nord

RUE DU
DELTA 229

Gare
de L'Est

RUE SAINT-DENIS/
PASSAGE GRAND-CERF 243

CITÉ DU WAUXHALL 234

17 RUE DE LA FONTAINE-AU-ROI 291

PLACE DU
CHÂTEAU D'EAU 240

RUE MONTORGUEIL 308

RUE DE LA FONTAINE-AU-ROI 241

Palais
Royal

SMALL BUILDING
IN CHARONNE 227

Pompidou
Centre

CIRQUE D'HIVER 234

MAIRIE
DU 11ÈME 239

MUR DES
FÉDÉRÉS 235

SAINT-MERRI 252

e du
e

RUE DES ROSIERS 235

Hôtel de Ville

Notre Dame

Opéra
Bastille

Palais du
Luxembourg

PANTHÉON 306

Gare
de Lyon

RUE GAY-LUSSAC 310

MAIRIE DU 12ÈME 235

Gare
d'Austerlitz

River Seine

BOULEVARD PÉRIPHÉRIQUE

A DE LOURCINE 254

LA BUTTE-
AUX-CAILLES 229

The Invention of Paris

A popular engraving from 1876 showing the pillory at the Carreau des Halles. 'At the centre stood a fountain and a pillory that was like an inverted Bentham panopticon, "an old octagonal stone tower with large windows at all sides of its upper level. In the middle of this tower was a rotating wooden device pierced with holes, for placing the head and arms . . ." ' (pp. 42–3).

'Course of the Bievre with Tanneries', taken sometime between 1858 and '78, by Charles Marville.

Fountain under the stairs of the Hôtel de Ville before the fire of 1871, by Charles Marville – 'it was the capture of the Hôtel de Ville that enabled an uprising to call itself a revolution' (p. 294).

Rue de la Montagne Saint-Geneviève, from Place Maubert, 1858. 'Of the Paris walks that is most weighty with meaning and memory is the climb up the Montaigne Saint-Geneviève from the Jardin de Plantes and the Statue of Lamarck' (p. 368).

The Paris arrondissements before 1860, with the suburban communes or villages. The first railway lines are shown, including the Ceinture.

In the 1880s, Huysmans wept over the disappearance of the Bièvre:

> Fundamentally, the beauty of a landscape consists in its melancholy. So the Bièvre, with its attitude of desperation and the thoughtful look of one who has suffered, charms me more than anything else and I deplore as the utmost crime the destruction of its gullies and its trees. This suffering countryside, this threadbare stream, these ragged plains were all that were left to us and now they're going to cut them to pieces. They're going to … fill in the marshes, level the roads, tear up the dandelions and briars, the whole flora of rubbish dumps and wasteland … Have they never ever looked at this strange river, that outlet for all kinds of filth, that bilge-water the colour of slate and molten lead, seething here and there with greenish eddies and spangled with cloudy spittle, which gurgles into a sluice-gate and disappears, sobbing, into a hole in the wall?[8]

The most recent stratum of Paris, that of the villages, was not built up in the same way as the earlier ones, for which the faubourgs served as mentors for a radial and centrifugal urbanization. Here there were communes that predated the annexation by many centuries. They formed a corona of satellites, some of which, such as Montmartre or Belleville, still maintain a somewhat distant relationship with the city. The Paris of villages was archaic by its rural origin, and modern by its industrial future, an ambiguity that still gives it in places a particular charm, even if the old factories are now few and far between, and if, to preserve their material traces and memory, a strange discipline had to be created, that of 'industrial archaeology'.

Of its 'modern' side, there persists in the ring of villages one element that has marked the landscape, drawn borders and defined quarters – that of the railway. The big Paris train stations were built in the years from 1835 to 1850 within the wall of the Farmers-General, some of them right up against it (Gare du Nord, Gare de Lyon), others closer in (Gare de l'Est, Gare Saint-Lazare). In order to leave Paris, the railway had in any case to cross the stratum of villages. Despite electrification, these metal crossings still survive as fragments of the nineteenth century in the city of today, whether you discover them from suspended balconies such as Rue d'Alsace above the platforms of the Gare de l'Est or the Square des Batignolles with its cantilever over the rails of Saint-Lazare, from high points such as the esplanade of the Bibliothèque de France, from where you look down on the immense steel plain of the Gare d'Austerlitz, or find yourself on an island surrounded by rails on all sides, such as the triangle of the Évangile

---

8   Huysmans, *Parisian Sketches*, p. 94.

between the tracks of the Gare de l'Est, the Gare du Nord, and the old Calberson warehouses, a kind of world's end linked to the mainland by the bridge of Rue Riquet – and it is only right that this long metal gangway thrown over the rails was named after the engineer who built the Canal du Midi in the eighteenth century.

Between La Chapelle and Barbès-Rochechouart, the overhead Métro that shakes and sparks on its metal bridges offers a double vista of the rails below and the glass roofs of the stations. As Paul Fargue wrote: 'The noise of the Dauphine-Nation line, like the sound of a Zeppelin, accompanies the traveller right to those quarters surrounded by factory chimneys, the lakes of metal into which Rue d'Aubervilliers hurls itself like a river of paint. The wails of lost trains are the foundation of the landscape.'[9] And what about those landscapes that are offered gratis to the passenger arriving in Paris by train? For those coming from Yerres or Choisy-le-Roi, you have the Entrepôts Frigorifiques, the Grands Moulins de Paris and, in the distance, just before the engine shed of the Gare d'Austerlitz, the dome of the Salpêtrière; for those coming from Villeparisis or Aulnay-sous-Bois, it is the canals, the heights of Buttes-Chaumont and the slopes of Montmartre. And the train always insinuates a certain disorder into the city, with piles of debris behind metal barriers, little abandoned triangles around signal boxes, where plants still grow that Huysmans saw on the banks of the Bièvre: 'dandelions and briars, the whole flora of rubbish dumps and wasteland'.

In the more remote regions, the metal fences of goods-yards preserve spaces from another age. The Gare de Bercy, formerly the Gare de Rungis, the ends of Rues Bobillot, de Tolbiac, de Vaugirard, des Batignolles, d'Aubervilliers and de la Chapelle – all these urban hiatuses where pensioned-off locomotives pull stray wagons towards a flock of trains, or obscure instructions may be read on faded signs, you can pass without noticing, without seeing that they represent the stubborn survival of an age when the railway was one of the great bastions of the imagination. Far still from any kind of productivism, the Ceinture railway round Paris, built within the fortifications soon after the annexation of the villages, was for a long time both a great means of transport and a source of entertainment. During the 1870 siege, the Goncourt brothers took a tour round Paris and noted in their *Journal*: 'An amusing spectacle, this vision rapid as steam, revealing, on emerging from the darkness of a tunnel, lines of white tents, lowered roads where guns are moving, the banks of a river with little crenellated parapets that have just been installed, canteens with their tables

---

9   Paul Fargue, 'Mon quartier', in *Le Piéton de Paris* (Paris: Gallimard, 1932).

and glasses open to the sky, with improvised waitresses who have sewn braid on the hem of their work jackets and skirts . . .'. Fargue, with friends at Auteuil, would take the train to return home: 'We could make music all night after we missed the old boiler of the Ceinture train.'[10] And Dabit, when his parents took him as a child to an aunt at Belleville on a Sunday:

> I gaily entered the station on Boulevard Ornano. A puffing engine arrived, pulling old carriages that struck me as splendid, even the third-class ones that we got into. The locomotive covered the landscape with smoke, and Mama told me to sit down: 'You'll get black as a coal-man.' Soon I asked her: 'Are we getting near?' She replied: 'Don't be silly, you know we have to go through the Buttes-Chaumont tunnel first.' . . . Suddenly, after the Belleville-Villette station, the train entered a cutting with a whistle, as if saying goodbye to the daylight. When we emerged from underground it was time to get up, we were reaching the Ménilmontant station.[11]

The remnants of the Petite Ceinture still punctuate village Paris – tracks in cuttings across the hills of Belleville and Ménilmontant, the metal struts of the bridges of Avenue Jean-Jaurès, Rue d'Avron or Rue de Vaugirard. Its stations have the look of the places it used to serve – pink and flowery Muette, down-at-heel Charonne with its café La Flèche d'Or, suspended over the tracks and frequented by the youth of the quarter. La Bédollière would be quite astonished, having written that, 'if Charonne is poor in buildings, it possesses one establishment that is a guarantee of future prosperity for this part of the capital: I mean the Ceinture railway. This important line, which makes a link between Bordeaux and Lille, Marseille and Cherbourg, has a station at Charonne that has already attracted a number of industries.'[12]

All these welcoming spaces are threatened today. There is talk of cover-ing them over and having the land this generates developed by semipublic companies. Such an operation has already been carried out above the TGV tracks at the Gare Montparnasse, constructing an 'Atlantic garden' whose principal merit is to be almost undiscoverable. The operation 'Seine–Rive-gauche' considered covering the tracks leading out of the Gare d'Austerlitz. This process has already been begun a little further out: between the Entrepôts Frigorifiques and Le Corbusier's Cité de Refuge a 'paved

10   Paul Fargue, 'Maurice Ravel', in *Refuges*.
11   Eugène Dabit, *Faubourgs de Paris* (Paris: Gallimard, 1933).
12   La Bédollière, *Le Nouveau Paris*.

garden' is currently being built above the rails. After so many horrors, one might think this very term would be proscribed, that for once the 'duty of memory' would be put to some use. But nothing of the kind; multicoloured posters surrounding the construction site proclaim that, under the direction of Christian de Portzamparc, the regime's official architect, the firm of Bruno Fortier has been commissioned to build a 'paved garden' that will crush everything that remains of the poor Rue du Chevaleret, its residences for African workers, its dilapidated flowering courtyards, its Doisneau-type charm. This is far from being the first assault on this sector in the name of town planning. The magazine *Potlach*, 3 August 1954: 'Rue Sauvage is being destroyed ... in the 13th arrondissement, despite its offering the most striking nighttime perspective of the capital, between the tracks of the Gare d'Austerlitz and a region of derelict land on the edge of the Seine.'[13] Just nearby, the cast-iron columns, steel beams and struts of the magnificent Rue Watt have recently been drowned in concrete. The principal arteries of the new quarter programmatically bear the names of Jean Anouilh, François Mauriac and Raymond Aron. Not Jean Genet, nor Samuel Beckett, nor Nathalie Sarraute, nor yet Jean-Paul Sartre, Michel Foucault or Gilles Deleuze. I recall the final catastrophic projects of Haussmann, which only the defeat of Sedan prevented: 'Rue de Rennes is to be extended in a straight line as far as the Seine, and, with the help of a new bridge, will link up with the old Rue des Poulies, which will be extended right into the Halles. The centre of Paris will thus not only be linked with the *banlieue*, but also with a whole group of departments, of which the nearer ones contribute to its provisioning.'[14] I also recall the great projects of Pompidou, the Vercingétorix radial designed to spill out at Denfert-Rochereau all the traffic from the south of Paris, the Left Bank expressway, the Canal Saint-Martin covered over and converted into a motorway. These follies were only avoided by illness and death. What disasters do we need in order to keep the Paris railways open to the sky?

THE LEFT BANK VILLAGES

Among the communes annexed in 1860, some, such as Auteuil and La Chapelle, have kept their name and their character. Other districts were simply absorbed and melted into the capital without keeping the traces of their village origins – in particular the intramural portions of those

---

13   *Potlach*, inspired in particular by Michèle Bernstein and Guy Debord, was the 'information bulletin of the French group of the Lettrist International'.
14   La Bédollière, *Le Nouveau Paris*.

communes cut in two by the *'fortifs'*. Not many people know that the Bibliothèque de France was built on a fragment of the old commune of Ivry, that the Parc Montsouris quarter belonged to Gentilly, or that the Ranelagh gardens and Rue Spontini were seized from the commune of Neuilly. Perhaps only the region between the Lion de Denfert and the Porte d'Orléans retained for many years the memory of its origins: 'I have settled now in Petit-Montrouge, in the 14th arrondissement', wrote Henri Calet,[15] a turn of phrase that would not have surprised my schoolfriends at the Lycée Louis-le-Grand who lived on Avenue d'Orléans in the 1950s.

But for one of the annexed villages to have kept a distinct identity, it is not enough that it was absorbed complete, as the examples of Vaugirard and Grenelle show *a contrario*, their past now being rather drowned in the monotony of the 15th arrondissement. Another condition was necessary, this being geographical. Either it was bordered and insulated by steep slopes, like Montmartre, Belleville–Ménilmontant–Charonne or the Butte-aux-Cailles – and it was not by chance that these were the main points of final resistance during the Bloody Week of May 1871. Or it was united and organized by an artificial element, such as the Ourcq canal for La Villette, or the railways for the Batignolles. Or finally, it was in an extreme position in relation to the city, as was the long and narrow peninsula formed by the villages of Passy and Auteuil between the Seine and the Bois de Boulogne.

Vaugirard and Grenelle

On the Left Bank, for these reasons, the quarters formed from the stratum of villages – more or less the 13th, the southern part of the 14th, and the 15th arrondissements – are not superimposed on the original communes, whose memory has been blurred. This region is a mixture of old quarters from the former *banlieue* (Javel, Plaisance, the Butte-aux-Cailles), recent nuclei formed around a pole of attraction (the quarter of Parc Montsouris), and phantoms like that of the Bièvre, today underground but in an earlier time terrible: 'The night of Wednesday, 1 April 1579, the river of Saint-Marceau, in the wake of the rain of the previous days, rose to a height of fourteen or fifteen feet, demolishing a number of mills, walls and houses, drowning many people surprised in

---

15   Henri Calet, *Le Tout sur le tout* (Paris: Gallimard, 1948). Avenue d'Orléans had not yet been given the name of Maréchal Leclerc, nor his unlikely image erected at the Porte d'Orléans.

their houses and beds, destroying a large quantity of cattle and causing tremendous damage.'[16]

For those unfamiliar with it, the 15th arrondissement amounts to an interminable walk down Route de Sèvres (now Rue Lecourbe) or Route d'Issy (Rue de Vaugirard), reminding us that Vaugirard was a street-village that stretched from the wall of the Farmers-General to the slopes of Issy and its windmills. Many do not know where the border between Vaugirard and Grenelle is situated – though this ignorance is not without its historic reasons, since Grenelle was part of the Vaugirard commune until 1830. The southern part, which is still Vaugirard, was in the late eighteenth century a region for holidays, where Parisians of a certain class had their country houses in fine parks, surrounded by vineyards and market gardens. Grenelle, on the contrary, was a large agricultural plain bordered by the Seine. This is where Parmentier undertook his first experiments in growing potatoes. On a map of 1813 there is no house to be seen, and only two roads cross the wide expanse of fields, the ancestors of Rue de Lourmel and Rue de la Croix-Nivert. In 1830, Théophile Gautier could still write to Arsène Houssaye: 'This morning I swum across the Seine to see my princess, who was waiting for me on the other bank, gathering cornflowers among the wheat of Grenelle.'[17]

Grenelle and Vaugirard developed in opposite directions. Vaugirard – today as formerly the region between Rue de la Croix-Nivert and the wall of the Farmers-General (Boulevards de Grenelle, Garibaldi and Pasteur) – became steadily more bourgeois. A guide of 1890 notes that the Saint-Lambert quarter, the old village of Vaugirard, was daily losing its original aspect, and taking on a Parisian look without any particular character. The same source indicates that two of the quarters in the 15th arrondissement, Grenelle and Javel, were covered with factories and chemical plants.[18] The chemical industry had long been present on the banks of the Seine: at the end of the ancien régime, industrialists supported by the Comte d'Artois had obtained authorization to establish a vitriol factory close to the Javelle mill. This was where the technique for manufacturing sodium

---

16 Pierre de L'Estoile, *Journal pour le règne de Henri III*. The Bièvre entered Paris through the postern of Les Peupliers, crossed Rue du Moulin-des-Près (there was a large water-mill there), and circled the southern slope of the Butte-aux-Cailles in a meander full of willows and poplars, before reaching the intersection of Rue Brillat-Savarin and Rue Vergniaud; it then bent again to the north, crossing the wall of the Farmers-General near Métro Corvisart, and enclosing the Square René-Le-Gall in two separate arms before reaching the Gobelins.

17 Cited in Lucien Lambeau, 'Grenelle', in *Histoire des communes annexées à Paris en 1859* (Paris: Leroux, 1914).

18 Martin, *Promenades dans les vingt arrondissements de Paris*.

thiosulphate was perfected, the famous *eau de Javel*. In 1792, Chaptal had an immense gunpowder plant built on the deserted plain, viewed as 'one of the bulwarks of the Republic'. Soon after 9 Thermidor, the plant exploded. The Jacobins were accused, and this was one of the arguments for closing their club and demolishing its premises. In 1796, it was the regiments stationed on the Grenelle plain that the remnant of the Montagnards tried to raise against the Directory. The plotters met at the inn of Le Soleil d'Or, in a house that still stands.[19] The attempt failed, and ten of its leaders were shot against the wall of the Farmers-General, where the Dupleix Métro station is now.

There was a lot of shooting on the Grenelle plain and against this wall. Under the Directory and the Consulate this was particularly the fate of émigrés, such as Armand de Chateaubriand, a cousin of François-René, who explains in his *Memoirs*: 'The day of the execution, I wanted to accompany my comrade to his last battlefield; I could not find a carriage, and hastened to the Grenelle plain on foot. I arrived in a sweat, a second too late. Armand was shot against the city wall of Paris. His head was broken, and a butcher's dog was licking his blood and his brains.' Under the Empire, it was the turn of General Malet, and later Louis XVIII had La Bédoyère shot in the same place, after he had rallied to Napoleon during the Hundred Days. His young widow had to pay the soldiers of the firing squad the sum of 36 francs – 3 francs per man. After the white terror, modern Grenelle was founded by an unusual developer, Léonard Violet, who in the 1820s bought and parcelled out a large quadrilateral bordered by what are now Rue de la Croix-Nivert, Rue Javel, Boulevard de Grenelle, the Quai de Grenelle and the Quai de Javel. He built a riverboat station and a wooden bridge that crossed the Île des Cygnes to link the new quarter to the Right Bank. It was at this time that the checkerboard pattern there was established, with street names – Rue du Commerce, Rue des Enterpreneurs – that reflect the optimism of the era. On the square that now bears his name, Violet built a mansion that still survives within the precinct of the fire station, but the new Grenelle was deliberately industrial and working-class. The bourgeois of Vaugirard, disturbed by these neighbours, asked to secede, and their request was granted by prefect Chabrol in 1830, a few days before the Trois Glorieuses.

Grenelle developed rapidly under the July monarchy. The Cail works, on the corner of the Quai and the Boulevard de Grenelle, with a dock on the Seine and a rail connection to the Ouest network, became one of the

---

19   26 Rue Vaugirard, now between a Chinese butcher and a discount store, in a courtyard two sides of which have been demolished.

main French locomotive works. (When the company left Paris in 1909, the Vel d'Hiv' took over this site,[20] for the better – the Six Jours cycle race, Cerdan, Piaf, and Yvette Horner's accordion – and eventually for the worse – Doriot's rallies, the roundup of Jews in July 1942 organized by the French police on the orders of René Bousquet.) It was also at Grenelle, and more particularly on Rue des Entrepreneurs, that the French aeronautics industry was born. Trials were conducted on a field close to Issy, and in the 1930s André Lurçat even proposed to transform the Île des Cygnes, widening it like an aircraft-carrier runway to make an aerodrome that he called Aéroparis. Meanwhile, André Citroën had converted the shell factory he had established during the First World War on the Quai de Javel into one of the most inventive brands in automobile history.

This past of smoke and steel has left only memories. The name of André Citroën has been given to a garden – undoubtedly the best thing built in the arrondissement in the twentieth century, compensating to some extent for the disaster of the Front de Seine. Vaugirard-Grenelle has become one of the most petty-bourgeois and provincial quarters of Paris. Its heteroclite fabric is a mixture of a few village houses, a few Art Nouveau gems, a good many characterless apartment blocks of the 1880s, and several groups of tower blocks from the 1960s and '70s. In this context of anonymity, Rue Santos-Dumont stands out all the more, with its individual houses with courtyards and gardens, likewise the little Village de l'Avenir at the end of Rue Castagnary – hurry there before they demolish it – the Lebaudy workers' housing estate on Rue de la Saïda, the artists' studios on Rue Pierre-Mille, the end of the Place du Commerce close by the old Grenelle *mairie*, the cedars of the Square Violet, and the apse of the Saint-Lambert church built on the site of a gigantic gasworks. Not forgetting the official celebrities of the quarter: the Objets Trouvés on Rue des Morillons, the Institut Pasteur, the artists' residence La Ruche on the Passage Dantzig, and L'Oiseau Lunaire, quite lost at the end of the little Square Blomet, where Miró and Masson had their studios, and where Artaud, Bataille and Limbour crossed paths with the young Dubuffet.

Plaisance

The 15th arrondissement is separated from the 14th – or, to put it another way, Vaugirard is separated from Plaisance – by the tracks of the Gare

---

20 This was in fact the second Vel' d'Hiv'. The first occupied the Galeries des Machines on the Champ-de-Mars, after the Exposition Universelle of 1900. Both were the work of Henri Desgranges, holder of the first recognized one-hour record and creator of the Tour de France.

Montparnasse, a fundamental element of the quarter until the construction of the new station in the late 1960s. Désirée and Céline, Huysmans's Vatard sisters, lived on the corner of Rue Vandamme and Rue du Château:[21]

> Their own room was situated at the back of the house overlooking the tracks of the Ouest rail line. A suspension bridge with a six-foot grillwork cut across the tracks at this particular spot. Beneath the bridge there was a passageway for vehicles, topped with a wooden tower ornamented with clocks … Bellowing and whistling piercingly, two locomotives manoeuvred on the tracks, searching their way … From time to time, a trumpet-like blast sounded, echoed, grew weak, and then once again blared. The gateman closed the barriers. An express train was approaching in the distance … The earth shook and in a white haze sprinkled with flashes of flame, a shower of dust and ashes, a gush of sparks, the long train shot into the railyard with a frightful din of clanking metal, shrieking boilers, and moving pistons. It filed past the window, its thundering gradually diminishing until only the three red lights of the caboose could be seen and only the jerky noise of freight cars jumping over rail switches could be heard.

Rue du Château and Rue de l'Ouest are the two original axes of the Plaisance development in the angle formed by Avenue du Maine and Rue Vercingétorix.[22] This was a wretched development, patched together without any overall plan, and carried out by petty speculators who had the idea of calling it Plaisance to attract clients whom the unpaved streets, which lacked lighting, drainage, and water hydrants, might have put off in the 1840s.[23] Though severely damaged by Ricardo Bofill (Place de Catalogne)

---

21   Rue Vandamme – which was called Chemin de la Gaîté until it was given the name of a general – still exists, but no longer runs as far as Rue du Château. Its last section has been replaced by Rue du Commandant-Mouchotte, the Sheraton-Montparnasse hotel, etc.

22   The third side was Route de Transit (now Rue d'Alésia). Rue du Château, originally known as Rue du Chemin-de-Fer, took its name from the Château du Maine, an estate occupying a large site between Rue de Vanves (now Raymond-Losserand), Rue du Château and Rue Didot. The present Rue Asseline corresponds to its entrance drive. Avenue du Maine takes its name from the Duc du Maine, who had it opened as a route from the Faubourg Saint-Germain to his residence at Sceaux.

23   Catherine Bruant, 'Plaisance et les Thermopyles', in *Montparnasse et le XIVe arrondissement* (Paris: Action artistique de la Ville de Paris, 2000). Some of these individuals – Bénard, Boyet-Barret – gave their names to streets in the quarter. They were successful enough to extend their operation eastward and open up Rues Didot, des Plantes, Hippolyte-Maindron, etc.

and the ravages at the beginning of Rue de l'Ouest, Plaisance still remains a plebeian quarter whose charm owes a great deal to its isolation: it is hardly connected to Avenue du Maine, and on the other side the roads are almost impossible to cross. On the transversal streets – Rue de la Sablière, Rue de Plaisance, Rue Pernety – the buildings are those of the original development: narrow, low, homogeneous and poor beneath their plaster rendering. The houses, workshops, little gardens and hydrangeas of Rue des Thermopyles – named on account of its narrowness that evokes the gorge in Thessaly – are a threatened rarity (Rue Léonidas, a few steps to the east, was disfigured in the 1970s). This is a quarter where individuals seeking quiet formerly took refuge – Marcel Duhamel, Jacques Prévert or Yves Tanguy, and Raymond Queneau at 54 Rue du Château, which in the 1920s formed the third apex of the surrealist triangle, along with Rue Blomet and Rue Fontaine.[24] In the 1950s, Alberto Giacometti had his studio on Rue Hippolyte-Maindron, and, among the hundreds of photographs taken of him, my favourite is that in which Cartier-Bresson captured him crossing the corner of Rue d'Alésia in the rain, with his raincoat pulled over his head.

Denfert-Rochereau and the 14th Arrondissement

> During these days of public-transport strike we have been forced, whether we like it or not, to retreat into ourselves rather more than we generally do ... It is in circumstances such as these that you notice how the arrondissement forms a little town of its own, quite complete within the city, a twentieth of the capital possessing its own *mairie*, its church, its markets and its cinemas. For my part, I have known for a long time that it is possible to live without leaving the *quatorzième* ... And by chance, this was the festival of the Lion of Belfort. We never failed to visit it on this occasion; we were very fond of it; it was our great fetish, and a kind of virility symbol for the surrounding inhabitants. In its paw it crushes an arrow, which may have a number of symbolic meanings.

That was the inimitable Henri Calet in *Combat*, on 28 October 1946. His own *quatorzième* fell into two parts: one sad and administrative, to the left as you come from the Lion de Belfort; the other, to the right, lived-in and busy, the dividing line being Avenue d'Orléans, 'formerly Rue d'Enfer, which was our open-air market hall, our Grands Boulevards,

---

24 No. 54 has disappeared, buried beneath the false columns and frontages of Ricardo Bofill on the Place de Catalogne.

our Champs-Élysées, our Broadway'.[25] Curiously enough, the 14th has not changed a great deal since 1945:

> I took the no. 8 bus, now known as the 38, the day it was brought back in service ... We had a pleasant ride, on pneumatic tyres, from one end of the line to the other. It seemed like a trip back in time; the Lion of Belfort, the Closerie des Lilas, Maréchal Ney who had also made his return (modern wars do not interest him; what he likes is the cavalry charge), the Tarnier clinic, the Luxembourg.[26]

From Rue Daguerre to the flea market of Vanves, from the Villa Seurat to the provincial Rues du Commandeur, Hallé, Ducouëdic and Sophie-Germain, nothing in his arrondissement escaped Calet. The reservoirs of the Vanne and the miraculously elevated streets that surround them (Rue Saint-Yves, Rue Gauguet, Rue des Artistes), the Montsouris park, the artists' villas on Rue Nansouty, the Cité Universitaire – he was at home everywhere, even at the hospital where he would happily end his days:

> I think I shall be in my place here. From the Tarnier clinic to the hospital of La Rochefoucauld, passing the Asile Maternel on Avenue du Maine, takes scarcely fifteen minutes. I have taken about forty years to make this journey; I have dawdled from one asylum to another ... To grow old on Avenue d'Orléans, then die without pain, simply putting a farewell letter in the post, is not asking the impossible, after all.

The 13th arrondissement, Butte-aux-Cailles, the Italie quarter

The 14th arrondissement, as a residential overflow from the very bourgeois Faubourg Saint-Jacques, escaped massive destruction. The 13th, on the other hand, the proletarian extension of the Faubourg Saint-Marceau, was one of the first to undergo the disasters of the postwar era, even before the bulldozers went to work on the heights of Belleville. As early as the 1950s, a start was made on destroying the Glacière quarter, then that of Maison-Blanche. This was followed by the Italie quarter, stretching broadly along Boulevard Vincent-Auriol. Today, demolition along the Seine is almost complete, where gloomy bistrots used to welcome bargemen and warehouse workers. (One of these on the Quai de la Gare, called La Maison Rouge, remained for many years standing alone like the Hôtel de Nantes on the Place du Carrousel).

---

25   Calet, *Le Tout sur le tout*.
26   Ibid.

There remain in the 13th arrondissement, scattered in a dislocated fabric, some fortunate islands such as the Place des Peupliers (now de l'Abbé-Hénocque) and the streets radiating out from it, bordered with little houses with pointed roofs, some half-timbered and others in brick, regularly arranged and showing great individual imagination. But among the micro-quarters of this arrondissement, the most famous is the Butte-aux-Cailles. You can reach this from Boulevard Blanqui, by steps that very properly bear the name of Eugène Atget. Or else from Place Paul-Verlaine, where Louis Bonnier built a swimming pool in the 1920s that could have been designed by Gaudí, filled from an artesian well. Or again climb along the side of Sainte-Anne's church to reach the Place de la Commune-de-Paris. With its fashionable restaurants and neo-Haussmannian street lights, the summit of the Butte-aux-Cailles lacks the guilelessness of the Plaisance quarter, but on its gentle slopes, fine paved passages bordered by low houses and gardens bring you down towards Rue Barrault, Rue Martin-Bernard or Rue Bobillot, named after a sergeant killed in Tonkin during the conquest of Indochina.

The Italie quarter escaped disaster by becoming the main Chinatown of Paris (it might be better to say Indochinatown, as the first Asian immigrants to settle there in the 1970s were 'boat people' from South Vietnam, though the majority of those now arriving from Southeast Asia are Chinese of the diaspora). Its limits – currently Rue de Tolbiac and the 'boulevards of the marshals', Avenue d'Italie and Rue Nationale – are slowly and steadily advancing, but the density of restaurants and shops is greatest at the corner of Avenues de Choisy and d'Ivry. There is nothing picturesque in the architecture or décor, unlike the large Chinatowns of New York, San Francisco or Singapore, whether because the ugliness of the tower blocks was seen as irremediable, or because of a preference to avoid difference that might have been due to our famous French hospitality. What is exotic is simply the population, and for anyone who likes not knowing where he has ended up, nothing can rival even the poorest supermarkets, where the shopkeepers do not speak French and the tins of preserves, videocassettes, vegetables and cakes are magnificently coloured but almost impossible to identify.

THE RIGHT BANK VILLAGES

On the Right Bank, from one extremity to the other of the Seine's mean-der, from the Point du Jour to Bercy, the arc of former villages is the most contrasting part of Old Paris. To pass from the *hameaux* of Auteuil to the *cités* at the top of Belleville, from Ranelagh to the Goutte d'Or, is to change planets. In the 1980s, Christof Pruskovski, a Polish photographer living in Paris, took several series of shots of different faces, each with all the negatives superimposed. These vague images often gave a disconcerting impression. In the Métro, for example, Pruskovski took a cumulative portrait of 'a hundred first-class travellers', and another of 'a hundred second-class travellers', two 'portraits' that could well have served to illustrate the morphological difference between the upper and lower classes in Lavater's *Physiognomie*. By combining in this way a hundred faces from Avenue Mozart with a hundred from Rue de Bagnolet, you certainly get two identikit portraits that are quite disturbing.

This contrast between the eastern and western villages, however, is not that old. In the early nineteenth century, both of them were characterized by vineyards, meadows, windmills, convents and lordly residences. But since the industrial revolution, the Commune, the arrival of foreign workers, the Resistance, and the massive demolitions of the 1960s, each step has deepened the gap between the favoured quarters and the rest. With the demolitions in particular, those who theorized them, decided on them and financed them kept them well away from their own districts.[27] The architectural treasures of Passy and Auteuil are intact, including, very fortunately, the building on Rue Nungesser-et-Coli where Le Corbusier lived and worked. The sectarian followers of the Athens Charter built their slabs and blocks as far away as possible, around the Place des Fêtes, Avenue de Flandre and Boulevard Mortier.

Passy and Auteuil

Like Vaugirard and Grenelle, or Belleville and Ménilmontant, Passy and Auteuil today seem like an old-established pair. What is specific to each of them has been rather submerged in the generic *seizième*, the arrondissement most charged with meaning of all the twenty in Paris, conjuring up a world of subscribers to *Le Figaro*, religious colleges, idyllic hamlets and masterpieces of Art Nouveau and Art Déco. But this has not always been the case; in the early twentieth century, you could still distinguish an elegant Passy from a rustic Auteuil: 'Auteuil is like the countryside of Passy, with its Boulevard de Montmorency, its quays, its viaduct, its Mouton-Blanc restaurant that is a historical curiosity, the former meeting-place of La Fontaine, Molière and Racine. People from Passy go to Auteuil on

---

27 There certainly were some horrific buildings constructed in the expensive quarters from the 1960s through to the '80s, but they most often respected the line of the street and the general scale. Besides, the materials used were generally of good quality.

Sunday as people from Rue Étienne-Marcel go to Brunoy.'[28] The border between the two was – and still is – marked by the parallel streets of Rue de l'Assomption and Rue du Ranelagh, where the Passy hill meets the plain of Auteuil. According to Jacques-Émile Blanche, 'the boundary post between the two communes was below the intersection of Rue Raynouard and Rue du Ranelagh, close to Rue de Boulainvilliers, below which was – as far as we can deduce – the park of Passy.'[29] This post has clearly been replaced by the Maison de la Radio.

The charm of Passy lies especially in the long descent from the Place du Trocadéro to the Seine through Rue Benjamin Franklin and Rue Raynouard, across what was once the park of the Château de Passy. There is here a kind of tradition of splendid luxury. When the domain belonged to Samuel Bernard, banker to Louis XIV, you could see orangeries, glasshouses, aviaries with gold filigree, grottos carpeted in greenery and terraces embellished with statues. In the eighteenth century, this is where the Farmer-General La Pouplinière received Rousseau, Rameau whose *Hippolyte et Aricie* was performed there, and Marmontel, as well as Chardin and Pigalle, Mlle Clairon and the Maréchal de Richelieu. Balzac, seeking wherever he could in Paris a residence worthy of his Polish lady, wrote to her on 7 September 1845: 'There is in Rue Benjamin Franklin, which is the road above the steep hill we so often climbed ... a house that is admirable and solidly built, situated on the crest of this rock that overlooks Paris and even all of Passy ... There is the most admirable view on all sides; first the whole of Paris, then the whole of the Seine basin.'[30] You still get this view over the river from the terraces of the apartments on Rue Raynouard, where pergolas, statues, fountains and floral parterres adorn sumptuous gardens in the 1930s style, suspended in the air. Rue de l'Alboni overlooks the Passy station, hidden behind chestnut trees and roses, and the tracks leading towards the Pont de Bir-Hakeim between the domes of the apartment buildings on the corner, famous from *Last Tango in Paris*. Lower down are the great blind walls bordering the steps of the Passage des Eaux, then Balzac's house, whose main

---

28 Fargue, *Le Piéton de Paris*. In his striking preface to Jacques-Émile Blanche's *Propos de peintres*, Proust recalled: 'As my parents spent spring and early summer at Auteuil, where Jacques-Émile Blanche spent the whole year, it was easy for me to go each morning to pose for my portrait.'
29 Jacques-Émile Blanche, 'Passy', in *Visages de Paris* (Paris: Éditions Pierre Lafitte, 1927).
30 This house, located near the top of Rue Paul-Doumer, should not be confused with that on Rue Raynouard where Balzac actually lived. Balzac has Corentin, the great policeman of *La Comédie humaine*, 'who was known there as a retired merchant passionately devoted to gardening', not very far from his own house, in 'one of the quietest and prettiest nooks of the little town of Passy' (*Scenes from a Courtesan's Life*).

entrance is on Rue Raynouard, but with an exit further down on Rue Berton, which has scarcely changed since the time of Atget or Apollinaire: 'If you pass Rue Berton at the time when it is at its finest, shortly before dawn, you can hear a harmonious thrush give a marvellous concert here, which thousands of other birds accompany with their own music; and, before the war, the pale and trembling flames of a few kerosene lamps lit up the lampposts here and have not been replaced.'[31] Close by, the Turkish embassy occupies the site of the park of Lauzun and the Princesse de Lamballe, where Émile Blanche – son of Esprit-Sylvestre Blanche who treated Nerval, and father of Jacques-Émile – received in his clinic Berlioz, Liszt, Gounod, Rossini, Delacroix 'and many others'.

Passy is more than just this enchanted hillside: in 1825 a new quarter baptised Élysée-Charles X was parcelled out and developed in the northern part, on the plain around the intersection that would become the Place Victor-Hugo. This was an immense quadrilateral whose limits today would be Avenue de la Grande-Armée, Avenue Kléber, Rue de Longchamp and Rues Spontini and Pergolèse.[32] The north of the 16th arrondissement, over-lapping Chaillot, Passy and La Muette, has been given by extension the name of Passy, but its true inhabitants are not deceived:

> Those who live beyond Rue Scheffer and the Trocadéro cemetery, or indeed on the even-numbered side of Avenue Henri-Martin – let us say, as far as the Square Lamartine – still boast of belonging to Passy, but we laugh at them: they are joking! The Passy of timid and sedentary bour-geois, the true, the unique, the incomparable, abdicated on this northern side its prerogative of an old village, and tried to ignore the zone in which such undesirables camped, i.e., beyond the Porte Dauphine, beyond the romantic shadows where the poet of *Jocelyn* meditated in his chalet, and where Jules Janin ended his career.[33]

Passy was already completely built up at the end of the nineteenth century, and there was scarcely any room for new architecture.[34] In Auteuil, on

---

31   Guillaume Apollinaire, *Le Flâneur des deux rives* (Paris: Éditions de la Sirène, 1918).

32   Across this quadrilateral, Haussmann drove two parallel roads towards the Bois de Boulogne: Avenue de l'Impératrice (now Foch) and Avenue de l'Empereur, today partitioned into Avenue du Président-Wilson, Avenue Georges-Mandel and Avenue Henri-Martin.

33   Blanche, 'Passy'.

34   Though there are two famous buildings, Perret's apartment block at 25 *bis* Rue Benjamin Franklin, and the Malet-Stevens fire station on Rue Mesnil.

the other hand, this 'charming village of 1,040 souls, half an hour from the *barrière*, between the Bois de Boulogne and the road to Versailles'[35] – though summer residences certainly proliferated in the 1830s, when the Boileau and Boulainvilliers hamlets were developed – was not yet the city in 1868, when the Goncourts settled on Boulevard de Montmorency: 'We are not even sure that we are not dreaming. This great tasteful toy for ourselves, the two drawing-rooms, the sun in the leaves, this bouquet of trees above, this corner of earth below, with birds flying overhead!' (Journal, 16 September 1868).[36]

In this Auteuil, which had only three streets at the time of its annexation – the Grand-Rue which became Rue d'Auteuil, Rue Molière (now Rémusat), and Rue La Fontaine which linked it to Passy – there was both free space and money, so that between the 1890s and the 1930s this was where masterpieces of Parisian Art Nouveau and Art Déco were constructed, as if arranged for today's visitor. From the Métro Jasmin, for example, Rue Henri-Heine is close at hand, with a late 1930 work by Guimard at no. 18, which I prefer to his more famous buildings, as the hesitation between the curves and countercurves of the two lower floors and the 'modernism' of the upper storeys creates a tension that is unusual in his work, and there is something rather moving in this doubt appearing in an old architect basking in his former glory. Two steps away, on Rue du Docteur-Blanche, there are two villas by Le Corbusier, and on Rue Mallet-Stevens – no. 5 here was published in the magazine *De Stijl*, along with projects from Van Doesburg and Van Eesteren, even a design by Malevitch – there is Patout's building of artists' studios, whose façade is covered with a material imitating sharkskin, not to mention the ten concrete storeys of the Ginsberg building, which together form an ensemble unique in Paris. Not far away, at 65 Rue La Fontaine, is the *Studiobuilding* by Henri Sauvage, an ensemble of studio residences for artists that is covered in grey and gold ceramic. And lower down again, at 42 Avenue de Versailles is another building by Ginsberg, 'brutalist' before the label (1933), the corner of which is topped by a glazed half-dome that serves as a foil to the play of curves of the entrance. But towards the later 1930s, creative architecture abandoned Auteuil. The promoters of apartment blocks of '*grand standing*' would from now on resort to mediocre architects, docile and interchangeable.

In the days when there were not just two French marques, but still ten

---

35 Henri Auguste Richard, *Le Véritable Conducteur parisien* (Paris, 1828).
36 The house still stands, at 67 Boulevard de Montmorency, now the premises of the Académie Goncourt.

or more, Avenue de la Grande-Armée was devoted to the automobile.[37] Today it is rather motorbike showrooms that you find here, but it still divides the 16th from the 17th arrondissement, an administrative border and also a sociological one: to the south, in the direction of Avenue Foch, Rue des Belles-Feuilles, and Avenue Bugeaud, the international bourgeoisie, corporate headquarters, and embassies; to the north, the more diverse population of Rue des Acacias, Rue du Colonel-Moll and the Place Saint-Ferdinand.[38]

Batignolles and Clichy

Beyond Rue de Courcelle begins the part of the 17th that continues along the Plaine Monceau towards the periphery, towards Place Wagram with its fine layouts, and the heavy apartment blocks on Boulevard Pereire that face each other above the tracks of the Ceinture railway, now converted into a flowery walk. Continuing east, you enter the sad and monotonous streets of the Batignolles, which acquire their real character around the tracks of Saint-Lazare, as is only to be expected for a quarter born along with the train. Les Ateliers des Batignolles on Avenue de Clichy, and Spies-Batignolles, the rival company to Eiffel, were the first factories – along with Cail at Grenelle – to manufacture railway locomotives in France. Léon-Paul Fargue, a student of Mallarmé's at the Collège Rollin, and later invited to the poet's Tuesdays, described 'the house chosen or suffered by him, opposite the metal fences of the railway, at the exit of the horrible Batignolles tunnel, whose diseased mouth blew catastrophes'.[39] On the other side of the tracks, on Rue Boursault, the room of Georges Duroy, *Bel-Ami*, 'on the fifth floor, looked down, as if

---

37   For those who may have forgotten them: Hotchkiss, Panhard and Levassor (whose factories were in the 13th arrondissement), Talbot, Rosengart, Salmson, Bugatti, Delahaye, Simca and Delage, without going all the way back to Voisin, De Dion-Bouton or Hispano-Suiza. On the other side of the Porte d'Asnières, Levallois-Perret was a district of garages, repair shops, and secondhand car dealers.

38   'At the bottom of our street, on the square, we had the statue of Serpollet. This was a fine stone monument; the breeze blew through the windshield, giving an effect of speed: individuals of both sexes saluted the man who had conceived the flash boiler as he stirred his stew, and was the first to ride from Paris to Saint-Germain at the wheel of a steam tricycle: Serpollet. A gentleman with a beard and stiff collar nervously hastened in front of the vehicle, at the risk of being run over by the monster whose driver seemed no longer to be in control' (Calet, *Le Tout sur le tout*).

39   Fargue, *Refuges*. The famous Batignolles tunnel was replaced in the 1920s by a cutting, after a train had caught fire in it.

over a deep abyss, onto the immense cutting of the railway of the Ouest,
just above the exit from the tunnel, close to the Batignolles station ...
At every moment, long or short blows of the whistle passed in the night,
some of them close, others hardly perceptible, coming from down there
on the Asnières side.'[40] Tastes change, and today one would find more to
admire in the landscape formed by the final curve of Boulevard Pereire,
the immense spread of the tracks of the Ouest expanded by the Gare
des Batignolles, the station of Pont Cardinet whose ogives and mosaics
are evocative of Otto Wagner, and the chestnut trees of the Square des
Batignolles.

The former commune of Les Batignolles continued along the east
side of Avenue de Clichy, forming a little quarter extending to Rues
Cavallotti and Forest, i.e., to the old Hippodrome so dear to Lautrec,
which then became the Gaumont-Palace, a great cinematic temple,
before ending up as an Ibis hotel and a Castorama. In this block, around
an immense brick garage dating from the 1930s, there are a number of
winding passages – the Impasses des Deux-Néthes and de la Défense,
Rue Capon, Passage Lathuille, Passage de Clichy – badly paved, bordered
with shacks, leading into courtyards cluttered with metal sheds and piles
of pallets: a disorder that is unlikely in the heart of Paris, and indeed
seriously threatened.

Passage Lathuille, Impasse de la Défense: these names evoke two glorious moments for these few metres of Avenue de Clichy. Manet, in order
to paint *Chez le père Lathuille* – seduction under the barrels – got Louis, the
son of the tavern landlord, to pose with the actress Ellen André. On the
same pavement, almost adjacent, the Café Guerbois was the rendezvous of
the friends who were still known as the Batignolles group.[41] Many years
previously, far more dramatic events had occurred at Père-Lathuille's: on
20 March 1814 this was Moncey's command post, directing the defence of
the Clichy barrier against the Cossacks:

> Paris hastened to take up arms, in an enthusiasm shared by bourgeois
> and people, children and old men – truly resolved, despite the defection
> of its natural protectors, to fight to the death. And this was a spectacle
> whose memory our fathers preserved, this frivolous city transformed into
> a camp in which women prepared bandages for the wounded, and inva-
> lids cast cannon balls to greet the invaders of their native soil. It was from

---

40 Maupassant himself lived just a couple of steps away when he was writing
this, on Rue Dulong.
41 Père-Lathuille was on the site that is now no. 7, and Guerbois at no. 9 (now
the Cinéma des Cinéastes).

hearing tales of that day – glorious despite the defeat – that I learned to hate oppression.[42]

This battle is an odd story, and singularly forgotten, apart from the monument to Moncey in the middle of the Place de Clichy, and the tiny Impasse de la Défense. It is one in a whole series that began in 1792 and ended in the years 1940–44 – its intermediate steps being precisely 1814, as well as 1871 – consisting of violent conflicts between a 'ruling elite' ready to capitulate and compromise with the enemy, and that section of the Paris people who are eternally rebellious.

Montmartre

Of all the villages annexed in 1860, Montmartre is the one that has retained most autonomy, despite being always very closely bound up with Parisian life. It is the only one to have a street bearing its name at the very heart of the city (indeed one of the oldest and most important), running right to the Halles and the apse of Saint-Eustache. The abbesses of Montmartre owned immense estates stretching down to the walls of Paris. Several of them gave their names to streets on the slopes of the 9th arrondissement: Louise-Émilie de la Tour d'Auvergne, Marie de Bellefond, Catherine de La Rochefoucault, Marguerite de Rochechouart – and one of the strangest couplings in the names of the Métro stations is that between this great name of French nobility and the professional revolutionary Armand Barbès.[43]

Montmartre is also the Paris quarter whose name has the largest number of different connotations. There is the Montmartre of village folklore – the '*Commune libre*', Poulbot, the Fête des Vendanges – which is included in, though does completely coincide with, tourist Montmartre, whose main attractions are the Sacré-Coeur and the Place du Tertre. There is the Montmartre of its heyday, whose story, told a thousand times, has its backdrops (the Moulin de la Galette, the Lapin-Agile, the Bateau-Lavoir), its heroes (Bruant, Apollinaire, Picasso), its chroniclers (Carco, Dorgelès, Mac Orlan, Salmon) and its painters (from Degas, Van Gogh and Lautrec to poor Utrillo). There is also Red Montmartre, its emblematic figure being Louise Michel, the schoolteacher from Rue Houdon, the inspiration behind the vigilance committee at 41 Chaussée de Clignancourt – I shall speak of her later on. And there is again, to take up the title of Louis Chevalier's book, the Montmartre of pleasure and crime. On 21 July 1938,

---

42   Delvau, *Histoire anecdotique des barrières de Paris*.
43   The Tour des Dames, incidentally, was the abbey's dovecote.

a few weeks before Munich, *Le Détective* carried the headline: 'From the Drama of the Rat-Mort to the Cannes Vendetta', announcing a report on the inexpiable hatred between the Foata and Stéfani clans. A world that was still very much alive in the 1950s – the Corsicans of Pigalle, Pierrot le Fou (the real one), the 'front-wheel drive gang' – evoked by one of the finest films on the underside of Paris, Jean-Pierre Melville's *Bob le Flambeur*.

In certain parts, these different meanings have built up in successive layers, but today they have melted into an indistinct general memory, though this has kept a certain sparkle despite the decline. On the semicircle of Place Pigalle, the fountain occupies the site of the square building constructed by Ledoux for the Montmartre *barrière*. The Café des Omnibus and the no. 67 bus stand recall the famous line from Pigalle to the Halle aux Vins. 'You find here', wrote Delvau in the 1860s, 'two temples to beer, the Café de la Nouvelle-Athènes, a meeting place for daubers and writers from the Breda quarter, and the Café de la Place Pigalle, a neighbour and competitor on this square widened by the demolition of the wall.' On Sunday mornings a fair for artists' models was held by the fountain: 'Italian girls musing around the basin waited, in sequined dresses and with tambourine in hand, for a painter keen on the past to invite them to pose.'[44] The Impressionists at the Nouvelle-Athènes – after the Guerbois – that was a whole chapter in the history of art and the legend of the quarter. George Moore, a regular there, explained to the English public Degas's painting *L'Absinthe*, which shows Deboutin seated in the Nouvelle-Athènes café:

> Look at the head of the old bohemian – the engraver Deboutin – a man whom I have known all my life, and yet he never really existed for me until I saw this picture ... The woman that sits beside the artist was at the Élysée Montmartre until two in the morning, then she went to the Rat-Mort and had a *soupe aux choux* ... she did not get up till half-past eleven; then she tied a few soiled petticoats round her ... and came down to the café to have an absinthe before breakfast.[45]

In this fin-de-siècle period, Pigalle was still peaceful at night. 'The Rat-Mort saw anarchists and authoritarians live side by side, artists and stockbrokers, writers and businessmen. But once the coffee was drunk, and the last glass of

---

44   Halévy, *Pays parisiens*.
45   George Moore, *Modern Painting* (London, 1893). The Rat-Mort was a tavern frequented among others by Courbet, Vallès and Manet (who painted George Moore at the Nouvelle-Athènes). It was located on the site that is now 7 Place Pigalle, and the Nouvelle-Athènes was at no. 9 – the building still stands, but is undoubtedly under serious threat.

beer swallowed, Good Night!, and everyone went their own way, making way for "ladies" who scorned the opinion of the few males still present.'[46] It was between the wars that things took a turn for the worse, when the '*milieu*' laid its hands on the place. Edith Piaf explained what life was like in Pigalle around 1930, when she was eighteen years old:

> I was obliged to take note, while I was singing in the streets, of the dance halls where there were very well-dressed women, with expensive necklaces and rings. In the evenings I reported what I had seen to Albert. On Saturday nights and Sundays, in his best suit, he went to the dance halls I had indicated. As he was very good-looking and self-assured, he always managed to seduce one of the women dancing. He took them all into Impasse Lemercier, a dark and deserted alley, and seized their jewellery and their money. I waited in the Café de la Nouvelle-Athènes. He bought me champagne for the rest of the night.[47]

It is memories such as these that give Pigalle and its surroundings today – Avenue Frochot, Impasse Guelma – the sadness and worn-out charm of a place 'aged and grown old in the glories and tribulations of life', as Baudelaire wrote in 'The Salon of 1859'.

Between Boulevard de Clichy and Boulevard de Rochechouart to the south, and Rues Caulaincourt and Custine to the north, the Montmartre hill inextricably mingles the best and worst – which, one has to say, are better and worse than elsewhere. 'Inextricably': the unusual contours, the cliffs, ravines, gorges and open quarries – one of which became the Montmartre cemetery – break up the hill into several separate geographical units, divided, joined and crossed by steps and hairpin bends. Fear of the worst, of the crowds and the tourist coaches, keeps many Parisians away from Montmartre. They do not know what they are missing, above all the joy of the hilltop. In the days of the Montmartre abbesses, there were only two ways of reaching the peak through the vineyards and windmills: from the Paris side was the Vieux-Chemin, now the route of Rue Ravignan, and from Saint-Denis the Chemin de la Procession, which has become Rue du Mont-Cenis. There is more choice today: the curves of Rue du Chevalier-de-la-Barre; Rue André-Antoine, which formerly bore the magnificent name Élysée-des-Beaux-Arts – after an adjacent dance hall – and leads from Place Pigalle to Rue des Abbesses past the hôtel of Maria Malibran;

---

46   Goudeau, a friend of Salis, the landlord of the Rat-Mort, in *Le Courrier français*, 24 October 1886. Cited by Chevalier in *Montmartre du plaisir et du crime*.
47   Cited by Chevalier in *Montmartre du plaisir et du crime*.

the steps of Rue Girardon, which, continuing through the workshops and gardens of Rue d'Orchampt, lead from the Place Constantin-Pecquer to the Bateau-Lavoir. Once at the top, when you find yourself on a fine winter morning in the square that holds the very essence of Montmartre, by Rue Cortot, Rue des Saules, Rue de l'Abreuvoir and the Maison Rose, the Allée des Brouillards dear to Nerval,[48] the vineyards, the Saint-Vincent cemetery, the Lapin-Agile, the magic curve of Avenue Junot – how can you not be struck by such splendour? And to end this talk of Montmartre, why ignore its pleasure, why not admit that the whole of literature, cinema and photography will never restore the happiness of a walk starting at the foot of Rue du Chevalier-de-la-Barre and ending at Stendhal's tomb in the Montmartre cemetery?

Clignancourt

Below Rue Caulaincourt and Rue Custine, the Butte Montmartre falls away sharply down to Rue Marcadet, followed by a more gentle slope to the edge of Paris, on Boulevard Ney. Certain points on this descent are extreme outposts of Montmartre: the Lamarck-Caulaincourt station, which you leave as if hurled into space, and the Place Jules-Joffrin, the only square in Paris where the *mairie* and the church stand face to face.[49] But the essential feature of this northern part of the 18th arrondissement is Clignancourt, an old quarter of artisans and small workshops, 'inhabited in 1860 by distillers, typefounders, mechanical sawyers, cleaners of bedding . . . It is in Clignancourt that Ignace Pleyel store wood and do their sawing, a company whose pianos rival those of Érard.'[50] Around the same time, on a fine spring afternoon, Germinie Lacerteux and her lover

> went up the Chausée Clignancourt and, with the stream of Parisians from the suburbs all in a hurry to drink in some fresh air, they walked towards the open stretch of sky which awaited them at the top of the rise, at the end of the long row of houses . . . At Château Rouge they

48 'What seduced me in this little space sheltered by the big trees of the Château des Brouillards was above all this remnant of vineyards . . . and the neighbouring watering-trough which is enlivened in the evenings by the spectacle of the horses and dogs that are washed there, and a fountain built in the antique style, in which women chat and sing while they do their washing, as in one of the early chapters of *Werther*' (Gérard de Nerval, 'Promenades et Souvenirs', *L'Illustration*, December 1854 to February 1855).
49 I exclude here the *mairies* of the 5th and 6th arrondissements, as the Panthéon and Saint-Sulpice are scarcely equivalent.
50 La Bédollière, *Le Nouveau Paris*.

came upon the first tree, the first leaves ... In the distance stretched the
country, sparkling and vague, lost in the golden haze of seven o'clock...
They walked downhill, followed the blackened pavement of the long
walls and lines of houses broken by the gaps of gardens ... The descent
came to an end, the paved road broke off ... And then Paris came to
an end and there began one of those dry landscapes which big towns
create around them, that first zone of suburbs *intra muros*, where Nature
is parched, the soil used up, the countryside sown with oyster-shells ...
Soon there rose before them the last street-lamp, hanging from a green
post ... Behind Montmartre they arrived at those big trenches, squared
excavations, with their criss-cross of small, worn, grey paths. At the end
of that, you turned to cross the railway-bridge, past that evil encampment of vagrants, the rough-walkers' quarter of lower Clignancourt.
They would pass quickly along by those houses built out of materials
stolen from demolitions, reeking of the horrors they concealed: these
hovels, half-shack, half-burrow, vaguely alarmed Germinie; she could
feel all the crimes of Night crouching there.[51]

The quarter grows increasingly noisy, and its population increasingly
colourful, as you approach Boulevard Ney. The Porte de Clignancourt
is animated by a more intense life than any of the other gates of Paris, the
majority of these now being little more than vast dislocated roundabouts
between the city and the suburbs, between the 'boulevards of the marshals'
and the no-man's-land beyond the Périphérique, unreachable on foot. At
Clignancourt, on the other hand, thanks to the neighbouring flea market,
this intermediate zone is chaotic and bustling, in the smoke of kebabs and
grilled maize, and the hellish noise of the Périphérique drowning the chants
of the three-card tricksters. Strange market stalls are ranged around dented
cars, amid sellers of tiger balm, pralines, luminous yo-yos and secondhand
jackets. Between Paris and Saint-Ouen is a piece of the Third World, an
oasis of disorder at the edge of a city that tolerates this less and less.

Goutte d'Or

For certain people, the Goutte d'Or – from the name of a white wine
much appreciated by Henri IV – is a part of Montmartre. It is a fact that

---

51   Edmond and Jules Goncourt, *Germinie Lacerteux* (New York; Grove, 1955),
p. 52ff. To my mind this is one of the finest 'descents' in the nineteenth-century
Parisian novel, along with that of Gavroche, from Ménilmontant to the barricade
on Rue de la Chanverie, and that of Guillaume and Pierre, from the Sacré-Coeur
to La Roquette for the execution of Salvat, at the end of Zola's *Paris*.

it continues along the hill eastward without interruption, exception made for the recent and artificial Boulevard Barbès. But the physical geography is not sufficient reason to combine two quarters whose differences are so apparent. The Montmartre streets run along the contours, and had to be linked by the famous steps, 'hard on the poor', as the song goes.[52] In the Goutte d'Or, the streets make a St Andrew's cross, giving them a gentler slope and making for a large variety of levels and cuts, sharp angles with buildings which have one entrance on an upper level and one on a lower, with long and narrow courtyards.

The two quarters also each have a quite different imaginary. Until the 1950s, the Goutte d'Or was dark and disturbing, a Paris equivalent of the Whitechapel of Jack the Ripper. As Carco puts it: 'It was not the girls I particularly liked, but above all the dark streets, the bars, the cold, the fine rain on the roofs, the chance encounters, and, in the bedrooms, a sense of shattering abandon that gripped my heart ... In the distance, beyond the Goutte d'Or, the gloomy land of the east like a storm cloud ready to burst and spill over us.'[53] Since then, the scenery has changed from *L'Assommoir* to *A Thousand and One Nights*. The Goutte d'Or has become a gateway to the East, an Arab quarter with 'piles of sequined fabrics, muslins, silks, lamés. And also the gleaming jewellery of countless gold objects, compli-cated necklaces and belts overloaded with pearls, hands of Fatima, etc. ... And still more than the pastry shops and their smells, still more than the shops selling records with Eastern rhythms, these shops selling jewellery and travel goods strike me as expressing in new forms, with new desires and dreams, what I would call in an old word the spirit of the place.'[54]

The Goutte d'Or was ravaged by a clumsy renovation in the late 1980s; the sharp edges of the corner buildings were smoothed, the *lavoir* on Rue des Islettes, which Zola had used as a model for that of Gervaise ('an immense shed with a flat roof, exposed beams, standing on cast-iron pillars and closed by large clear windows'), has been demolished, and the contours that were so specific to the place have been levelled to build playing fields that are always deserted. The atmosphere of the old quarter can still be found, however, around the Saint-Bernard church, Rue Léon and its Théâtre du Lavoir, and Rue Cavé, still bordered by little houses, between which there even remains some open ground.

As you descend towards Rue des Poissonniers, passing the mosque on the corner of Rue Polonceau, you suddenly leave the Maghreb for Black

52   Maurice Culot, in *La Goutte d'Or, faubourg de Paris*, with a preface by Louis Chevalier (Paris/Brussels: AAM and Hazan, 1988).
53   Carco, *De Montparnasse au Quartier Latin*.
54   L. Chevalier, preface to *La Goutte d'Or, faubourg de Paris*.

Africa: Rue Myrha with its shops selling clothes, hairpieces and cosmet-
ics, the fabulous market in Rue Dejean that displays all the vegetables and
fish of the Gulf of Guinea – Senegal captain, thiof, tilapia and shark. You
are here on the uncertain border between the Goutte d'Or and something
that is not really a quarter but keeps a prestigious name: Château-Rouge.
This was a large domain, which would today be bordered by Rue Ramey,
Rue Christiani, Rue des Poissoniers and Rue Doudeauville (on either
side of Boulevard Barbès, just as today are Rue Myrha, Rue Poulet and
Rue Doudeauville, built before the boulevard). It took its name from a
fine dwelling of brick and stone built on the Chaussée de Clignancourt.[55]
In the 1840s, this was the site of what would become one of the largest
public dance halls in the north of Paris – along with the Grand-Turc in La
Chapelle – the Bal du Château-Rouge, also known as the Nouveau Tivoli.
This is where, on 9 July 1847, over a thousand people gave the starting
signal for the 'banquets campaign', the long prologue to the revolution of
February 1848.

La Chapelle and La Villette

The gap between the last foothills of the Goutte d'Or and the first slopes
of Buttes-Chaumont serves as a passage for the trains of the Nord and Est
lines, the canals, and the roads to Saint-Denis, Flanders and Germany; this
was the triumphal return route for victorious kings of France, as well as
the route of successive invasions: Blücher, Moltke, the Panzers of 1940.
From below, you do not get the feeling of being in a hollow between two
hills, but from a promontory of Buttes-Chaumont that you reach via the
hairpin bends of Rue Georges-Lardennois, the contours are as visible as
on a map: in the foreground a hillside of gardens and vineyards, then the
valley, and behind this Montmartre, seen in profile as it cannot be from
anywhere else.

There are two quarters in this plain, two major centres of industrial
Paris, which has steadily extended towards the north and is still doing so:
La Chapelle and La Villette. In the early twentieth century, when young
Eugène Dabit, leaving school with his friends, reached the Marcadet bridge:

> In this part the houses were darker, and so too were the men who entered
> them, all railwaymen. The factory sirens sounded, and suddenly the street

---

55   In Joanne, *Paris illustré en 1870*, this is described as 'a charming construction
that dates from the reign of Henri IV'. For Hillairet, it was a folly dating from
1780. La Chope du Château-Rouge, where Rue de Clignancourt goes over the
hill, keeps its memory.

was full of workers. Some of them said 'Hullo, kids' in a listless voice. There was something sad behind their look, a dejection in their attitude, and black cuts in their open hands ... We started to run, we crossed Rue de la Chapelle where you came across the carts of market garden-ers, cattle, flocks of sheep, and almost reached La Villette. We would see warehouses, the smoky lines of the Est railway; the rumbling of trains sounded like a muffled song.[56]

These two neighbouring quarters had different vocations. La Chapelle, organized around the railway, was a district of factories, dark and poor. La Villette, on the other hand, built around the Canal d'Ourcq and the Canal Saint-Denis, was a district of fairly thriving warehouses. The commune here had been particularly hostile to its annexation by Paris, which is understandable: 'Thanks to its basin, the proximity of the stations, and the platforms of the Ceinture railway, La Villette is a major entrepot for wine, spirits, timber for building and carts, coal and charcoal, grain and flour, oil, glassware, cast-iron, etc. The docks here receive ten thousand ships each year, with a total load of around 1,100,000 tons, which places La Villette above Bordeaux.'[57]

This difference is still visible. La Chapelle is the end of the world, lost between the overhead Métro, the tracks of the Nord and Est rail-ways, and the big warehouses on Boulevard Ney, along which young women hailing from Black Africa and Eastern Europe are busy attract-ing the attention of lorry drivers parked in the side streets. This is the most deprived part of Paris. Its main artery, Rue de la Chapelle (Rue Marx-Dormoy in its southern half) is dusty and rutted like any of the main roads in the old villages would have been – known here before the annexation as Grand-Rue, and elsewhere as Rue de Paris. But the very old church of Saint-Denis-de-la-Chapelle, whose façade bears one of the five Paris statues of Joan of Arc, seems to have been buried in a cape of sick concrete.[58] One night on Rue Pajol, parallel to Rue de la Chapelle, André Breton was following a young woman: 'I have since had the opportunity on several occasions to see again the dilapidated façade,

---

56   Dabit, *Faubourgs de Paris*. The Marcadet bridge is where Rues Marcadet and Ordener merge and cross the tracks of the Nord railway.
57   La Bédollière, *Le Nouveau Paris*.
58   The other statues are that by Frémiet on Rue des Pyramides, and those on Rue Jeanne d'Arc, the esplanade of the Sacré-Coeur, and the parvis of Saint-Augustin, not counting the head of the Maid of Orleans on Rue Saint-Honoré, where a plaque commemorates her being wounded by an English arrow in front of the Porte Saint-Honoré.

blackened by smoke, of the house on Rue Pajol … I have never known a more saddening frontage.' But like this woman who aroused Breton's astonishment,[59] La Chapelle retains a hidden charm, around the Place de Torcy in the little Chinese quarter which is one of the oldest in Paris, in the welcoming cafés on Rue l'Olive, and in its covered market, whose clientele is a reflection of every continent on earth. The landscape beyond Rue Riquet, where the bridge crosses the tracks of the Est railway, is for me one of the most beautiful in Paris, with an immense all-round vista towards the Rue d'Aubervilliers and the disused building of the Pompes Funèbres Municipales, designed by a belated imitator of Ledoux, towards the repair shops for rolling stock of the Nord railway, whose semiconical nesting roofs suggest the scales of a prehistoric reptile.

'It is via the beautiful and tragic Rue d'Aubervilliers that Debord and Wolman continue their northward progress.'[60] Beautiful and tragic it still is, and when the setting sun lights up its frontages, it has the sparkle of a southern port – Algiers, Palermo or Alexandria. Further on, you enter La Villette by the Place du Maroc:

> when I happened on it one Sunday afternoon, not only a Moroccan desert but also, and at the same time, a monument of colonial impe-rialism; topographic vision was entwined with allegorical meaning in the square, yet not for an instant did it lose its place in the heart of Belleville. But to awaken such a view is something ordinarily reserved for intoxicants. And in such cases, in fact, street names are like intoxicat-ing substances that make our perceptions more stratified and richer in spaces.[61]

This is indeed the secret of the excitement that affects anyone who stum-bles on Rue de Pali-Kao, the Passage du Roi d'Alger, or the Villa de Cronstadt.

In La Villette, there is nothing good to expect from the major centrifu-gal arteries, Avenue de Flandre and Avenue Jean-Jaurès. It is in the cross streets that past beauty can still be glimpsed: at the end of Rue Curial, in the

---

59   An amazement that 'no longer knew any bounds, when she deigned to invite me to accompany her to a neighbouring *charcuterie* where she wanted to buy some gherkins' (Breton, *Communicating Vessels*).

60   'Relevé d'ambiances urbaines au moyen de la dérive', in *Les Lèvres nues*, 9, November 1956.

61   Benjamin, *The Arcades Project*, p. 518. Benjamin has the Place du Maroc in Belleville, which is not correct, but clearly doesn't matter.

passages where garages, single-storey hotels, and metal-roofed workshops housing obscure activities press tightly together; in the almost African little shops of Rue de l'Ourcq, beneath the arches of the Ceinture railway. The heart of the quarter, the Bassin de La Villette, has indeed been improved by making use of what it was designed and built for in the port's heyday: the wheels of the lifting bridge on Rue de Crimée so often photographed by Atget, Brassaï and Doisneau; the warehouses; the Saint-Jacques-Saint-Christophe church that would be ugly anywhere else but here strikes just the right note, between the square, the fire station, and the waterfront market. Further along, the basin widens, dividing into two branches with different qualities. The Canal de l'Ourcq, which until the 1970s separated the cattle market and the abattoirs, today waters the Parc de la Villette in which footballers, tourists, cineastes and young mothers (veiled or not) spend Sundays harmoniously by the waterside. The Canal Saint-Denis, for its part, runs modestly out to the industrial wastelands of the north, hidden beneath Avenue Corentin-Cariou, Boulevard Macdonald, and the Périphérique, proletarian and a bit dirty, like the '*petits enfants d'Aubervilliers*' in the song by Prévert and Kosma.

Buttes-Chaumont

The streets bordering the Parc des Buttes-Chaumont bear the names of heroes of national liberation struggles – Manin who was president of the short-lived republic of Venice in 1848, Botzaris who defended Missolonghi together with Byron, and Simon Bolivar. This has not prevented the quarter from today being a bourgeois island between La Villette and Belleville, with apartment blocks as substantial as those of Auteuil. But for many years this was a fearsome place for the working and dangerous classes. The Montfaucon gibbet was erected on the southwestern slope. In *The Last Day of a Condemned*, Victor Hugo – who, as we have seen, denounced the secret nighttime executions at the Barrière Saint-Jacques – exclaims: 'Give us back Montfaucon, its caves of bones, its beams, its crooks, its chains, its rows of skeletons; give us back, in its permanence and power, that gigantic outhouse of the Paris executioner!' The famous 'sixteen pillars' of Montfaucon were connected by three levels of transverse beams, so that on certain days you could see up to sixty individuals swinging there. The Montfaucon gibbet was in operation until the opening of the Saint-Louis hospital in the 1610s, after which the site was used for a *voirie*, i.e., a depository for the rubbish of the city, and a knacker's yard where old and sick horses ended up:

The place was a horrible one, on account of the dead flesh always on display. The bones rotted on the spot, heaped four or five feet high, until the time came for ploughing, when peasants came to look for fertilizer ... The skins were removed every two or three days by the tanners of the Bièvre. But all around there were gut-dressers and workshops for chemical products, whose waste ran through the marshes and in the open towards Rue de la Grange-aux-Belles ... Around the knacker's yard there were so many rats that, if the carcasses of the horses slaughtered during the day were left out in a corner of the premises, by the next morning they would be completely stripped.[62]

At the foot of Buttes-Chaumont, just above the refuse dump, there were two large holes in the hillside – the tunnel of the Ceinture railway, and the mouth of the chalk pit known as the Amérique quarry.[63] From these vast excavations rose the smoke of gypsum kilns. The blocks were taken out of the kilns by *chaufourniers* (a street in the quarter bears their name, and there is also the Passage des Four-à-Chaux). The immense underground caverns, which remained relatively warm, sheltered a nighttime population of vagabonds. Rumour spread that a new court of miracles had arisen in the Amérique quarries. Regular expeditions by the police, and even the army, were organized to the 'dark and gloomy caverns',[64] to hunt out these unfortunate victims of the industrial revolution. In November 1867, *La Gazette des tribunaux* condemned the 'still growing audacity of the prowlers who infest

---

62   Chevalier, *Classes laborieuses et classes dangereuses*. The *voirie* and the knacker's yard was removed in 1849 to the Bondy forest. On the rats: 'In a book by Théophile Gautier, *Caprices et zigzags*, I find a curious page. "A great danger threatens us," it says. "The modern Babylon will not be smashed like the tower of Lylak; it will not be lost in a sea of asphalt like Pentapolis, or buried under the sand like Thebes. It will simply be depopulated and ravaged by the rats of Montfaucon." ... The rats of Montfaucon ... have not endangered Paris; Haussmann's arts of embellishment have driven them off ... But from the heights of Montfaucon the proletariat have descended, and with gunpowder and petroleum they have begun the destruction of Paris which Gautier foresaw' (Max Nordau, *Aus dem wahren Milliardenlande: Pariser Studien und Bilder* [Leipzig, 1878], vol. 1, pp. 75–6; cited by Benjamin, *The Arcades Project*, p. 91).
63   La Bédollière, *Le Nouveau Paris*. He repeats the idea that this 'Amérique' took its name because 'production from it was exported far away: a large part was embarked on the canal, then transshipped at Le Havre for the other side of the Atlantic'. But this seems to be simply a legend, 'Amérique' being no more than a place name.
64   *Mémoires de M. Claude*, commissioner of police for the quarter, cited in Simone Delattre, *Les Douze Heures noires*.

this zone of Paris, and seem to have chosen the said quarries as their headquarters'.[65]

And so 'this famous vale of rubble constantly about to fall, the streams black with mud', as Balzac writes on the first page of *Old Goriot*, was built with its own subsoil, stones from the south and chalk from the north.[66] It was the tunnels of these immense quarries that fuelled the imaginary underground of Paris, more developed than in any other capital, even bearing in mind the final chase in *The Third Man* and the battles of the Warsaw uprising. The first chapter was that of the Catacombes, which are the quarries of Montrouge and Montparnasse where remains from the Innocents cemetery were transferred. Nadar, who managed to photograph there in the 1860s using artificial light, described 'those skeletons piled pell-mell and disintegrating ... the ribs, vertebrae, sternums, wrist and ankle bones, metacarpals and metatarsals, etc. ... the whole menu of bones ... pressed together and heaped in more or less cubic masses below the crypts ... and maintained in front by skulls chosen from the best preserved'.[67]

But the fantasy of an underground city was not just a matter of bones; there was always an element of threat attached to it. The metaphor of the social underground is developed in a marvellous chapter of *Les Misérables* (Volume V, book 2, ch. 2), 'Ancient History of the Sewer':

> The sewer is the conscience of the city. Everything there converges and confronts everything else. In that livid spot there are shades, but there are no longer secrets ... All the uncleannesses of civilization, once past their use, fall into this trench of truth, where the immense social sliding ends ... The Saint-Barthelemys filters through there, drop by drop, between the paving stones. Great public assassinations, political and religious butcheries, traverse this underground passage of civilization, and thrust their corpses there ... Beneath these vaults one hears the brooms of spectres. One there breathes the enormous fetidness of social catastrophes.

---

65 Ibid.

66 'Paris is growing, and faubourgs have been heedlessly built over old quarries; with the result that everything you see above the ground basically lacks the foundations of a town in the earth. ... A matter for reflection, considering how this great city is formed and supported by absolutely contrary means! These church towers, these temples, are so many signs that say clearly: what we see in the air is lacking under our feet' (Mercier, *Tableau de Paris*).

67 Félix Nadar, *Quand j'étais photographe* (Paris: Flammarion, 1900).

And, as an echo, during Bloody Week of 1871, the rumour spread that the Communards had taken refuge in the Catacombes and sewers and were preparing to blow up Paris.

The Métro never aroused such terror, and it was only in irony that Walter Benjamin took up the traditional image of an underground hell:

> But another system of galleries runs underground through Paris: the Métro, where at dusk glowing red lights point the way into the under-world of names. Combat, Élysée, Georges V, Étienne Marcel, Solférino, Invalides, Vaugirard – they have thrown off the humiliating fetters of street or square, and here in the lightning-scored, whistle-resounding darkness are transformed into misshapen sewer gods, catacomb fairies. This labyrinth harbours in its interior not one but a dozen blind raging bulls, into whose jaws not one Theban virgin once a year but thousands of anaemic young dressmakers and drowsy clerks every morning must hurl themselves ... Here each name dwells alone; hell is its demesne. Amer, Picon, Dubonnet are guardians of the threshold.[68]

There is a further consequence of the abundance of chalk in the hills north of Paris, and one not at all in the realm of the imaginary. Under Philippe le Bel, a decree was promulgated that obliged every new house built in Paris to be covered with plaster. As an excellent fire-resistant and insulator, plaster certainly saved Paris from burning as London did, and it was this measure, enforced for several hundred years, that gave the city its unity of material and colour. Descending from the Place des Fêtes to the Hôtel de Ville through Rue de Belleville, Rue du Faubourg-du-Temple and Rue du Temple, or leaving Barbès-Rochechouart and taking Rue du Faubourg-Poissonière, Rue Poissonière, Rue des Petits-Carreaux and Rue Montorgeuil to reach Les Halles, you pass monuments and large buildings made of cut stone, brick, concrete, glass, plastic and metal. But the connecting tissue, which does not strike the eye but whose great importance is recognized as soon as it is missing, is plaster-covered front-ages, in which the close repetition of tall and narrow windows creates a continuous vertical rhythm. No ornaments, no balconies, no shutters, and windowsills scarcely visible in the frames, no relief apart from the thin string-courses on the lower edges of windows, often protected from the rain by a thin zinc strip – also a very Parisian material, both on bistro counters and on roofs to which it gives a grey tint and a very particular ribbing.

---

68   Benjamin, *The Arcades Project*, p. 84.

These modest façades are an essential part of older buildings in the working-class districts on the periphery. In the centre they accompany aristocratic dwellings in the same way as the left hand on the piano supports the melody. They were certainly applied to constructions that differed according to time and place: in Old Paris, these are houses on narrow plots – eight metres wide, allowing for just two rooms. As you go through the front door, you almost immediately reach the far end of the corridor, and a little courtyard with dustbins is shared with a building giving onto the next street. In the villages of the crown, on the other hand, frontages were wider, up to five or six spans, and behind the buildings facing the street could be a long succession of courtyards, reproducing the outside arrangement on a simpler scale.[69] But the construction process was the same: a timber frame, rubble filler, and plaster rendering. This technique was used until much later in the plebeian quarters ('Cut stone is too heavy and too dear! Plaster, if you please! Tell me about it! It looks good, it's light, it's suited for all kinds of decoration – and besides, it's not expensive!'[70]) Just as the Gothic style was still used in Paris in the seventeenth century (Saint-Eustache), and neoclassicism marks many features in the most Haussmannian of constructions (Place Saint-Michel), so buildings in the outlying districts were made of timber framing covered with plaster until the end of the nineteenth century, when the *beaux quartiers* were already into Art Nouveau. It is amazing how the plaster tradition was handed down by the builders who constructed Paris and continue to do so – formerly from the Creuse or Italians, today Portuguese or Malians – preserving the shades of grey that are so particular to the city, varying sometimes towards a very light yellow-pink, and sometimes towards colder and almost bluish tones, but always very discreet and in keeping with the general harmony of the street.

In the late 1860s there still stretched between the Buttes-Chaumont and the boulevards separating Paris from Le Pré-Saint-Gervais a wide and unpopulated zone fissured with ravines. After the old quarry workings were filled in, a horse market was established around the Place du Danube (Rhin-et-Danube since Liberation), which very quickly collapsed. On this land, between Rue David-d'Angers, Rue de la Mouzaïa and Rue de Bellevue, little flowery streets were built, bordered with suburban villas, shacks, and workers' allotments. These bear the names Égalité, Liberté, Solidarité and Prévoyance, resuscitated for the centenary of 1789 on the occasion of an

---

69 On all these questions, see Loyer's incomparable *Paris XIXe siècle, l'immeuble et la rue*.

70 Delvau, *Histoire anecdotique des barrières de Paris*.

Exposition Universelle famous for its inauguration, at the other end of Paris, of the Eiffel Tower. These streets fall sharply down towards Boulevard Sérurier and Boulevard d'Algérie, whose curves surround the Square de la Butte-du-Chapeau-Rouge, a magnificent promontory that overlooks the whole of the eastern suburbs, from Pantin to Les Lilas, with the hills of Romainville behind.

Belleville and Ménilmontant

Certain quarters of Paris have a character that owes most to history and architecture, others to their economic activity, and others again to geography. None of these criteria, however, is quite suitable for characterizing the hills stretching from Buttes-Chaumont to Père-Lachaise, and defining what makes Belleville and Ménilmontant unique. For my part, I am convinced that these are quarters whose identity is largely an emotional one. I don't mean by this the debut of Maurice Chevalier at the Élysées-Montmartre, nor the plaque on 72 Rue de Belleville indicating that 'it was on the steps of this building, on 19 December 1915, in the greatest destitution, that Édith Piaf was born, whose voice would later shake the world'. By 'emotional', I mean – misguidedly, perhaps – 'arousing the emotions'. Here these are emotions of affection for many people, but there are others as well. If you climb Rue des Solitaires, and reach on foot the immense tower blocks constructed on what was once the Place des Fêtes, it is clear that the managers of domination had a score to settle with Belleville. Architectural aberration and the concern for profit are not enough to explain this brutality; they must have felt towards the quarter the same emotion as those who, a century earlier, wiped the Faubourg Saint-Marceau off the map.[71] Fortunately, as Raymond Queneau predicted, 'one day these lovely modern buildings will be demolished/their plexiglass windows broken/their boilers designed at the polytechnique dismantled/their collective tv aerials severed/their lifts unscrewed/their water-heaters crunched/their fridges crushed/when these blocks grow old/with the infinite weight of the sadness of things.'[72]

---

71   On this subject, a friend of mine recently pointed out to me a magnificent passage from Guy Debord's *Panégyrique*: 'I believe that this town was ravaged somewhat before others because its ever recurring revolutions disrupted and shocked the world all too greatly; and because they unfortunately always failed. So we were eventually punished by a destruction as complete as that which the Brunswick manifesto had formerly threatened, or the speech of the Girondin Isnard: with a view to burying so many fearsome memories, and the great name of Paris.'
72   Raymond Queneau, *Courir les rues* (Paris: Gallimard, 1967).

Belleville and Ménilmontant have a western slope that looks towards Paris, and an eastern one, less steep and shorter, that looks to the outer suburbs. The north–south line of the ridge that divides them follows Rue Pelleport, which, like Rue Compans, Rue Rébeval, and Avenue Secrétan, bears the name of one of the officers who commanded the Paris National Guard, the students of the École Polytechnique and what remained of the regular forces against the Prussian royal guard in the battle of Paris, on 30 March 1814.[73] Rue Pelleport begins from Rue de Belleville close to the Télégraphe Métro station, the culminating point of the eastern hills, where Chappe installed the optical telegraph that brought Parisians news of the victories of Fleurus and Jemmapes. Later on, the third – and present – cemetery of the village was located there, and the reservoirs accompanied by twin water towers whose silhouette is part of the Belleville landscape.

Between Rue Pelleport and the 'boulevards of the marshals' – here called after Mortier, another hero of the battle of Paris, who ended up as one of the victims in Fieschi's attempted assassination of Louis-Phillipe on Boulevard du Temple[74] – there is an undifferentiated band in which it is impossible to distinguish the part belonging to Belleville from that belonging to Ménilmontant. This was formerly an immense estate, from Rue Pelleport to the far side of Boulevard Mortier.[75] The château and the park, which encroached substantially on both villages, belonged to a family of the *noblesse de robe*, Le Peletier, also known as de Saint-Fargeau as they owned a domain of that name close to Auxerre.[76] This great aristocratic fiefdom corresponds today to the most deprived part of the hill, where the brick public housing of the 1920s alternates with the tower blocks of the 1960s, *cités* as they are termed, using this ancient word with its sense of common

---

73   The only one who does not have a street here is Marshal Marmont, despite the fact that he fought valiantly on that day. But history has condemned him for signing the capitulation of Paris, and no doubt also for commanding the royal forces in July 1830.
74   Fieschi and his accomplices tried out their explosive device in a meadow in Ménilmontant, close to what is now Rue d'Annam.
75   And in the other direction, from Rue du Surmelin to Rue de Romainville, whose curious bend is due precisely to its circling this domain.
76   Rue Le Peletier, which comes out on Boulevard des Italiens, is named after Claude Le Peletier, provost of merchants under Louis XIV. The illustrious Louis Le Peletier de Saint-Fargeau, a deputy for the nobility to the Estates-General, then a member of the Convention who voted for the death of the king and was assassinated for this reason on 20 January 1793, had a daughter who was made a ward of the nation. It was she who started to divide up the estate for development, and sold the old château. By the 1850s there was nothing left of the domain except perhaps a few trees in the Belleville cemetery.

life to denote a world of disintegration of the public space. You can find a certain charm around the reservoirs of Ménilmontant, at the pretty Art Déco stations of the 3 *bis* Métro line – it actually has only two stations of its own, Pelleport and Saint-Fargeau – and Rue du Groupe-Manouchian, both in its name and its little houses, but there is nothing really worth visiting in the long rectangle that stretches from the proletarian shacks along Rue Mouzaïa to the little English-style quarter around Rue Étienne-Marey near the Porte de Bagnolet.

It is rather on the western slope of the hill, the Paris side, that Belleville and Ménilmontant display themselves. The boundary between them used to be marked by a place called the Haute-Borne, where the famous tavern of Le Galant-Jardinier was located. It is said that Cartouche was arrested at the Haute-Borne, and it was here on Thursday, 24 October 1776 that Jean-Jacques Rousseau was knocked over by a huge Great Dane, with the terrible results that are well known. ('It was almost night when I regained consciousness . . . They asked me where I lived; it was impossible for me to say. I asked where I was; they told me: "at the Haute-Borne". They might just as well have said: "on Mount Atlas".'[77]) Even if Rue des Couronnes is still a plausible border, the division of the hill between Belleville and Ménilmontant is a shifting one, and old inhabitants have different opinions on this subject. Some give the Belleville limits as 'Boulevard de Belleville, Rue de Belleville, Rue des Pyrénées, Rue de Ménilmontant . . . you see, it's a quadrilateral. The heart was Rue de Tourtille, Rue Ramponeau, Rue de Pali-Kao, Rue des Couronnes'. An old lady says: 'We were born in Ménilmontant, you know, it's a part of Belleville.' And another man: 'Everyone has their own Belleville. Mine is bounded by Rue Rébeval, it climbs up in a bend to Rue de Belleville, and then on the other side of the street towards Rue Vilin, and down towards Rue des Couronnes.'[78]

The opposition between the two quarters is an old one:

There was a great difference between the clientele of the taverns of Courtille and the regulars of the taverns of Ménilmontant; in the latter, in fact, families would come to spend Sundays, and the artisan of the last century would get to know his intended at the dances of the Galant

---

77   Rousseau, *The Reveries of a Solitary Walker*, 'Second Walk'. The quadrilateral of the Haute-Borne, bounded by Boulevard de Belleville, Rue Julien-Lacroix, Rue des Couronnes and Rue de Ménilmontant, was totally ravaged in the 1960s.
78   Françoise Morier (ed.), *Belleville, belle ville, visage d'une planète* (Paris: Creaphis, 1994). The old lady is right to say that Ménilmontant is a 'part', as it belonged to the commune of Belleville when this was annexed to Paris, which explains the topographical uncertainties.

Jardinier or the Barreaux Verts. At Courtille, on the other hand, the dance halls of the Boeuf Rouge, the Sauvage and the Carotte Filandreuse were frequented mainly by drunkards and girls of easy virtue. At Ménilmontant, therefore, modest lovers and well-behaved diners under the arbour; at the Belleville dances, orgies and battles, with people using knives and biting each other like bulldogs.[79]

In *L'Apprentie,* a novel by Gustave Geffroy set in Belleville in the wake of the Commune, old Pommier takes his daughters, Céline and Cécile

as far as the lake of Saint-Fargeau, where splendid poplars shade the peaceful waters of a pond ... and to the dance halls of their old quarter [i.e., Ménilmontant], the Barreaux Verts on the Chausée and the Élysée-Ménilmontant on Rue Julien-Lacroix. The latter place was quite special: a garden with fine chestnut trees, and an almost family welcome. Traditions were kept up there, the clientele and their behaviour were not at all like that in the dance halls of the outer boulevards. Young girls who went down to Paris were nostalgic for this greenery, this music, this décor of first confessions and first revelations.[80]

In the 1950s you could still hear almost the same words: 'For me, Belleville and Ménilmontant were two different quarters. If you said at the time that you were from Belleville, you were seen as a bit rough ... While if you were from Ménilmontant, that was better ... That's how it was.'[81]

Rue de Belleville begins at the former *barrière,* now the meeting point of four arrondissements. Haussmann had cut Belleville in two, so that the 10th, 11th, 19th and 20th arrondissements touch each other here – like New Mexico, Arizona, Colorado and Utah on the San Juan River. In *L'Apprentie,* it is

a busy quarter, noisy and working-class, commercial during the daytime. It was hard to move between the throng of cabs and buses, trolleys and carts ... The pavement was just as cluttered. The crowd moved, stopped, chatted and made their purchases between the shops and the vegetable stalls ... The high street of Belleville was not like Montrouge or Montmartre, the Faubourg Saint-Antoine or even nearby Ménilmontant. The first houses, with their wine-merchants' saloons

---

79   La Bédollière, *Le Nouveau Paris.*
80   Gustave Geffroy, *L'Apprentie* (Paris: Fasquelle, 1904). The outer boulevards here meant Boulevards de Belleville, Ménilmontant, etc.
81   Morier (ed.), *Belleville, belle ville.*

filled with enormous counters, their concerts and dances, their hotels with transparent screens brightly lit up by gas – these first houses did not suggest a neighbourhood of work, but conjured up the night-time underworld of prostitution and gangsters, and the memory of Milord l'Arsouille and the 'descent from the Courtille'.

At the beginning of the century, Dabit saw there 'a provincial shop, a bespoke tailor, the Cocorico cinema, cafés: the Point du Jour, the Vielleuse with its ten billiard tables, surrounded from six in the morning by players in their shirtsleeves. Hawkers unpacked their wares, street urchins cried the morning papers; sometimes a giant with a tattooed body juggled with 20-kilo weights. You got off at this crossroads as if at a port.'[82] Everything has changed today except the spirit of the place, so that at bottom it is all still the same. Le Point du Jour has been removed along with the left side of Rue de Belleville. La Vielleuse is still in existence, but in a modern building that has taken the place of the house that Vallès/Vingtras depicts on the night of Saturday-Sunday 27–28 May 1871: 'We responded with musket and cannon to the terrible fire directed against us. At the windows of the Vielleuse, and of all the houses on the corner, our people put up mattresses, whose stuffing smoked under the hail of projectiles.'[83] These two cafés are nicely depicted on one of the itinerant stalls on the central reservation of the boulevard. Three days each week the market reaches up to the Métro station. Every day, the horns, the merry-go-rounds, the crowd around the Métro entrance, the chants of Arab beggars, the sellers of grilled maize, chestnuts, flowers, mechanical toys running around on the pavement, plastic covers for identity papers, and double lines of vans unloading boxes outside Chinese supermarkets: the great port of Belleville is still very active.

The steam funicular, 'which made a stately descent from the Saint-Jean-Baptiste church to the Place de la République, climbed slowly up again, and, creaking and grating, took you along Rue du Faubourg-du-Temple and Rue de Belleville for ten centimes', has been replaced by the no. 11 Métro line, a good deal less picturesque.[84] But alongside Chinese restaurants and grocers, the bottom of Rue de Belleville keeps some vestiges of its old glory, like the Café des Folies-Belleville that evokes the music hall where Mayol, Dranem, Damia, Georgius, Fréhel and Maurice Chevalier

---

82   Dabit, *Faubourgs de Paris*.
83   Jules Vallès, *L'Insurgé* (1884).
84   Dabit, *Faubourgs de Paris*. In the late 1990s, the corner of Rue du Faubourg-du-Temple and Avenue Parmentier was occupied by a shoe shop, Au Funiculaire, since replaced by a mobile phone dealer.

performed. The Théâtre de Belleville was a few metres up. To quote Lucien Daudet:

> I went several times to this theatre, together with Eugène Carrière, Geffroy and Rodin. We took four places in the circle, after a good dinner at a rotisserie in the same street, where you could see your chicken being grilled and buy bread on the side, and we enjoyed the physiognomies, heads and faces gathered there, leaning forward and drinking them in with our eyes, a spectacle very much in the style of Daumier.[85]

The theatre was later transformed into a cinema, one of the dozen you could count in the interwar years between the Boulevard and the Belleville church, specializing in horror films. The Floréal, for its part, showed gangster films with Edward G. Robinson and James Cagney, the Paradis was for musical comedies, westerns at the Alhambra and the Cocorico, and Soviet and Yiddish films at the Bellevue.[86]

The omnipresent Chinese are only the latest in a long series of immigrants who arrived in Belleville in successive waves, starting with the Russian and Polish Jews who fled from the pogroms of the early years of the century to establish at the foot of the hill their tradition of textile and clothing work learned in the factories of Lodz, Minsk or Bialystok. In the 1920s, Belleville had a CGT hatters' branch whose banner carried its name in Yiddish. There were leather workers and furriers, also seen as Jewish trades. Yiddish was spoken in the synagogue on Rue Julien-Lacroix, and at the Lumière de Belleville restaurant the menu offered *gefiltefish* and *pickelfleish* just as in Warsaw. Later came the Armenians fleeing Turkey in 1918. Their community was grouped around Rue Jouye-Rouve and Rue Bisson, and their speciality was shoemaking. Then came Greeks expelled from Asia Minor, German Jews in 1933 and Spanish Republicans in 1939. The Jewish concentration remained so strong that the French police had no trouble in carrying out a nice raid here in July 1942: the number of those taken from Belleville via Drancy to Auschwitz is estimated at eight thousand.

After the war it was the turn of the Algerians, needed to rebuild the

---

85 Daudet, *Paris vécu*. The Folies-Belleville was at 8 Rue Belleville, and the theatre at no. 46. Geffroy described the theatre at length in *L'Apprentie*: 'There were animosities, and insults sometimes exchanged between the different social classes of this little town. The noise of the upper galleries annoyed the peaceful occupants of the stalls and the boxes. Overly coquettish *toilettes* made everyone's flesh creep and were sometimes the object of a word or a projectile.'

86 Clément Lépidis, 'Belleville mon village', in *Belleville* (Paris: Veyrier, 1975).

country. Along with La Chapelle, Belleville was one of the main strong-holds of the FLN during the Algerian war, which did not prevent the *pieds noirs*, and Tunisian Jews in particular, from establishing themselves here on a massive scale in the 1960s. On the boulevard, between Rue de Belleville and Rue de Ménilmontant, there is something of a boundary line at Rue Bisson and Rue de la Fontaine-au-Roi. On the Belleville side, spilling into Rue Lemon, Rue Ramponeau and Rue de Pali-Kao are the kosher restaurants, patisseries and grocers run by Jews. On the Ménilmontant side you have travel agents specializing in the Maghreb, Islamic bookshops, Kabyl cafés – including the marvellous Soleil, close to the Métro. This frontier, visible from the shop signs, does not prevent the population of the quarter from mingling peacefully on the boulevard, old Jewish ladies drinking tea on the patisserie terraces, young Black mothers in African robes, a baby on their back, walking up from the boulevard to do their shopping in the market, orthodox Jewish men with black hats as worn in Vilnius, groups of retired workers basking in the sun, conversing in Arabic or Kabyl, whom you imagine to be full of tolerance and humanity.

The place where the boulevard stops being Belleville and becomes Ménilmontant does not have a name. The elegant semicircular line of the apartment blocks on the side facing the city, Ménilmontant station under the catalpas of its little square, the emptiness of the boulevard's central island, form an ensemble that is much quieter than the Belleville *barrière*. Rising in a gigantic and absolutely straight line, Rue de Ménilmontant offers a view to the hilltop, and Rue Oberkampf plunges down to the centre of Paris:

> Giacometti and I – and some Parisians too, I'm sure – know that there exists in Paris, where she has her dwelling, a person of great elegance, fine, haughty, vertical, singular and grey – a very tender grey – known as Rue Oberkampf, who cheekily changes her name and is called higher up Rue de Ménilmontant. Beautiful as a needle, she rises up to the sky. If you decide to explore her by car, starting from Boulevard Voltaire, she opens up as you climb, but in a singular manner: instead of retreating, the houses converge, offering very simple frontages and gables, quite commonplace but which, truly transfigured by the personality of this street, take on the quality of a kind of goodness, familiar and distant.[87]

If Belleville has certain aspects of a larger town – around the church, in particular, where drapers, cake shops, cheesemongers and bookshops are

---

87   Jean Genet, *L'Atelier de Giacometti* (Paris: L'Arbelète, 1963).

grouped like in the provinces – Ménilmontant has retained more of a country feel. Rue de la Chine, between the Tenon hospital and the *mairie* of the 20th arrondissement, certainly lacks the 'joyous aspect of a country road' that Huysmans found there. The times have certainly changed a lot since:

> In this huge *quartier* where meagre wages doom women and children to eternal privations, Rue de la Chine and those streets which join and cross it, such as Rue des Partants and the amazing Rue Orfila, so fantastic with its windings and its sudden turns, with its badly squared-off enclosures of trees, its abandoned summerhouses, its deserted gardens returning to a state of nature and abounding in untamed shrubs and wild grasses, give off a unique note of peace and calm.[88]

But you still find in Ménilmontant waste ground where 'wild bushes and crazy weeds' sprout, cobbled passages bordered with little gardens, streets whose names evoke the northern streams that supplied Paris with water for hundreds of years – Rues des Cascades, des Rigoles, de la Mare, de la Duée, de la Cour-des-Noues, old French words that all mean spring or stream. You pass along stone walls covered with moss, and views of the old conduits – the finest of which, on Rue des Cascades at the top of Rue de Savies, dates from the reign of Henri IV. Near the Passage des Saint-Simoniens, Rue Taclet, the Villa Georgina and the Villa de l'Ermitage have not changed much since Père Enfantin attempted to practise in this quarter, away from the world, the thought of the dead master.

Père-Lachaise and Charonne

Between Ménilmontant and Charonne, Père-Lachaise is an unspoiled beauty, protected against commerce and fashion – in cemeteries the spirit of place always prevails over the spirit of time. The administrative boundary between the old villages of Belleville and Charonne used to pass further to the west (Rue des Partants, Rue Villiers-de-l'Isle-Adam), but today it is Père-Lachaise, belonging neither to the one nor to the other, that marks their separation. In the eighteenth century, Charonne, with its south-facing hillside, was entirely planted with vineyards and had all kinds of *guinguettes* – a word that, according to Jaillot, 'apparently derives from the fact that in these taverns the only wine sold is a little green one known

---

88   Huysmans, *Parisian Sketches*, p. 102.

as Guinguet, grown in the surroundings of Paris'.[89] Several streets in the
Charonne quarter recall its agricultural past: Rues des Haies, du Clos,
des Grands-Champs, de la Plaine; Rues des Maraîchers, des Vignoles,
des Orteaux – the latter mysteriously deriving from the Latin *hortus*. It
is perhaps this rural background and the consequent absence of remarkable buildings or historic events that have left Charonne with a deficient
identity – despite having given its name to a major street, a boulevard, and
a Métro station. Few people say that they live in Charonne; these are to
be found almost entirely at the centre, on the site of the former château
and around the church, in the little hamlet that you could find 'coming
down from Belleville via the Ratrait, two kilometres further on, a village
of houses interspersed with gardens, dominated in the foreground by a
rustic bell tower'.[90]

It is rather better to reach Charonne from above, for example through
Rue Stendhal (curiously described as a '*littérateur*' on the blue and white
plaque). This is a street that Queneau found sad: 'Among the saddest streets
of Paris/one could mention Rue Villiers-de-L'Is/le-Adam, Rue Baudelaire
(Charles)/and Rue Henri-Beyle known as Stendhal/these really haven't
been spoiled/you even start thinking/they have rather been punished/by
naming such sad streets after them.'[91] And yet the acute angle made by
Rue Stendhal when it forks off from Rue des Pyrénées is occupied by a
dispensary from the 1910s devoted to 'diseases of the chest', and, on the
gable wall that drops down to it you can still read, above an almost oblit-
erated advertisement for Saint-Raphaël, a slogan for '*Cadorcin, shampoing
à l'huile*', these few metres being almost a condensation of the first half of
the twentieth century in Paris, from the BCG vaccination and the anti-TB
stamp through to André Kertész and the Poste Parisien (a private radio
station belonging to the newspaper *Le Petit Parisien*). Further along, the
tall chestnut trees of the cemetery appear on the hillside, together with the
pointed bell tower of the church of Saint-Germain-de-Charonne. Crossing
the grass that covers the Charonne reservoirs, you reach an immense garage
bordering on Rue Lucien-Leuwen. Although this is a cul-de-sac, it is the
only street in Paris to bear the name of the hero of a novel. (Likewise

89   Jaillot, *Recherches critiques, historiques et topographiques*.
90   La Bédollière, *Le Nouveau Paris*. The Château de Charonne, built in
the seventeenth century, had a large park that was bounded, according to
Hillairet, by Rue de Bagnolet from Rue de la Réunion to Rue des Prairies,
then along this street, and by Rue Lisfranc and two lines that would continue
Rue Lisfranc and Rue de la Réunion to meet inside Père-Lachaise by the Mur
de Fédérés.
91   Queneau, *Courir les rues*.

unfinished; there is also, not far from here, the Rue Monte-Cristo, but this was an island before becoming a character.) It is high time that all those shameful names of the Second Empire were replaced by characters from novels: Avenue Mac-Mahon – capitulationist general, well-known idiot, and seditious president – could become Avenue Manon-Lescaut (perhaps an exception could be made here, calling this Avenue Anna-Karina to honour the historic New Wave cinema); Avenue Bugeaud could become Avenue du Prince-Mishkin; Boulevard de Magenta, Boulevard Eugène-Rastignac; Avenue de Malakoff, Avenue Charles Swann; the Pont de l'Alma, Pont Jean-Valjean; and Rue de Turbigo, Rue Moll-Flanders. This would mean a lot of work, as I have counted thirty-one Paris streets named after the glorious campaigns of Napoleon III in Italy, the Crimea and Mexico. Not counting those that remind us of great deeds in the colonies, and their heroes both imperial and republican.

Opposite Rue Lucien-Leuwen, in Rue du Parc-de-Charonne, a small gate gives access to the cemetery. The standing statue of a man in a three-cornered hat, holding his cane in one hand and a bunch of flowers in the other, has recently been taken away – for restoration, I hope. This could be a secretary of Robespierre's, with a new interest in horticulture. The tomb of Robert Brasillach (6 February 1945) has not been removed, but joined in 1998 by his brother-in-law Maurice Bardèche. At the foot of the hill the very old Charonne church, on its raised platform, overlooks Rue de Bagnolet and the vista of Rue Saint-Blaise, the former village high street. ('Saint Blaise, one of the great miracle workers of the East, bishop of Sebaste in Armenia according to some, of Caesarea in Cappadocia according to others, died 316, was particularly invoked to deal with vipers and sore throats.'[92])

On the last foothills of Charonne, between Rue de Bagnolet – from where you glimpse the tops of the trees in Père-Lachaise, across the walls at the end of ravishing cul-de-sacs – and the very proletarian Rue d'Avron that marks your arrival on the plain, more recent streets cut across village streets that are, along with the periphery of La Chapelle, what is most 'away from it all' in Paris: Rue des Maraîchers that parallels the tracks of the Ceinture railway, with its wild wood, Rue Fernand-Gambon from where you look over the ruins of a Magritte-type station covered in ivy, the warehouses of Rue du Volga (sic) and Rue des Grands-Champs, and my favourite, Rue des Vignoles. There are little passages here between all the houses – the Impasses des Souhaits, de la Confiance, des Crins, de Bergame, even Impasse Satan opposite Passage Dieu, and a nameless blind

---

92   Amédée Boinet, *Les Églises parisiennes*, vol. 1 (Paris: Minuit, 1958).

alley with the black-and-red flag of the anarchist Confédération Nationale du Travail. These are not two metres wide, and end up at fences, workshops, broken doors. It is here – and here alone in Paris – that you can still see what Huysmans described so tenderly about Rue de la Chine:

> Everything here is crooked: there are no walls, no bricks, no stones, but on each side, lining an unpaved road furrowed down the middle by a ditch, stretches a picket fence from old boat timbers, marbled with green moss and veneered with golden-brown tar, which leans, dragging down a whole cluster of ivy, and almost taking with it a gate, clearly bought in a lot from some demolition yard, embellished with mouldings whose delicate grey still shows through under a brown layer of tan deposited by the successive touch of dirty hands.[93]

Bercy

Across the Cours de Vincennes, the world changes as you enter the section of the 12th arrondissement annexed at the expense of the commune of Saint-Mandé. In this district, the wall of the Farmers-General forms a salient – Boulevard de Picpus, Boulevard de Reuilly, Place Félix-Éboué (Métro Daumesnil) – curious on the map but whose reason is clear enough on the ground: the wall followed the edge of a plateau that overlooks the Seine and the Bois de Vincennes. (La Bédollière: 'The Bel-Air is the name of an avenue that connects the Place du Trône with the Avenue de Saint-Mandé. The name is justified by the pureness of the air that you breathe on this plateau, on which boarding-schools, clinics and convents proliferate.') Rue Claude-Decaen goes sharply uphill from Daumesnil towards the Bois, and Rue Taine down towards Bercy and the river.[94] At the bottom, in the valley, Rue de Charenton, parallel to the tracks from the Gare de Lyon, ends its long trajectory from the Bastille. In its final stretch, on the corner of the 'boulevard of the marshals' which has here the name of Poniatowski, this bridges the rusty tracks of the Ceinture railway. From this spot, opposite the gate of the little Bercy cemetery that is the only old enclave in this remote corner, you have – over the landscape of the southeastern suburbs, an endless sea of concrete – the 'terrible view of the plains that lie, harassed, at the feet of the city', as Huysmans put it.

Between Rue de Charenton and the Seine, once the Lyon tracks are

---

93   Huysmans, *Parisian Sketches*, pp. 101–2.
94   The fountain of the Place Daumesnil was, we may recall, the second fountain on the Place du Château-d'Eau (now Place de la République). Rue Claude-Decaen was formerly the Chemin de Reuilly.

crossed (no easy business), is Bercy, which is completely different. The park of the Château de Bercy was bordered by the Seine and Rue de Charenton:[95]

> The Château de Bercy is a building of very regular shape, raised according to the designs of François Mansart, and under his direction. Its vistas extend very far in each direction, and make a very agreeable effect. It is endowed with singular and valuable paintings ... The gardens are spacious, and have been improved since 1706 by a number of avenues, statues, and a long terrace along the river. This magnificent château belonged to Monsieur de Bercy, the former royal *intendant* of finances.[96]

Along the Seine, downstream from the domain of Bercy, financiers and great lords built country houses under the Regency, the most famous of these being that of the Pâris brothers, whom the people called the Pâté-Paris. There were also taverns specializing in fried fish and *matelote*, as at the Point du Jour at the other end of the city.

Bercy had two river ports, one for gypsum and timber, the other for wine. After the Revolution, the warehouses of the wine merchants gradually encroached on the Bercy estate, until the château was finally demolished in 1861. By this time, Thiers's fortifications had already cut the park in two (one part remaining outside Paris), and the tracks of the Lyon railway cut through in the other direction. That was the end of this place whose splendour was compared with that of Versailles – or perhaps more accurately with Christopher Wren's Greenwich on the banks of the Thames. The new Bercy park, on the site of the wine warehouses, has a rather awkward shape, but presumably the terrain did not allow anything better, and the elements preserved – cobblestones, railings, pavilions, old plane trees – have been integrated with tact. The high terrace that separates the park from the expressway along the Seine has been laid out well, and, on the other side of the river, the new housing blocks make it possible to measure the progress of architecture in Paris since the years of the Front de Seine and upper Belleville.

---

95   It extended into Charenton proper, which was then known as Conflans. The park's boundaries were Rue de la Grange-aux-Mercier (now Nicoläi) and Rue de la Liberté at Charenton.

96   Hurtaut and Magny, *Dictionnaire historique de la ville de Paris*. But they are mistaken here: the château was by Louis Le Vau and not François Mansart. Bercy's links with finance are thus not just recent. The greed of the lords of Bercy was well-known, as attested by this verse from 1715: 'Let Bercy satisfy its greed/ in melted gold/ and despite the horror of its suffering/ die after rendering it.'

The Zone

On 19 April 1919, a victorious France voted the 'declassification' of the fortified walls of Paris, in other words their demolition. Like the wall of the Farmers-General, these had lasted for eighty years, but their military role had sterilized the land around them, making it into a *zone*, a non-place very different from the joyous bazaar along the wall of the Farmers-General. In Flaubert's *A Sentimental Education*, Frédéric enters the city in 1848, just after the fortifications had been completed:

> He was awakened by the dull sound of wheels passing over planks: they were crossing the Pont de Charenton; it was Paris ... In the distance, tall factory chimneys were smoking. Then they turned into Ivry. They went up a street, and all of a sudden he caught sight of the dome of the Panthéon. The plain had changed beyond recognition and looked like a town in ruins. The fortifications crossed it in a horizontal ridge, and on the unpaved paths edging the road stood small branchless trees protected by battens bristling with nails. Chemical factories alternated with timber-merchants' yards ... Long-fronted, dull-red taverns displayed a pair of crossed billiard cues in a wreath of painted flowers between their first-floor windows ... Workmen in smocks went by, and also brewers' drays, laundry vans, and butchers' carts ... They stopped at the city gate for a long time, for it was blocked by poultry-farmers, carriers, and a flock of sheep. The sentry, his hood thrown back, walked up and down in front of his box in order to keep warm. The toll-clerk clambered on to the top of the coach, and a fanfare on a cornet rang out. They went down the boulevard at a brisk trot ... and finally reached the iron gate of the Jardin des Plantes.[97]

Between this prehistory and the building of the ring of social housing in the 1920s and '30s, the zone gave rise to a populist literature that was somewhat conventional, and it is rather in photography that one should seek the traces of its melancholic poetry. Atget, above all, showed families of zone-dwellers on the steps of their caravans at the Porte d'Italie, shacks made out of metal and wood perched on the bushy escarpments of the Poterne des Peupliers, the snowy banks of the Bièvre at the entry to the city, ragpickers pushing their barrows along Boulevard Masséna, the ditches by the Porte de Sèvres, the vegetable tangle at Porte Dauphine, a silent world in which nature is weary and no longer able to afford a welcome to the poor. Long

---

97   Gustave Flaubert, *A Sentimental Education* (Oxford: OUP, 2000), p. 112.

after the 'fortifs' had disappeared, this sadness persisted. 'MUR de la MORT':
a clumsy inscription on a fairground caravan in the fog and mud of a waste
ground near the Porte de Clignancourt – this is a photograph by Robert
Frank dating from 1951, depicting the dangerous spectacle, since banned,
in which motorcyclists climb and turn in a gigantic vertical cylinder, which
they only adhere to by centrifugal force.

On the site of the demolished fortifications, the 'boulevards of the
marshals' and the blocks of social housing that border them have little to
remind us of the zone of Flaubert, Atget or Carco, but a tour of Paris by this
route does not have the monotony and homogeneity of the Périphérique.
These boulevards are as varied as the quarters that border them. The desert
of Boulevard Macdonald, in a straight line along the wasteland that has
replaced the Claude-Bernard hospital, the disjointed space of Boulevard
Ney between the Porte d'Aubervilliers and the great intersection of La
Chapelle, the barracks on Boulevard Bessières continued by the grey
concrete mass of the Lycée Honoré-de-Balzac, have nothing in common
with the little hôtels particuliers on Boulevard Berthier, the clever use of
polychrome brick by the Porte Champerret, or the apartment blocks along
Boulevard de la Somme that seem to have been built by a pupil of Loos.
Towards the Bois de Boulogne there is no more social housing. The
Boulevards Lannes and Suchet display the luxury of 1910 on the city side
– monumental masses, sculpted corner rotundas, colossal pilasters, stone
balustrades – while on the side of the Bois there are the marble, bronze, and
statues of the 'return to order' of the 1930s. It would need a Hugo to make
the comparison between the Porte de la Muette with its pink chestnut
trees, a sumptuous embarkation for Cythera, and the Porte de Pantin, an
uncrossable barrage of concrete and noise, where the Périphérique passes at
eye level, with Boulevard Sérurier beneath it engulfed in a hideous cutting
in which the scrawny grass of the central reservation is littered with greasy
wrappers and beer cans, and where the only human beings on foot are
natives of L'viv or Tiraspol trying to survive by begging at the traffic lights.
A very Parisian antithesis, in the end.

PART TWO

Red Paris

Your metal domes fired by the sun,
Your theatre queens with enchanting voices,
Your bells, cannons, deafening orchestra,
Your magic cobbles erected into fortresses,
Your little orators with baroque turns of phrase
Preaching love, and then your sewers full with blood,
Pouring into hell like so many Orinocos.
      – Baudelaire, projected epilogue to the
         1861 edition of *Les Fleurs du Mal*

5

Red Paris

The small building in Charonne, on the corner between Rues Saint-Blaise and Riblette, has an entrance like thousands of others, except for two marble plaques that face each other in the doorway. The one on the left reads:

Here lived
Cadix Sosnowski
F.T. P. Français.
Shot by the Germans
at the age of 17.
Died for France
26 May 1943.

On the right side, framing the serious face of a boy of about fifteen, the inscription recalls:

The home of
Brobion Henri,
F.T. P. F.
Soldier with the Fabien brigade.
Fallen on the field of honour
18 January 1945
at Habsheim, Alsace.

It was perhaps Cadix who brought his friend Henri into the Resistance – I imagine him with the insolent look and fine Slavic features of Marcel Rajman on the 'red poster' ('The killer is a Polish Jew, age 20, seven attacks', including the execution of the SS general Julius Reitter in the heart of Paris, close to the Trocadéro). His parents had probably arrived from Poland in the 1920s, like so many others living in Belleville-Ménilmontant:

My father was what you call a gentleman's outfitter. He could make a jacket, a suit, a man's waistcoat, he could make an overcoat ... This was a trade that Frenchmen didn't follow. At the Ramponeau school we were all little reds. We didn't know what the words 'Communist' and 'popular front' meant, but see a red flag, and all the kids would line up behind it! All our brothers and sisters, who'd arrived from Poland illegally, without papers, language, resident permit, trade or money, went to work on the sewing machine.[1]

It was only natural that the children of these immigrants should join the Resistance:

I spent my childhood there, Rue des Cendriers, my childhood until the age of eighteen, when I was wanted by the Vichy police and left for the unoccupied zone in order to hide and do forestry, as I was wanted for Resistance activities. In other words: distribution of leaflets, scattering leaflets in cinemas in Rue de Ménilmontant – the Phénix, the Ménil-Palace ... There were two of us, me and André Burty, who was shot. My group was decimated and came to an end. There were three or four survivors out of a group that had sections in each of the four quarters of the 14th arrondissement: Belleville, Père-Lachaise, Pelleport and Charonne ... It's a miracle, to have survived all that we went through in those days. One evening, we released a red flag with a system of metal hooks that fastened to the electric line above some waste ground between Rue des Panoyaux and Rue des Cendriers, and it was only the next day that the firemen came to remove it.[2]

Poles – whether Jewish or not – were a regular part of the scene in Red Paris. The two best generals of the Paris Commune were Poles.[3] Dombrowski,

---

1 Étienne Raczymow, in *Belleville, belle ville*.
2 Laurent Goldberg, in ibid.
3 'The Commune admitted all foreigners to the honour of dying for an immortal cause. Between the foreign war lost by their treason, and the civil war fomented by their conspiracy with the foreign invader, the bourgeoisie had found the time to display their patriotism by organizing police-hunts upon the Germans in France. The Commune made a German working man [Leo Frankel] its Minister of Labour. Thiers, the bourgeoisie, the Second Empire, had continually deluded Poland by loud professions of sympathy, while in reality betraying her to, and doing the dirty work of, Russia. The Commune honoured the heroic sons of Poland by placing them at the head of the defenders of Paris' (Karl Marx, 'The Civil War in France', *The First International and After* [Harmondsworth: Penguin, 1974], p. 217).

whom the Russians had condemned to death after the Warsaw uprising, was in command of the forces on the Right Bank at the moment when everything collapsed. Louise Michel, on the barricade of Rue Delta, found a phrase worthy of Victor Hugo to relate his end: 'Dombrowski passed with his officers. "We are lost," he told me. "No," I replied. The next time he passed he was on a stretcher; he was dead.'[4] It was 23 May when Dombrowski was struck down on the barricade of Rue Myrha. His body was taken to Père-Lachaise to receive its honours, but during the procession, 'the Fédérés stopped the cortège and placed the corpse at the foot of the July column; some men, torches in their hands, formed into a circle, and all the Fédérés, one after the other, came to place a last kiss on the brow of the general'.[5]

Wroblewski, likewise a career officer and a participant in the Warsaw insurrection, led the only counterattack during Bloody Week, from the Butte-aux-Cailles which he defended with the 101st battalion, 'all citizens of the 13th arrondissement and the Mouffetard quarter, undisciplined, undisciplinable, wild, rough, their clothes and flag torn, obeying only one order, that to march forward, mutineering when inactive, when hardly out of fire rendering it necessary to plunge them in again'.[6]

Thanks to plaques showing where those who were shot or deported lived and met, it is possible to sketch the outline of a Resistance Paris, northeast of a line running from the Porte de Clignancourt to the Porte de Vincennes, passing through the Gare Saint-Lazare, the République and the Bastille, and spilling broadly out into the banlieue, from Saint-Ouen and Gennevilliers to Montreuil and Ivry.

If certain places are ambivalent in this respect – such as the Latin Quarter where Cavaillès could frequent the same café as Carcopino, or Saint-Germain where Antelme could have passed (and greeted?) Drieu La Rochelle in Rue Jacob – the other Paris, that of the Germans and their collaborators, closely corresponds to what it is customary to call the *beaux quartiers*. The Kommandantur Gross-Paris was on Place de l'Opéra, at the corner of Rue du Quatre-Septembre. The Gestapo had its headquarters in a private hotel on Avenue Foch, close to the Porte Dauphine, with a number of offices across the city, the most important of these being on Rue des Saussaies, in the premises of the Sûreté Générale. Its French

---

4   Louise Michel, *La Commune, histoire et souvenirs* (Paris: La Découverte, 1999).
5   Prosper-Olivier Lissagaray, *A History of the Paris Commune of 1871*, trans. Eleanor Marx.
6   Ibid. Wroblewski managed to escape from this hell, reached London and joined the General Council of the International.

acolytes, the notorious Bonny and Lafont, established themselves on Rue Lauriston, near the Trocadéro. For some people, the very words Rue Lauriston or Rue des Saussaies still raise a shudder: 'Certain streets in Paris are as degraded as a man covered with infamy,' as Balzac wrote at the start of *Ferragus*. The Propaganda-Staffel, where Ernst Jünger worked, was in the Hôtel Majestic, on Rue Dumont-d'Urville near the Étoile. General Speidel stayed at the Hôtel George-V. The pass office was a couple of steps away, on Rue Galilée. The German military tribunal[7] was on Rue Boissy-d'Anglas, and the recruitment office for the Waffen SS on Avenue Victor-Hugo. The (French) commissariat for Jewish affairs was on Rue des Petits-Pères, behind Place des Victoires. Brinon, 'Paris delegate of the vice-president of the council of ministers', had his offices in the Hôtel Matignon, and he lived in a 'little palace' on Avenue Foch.[8]

'When I think that I passed on my way the church of Saint-Roch, on the steps of which César Birotteau was wounded, and that at the corner of Rue des Prouvaires the pretty salesgirl Baret took Casanova's measurements in the back of her shop, and that these are just two tiny facts in an ocean of real or fantastic events – I am overwhelmed by a kind of joyous melancholy, a painful pleasure', Jünger wrote on 10 May 1943. Few Parisians would have been capable of such a diary entry, so disenchanted and accurate. But Jünger also limited his customary itineraries to the elegant quarters of the Right Bank and the Faubourg Saint-Germain. He stayed at the Raphaël on Avenue Kléber, and frequented such luxury establishments as the Pâtisserie Ladurée on Rue Royale (3 June 1941), the Ritz, 'along with Carl Schmitt who gave a lecture yesterday on the significance, from the point of view of public law, of the distinction between land and sea' (18 October 1941), and the Brasserie-Lorraine on the Place des Ternes, 'after returning up Rue du Faubourg-Saint-Honoré where I always experience a feeling of well-being' (18 January 1942). He dined at Prunier's (6 March 1942), at Lapérouse's (8 April 1942), at Maxim's ('where I was invited by the Morands. We spoke among other things of American novels, in particular *Moby Dick* and *A High Wind in Jamaica*': 7 June 1942), and at the Tour d'Argent 'where Henri IV

---

7   The French authorities, for their part, had established special sections attached to the appeal courts to judge those arrested by the French police for 'any offence promoting communism, anarchy, social and national subversion, or rebellion against the legally established social order'. The Paris special section had its offices in the Palais de Justice.

8   'At midday, with Speidel, to Brinon's embassy on the corner of Rue Rude and Avenue Foch. The little palace where he received us is said to belong to his wife who is Jewish, which did not prevent him from making fun of "*youpins*" at the lunch table' (Ernst Jünger, 8 October 1942, *Journal de guerre* [Paris: Christian Bourgois, 1979–80]).

already ate heron pâté' (4 July 1942). He walked to the Bagatelle, where a French woman friend told him how 'students are now being arrested for wearing yellow stars with various inscriptions such as "idealist" ... These individuals do not yet know that the time for discussion has passed. They also imagine that the adversary has a sense of humour' (14 June 1942).

In the western part of the city, therefore, cultivated German officers, Francophile and even anti-Nazi, signed orders for the execution of young people who, in the eastern part, were making posters and throwing leaflets in the Ménilmontant cinemas.[9]

The Champs-Élysées was the major axis of Paris collaboration, following an established tradition. Back in 1870, Louise Michel noted how café chairs and counters were broken there, after they had been the only cafés in Paris to open to the Prussians.[10] After the Popular Front, 'the elegant crowd acclaimed Hitler in the Champs-Élysées cinemas at 20 francs a seat ... The culmination of ignominy was perhaps reached in 1938, on this *cagoulard* Champs-Élysées where elegant ladies acclaimed Daladier's horrendous triumph and squealed: "Communists, pack your bags; Jews, off to Jerusalem".' Later on, 'the whole *cagoulard* elite of the country, hurrying back to its Champs-Élysées and its Boulevard Malesherbes, went into ecstasy over the politeness of the big blond Aryans. On this point there was only one cry from Auteuil to Monceau: the gentleman-executioners were correct, and even men of the world in their own way.'[11] The changing of the Wehrmacht guard took place on the Champs-Élysées every day for four years: at midday, starting from the Rond-Point, the new guard paraded to music up to the Étoile, where it passed in review, before dispersing to the palaces of the general staff.

This political division of Paris goes back a long way. On 20 May 1871, just before the Versaillais entered Paris, Lissagaray took an imaginary friend, 'one of the most timid men from the timid provinces', on a walk through the city. In the popular quarters – on the Place de la Bastille, 'gay, animated by the gingerbread fair', at the Cirque Napoléon (Cirque d'Hiver) where five thousand people filled the place from the arena to the dome – the revolutionary festival continued despite (or because of?)

---

9 Jünger, on the Propaganda-Staffel, did not have to sign such orders, but Heinrich von Stülpnagel, the general in command, with his 'nice way of smiling' (ibid., 10 March 1942) and his great knowledge of Byzantine history, did indeed – though he committed suicide after the bomb attempt on Hitler in July 1944.
10 Michel, *La Commune, histoire et souvenirs*.
11 Vladimir Jankélévitch, 'Dans l'honneur et la dignité', *Les Temps modernes*, June 1948.

imminent catastrophe. The fashionable quarters were silent, plunged in darkness – even though, by an irony of fate, it was here that the shells fired by the Versaillais from Mont Valérien and Courbevoie fell, and the arch of the Arc de Triomphe had to be walled in against the gunfire coming up the Champs-Élysées. Their inhabitants, who only yesterday had animated the salons of the Empire, in the Tuileries and at Compiègne, expressed their feelings with no beating about the bush. Edmond de Goncourt, in the first few days: 'The quay and the two large streets leading to the Hôtel de Ville are closed by barricades, with lines of National Guard in front of them. One reacts with disgust at the sight of their stupid and abject faces, on which triumph and drunkenness have the shine of a radiant villainy.'[12] And later, while Thiers was bombarding Paris: 'Still waiting for the attack, for the deliverance that does not come. It is impossible to depict the suffering we experience, amid the despotism on the streets of this scum disguised as soldiers.'[13]

For Maxime Du Camp, awarded the cross of the Légion d'Honneur for his conduct at the time of the 'criminal insurrection' of June 1848, the Commune was 'a fit of moral epilepsy; a bloody bacchanalia; a debauchery of petroleum and cheap spirits; a tempest of violence and drunkenness that made the capital of France into the most abject of swamps'.[14] For Théophile Gautier:

> Under all the great cities there are dens for lions, cellars sealed with thick bars in which savage, stinking, poisonous beasts are kept, all the refractory perversities that civilization has been unable to tame, those who love blood, those who enjoy real fires as if they were fireworks, those with the taste for theft, those for whom an assault on modesty represents love … One day it so happened that the distracted keeper forgot the keys to the menagerie doors, and the wild animals spread out across the city with savage cries. It was from these opened cages that the hyenas of 1793 and the gorillas of the Commune broke loose.[15]

Two subjects aroused particular hatred: women, and Gustave Courbet. Arsène Houssaye held that 'with a kick to their skirts we should cast into the hell of malediction all these horrible creatures who have dishonoured

---

12   E. & J. de Goncourt, *Journal*, 19 March 1871.
13   Ibid., 15 May 1871.
14   Du Camp, *Les Convulsions de Paris*.
15   Cited in *Les Reporters de l'Histoire. 1871: la Commune de Paris* (Paris: Liana Levi / Sylvie Messinger, 1983). Quotations without other reference in the following pages are taken from this book.

women in the saturnalias and impieties of the Commune'. For another writer:

> Their women, these nameless harpies, roamed the streets of Paris for a whole week, pouring petrol into cellars and lighting fires everywhere. They are hunted down with muskets like the wild beasts that they are . . .[16] This infamous Courbet, who wanted to burn the Louvre museum, not only deserves to be shot if he has not been already, but the filthy pictures that he sold to the state should also be destroyed.

It was Leconte de Lisle who expressed himself in these terms. And Barbey d'Aurevilly, in *Le Figaro* for 18 April 1872:

> The atrocious bandits of the Commune, with Monsieur Courbet as their clown, are not political enemies. They are the enemies of any society and any order. Can you say what their political ideal is? Of course not! Any more than you can say what is Monsieur Courbet's aesthetic ideal. Their ideal is to steal, and to kill and burn if need be, just as his ideal is to brutally paint the concrete fact, the vulgar and even abject detail.

In the great tradition of intelligence with the enemy against Red Paris, the Versaillais right were collaborators. The same men who pressed for the capitulation of Paris in the face of an army of inferior numbers, begged the Prussians to assist them against the Commune. Bazaine, under siege in Metz, wrote to Bismarck that his army was the only force that could control the anarchy – and indeed, it was the arrival of prisoners freed by the Prussians that gave the Versaillais, from the first days of May, a decisive advantage. On 10 March, even before the uprising of the Commune, Jules Favre wrote to Thiers:

> We have decided to put an end to the strongholds of Montmartre and Belleville, and we hope this will be done without spilling blood. This evening, judging a second category of those accused for the events of 31 October, the council of war condemned Flourens, Blanqui, and Levrault

---

16   Nor were children forgotten here: 'All these stunted and unhealthy creatures, half wolf and half ferret, who have been prematurely depraved by a free collective life that poorly inspired poets have sought to glorify [Victor Hugo!], who draw the etymology of their common name from the public way where they roam like errant dogs, all these "*voyous*", in a word, threw themselves into battle with the curiosity, recklessness and impetus of their age' (Du Camp, *Les Convulsions de Paris*).

to the death penalty in their absence; and Vallès, present, to six months in prison. Tomorrow morning, I shall go to Ferrières to meet with the Prussian authorities on a number of points of detail.[17]

Flaubert, though very hostile to the Commune, wrote to George Sand on 31 March: 'Many conservatives who wanted to preserve the republic [in 1851] will regret Badinguet. And call on the Prussians with all their hearts.' And on 30 April: '"Thank God the Prussians are here" is the universal cry of the bourgeoisie.' In *Le Drapeau tricolore* for 2 May, you could read that the Germans were 'good people who are slandered. The rumour went round, a week ago, that they were leaving. No more Prussians, no more police, no more order, no more security!' Collaboration did not stop at sentiments such as these, there was also military collaboration. The Fédérés believed that the Versaillais would not attack from the side held by the Prussians.[18] But the Prussians who occupied the northern and eastern forts let the Versaillais advance in a sector that was forbidden them by the armistice, thus enabling them to seize the defences of Paris from behind.

When it was all over, in September, Francisque Sarcey noted that

> the bourgeoisie found themselves, not without a certain melancholy, between the Prussian feet on their throat and those whom they called the Reds, and could only see as men armed with daggers. I do not know which of these two evils frightened them most; they hated the foreigner more, but they feared more the people of Belleville.

This metonymy is justified if we take 'Belleville' in the broad sense, as stretching to Ménilmontant on the one side, to the Popincourt quarter and the Faubourg du Temple on the other, and spilling into the 10th arrondissement along the Canal Saint-Martin. The central committee of the National Guard was formed at two popular meetings held during the siege, the first at the Cirque d'Hiver and the second in the Wauxhall on Rue de la Douane (now Léon-Jouhaux) close to the canal – in the course of which Garibaldi was appointed an honorary general of the National Guard by popular acclamation. It was in front of the *mairie* of the 12th

---

17   Cited by Michel, *La Commune, histoire et souvenirs*.
18   'If only the Commune had listened to my warnings! I advised its members to fortify the northern side of the heights of Montmartre, the Prussian side, and they still had time to do this; I told them beforehand that they would otherwise be caught in a trap . . .' Karl Marx, letter to E. S. Beesly, 12 June 1871.

arrondissement that the guillotine was burned by the 137th battalion, in a great moment of joy – 'that shameful machine of human butchery', as Louise Michel called it. This Red Paris was constantly crossed by fighters on their way to the forts:

> Like figures in a dream, the Commune's battalions went past – Flourens's Vengeurs, the Commune's *zouaves*, the Fédéré scouts who looked like Spanish guerrilleros, the Enfants Perdus who leapt from trench to trench with such gusto, the Commune's Turcos, the Montmartre terrors.[19]

It is true that the Commune began not in Belleville but Montmartre. This was where the artillery of the National Guard had been parked, at the top of Rue des Rosiers (now du Chevalier-de-la-Barre). Victor Hugo relates this first confrontation in his inimitable fashion. He was in Brussels, having resigned his seat in the Chamber of Deputies – that 'assembly of rurals' who booed and manhandled him in Bordeaux when he defended Garibaldi, and 'at the first session, could not make himself heard, the abuse drowning his voice when he offered his sons to the Republic'.[20]

> The moment chosen is a dreadful one.
> But was the moment really chosen?
> Chosen by whom?
> Let us examine the matter.
> Who acted on 18 March?
> Was it the Commune?
> No. The Commune didn't exist.
> Was it the central committee of the National Guard?
> No. This seized the opportunity, but did not create it.
> So who acted on 18 March?
> It was the National Assembly; or strictly speaking, its majority.
> An attenuating circumstance is that it did not act deliberately.
> The majority and its government simply wanted to remove the cannon from Montmartre. A small motive for such a great risk.
> That's it. Remove the cannon from Montmartre.
> That was the idea; how did they set about it?
> Cleverly.
> Montmartre was asleep. Soldiers were sent in the night to seize the cannon. When the cannon were seized, it was realized that they had to

19   Michel, *La Commune, histoire et souvenirs*.
20   Ibid.

be taken away. This needed horses. How many? A thousand! Where to find them? No one had thought about that. What to do? Send people to look for them. Time passed, the day broke, Montmartre woke up; the people came running and wanted their cannon; they had almost stopped thinking about them, but because the cannon had been seized, they demanded them; the soldiers gave in, the cannon were taken back, an insurrection broke out, a revolution began.

Who did that, then?

The government, without wanting to or knowing what it was doing.

This innocent party really is guilty.[21]

Louise Michel expressed the spirit that prevailed in Montmartre during these weeks better than anyone else.[22] During the siege by the Prussians, 'Montmartre, the *mairie*, the vigilance committees, the clubs and inhabitants, were along with Belleville the nightmare of the party of Order'. The vigilance committee of the 18th arrondissement met at 41 Chaussée de Clignancourt, 'where we warmed ourselves more often with the fire of ideas than with logs'. When Louise chaired the meetings, either there or at the club La Patrie en Danger, or again at the Reine-Blanche, she had beside her 'on the desk a little old pistol without a hammer, which, positioned right and grasped at the right moment, often stopped the Order crowd'. During the Commune, she only left Montmartre to go and fight at the fortifications. She read Baudelaire with a student in a trench outside Clamart while the bullets were whistling past, she shot with the defenders of the fortress of Issy ('The fortress is magnificent, a spectral fortress ... I spend a good part of the time with the gunners, we've been visited there by Victorine Eudes ... she also doesn't shoot badly'), she worked with an ambulance 'in the trenches of the Hautes-Bruyères, where I got to know Paintendre, the commander of the Enfants Perdus. If ever that name was justified, it is by him, by all of them; they were so bold that it no longer seemed possible they could be killed':

On 22 May, when all was lost, the Fédérés of the 61st battalion joined us at the *mairie* [of the 18th arrondissement]. 'Come with us', they said to me, 'we're going to die, you were with us on the first day, you must be with us on the last.' ... I set off with the detachment to the Montmartre cemetery, where we took up our position. Although there

21   Victor Hugo, letter to C. Vacquerie, Brussels, 28 April 1871.
22   All the following quotations are taken from Michel, *La Commune, histoire et souvenirs*.

were very few of us, we thought we could hold out a good while. In some places we had crenellated the walls by hand. Shells struck the cemetery with increasing frequency . . . This time the shell fell close to me, coming down through the branches and covering me with flowers, close to Murger's tomb. The white figure throwing marble flowers on this tomb made a charming effect . . . There were ever fewer of us; we fell back on the barricades, which still held out. The women passed by, red flag at their head; they had their barricade on the Place Blanche . . . More than ten thousand women fought for freedom in those May days, mixed or together.

At the moment when the Versaillais entered Paris, a remarkable turnaround took place. The Fédérés, tired of being pinned down in the forts and trenches, were almost happy to find themselves back on their home ground, in their cobbled streets. Delescluze,[23] who a few days before had been appointed delegate for war, drafted a declaration on 22 May which the Barcelona anarchists of summer 1936 would not have disavowed:

> Enough of militarism! No more staff-officers with their gold-embroidered uniforms! Make way for the people, for the combatants bare-armed! The hour of the revolutionary war has struck . . . The people know nothing of learned manoeuvres. But when they have a gun in their hands,

---

23 Charles Delescluze was a law student when he was wounded in 1830 in a republican uprising. He took part in all the insurrectional *journées* under the July monarchy, and had to go into exile in Belgium until 1840. In 1848, having sided with the June insurgents, he was sentenced to a fine of 11,000 francs and three years in prison for articles against Cavaignac and the massacres. After staying in England, he returned secretly to Paris in 1853, was captured, deported to Belle-Île in Corsica and then to Cayenne. After his return in 1860, he founded *Le Réveil*, whose first issue brought him a fine and a further prison sentence. In August 1870 he was once more imprisoned, and his paper suspended, for having protested against the declaration of war. With the fall of the Empire he was elected mayor of the 19th arrondissement, but resigned in protest at the cowardice of the provisional government. The failure of the January 1871 uprising led once more to the suspension of his paper and his imprisonment, but with the legislative elections he was triumphantly elected in Paris with over 150,000 votes. During the Commune, he was one of the few representatives of the 'Jacobin' tendency to take the side of the revolution against that of the Assembly, of Paris against Versailles – as opposed to Ledru-Rollin, Louis Blanc, and Schoelcher. Elected to the council of the Commune by the 9th and 19th arrondissements, he resigned his seat in the Assembly. He was on the commission for foreign relations, the committee of public safety, and finally, on 11 May, when the situation became critical, he agreed to become the delegate for war.

and paving-stones under their feet, they fear not all the strategists of the monarchical school.[24]

The barricades sprung up with all haste.

That of Rue de Rivoli, which was to protect the Hôtel de Ville, was erected at the entrance of the Place Saint-Jacques, at the corner of Rue Saint-Denis. Fifty workmen did the mason-work, while swarms of children brought wheelbarrows full of earth from the square ... In the 9th arrondissement, Rues Auber, de la Chaussée-d'Antin, de Châteaudun, the crossroads of the Faubourg Montmartre, of Notre-Dame-de-Lorette, la Trinité and Rue des Martyrs were being unpaved. The broad approaches, La Chapelle, Buttes-Chaumont, Belleville, Ménilmontant, Rue de la Roquette, the Bastille, the Boulevards Voltaire and Richard-Lenoir, the Place du Château-d'Eau [now Place de la République], the Grands Boulevards especially from the Porte Saint-Denis; and on the Left Bank the whole length of the Boulevard Saint-Michel, the Panthéon, Rue Saint-Jacques, the Gobelins, and the principal avenues of the 13th arrondissement.

'On the Place Blanche,' Maroteau wrote the following day in *Le Salut public*, 'there was a barricade completely constructed and defended by a women's battalion of around a hundred and twenty. At the moment that I arrived, a dark form detached itself from a carriage gate. It was a girl with a Phrygian bonnet over her ear, a musket in her hand, and a cartridge-belt at her waist: "Halt, citizen, you don't pass here." '[25]

But the majority of these fragile barricades were quickly taken. The Commune had to evacuate the Hôtel de Ville, and the fighting focused around the Place du Château-d'Eau and the Bastille. The Versaillais 'went to occupy the Saint-Laurent barricade at the junction of the Boulevard Sébastopol, erected batteries against the Château d'Eau, and reached the Quai Valmy by the Rue des Récollets ... In the 3rd arrondissement they were stopped in the Rue Meslay, Rue Nazareth, Rue du Vert-Bois, Rue Charlot and Rue de Saintonge. The 2nd arrondissement, invaded from all sides, was still disputing its Rue Montorgueil.' On 26 May, in the Place de la Bastille, 'at seven o'clock the presence of soldiers at the top of the faubourg was announced. The Fédérés hurried thither with their cannon. If they do not hold out, the Bastille will be taken. They did hold out. The

---

24   Cited from Lissagaray, *A History of the Paris Commune.*
25   Ibid.

Rue d'Aligre and the Avenue Lacuée vied with each other in devotion ...
The house at the corner of the Rue de la Roquette, the angle of the Rue
de Charenton, disappeared like the scenery of a theatre.'[26]

What remained of the Commune and the central committee fell back on
the *mairie* of the 11th arrondissement. On the steps of the staircase, women
silently sewed sacks for the barricades. In the main hall, the Commune was
in session: 'Everyone mingled together, officers, ordinary guards, NCOs of
various ranks, belts with white or yellow tassels, members of the Commune
or the central committee – and all took part in the deliberations.'[27] In this
dramatic confusion, it was Delescluze who spoke. Everyone listened in
silence, for the slightest whisper would have drowned out his almost lost
voice.

When Oscar Wilde was asked what had been the saddest event of his
life, he replied that it was the death of Lucien de Rubempré in *Scenes from
a Courtesan's Life*. If I had to answer the same question, I would choose the
death of Delescluze on the barricade of the Château d'Eau. In the account
Lissagaray gives, he rises to the level of Plutarch:

> He said all was not lost; that they must make a great effort, and hold out
> to the last ... 'I propose', said he, 'that the members of the Commune,
> engirdled with their scarfs, shall make a review of all the battalions that
> can be assembled on the Boulevard Voltaire. We shall then at their head
> proceed to the points to be conquered.' The idea appeared grand, and
> transported those present ... The distant firing, the cannon of the Père-
> Lachaise, the confused clamours of the battalions surrounding the *mairie*,
> blended with, and at times drowned his voice. Behold, in the midst of
> this defeat, this old man upright, his eyes luminous, his right hand raised
> defying despair, these armed men fresh from the battle suspending their
> breath to listen to this voice which seemed to ascend from the tomb.
> There was no scene more solemn in the thousand tragedies of that day.

Of course, things very quickly took a turn for the worse:

> The Place du Château-d'Eau was ravaged as by a cyclone ... At a
> quarter to seven ... was saw Delescluze, Jourde, and about a hundred
> Fédérés marching in the direction of the Château-d'Eau. Delescluze
> wore his ordinary dress, black hat, coat, and trousers, his red scarf,
> inconspicuous as was his wont, tied round his waist. Without arms,

---

26   Ibid.
27   Vallès, *L'Insurgé*.

he leant on a cane. Apprehensive of some panic at the Château-d'Eau, we followed the delegate. Some of us stopped at the Saint-Ambroise church to get arms … Vermorel, wounded by the side of Lisbonne, whom Theisz and Jaclard were carrying off on a litter, leaving behind him large drops of blood. We thus remained a little behind Delescluze. At about eight yards from the barricade the guards who accompanied him kept back, for the projectiles obscured the entrance of the boulevard.

Delescluze still walked forward. Behold the scene; we have witnessed it; let it be engraved in the annals of history. The sun was setting. The old exile, unmindful whether he was followed, still advanced at the same pace, the only living being on the road. Arrived at the barricade, he bent off to the left and mounted upon the paving-stones. For the last time his austere face, framed in his white beard, appeared to us turned towards death. Suddenly Delescluze disappeared. He had fallen as if thunderstruck on the Place du Château-d'Eau.

Just to make sure, the Versaillais had him condemned to death in his absence in 1874.

The two last days, Saturday 27 and Sunday 28 May, in superb weather, Red Paris was slowly reduced to the Faubourg du Temple. On Saturday evening, the Versaillais were installed on the Place de Fêtes, Rue Fessart, and Rue Pradier as far as Rue Rébeval, where they were contained. The Fédérés occupied a quadrilateral between Rue du Faubourg-du-Temple, Rue de la Folie-Méricourt, Rue de la Roquette and Boulevard Belleville. By Sunday morning, resistance was reduced to the small square formed by the Rues du Faubourg-du-Temple, des Trois-Bornes, des Trois-Couronnes, and the Boulevard de Belleville. Which was the last of the Commune's barricades to hold out? In Lissagaray's account, it was that on Rue Ramponeau: 'For a quarter of an hour, this was defended by a single Fédéré. Three times he broke the pole of the Versaillais flag displayed on the barricade of Rue de Paris [now de Belleville]. As reward for his courage, this last Commune soldier managed to escape.' Legend has it that this was Lissagaray himself. For others, the last barricade was on Rue Rébeval. But that most often cited is that on Rue de la Fontaine-au-Roi. Louise Michel:

An immense red flag floated over the barricade. The two Ferré's were there, Théophile and Hippolyte, J. B. Clément, the Garibaldian Cambon, Varlin, Vermorel, Champy. The barricade on Rue

Saint-Maur had just fallen, that on Rue de la Fontaine-au-Roi stubbornly held, spitting fire in the bloody face of the Versaillais ... The only ones still standing, when the Père-Lachaise cannon fell silent, were those of Fontaine-au-Roi. At the moment that they fired their last shots, a young girl coming from the barricade on Rue Saint-Maur arrived, offering to help. They told her to go away from this place of death, but she remained despite them. It was to this ambulance girl of the last barricade and the last hour that J. B. Clément dedicated, much later, his song *Le Temps des Cérises*.

When you think of the Commune, the first image is that of the barricade, although the 'magic cobbles' only arose in the last week of its brief existence. But if the Commune became a paradigm of revolution in its purest form, it was by the way it faced death on the barricades rather than by the measures it took, however strong their political and poetic charge. The barricade, in fact, had never been effective as a fighting instrument. In the ascending phase of uprisings, erected in a few minutes with whatever came to hand – an upturned cart, a couple of cupboards, a few barrels hoisted onto a heap of paving-stones – it was not defended for long, but was there simply to impede the movement of regular troops, weighed down with their kit, and to make their horses stumble. When it became a major defensive work, like 'the Charybdis of the Faubourg Saint-Antoine and the Scylla of the Faubourg du Temple' in June 1848, described at the start of Volume Five of *Les Misérables*, or the gigantic redoubt constructed to block Rue de Rivoli at the level of Rue Saint-Florentin in May 1871, it only held out a few hours, as after June 1832 the forces of order no longer had any hesitation in using cannon.

Right from the start, the barricade played a role that doubled its fighting status with that of a stage set. A comic scene, when the fighters on both sides called out to one another, insulting each other as under the walls of Troy, or trying to convince the other side, either to capitulate before they were massacred, or, conversely, to join the ranks of their brothers. A tragic scene, *all' antica*, in which the hero descends from the barricade and walks alone towards the soldiers, in a final effort of persuasion or simply to avoid experiencing defeat, to end it along with life. It is this theatrical role of the barricade that explains its resurgence in the twentieth century, from St Petersburg to Barcelona, from Spartakist Berlin to Rue Gay-Lussac, even when its military effectiveness has fallen asymptotically over time to nearly zero.

The Birth of the Barricade

Even if several streets of Old Paris keep the memory of risings and insurrections, going back at least to Étienne Marcel, even if one could recall a 'Red' Paris stretching across centuries, I have decided to focus this narrative on the heyday of that great symbolic form of Parisian revolution that is the barricade, in other words on the nineteenth century.

The barricade made its reappearance in Paris in the late 1820s, after two centuries of absence. There had been time to forget the 'day of the barricades' in May 1588, when, against the troops that Henri III had deployed in the city, 'all men hastily took up arms, set out through the streets and sections, and in no time brought chains and made barricades at the street corners'.[28] Far back too were the barricades of the Fronde, erected on an August night in 1648, which Cardinal de Retz describes in terms strangely familiar for anyone who has read Lissagaray:

> The movement was like a sudden and violent fire, which spread from the Pont-Neuf to the whole city. Everyone without exception took up arms. You could see boys of five or six years with daggers in their hands, and mothers who brought these themselves. In Paris there were more than twelve hundred barricades in less than two hours, decorated with flags and with all the weapons that the League had left intact.

Since then, there had indeed been the barricades of the Faubourg Saint-Antoine during the days of Prairial, but this was not much in the great annals of revolutionary events. And if Chateaubriand noted in his *Memoirs* that 'for the rest, the barricades are retrenchments that belong to the Paris spirit: they are found in all our disturbances, from Charles V to our own day', there was none the less a long hiatus in the history of the barricade between the baroque and the romantic age.

The barricade made its reappearance on 19 November 1827.[29] This was an election day. Two weeks previously, had dissolved the Chamber of Deputies and named seventy-six new peers so as to keep control of the upper house. The Liberal opposition won a great success in Paris. On the evening of the

28   Pierre de L'Estoile, *Journal pour le règne de Henri III*.
29   See Alain Corbin and Jean-Marc Mayeur (eds), *La Barricade*, proceedings of a colloquium organized on 17–18 March 1995 by the Centre de Recherches en Histoire du XIXe Siècle and the Société d'Histoire de la Révolution de 1848 et des Révolutions du XIXe Siècle (Paris: Publications de la Sorbonne, 1997). The following unreferenced quotations are taken from this work.

18th, the newly elected deputies held banquets and lit up their windows. The director-general of the police warned his prefect: 'Since it is possible that the movement led by the revolutionaries may go further than we had envisaged, I urge that preparations be made to suppress any disorder ... I have arranged with the major of the royal guard that three hundred cavalry will remain on duty to be available as soon as they are needed.' And indeed, on the evening of the 19th, in Rue Saint-Denis, a police informer noted that 'rockets and petards are being thrown on the public way; men, mainly sales clerks, are walking about with an unfurled umbrella in their hand, topped with a lighted candle. Every now and then, musket or pistol shots can be heard fired from within buildings; in a word, in the streets above mentioned where the crowd is assembled, there is a repetition of all the scandalous scenes that took place when the law on the license of the press was withdrawn.' At ten in the evening the crowd attacked a police station on the Rue Mauconseil. The prefect sent fifty mounted police to disperse them. The officer in command later explained to the commission of inquiry that 'when the troops arrived, they found Rue Saint-Denis without cobbles in many places, and four barricades in succession, behind which a large number of bad characters had assembled, armed with stones'. From the tallest barricade, where the Passage du Grand-Cerf opens into Rue Saint-Denis, came a hail of bullets. The police finally reestablished order. In withdrawing, they fired into Rue aux Ours and wounded several people including a twenty-two-year-old student, Auguste Blanqui, who received a bullet in the neck.

The following evening, several bands again roamed Rue Saint-Denis and its surroundings. The investigation of the high court indicated that

> unknown individuals broke into the houses under construction in front of the Saint-Leu church and the Passage du Grand-Cerf, removing the fences; to erect barricades they seized tools and materials that had been used the previous day and which had been locked up in the houses instead of being taken away. The new barricades were constructed with greater care and intelligence than the day before. This work, performed by young people mostly between fifteen and eighteen, continued for two hours without meeting any obstacle, or any public force being commissioned to prevent it.

At eleven o'clock, Colonel de Fitz-James, who commanded the regular troops, reached Rue Saint-Denis via Rue Greneta:

> At a distance of about fifty yards we perceived a strong barricade, from behind which the crowd's shouts could be heard, and before we could

clearly make out the insults and provocations, stones began to reach the advance squad and gave us positive warning of the intentions of those behind the barricades.

The troops fired and killed four people. The adjacent streets were cleared by cavalry. *Le Journal des débats* for the next day, 21 November, deemed that the forces of order had shown insufficient vigour: 'It is impossible to regret too much that this mob were not hunted down and arrested by the troops.' But the prefect of police maintained that 'the events of this evening inspired in the quarter a salutary fear that we must hope will prevent the return of similar disorders'.

This hope was not to be realized. In the course of the half-century between the anonymous nighttime barricades of November 1827 and the seventy sunny days of the Commune, the list of Paris demonstrations, riots, coups, uprisings and insurrections is so long that no other capital can claim anything similar. Their geography, and their distribution between the quarters of Paris, reflects the industrial revolution, the new relationship between bosses and workers, the centrifugal migration of the labouring and dangerous population, the development of major works, and the 'strategic embellishment' of the city. The same street names, and the same quarters, return constantly throughout the century, but we do see the centre of gravity of Red Paris shift slowly to the north and east, with interruptions and accelerations that stamp on the map of the city the mark of an old notion now fallen into disrepute, that of class struggle.

The unfurling of Paris insurrections in the nineteenth century is well known, but the story is often presented as a succession of *images d'Épinal* – Delacroix and his *Liberty*, Lamartine with his tricolour, Hugo's *Chastisements* and his rock, Gambetta's balloon. This constructs an ideal republican genealogy, complete with names of Métro stations and fictionalized biographies, which gives a reassuring version of what was in reality a series of bloody and pitiless confrontations. The care taken to give all this the most bowdlerized presentation is still more manifest today, when, in the name of rejecting the archaic, we are pressed to abandon the 'dusty philosophical and cultural corpus' of the nineteenth century.[30] I shall try to retrace the stages of this insurrectionary history, limiting myself to what happened in the streets and quarters of Red Paris, but without forgetting that these events served as

---

30 As described by Jacques Rancière, *On the Shores of Politics* (London: Verso, 2007), p. 5.

calls to action for the whole of Europe, as theoretical models and reasons for hope.

On 27 July 1830, the day after the publication of decrees on the press and the electoral law, the police turned up at *Le Temps*, on Rue de Richelieu, to break up the presses.[31] The printers in this quarter, fearing unemployment, dismissed their workers:

> The printing workers never worked on Mondays. Now, it was precisely Monday 26 July that they learned of the publication of decrees that deprived them of bread by undermining the freedom of the press ... They left the city, spread out beyond the barriers and dined in the taverns there, with the avowed intention of neglecting nothing to move the minds of builders, carpenters, locksmiths and other workers.[32]

The following day they mingled with students, including those of the École Polytechnique, crying: 'Down with Polignac!' At the Palais-Royal, stones were thrown at the gendarmes. An infantry company opened fire on the crowd; one demonstrator fell. Immediately, men surged forward as if from nowhere and seized the body, which they paraded with cries of revenge. The inflamed crowd began to raid the armourers, and erected a barricade on Rue de Richelieu. Yet by the evening Paris seemed calm, the deputies had gone to ground, there seemed to be neither leaders nor organizations. These appeared during the night. The Carbonari and officers on half-pay formed twelve directing committees, seized and distributed weapons and took control of the Imprimerie Royale. On the morning of the 28th, the royal army found itself facing on the barricades former soldiers of the Empire who taught the Parisians how to fight. Paris was at boiling point:

> They dragged down and burnt the arms of France; they hung them from the cords of broken street-lamps; they tore the fleur-de-lis badges from

---

31 'The first decree established the suppression of press freedom in its various forms; it was the quintessence of all that had been elaborated in the cubbyholes of the police department over fifteen years. The second decree reworked the electoral laws. Thus the two primary freedoms, the freedom of the press and electoral freedom, were radically harmed; this emanated not from an iniquitous though legal action of a corrupt legislative authority, but by decree, as in the days of royal whim' (François-René de Chateaubriand, *Memoirs*, Book 31, chapter 8).

32 Letter from a Paris bookseller of the time, cited in Paul Chauvet, *Les Ouvriers du livre en France, de 1789 à la constitution de la Fédération du livre* (Paris: PUF, 1956).

the postmen's uniforms; the notaries took down their escutcheons, the bailiffs removed their badges, the carriers their official signs, the Royal suppliers their warrants. Those who had previously covered their oil-painted Napoleonic eagles with Bourbon lilies in distemper only needed a sponge to wipe out their loyalty; nowadays empires and gratitude are effaced with a little water.[33]

At midday, the state of siege was proclaimed. Marshal Marmont, major-general of the guard, 'a man of intellect and merit, a brave soldier, and a wise but unlucky general, proved for the thousandth time that military ability is insufficient to handle civil disturbances; any police officer would have had a better idea than he what should be done ... He had only a handful of men with him, but devised a plan which would have needed thirty thousand soldiers for its execution.'[34] This plan was to send four columns out from the Louvre: one via the boulevards towards the Bastille, another to the same destination but along the quays, an intermediary column towards the Innocents market (Les Halles) and a fourth up Rue Saint-Denis.[35] 'As they advanced, the communications posts established en route, being too weakly defended and too far apart, were isolated by the mob, and separated from one another by fallen trees and barricades.'[36]

On the morning of the 29th, a column of insurgents left the Panthéon in the direction of the Louvre, defended by the Swiss guards. Along the way, two regular regiments who were occupying the Place Vendôme went over to the side of the people. Marmont was forced to remove guards from the Louvre. Students scaled the façade, the Swiss retreated, and Marmont's forces surged back in disorder towards the Champs-Élysées. Charles X had to flee, for, as Benjamin Constant replied to emissaries seeking a compromise: 'I will only say that it would be all too convenient for a king to open fire on his subjects and then be quit of it by claiming: *He did nothing.* The statue of Henri IV on the Pont-Neuf held a tricolour flag, like

33   Chateaubriand, *Memoirs*, Book 32, ch. 3.
34   Ibid. Tocqueville criticized General Bedeau in 1848 in the following terms: 'I have always noted that the men who most easily lose their head and generally show themselves the weakest in days of revolution are men of war.'
35   Dubech and D'Espezel (*Histoire de Paris*, Paris, 1926) note that the route of Marmont's three main columns corresponds to the course of the major works undertaken by Rambuteau under Louis-Philippe: widening and levelling of the boulevards, cutting of Rue Rambuteau to connect the Innocents to the Bastille, and improvement of the quays along the Seine. Haussmann did not invent the 'strategic embellishment' of Paris.
36   Chateaubriand, *Memoirs*, Book 32, chapter 3.

a standard-bearer of the League. Men of the people said, looking at the bronze king: "You would never have done anything so stupid, you old rascal."[37]

A lithograph by Granville, titled *Révolution de 1830*, shows a clutch of terrifying beings – animals with nightmarish heads, dressed in bourgeois frock-coats – attacking a flight of stairs on top of which a bizarre creature is enthroned, apparently made up of banknotes. It bears the epigraph: 'The people are victorious, these gentlemen are sharing out the spoils.' The streets of Paris were not yet cleared of the heaped-up cobbles and felled trees, but the people were already expressing their discontent at the musical-chairs trick that had brought to the throne the 'best of republics' in the person of Louis-Philippe. On 6 August, a week after the fighting had ended, a procession of several thousand students, led by Ulysse Trélat and François Raspail, doctors to the poor, set out from the Latin Quarter to take an address to the Palais-Bourbon, refusing constituent power to the Chamber elected under Charles X.[38]

At the end of August, the Société des Amis du Peuple,[39] inspired by Trélat, sent a battalion to fight alongside the Belgian revolutionaries against the Dutch. In November, the students of the *grandes écoles* formed brigades to go and support the uprising in Warsaw.

On 21 September, an immense crowd came into the streets to commemorate the anniversary of the execution of Jean-François Borie and the three other sergeants of La Rochelle, executed on the Place de Grève eight years before. The new school year at the École Polytechnique was so agitated that the minister was forced to appoint François Arago, very popular with the students, as director of the school.

On 10 December, the funeral carriage of Benjamin Constant, drawn to Père-Lachaise by the students, was followed by all the republican leaders.

---

37   Ibid.
38   'The Nation ... cannot recognize as constituent power either an elective chamber appointed during the existence and under the influence of the dynasty that has been overthrown, or an aristocratic chamber which as an institution is directly opposed to the sentiments and principles that have put arms in its hand' (*La Révolution*, 8 August 1830, cited by Jeanne Gilmore, *La République clandestine, 1818–1848* [Paris: Aubier 1997]).
39   'There were present fifteen hundred men well packed together in a small hall which had the appearance of a theatre. The citizen Blanqui, son of a member of the Convention, made a long speech against the *bourgeoisie,* the shopmen who had elected as king Louis-Philippe, "*la boutique incarnée*", and that in their own interests, not in those of the people – *du peuple qui n'était pas complice d'une si indigne usurpation*. It was a speech full of wit, honesty and anger' (Heine, *Letters from Paris*).

Trélat gave a speech at the graveside: 'Friends of the people, let us all swear that our July days, so dearly bought by the lives of our brothers, will not be lost.'[40]

In December again, a riot broke out in front of the Luxembourg, where the trial of Charles X's ministers was under way. The crowd, who had liter-ally waited for days, expressed its fury at sentences limited to prison terms. The repression was violent. Those wounded included a law student aged twenty-two, Charles Delescluze.

On 13 February 1831, the Legitimists celebrated a mass at Saint-German-l'Auxerrois, for the anniversary of the assassination of the Duc de Berry. A collection was organized for the benefit of the Swiss guards wounded during the July days.[41] When news got round, the crowd invaded and sacked the church. The following day, the archbishop's residence was attacked and completely devastated. In *The Atheist's Mass*, a little masterpiece from 1836, Balzac used the event – a memorable one, therefore, even if Martin Nadaud sees it as a police provocation[42] – to date the meeting that serves as a coda to his story: 'At last, seven years later, after the Revolution of 1830, when the mob invaded the Archbishop's residence, when Republican agita-tors spurred them on to destroy the gilt crosses which flashed like streaks of lightning in the immensity of the ocean of houses; when Incredulity flaunted itself in the streets, side by side with Rebellion...' Following this explosion of anticlerical fury, the king was forced to remove the fleur-de-lis from the French coat of arms, and ceased attending mass in public. (But this was not without precedent: in January 1815 the people had ravaged the

---

40   Georges Weill, *Histoire du parti républicain en France, 1814–1870* (Paris: Alcan, 1928). Attending the funeral of Casimir Perier, who died of cholera in 1832, Heine wrote: 'My neighbours who saw the procession spoke of the obsequies of Benjamin Constant. As I have been only a year in Paris, I only know the grief which the people felt on that day from description. Yet I can imagine what such popular suffering must be, as I had not long before seen the burial of the former bishop of Blois, or the Grégoire of the Convention. There were, indeed, no grand officials, no infantry or cavalry... no cannon, no ambassadors with gay liveries, no official pomp. But the people wept. There was the suffering of sorrow on every face, and though it rained like bucketsful from heaven, all heads were uncovered, and the crowd harnessed itself before the hearse, and drew it to Montparnasse' (*Letters from Paris*, 12 May 1832).

41   'The Royalists, full of excellent qualities, but sometimes foolish and often provocative, never considering the consequences of their actions, always thinking to re-establish the Legitimacy by choosing to wear a coloured cravat or a flower in their buttonhole, caused deplorable scenes' (Chateaubriand, *Memoirs*, Book 34, chapter 2).

42   Martin Nadaud, *Léonard, maçon de la Creuse* (Bourganeuf, 1895; republished Paris: La Découverte, 1998).

church of Saint-Roch – where the priest had refused to conduct a funeral service for an actress of the Comédie-Française, Mlle Raucourt – to the cry of 'Death to the priests!')

7 September 1831 brought the capitulation of Warsaw, under siege by the troops of Paskievitch. When the news reached Paris, a crowd gathered on Boulevard des Capucines in front of the foreign ministry, to cries of 'Long live Poland! Down with the ministers!' Dispersed by dragoons, the rioters reached the Porte Saint-Denis, pillaging on their way an armourer on Boulevard Bonne-Nouvelle. The next day, barricades were erected on Boulevard Montmartre, and it took the troops and the National Guard three days to reestablish order.

Such agitation was constant. George Sand, who had been in Paris for a few weeks, wrote on 6 March 1831: 'It really is very funny. The revolution is in permanent session, like the Chamber; and we live as merrily, in the midst of bayonets, riots and ruins, as if there was complete peace.'[43] Political refugees flocked in from all countries where insurrections, launched in the wake of Paris, were crushed one after the other.[44] Casimir Perier, the energetic prime minister appointed after the Saint-Germain-l'Auxerrois affair, banished them to zones of residence where they were subject to all kinds of political harassment, and were not allowed to change their domicile or their employer without administrative authorization.

Early in 1832, just after the first insurrection of the Lyon silk-workers had been crushed by a regular army under the command of Marshal Soult, Paris was gripped by cholera. On 13 February, the disease struck down a porter in Rue des Lombards, then a little girl from Rue du Haut-Moulin on the Île de la Cité, then a street salesman on Rue des Jardins-Saint-Paul, then an egg-seller on Rue de la Mortellerie.[45] By March, some eight hundred people were dying each day. The nature of the disease and the way it spread were as mysterious as at the time of the Black Death five centuries earlier. After a study trip to London, Magendie decided that the disease was not contagious. At the Hôtel-Dieu, directed by Broussais – a

---

43 George Sand, *Correspondance* (Paris: Garnier), vol. 1.

44 'Brussels expelling the Nassaus as Paris did the Bourbons, Belgium offering herself to a French prince and giving herself to an English prince, the Russian hatred of Nicolas, behind us the demons of the South, Ferdinand in Spain, Miguel in Portugal, the earth quaking in Italy, Metternich extending his hand over Bologna, France treating Austria sharply at Ancona, at the North no one knew what sinister sound of the hammer nailing up Poland in her coffin . . .' (Hugo, *Les Misérables*, Volume Four, book 1, chapter 4).

45 Chevalier, introduction to *Classes laborieuses et classes dangereuses*.

convinced republican but a dangerous doctor – the mortality was frightful. The hearse of his most famous patient, Casimir Perier, took with it the master's 'physiologism'.[46] Heinrich Heine, 19 April 1832:

> Many disguised priests are now gliding and sliding here and there among the people, persuading them that a rosary which has been consecrated is a perfect preservative against the cholera. The Saint-Simonists regard it as an advantage of their religion that none of their number can die of the prevailing malady, because progress is a law of nature, and as social progress is specially in Saint-Simonism, so long as the number of its apostles is incomplete none of its followers can die. The Bonapartists declare that if any one feels in himself the symptoms of the cholera, if he will raise his eyes to the column of Place Vendôme he shall be saved and live.

The epidemic harshly showed up social inequality in the face of death: Jules Janin referred to 'this plague of a population that is the first and only one to die, formidably giving the lie by its bloody death to the doctrines of equality that have been preached to it for half a century'. Hatred broke out in the city. The bourgeois accused the poor of having unleashed and spread the plague: 'All individuals affected by this epidemic disease', you could read in *Le Journal des débats* for 28 March 1832, 'belong to the class of the people. They are shoemakers and those working on the manufacture of woolen garments. They live in the dirty and narrow streets of the Île de la Cité and the Notre-Dame quarter.' The people, for their part, accused the government of poisoning the public water-sources, the barrels of the water-carriers, the sick in the hospitals. Heine noted how 'the multitude murmured bitterly when it saw how the rich fled away, and, well packed with doctors and drugs, took refuge in healthier climes. The poor note with discontent that money has also become a protection against death.'

'The great city is like a piece of artillery. When it is loaded, a spark need only fall and the gun goes off. In June 1832, the spark was the death of General Lamarque.'[47] Maximilien Lamarque, deputy for the Landes, had defeated Wellington in Spain and was popular among the young. On 5

---

46   See Georges Canguilhem, *Idéologie et Rationalité dans l'histoire des sciences de la vie* (Paris: Vrin, 1988). It is not hard to understand this phenomenon. Cholera patients generally died from dehydration. Broussais's 'anti-inflammatory' methods (leeches, bloodletting) could only be disastrous.

47   Hugo, *Les Misérables*, Volume Four, book 10, chapter 3. Hugo wrote a long time after the events, but he drew closely on the documentary sources, and his account corresponds to contemporary witnesses such as Rey-Dussueil.

June, an immense crowd followed his coffin, which was being taken to Mont-de-Marsan. The procession mingled Bonapartists and republicans, with students from the Alfort veterinary school and the Polytechnique at its head. (Lucien Leuwen, we recall, 'had been expelled from the Polytechnique for having gone for an inappropriate walk, on a day that he and all his fellow students were detained: that was the time of one of the famous days of June, April or February 1832 or 1834'.) Setting out from Rue d'Anjou, the hearse reached the Madeleine and followed the boulevards as far as the Bastille. Here, 'a circle was formed around the hearse. The vast throng was hushed. Lafayette spoke, and bade Lamarque farewell ... All at once a man on horseback, dressed in black, appeared in the middle of the group with a red flag.'[48]

Heine also noted how 'there was indeed some mysterious influence in this red flag with black-fringed border, in which were in black the words "*La Liberté ou la Mort!*" and which rose like a banner of consecration to death above all heads on the Pont d'Austerlitz'.[49] Tradition has it that this was the first appearance of the red flag on the side of the uprising, in a remarkable turnaround since it had served until then as the final warning given by the forces of order before the unleashing of repression ('At the signal of the red flag, any assembly becomes criminal and must be dispersed by force' – such had been the law since October 1789).

> Meantime, the Municipal cavalry galloped along the Left Bank to bar all passage of the Pont d'Austerlitz, while on the Right Bank the dragoons came from the Célestins and deployed along the Quai Morland.[50] The people ... suddenly perceived them ... and cried: 'The dragoons!' The troops advanced at a walk, silently, with their pistols in the holsters, their swords in their scabbards, their muskets slung in their leather sockets, with an air of gloomy expectation.

Where did the first shots come from? History does not say, but what had to happen did happen:

---

48   Ibid.

49   Heine, *Letters from Paris*, 16 June 1832.

50   The Célestins barracks, rebuilt at the end of the nineteenth century, still houses the cavalry of the Republican Guard. The Île de Louviers was not at that time connected to the Right Bank (it corresponds today to the land surrounding the administrative building of the Ville de Paris, between Boulevard Morland and the Quai des Célestins). This was a yard for timber brought down the Seine for construction and firewood. Boulevard Morland was then a quay and the Arsenal was on the water's edge.

The tempest was unchained, stones showered, the fusillade burst forth. Many rushed to the water's edge, and crossed the small arm of the Seine, which is now filled in. The timber-yards on the Île de Louviers, that ready-made citadel, bristled with combatants; stakes were pulled up, pistols were fired, a barricade began. The young men, driven back, crossed the Pont d'Austerlitz with the hearse at a run, and charged the Municipal Guard. The carabineers galloped up, the dragoons cut and slashed, the crowd dispersed in all directions; a rumour of war flew to all four corners of Paris . . . Passion spread the riot as the wind does fire.[51]

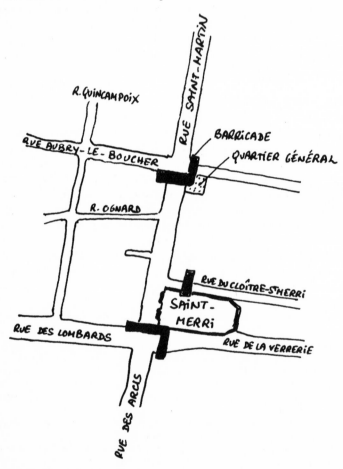

---

51   Hugo, *Les Misérables*, Volume Four, book 10, chapter 3.

In the evening, the crowd roamed the Marais, and the Saint-Martin and Saint-Denis quarters, calling out: 'To arms! Long live liberty! Long live the Republic!' In Rues Saint-Martin and Saint-Denis, lampposts were broken and barricades erected. The police stations on the Place du Châtelet, Rue de la Verrerie and Rue Mauconseil were disarmed, and the armourer Lepage on Rue du Bourg-l'Abbé pillaged.[52] At seven o'clock the insurgents were in control of the Châtelet, the Quai de la Mégisserie and the Quai de Gesvres, but the government had gathered 25,000 soldiers in Paris and this time the National Guard were on its side – except for the artillery which refused to fire on the people.[53] The following day, 6 June, the insurgents had to abandon almost all their positions, and the fighting centred on the Saint-Merri cloister, a labyrinth of little streets where the Centre Beaubourg is now, along with its esplanade and the Horloge quarter. Rey-Dussueil:

> Within less than an hour they improvised a fortress. A house facing Rue Aubry-le-Boucher was their headquarters, and a barricade five feet high defended its approaches ... Two lit stoves were placed outside the door; molten lead was poured into moulds to be rounded into bullets, each one of which seemed to have a ready destination.[54] To the south, in front of the Saint-Merri church, piled-up stones closed off Rue de la Verrerie and Rue des Arcis; behind, another barricade stopped any enemy who sought to advance through Rue de Cloître. There was no way out to the north, nor through Rue Maubuée, nor the Passage de Venise, nor Rue de la Corroierie. It was necessary to attack either from the front through Rue Aubry-le-Boucher, or from behind through Rue Saint-Martin ... This Thermopylae did not occupy, in length, a space of more than a hundred paces; its width was that of Rue Saint-Martin.[55]

---

52 This armourer showed resilience, as his shops were pillaged at each insurrection. In *Things Seen*, Hugo tells how on 24 February 1848 'forty men at a time pushed the bus in one fell swoop against the shop-window.' There is still a Lepage armourer on the Place du Théâtre-Français.

53 Its uniform was black, with a red pompom on the shako. Young people were attracted by this elegant costume, and as they were less petit-bourgeois than their elders, the artillery of the National Guard had to be dissolved on several occasions during those years.

54 Baudelaire: 'You whose clear eye sees the deep arsenals/Where the tribe of metals sleeps in its tomb' ('The Litany of Satan').

55 Rey-Dussueil, *Le Cloître Saint-Merry* (Paris: Ambroise Dupont, 1832). Rue des Arcis is Rue Saint-Martin south of the transverse axis of Rue de la Verrerie–Rue des Lombards. It was certainly the great barricade of Saint-Merri that served as a model for the barricade of Rue de la Chanvrerie in *Les Misérables*, that which Jean

This fortress could not be taken without artillery. A gun battery was accordingly installed on Rue Saint-Martin, which it enfiladed from the church of Saint-Nicolas-des-Champs. Another battery fired from the Innocents market through Rue Aubry-le-Boucher. This was the first time that artillery was used against the people of Paris, and these days of June 1832 thus saw two innovations with a great future – the red flag of the people, and the cannon of the party of order. On the evening of the 6th, the central barricade was demolished by a convergent attack of overwhelming force from both north and south of Rue Saint-Martin. The barricade leader, a workman named Jeanne who had been one of the July insurgents, went down in legend for refusing to surrender, and single-handedly opening a passage with his bayonet through the battalions of the 4th legion of the National Guard. Heine:

> It was the best blood of France which ran in Rue Saint-Martin, and I do not believe that there was better fighting at Thermopylae than at the mouth of the alley of Saint-Merri and Aubry-le-Boucher, where at the last a handful of some sixty Republicans fought against sixty thousand troops of the line and National Guards, and twice beat them back ... the few who remained alive in no wise asked for mercy ... they rushed with bared breasts before the enemy, offering themselves to be shot.

Martial law was proclaimed the next day, and to identify the dead 'many people visited the Morgue, where there was a queue like that at the Opéra when *Robert le Diable* is performed.' Anger mounted in these lines waiting outside the Morgue:

> As remedy for the long series of ills they have visited on us, as consolation for their order of things in which everything goes to despair, they open wide to us the doors of the morgue, and their police push us in with their swords in our sides! The day is not far off when they will be afraid to confess the crimes of the night; there will be talk of massacre, bridge, and river, and the rest will be passed over in silence.[56]

In April 1834, Thiers, interior minister in the Soult government, had a law passed on the subject of public criers and hawkers, which immediately deprived the people of their main source of information, as well as a further

---

Valjean defends and where Gavroche dies. See Thomas Bouchet, 'La barricade des Misérables', in Corbin and Mayeur (eds) *La Barricade*. It was also at Saint-Merri that the republican Michel Chrestien died a heroic death in *Lost Illusions*.
56   Rey-Dussueil, *Le Cloître Saint-Merry*.

law requiring preliminary authorization for any associations: 'Hardly was this monstrous law promulgated, than it was right away applied; clubs were closed, the sale of newspapers was banned on the public way, and, as the high point of infamy, the right of assembly was completely suppressed, since for more than twenty-one citizens to gather without authorization in any place was a crime.'[57] Lyon then rose in a second insurrection, while the leaders of the first one were being tried. The workers of La Croix-Rousse were massacred by cannon fire, and on 10 April, Soult was able to make a second triumphal entry into the city in the company of the crown prince, the Duc d'Orléans.

In Paris on 12 April, Armand Marrast, publisher of the republican newspaper *La Tribune*, printed a special issue calling the sixty-three sections of the Société des Droits de l'Homme to come out in the streets. The police raided the print works, seized the paper and arrested Marrast and his deputy. Too late: on the night of the 12th, barricades arose once more in the quarter that was still called Maubuée: Rue Beaubourg, Rue de Montmorency, Rue Aubry-le-Boucher, Rue Transnonain, Rue Geoffroy-Langevin, Rue aux Ours and Rue du Grenier-Saint-Lazare. But the few hundred insurgents were rapidly overwhelmed by the soldiers of the 25th regiment of the line. When the fighting was over, someone fired a musket from a window in 12 Rue Transnonain, where the barricade had resisted longer than elsewhere.[58] The soldiers entered the house and massacred all its inhabitants – men, women and children. In his *Grand Dictionnaire universel du XIXe siècle*, Pierre Larousse states that 'the regiment that had sullied the glorious French uniform by this crime was an object of horror in its various garrisons for the rest of Louis-Phillipe's reign'.[59] And Bugeau, who commanded these troops in their application of techniques perfected in Algeria, would always remain 'the butcher of Rue Transnonain'. Repression came down hard on the republican leaders. A big trial, with 121 accused, was held in

---

57 Nadaud, *Léonard, maçon de la Creuse*.
58 Rue Transnonain disappeared with the cutting of Rue de Turbigo and the widening of Rue Beaubourg, but some of its houses were absorbed in the latter, on the even-numbered side.
59 Under 'April 1834, days of'. In 'Some French Caricaturists', which dates from 1857, Baudelaire describes the famous lithograph by Daumier: 'In a poor, mean room, the traditional room of the proletarian, with shoddy, essential furniture, lies the corpse of a workman, stripped but for his cotton shirt and cap; he lies on his back, at full length, his legs and arms outspread. There has obviously been a great struggle and tumult in the room, for the chairs are overturned, as are the night-table and the chamber-pot. Beneath the weight of the corpse – between his back and the bare boards – the father is crushing the corpse of his little child. In this cold attic all is silence and death' (Baudelaire, *The Mirror of Art*), p. 163.

April 1835, before the Court of Peers sitting in the Luxembourg palace. All those who had not managed to take flight were imprisoned. In July 1835, Armand Carrel, publisher of *Le National*, was killed in a duel by Émile de Girardin. As his friend Chateaubriand wrote, 'it seemed there was never enough danger for him'.[60] His death weakened the republican camp further, and the days of April 1834 were its last armed uprising until 1848.

But there was still Blanqui. If he took part in most of the *journées* of the 1830s, this was without the slightest illusion as to the manner in which the republican bourgeoisie conceived equality and fraternity. In January 1832, before the court of assizes where he was accused of infringing the press laws, the procurer asked his profession. He replied: 'proletarian'. The procurator objected that this was not a profession. Blanqui responded: 'It is the profession of the majority of our people, who are deprived of political rights.'[61] The magistrates acquitted Blanqui for the press offence, but condemned him to a year in prison for insulting the court. Early in 1834, after serving this sentence, Blanqui established *Le Libérateur, journal des opprimés*, in which he wrote, by way of programme: 'Our flag is equality ... The Republic means the emancipation of the workers, the end of the reign of exploitation, the coming of a new order that will free labour from the tyranny of capital.' There were not many people who could express these thoughts in 1834, either in France or elsewhere. (Marx was sixteen years old at this time. Much later, he would say that he learned these essentials from the Paris workers, who were largely Blanquists.)

In 1835, Blanqui and Barbès, who had not yet quarrelled, founded the Société des Familles. In 1836 they were arrested for having established, on Rue de Lourcine, a workshop for making gunpowder. After being amnestied, Blanqui organized the Société des Saisons, and early in 1839, cadres were prepared for the army of revolt.[62] The day was fixed for 12 May, a Sunday, as Paris was then relatively empty of police, and the bourgeois were at the races in Neuilly. The thousand men whom Blanqui counted on to start the uprising were to gather between Rue

---

60   This strange friendship (Armand Carrel had been a volunteer with the Spanish republicans in 1823, and had thus fought the French troops that Chateaubriand had been involved in sending) is one of many signs that Chateaubriand was not a run-of-the-mill reactionary as is often believed.

61   Rancière, *On the Shores of Politics*.

62   'The groups were divided into Weeks and Months. The three Months that formed a Season received their orders from a leader who was known as Spring. Each month comprised four Weeks led by a July. The weeks were made up of six members under the leadership of a Sunday. The leaders went unseen, and Blanqui did not attend the general meetings ... This was the hidden conscription and secret recruitment of the army of revolt' (G. Geffroy, *L'Enfermé*).

Saint-Denis and Rue Saint-Martin, in the back rooms of wineshops, and in buildings near the store of the armourer Lepage on Rue du Bourg-l'Abbé. Around midday, Blanqui arrived at the café on the corner of Rue Mandar and Rue Montorgueil. He briefly announced the object of his summons. Everyone came out, his supporters thronged into the neighbouring streets, and the cry 'To arms!' was heard. The doors of Lepage's establishment were broken down, Barbès and Blanqui handed out muskets and cartridges through the windows. But the affair got off to a bad start, and Parisians watched in bemusement as these armed groups passed by. Victor Hugo:

> Towards three o'clock two or three hundred young men, poorly armed, suddenly broke into the *mairie* of the 7th arrondissement, disarmed the guard, and took the muskets. Thence they ran to the Hôtel de Ville and performed the same freak ... When they had the Hôtel de Ville, what was to be done with it? They went away ... At this moment barricades are being made in Rue des Quatre Fils, at the corner of all the little Rues de Bretagne, de Poitou, de Touraine, and there are groups of persons listening ... It is seven o'clock; from my balcony in the Place Royale platoon-firing is heard.[63]

The insurgents had not been understood and supported. They returned to the Saint-Martin quarter, to Rues Simon-le-Franc, Beaubourg and Transnonain. Blanqui and Barbès found three barricades in Rue Greneta as defence against the National Guard. But very soon they had to retreat to Rue du Bourg-l'Abbé under a hail of bullets. The last barricade, in the Saint-Merri quarter, was taken, and the uprising was over. At the trial of nineteen insurgents, in June, Barbès and Blanqui were condemned to death – Blanqui in his absence, as he had managed to escape, though he was captured not long after. Both men had their sentences commuted, and spent long years in Mont Saint-Michel. This was the end of Parisian uprisings for a long time. Heine wrote on 17 September 1842:

> A very great calm reigns here. All is as silent as a winter night wrapped in snow. Only a little mysterious and monotonous noise, like falling drops. This is the interest on capital, falling into the strongboxes of the capitalists and almost spilling over. The continual swell of the riches of the rich can be distinctly heard. From time to time there is mixed with this dull ripple

the sob of a low voice, the sob of poverty. Sometimes you can also hear a light metallic noise, like that of a knife being sharpened.[64]

The knives would emerge from their sheaths in 1848, on the occasion of a banquet that did not actually take place. To close the election campaign going on in the provinces, the opposition had prepared an enormous banquet in Paris, organized by the 12th legion of the National Guard (the legion of the Faubourg Saint-Marceau under the command of François Arago), along with the students of the Latin Quarter who were in ferment: Michelet and Quinet had been suspended from lecturing, and on 4 and 6 January the students demonstrated en masse to demand their recall. On 14 January, Guizot banned the banquet. After much hesitation, the opposition decided to go ahead. On 19 February, Le National affirmed that this would be held at noon on the 22nd. Rodolphe Apponyi, an attaché at the Austrian embassy, wrote in his diary on the 18th:

In the last few days, all the talk is of this famous banquet that is to be held. We do not yet know either the time or the place, but the very idea of such a gathering, to which not only the rioters of Paris are invited, but also those of towns a hundred leagues around, makes one tremble. The sponsors themselves are afraid, since if the head of the procession, which is supposed to cross the whole of Paris, keeps calm, it is by no means sure that the tail will do the same.[65]

Tocqueville wrote in his Recollections: 'On the 20th February almost all the opposition newspapers published a programme for the forthcoming banquet, which was really a proclamation calling on the schools and the National Guard itself to attend the ceremony as a body ... One might have taken it for a decree of the Provisional Government, which was formed three days later.'[66] This 'programme' envisaged that the deputies,

---

64 Heinrich Heine, Lutèce (Paris: Michel Lévy, 1855). Another foreigner in Paris, Alexander Herzen, gave a similar diagnosis: 'Capital gave its votes to the government, and the government lent its bayonets to the defence of all the abuses of capital. They had a common enemy: the proletariat, the worker ...' (Lettres de France et d'Italie, 10 June 1848).
65 Rodolphe Apponyi, De la Révolution au coup d'État, 1848–1851 (Paris: Plon, 1913; republished Geneva: La Palatine, 1948). Apponyi was from an old Hungarian family, and the cousin of the Austrian ambassador to Paris. As secretary to the embassy, he lived in Paris from 1826 to 1852. His diary, very lively and written in impeccable French, gives the point of view of a worldly and cultivated diplomat, a champion of order but lacking in ferocity.
66 Alexis de Tocqueville, Recollections (London: Macdonald, 1970), p. 26.

peers, and other guests at the banquet would assemble at eleven o'clock at the regular gathering place of the parliamentary opposition, on the Place de la Madeleine. The procession was to go via the Place de la Concorde and the Champs-Élysées, ending at Chaillot where the banquet would be held.

The 22nd was a rather well-behaved *journée*. At nine o'clock the students gathered without weapons at the Panthéon, where they were joined by workers from the Faubourgs Saint-Marceau and Saint-Antoine. The procession reached the Madeleine at around eleven. After a little scuffle with the local police, it headed down Rue Royale, crossed the Place de la Concorde, pushed aside the Municipal Guards defending the bridge and invaded the courtyard of the Palais-Bourbon. The dragoons and gendarmes cleared the Assembly, it rained throughout, and the *journée* was over.

In the morning of the 23rd, it was still raining. Duchâtel, the interior minister, ordered two battalions of each legion of the National Guard to occupy strategic zones: the Place de la Bastille, the Place de l'Hôtel-de-Ville, the Tuileries, the Place de la Concorde, the Place des Victoires, the Pointe Saint-Eustache and the Porte Saint-Denis. In the morning, however, the majority of these legions, far from attacking the barricades that were rising throughout the city centre, refused to fight, shouted 'Long live Reform, down with Guizot!', and interposed themselves between the regular troops and the insurgents. On hearing this news, Louis-Philippe, who up till then had been optimistic − 'You call a carriage turned upside down by two ruffians a *barricade*', he said − collapsed. He dismissed Guizot and replaced him with Molé.[67] News of this led to celebrations throughout Paris.

> The boulevards took on a fairyland appearance. A long garland of multi-coloured lights, hanging from every floor, linked the buildings as a joyful emblem of the union of hearts. From time to time, you could see groups pass along the road carrying flags and allegorical streamers, and singing the *Marseillaise* in chorus ... Towards half past nine a much larger group appeared, a long column waving torches and a red flag, on the boulevards at the crossing of Rue Montmartre. This came from the depths of the Faubourg Saint-Antoine ... Attracted by the beauty of the chanting, a large number of curious persons joined in this demonstration, which

---

67 'It was three o'clock when M. Guizot appeared at the door of the House. He entered with his firmest step and haughtiest bearing, silently crossed the gangway and mounted the tribune, almost throwing his head over backwards for fear of seeming to bow it; in two words he announced that the king had entrusted M. Molé with the formation of a new government. I have never seen such a piece of melodrama' (Tocqueville, *Recollections*, p. 32).

seemed inoffensive. In the effusion of this common festival, bourgeois
and proletarians clasped each other's hands.[68]

The republican leadership, however, were not satisfied with this conclusion, which they saw as a comic dénouement. This party's men of action
kept their weapons and prepared fortifications in the old centre of popular
uprisings, Rues Beaubourg, Transnonain, etc.

The course of the revolution quickened on the night of 23 February.
Apponyi had a grandstand view. He had left the Princesse de La Trémoille
in the Faubourg Saint-Germain and was on his way home:

> The boulevards were filled with promenaders: women, children, those
> simply curious like myself. But the foreign ministry building was so well
> guarded that there was no more room to walk by; you had to go down
> to Rue Basse-du-Rempart, which was still more filthy than usual.[69] A
> crowd of young people, most of them in workers' clothes, were advanc-
> ing down the boulevards, preceded by lanterns in red and yellow paper
> that were carried on long poles. This jubilant mob wanted to enter Rue
> de la Paix, but the soldiers stationed there prevented them and they came
> towards us. To avoid finding myself in the midst of this mass of proletar-
> ians, whose attitude was in no way reassuring for an individual armed
> only with an umbrella, I thought it best to walk as close as possible to
> the metal railing that runs along Rue Basse-du-Rempart at that point. I
> had not taken more than a few steps towards the crowd, when all at once
> the regiments of the line opened platoon-fire on us, and there we were,
> a hundred persons, lying, falling, rolling on the ground; on top of one
> another, with cries and whimpers … The two little women [whom he
> had described talking with some minutes before] were now dead bodies,
> along with more than fifty others struck by a second round of firing
> before those wounded in the first had time to stand!

What followed is one of the most famous revolutionary images: the cart
pulled by a white horse, the heap of bodies lit up by a torch held by a
child, the circuit round the centre of Paris to shouts of 'Revenge! They're
butchering the people!' On the morning of the 24th, 'the troops, who had

68   Daniel Stern (the Comtesse d'Agoult), *Histoire de la Révolution de 1848* (Paris:
Librairie internationale, 1850–3).
69   Guizot lived in the Hôtel des Affaires Étrangères, on the corner of Rue des
Capucines and Boulevard des Capucines; hence the guard that evening. Rue
Basse-du-Rempart, as we have seen, ran parallel to Boulevard des Capucines at a
lower level, divided from it by a small wall and a metal railing.

bivouacked in the rain with their feet in the mud, their minds troubled and their bodies numb with cold, perceived with the first glimmers of dawn a bold and resolute multitude, flocking in through Rues Saint-Martin, Rambuteau, Saint-Merri, du Temple and Saint-Denis, where barricades had been raised at a number of places'.[70]

Tocqueville, who had heard nothing of this, left home in the early morning.

> As soon as I had set foot in the street I could for the first time scent revolution in the air ...The boulevard along which we passed presented a strange sight. There was hardly anyone to be seen, although it was nearly nine o'clock in the morning; no sound of a human voice could be heard; but all the little sentry boxes the whole way along that great street seemed on the move, oscillating on their bases and occasionally falling with a crash, while the great trees along the edge came tumbling into the road as if of their own accord. These acts of destruction were the work of isolated individuals who set about it silently, methodically and fast, preparing materials for the barricades that others were to build ... Nothing that I saw later that day impressed me so much as that solitude in which one could, so to speak, see all the most evil passions of humanity at work, and none of the good ones.[71]

It is clear here what Tocqueville saw as the 'good passions'. A little later, he crossed an infantry column retreating to the Madeleine: 'Their ranks were broken and disorderly, and they marched with hanging heads, shamefaced and frightened. Whenever one of them left the main body for an instant, he was immediately surrounded, caught, clasped, disarmed and sent back; all this in the twinkling of an eye.'[72] These were the troops of General Bedeau, falling back from the Bastille to the Tuileries via the boulevards. On that day, at nine in the morning, the insurgents held four of the strategic points that the forces of order were supposed to defend at any price: the Bastille, the Porte Saint-Denis, the Place des Victoires and the Pointe Saint-Eustache. The Prefecture of Police and the Hôtel de Ville were taken without a struggle. Only a company of the 14th Regiment of the line, badly informed about the development of events, got themselves killed at the Palais-Royal. Turgenev noted that the only serious fighting in the February days was on the Place du Palais-Royal.[73] 'Two companies of regular army

70 Stern, *Histoire de la Révolution de 1848*.
71 Tocqueville, *Recollections*, p. 36.
72 Ibid., p. 39.
73 Ivan Turgenev, 'Monsieur François', *The Fortnightly Review*, 1 Nov 1911, pp. 946–961.

regiments occupied the position that forms the left wing of the Château d'Eau. This building ... could only be destroyed by cannon. It was from there that the troops fired on the people positioned opposite in the court-yard of the Palais-Royal, and whose own shots only hit the stonework ... Finally, they made their way into the royal stables, carriages were rolled under the windows of the army post and set on fire.'[74] By one o'clock, the king had abdicated and left the Tuileries for Saint-Cloud, repeating in a daze: 'Like Charles X, like Charles X!' The insurgents invaded the Tuileries, the royal throne was carried to the Bastille and burned. This was the end of the first phase of the revolution, which for Tocqueville was 'the shortest and the least bloody that the country had known'.

Throughout the following days, calm reigned in the streets. 'I went around very easily in a cab,' Apponyi noted on 27 February, 'the barri-cades were still in place, but a wide enough space was left for a carriage to pass. So I could go to Rothschild's; it would be impossible to depict the terror of the bankers and notaries, they were in a deplorable state.' The self-proclaimed Provisional Government met in the Hôtel de Ville, in unprecedented conditions:[75] for two weeks, until 5 or 6 March, it delib-erated under the direct pressure of the crowd that massed there. Every minute the debates were interrupted by the clamour of popular delegates. The nascent power was beset by mistrust, the swindle of July 1830 was still too close to be forgotten. It was in these conditions that the affair of the red flag developed on the evening of the 25th, suddenly revealing the hidden antagonisms. Lamartine:

> The arches, the courts, the steps of the great staircase, the Salle Saint-Jean, were strewn with dead bodies ... Bands of senseless men and ferocious boys sought here and there for the dead bodies of horses, drowned in

---

74 Louis Ménard, *Prologue d'une révolution, février-juin 1848* (Paris: Au Bureau du peuple, 1848).

75 This was formed by the deputies Dupont de l'Eure, François Arago, Lamartine, Ledru-Rollin, Garnier-Pagès, Crémieux and Marie, and three non-parliamentar-ians, Louis Blanc, Flocon and Albert – an engineer, member of the Société des Nouvelles Saisons and 'a representative of the working class' (Marx). 'Why had the fate of the people, only liberated just a moment ago, fallen precisely into the hands of these men? Did they know anything of the needs and aspirations of the people, had they risked death for them, was it they who had won the victory? Or perhaps they had some new and fertile thought? No, a hundred times no. They occupied these positions because they were bold enough to claim them, not on the barricades but in a newspaper office, not on the place of struggle but in the conquered Chamber of Deputies' (Alexander Herzen, *Lettres de France et d'Italie*, 10 June 1848).

the pools of blood. They passed cords around their breasts, and dragged them, with laughter and howling, over the Place de Grève, and then threw them into the vault at the foot of the staircase [of the Hôtel de Ville].[76]

At the head of the 'seditionists', a worker named Marche spoke:

His face, blackened by the smoke of powder, was pale with emotion; his lips trembled with rage; his eyes, sunk beneath a prominent brow, flashed fire ... He rolled in his left hand a strip of ribbon or red stuff. He held in his right hand the barrel of a carbine, the butt-end of which he struck with force upon the floor at every word ... He spoke not as a man, but in the name of the people, who wished to be obeyed, and did not mean to wait ... He repeated ... all the conditions of the programme of impossibilities which the tumultuous cries of the people had enjoined it to accept and to realize on the instant: the overthrow of all known society; the destruction of property and capitalists; spoliation; the immediate installation of the proletarian into the community of goods; the proscription of the bankers, the wealthy, the manufacturers, the bourgeois of every condition above the wage-earners; a government, with an axe in its hand, to level all the superiorities of birth, competence, inheritance, and even of labour; *in fine*, the acceptance, without reply, and without delay, of the red flag, to signify to society its defeat; to the people, their victory; to Paris, terror; to all foreign governments, invasion: each of these injunctions was supported by the orator with a blow of the butt of his musket on the floor, by frantic applause from those who were behind him, and a salute of shots fired on the square.[77]

Lamartine, who speaks of himself in the third person in this *History*, ends up making his famous speech – an essential marker in republican genealogy – on the red flag, 'which had only made the tour of the Champs-de-Mars, drawn through the blood of the people', whereas the tricolour 'has made the circuit of the world, with the name, the glory, and the liberty of the country'. Apponyi was very grateful to him for having carried the day: 'We owe this victory to the courage and unheard-of devotion of M. de Lamartine, who spent sixty hours without eating or drinking, without sleeping ... he was everything and did everything with a miraculous force

76 Alphonse de Lamartine, *History of the French Revolution of 1848* (Boston: Phillips, Sampson, 1854), trans. Durivage & Chase.
77 Ibid. (Translation modified.)

of mind and body.' It was in this way, wrote Herzen, that 'the flag of the people, waved under fire, the flag of democracy, of the future Republic, was rejected ... and the flag that served as shop-sign for seventeen years to Louis-Philippe, the flag behind which the Municipal Guard fired on the people, the flag of the royalist bourgeoisie, was taken as the standard of the new republic ... As soon as the bourgeoisie learned of the affair of the tricolour flag, the shops opened, and they were lighter of heart. For this concession, they had to make one in return, and agreed to recognize the Republic.'[78]

The confrontation rapidly moved to new ground, and the big affair became the date of the election to the Constituent Assembly. The bourgeois parties tried to have the vote set for as early as possible, whereas the republican left wanted time for an election campaign that would address the new electors, especially in the provinces.[79] On 17 March, 150,000 demonstrators came to calmly demand the postponement of the elections: 'From every quarter, from every faubourg, from the whole banlieue, groups of workers converged on the Place de la Révolution [de la Concorde]. They had neither the dress nor the physiognomy of men torn from their workshops by riot ... Soon an enormous organized column covered the great avenue of the Champs-Élysées, from the railings of the Tuileries to the barrier of the Étoile.'[80] The procession, in which the flags of Poland, of Italian and German unity and the green flag of Ireland could be seen, set out for the Hôtel de Ville along the quays of the Seine. Some fifty delegates, including Blanqui, Raspail, Cabet and Barbès, were received by the Provisional Government. Blanqui spoke, demanding the removal of troops and the postponement of elections. Lamartine eloquently lied: 'There are no troops in Paris, aside perhaps for some fifteen hundred or two thousand men, divided between the external positions, to protect the city gates and the railways, and it is false that the government has any thought of bringing them into Paris ... The Republic, internally, wants no other defenders than the armed people.'[81] Louis Blanc, hesitating between the people and the government, succeeded in aborting the movement that had begun,

---

78 Herzen, *Lettres de France et d'Italie*, 10 June 1848.
79 The new electoral law provided for universal (male) suffrage, which meant millions of new electors. 'M. Ledru-Rollin did not find France republican enough. He wanted to have the time to inflate from all sides, by the organ of his clubs, the spirit of demagogy' (*Histoire de la chute du roi Louis-Philippe, de la République de 1848 et du rétablissement de l'Empire, 1847–1855* [Paris: Plon, imprimeur de l'Empereur, 1857]).
80 Garnier-Pagès, *Histoire de la Révolution de 1848* (Paris: Pagnerre, 1861–72).
81 Ménard, *Prologue d'une révolution*.

by siding with the established power. Proudhon remarked that he used the same terms as Guizot to characterize the demonstrators.[82] Finally, the ballot would only be delayed for two weeks, an insufficient time to 'call the people to meetings, enlighten them, conduct their political education', as Blanqui said during the Bourges trial.

On Sunday, 16 April, a week before the date set for the elections, a crowd of workers gathered on the Champ-de-Mars to choose its officers for the National Guard. Here and there the question of elections was heatedly discussed. A delegation left for the Hôtel de Ville, to take the proceeds of a collection, but Ledru-Rollin had sounded the call to arms, and the astonished workers had to pass between the bayonets of the bourgeois National Guard and the Mobile Guard to reach the Maison du Peuple. In the evening, the National Guard of the *beaux quartiers* patrolled the streets with shouts of 'Down with the communists! Death to Blanqui! Death to Cabet!'

But there was a section of the elegant bourgeoisie that had learned their habits from Blanqui's club, the Société Républicaine Centrale, in the hall of the Conservatoire des Arts et Métiers:

> Parisian society, after the first reaction of consternation, and still too disturbed to renew its customary gatherings and pleasures, ran from club to club ... Blanqui's club was in favour with people who had this kind of curiosity. The boxes and galleries where in previous years people had come to hear in rapt communion the masterpieces of musical art, were besieged every night by a singularly mixed and noisy crowd. They recognized each other at a distance, and greeted one another with a hasty gesture, lost as they were in this crowd in workmen's clothes whom many believed to be armed.[83]

The members of the Société Républicaine Centrale included Charles Baudelaire, who published in March, together with Champfleury and

82 Geffroy, *L'Enfermé*. In his *Pages d'histoire de la révolution de Février*, Louis Blanc wrote: 'I perceived among those attending unknown figures whose expression had something sinister about it.'

83 Stern, *Histoire de la Révolution de 1848*. In the long list of clubs that opened up at that time, the most important were that of Barbès (Club de la Révolution), which met at the Palais-National (former Palais-Royal), that of Raspail (Club des Amis du Peuple) in the Marais and that of Cabet on Rue Saint-Honoré. But there were many more, such as the Club des Amis des Noirs, the Société Démocratique Allemande, the Club des Blessés et Combattants de la Barricade Saint-Merri, the Club des Condamnés Politiques, those of the Démocrates de Belleville, the Émigrés Italiens, the Français non Naturalisés and the Fraternité du Faubourg Saint-Antoine, as well as the Vésuviennes, the only club reserved for women.

Toubin, the two issues of *Le Salut public*. It was certainly in this hall that Baudelaire drew the pencil portrait of Blanqui that Walter Benjamin mentions, in the singular intuition that leads him to compare the poet and the man in black: 'The solitude of Baudelaire as a counterpart to that of Blanqui'; 'the enigmatic stuff of allegory in one, the mystery-mongering of the conspirator in the other'. And in Baudelaire's 'The Litany of Satan': 'You who give the outlaw that calm and haughty look/That damns the whole multitude around his scaffold', Benjamin sees 'the dark face of Blanqui shine through between the lines'.

A few days later, after the feast of Fraternité, Blanqui predicted that 'the fruit of this fraternity between the bourgeoisie and its army will be a Saint Bartholemew of the proletarians'.[84] The *journée* of 15 May was a prelude to this – along with the events in Rouen, where the National Guard fired on an unarmed demonstration of workers. The clubs had decided on a big demonstration in support of Poland. Blanqui was opposed to this, as the proceedings of the Bourges trial note:

> M. Blanqui ... explained that after having resisted the demonstration, he was forced to accept it and took part. 'The point is,' he said, 'that handling the popular element is not like commanding a regiment that stands ready, arms in hand, to which you say "march" and it marches, "stop" and it stops. No, gentlemen, it isn't like this at all, and I had to accept this popular invasion in support of Poland.'

Setting off from the Bastille, the demonstration headed towards the Madeleine via the boulevards, crossed the Place de la Concorde, and reached the Palais-Bourbon where the new Constituent Assembly had met for the first time a week or so ago. Blanqui, Barbès and Raspail were there; Tocqueville as well, who had been elected deputy for the Manche in his constituency of Valognes:

> The sitting began like any other; and, what was very odd, twenty thousand men had surrounded the Chamber before any sound from outside had indicated their presence. Wolowski was at the rostrum; he was mumbling between his teeth some platitude or other about Poland when the people suddenly demonstrated how close they were by a terrible shout which, bursting through all the windows at the top of the Chamber, left open on account of the heat, fell upon us as if it came from the sky ... the doors of the galleries burst open with

---

84   Ménart, *Prologue d'une révolution*.

a crash; a flood of people poured into them, filled them, and soon overflowed them. Pressed forward by the crowd following them ... the first arrivals climbed over the balustrades ... they let themselves down at the sides of the walls and jumped the last five or six feet into the middle of the Assembly ... While one group of the people fell into the hall, another, composed mainly of the leaders of all the clubs, invaded us through every door. These latter carried various emblems of the Terror, and they waved a lot of flags, some of them with a red cap on top ... Some of our invaders were armed ... but not one seemed to have a fixed resolve to strike us ... there seemed to be no obedience to a common leader; it was a rabble, not a troop. I did see some drunks among them, but most of them seemed to be prey to a feverish excitement ... they were dripping with sweat, although the nature and state of their clothing should have made the heat not particularly disagreeable, for sometimes a good deal of naked skin was showing ... Throughout this disorder the Assembly remained passive and motionless on its benches, neither resisting nor giving way ... Some members of the Mountain fraternized with the people, but furtively and in whispers.[85]

Raspail read from the tribune a petition in support of Poland, amid great confusion. The president rang his bell. But suddenly silence fell, Blanqui was about to speak:[86]

It was at that moment that I saw a man go up onto the rostrum, and, although I have never seen him again, the memory of him has filled me with disgust and horror ever since. He had sunken, withered cheeks, white lips, and a sickly, malign, dirty look like a pallid, mouldy corpse; he was wearing no visible linen; an old black frockcoat covered his lean, emaciated limbs tightly; he looked as if he had lived in a sewer and only just come out. I was told that this was Blanqui.[87]

---

85 Tocqueville, *Recollections*, pp. 115–8.
86 In the proceedings of the Bourges trial, Blanqui explains: 'It is certainly true that I had come despite myself, shrugging my shoulders, and that even so I had given a speech with perfect composure. A man of politics is always able to do this. ... If we had wanted to overthrow the Assembly, I beg you to believe that we would have acted quite differently. We have some experience of insurrections and conspiracies, and I assure you that we would not have spent three hours chatting in an Assembly that we intended to overthrow.'
87 Tocqueville, *Recollections*, p. 118.

This description is worth dwelling on. Blanqui had just spent eight years in the worst prisons; his health was ruined, he spat blood, his wife had died, and one might well believe that these cruel tests had marked him. On top of this, he can hardly have been at his best that day, forced into a confrontation that he did not want. But in Tocqueville's words there is hatred, the same as he expresses towards the mob, the *ochlos*, these 'disgustingly sweaty and quite ragged' men – the same as he would soon express for the June insurgents. Tocqueville, that cynosure of the Institut des Sciences Politiques and the late lamented Fondation Saint-Simon, the idol of the liberals, was literally possessed by a hatred for the people, and though highly polite in general, he expresses himself in a vulgar fashion, to use one of his own adjectives.[88]

The affair turned disastrously wrong. Blanqui was not very convincing, wavering between Poland and the situation in France. Barbès spoke after him, undoubtedly in a fit of crazy outbidding directed against Blanqui, now that they had become enemies, and demanded an immediate tax of a billion francs on the rich. A certain Huber – who turned out to be an agent provocateur – proclaimed the dissolution of the Assembly, amid total chaos. The majority of deputies left the chamber. Soon the call to arms was heard, and the Mobile Guards arrived and expelled the demonstrators; the *journée* was over. In the evening, Barbès, Albert and Raspail were arrested. The clubs of Blanqui and Raspail were closed. Blanqui himself went underground, but was arrested on 26 May along with his faithful friends, the chef Flotte and the doctor Lacambre. The most evident result of this *journée* was that of depriving the Paris proletariat of its leaders at the very moment when it had most need of them.

'Rather an end with terror than a terror without end!' – this was the cry that the bourgeois 'madly snorted at his parliamentary republic'.[89] During

---

88   It is interesting to compare Tocqueville's description with that of another opponent of Blanqui, Victor Hugo: 'Blanqui had stopped wearing a shirt at this point. He wore the same clothes as he had for twelve years, his prison clothes, rags that he displayed at his club with a sombre pride. He only renewed his shoes, and his gloves which were always black ... There was in this man something of a broken aristocrat trampled underfoot by a demagogue ... A fundamental aptness; no hypocrisy. The same in private and in public. Rough, hard, severe, never laughing, repaying respect with irony, admiration with sarcasm, love with disdain, and inspiring extraordinary devotion. A sinister figure ... At certain moments this was no longer a man, but a kind of gloomy apparition that seemed to embody all the hatreds born from all the miseries' (*Things Seen*).

89   Marx, 'The Eighteenth Brumaire of Louis Bonaparte', *Surveys from Exile*, p. 228.

the five weeks that elapsed between the *journée* of 15 May and the June insurrection, the bourgeoisie made preparations for this 'end with terror'. A *union sacrée* came into being against Red Paris – Orleanists, Legitimists, republicans of all shades, including the quasi-totality of socialists, had only one idea in mind: to put an end to all this. Discordant voices were very rare, such as that of Pierre Leroux in the Assembly on 10 June: 'You have no other solution than violence, threats and blood, the old, false, absurd political economy. There are new solutions, socialism can bring them, allow socialism to let humanity live!' Daniel Stern noted how 'nothing could appear more singular to this Assembly, which was beginning to find that it was a bit too republican, after hearing that it was not republican enough'.

The preparations for the battle against the Paris proletariat were made in the broad light of day. Lamartine presented the general lines of these to the Executive Commission, which had replaced the Provisional Government in May:

> I do not wish to take upon my name the responsibility of a position of weakness, and of disarming society, which may degenerate into anarchy. I demand two things: laws of public security respecting the rioters, the clubs, the abuses of complaint in anarchical journals, the power of banishing from Paris to their communes the agitators convicted of public sedition, and lastly a camp of twenty thousand men, under the walls of Paris, to assist the army of Paris and the National Guard in the certain and imminent campaign which we would inevitably have to make against the National Workshops, and against the more guilty factions which might arise and become masters of this army of all the seditions.[90]

This gentle elegiac poet, the head of the angelic school as Balzac ironically called him, would obtain satisfaction of his demands – a law against rioting, with a penalty of twelve years in prison and withdrawal of civil rights for any citizen taking part in an armed riot that did not disperse at the first summons. Thanks to this law, 'the prisons of the Republic opened again for those who had grown old in the prisons of the monarchy'.[91]

The memories of February were still fresh. The party of Order knew that the military could change sides and that the National Guard from the popular arrondissements was unreliable. A new body was therefore created, specially recruited and trained for repression: the Mobile Guard, recognizable by its

---

90 Lamartine, *History of the French Revolution of 1848*.
91 Ménard, *Prologue d'une révolution*.

green epaulettes. It was in relation to this force that Marx used for the first time, I believe, the term 'lumpenproletariat'. According to Victor Marouk, this was formed from 'people with no allegiance'; in Hippolyte Castille's words, 'the scum of Paris'. For Louis Ménard, 'since no precautions were taken with recruitment, this floating population that pullulates in the big cities had no trouble in joining'.[92] These were very young men, including a large unemployed number of working-class origin, who were attracted by the pay of 30 sous a day, and by uniform and adventure.[93] The bourgeoisie was unsure until the last moment whether they would not betray it. Tocqueville expressed this fear at the feast of Concorde on the Champs-de-Mars, a sinister parody of the feast of the Fédération of 1790:

> The sight of those two hundred thousand bayonets will never leave my memory ... Only the rich sections sent out any large number of the National Guard wearing military uniform ... Among the legions from the suburbs, which by themselves stretched out into whole armies, one saw little but jackets and blouses, although that did not prevent them marching with very warlike expressions. Most of them, as they came by us, shouted, 'Long live the democratic Republic!' or sang the *Marseillaise* or the Girondins' song ... The various exclamations which we could hear from the battalions of the Garde Mobile left us full of doubts and anxiety about the intentions of these young men, or rather children, who, more than anybody else at that time, held our destinies in their hands. The regiments of the line, who closed the review, marched past in silence. My heart was filled with sadness as I watched this prolonged spectacle ... I felt that these were the two armies of the civil war that we were just beginning.[94]

The proletariat was also preparing for battle in its workshops. This was above all a question of manufacturing gunpowder and firearms, as weapons were not lacking. Even a cannon was constructed in the Faubourg du Temple. In July, a certain Allard, police chief in charge of public security, testified before the parliamentary commission of inquiry:

92 Ibid.
93 Pierre Gaspard, 'Aspects de la lutte des classes en 1848: le recrutement de la garde nationale mobile', *La Revue historique*, 511, July–September 1974. Through an irony of history, their uniforms were manufactured by the Association Fraternelle des Tailleurs, two thousand tailors who had come from all sides and worked in the abandoned premises of the debtors' prison of Clichy (Rancière, *The Nights of Labor*).
94 Tocqueville, *Recollections*, p. 130.

I had the houses searched on the right and left sides of the whole length of Rue de Charenton. We were sometimes forced to knock down the doors. We found muskets that were still hot, and hands black with powder. But what caught our attention above all was a veritable factory for gunpowder and other ammunition in a small passage on Rue du Chantier, between Rue de Charenton and Rue du Faubourg Saint-Antoine ... Here, at no. 10, was a locksmith's foundry where gunpowder, bullets and cartridges were being made. Bullets were moulded in thimbles, others in musket barrels. The lead ingots produced in these were then cut into sections.[95]

To make an end a pretext was needed, and this was provided by the National Workshops. Established in the wake of the February revolution, after an idea of Louis Blanc, these were supposed to relieve poverty by organizing new forms of work. But very soon the enormous demand transformed these cooperative and generous projects into meaningless tasks; by May-June, more than 100,000 men were employed, and 20,000 women, with all trades mixed together and functioning as navvies or seamstresses; 2 francs per day for men, and 1 franc for women.[96] There was no money left to finance the major works originally envisaged, as the economic crisis that had begun in 1846 was aggravated by a flight of capital.[97] The overwhelming majority of the National Assembly wanted the immediate closure of the National Workshops, as not only did they cost a great deal, but they aroused fear. Daniel Stern:

> This confused and floating population that had been pressed here to clear the public space was tacitly inspired by a common spirit. It was disciplined and organized by its own strength; it constituted a veritable army

95 *Rapport de la Commission d'enquête sur l'insurrection qui a éclaté dans la journée du 25 juin et sur les événements du 15 mai.*
96 For the sake of comparison, a correspondent of Eugène Sue wrote to him: 'Your Chourineur ... earns too little. If you were well informed, you would know that a good barge-worker earns 7 or 8 francs per day, and that 35 sous [1.75 francs] is what is paid to a streetsweeper' (Cited by Chevalier, *Classes laborieuses et classes dangereuses*).
97 'Business went from bad to worse; Lamartine was completely overwhelmed, the public finances were in a deplorable state, bankruptcies followed one another at an inconceivable rate, metallic currency became so rare that every effort was made to obtain it ... What also struck several people here was the lack of money to travel, for with the exception of Rothschild, no banker paid out any more, and even the richest people had only one or two hundred francs at their disposal' (Apponyi, *De la Révolution au coup d'État*).

... which elected leaders of its own choice that would be the only ones obeyed on the decisive day. But if some spirits, taking account of circumstances, sought a mode of slow and managed dissolution which would not suddenly cast into distress the families of valiant workmen whose only wrong was to lack employment, others on the contrary treated the equity of the former as culpable complicity, and wanted immediately, without transition or arrangement, to expel these *lazzaroni*, these *janissaries* – as they called them in terms both unjust and imprudent – from Paris and disperse them at any cost, without worrying about where they would find bread.

Under the influence of Falloux, chair of the labour committee, the Assembly and the Executive Commission decided to act quickly. On 20 June, Victor Hugo demanded the dissolution of the National Workshops in terms very close to those of Falloux, to whom he specifically referred: 'Independently of the dismal effect that the National Workshops have on our finances, these Workshops in their present form, and as they threaten to continue, could in the long term – a danger that has already been pointed out to you – seriously alter the character of the Parisian worker.' On 21 June, the Commission decreed that all male workers between 18 and 25 years of age would be immediately enrolled in the army. Others would be sent to provincial departments that would be allocated them, to do navvying work. The first contingent was to leave Paris for the swamps of the Sologne the next day, 22 June. This decree fell on a city that was already in ferment: 'On 6 June, new rioting on Rue Saint-Denis, constantly increasing. At ten o'clock there was a compact crowd on the boulevard ... detachments of National Guard, Mobile Guard and regular forces arrived from all sides ... Same rioting on the 8th. The crowded is bigger every day, the repression more energetic ... On the 11th the agitation continued, and 134 seditionists were arrested.'[98]

By the evening, groups of hungry people roamed the streets calling out in a low voice: 'Bread or lead, bread or lead', a dark and contracted version of the battle cry of the Lyon silk-workers: 'Live working or die fighting'.

The Executive Commission's provocation would trigger the June insurrection, which Tocqueville saw as:

the greatest and the strangest that had ever taken place in our history, or perhaps in that of any other nation: the greatest because for four days more

---

98   Maurice Vimont, *Histoire de la Rue Saint-Denis* (Paris: Les Presses modernes, 1936).

than a hundred thousand men took part in it, and there were five generals killed; the strangest, because the insurgents were fighting without a battle cry, leaders, or flag, and yet they showed wonderful powers of coordination and a military expertise that astonished the most experienced officers. Another point that distinguished it from all other events of the same type during the last sixty years was that its object was not to change the form of the government, but to alter the organization of society. In truth it was not a political struggle (in the sense in which we have used the word 'political' up to now), but a class struggle, a sort of 'Servile War'.[99]

On 22 June, when news of the decree reached them, tens of thousands of workers came out in the streets, crying: 'Down with Marie! Down with Lamartine!', and chanting in unison: 'We won't leave, we won't leave.' A procession made its way to the Luxembourg, where the Executive Commission and the labour committee were in session, to ask for the suspension of the decree. A delegation led by Pujol, an official of the National Workshops, was received by Marie, the minister of public works. The tone grew rapidly heated, and Marie ended up uttering the fatal words: 'If the workers are unwilling to leave for the provinces, we shall compel them by force.' The delegates left the Luxembourg in a fury, and headed for the Place Saint-Sulpice, where Pujol, standing on the fountain, informed them of the response of the government and summoned the workers to the Panthéon that same night.

During the evening, an immense crowd of men and women from the working-class quarters, the Faubourg du Temple and the Faubourg Saint-Antoine, made their way up Rue Saint-Jacques and massed around the Panthéon. Pardigon, a law student who was to take part in the insurrection, recalled:

Several speakers spoke at once, but without leading to confusion. Each of them had their own audience. At certain moments, low murmurs and oscillations among these groups, in which even faces could not be distinguished, showed that all minds were moved by a single thought, a thought as cold and severe as it was passionate, for the shouts, cheers, applause and enthusiasm customary at popular meetings were lacking ... The spectre of the Sologne was present in everyone's mind, like a French Siberia, to which the workers of the National Workshops were to be exiled, thus putting an end to the question of the Right to Work and ridding Paris of its revolutionary forces.[100]

99 Tocqueville, *Recollections*, p. 136.
100 F. Pardigon, *Épisodes des journées de juin* (London, 1852).

Finally, Pujol, perching on a fence post, invited the workers to assemble the next day in the same place. 'Acclamations greeted his incendiary words, the torches were extinguished, the crowd melted away, and the night passed in dull and horrible preparations.'[101]

That night, the prefect of police received the order to occupy the Place du Panthéon and arrest the fifty-six delegates of the National Workshops of the 12th arrondissement, which housed what Lamartine called the 'famished masses', along with those of the Latin Quarter and the Faubourg Saint-Marceau. This order was not carried out, and at six in the morning several thousand workers massed on the Place du Panthéon. Coming down through Rue Saint-Jacques and Rue de la Harpe, they erected barricades in the little streets around the church of Saint-Séverin, occupied the Petit-Pont, and built fortifications in the labyrinth of the Île de la Cité, where they threatened the police prefecture.[102]

At the same time, another mass of insurgents gathered at the Poissonière and Saint-Denis barriers (now the Barbès-Rochechouart and La Chapelle crossroads) and in the Clos Saint-Lazare – the construction site of the Louis-Philippe (now Lariboisière) hospital. This group built fortifications around the new church of Saint-Vincent-de-Paul and on the Place La Fayette (now Franz-Lizst). On Rue de Bellefond, Rue Rochechouart and Rue du Faubourg-Poissonière, railway engineers erected barricades.

The third focus of insurrection was the Faubourg Saint-Antoine. This joined the Faubourg du Temple in the Popincourt quarter, and established its forward positions right against the Hôtel de Ville, fortifying the little streets around the church of Saint-Gervais:

> In all the little streets around that building [the Hôtel de Ville] I found the people busy constructing barricades. They went about the work with the methodical skill of engineers, not taking up more paving-stones than were needed to provide squared stones for a solid and even fairly tidy wall, and they usually left a narrow opening by the houses to allow people to circulate.[103]

The Place du Panthéon and the Clos Saint-Lazare, on the Left and Right Banks respectively, were thus the two outer strongholds of the insurrection.

---

101   *Histoire des journées de juin*, anonymous pamphlet (Paris: Martinon éditeur, 5 Rue du Coq-Saint-Honoré, 1848).

102   This was then on Rue de Jérusalem, a small street on the Île de la Cité that disappeared under Haussmann. People said 'Rue de Jérusalem' to mean the police, as we say today 'the Quai d'Orsay' or 'the Élysée'.

103   Tocqueville, *Recollections*, p. 138.

They were linked to the Faubourg Saint-Antoine which was its headquarters – the former through the Place Maubert, the Cité, and the Hôtel de Ville quarter, and the second via the Faubourgs Saint-Martin and du Temple and their respective boulevards. In this way, the insurrection controlled a great semicircle in the eastern part of Paris, the most populous and the poorest, where the narrow streets and the nature of the buildings made any attack very problematic:

> Once in control of this broad space, and having expanded its ranks with the whole working population of these quarters, the insurrection could advance on the Right and Left Banks simultaneously, through the boulevards and along the quays, towards the other half of Paris that was richer and less populated, that containing the Tuileries, the Palais-Royal, the ministries, the National Assembly, the Bank, etc.[104]

But an offensive of this kind required a strategic conception, and this was lacking. 'The June insurrection was made without an overall plan, without a conspiracy in the strong sense of the term, without a headquarters, but it was certainly not made without work by the people on itself, without advance agreement', writes Pardigon. Louis Ménard thought likewise: 'The leaders of the democratic forces played no part in the insurrection. The most talented and energetic of them were imprisoned at Vincennes. The others lacked boldness and faith; hence, in the party of the People, this absence of unity, of overall plan, that made possible the victory of its enemies.'[105]

At all events, by midday on the 23rd, half of Paris was in the hands of the people without a shot being fired. In the afternoon, the Executive Commission transferred all military power to the minister of war, General Cavaignac ('Lamartine's fireworks have turned into Cavaignac's incendiary rockets', Marx wrote in the *Neue Rheinische Zeitung*). The son of a member of the Convention, a student at the Polytechnique when the school was a focus of republicanism, and the brother of Godefroy Cavaignac who had been a leading light in the republican opposition ('our Godefroy', Delescluze called him), there was something ambiguous about this character, but it was the African general in him who carried the day: 'This time they will not escape us ... I am charged with crushing the enemy and I shall act massively against him, as in

---

104 *Histoire des journées de juin.*
105 Ménard, *Prologue d'une révolution.*

war. If need be, I shall attack in the open country and I shall succeed in defeating him.'[106]

Cavaignac's forces were made up of three bodies, designed to operate, as he put it, in compact masses, so as to avoid fragmentation and demoralization when they came in contact with the insurgents:

> The three headquarters were: 1) the Porte Saint-Denis, to act against the Clos Saint-Lazare, the Faubourg Saint-Martin and the Faubourg du Temple; M. de Lamoricière, in command of this side, would distinguish himself by the swiftness of his vision and his brilliant courage; 2) the Hôtel de Ville, where Duvivier prepared operations against the Saint-Antoine quarter and faubourg; 3) the Sorbonne, from where Bedeau and Damesne, commanding the Mobile Guard, were to act against the Panthéon and the Faubourgs Saint-Jacques and Saint-Marceau.[107]

The first engagement was late in the morning of the 23rd, at the Porte Saint-Denis:

> The detachment that set out from the Clos Saint-Lazare to occupy the Porte was made up of a force of young men with a drum at their head. As this force was arriving, a voice cried out: 'To the barricades!' 'To arms!', a thousand other voices replied. From every house, men, women and children came out into the streets, seizing vehicles, tearing up cobbles, and in a few minutes erecting a formidable barricade. One woman hoisted to the top of the barricade a flag with the words: 'National Workshops, 4th arrondissement, 5th section'.[108]

The Rue and the Faubourg Saint-Denis, Rue Sainte-Apolline, Rues d'Aboukir and de Cléry were all covered with barricades. The railings and fences of Boulevard de Bonne-Nouvelle were torn up. Suddenly a detachment of National Guard came down the boulevards. When they saw the barricade, they opened fire without reading the summons. The insurgents

---

106   Cited by Maïté Bouyssy in his introduction to Maréchal Bugeaud, *La Guerre des rues et des maisons* (Paris: Jean-Paul Rocher, 1997). Soldiers were not alone in their humanist vision of colonial war. Tocqueville: 'I have often heard in France, from men whom I respect but do not approve of, that they find it bad to attack unarmed men, women and children. In my view, these are unpleasant necessities, but ones that any people that wants to make war on the Arabs will be obliged to accept' (Cited by A. Brossat, *Le Corps de l'ennemi*, Paris: La Fabrique, 1998).
107   *Histoire des journées de juin.*
108   Ibid. The 4th arrondissement at that time was the Les Halles quarter.

responded, and the Guards fled. Then came a battalion of the 2nd Legion and a company of the 3rd. The leader of the insurgents who was directing the fire was struck by a bullet and fell. A woman took up the flag:

> with thin hair and bare arms, in a strikingly coloured dress, she seemed to defy death. On seeing her, the National Guard hesitated to fire; they shouted to the young woman to get back; she remained undaunted, and provoked the attackers with her gestures and voice; a shot was fired, and she staggered and collapsed. But another woman suddenly rushed to her side; with one hand she supported the bloody body of her friend, with the other she hurled stones at the attackers. A new volley of shots echoed, and she fell in her turn on to the body that she was embracing.[109]

The barricade was taken. At the same time, the head of the column led by Lamoricière appeared on the boulevard, coming from the Madeleine – troops of the line and Mobile Guards – to take up position at the Château d'Eau. It swept the boulevards, the Faubourgs Saint-Denis and Saint-Martin, and advanced northward through the Faubourg Poissonière, where it stormed the barricades erected on Rue Richer and Rue des Petites-Écuries. But it was brought to a halt at the gigantic defences on the Place La Fayette, commanded by the industrial designer Legénissel, a captain in the National Guard who had gone over with his company to the insurrection. Lamoricière had to retreat towards the Porte Saint-Denis.

That Friday 23rd, the first of four days of fighting, the insurgents succeeded in securing their positions:

---

109   Stern, *Histoire de la Révolution de 1848*. Remember that this author was a woman, the Comtesse d'Agoult. In *Things Seen*, Hugo describes this episode in a manner both intimate and hostile: 'The National Guard, irritated more than intim-idated, advanced in a rush to the barricade. At that moment, a woman appeared on top of the barricade, young, pretty, wild-haired and terrible. This woman, who was a prostitute, lifted her dress up to her belt and shouted to the National Guards, in the horrible brothel language that one always has to translate: "Cowards, fire on the belly of a woman if you dare!" Events now took a terrifying course. The National Guard did not hesitate. A platoon-fire toppled the wretched woman; she fell with a loud scream. There was a horrible silence, both on the barricade and from the attackers. Suddenly a second woman appeared. This one was still younger and prettier: almost a child, scarcely seventeen years old. What a wretched situ-ation! She too was a prostitute. She lifted her dress, showed her belly, and cried: "Shoot, you brigands!" They shot. She fell in a hail of bullets on the body of the first. It was thus that the war began.'

The Clos Saint-Lazare, the barriers of Poissonière, La Chapelle, La
Villette and Temple, the communes of Montmartre, La Chapelle, La
Villette and Belleville, the Faubourg du Temple, the Popincourt quarter, the Faubourg and Rue Saint-Antoine, the quarters of Saint-Jacques
and Saint-Victor, were entirely controlled by the insurrection … In
the Saint-Martin quarter as well, which was cut off from the three
main centres of rebellion, barricades were raised in Rues Rambuteau,
Beaubourg, Planche-Mibray, etc. A portion of the National Guard of the
8th, 11th and 12th arrondissements were installed behind the barricades.[110]

At the Panthéon, it took very little for two legions of the National Guard to
come to blows. The 11th Legion, commanded by Edgar Quinet, was mainly
on the side of order. The 12th Legion, which had gone over to the side of
the people, demanded that the 11th should return to the limits of its own
arrondissement. 'Some thirty students from the École Normale Supérieure,
in their new uniforms and armed with muskets, intervened to prevent the
spilling of blood. They deplored the insurrection, but were not hostile to
it.'[111] The mayor of the 12th arrondissement, a very popular doctor, was
negotiating with the people on the barricades when suddenly a detachment led by the elderly François Arago arrived from the Luxembourg and
stopped at the barricade barring Rue Soufflot. Arago furiously asked the
insurgents why they were fighting against the Republic. An old insurgent
reminded him: 'We were together at the time of Rue Saint-Merri.' After
summoning those present to disperse, the barricade was attacked and taken.
On the Place de Cambrai and Rue Neuve-des-Mathurins, new barricades
went up, and this time Arago gave orders to use cannon.[112]

Quinet and Arago – how did these old republicans arrive at bombarding
the people?

These men, who had spent their whole life fighting for the progress of
democratic ideas … were persuaded on this occasion that the people, by
rising up against the national representation, would drown not only law
and right, but the Republic and perhaps even the state in their calamitous
victory, and with a shattered heart but a firm spirit, they set out against

---

110   *Histoire des journées de juin.* The 8th arrondissement comprised the northern
part of the Marais, the 11th the Luxembourg, and the 12th, as we have seen, the
Latin Quarter and the Faubourg Saint-Marceau.
111   Pardigon, *Épisodes des journées de juin.*
112   The Place de Cambrai was in front of the Collège de France, before Rue des
Écoles was driven through. Rue Neuve-des-Mathurins was off Rue Saint-Jacques,
not far from this.

this strange enemy whose emancipation had been the goal of their efforts for more than twenty years.[113]

Perhaps also, in the face of this proletariat of which they had previously had only an abstract vision, their class instinct took the upper hand over their generous ideas.

In the afternoon of the 23rd, General Bedeau left the Hôtel de Ville with two columns to attack the Montagne Saint-Geneviève. One column crossed the Seine by the Pont d'Arcole, the other by the Pont Notre-Dame. An artillery battery was installed in the Hôtel-Dieu to support them.[114] The Guards easily stormed the barricade of the Petit-Pont on the Île de la Cité, but on the other side, the one blocking entrance to Rue Saint-Jacques remained. This was defended by old republicans who had been in prison under Louis-Philippe together with Guinard, the officer now commanding the artillery opposite them. 'Citizen Guinard was at the head with his gunners, though not all of them, as some were on the barricade, so that they could recognize one another and call out to each other by name.'[115] As happened very often in the course of these days, it was the arrival of the Mobile Guard that decided things. The barricade was taken. The insurgents took refuge in a draper's shop at the bottom of Rue Saint-Jacques, 'Aux Deux Pierrots':

> Belval, their leader, an energetic man of great composure, wanted to demolish the staircase and fight from the upper floors. He was not listened to, and got angry with his companions. The Mobile Guard began a terrible carnage. The workers, hidden behind display cases, under the counters, in the eaves and the cellars, were killed with bayonet thrusts, to the savage laughter of the murderers. Blood ran in streams.[116]

Tocqueville had no reason to be worried about the behaviour of the Mobile Guards:

> The bravery of these youngsters of the Mobile Guard, in this first and terrible test, could not even be imagined by those who did not witness

---

113   Stern, *Histoire de la Révolution de 1848*.
114   The old Hôtel-Dieu, on the edge of the small arm of the Seine, in the square where Charlemagne's statue now stands, had an extension on the Left Bank, to which it was joined by a covered bridge. This is no doubt where the battery was placed.
115   Pardigon, *Épisodes des journées de juin*.
116   Marouk, *Juin 1848*.

it. The noise of the firing, the whistling of bullets, seemed to them a new and joyful game. The smoke and the smell of powder excited them. They ran to the attack, climbed up the falling cobblestones, clung to every obstacle with a marvellous agility. Once on their way, nothing could hold them back; they were seized by a desire for emulation which drove them on in the face of death. To seize a musket from the bloody hands of an enemy, to press the barrel of a carbine against a naked breast, to dig the point of a bayonet in quivering flesh, to trample corpses underfoot, to be the first to stand on top of the barricade, to receive mortal attacks without flinching, to laugh at one's own blood flowing, to seize a flag and wave it about one's head, defying the enemy bullets – all this was, for these foolish and heroic youngsters of Paris, unknown bliss that made them insensitive to everything. Not much else was needed for this transport of youth and madness for glory, supported by the brilliance and calmness of army officers, to lead the regiments and the mass of the National Guard. If the Mobile Guard had gone over to the insurrection, as was feared, it is almost certain that victory would have gone over with them.[117]

After this success, General Bedeau attacked up Rue Saint-Jacques, but fire came from every window, the troops ran out of ammunition, barricades multiplied as they climbed, and the losses were enormous. Night fell, and there was no longer any question of reaching the Panthéon. The troops fell back on the Hôtel de Ville. 'So many dead and wounded, such disproportionate losses for the slim advantages won, cast a great sadness into the mind of General Bedeau.'[118] On the other flank of the Montagne, towards the south, the situation for the forces of order was no better. The Mobile Guard had experienced very heavy losses, and one company had been disarmed on Rue Mouffetard. On the Left Bank, the insurrection was still unvanquished on the night of the 23rd.

On the Right Bank, Cavaignac and Lamartine directed operations on horseback, accompanied by Pierre Bonaparte. ('This intrepid young man', wrote Lamartine in his *History*, 'inherited the republicanism of his father.' Twenty-two years later Pierre Bonaparte would murder the journalist Victor Noir, bringing all of Paris into the street for the first time since the coup d'état.) During a rainstorm, they attacked the Faubourg du Temple. 'Many representatives who were present during the day had already received gunshot wounds, when Monsieurs Cavaignac and Lamartine put

---

117   Stern, *Histoire de la Révolution de 1848*.
118   Ibid.

themselves at the head of the assault columns that successively attacked all the barricades.'[119] Cavaignac and his seven battalions were halted by an immense barricade on the corner of Rue de la Fontaine-au-Roi and Rue de la Pierre-Levée – the very place where the last barricade of the Commune would later hold out. Cavaignac had the 20th Battalion of the Mobile Guard lead the assault, but it was stopped short by a tremendous volley of gunfire. A second battalion suffered the same fate, and all seven were repulsed one by one:

> Then Cavaignac had the cannon brought up. Alone on horseback, in the middle of the roadway and completely composed, he remained immobile and gave orders with a perfect sang-froid; two-thirds of the men operating the guns were killed or wounded at his side. The general sent several detachments through side streets to try and get round the barricade. But it was all in vain. Hours passed, ammunition ran out. Cavaignac, who had come to bring reinforcements to Lamoricière, was forced to ask him what to do. Night was falling. It was only after a battle lasting five hours that the barricade was finally taken by Colonel Dulac, at the head of the 29th Regiment of the line ... Cavaignac, his heart shattered by this sad success [so highly sensitive, these generals: E.H.], headed back to the Palais-Bourbon.[120]

The next day, the barricade was rebuilt.

Around the Hôtel de Ville, in the evening of the 23rd, the party of Order was in no better position: 'The taking of the town hall, which was the traditional seat of popular government, would give a kind of legal character to the insurrection; so the insurgents made unheard-of efforts to seize it.'[121] Barricades surrounded the Hôtel de Ville, on the Île de la Cité, Rue Saint-Antoine, the little streets around Saint-Gervais and Rue du Temple. The troops were harassed by sniper fire from buildings between the Place de l'Hôtel-de-Ville and the Place du Châtelet.

In the Assembly, that evening, the atmosphere was gloomy and tense:

> When the sitting resumed, we learned that Lamartine had been received with fire at every barricade he had approached; two of his colleagues, Bixiou and Dornès, had been mortally wounded attempting to harangue

---

119   *Histoire des journées de juin.*
120   Stern, *Histoire de la Révolution de 1848.*
121   Ibid.

the insurgents. Bedeau got a bullet through his thigh at the turning into the Faubourg Saint-Jacques; many distinguished officers were already killed or put out of action ... Towards midnight Cavaignac appeared ... In a jerky, abrupt voice and using simple, exact words, Cavaignac recounted the main events of the day. He announced that he had given orders for all the regiments along the line of the railway to converge on Paris, and that all the National Guards in the outskirts had been called up.[122]

The next day, Saturday, 24th June, Victor Hugo, who had just been told (wrongly) that his house on the Place des Vosges had been burned during the night, witnessed the death agony of the Executive Commission:

> I suddenly found myself face to face with all those men who were the established authority. It was more like a cell in which the accused await their condemnation than a council of government ... M. de Lamartine, standing against the frame of the left-hand window, was chatting with a general in full-dress uniform, whom I saw for the first and last time; this was Négrier. Négrier was killed in front of a barricade on the evening of that same day. I hastened to Lamartine who took a few steps towards me. He was pale, untidy, with a long beard, his coat not brushed and all powdery. He stretched out his hand: 'Ah, good day, Hugo.' ...
>   'What is happening, Lamartine?'
>   'We're f...'
>   'What do you mean by that?'
>   'I mean that in a quarter of an hour the Assembly will be invaded.'
>   'How on earth? And the troops?'
>   'There are no troops.'[123]

But the Assembly, by a parliamentary coup d'état fomented by the royalists in alliance with the right-wing republicans, declared Paris in a state of siege and gave full powers to General Cavaignac to restore order. Only sixty deputies voted against the decree (including Tocqueville, though he later admitted that he was mistaken). The Executive Commission resigned amid general indifference: 'It was resolved that sixty members of the Chamber, selected by the committees, should disperse through Paris to inform the National Guards of the various decrees just passed by the

---

122   Tocqueville, *Recollections*.
123   Hugo, *Things Seen*.

Assembly and thereby restore their confidence, for they were said to be hesitant and discouraged.'[124] Among them were Tocqueville and Victor Hugo.

From three a.m. on the 24th, the fighting recommenced with extreme violence. On the Left Bank, the church of Saint-Séverin, the Place Maubert and the barricades on Rue Saint-Jacques were stormed in turn. The troops arrived on the Place du Panthéon, where the insurgents had occupied the building, the law school and the neighbouring houses. Pardigon, familiar with these places and himself involved in the battle, recalled:

> The insurgents, retrenched beneath the porticos of the Panthéon and in its wings, showed great skill in manoeuvring and defending themselves. Two barricades, as strong as bastions, flanked the monument. One of them dominated Rue d'Ulm ... The troops' cannon fired from Rue Soufflot. Their shells passed through the church from end to end: one of them broke off the head of the statue of Immortality that stands on the steps of the choir. The platoon-fire of the insurgents rivalled in precision that of the troops, and left the officers of the National Guard quite amazed.

But the soldiers succeeded in gaining entrance to the law school through a back door. They fired on the insurgents from the windows, and were fired on themselves from the dome of the Panthéon and the *mairie*. General Damesme – who was subsequently wounded in the thigh and died a few days later – managed to get a gun battery into the middle of Rue Soufflot. The door of the Panthéon was broken down and the building saw hand-to-hand fighting; prisoners were shot on the spot. The troops then attacked Rue des Fossés-Saint-Jacques and Rue de l'Estrapade. In the evening, General Bréa, who had replaced Damesme, made his way down the southern slope of the Montagne along Rue Mouffetard, and captured the barricades of the Faubourg Saint-Marceau and the surroundings of the Jardin des Plantes.

On the side of the Hôtel de Ville, the insurgents had retaken during the night Rues Planche-Mibray, des Arcis, de la Verrerie and Saint-Antoine. General Duvivier tried to reach the building, but in order to capture the block of houses around Saint-Gervais he had to use cannon, and the fighting was house by house. 'On the Place Baudoyer, despite the cannon deployed against the barricades, resistance was so strong that

---

124 Tocqueville, *Recollections*, p. 148.

when night fell it was decided to bring troops up to the surroundings of the Hôtel de Ville.'[125]

In the northern faubourgs, fighting was centred around the Place La Fayette, where engineering workers from La Chapelle and Saint-Denis had constructed an immense barricade, supported by the houses on the corner of Rues La Fayette and d'Abbeville. This fortification resisted for several hours, but in the evening the great barricade was finally taken after hours of cannon fire. The workers fell back to the Clos Saint-Lazare. In the Faubourg Saint-Denis, the troops unsuccessfully attacked barricades defended by workers of the Nord railway. The two generals commanding the artillery, Korte and Bourgon, were both wounded, the latter mortally.

On Sunday morning, the 25th, the insurgents were reduced to isolated quarters: in the north, the Clos Saint-Lazare and the adjacent section of Faubourgs Poissonière and Saint-Denis; in the centre-east, the greater part of the Faubourg du Temple and the Faubourg Saint-Antoine; and in the south, the periphery of the Faubourg Saint-Marceau towards the Fontainebleau barrier (now Place d'Italie). Cavaignac posted up his proclamation, with such a generous ending that it might have been written by Lamartine: 'Come to us, come as brothers repentant and subject to the law, and the arms of the Republic are quite ready to receive you.' As Marouk writes, these arms were quite ready to receive the insurgents, but only to murder them. Fighting began again at dawn. Around the Hôtel de Ville, the troops managed this time round to break the encirclement, and by the end of the morning they reached the Bastille. In the south, Bréa arrived at a great barricade by the Fontainebleau barrier, defended by two thousand men. He was shot there in circumstances that are rather unclear, and his death, along with that of Monsignor Affre, the archbishop of Paris, the same day in the Faubourg Saint-Antoine, would serve as justification – even in some educational textbooks – for the massacres that followed the defeat (the hostages of Rue Haxo played the same role in the history of the Commune). As Granier de Cassagnac explains in choice terms: 'Towards men guilty of the greatest excesses, of many of the most serious crimes, all the moderation was used that victory counsels and that the state of society permits ... The seditionists, who completely dispense with all laws, will always be ready to complain of the victors who dispense with some formalities.'[126]

That Sunday, the balance of forces was reversed, as 'down all the roads not held by the insurgents, thousands of men were pouring in from all parts

---

125   *Histoire des journées de juin.*
126   *Histoire de la chute du roi Louis-Philippe, de la République de 1848.*

of France to aid us. Thanks to the railways ... These men were drawn without distinction from all classes of society; among them there were great numbers of peasants, bourgeois, large landowners and nobles, all jumbled up together in the same ranks.'[127]

With the fall of the Barrière d'Italie the Left Bank was lost. That morning, Tocqueville, who played his role of representative of the people to the armed forces with sufficient courage, was at the Château d'Eau, from where Lamoricière was attacking the Faubourg du Temple:[128]

I eventually reached the Château d'Eau, where I found a large body of troops from different branches of the army congregated. At the foot of the fountain was a cannon trained down Rue Samson [now Léon-Jouhaux]. At first I thought the insurgents were answering our fire from a gun of their own, but I finally saw my mistake; it was the echo of our own firing that made the frightful noise. I have never heard anything like it; one would have thought one was in the midst of some great battle. But in fact the insurgents answered only with infrequent but deadly musket fire ... Behind the fountains, Lamoricière, astride a large horse and in range of the guns, gave his orders amid a rain of bullets. I found him more excited and more talkative than I would have supposed a general in command should be at such a moment ... and I would have admired his courage more had it been calmer ... I had never imagined war was like that. As the boulevard [du Temple] seemed clear beyond the Château d'Eau, I could not see why our columns did not advance, or why we did not capture the large house facing the street at a rush, instead of remaining so long subject to the murderous fire from it. Yet nothing could have been easier to explain: the boulevard that I supposed free ... was not so; there was a bend in it, and after that point it bristled with barricades the whole way to the Bastille. Before attacking the barricades, we wanted to control the streets that would be behind us, and in particular to get control of the house facing Rue Samson, which dominated the boulevard and would have harassed our communications badly; finally, we could not take that house by assault because the canal stood in the way, but I could not see that from the boulevard ... As the insurgents had no guns, this battlefield must have been less terrible to contemplate than one ploughed up by cannon balls. The men struck down before my eyes seemed transfixed by an invisible shaft; they staggered and fell with no more to be seen at

127   Tocqueville, *Recollections*.
128   To understand his account, you have to imagine these places before the opening of the Place de la République, the Boulevard Voltaire, etc.

first than a little hole in their clothes ... It was indeed a strange and a terrifying thing to see the quick change of expression, the fire of life in the eyes quenched in the sudden terror of death ... I noticed that the soldiers of the line were the least eager of our troops ... Without any doubt the keenest were those very Gardes Mobiles whose fidelity we had questioned so seriously and, I still say, even after the event, so rightly, for it would have taken very little to make them decide against us instead of for us.[129]

A few hours later, the troops had advanced to the Bastille. Victor Hugo was on the boulevard:

The insurgents fired from the top of the new houses all along Boulevard Beaumarchais ... They had put dummies in the windows, bundles of straw dressed in blouses and with caps on top. I could clearly see a man there defended by a small brick barrier, at the corner of the fourth-floor balcony on the house opposite Rue du Pont-aux-Choux. He kept up his fire for a long while and killed several people. It was three o'clock. The soldiers and the Mobile Guard were on the roofs of Boulevard du Temple and responded to his fire ... I believed that I had to make an effort to try and stop the flow of blood, if this was at all possible, and I pressed forward to the corner of Rue d'Angoulême [now Jean-Pierre-Timbaud]. As I was passing the little tower at that point, a volley of shots came in my direction. The tower behind me was riddled with bullets. It was covered with theatre posters shredded by the musket-fire. I pulled off a strip of paper as a souvenir. The poster this was from advertised a fête at the Château des Fleurs that very Sunday, with 'ten thousand Chinese lanterns'.[130]

By Sunday afternoon, the insurgents held on only to the Clos Saint-Lazare and the Faubourg Saint-Antoine. Cavaignac decided to deal first with the former, so that he could then bring all his forces to bear on the latter. Lamennais wrote in his newspaper, *Le Peuple constituant*: 'In the Clos Saint-Lazare, the struggle took enormous proportions: to speak only of the National Guard, it was a complete battle, with all the features of bold hero-ism and sublime death. Whether or not these men were seditionists, anyone who saw them fall under the hurricane of shot that ploughed through them from all four sides at a time could not prevent an involuntary admiration.'

129   Tocqueville, *Recollections*, p. 158.
130   Hugo, *Things Seen*.

When all was over, the leader of the insurgents there, a journalist by the name of Benjamin Laroque, one of the few intellectuals engaged in the battle on the side of the people, ended up marching forward to his death, in Roman style, as Baudin would later do in the Faubourg Saint-Antoine and Delescluze on the Place du Château-d'Eau in 1871.

By the morning of the 26th, the Faubourg Saint-Antoine remained alone. An attempt at mediation by three deputies was rebuffed by the army command. 'The African generals were unwilling to release their prey. The Faubourg Saint-Antoine could not escape the fate of the other working-class quarters. The army's *honour* demanded this.'[131] Lamoricière's column emerged from the Popincourt quarter through Rues Saint-Maur and Basfroi, at the same time as the troops massed around the Bastille drowned the faubourg with a formidable artillery fire. The battle did not last long, but was terribly violent. At ten o'clock, the faubourg capitulated. A few insurgents resisted until the evening at the Amandiers barrier (now Boulevard de Charonne, at the western corner of Père-Lachaise), but at two in the morning, Sénart, the president of the Assembly, was able to exclaim: 'It is all over, gentlemen, thank God!'

'Shoot, gentlemen, but don't slander!' Blanqui demanded from the depths of his prison.[132] The winners of June had already begun to apply the first part of this exhortation when the fighting was still in progress. In this respect, as in many others, June 1848 stood in sharp contrast to the insurrections of the 1830s. Certainly, it had not been very safe to be caught with weapons in hand in the Saint-Merri cloister or Rue Transnonain, and for those who did escape the courts of the July monarchy were not inclined to be lenient. But the banker Leuwen could not ignore that his dear Lucien was fighting on the other side, with his fellow students of the École Polytechnique. A section of the sons of the republican bourgeoisie were then behind the barricades with the workers, which ruled out the prisoners being shot en masse. There was no concern of this kind in 1848. Ménard, Pardigon and Castille speak of rivers of blood, mountains of piled-up corpses, punctured and bleeding flesh, manhunts, public gardens turned into slaughterhouses – and these were not just metaphors. Insurgents captured with weapons were shot on the spot:

The majority of workers caught on the barricade of Rue des Noyers and other barricades on Rue Saint-Jacques were taken to the police station

---

131   Marouk, *Juin 1848*.
132   Auguste Blanqui, 'Adresse au banquet des travailleurs socialistes', 3 December 1848.

on Rue des Mathurins, or the Hôtel de Cluny, and shot ... When the proclamation [of Cavaignac, promising to spare the lives of insurgents who surrendered] became known to the workers, a large number gave themselves up. Some were then shot on the spot, others taken to the Hôtel de Ville and some other points that were particularly used for slaughter. On the Pont d'Arcole, prisoners fell under the crossfire of the Mobile Guards placed on the two quays. On the Pont Louis-Philippe, more than forty were thrown into the water. Others were taken to the Quai de l'Hôtel-de-Ville and thrown into the river, where they were shot. Most often they fell on the bank, and other Mobile Guards finished them off with musket fire.[133]

The insurgent city was transformed into a charnel house. The cobbles and the earth in the gardens were red. 'It was only when a rainstorm came that the pools of blood were washed away.'[134] The dead were heaped up in pits, thrown into the Seine, piled into hastily dug common graves.

In the Place du Carrousel, on the night of the 24th the National Guard, all the more savage in that they had not performed too brilliantly during the fighting, murdered a column of prisoners who were being taken to the cellars of the Tuileries. Pardigon was among them:

My knee had hardly grazed the ground when a terrible gunfire, from just in front of us, burst like a shell. The hurricane toppled us. The head of the column was swept by shots ... A few weak cries could be heard, several men fell back heavily in silence, they died as soon as they were hit. The wounded and living were left among the dead and dying ... The hail of bullets continued. I myself fell with my face against the ground, I was hit ... Stray bullets crossed the fence towards the Louvre, on the side of Rue de Rohan, in fact all around. National Guards were posted in these different places. When they were struck by bullets they thought they were under attack, and responded. Then thousands of bullets converged on us from all sides. This dark mass of men, lit up only too brightly by the lampposts in the square, became the general target.

And he concludes: 'There were the dead, the only question now was to remove them. The wounded dragged themselves along and were tied up. Some survivors had fled, but they would be caught. It was not all over,

---

133   Ménard, *Prologue d'une révolution*. On the role of the Mobile Guards in this repression, Hippolyte Castille notes: 'The little men with green epaulettes resembled weasels with their snouts in blood' (*Les Massacres de juin* [1857]).
134   Ménard, *Prologue d'une révolution*.

now would come revenge!' This affair made a great impression right across Europe. Even the Russians in Warsaw or the Austrians in Milan had not done any better. A dozen years later, Baudelaire recalled the massacre as explicitly as the censorship would permit, in *Les Fleurs du mal*. In 'The Swan', the final evocation of the Place du Carrousel ends on a thought, 'Of the captives, of the vanquished! ... of many others too', and the final stanzas of 'The Flawed Bell' are like an echo of Pardigon's account: 'I, my soul is flawed, and when, a prey to ennui,/She wishes to fill the cold night air with her songs,/It often happens that her weakened voice/Resembles the death rattle of a wounded man,/Forgotten beneath a heap of dead, by a lake of blood,/Who dies without moving, striving desperately.'[135]

After the killing there began the great hunt – searches, denunciations, arrests. The Procurator-General gave the police 'instructions on the means to discover the June fighters'. He advised 'checking whether prisoners have their lips or hands blackened by powder. Grains of powder may remain in the wrinkles or crevices of calloused hands. A thumb that has been used to load the musket hammer will sometimes bear a burn, and most often at least a bruise ... Pockets must be scrupulously examined; they may contain some grains of powder or explosive caps. It is said that if you place your face close to the butt of a musket you can smell the scent of powder a full week after it has been fired.'[136]

The captives were imprisoned in forts, barracks, in the Luxembourg (a real headquarters of butchery),[137] in the cellars of the Hôtel de Ville and the Tuileries, where they were left to die of hunger. If they made a noise or asked for anything, the guards fired at the heap of prisoners through the bars. Pardigon's account ('They also fired through the grill, along the cellar. This firing was no longer haphazard, but deliberate') prefigures Père Roque's famous gesture in *A Sentimental Education*:

Other prisoners present themselves at the vent-hole, with their bristling beards, their burning eyeballs, all pushing forward, and yelling: 'Bread!'

---

135   On the echoes of the June days in literature, see Oehler, *1848. Le Spleen contre l'oubli*.

136   Cited by Marouk, *Juin 1848*. These directives were indeed applied: 'In the little wood close to the Passage Ronce [in Ménilmontant], unarmed men were shot on the pretext that their hands smelled of powder' (Ménard, *Prologue d'une révolution*).

137   'Right from the first night of the battle, massacres were organized in the Luxembourg. Captured insurgents were brought there in batches of twenty. They were forced to their knees and then shot. After these executions, the garden was closed for two weeks. The pools of blood that gave evidence of the slaughter had to be well hidden' (Marouk, *Juin 1848*).

Père Roque was indignant at seeing his authority slighted. In order to frighten them he took aim at them; and, borne backward into the vault that nearly smothered him, the young man, with his eyes staring upward, once more exclaimed: 'Bread!' 'Hold on! Here it is!' said Père Roque, firing a shot from his gun. There was a fearful howl, then silence.[138]

In this catastrophe, the Paris proletariat stood alone. Those who should have supported them, 'that party that dared to call itself the Mountain', as Louis Ménard put it, did not lag behind in shooting them down. Ledru-Rollin, minister of the interior, left the repression to Cavaignac when he resigned from the Executive Commission, but just before this, 'he took it upon himself to use the telegraph to ask for regiments of the line, the National Guards of the departments, and even sailors from Brest and Cherbourg, to be brought in as rapidly as possible by rail'.[139] Louis Blanc, 'accused of supporting the insurrection, would maintain in August: "No one could have been more foreign than myself to these unhappy events, no one mourned more deeply than I did this deplorable conflict, the first news of which was given me by my concierge."'[140] Few indeed dared to publicly protest against the massacres – Pierre Leroux, Victor Considérant, and Proudhon.[141] Announcing the closing

---

138   Some recent writers, such as Dolf Oehler, have drawn on this passage (and others) to present Flaubert as vaguely sympathetic to the insurgent workers. I believe however that his political ideas are shown very well on the same page of *A Sentimental Education*: 'Aristocracy had the same fits of fury as low debauchery, and the cotton cap did not show itself less hideous than the red cap.' He expressed his disgust of the people still more strongly at the time of the Commune (see his letters to George Sand).

139   Stern, *Histoire de la Révolution de 1848*. In *Le Prolétariat*, Victor Marouk commented on the inauguration of the statue of Ledru-Rollin in 1885, on the Place Voltaire (now Léon Blum): 'Speeches will be delivered, recalling the titles of this famous republican to public honour. Newspapers ... will tell us of the tribune and his superb speeches, of the member of the Provisional Government, the father of universal suffrage, the defender of the Constitution, banished under the Empire. Orators and journalists will certainly refrain from mentioning the Ledru-Rollin of reaction and the firing squads, the Ledru-Rollin of 16 April 1848 and the June days.' And he concluded: 'The sons of those shot will keep their distance from this apotheosis of the man of the firing squad.'

140   Cited in Marouk, *Juin 1848*.

141   'Out of parliamentary stupidity, I failed in my duty as representative. I had eyes to see, and I did not see ... Elected by the people, and a journalist of the proletariat, I should not have left this mass without leadership and advice. A hundred thousand fighting men deserved that I should have concerned myself with them. That would have been better than to bury myself in your offices' (P. Proudhon, *Confessions d'un révolutionnaire* [Paris: Lacroix & Verboeckhoven, 1868]; written between 1849 and 1851).

down of his newspaper, old Lamennais was almost alone in showing that he understood it all:

> *Le Peuple constituant* began with the Republic, and is ending with the Republic. For what we are seeing is certainly not the Republic, it is not anything that has a name. Paris is in a state of siege, delivered to a military power, which is itself handed to a faction that has made it its instrument; the jails and fortresses of Louis-Philippe are filled with 14,000 prisoners, in the wake of an atrocious butchery; mass transportations, banishments unequalled by those of 1793, laws curtailing the right of assembly, in practice destroyed, the enslavement and ruin of the press ... the People decimated and repressed in their misery, more deeply than ever before – no, once again, this is certainly not the Republic; but around its bloody tomb the saturnalia of reaction.

The Paris Commune, repression of which involved far more shootings, deportations and banishments than the June days of 1848, ended up by being integrated into consensual republican history, thanks to Hugo, Jaurès and Péguy, to the point that it is sometimes overlooked how in 1871 the social democrats were in Versailles and not in Paris. A plaque at 17 Rue de la Fontaine-au-Roi, notes: 'The last barricade of the Commune resisted in the Rue de la Fontaine-au-Roi. A hundred and twenty years later, the Socialist party and its first secretary Pierre Mauroy render homage to the people of Paris who sought to change their lives, and to the 30,000 dead of the Time of Cherries.' This trumpery makes short work of history, for Louis Blanc, the Mauroy of his day, maintained that 'this insurrection is completely to be condemned, and must be condemned by any true republican'.

If textbooks dispatch the June days in a few short lines, if the hundred and fiftieth anniversary of 1848 went by quite unnoticed and the only monograph devoted to them, that of Marouk, goes back a hundred and twenty years, it is because their ghost is still as troublesome as it was then. Already at that time, the clearest minds had grasped that June was a fundamental rupture, that these days marked the end of an era, the end of the illusion that had underpinned all the struggles since the Restoration, in other words that the bourgeoisie and the people, hand in hand, would finish what had been started in 1789.

The seventy days of the Commune gave time for many joyful episodes, in which men and women spoke to each other in the street, and embraced without knowing each other. Above all, despite Engels's famous phrase on the 'dismal solo' played by the proletariat during the Commune, the

Paris workers were not alone in 1871. There was with them a whole literary and artistic *bohème* – Courbet and Vallès were not isolated cases – and such major figures as the scientists Flourens and Élisée Reclus. There were foreigners, Garibaldians, Poles, Germans. There were republicans who had broken with their own party, such as Delescluze, the doctor Tony-Mollin, and Millière who was shot on the steps of the Panthéon, shouting: 'Long live humanity!'

Nothing of that in June 1848, but a desolation that struck even the least sentimental. For Blanqui, '26 June was one of those days that the Revolution claims in tears, like a mother claiming the body of her son'.[142] And for Marx, 'the June revolution is the *ugly* revolution, the repulsive revolution, because realities have taken the place of words, because the republic has uncovered the head of the monster itself by striking aside the protective, concealing crown ... Woe unto June!'[143] It was in stupefaction that the bourgeoisie saw these threatening savages surge forward from nowhere, these new barbarians, these wild beasts, these beings towards whom Lamartine, Musset, Tocqueville, Mérimée, Dumas, Berlioz and Delacroix expressed their disgust and terror. Hugo, in his speech of 20 June on the National Workshops, launched into a flight of oratory: 'Take care! Two plagues are at your gate, two monsters are waiting and roaring, there in the shadows behind us and behind you: civil war and servile war, the lion and the tiger.' The June insurgent, whether a recent industrial worker, an unemployed builder or an uprooted artisan, was Agamben's *Homo sacer*, who could be rightfully killed without this being a crime or a sacrifice.[144] To shoot or deport them no legal process was needed, or else a purely derisory one: 'Opposite Rue des Mathurins, the Mobile Guards put up trestles to form a kind of tribunal; they simulated a council of war and handed out death sentences that were carried out on the spot.'[145]

These barbarians who emerged from the shadows had no known commander. Thirty years later, Marouk summoned up the memory of some of the barricade leaders:

> Legénissel, a draughtsman and former deserter, captain of the National Guard, directed the defence of the Place La Fayette. The Clos

---

142   Blanqui, *Adresse au banquet des travailleurs.*
143   Marx, 'The Class Struggles in France', *Surveys from Exile*, p. 60.
144   Giorgio Agamben, *Homo Sacer* (Palo Alto: Stanford Univ. Press, 1998). Compare Pardigon's exclamations: 'Prisoners so despised and execrated! Surplus men, whose valueless lives are hurled randomly into the ocean of destruction.'
145   Stern, *Histoire de la Révolution de 1848.*

Saint-Lazare was headed by a journalist, Benjamin Laroque. An old shoemaker of sixty, Voisambert, commanded Rue Planche-Mibray. A young engineering worker, Bartélemy, was in charge of the barricades on Rue Grange-aux-Belles. In the Faubourg Saint-Antoine you would find Pellieux, the worker Marche,[146] Lacollonge, editor of *L'Organisation du travail, journal des ouvriers*, and the naval lieutenant Frédéric Cournet. The engineering worker Racary commanded the Place des Vosges. Touchard, formerly of the Montagne, was in charge in Rue de Jouy, and Hibruit, a hat-maker, Rues des Nonnains-d'Hyères, du Figuier and Charlemagne. Raguinard was at the Panthéon, and the builder Lahr at the Barrière d'Italie, supported by the horse-dealer Wappreaux, Choppart and Daix.[147]

The June heroes were anonymous and unknown – shoemakers, engineering workers, people with nothing. The reason for their repression, for hiding the dark monument of the June days, is clear enough: it is that this constituted the real and deep fracture in the history of nineteenth-century France, that it disturbs the republican consensus by shattering for a brief but explosive moment the order of the arrangement of bodies in the community, that order which Rancière calls 'the police'.

The disruption of the June days can also be read in a different way: as an insurrection that did not unfold – at least not entirely – in the traditional centres of Paris uprisings. Preindustrial Red Paris, that of the 1830s, one would say of *La Comédie humaine* if Balzac had not been silent on this subject, was the heart of the old city, a quadrilateral bordered by the Tuileries, the Bastille, the Boulevards and the Seine. The main battleground was still more restricted, centred on the lower part of Rues Saint-Denis and Saint-Martin where the quarters still kept their medieval names, from the Marches, in other words Les Halles, to the Arcis around the Hôtel de Ville. The same streets turn up time and again in police reports, eyewitness accounts, and parliamentary inquiries: Rues Mauconseil, du Bourg-l'Abbé, Greneta, Tiquetonne; Rues Beaubourg, Transnonain, des Gravilliers, au Maire; Rues Aubry-le-Boucher, Maubuée, Neuve-Saint-Merri; Rue de la Verrerie, and Rue Planche-Mibray where there was always fighting, as it

---

146 The man who had stood up to Lamartine at the time of the red flag affair.
147 Lahr – a German – and Daix were guillotined on 17 March 1849 for the 'murder' of General Bréa. The next day, Delescluze wrote in his newspaper, *La Révolution démocratique et sociale*: 'Crazy people! They've erected a new political scaffold...'

gave access to the Pont Notre-Dame.[148] Even if this was not always where things started, even if the first shots were fired on the Pont d'Austerlitz or Boulevard des Capucines, the main fighting always took place in this labyrinth.

This constant is not just explained by symbolism, even if it was the capture of the Hôtel de Ville that enabled an uprising to call itself a revolution. It also had strategic reasons, derived from the interlacing and narrowness of the streets (you have to imagine these quarters without Boulevard de Sébastopol, or the present Rues de Rivoli and Beaubourg, or Avenue Victoria, and remember that the only spaces that were somewhat more open were the Place du Châtelet and the Place de Grève, still smaller then than they are today). Rey-Dussueil:

> In the heart of old Paris, where the narrow streets cross and interweave in a thousand directions, an inextricable labyrinth that so bristles with tall and dark houses that the road does not seem wide enough for those taking it, is the church of Saint-Merri whose modest spire scarcely rises above the roofs ... This is where good folk come to a halt, this is the road leading to the Hôtel de Ville, and this labyrinth of streets and ruined monuments offers a thousand means of attack and defence.

There are two remarkable technical works on this war in the old quarters, *La Guerre des rues et des maisons* by Marshal Bugeaud, and August Blanqui's *Instructions pour une prise d'armes*.[149] The former was written immediately after June 1848, from a concern to oppose to Cavaignac's costly and clumsy strategy, which Bugeaud detested, the science that he had himself demonstrated in repressing the uprising of 1834. Blanqui's *Instructions* date from the late 1860s, after his long passage through obscurity, prison and exile. There is a striking affinity between these two manuals, written by men whose only exchange had been of bullets. Both insisted on the organization and concentration of forces. Blanqui:

> [T]he vice of the popular tactics is responsible for some of its disasters ... no point of leadership or overall command, not even consultation

---

148 The present Rue Saint-Martin, formerly Rue des Lombards, first became Rue des Arcis, then between the Tour Saint-Jacques and the Seine it was Rue Planche-Mibray, a medieval name derived from the planks put down to cross the *bray*, i.e., the mud of the streets.

149 Maréchal Bugeaud, *La Guerre des rues et des maisons*; Auguste Blanqui, *Instructions pour une prise d'armes; L'Éternité par les astres, et autres textes*, edited by Miguel Abensour and Valentin Pelosse (Paris: La Tête de Feuilles, 1972).

between the fighters. Each barricade has its particular group, more or less numerous but always isolated ... Often there is not even a leader to direct the defence... The soldiers just do what they like. They remain, they leave, they return, as they see fit. At night they go home to sleep ... No one knows anything of what is going on elsewhere, and they don't see this as a problem ... They calmly hear artillery and gunfire while drinking at the bar of a wine-merchant. As for bringing support to the positions under attack, the very idea doesn't occur to them. 'Let each defend his post, and all will go well', the most solid ones say. This singular reasoning derives from the fact that the majority of insurgents fight in their own quarter, a capital fault that has disastrous consequences after defeat, in particular in terms of denunciation by neighbours.

Bugeaud also warns against dispersion:

What is most compromising, most dangerous, most paralysing for the public forces, is to let themselves be closely hemmed in by the rioting multitude ... Thus, when they reach a boulevard or a square, it is necessary to have the terrain to be occupied completely evacuated, and then not let anyone enter. The energetic word of officers is generally enough to effect this suppression, especially when these words are supported by the steps of the troops deployed so as to fill the whole space.

Like Bugeaud, Blanqui held that 'the real fighting position is at windows. From here, hundreds of snipers can direct a deadly fire in all directions.' And he describes an imaginary system of battle on the upper floors – just as Bugeaud proposed to transform a series of strategic buildings into urban fortresses, with a view to avoiding any future uprising:

One would select buildings that command several streets, bridges and the main arteries of the faubourgs ... Openings with a view on the streets would be walled in and fortified ... Entrance doors would be reinforced with metal ... These buildings should be considered as little fortresses. They would be equipped with the same regularity as in the plans of war ... Each building would have supplies of thirty or forty thousand rations of biscuits, spirits, and thirty thousand cartridges.

Both writers agreed that artillery was of limited use, showing how their respective instructions bore on the street fighting they had themselves experienced in the tortuous streets of the medieval city. When Blanqui presents a practical example, he describes a defensive front on Boulevard de Sébastopol to adapt his argument to the modern city, but it is in the adjoining medieval labyrinth that he organizes the defence, describing in his characteristically obsessive manner the disposition of barricades, coun-ter-guards, and firing points.

The predilection of the risings of the 1830s for the central quarters of the Right Bank also had other nonstrategic reasons. The population of these old streets still found men, women and children prepared to join an insurrection. These were immigrant quarters, which had the highest proportion of single male lodgers in Paris, and the lowest proportion of women.[150] They came from the agricultural regions of the Paris basin and the Nord, from Lorraine and the Massif Central. They were porters, casual workers, water-carriers like Bourgeat, that generous fellow from the Auvergne, friend of the teacher Desplein in *The Atheist's Mass*; they were builders, often from the Creuse like Martin Nadaud, living ten to a room on Rue de la Mortellerie – the street of mortar mixers – in the squalor that was said to have brought cholera to Paris.[151] It was also said that they smelled bad, that they were lazy and thieving, that they didn't even speak French, and that they took work from true Parisians at these times of crisis and unemployment. 'On Sundays', wrote La Bédollière, 'the Auvergnat water-carriers go dancing, but to their own Auvergnat dances, never the French ones; for these Auvergnats adopt neither the manners, nor the tongue, nor the pleasures of Paris. They remain isolated like the Hebrews in Babylon.'[152] *Le Journal de débats* for 10 July 1832 regretted 'the frightful racket that the opposition made a few months ago on the subject of a mere word, that of "barbarians", which we applied to a class of men whose lack of education and precarious living lead them in fact to a state of dangerous hostility towards society'. Measures were needed to halt this invasion. In the Chamber of Deputies, in the days following the revolution of 1830, Baron Dupin demanded that, in navvying work, 'preference should be given to fathers of families, and to workers domiciled in Paris ... The government should seek the means to return voluntarily to their own departments the overabundant class of workers that are found in Paris.' (Loud murmurs: 'And liberty?') Dupin continued: 'I also support the maintenance of order in asking that for

---

150   Chevalier, *Classes laborieuses et classes dangereuses.*
151   Even apart from epidemics, Villermé notes how 'Rue de la Mortellerie has four and a half times as many deaths as the quays of the Île Saint-Louis, where the inhabitants live in roomy and well-ventilated apartments' (*La Mortalité en France dans la classe aisée, comparée à celle qui a lieu parmi les indigents* [Paris, 1827]).
152   La Bédollière, *Les Industriels* (Paris, 1842).

public works in the capital, preference should be given to workers domiciled in the capital (Prolonged interruption).'[153]

These savages who had nothing to lose were not the only bad subjects in these quarters. In the settled population, among artisans, drapers, haberdashers, goldsmiths, gold-beaters, porcelain workers and typographers, 'there are a very large number of men with a position between that of master and worker; in other words they have characteristics of both, as they work for masters and are treated by them as workers, while they in their turn are treated as masters by the workers they employ'.[154] Both masters and workers from this preindustrial population could often be found on the barricades, joined there by shop clerks, who were ready to seize the opportunity to lift cobbles. We already met them in November 1827, preparing evil deeds in the night, 'an unfurled umbrella in their hand, topped with a lighted candle'.

To this medley of undesirable folk were added roaming children. It was not by chance that Gavroche became a generic term, a type in the same sense as Don Juan or Don Quixote. He was there already, brandishing his pistols, in Delacroix's famous painting. Canler, a former prefect of police, recalls in his *Mémoires* how, just after the insurrection of June 1832 (the one in which Victor Hugo's Gavroche died), 'a boy of twelve or so years old, clad in a coloured jacket of the Auvergne style, was thrust to the front rank, whether willingly or no. Everyone knew this breed of Paris *gamin*, who always uttered seditious shouts in these gatherings, brought the first cobbles to the barricade in the uprisings, and almost always fired the first shots.'[155] On the barricade in Rue Saint-Merri, the flag of the Société des Droits de l'Homme was waved for a long time by a boy of sixteen. Rey-Dussueil has little Joseph as one of the main characters in his *Saint-Merri*, and this description possibly influenced Hugo. Joseph hides behind the elephant on the Place de la Bastille – the same spot as Gavroche – to throw stones at the National Guard; and when the men ask him to go and post a letter, to get him away from the barricade, his reply, 'Very sorry, but I haven't the time', is pure Gavroche.

These *gamins* were an abomination to the party of Order, just as the '*pétroleuses*' of the Commune would be later on. The critic of *La Revue des Deux Mondes*, commenting on a painting by Adolphe Leleux titled *The Password*, in which a boy in the centre of the group carries a long musket, asks: '*The Password* certainly has solid qualities, life, movement and

---

153 *Le Journal des débats*, 27 August 1830.
154 Report by Achille Leroux, BNF, Fonds Enfantin, MS 7816, cited by Rancière, *The Nights of Labor*.
155 Cited by Chevalier, *Classes laborieuses et classes dangereuses*.

harmony; but for God's sake! What does the choice of such a subject mean?
. . . The Paris street-urchin is a type which should not tempt any artist. He
is generally ugly, small, sickly . . . in our filthy mud, poverty is disgusting
and rags are horrible. Since M. Leleux likes rags and tatters, I advise him to
keep to those of Spain and the Orient.'[156]

During the 1830s there was scarcely any fighting in the faubourgs, and still
less in the fields and vineyards of the surrounding communes – Belleville,
Montmartre or Charonne. Since the Revolution of 1789, the population
of the working-class faubourgs traditionally came to fight in the centre of
Paris. But during the ten years that passed between the action of *Cousine
Bette* and that of *A Sentimental Education*, the faubourgs and banlieue were
transformed. To the north and east of Paris, factories, warehouses and workers' housing drove out market gardeners, winegrowers and cattle dealers.
('The industrial revolution . . . had attracted a whole new population of
workers within its walls, to which the works of fortification had added a
further population of cultivators now without work.').[157] There was very
little difference between the population of the villages of La Villette or
La Chapelle, and that of the Faubourg Poissonière or the Faubourg du
Temple. At the same time, workers began to be driven out of the old streets
of the city centre, whose destruction had been begun by Rambuteau. The
7th arrondissement of that time, i.e., the Marais, 'has quarters that are poorly
built, unhealthy and poorly inhabited. The worst of these is the Quartier
des Arcis, which, except for the Quai Pelletier [between the Pont Notre-
Dame and the Pont d'Arcole], is occupied largely by monthly and nightly
boarders, and by the population that this class of establishment attracts.
Thanks to the new Rue Rambuteau, the Beaubourg quarter which was in
no less disturbing a situation will receive a little sunlight. The main streets
of this arrondissement are commercial, and have no need to be widened to
become still more so.'[158] Some of these expelled workers crowded into the

---

156   Cited by T. J. Clark, *The Absolute Bourgeois, Artists and Politicians in France,
1848–1851* (London: Thames and Hudson: 1973), p. 29. Leleux's painting was
exhibited at the Salon of 1849.
157   Tocqueville, *Recollections*. This passage deserves to be quoted at greater
length: 'the eagerness for material enjoyment that, spurred by the [republican]
government, increasingly excited this multitude, and the democratic malaise of
envy that was silently at work; the economic and political theories that began to
come to light and tended to give the impression that human misery was the work
of laws and not of Providence, and that poverty could be abolished by changing
the basis of society'.
158   'Rapport de la Commission des Halles', 1842. Cited by Chevalier, *Classes
laborieuses et classes dangereuses*.

neighbouring quarters – the centre of the Île Saint-Louis, 'so well populated in previous times, but which now has no more of a middle-class
population than do the houses that border the quays', the surroundings of
the Place Maubert, already dangerous – but others left to settle further out,
in Belleville or the northern slopes of Montmartre.

The insurrection of June 1848 took place in an unusual setting, and this
new topography reflects the great changes of the industrial age. Though
it began around the Panthéon, this was not because the workers hoped
to bring with them the youth of the schools. On that memorable night
of 22 June, when, despite the torches, the faces of the tremendous crowd
remained drowned in shadow as in Daumier's drawing *L'Émeute*, they only
met on the big square there because it was familiar: every evening since
February this was where the wages of the National Workshops had been
paid. In the ascending phase of the insurrection, it is true, the workers
invaded the centre of Paris and crossed the traditional quarters of revolt
quite close to the Hôtel de Ville. But this offensive was made from bases in
the faubourgs to the north, east and south. It was to these quarters that they
retreated when the push towards the centre failed, and it was there that they
fought to the bitter end. During the final week of May 1871, despite the
further transformations of the city in the meantime, the Fédérés defended
themselves in the same streets, the same squares and the same crossroads,
and perhaps it was even the same cobbles that were used twice over to
build barricades described in the same terms at an interval of twenty-three
years, on Rue Saint-Maur, Rue de la Fontaine-au-Roi, the Barrière des
Amandiers or the entry to the Faubourg Saint-Antoine.

Victor Hugo's Redemption

In the final number of *Le Peuple constituant*, in the aftermath of June 1848,
Lamennais predicted that 'the men who have become ministers of reaction,
its devoted servants, will not delay in reaping the reward held out to them,
which they have only too richly deserved. Expelled with contempt, bent
under shame, cursed in the present and the future, they will go and join the
traitors of all centuries.' This was a keen observation. The Second Republic
was now on life support. In its two final somersaults, the first marking the
end of the parliamentary regime and the second a hopeless struggle against
Louis Bonaparte's coup d'état, 'the people were at the windows, only the
bourgeois in the street', as Baudelaire's friend Hippolyte Babou put it.[159]

---

159 Hippolyte Babou, *Les Prisonniers du 2 décembre, mes émotions, mes souvenirs*
(Paris, 1876).

The first of these *journées*, 13 June 1849 – a date chosen not entirely by chance – was a simulacrum of insurrection led by the bourgeois-radical Montagne party, increasingly disturbed by the attitude of the president of the Republic elected in December 1848, Louis Bonaparte. Its pretext was the expedition to Rome.[160] On 11 June, Ledru-Rollin demanded the prosecution of the president of the Republic and his ministers for having violated the constitution by attacking the liberty of another people. The royalist-clerical majority of the Legislative Assembly rejected the demand. The Montagne then decided on a nonviolent demonstration. Its supporters gathered without weapons at the Château d'Eau, at midday on the 13th, and set off via the Boulevards towards the Assembly. But when they reached Rue de la Paix, Changarnier's cavalry arrived to disperse them. The leaders of the Montagne then met at the Conservatoire des Arts et Métiers and decided to establish there a 'National Convention', under the protection of the artillery of the National Guard commanded by Guinard, the same man who had directed the cannon fire against the insurgents in Rue Saint-Jacques the previous year. Attempts to start a real insurrection in the neighbouring streets failed, and by the late afternoon the whole business ended in confusion and ridicule. The Montagne was proscribed, Ledru-Rollin, Considérant and Louis Blanc fled abroad, and other leaders were brought before the High Court. June 1849 was, as Marx put it, the nemesis of June 1848.

The resistance to the coup d'état of 2 December 1851 was a far more serious affair, in which many people were killed, contrary to the impression given by the relativist historiography of today, which is completely oriented to the rehabilitation of Louis Bonaparte. The events can be followed hour by hour, thanks to a prodigious historic document from one of the leaders of the resistance: Victor Hugo's *The History of a Crime*, written in Brussels between December 1851 and May 1852, 'with a hand still hot from the struggle against the coup d'état', and subtitled 'the testimony of an eyewitness'.[161]

---

160   Before dispersing, the members of the Constituent Assembly had voted a credit for sending an expeditionary force to Italy, with the mission of supporting the Italian republicans in their revolt against Austria. But this little army, commanded by Oudinot, was then used to attack the Roman republicans and restore the power of the pope.

161   The book was published by Calmann-Lévy, in the midst of the Mac-Mahon affair. Hugo placed at the start of the book the words: 'This book is more than topical; it is urgent. I am publishing it. V.H., 1 October 1877.' The first printing was of 165,000 copies.

On the subject of Hugo, I am convinced that his political trajectory, the opposite of the customary progress from generous youth to reactionary old age, was determined by the June days. Hugo had been a royalist when he wrote *Hernani*, a peer of France under Louis-Philippe, and when he was elected very young to the Académie Française he referred disparagingly in his acknowledgement speech to the *populace*, as opposed to the *people* – 'the ochlocracy rises against demos', as he would later write about the June days.[162] At the decisive moment, he joined the supporters of a show of strength, demanding that the National Workshops be closed. But during the days of insurrection, Hugo, usually so quick to seize the opportunity for writing, showed astonishing discretion, describing only two episodes of the struggle among those most often cited, and in fairly conventional terms. Almost nothing on the repression, a more or less passing note on the famous cellars of the Tuileries, those of Pardigon and Père Roque. And on his personal role – he was as we saw one of the deputies charged with going to the firing line to support the failing morale of the bourgeois National Guard – Hugo was evasive. He still insisted that efforts of mediation should be made. On Boulevard Beaumarchais, 24 June, 'I believed I had to make an effort to cease, if it were possible, the flow of blood'.[163] Or again: 'I was one of the sixty Representatives sent by the Constituent Assembly into the middle of the conflict, charged with the task of everywhere preceding the attacking column, of carrying, even at the peril of their lives, words of peace to the barricades, to prevent the shedding of blood, and to stop the civil war.'[164]

But the reality seems to have been rather different. In September 1848, before the second council of war in Paris, Hugo testified: 'We had just attacked a barricade on Rue Saint-Louis [now Rue de Turenne] from where very vigorous firing had been directed since the morning, costing us a number of brave men; when this barricade was taken and destroyed, I went alone to another barricade, placed across Rue Vieille-du-Temple, and very strong.'[165] *Le Moniteur* reported on 11 July 1848:

Today, M. Victor Hugo and M. Ducoux brought to the National Assembly and presented to the president an intrepid National Guard of the 6th legion, M. Charles Bérard, wounded in taking the flag of the barricade at the Barrière des Trois-Couronnes [now the site of the Couronnes

162   Hugo, *Les Misérables*, Volume Five, book 1, chapter 1.
163   Ibid.
164   Hugo, *The History of a Crime*, chapter 17, trans. Joyce and Locker.
165   Victor Hugo, *Actes et paroles*, I, 'Avant l'exil', in *Politique, Notes Annexes de V. Hugo* (Paris: Laffont).

Métro station]. Charles Bérard was one of those who had accompanied Messrs Victor Hugo and Galy-Cazalat last Saturday in attacking and taking the barricades of the Temple and the Marais, an attack that only took place, as is known, after M. Victor Hugo had exhausted all efforts at mediation.

Thus, after his efforts to get the insurgents to capitulate by the power of his words, Hugo took part in the fighting, without however actually ordering charges and volley-fire, like Lamartine or Arago. He witnessed the shooting of prisoners, the mass arrests, and the manhunts in the streets. But he says not a word about any of this, and I see this silence as expressing a sense of guilt for having been on the side of the murderers in what he would call the 'fatal' June days. And the rest of his political life can be seen as one long effort to restore himself in his own eyes.

First of all there was that extraordinary series of speeches, from July 1848 in the Constituent Assembly, then in the Legislative Assembly: for the freedom of the press, against the state of siege, against the death penalty, for secular education,[166] against the deportations,[167] on poverty:

> There are in Paris, in these faubourgs of Paris that the wind of revolt used to arouse so readily, there are streets, houses, sewers, in which families, whole families, live on top of each other, men, women, girls and boys, only having for bedding, for covering, I almost said for clothing, infected and fermenting rags, gleaned in the outlying mud, the dunghill of the city, where human creatures bury themselves alive to escape the winter cold.

In *Les Misérables*, which Hugo began in 1845, abandoned in 1848 because of the revolution, took up again in 1860 and finished at Hauteville House in 1862, the fifth volume opens with a chapter titled 'The Charybdis of the Faubourg Saint-Antoine and the Scylla of the Faubourg du Temple'. Hugo apologized for this insertion, totally foreign to the rest of the book: 'The two most memorable barricades which the observer of social maladies can name do not belong to the

---

166   'Your law is a law with a mask ... That is your custom. When you forge a chain, you say: "Here is a freedom!" When you make a proscription, you cry: "Here is an amnesty!" ... You are not believers, but sectarians of a religion that you do not understand. You are presenters of holiness. Don't involve the church in your affairs, your tricks, your doctrines, your ambitions.'
167   'But rise up then, Catholics, priests, bishops, men of religion sitting in this Assembly; rise up, it is your role! What are you doing on your benches?'

period in which the action of this work is laid.' There follows the parallel between the two fortresses, that at the entrance to the Faubourg Saint-Antoine, 'ravined, jagged, cut up, divided, crenellated, with an immense rent, buttressed with piles that were bastions in themselves throwing out capes here and there, powerfully backed up by two great promontories of houses of the faubourg, it reared itself like a cyclopean dike at the end of the formidable place which had seen the 14th of July' – and that of the Faubourg du Temple, where 'it was impossible, even for the boldest, not to become thoughtful before this mysterious apparition. It was adjusted, jointed, imbricated, rectilinear, symmetrical and funereal. Silence and gloom met there. One felt that the chief of this barricade was a geometrician or a spectre. One looked at it and spoke low.' The only reason for this extraordinary chapter is a homage to the June insurgents, to their cause and their courage ('"The cowards!" people said. "Let them show themselves. Let us see them! They dare not! They are hiding!" The barricade of the Faubourg du Temple, defended by eighty men, attacked by ten thousand, held out for three days . . . Not one of the eighty cowards thought of flight, all were killed there.'). And Hugo delivers, as a confession, his feeling about his own role in June: 'This is one of the rare moments when, while doing that which it is one's duty to do, one feels something which disconcerts one, and which would dissuade one from proceeding further; one persists, it is necessary, but conscience, though satisfied, is sad, and the accomplishment of duty is complicated with a pain at the heart.'

It is this Hugo who would play such a major role in the resistance to Louis Bonaparte's coup d'état. A price was put on his head, which did not displease him, as he held it his duty to get himself killed during these *journées*. He says this briefly and without self-glorification: 'He [Jules Simon, at the moment of the massacre on Boulevard Montmartre] stopped me. "Where are you going?" he asked me, "You'll get yourself killed. What do you want, then?" "Just this," I said. We shook hands and I continued to advance.' But due to an error of timing, it was Baudin who died in his place on the barricade of the Faubourg Saint-Antoine. That is what would always haunt him; Baudin was his other self.

Dark as a December night, without the accusing rhetoric of *The Chastisements* or *Napoleon the Little*, *The History of a Crime* can be read at three different levels. The first is that of a historical description of the events of 2nd to 6th December 1851. The starting point ('The Ambush') is one of surprise: the rumour of a coup d'état has been going for so long that no one still believes it. 'People laughed at the notion. They no longer said "What a crime!"

but "What a farce!"'[168] But on the night of 1 December, regiments that had gone over to Bonaparte took up positions around the Assembly. The prefect of police summoned the forty-eight police commissioners of Paris: 'It was a question of arresting at their own homes seventy-eight Democrats who were influential in their districts, and dreaded by the Élysée as possible chieftains of barricades. It was necessary, a still more daring outrage, to arrest at their houses sixteen Representatives of the People.' The Imprimerie Nationale was requisitioned in order to print posters announcing the decree dissolving the Assembly: 'The compositors were in waiting. Each man was placed between two gendarmes, and was forbidden to utter a single word, and then the documents which had to be printed were distributed throughout the room, being cut up in very small pieces, so that an entire sentence could not be read by one workman.' At six in the morning, the troops began to mass on the Place de la Concorde. The arrested deputies and the tricolour republican generals, the killers of June 1848 – Cavaignac, Lamoricière, Bedeau – crossed the deserted city in a police van en route to the prison of Mazas, 'a lofty reddish building, close to the terminus of the Lyon railway, [which] stands on the waste land of the Faubourg Saint-Antoine'.

In the course of the morning, the troops invaded the Assembly and expelled the deputies. Some sixty representatives of the left, including Hugo, met in an apartment on Rue Blanche and proclaimed Bonaparte outside the law. The right, a larger group, met in its own headquarters, the *mairie* of the 10th arrondissement, and voted the deposition of Bonaparte. ('The decree of deposition taken up and countersigned by us added weight to this outlawry, and completed the revolutionary act by the legal act ... Some of those men who were termed "men of order" muttered while signing the degree of deposition, "Beware of the Red Republic!" and seemed to entertain an equal fear of failure and of success.') The Vincennes chasseurs came and took away the two hundred and twenty representatives – Hugo gives a list of names – from the *mairie* to the Orsay barracks. 'Thus ended the party of Order, the Legislative Assembly and the February revolution.'[169] During this time, the left deputies, who had spent the whole day wandering from one refuge to another, decided to raise the Faubourg Saint-Germain the next day. ('The evening wore a threatening aspect. Groups were formed on the Boulevards. As night advanced they grew larger and became mobs,

---

168   On the morning of 2 December, Babou and a group of his friends met Pierre Leroux, who said to them: 'You young people! Laugh like we do and buy whistles; the coup d'état will end up in ridicule' (*Les Prisonniers du 2 décembre*).
169   Marx, 'The Eighteenth Brumaire of Louis Bonaparte', *Surveys from Exile*, p. 233.

which speedily mingled together, and only formed one crowd. An enormous crowd, reinforced and agitated by tributary currents from the side streets, jostling one against another, surging, stormy, and whence ascended an ominous hum.') The following day ('The Massacre'), 'Louis Bonaparte had not slept. During the night he had given mysterious orders; then when morning came there was on this pale face a sort of appalling serenity.' The centre of Paris, the Marais, the Saint-Honoré quarter and that of Les Halles were covered with barricades. The coup d'état seemed to be stalling. But suddenly in the afternoon there was carnage on Boulevard Montmartre. ('In the twinkling of an eye there was butchery on the boulevard a quarter of a league long ... A whole quarter of Paris was filled with an immense flying mass, and with a terrible cry. Everywhere sudden death. A man is expecting nothing. He falls ... To be in the street is a Crime, to be at home is a Crime. The butchers enter the houses and slaughter ... One brigade killed the passers-by from the Madeleine to the Opéra [Rue Le Peletier], another from the Opéra to the Gymnase; another from Boulevard Bonne Nouvelle to the Porte Saint-Denis; the 75th of the line having carried the barricade of the Porte Saint-Denis, it was no longer a fight, it was a slaughter. The massacre radiated – a word horribly true – from the boulevard into all the streets ... Flight? Why? Concealment? To what purpose? Death ran after you quicker than you could fly.') The fourth day ('The Victory') saw the end of a hopeless struggle, the death of Denis Dussoubs at a barricade on Rue du Cadran, the continuation of massacres and pursuit, the prisoners piled up – yet again – in the Tuileries cellars, below the terrace along the waterfront ('They called to mind that in June, 1848, a great number of insurgents had been shut up there, and later on had been transported'), from where three hundred and thirty-seven would be taken out the next day to be shot in the courtyard of the École Militaire.

The History of a Crime can also be read as a personal adventure. A grand bourgeois, an illustrious writer, an Academician and deputy, becomes in the space of a few hours a clandestine fugitive. Bonaparte's police is at his heels. He spends the night in the backrooms of local cafés, and apartments of friends met by chance. By day, he runs from one meeting to another, through those quarters that were so well pacified three years previously, Rue de la Cerisaie, Quai de Jemmapes, Rue de Charonne. At 82 Rue Poincourt, 'we entered into a blind alley of considerable length and dimly lighted by an old oil lamp – one of those with which Paris was formerly lighted – then again to the left, and we entered through a narrow passage into a large courtyard encumbered with sheds and building materials. This time we had reached Cournet's.' Cournet! The very same who, in Les Misérables and in reality, commanded the Charybdis of the Faubourg

Saint-Antoine, 'intrepid, energetic, irascible, stormy; the most cordial of men, the most formidable of combatants'. Hugo never misses the opportunity to make a connection between the December days of 1851 and the past and future of Red Paris, 1848 and the Commune. In a disturbing contraction of time, two men who were to die under fire, Baudin and Millière, meet each other at 70 Rue Blanche. 'Millière ... I can still see that pale young man, that eye at the same time piercing and half closed, that gentle and forbidding profile. Assassination and the Panthéon awaited him[170] ... Millière went up to him. "You do not know me", said he. "My name is Millière; but I know you, you are Baudin."' And Hugo concludes: 'I was present at the handshaking between these two spectres' – words that give me a shiver.

As if the danger was not great enough, Hugo adds to it by provocation. The first day, he is on the way to the centre of Paris:

> As the omnibus entered into the cutting of the Porte Saint-Martin a regiment of heavy cavalry arrived in the opposite direction ... They were cuirassiers. They filed by at a sharp trot and with drawn swords ... Suddenly the regiment halted ... By its halt it stopped the omnibus. There were the soldiers. We had them under our eyes, before us, at two paces distance ... these Frenchmen who had become Mamelukes, these citizen soldiers of the Great Republic transformed into supporters of the degraded Empire ... I could no longer restrain myself. I lowered the window of the omnibus. I put out my head, and, looking fixedly at the dense line of soldiers which faced me, I called out, 'Down with Louis Bonaparte. Those who serve traitors are traitors!' Those nearest to me turned their heads towards me and looked at me with a tipsy air; the others did not stir, and remained at 'shoulder arms', the peaks of their helmets over their eyes, their eyes fixed upon the ears of their horses.

The following day, hurrying towards the barricade on which he arrived too late to be killed, Hugo passed the Bastille in a cab (the cab drivers of that time were singularly courageous):

---

170   Millière was shot on the steps of the Panthéon on 26 May 1871. He had refused to kneel, and died shouting: 'Long live humanity!' In *The History of a Crime*, published in 1877, this passage is clearly a later addition. I read many years ago the memoirs of a Soviet writer of the great era – I can't remember which – who recalled how much that cry of 'Long live humanity!' had struck him as a young man.

Four harnessed batteries were drawn up at the foot of the column. Here and there knots of officers talked together in a low voice, – sinister men ... The emotion which I had felt on the previous day before a regiment of cuirassiers again seized me. To see before me the assassins of the country, at a few steps, standing upright, in the insolence of a peaceful triumph, was beyond my strength: I could not contain myself. I drew out my sash. I held it in my hand, and putting my arm and head out of the window of the fiacre, and shaking the sash, I shouted, 'Soldiers! Look at this sash. It is the symbol of Law, it is the National Assembly visible ... You are being deceived. Go back to your duty ... Louis Bonaparte is a bandit; all his accomplices will follow him to the galleys ... Look at that man who is at your head, and who dares to command you. You take him for a general, he is a convict.'

Someone murmured that he would get himself shot, but Hugo would not listen, and continued: "'You, who are there, dressed up like a general, it is you to whom I speak, sir. You know who I am ... and I know who you are. I have told you you are a criminal. Now, do you wish to know my name? This is it." And I called out my name to him. And I added, "Now tell me yours." He did not answer. I continued, "Very well, I do not want to know your name as a general, I shall know your number as a galley slave."'

The third level of *The History of a Crime* is that of political analysis, where Hugo joins Marx – whose name he perhaps never heard – in asking: 'Why did the Paris proletariat not rise in revolt after 2 December? ... Any serious proletarian rising would at once have revived the bourgeoisie, reconciled it with the army, and ensured a second June defeat for the workers.'[171] For Hugo, the truth came from the mouth of an old woman, the very first day, in a scene in which the ghost of the June days appears: 'At the corner of Rue du Faubourg Saint-Antoine before the shop of the grocer Pépin, on the same spot where the immense barricade of June 1848, was erected as high as the second storey, the decrees of the morning had been placarded. Some men were inspecting them, although it was pitch dark, and they could not read them, and an old woman said, "The 'Twenty-five francs' are crushed – so much the better!"'[172] In a chapter with the explicit

171   Marx, 'The Eighteenth Brumaire of Louis Bonaparte', p. 235.
172   'The Twenty-five francs': an expression of contempt denoting the deputies by their daily remuneration. The wage paid by the National Workshops, we recall, was two francs for a man and one franc for a woman. The following day, to the workers of the faubourg who asked him if he really thought that they would get themselves killed to keep him in his twenty-five francs, Baudin made the famous reply before climbing on to the barricade: 'You will see how someone dies for twenty-five francs.'

title 'The Rebound of the 24th June, 1848, on the 2nd December, 1851',
Auguste, the wineseller in Rue de la Roquette whose life Hugo had saved
in June, lucidly explains that 'the people were "dazed" – that it seemed to
all of them that universal suffrage was restored; that the downfall of the law
of the 31st of May was a good thing':[173]

> To tell the whole truth, people did not care much for the Constitution,
> they liked the Republic, but the Republic was maintained too much by
> force for their taste. In all this they could only see one thing clearly, the
> cannons ready to slaughter them – they remembered June, 1848 – there
> were some poor people who had suffered greatly – Cavaignac had done
> much evil – women clung to the men's blouses to prevent them from
> going to the barricades – nevertheless, with all this, when seeing men like
> ourselves at their head, they would perhaps fight, but this hindered them,
> they did not know for what.

All Hugo's efforts and those of his friends to arouse the faubourgs were in
vain. After the death of Baudin:

> On leaving the barricade of Rue Sainte-Marguerite, De Flotte went to
> the Faubourg Saint-Marceau, Madier de Montjau went to Belleville,
> Charamaule and Maigne proceeded to the Boulevards. Schoelcher, Dulac,
> Malardier, and Brillier again went up the Faubourg Saint-Antoine by the
> side-streets which the soldiers had not yet occupied. They shouted, 'Vive
> la République!' They harangued the people on the doorsteps ... They
> even went as far as to sing the *Marseillaise*. People took off their hats as
> they passed and shouted 'Long live the Representatives!' But that was all.

A reason had to be given. 'It was clear that the populous quarters would
not rise, we had to turn to the commercial quarters, abandon trying to stir
the extremities of the city and agitate the centre.' This strategy of going
back in time, in the opposite direction to the sociology of Parisian revolution, meant the defeat of the resistance. The last shots were fired on Rue
Montorgueil, a musket-shot away from the place where the barricades had
made their first reappearance in November 1827. For Red Paris, a hiatus of
twenty years would now begin.

---

173 This law of 31 May 1850 abolished in practice the universal suffrage
proclaimed in February 1848: to be an elector now needed a permanent house-
hold, whereas the majority of workers were migrants. The posters of the coup
d'état promised the return of universal suffrage.

In this whole century of barricades, all the Paris uprisings and revolutions were thus defeats, either immediate or delayed. It was in no way surprising, therefore, that the old Blanqui, in 1871, developed in his cell in the Taureau fortress a cosmogony that reflects his disarray in the face of the eternal recurrence of defeat:

> All worlds are engulfed, one after another, in the revivifying flames, to be reborn from them and consumed by them once more – monotonous flow of an hourglass that eternally empties and turns itself over. The new is always old, and the old always new ... Here, nonetheless, lies a great drawback: there is no progress, alas, but merely vulgar revisionist reprints ... Men of the nineteenth century, the hour of our apparitions is fixed forever, and always brings us back the very same ones, or at most with a prospect of felicitous variants. There is nothing here that will much gratify the yearning for improvement. What to do? There I have sought not at all my pleasure, but only the truth.[174]

But if we explore the surroundings of this notion of 'defeat', beyond the summary executions, the banishments and mass deportations, what remains is an immense truth effect. The defeat brings to light that which did not take place. Where illusion had reigned – of republican fraternity, of the neutrality of right and law, of the emancipation of universal suffrage – defeat suddenly reveals the true nature of the enemy, it dissolves the consensus, dismantles the ideological mystifications of domination. No political analysis, no press campaign, no electoral struggle, so clearly bears a message as the spectacle of people being shot in the street.

For the century from 1871 to 1968, the pacification of political manners – in other words, the continuation of civil war by other means – favoured the return of the illusion. In efforts that would be laughable if they did not lead to such weakening, those who, despite themselves, were the heirs of the Montagnards of 1848 and the Versailles socialists of 1871, constantly worked to plaster over the old prison house that was supposedly democratic and republican. In May 1968, those who had envisaged and prepared revolution placed themselves explicitly in the continuity of the disorders of the nineteenth century. The *Internationale situationniste* wrote in 1961 that 'we must take up again the study of the classical workers' movement in a disabused fashion, disabused firstly in respect to its various kinds of political

---

174 Auguste Blanqui, *L'Éternité par les astres, hypothèse astronomique*, cited by Benjamin, *The Arcades Project*, p. 114.

or pseudo-theoretical heirs, since they only possess the inheritance of its defeat'. And a short while after, when barricades appeared in the night of 10 May 1968 on Rue Gay-Lussac, the extraordinary idea of taking up the cobbles from the street was not a residue of collective memory and still less accidental. It was a deliberate and experimental attempt to shatter the mechanisms of domination by raising up from the ground the great spectral figure of revolution, only modernized a little by setting fire to cars. Of course, these 'magic cobbles' were less effective than ever strategically, and when Malraux and company maintained that tanks would have occupied Rue Gay-Lussac more quickly than the gendarmerie, they were quite right. But it was by this symbolic wager that the uprising of Red Paris in May 1968 was able to set fire – as in July 1789, July 1830, and February 1848 – not only to just Europe this time round but to the whole planet, from Tokyo to Mexico, something that the Berkeley students had not managed to do, precisely for lack of historical anchorage. The Paris insurgents, however, were able to avoid both archaic seductions and the pitfalls of romanticism. They did not storm the police stations, they did not pillage armourers, nor try to seize the buildings of the state (remember the astonishment of journalists when the demonstrators passed the Palais-Bourbon without noticing it). This was not simply from a correct evaluation of the balance of forces: no doubt, if bullets had been mixed with the cobbles and the oddly named 'Molotov' cocktails, we would have seen just how far the humanism of Prefect Grimaud stretched, or the republican spirit of the generals who had won their stars in Algeria, just like Lamoricière and Cavaignac. There was no massacre because May 1968 was the first modern revolution: it did not aim at taking power. Informed by all the disasters of the century, it unfolded in the mode of a defeat programmed in advance, the devastating effects of which on the old world are still being studied. None of the mechanisms of domination were able to operate after May as they did before. The two rival organizations of Gaullism and the 'Communist' party, in solidarity with one another in the police order of the time, only appeared to triumph with the demonstration of the Champs-Élysées and the Pompidou-Séguy agreements at Grenelle. They did not realize that they were already running on empty, like those characters in comic books who continue their chase beyond the edge of the cliff. It took a bit of time to look at the ground and begin the famous nosedive.

The May revolution has not generally been called by its true name. It is denoted by the vague and cowardly term of 'events'. This denial serves to argue – most often implicitly – that it is inappropriate to give this student affair the same dignity as 1793 or 1917. The CGT never stopped opposing the 'seriousness' of the striking workers to the festival of the bourgeois-student youth. It is certainly a fact that it was the students who imagined and programmed May, that the Latin Quarter was from one end to the other the headquarters of operations. The great demonstration of 13 May had its rallying point in the Place de la République, but what is remembered above all is its passage along Boulevard Saint-Michel and in Montparnasse. Not much happened in May on the Right Bank, except of course the rather unconvincing attempt to set fire to the Bourse. The traditional quarters of Parisian revolutions – the Faubourg Saint-Antoine, the Faubourg du Temple, Belleville – did not move. They had been ravaged during the Pompidou years, plunged into the depths of deindustrialization and renovation. Unstructured building, populations expelled, the working-class tradition wiped out – that was plebeian Paris of the late 1960s. The reconstitution of a mixed population, made up of what remained of the Paris proletariat, together with immigrants and an intellectual but nonuniversity youth, was a reconquest that had not yet begun.

Outside the occupied factories and in their immediate surroundings, the communes of the 'red belt', Ivry and Villejuif on the one side, Saint-Denis and Gennevilliers on the other, did not move either, solidly held as they were by the 'Communist' party, whose descent into hell began at this time with its pathetic efforts to maintain order. But what has always been carefully obscured, glossed over in commemorations and anniversaries (the thirtieth anniversary was exemplary in this respect), is that *thousands* of young workers, fringe elements, unemployed and foreigners came running to the Latin Quarter. They were not often heard in the general assemblies, but when it was a question of elegantly swinging a cobblestone, overturning and burning police cars, or throwing back tear-gas grenades, they were first in line, with the poise of people who had spent their whole life on the barricades. The bureaucrats of the various 'revolutionary youth' organizations tried to keep them at a distance, and they were not seen on television, except when it was necessary to show the terrified provinces the *'casseurs'* who had been arrested. Why were they unwanted? All they did was test in anticipation the idea that 'what gives an action a political character is not its object or the place where it is performed, but solely its form, that which inscribes the verification of equality in the institution of a dispute, of a community that exists only in division'.[175]

Those who rejoice to see the city so calm today, stuck in the continuum of the Bergsonian time of domination and boredom, could still find themselves in for a shock one day. Better than any other, the history of Red

---

175 Jacques Rancière, *Disagreement: Politics and Philosophy* (University of Minnesota Press, 1998).

Paris illustrates Benjamin's remark that the time of the oppressed is by nature discontinuous. In the course of the battles of July 1830, stupefied observers agreed in maintaining that in many districts of Paris the insurgents had set fire to the clocks on monuments.

PART THREE

Crossing the Swarming Scene

Crossing the swarming scene that is Paris . . .
– Baudelaire, 'Little Old Ladies', *Les Fleurs du mal*

6

Flâneurs

But the majority of men make their way through Paris in the same manner as they live and eat, that is, without thinking about it . . . Ah! to wander over Paris! What an adorable and delightful existence is that! Flânerie is a science; it is the gastronomy of the eye. To take a walk is to vegetate; flânerie is life.

— Balzac, 'The Physiology of Marriage'

'There gathers here everything that is great in terms of love or hate, of emotion and of thought, of knowledge and of power, of both happiness and unhappiness, of the future and of the past . . . Here is created a new art, a new religion, a new life; it is here that the creators of a new world are merrily at work.' In his Paris chronicles for the *Augsburger Allgemeine Zeitung*, Heine heightens the colours of Paris to contrast with the darkness of Austro-Prussian reaction; but for all that, Paris of this time was indeed the first city of the Western world, and it was no accident that another immigrant German Jew would pursue the traces of this a century later, and title the exposé of the great work that he projected, 'Paris, Capital of the Nineteenth Century'.[1]

During Heine's Paris years — between *Adolphe* and *Madame Bovary*, between Géricault's *Wounded Hussar* and Manet's *Dead Toreador*, between the completion of the Madeleine and of the Gare du Nord — the system of literature that had held sway in France for the last two centuries, and was already beginning to crack, splintered completely. I shall try here to trace the stages, over a period of something under a century, of this general rejection of genres, boundaries and hierarchies, a rejection in which Paris represents far more than a context, a mere favourable milieu. As the para-

---

1 Of Walter Benjamin's two exposés of his project, that of 1935 was titled 'Paris, the Capital of the Nineteenth Century', and that of 1939, written in French, 'Paris, Capital of the Nineteenth Century'.

digm of the 'modern' city in which 'the obelisks of industry spew against the firmament their coalitions of fumes', whose population was constantly growing, where gas lighting was replacing oil lamps and old streets were being mercilessly destroyed, Paris played at this time the role of detonator. Formerly, when the action of a book was set in Paris, the city simply served as an abstract or stylized backdrop: you could search in vain for precise details of Paris locations in *The Princess of Cleves, Manon Lescaut* or *La Vie de Marianne.* But now, in streets that were named and described – which was already a decisive break in the literary status of the metropolis – a red-haired beggar-woman might cross paths with an adulterous countess, a great surgeon, an Auvergnat water-carrier, a ragpicker, a future minister or a policeman (Vidocq, Javert, Peyrade), not to mention a bankrupt lawyer. The hierarchy of genres, according to which certain forms were naturally designed for particular social strata, could no longer hold out. Through newspaper supplements that were sold in the streets, the novel invaded fashionable salons, libraries, and the back rooms of wineshops. Everything could become the subject of drama, verse, story or song, and all subjects were equal here, so much so that there was no longer any compulsory relationship between form and content. Vague intermediate zones would disrupt the borders between art and what was traditionally not accepted as art. In 1857, Hippolyte Babou could write without blaspheming that 'when Balzac lifts the roofs or penetrates the walls in order to clear a space for observation ... you speak insidiously to the porter, you slide along fences, you make little holes in partitions, you listen at doors, you focus your eye-glasses at nighttime on the silhouettes dancing in the distance behind lighted windows; you act, in a word, what our prudish English neighbours call the "police detective".'[2] And it was 'in an obscure library in Rue Montmartre' that the narrator of *The Murders in the Rue Morgue* met a certain Dupin, the first amateur detective in literature – not in London nor in New York, but in Paris where Poe had never set foot.

It was flâneurs who erected the metropolis into a theoretical object, an instrument of rupture with the forms of the past. The forerunners of this phenomenon that initiated modernity – the big city as raw material, roaming it as support for artistic creation – could already be found in the late eighteenth century.[3] The elderly Rousseau, for example, setting out each

2   In *La Vérité sur le cas Champfleury* (Paris, 1857). Cited by Walter Benjamin in 'Charles Baudelaire, a Lyric Poet in the Era of High Capitalism', *The Writer of Modern Life: Essays on Charles Baudelaire* (Cambridge, MA: Harvard, 2006).
3   I use 'modernity' here in Baudelaire's sense: 'Modernity is the transitory, the fugitive, the contingent – half of art, the other half being the eternal and unchanging'

day from Rue Plâtrière (now Jean-Jacques Rousseau), crossing Paris on foot
to go botanizing. 'I could never do anything', he wrote in his *Confessions*,
'sitting pen in hand at my table and paper'. And in his 'Notes Written on
Playing Cards', 'My whole life has been just one long reverie divided into
chapters by daily walks'. In his *Essai sur Jean-Jacques Rousseau*, Bernadin de
Saint-Pierre describes him, impeccably dressed, when

> at seventy years of age he would go to the Pré-Saint-Gervais in the after-
> noon, or take a turn in the Bois de Boulogne, without seeming tired at
> the end of this walk ... He had two star-shaped holes cut in the soles
> of his shoes, because of the corns that troubled him ... He dined at
> half past twelve. At half past one he would often take coffee at the Café
> des Champs-Élysées, where we would arrange to meet. He then went
> off botanizing in the countryside, his hat under his arm in the bright
> sunshine, even during a heat wave.

Rousseau was able to find the countryside even within Paris: 'The weather
being quite nice, though cold, I went for a walk all the way to the École
Militaire, expecting to find some mosses in full bloom there.' Another
day, 'having gone for a walk in the vicinity of Nouvelle-France, I pressed
further on; then veering left and wanting to circle Montmartre, I crossed
the village of Clignancourt'. (This is followed, in the 'Ninth Walk', by the
famous passage on the 'little child of five or six squeezing my knees with all
his might while looking up at me in such a friendly and affectionate manner
that I was inwardly moved'.) Or again: 'One Sunday my wife and I had
gone to dine at Porte Maillot. After dinner we crossed through the Bois
de Boulogne as far as the Château de la Muette. There we sat down in the
shade on the grass and waited for the sun to get lower so as to return quite
easily through Passy afterwards.' (This is where the episode of the wafers
offered to the little girls comes in, and 'that afternoon was one of those of
my life which I remember with the greatest satisfaction'.)

Rousseau stressed the harshness of the metropolis, and in his *Reveries of
a Solitary Walker* you can hear as a background noise the terrible misery
of pre-Revolutionary Paris. The little boy he meets close to the Barrière
d'Enfer in the 'Sixth Walk', 'a very nice, but lame little boy who, hobbling
along on his crutches, goes about quite graciously asking passersby for

---

(*The Painter of Modern Life*, 'Modernity'). For an analysis of present-day fluctuations
in the use of the word, see Jacques Rancière, *The Politics of Aesthetics* (London:
Continuum, 2004). An editorial in the 18 May 2000 issue of *Libération* began with
the words: 'The first alarm aroused by mobile phones was almost contemporary
with the appearance of this symbolic object of modernity.'

alms', belonged to that population of abandoned or lost children who are so common in the police reports. On 19 October 1773, a police commissioner by the name of Mouricaud noted:

> There appeared in court Jean Louis Paillard known as Larose dwelling at the Porte Saint-Paul with Madame Blin the wine-seller who stated that last Friday Savary an agent for wet nurses gave him on getting out of the coach from Sens around four o'clock two children returned from the nurse to be taken to their fathers and mothers, one of these being of male sex whose parents lived at La Courtille, and the other of female sex who according to the address given to him by Savary was to be taken to Monsieur Le Roi at the Porte Saint-Martin and that being unable to read various persons read the address to him; that having been unable to find the father of the child either at the Porte Saint-Martin or at the market, he took this child with the other to La Courtille, and after having returned the boy to his father took the girl home with him where she ate and slept.[4]

Rousseau's shadowy and dilapidated double, whom contemporaries nicknamed Jean-Jacques des Halles, the perverted and fetishistic Restif, was an informer for the police of Sartine and Lenoir, and it was his connections in high places and the blue suit under his overcoat that enabled him to explore the most dangerous places.[5] 'Owl!' he exclaims at the start of the first of his three hundred and eighty-eight *Nuits de Paris*, subtitled 'Le Spectateur nocturne', 'how many times have your funereal cries made me shudder in the dark of the night! Sad and solitary like you, I wandered alone in the dark through this immense capital: the glow of lampposts cutting across the shadows does not destroy them, it makes them more clear: this is the chiaroscuro of great painters!' Restif lived in the wretched quarter between the Place Maubert and the Seine, on Rue de la Harpe, Rue de Bièvre, Rue des Bernadins and finally Rue de la Bûcherie. He had a little printing press there which enabled him to resume the trade of his youth and to publish

---

4   Arlette Farge, *Le Cours ordinaire des choses dans la cité du XVIIIe siècle* (Paris: Le Seuil, 1994).
5   The parallel between Rousseau and Restif (also known as Rétif de la Bretonne) was taken up by Maurice Blanchot: 'To write without care, without awkwardness or effort, is not so easy, as Rousseau shows by his own example. It could only be expected that, by the law of historical duplication, the tragic Jean-Jacques would be followed by a comic one, for lack of care or awkwardness, as well as chatting, finally took its place in literature with Restif, and the result was not very convincing' (*Le Livre à venir* [Paris: Gallimard, 1959]).

his own works: 'He only typeset his own works, and he was so productive that he no longer took the trouble to write them first: standing before his type-case, the fire of enthusiasm in his eyes, he assembled letter by letter in his composing-stick these pages, inspired and full of mistakes, on whose bizarre spelling and calculated eccentricities everyone remarked.'[6]

Restif's field of action was above all the Marais and the Île Saint-Louis. Emotional ties attracted him to Rue de Saintonge and Rue Payenne ('Very late in the evening – as I had been writing until a quarter past eleven, after my manual work – I went to Rue Payenne; I had taken the longest route: it was now half past twelve. The Marquise was at her window . . .') But he also haunted Les Halles and the Boulevards:

> In the evening, after leaving work, I wandered in the surroundings of the Marquise's quarter, but it was not yet time to see her. I went as far as Rue de la Haute-Borne . . . I retraced my steps and entered a wretched beer hall on Rue Basse-du-Rempart, behind the Ambigu-Comique and the Danseurs de Corde: I asked for a light, a pot of wine, and six *échaudés*;[7] I took out my paper and my writing case and I wrote *L'Homme de nuit*.

Ever ready to rescue young women in danger, especially if they were pretty, Restif was undoubtedly the first to describe the pleasure of night-time wandering in this Paris populated by beggars, whores and thieves, the intoxication that takes hold of someone who has walked for a long while quite alone, and aimlessly, just following the streets.

It was Gérard de Nerval who carried this exploration of nocturnal Paris to an extreme, and Nerval had a very high opinion of Restif. 'Rousseau's example', he wrote, 'has no bolder imitator than Restif . . . No writer perhaps has ever before possessed to such a high degree the precious qualities of imagination. Diderot may well have been more correct, Beaumarchais more fluent, but did either of them have even half this wild and quivering

---

6 Gérard de Nerval, 'Les Confidences de Nicolas', first published in *La Revue des Deux Mondes* (15 August, 1 and 15 September 1850), and later included in *Les Illuminés*. Restif's typographic eccentricities would have enchanted Perec: 'Sometimes he liked to try a new system of spelling; he suddenly warned the reader by a parenthesis, then continued his chapter, either suppressing some of the vowels in the Arab style, or throwing the consonants into disorder by replacing "c" by "l", "l" by "t", "t" by "ç", etc. – always following rules that he explained at length in notes' (ibid).

7 For the Haute-Borne, see above, p. 213; an *échaudé* was a triangular cake (p. 100).

verve, which does not always produce masterpieces, but without which masterpieces would not exist?'[8] Nerval's *Les Nuits d'octobre*, a more high-flown version of Restif's *Nuits*, begins with a realist profession of faith. His chapter on 'The Halles' is the first precise description of the atmosphere of that quarter, which would remain unchanged until the 1970s: the arrival of produce early in the night ('The little square of the markets begins to grow animated. The wagons of the market-gardeners, the fish merchants, the dairymen and greengrocers constantly cross one another. When the wagoners reach their destination, they refresh themselves in the cafés and bars, which remain open here the whole night'); the sales agents (' "These men in work clothes are richer than us", my companion tells me. "They disguise themselves as peasants. Under their smocks or overalls they are perfectly dressed, and tomorrow will leave their blouse at the tavern and return home in a Tilbury"'); the saleswomen ('One of them cries: "My little cabbages, make your ladies flower!" And, as it is only wholesale at this time, a large number of ladies would have to "flower" to buy so many bouquets. Another chants the song of her position: "Reinette and Lady apples!" "Red and white Calvilles!"'). Nerval and his friend enter an elegant restaurant ('The custom here is to order Ostend oysters with a little stew of chopped shallots in vinegar and pepper ... Then it is onion soup, which is cooked admirably at the Halles, and into which the more refined toss grated Parmesan'), then a wretched dive ('An immense counter divides the room in two, and seven or eight women ragpickers, regulars in this place, make a display on a bench opposite the counter. The back is occupied by a fairly motley crowd, who often erupt in quarrels'). But Nerval does not stick to his 'realism' for too long. Already, when his steps lead him to Montmartre, his other district of choice, it is the quarries that he depicts, a place of fantasy par excellence. And at the end he walks in his dream down 'corridors, endless corridors', a nightmare that prefigures the hallucinated wandering at the end of *Aurélia*:

> The stars shone in the firmament. Suddenly it seemed to me that they had just gone out, like the candles I had seen in the church. I believed the end of time had arrived, and we were coming to the end of the world heralded in the Apocalypse of St John. I thought I was seeing a black sun in the deserted sky, and a red globe of blood above the Tuileries. I said to myself: 'Eternal night is beginning, and it will be terrible. What will happen when men perceive that there is no more sun?'

---

8   G. de Nerval, *Les Confidences de Nicolas*.

These first solitary explorers of the city night have a whole line of descend-
ants: Villiers, Huysmans, Apollinaire, Breton – who preferred Restif to
Rousseau, and ranked Nerval among those 'who had heard the voice of
Surrealism'.[9] But alongside this dark and silent Paris still imbued with the
feel of nature, a different city was emerging in the 1830s, a city in which
'three thousand shop-fronts sparkle, and the great poem of display sings its
strophes of colour from the Madeleine to the Porte Saint-Denis'.[10] This
brilliantly lit city, in which the flâneur swims with the crowd, in which
vice, fashion and money display themselves on the Boulevards along with
goods for sale, is that of Balzac. This attribution should be taken in the
strong sense: the relationship between *La Comédie humaine* and the Paris of
the July monarchy is not just one between a work of art and its model. The
echo of the regime could not but influence the physiognomy of a work
such as Balzac's, as reflected in the fact that certain Russian aristocrats are
said to have divided up the roles of Balzac's *Scenes from a Courtesan's Life*
and fashioned their lives after those of the characters they had selected. In
his *Grand Dictionnaire universel du XIXe siècle*, Pierre Larousse, a Voltairean
and republican, who hated Balzac as a defender of throne and altar, judged
that 'his influence on the literature of his time has been no less than his
influence on manners in a certain class of society, and in many respects it
has been no less deplorable'.

At first glance, Balzac is no less severe towards Paris than was Rousseau.
In the preface to *Ferragus* the words 'monster' and 'monstrous' recur several
times, and he notes how 'every man, every fraction of a house is a lobe
of the cellular tissue of that great courtesan', a metaphor that came very
naturally to an admirer of Broussais and Geoffroy Saint-Hilaire. At the start
of *The Girl With the Golden Eyes*, the motif of 'gold and pleasure' is taken
'for a lantern ... to explore that great stucco cage, that hive with its black
gutters', and the reader is warned: 'it is not in mere sport that Paris has been

9   'Alongside him [de Sade], and yet offering a higher literary interest, it is
correct to rank Restif de la Bretonne, whose books *Le Paysan et la Paysanne perver-
tis* and *Monsieur Nicolas* appear today as more important works than Rousseau's
Confessions, already in your library catalogue' ('Projet pour la bibliothèque de
Jacques Doucet', in *Oeuvres complètes*, vol. 1 [Paris: Gallimard]). And on Nerval,
'we could no doubt have seized on the word SUPERNATURALISM, which
Gérard de Nerval used in the dedication to *Les Filles du Feu*. It seems in fact that
Nerval possessed to a remarkable degree the spirit that we ourselves claim ...'
This term, used by Nerval in the dedication of his work to Alexandre Dumas ('this
state of super-naturalist reverie, as the Germans call it'), is a reference to his friend
Heine, who on many occasions defined himself as a 'super-naturalist' – for example in 'Le Salon de 1831'.
10   H. de Balzac, 'Histoire et physiologie des boulevards de Paris'.

called a hell ... There all is smoke and fire, everything gleams, crackles, flames, evaporates, dies out, then lights up again, with shooting sparks, and is consumed.' But right in the midst of such moralizing reflections, Balzac lets escape, like a confession, his love for the great city. The same is true in *Ferragus*, where he suddenly exclaims: 'O Paris! he who has not admired your gloomy passages, your gleams and flashes of light, your deep and silent cul-de-sacs, who has not listened to your murmurings between midnight and two in the morning, knows nothing as yet of your true poesy, nor of your broad and fantastic contrasts.' And, after the long opening of *The Girl With the Golden Eyes*, in which the population of the city, 'wan and colourless', is 'like the faces of those houses upon which all kinds of dust and smoke have blown', we suddenly hear an elegiac note: 'Upon one of those fine spring mornings, when the leaves, although unfolded, are not yet green, when the sun begins to gild the roofs, and the sky is blue, when the population of Paris issues from its cells to swarm along the Boulevards, glides like a serpent of a thousand coils through Rue de la Paix towards the Tuileries, saluting the hymeneal magnificence which the country puts on; on one of these joyous days, then ...' It is then, in the broad avenue of the Tuileries, that Henri de Marsay catches the eye of an unknown girl, 'whose rays seemed akin to those which the sun emits, and whose ardour set the seal upon that of her perfect body, in which all was delight'.

Several writers have described how, starting with *The History of the Thirteen* and *Old Goriot*, the stories that make up *La Comédie humaine* are interlinked, the principal and secondary characters reappearing from one book to another and giving the whole construction its unity. But this network or concatenation does not just link people, but also places, as Walter Benjamin noted:

> Balzac has secured the mythic constitution of his world through precise topographic contours. Paris is the breeding ground of his mythology – Paris with its two or three great bankers (Nucingen, du Tillet), Paris with its great physician Horace Bianchon, with its entrepreneur César Birotteau, with its four or five great cocottes, with its usurer Gobseck ... But above all, it is from the same streets and corners, the same little rooms and recesses, that the figures of this world step into the light. What else can this mean but that topography is the ground plan of this mythic space of tradition, as it is of every such space, and that it can become indeed its key.[11]

---

11   Benjamin, *The Arcades Project*, p. 83.

And moreover, what forms the connecting tissue of *La Comédie humaine*, far more than the return of the main characters in their favoured locations, is the wealth of its secondary ties, 'those indications of kinship, neighbourly relations and friendship, references to business deals and clients, records of addresses that seem borrowed from the registers of civil status or commercial directories, in the dryness and barrenness of which history seeks its most intense and surest evocations'.[12]

As far as Balzac's personal and physical relationship with Paris is concerned, what is always quoted is the beginning of *Facino Cane*, where the narrator follows a couple of workers coming back from the Ambigu-Comique: 'As I listened, I could make their lives mine, I felt their rags on my back, I walked with their gaping shoes on my feet; their cravings, their needs, had all passed into my soul, or my soul had passed into theirs. It was the dream of a waking man.' I don't think that Balzac really ever did proceed in this way. The fact that he cites in this passage Rue Lesdiguières where he had lived, and uses the first person singular, is not enough to make this autobiographical information. It is a prelude like any other of Balzac's, and he never began without a kind of tuning-up. He was either unable or unwilling to start *in media res*, like the beginning of Stendhal's *Lucien Leuwen* that we cited in the previous chapter, or the clash of cymbals that opens *The Charterhouse of Parma*.

A Balzac who slept by day and worked by night, the dressing gown, the cut goose-quills, the coffee pot – that legend certainly contains an element of truth. But Balzac was not a recluse like Proust in his final years. He spent a great deal of time out and about, seeking out a residence worthy of the 'Foreigner', buying his particular mixture of coffees – *bourbon* on Rue de la Chausée-d'Antin, *martinique* on Rue des Haudriettes, and *moka* on Rue de l'Université. Théophile Gautier, who often accompanied him, wrote:

How he loved and knew this modern Paris, at a time when lovers of local colour and the picturesque still failed to appreciated its beauty! He crossed it in every direction, by night and by day ... He knew everything about his beloved city; it was for him an enormous monster, hybrid and formidable, an octopus with a hundred thousand arms that he heard and saw living, and which in his eyes had a kind of immense individuality. You could often have seen him, especially in the mornings, when he rushed to the printer's to take in copy and collect his proofs. You would remember his green hunting jacket, his black-and-grey check trousers ... he walked buried in large shoes with flaps, a red scarf drawn in a knot

---

12 Chevalier, *Classes laborieuses et classes dangereuses*.

around his neck. Despite the disorder and poverty of this attire, no one could have been tempted to take this great man whom they passed as a common unknown, swept as he was by his dream like a whirlwind.[13]

Gozlan was a companion of Balzac with whom he rambled the centre of Paris in all directions, seeking a name on a shop sign to use for the hero of his latest novel. They walked for hours. 'Let's just continue as far as Saint-Eustache', Balzac asked Gozlan:

> That was only a pretext to get me to measure the whole length of Rues du Mail, de Cléry, du Cadran, du Faubourg-Montmartre and the Place des Victoires, peppered with magnificent Alsatian names that conjure up the taste of the Rhine. Until in Rue du Bouloi – and this I shall never forget in my whole life – after raising his gaze above a poorly marked gate in the wall, an oblong, narrow, dilapidated gate opening into a damp and dark alley, he suddenly changed his tone and, with a shiver that passed from his arm to mine, uttered a cry and said: 'There! There! There! Read it, read it!' His voice broke with emotion. And I saw the name MARCAS.
> 'Marcas! What do you think? Marcas! What a name! Marcas!'
> 'I don't see . . .'
> 'Stop it! Marcas!'
> 'But . . .'
> 'Stop it, I tell you. It's the name of names! We won't look for another. Marcas can be a philosopher, a writer, a great politician, an unknown poet, everything. Marcas, and I'll call him Z. Marcas, to add a certain flame, a sparkle, a star!'[14]

The quarters of Paris where the characters of La Comédie humaine live were chosen with the same care as their names, and the same goes for their clothing and their domestic surroundings. The Left Bank, apart from the Faubourg Saint-Germain, was the realm of déclassés, marginaux, victims of life – or of those who made a business of living among them, such as the good judge Popinot in The Commission in Lunacy (his house was on Rue du Fouarre, 'always damp, from the stream that carried towards the Seine the dark waters of some dye-works'), or else troublesome policemen such as Peyrade, who lived with his daughter on Rue des Marais-Saint-Germain (now Visconti), where Balzac had his printing press, and Corentin

---

13   Théophile Gautier, Honoré de Balzac (Paris: Poulet-Malassis, 1859).
14   Léon Gozlan, Balzac en pantoufles (Paris: Michel Lévy, 1862).

who lived on Rue Cassette, where Carlos Herrera established himself with Lucien de Rubempré. Also in *The Commission in Lunacy*, the poor Marquis d'Espard, stripped of everything by his wife, who pretended he was spoiled, lived with his two sons on the Montagne Saint-Geneviève, 'in an apartment whose destitution was unworthy of his name and social position'. At the start of *The Black Sheep*, Mme Bridau, an elderly widow without a penny, comes to live in 'one of the most horrible corners of Paris', 'that portion of Rue Mazarine which runs from Rue Guénégaud to the point at which it joins Rue de Seine'. Rue des Quatre-Vents (also 'one of the worst streets in Paris', according to *The Atheist's Mass*), in the shadow of Saint-Sulpice, successively housed – in one of those buildings 'of which the narrow door opens into a passage with a winding staircase at the end, with windows appropriately termed "borrowed lights"' – two young people at the time still poor and unknown: Arthez, the great writer of the Cénacle, one of Balzac's 'doubles', and Desplein, who ended up as surgeon-in-chief at the Hôtel-Dieu, like his model the great Dupuytren.

Further out, in the Faubourg Saint-Marceau, the poverty was still worse. Colonel Chabert, the hero of the battle of Eylau, who was taken for dead and had no legal existence, lodged in Rue du Petit-Banquier (now Watteau), and the good Derville, the lawyer who visits him, was forced to go on foot, as his coachman refused to enter an unpaved street whose ruts were too deep for the wheels of a cabriolet.

On the Right Bank, the Marais, then at its nadir, was a quarter of characters who were humble but worthy. Cousin Pons, leader of an orchestra in a little theatre on the Boulevards, who gave music lessons in a few boarding schools for girls so as not to die of hunger, lived, as we have seen, on Rue de Normandie. In *The Wrong Side of Paris*, Mme de la Chanterie, at the age of seventeen, 'found herself obliged to live, along with the little girl that she cared for, from the work of her hands, in an obscure quarter to which she had retreated'; during the Revolution this ruined noblewoman exercised the demanding profession of corset-marker in Rue de la Corderie-du-Temple.

Very different from these fallen nobles, the characters whom Balzac places around the Place Vendôme, Rue Saint-Honoré and Les Halles belong to the world of business. When he was in Paris, the illustrious Gaudissart, 'one of those profound dealers who speak in the name of calicots, jewellery, cloth and wine, and are often more clever than ambassadors, who generally know only conventions', lived in the Hôtel de Commerce, at the end of Rue des Deux-Écus. 'La Reine des Roses', the perfumery where César Birotteau perfected his 'Double Paste of Sultans' and 'Carminative Balm', was on Rue Saint-Honoré, close to the church of Saint-Roch where he had been wounded on 13 Vendémiaire (which enabled him to make 'solid reflections on the absurdity of an alliance between politics and perfumery'). Popinot, his former clerk who was now his son-in-law, set up home on Rue des Cinq-Diamants (now Quincampoix). Gobseck's colleague, the usurer Gigonnet who plays a role in Birotteau's financial collapse (many writers have stressed how meticulously this is described, with fraudulent manoeuvres at the Tribunal of Commerce – in matters of bankruptcy Balzac was of course in his element), lived on Rue Greneta, 'on the third floor of a house whose window-sashes, with small and very dirty panes, swung by the middle, on pivots ... The stairs were covered with filth. Each landing of this noisome stairway bore the names of the occupants in gilt letters on a metal plate, painted red and varnished, to which were attached specimens of their craft.'

But the most Balzacian quarter of all was the Nouveau Paris beyond the Boulevards, the arc between the Faubourg Saint-Martin and the Champs-Élysées.[15] When Balzac was attempting to buy a house, this was the region that he explored. On 4 December 1845, he wrote to the 'Foreigner':

> Tomorrow I am going to see in Rue des Petits-Hôtels, Place Lafayette [now Franz Liszt] as you know, a little hôtel for sale, just beside the church of Saint-Vincent-de-Paul that we went to see ... Rue des Petits-Hôtels opens into Rue Hauteville, which comes down to the boulevard by the Gymnase, and into the Place Lafayette, which reaches Rue Saint-Lazare and Rue de la Pépinère via Rue Montholon. You are at the heart of that part of Paris known as the Right Bank, where all the theatres, boulevards, etc. are; it's the quarter of the big banks.

And indeed, Keller's bank in *La Comédie humaine* is on Rue Taitbout – also where the painter Théodore de Sommervieux[16] lived, and for a while Rastignac as well. Claparon's bank is on Rue de Provence, and Mongenod's bank on Rue de la Victoire, in a magnificent hotel with courtyard and garden. Of Old Goriot's two daughters, Mme de Restaud lived on Rue de Helder, and Delphine de Nucingen on Rue Saint-Lazare, in 'one of

---

15   No major character in *La Comédie humaine* lives in the east of Paris. If the Faubourg Saint-Antoine is often mentioned, this is only in a metaphorical sense (as when Madame Madou 'bore down like an insurrectionary wave from the Faubourg Saint-Antoine'). The Faubourg du Temple only makes an appearance because Birroteau 'hired some sheds, with the ground about them, in the Faubourg du Temple, and painted upon them in big letters, "Manufactory of César Birotteau"'.
16   Honoré de Balzac, *At the Sign of the Cat and Racket*.

those many-windowed houses with a mean-looking portico and slender columns, which are considered the thing in Paris, a typical banker's house, decorated in the most ostentatious fashion; the walls lined with fine stucco, the landings of marble mosaic'. Her garden bordered that of the Hôtel de Saint-Réal, where the Marquise hides away the Girl With the Golden Eyes. On Rue de la Chausée-d'Antin, Camille Maupin 'purchased for one hundred and thirty thousand francs one of the finest houses in the street'.[17] Rue Saint-Georges was less elegant: this was the street of the *lorettes*, the world of 'Fanny Beaupré, Suzanne du Val-Noble, Mariette, Florentine, Jenny Cadine, and their kind'. It was here that the Baron de Nucingen installed poor Esther, and that later Du Tillet – the little thief who had become a big banker and a centre-left deputy – would lodge 'the illustrious Carabine, whose lively mind, cavalier manners, and brilliant lack of shame formed a counterweight to the works of his domestic, political, and financial life'.[18]

Another region of venal love, the Quartier de l'Europe, was still under construction:

Without the Aspasias of the Notre-Dame de Lorette quarter, far fewer houses would be built in Paris. Pioneers in fresh stucco, they have gone, towed by speculation, along the heights of Montmartre, pitching their tents in those solitudes of carved free-stone, the like of which adorns the European streets of Amsterdam, Milan, Stockholm, London, and Moscow ...The situation of these dames is determined by their location in these apocryphal regions. If the house is near the line traced by Rue de Provence, the woman has an income, her budget prospers; but if she approaches the farther line of the *boulevards extérieurs* or rises towards the horrid town of Batignolles, she is without resources. When Monsieur de Rochefide first encountered Madame Schontz, she lived on the third floor of the only house that remained in Rue de Berlin; thus she was camping on the borderland between misery and its reverse.[19]

The Faubourg Saint-Honoré and the Champs-Élysées were clearly the realm of the aristocracy – along with the Faubourg Saint-Germain, but we have seen how Balzac, as later also Proust, drew the borders of this more in terms of symbolism than geography. The Marquise d'Espard, former wife of Colonel Chabert, lived close to the Élysée, and the beautiful Duchesse de

---

17 Balzac, *Beatrix*.
18 Balzac, *The Unconsicous Comedians*.
19 Balzac, *Beatrix*.

Maufrigneuse, one of the queens of Parisian society, occupied the immense Hôtel de Cadignan, right at the top of the quarter. But in these parts one could also meet more recent fortunes, and not always well acquired: 'Though without a family, a parvenu, Du Tillet had married in 1831 – God knows how! – the youngest daughter of the Comte de Granville, one of the most famous names in the French judiciary.' This enabled him to live 'in one of the finest hôtels on Rue Neuve-des-Mathurins'.[20]

Thus the links of the chain cast across the city both host and connect the Paris episodes of *La Comédie humaine*. Balzac's extraordinary innovation of using the ties in this network to construct the 'themes' of his characters would become one of the hallmarks of French narrative, from Eugène Sue to Georges Simenon, with *Les Misérables* and Zola's Paris novels as steps on the way. And if Proust most frequently has the key locations for his characters away from Paris, if Oriane brings in the Vivonne and its water lilies, and Albertine the Balbec seawall, his procedure is the same, and this is not the least of the borrowings that *À la recherche du temps perdu* makes from *La Comédie humaine*.

'The Paris Prowler', 'The Solitary Walker' and 'Glows and Smoke' were among the titles Baudelaire had considered before Banville and Asselineau judiciously chose *Le Spleen de Paris* for the original posthumous edition of his 'little prose poems'. It needed the combination of a poet's unhappiness and a great unsteadiness of the city itself for the elaboration 'with fury and patience' of a work that is complex to the point of sometimes being perceived, either as 'this buried temple … in which he wildly illuminates an immortal pubis', as 'the work that bends the curve stretching from the *taedium vitae* of the Romans to the "modern style"', or again as 'the transfiguration of absolute commodification'.[21] His contradictions and divergences, which for so long were criticized, are precisely what brings him so close to us, contributing to establish that 'sudden coincidence' in which nineteenth-century Paris focuses on itself and gathers itself up before erupting anew. In the allegories that Baudelaire reprises, radically transforming their character with the help of the same 'cruel demon' that he saw at work in the etchings of Meryon, he combines and goes beyond the visions of the big city that Nerval, Balzac or Poe had, and on 19 February 1859 he could with all justice write to Poulet-Malassis: 'Finished *Nouvelles Fleurs*. It will break everything, like a gas explosion in a glazier's.'

'It always seems to me that I should feel well in the place where I am not, and

---

20   Honoré de Balzac, *A Daughter of Eve*.
21   Stéphane Mallarmé, *Le Tombeau de Charles Baudelaire*; Benjamin, *The Arcades Project*; Giorgio Agamben, *Stanze* (Paris: Christian Bourgois, 1981).

this question of removal is one which I discuss incessantly with my soul.'[22] Rue de l'Estrapade, Quai de Béthune, Rue Vaneau, Hôtel Pimodan on the Quai d'Anjou, Hôtel Corneille on Rue Corneille, Hôtel de Dunkerque et Folkestone on Rue Lafitte, Rue de Provence, Rue Coquenard (now Lamartine), Rue de Tournon, Rue de Babylone, Rue Pigalle, Rue des Marais-du-Temple (now Yves-Toudic), Boulevard de Bonne-Nouvelle, Hôtel d'York (now Hôtel Baudelaire) on Rue Saint-Anne, Hôtel du Maroc on Rue de Seine, Hôtel de Normandie on Rue des Bons-Enfants, Rue d'Angoulême (now Jean-Pierre-Timbaud), Hôtel Voltaire on Quai Voltaire, Rue Beautreillis, Hôtel de Dieppe on Rue d'Amsterdam, Hôtel du Chemin de Fer du Nord on the Place du Nord – from the Lycée Louis-le-Grand to Dr Duval's hydrotherapy establishment on Rue du Dôme, Baudelaire's last staging post before the Montparnasse cemetery, his Paris dwellings map an archipelago whose main two islands are the Latin Quarter and Nouveau Paris between the Boulevards and the northern *barrières*. Its geography would certainly not be very different it we actually knew all the places where Baudelaire slept. On 5 April 1855 he wrote to his mother: 'In just ONE MONTH I have been forced to move SIX times, living in wet plaster, sleeping with fleas – my letters (the most important ones) returned, or forwarded from one hotel to the next; I took a big decision, lived and worked at the printer's,[23] as I could no longer work where I lived.' In 'My Heart Laid Bare', he noted: 'Study of the great Disease of horror of being Settled. Reasons for the Disease. Steady increase of the Disease.'

Baudelaire, Walter Benjamin wrote, 'was forced to claim the dignity of a poet in a society that no longer had any kind of dignity to offer. Hence the buffoonery of his attitude.'[24] Baudelaire belongs to that line of artists who, from Byron on, worked at their physical character to the point of making this an integral part of their work – a part that would later become preponderant, with Duchamp, Warhol, or Beuys. As so often, the ideal that he seeks to attain he describes in someone else: 'His manners, a singular mixture of hauteur with an exquisite gentleness, were full of certainty. Physiognomy, approach, gestures, movements of the head, everything designated him as a chosen creature, above all on his good days.'[25] Here it is

---

22   Baudelaire, 'Anywhere Out of the World', *Paris Spleen*.
23   He was working on his translation of Edgar Allan Poe.
24   Benjamin, 'Charles Baudelaire, a Lyric Poet in the Era of High Capitalism'.
25   Charles Baudelaire, *Edgar Poe, His Life and Works*. In 1864, in a letter to Thoré who had accused Manet of imitating Spanish painting, Baudelaire wrote: 'Well, I myself am accused of imitating Edgar Poe! Do you know why I've translated Poe so patiently? Because he was like me. The first time I opened one of his books, I saw, with horror and delight, not only topics I'd dreamed of, but *sentences* I'd thought of, and that he had written twenty years before' (*Selected Letters*, p. 204).

Edgar Allan Poe, whom he made into a kind of complete double of himself. Undoubtedly too great an importance has been placed on Baudelaire's judgements on photography, and not enough on the number and quality of the photographic portraits we have of him, so poignant that even the talent of Nadar or Carjat is not sufficient explanation. First of all, in very studied poses, we see a handsome young man with an insolent look – like Rembrandt in his first self-portraits. Twenty years later, the series ends with a photograph taken in Brussels and inscribed to Poulet-Malassis, 'the only being whose laughter relieved my sadness in Belgium', an image in which the long greying hair and tired eyes express 'the mortal fatigue that precedes death' which Proust speaks about, precisely apropos Baudelaire.[26]

At Levêque and Bailly's *pension* on Rue de l'Estrapade, where Baudelaire was supposedly preparing for the École des Chartes, his friend Prarond describes him descending the stairs, 'thin, his collar open, a very long waistcoat, full cuffs, a light gold cane in his hand, with a supple, slow and almost rhythmic step'.[27] Later, Nadar tells of meeting him near the Hôtel Pimodan on the Île Saint-Louis: 'Black trousers drawn well above his polished boots; a blue workman's blouse, stiff in its new folds; his black hair, naturally curly, worn long his only coiffure; bright linen, strictly without starch … rose-coloured gloves, quite new … Baudelaire walked about his *quartier* of the city at an uneven pace, both nervous and languid, like a cat, choosing each stone of the pavement as if he had to avoid crushing an egg.'[28] Baudelaire entering the editorial office of *Le Corsaire-Satan*: 'You then saw his fantastic black suit appear on the boulevard, the cut that he had imposed on the tailor insolently going against the prevailing fashion – long and buttoned, opening at the top like a horn and ending in two narrow pointed lapels, like a whistle, as Petrus Borel supposedly said.'[29] In 1848, 'you would see him … on the outer boulevards, dressed either in a loose jacket or a blouse; but as irreproachable, as correct in this democratic outfit as in

---

26   This photograph, taken by Charles Neyt, is reproduced in the catalogue *Baudelaire Paris*, with a preface by Yves Bonnefoy and texts by Claude Pichois and Jean-Paul Avice (Paris: Paris-Musées, 1993). The Proust quotation is from 'À propos de Baudelaire', *Nouvelle Revue française*, 1 June 1921: 'Perhaps it is necessary to have experienced the mortal fatigue that precedes death, in order to be able to write about it the enchanting line that Victor Hugo would never have found: "And who makes the bed of the poor and the naked".' Proust died on 18 November 1922, and had already long been familiar with this 'mortal fatigue'.

27   Cited in François Porché, *Baudelaire, histoire d'une âme* (Paris: Flammarion, 1944).

28   Firmin Maillard, *La Cité des intellectuels* (Paris: 1905), cited in Benjamin, *The Arcades Project*, p. 230.

29   Charles Asselineau, *Charles Baudelaire* (Paris: Lemerre, 1869; republished Paris: Cognac, 1990).

the black suit of more prosperous times'.[30] Two months after the trial over *Les Fleurs du mal*, in October 1857, the Goncourts, never short on low comments, were dining at the Café Riché on Rue Le Peletier: 'Baudelaire was having his supper alongside us, tieless, bare neck, shaved head, as if dressed for the guillotine. Just one refinement: little washed hands, cleaned and manicured. The head of a madman, a voice sharp as a blade. A pedantic manner of speech: the look of Saint-Just or a practical joker. He defends himself, quite stubbornly and with a certain rough passion, against the charge that his verses caused outrage to good manners.'

Baudelaire described himself on several occasions as a 'dandy' or 'flâneur', and these terms have since been constantly applied to him. This is clearly not without good reason, and yet they should be used only with a double filter, as it were, made necessary both by Baudelaire's own taste for mystification, and by the shift in the meaning of these words in the century and a half that divides us from *Les Fleurs du mal*. Baudelaire certainly was a Parisian *dandy* in the sense of refinement of dress, cool insolence, the affectation of impassibility. In *My Heart Laid Bare*, provocations proliferate: 'Woman is "natural" – that is to say, abominable. Moreover, she is always vulgar – that is to say, the opposite of the dandy.' Or again: 'The dandy should aspire to be sublime, continually. He should live and sleep in front of a mirror.' Or more ambiguously: 'The eternal superiority of the dandy. What is a dandy?' Finally, almost revealing himself: 'A dandy does nothing. Can you imagine a dandy speaking to the people, unless to scoff at them?'[31]

And yet to grasp the root of his thinking, there is in his portrait of Monsieur G., 'The Painter of Modern Life', this passage in which it is impossible that Baudelaire did not have himself in mind:

> I might perhaps call him a dandy, and I should have several good reasons for that; for the word 'dandy' implies a quintessence of character and a subtle understanding of the entire moral mechanism of this world; with another part of his nature, however, the dandy aspires to insensitivity, and it is in this that Monsieur G., dominated as he is by an insatiable passion – for seeing and feeling – parts company decisively with dandyism ... The dandy is blasé, or pretends to be so, for reasons of policy and caste. Monsieur G. has a horror of blasé people.[32]

30   Ibid.
31   Charles Baudelaire, *My Heart Laid Bare and Other Prose Writings* (London: Soho Book Company, 1986), pp. 176–80 (translation modified).
32   Charles Baudelaire, *The Painter of Modern Life and Other Essays* (London: Phaidon Press, 1964).

And when Baudelaire wrote to his mother: 'How often I've told myself, "Despite my nerves, despite my terrors, despite the creditors, despite the horrors of solitude, I must pull myself together ...!"' (1 January 1865), or again: 'I'm attacked by a frightful illness, which has never played such havoc with me as in this year – I mean my reveries, my depression, my discouragement, my indecision' (31 December 1863). This was far indeed from the elegant display on the steps of Tortoni's.

The term 'flâneur' today is inseparable from the notion of idleness; flânerie is perceived as an unproductive way of spending time. But what Baudelaire feared more than anything was precisely his tendency to idleness. On 4 December 1847 he wrote to his mother: 'The absolute idleness of my apparent life, in contrast with the perpetual activity of my ideas, throws me into unheard-of fits of rage.' When he let himself go, this was not in the street but at home when there was nothing to be done: 'On occasion I've had to spend up to three days in bed, sometimes because I had no clean linen, sometimes because there was no wood ... To be honest, laudanum and wine are of little help against sorrow. They make the time pass but they don't change one's life.'[33] For Baudelaire, therefore, there was nothing passive about flânerie. He reflects on its function in poetic work in relation to a major figure of his day, and even if his feelings towards the man are ambivalent, to say the least, this is still impressive:

> For many years now Victor Hugo has no longer been in our midst. I remember the time when his figure was one of those most frequently encountered among the crowds, and many times I wondered, seeing him appear so often amid holiday excitement or in the silence of some lonely spot, how he could reconcile the needs of his incessant work with the sublime but dangerous taste for strolling and for reverie. This apparent contradiction is evidently the result of a well-ordered life and of a strong spiritual constitution which permits him to work while walking, or rather to be able to walk while he is working.[34]

And in 'The Painter of Modern Life', Baudelaire focuses and develops his theory of flânerie:

> For the perfect flâneur, for the passionate spectator, it is an immense joy to choose to set up house in the heart of the multitude, amid the ebb

---

33   *Selected Letters of Charles Baudelaire*, p. 31.
34   'Reflections on Some of My Contemporaries', in *Baudelaire as a Literary Critic* (Pennsylvania State Univ. Press, 1964), p. 235.

and flow of movement, in the midst of the fugitive and the infinite. To be away from home and yet to feel oneself everywhere at home; to see the world, to be at the centre of world, and yet to remain hidden from the world – such are a few of the slightest pleasures of those independent, passionate, impartial natures ... the lover of universal life enters into the crowd as though it were an immense reservoir of electrical energy. Or we might liken him to a mirror as vast as the crowd itself; or to a kaleidoscope gifted with consciousness, responding to each one of its movements and reproducing the multiplicity of life and the flickering grace of all the elements of life.[35]

It was not just reasons of a poetic order that drove Baudelaire into the streets of Paris. His removals were conducted in a handcart, and he never had with him what he needed for his work. 'At the Hôtel Pimodan,' Banville recalls, 'when I went there for the first time, there were no dictionaries, no desk, no table with what he needed for writing, let alone cupboards and dining room, nor anything that recalled the compartmentalized arrangement of a bourgeois apartment.'[36] It was worse when he lived with Jeanne, who made life quite impossible. On 27 March 1852, at two in the afternoon, he wrote to his mother: 'I am writing this in a café opposite the long-distance post office, in the midst of noise, card games and billiards, so as to be calmer and be able to think more clearly ... Sometimes I escape from my rooms in order to write and I go to the library or to a lending library, or a wine shop or a café, as I'm doing today. The result of all this is that I live in a state of constant rage.'[37]

The Paris street, for Baudelaire, had two distinct functions. The first of these was something like a search. It was not a question of accumulating documentary material, like Zola later on walking through the Goutte d'Or or along the Rue de Seine with notebook and pencil: Baudelaire was never short of sarcasm towards 'a certain literary procedure known as "realism" – a disgusting insult thrown in the face of all analysts, a vague and elastic word that for the vulgar means not a new method of creation but a meticulous description of accessories'. Nor does he set great store by what he calls 'observation'. When he evokes 'Honoré de Balzac, that prodigious meteor who would cover our country with a cloud of glory', he is amazed 'that his great glory was to pass for an observer; it has always seemed to me that his chief merit was to be a visionary, and a passionate one at that'.[38] What

---

35 Baudelaire, *The Painter of Modern Life*, pp. 9–10.
36 Théodore de Banville, *Mes souvenirs* (1882).
37 *Selected Letters of Charles Baudelaire*, pp. 47–8.
38 Charles Baudelaire, '*Madame Bovary* par Gustave Flaubert', published in *L'Artiste*, 18 October 1857.

Baudelaire sought in the crowds was the shock of encounter, the sudden vision that kindled his imagination, creating the 'mysterious and complex enchantment' that was the essence of poetry.

There are certain texts in which he reveals his manner of keeping abreast of 'this marvellous world that envelops and drenches us like the atmosphere':

> One day on a pavement I saw a large gathering; I managed to lift my eyes above the shoulders of the gawpers, and this is what I saw: a man lying on his back on the ground, his eyes open and fixed on the sky, another man standing in front of him and speaking only in gestures, the man on the ground responding only with his eyes, both with the animated air of remarkable goodwill. The gestures of the standing man said to the understanding of the man lying down: 'Come on then, happiness is just two steps away, on the corner of the street. We have not completely lost sight of the shore of dejection, we have not yet reached the high sea of dreams; so courage, my friend, tell your legs to satisfy your thought.'

The other, who clearly had already 'reached the high sea', did not want to listen, and his friend,

> still full of indulgence went off to the tavern by himself, then returned with a rope in his hand. He certainly could not suffer the idea of sailing and running after happiness alone; and so he came to collect his friend in a carriage. The carriage was this rope, and he passed the carriage around his friend's waist. The friend, still lying down, smiled; he certainly understood this motherly thought. The other made a knot; then he started walking, like a gentle and well-behaved horse, and pulled his friend to the rendezvous of happiness.[39]

The other reason why Baudelaire was to be found more often outdoors than at home is that the slow elaboration of his poems was made while walking. 'For my part, I saw him composing verses on the hoof while he was out in the streets; I never saw him seated before a ream of paper', wrote Prarond. And for Asselineau: 'Baudelaire worked slowly and unevenly, going twenty times over the same passage, spending hours in conflict with himself over a word, and stopping in the middle of a page to go and "cook" his thought in the oven of flânerie and conversation ... In sum, flânerie (slowness, unevenness) was for him a condition of perfection and a neces-

---

39   Charles Baudelaire, 'Le Vin', in *Du vin et du haschisch*.

sity of his nature.'[40] The first verse of 'The Sun' is reminiscent in this respect of Descartes' preface to *The Discourse of Method*:

> When the cruel sun strikes with increased blows
> The city, the country, the roofs, and the wheat fields,
> I go alone to try my fanciful fencing,
> Scenting in every corner the chance of a rhyme,
> Stumbling over words as over paving stones,
> Colliding at times with lines dreamed of long ago.

One may well ask whether Proust – who knew *Les Fleurs du mal* by heart[41] – was not remembering these paving-stone words over which Baudelaire stumbles when, at the end of *Time Regained*, the narrator stumbles over a cobble in the courtyard of the Hôtel de Guermantes, and collides, not with 'lines dreamed of long ago', but rather with something that is not so distant, a 'dazzling and indistinct vision' of Venice, that 'a chance happening had caused ... to emerge, in the series of forgotten days'.[42] And a few seconds before finding himself plunged into the final party, it is again Baudelaire who comes to the Narrator's mind:

> Above all in Baudelaire, where they are more numerous still, reminiscences of this kind are clearly less fortuitous [than in Nerval] and therefore, to my mind, unmistakable in their significance. Here the poet himself, with something of a slow and indolent choice, deliberately seeks, in the perfume of a woman, for instance, of her hair and her breast, the analogies which will inspire him and evoke for him *'l'azur du ciel immense et rond'* and *'un port rempli de flammes et de mâts'*. I was about to search in my memory for the passages of Baudelaire at the heart of which one may find this kind of transposed sensation, in order once and for all to establish my place in so noble a line of descent and thus to give myself the assurance that the work which I no longer had any hesitation in undertaking was worthy of the pains which I should have to bestow upon it.[43]

---

40 Alphonse Séché, *La Vie des Fleurs du mal* (Amines, 1928), cited by Benjamin, *The Arcades Project*, p. 231; Asselineau, *Charles Baudelaire*.
41 In 'À propos de Baudelaire', where he cites several verses, Proust inserts a note: 'When I wrote this letter to Jacques Rivière, I did not have a single book beside my sick-bed. You will therefore excuse the possible inexactness, which is easy to correct.'
42 Proust, *Time Regained*, *Remembrance of Things Past*, vol. 3, pp. 899–900.
43 Ibid., p. 959.

These simple words, 'something of a slow and indolent choice', could serve as an epigraph for any reflection on Baudelairean flânerie.

Apart from the Louvre and the Carrousel in 'The Swan', Baudelaire does not name or describe any place, but this does not prevent each one of his Paris poems, in verse or in prose, from being very precisely located. He either moves in the elegant quarters where women have the lightness of the women of Constantin Guys, or else, in the bustle of the Boulevards, he meets the 'Passerby', the 'Mendicant Redhead', and also – 'in the explosion of the New Year: chaos of mud and snow, crossed by a thousand carriages' – the 'Pleasant', that idiot 'who seemed to me to concentrate the entire spirit of France'. (Baudelaire speaks of France as Nietzsche would do of Germany, which is not their only point in common.)

But often – and this is the Paris of his 'fanciful fencing', of his favourite walk along the banks of the Canal Saint-Martin – he spent hours in the faubourgs. The word often recurs in *Les Fleurs du mal* and *Paris Spleen*, sometimes in its strict sense ('Along the old street [*faubourg*] on whose cottages are hung/The slatted shutters which hide secret lecheries'), where 'along' conjures up a street like Rue du Faubourg-du-Temple, which Baudelaire certainly strolled when he lived on Rue des Marais-du-Temple and Rue d'Angoulême), and sometimes in its more general sense of the urban periphery: 'January, irritated with the whole city,/Pours from his urn great waves of gloomy cold/On the pale occupants of the nearby grave-yard/And death upon the foggy slums [*faubourgs*]'). In 'The Rag-Pickers' Wine' ('In the heart of some old suburb [*faubourg*], muddy labyrinth,/ Where humanity crawls in a seething ferment'), in 'The Seven Old Men' ('I was following, steeling my nerves like a hero,/Arid arguing with my already weary soul/A squalid street [*faubourg*] shaken by the heavy dump-carts'), in the strange 'Miss Bistouri' ('As I came to the end of the suburb [*faubourg*] under the gaslight I felt an arm slipped gently under mine'), or in the marvellous projected epilogue to the 1861 edition: ('Your bombs, your daggers, your victories, your feasts,/Your melancholy faubourgs/ Your boarding-houses'), the Paris faubourgs are always for Baudelaire a place of misery and death. The colours here no longer have anything of the reds and greens that he admired in Delacroix, or of what enchanted Proust there – the wide doorways, marine suns, gold and shimmering antique cities, 'and the scarlet colour that they bring here and there into his work', as he writes in the letter to Rivière. Baudelaire's faubourgs, for their part, are unrelieved grey. They are rainy as they should be in autumn, and, despite the enormous body of images accumulated since Hesiod on this season of the year, Baudelaire's verses on 'the ends of seasons charged with enervating splendours' read as if no one had spoken of them before him. The first lines of 'Mists and Rains': 'O ends of autumn, winters, springtimes drenched with mud,/Seasons that lull to sleep . . .'; or of 'Autumn Song': 'Soon we shall plunge into the cold darkness;/Farewell vivid brightness of our short-lived summers!/Already I hear the dismal sound of firewood/ Falling with a clatter on the courtyard pavements'; or the opening of 'The Confiteor of the Artist': 'How penetrating is the end of an autumn day! Ah, yes, penetrating enough to be painful even; for there are certain delicious sensations whose vagueness does not prevent them from being intense; and none more keen than the perception of the Infinite.'

This 'melancholy faubourg' is the Paris of the poor. This is where you meet 'The Good Dogs' ('the filthy dog, the poor dog, the dog without a home, the loafing dog, the mountebank dog'), and their masters, the 'Rag-Pickers': 'Yes, these people harassed by domestic worries,/Ground down by their work, distorted by age,/Worn-out, and bending beneath a load of debris,/ The commingled vomit of enormous Paris'. The two 'crepuscule' poems are populated by the poor: 'Twilight' ('It is now that the pains of the sick grow sharper!/Sombre Night grabs them by the throat; they reach the end/ Of their destinies and go to the common pit'); and 'Dawn' ('It was the hour when amid poverty and cold/The pains of women in labour grow more cruel;/The cock's crow in the distance tore the foggy air/Like a sob stifled by a bloody froth'). Towards the sick, the lame and the dying who people *Les Fleurs du mal* and *Paris Spleen*, towards the beggars, old men in rags, wrinkled old women, ragpickers, prostitutes wandering 'past the lights shaken in the wind', the frightful blind, 'the poor women, dragging their thin cold breasts', Baudelaire never shows pity, nor − still worse − charitable tenderness, sentiments so widespread at the time, and that drive him into a rage (from 'The Devil and George Sand': 'If I met her, I would be unable to refrain from throwing a stoup of holy-water at her head.')[44] He is saved from this by his Satano-dandyism, but above all, what he experiences towards these down-and-outs is fraternity. When all is said and done, he feels himself one of them. At the end of 'Little Old Women', after 'My anxious eyes are fixed on your uncertain steps,/As if I were your own father; how wonderful!', he utters this amazing cry: 'Ruins! My family! O kindred minds!'[45] On another day, in the midst of a travelling fair, he sees

---

44 Baudelaire, *My Heart Laid Bare*, p. 185.
45 In 'Against Saint-Beuve', Proust, addressing his mother who did not like Baudelaire, wrote: 'Certainly, in a sublime poem like "Les Petites vieilles" not one of their sufferings eludes him. It is not only their immense sorrows: he is inside their bodies, he shudders with their nerves, shivers with their debilities' (Marcel Proust, *Against Saint-Beuve* [Harmondsworth: Penguin 1988], pp. 40−1).

a pitiful acrobat, stooped, obsolete, decrepit, a human ruin, backed against one of the posts of his shack ... He was not laughing, the wretched man! He was not crying, he was not dancing, he was not gesturing, he was not shouting; he was singing no song, neither jolly nor woeful, he was not beseeching. He was mute and motionless. He had given up, he had abdicated. His destiny was done ... And, turning around, obsessed by that vision, I tried to analyse my sudden sorrow, and I told myself: I have just seen the image of the old writer who has survived the generation whose brilliant entertainer he was; of the old poet without friends, without family, without children, debased by his wretchedness and the public's ingratitude, and whose booth the forgetful world no longer wants to enter![46]

It is this identification with the oppressed that defined Baudelaire's political position throughout his life, and not his provocative and contradictory declarations, on which subject we should never forget what he wrote of his ideal model: 'Poe was always great, not only in his noble conceptions, but even as a jester.'[47] Those who have spread the legend of a Baudelaire who retracted his revolutionary errors of February and June 1848, the good Catholic seriously won over to the doctrines of Joseph de Maistre, are the heirs of those who despised and persecuted him all his life. It was a mask he put on when he wrote in *My Heart Laid Bare*: 'I have no convictions, as such things are understood by my contemporaries, because I have no ambition.'[48] A few lines further on, this mask is raised a little. Walter Benjamin, in the parallel that we have seen him make between Baudelaire and Blanqui, shows the extent to which the former's position after June 1848 was one of camouflage:

Behind the masks which he used up, the poet in Baudelaire preserved his incognito. He was as circumspect in his work as he was capable of seeming provocative in his personal associations ... His prosody is comparable to the map of a big city in which it is possible to move around inconspicuously, shielded by blocks of houses, gateways, courtyards. On this map the places for the words are clearly indicated, as the places are indicated for conspirators before the outbreak of a revolt ... His images are original by virtue of the inferiority of the objects of comparison ... *Les Fleurs du mal* is the first book that used in poetry not only words of ordinary

---

46   'The Old Acrobat', *Paris Spleen* (University of Georgia Press, 1997), p. 29, trans. Kaplan.
47   Charles Baudelaire, *Notes nouvelles sur Edgar Poe*.
48   Baudelaire, *My Heart Laid Bare*, p. 178.

provenance but words of urban origin as well ... He uses *quinquet, wagon* or *omnibus*, and does not shrink from *bilan, réverbère*, or *voirie*. This is the nature of the lyric vocabulary in which an allegory appears suddenly and without prior preparation ... Where *la Mort* or *le Souvenir, le Repentir* or *le Mal* appear, centres of poetic strategy are indicated. The flash-light appearance of these figures, recognizable by their majuscule, in a text which does not disdain the most banal word betrays Baudelaire's hand. His technique is the technique of the *putsch*.[49]

---

49   Benjamin, 'Charles Baudelaire: A Lyric Poet in the Era of High Capitalism', pp. 98–100.

7

The Visual Image

Paris is striped: the thin tall chimneys that rise above the flat chimneys, all the little chimneys shaped like flower pots, the old gas candelabras that are completely silent, the horizontal stripes of the blinds ... the little chairs that you see out in the open and the little café tables whose legs are lines, the public gardens whose railings have gilded points.

— Franz Kafka, *Diaries*

Paris is the city of mirrors. The asphalt of its roadways smooth as glass, and at the entrance to all bistros glass partitions. A profusion of windowpanes and mirrors in cafés, so as to make the inside brighter and to give all the tiny nooks and crannies, into which Parisian taverns separate, a pleasing amplitude. Women here look at themselves more than elsewhere, and from this comes the distinctive beauty of the Parisienne.

— Walter Benjamin, *The Arcades Project*

A striped city, a city of mirrors, a black-and-white city in any case: it is perhaps in this direction that we should seek the reasons for the particular connection between Paris and photography, so close that it could almost be said to be a family tie. Not simply because photography began in Paris, with Niepce's *La Table de Déjeuner* as its prehistory by the Saône. But also because there are moments in the city's history for which photography, almost single-handedly, can restore reality with the precision of poetry. Neither novels (despite Calet), nor cinema despite the news, nor songs despite Prévert and Kosma, give a real idea of the era that followed Liberation in 1945. The last bus lines denoted by letters, with their solid tyres, the dark winter of 1946, the queues in the snow, the bread tickets, the American soldiers, the poor children without shoes, the barges caught in the ice on the Canal Saint-Martin, the steam engines on the Petite Ceinture, the Renault Juvaquatre, the *zazous* [hep cats], the copper of the percolators, the return of travelling fairs – you have to go to Doisneau to find the trace of these things, far more exact than history books that focus on the sinister clowns of tripartism.

The first picture of a human being taken in Paris dates from 1838, the year that Balzac began *Scenes from a Courtesan's Life*. To capture this image, Daguerre climbed to the top of his diorama, on Boulevard du Temple.[1] Since this mythical view was taken from this particular building, and by a landscape painter and theatre designer, it can be seen as a condensation of the relationship between the new invention, painting, and literature, an anticipation of what Baudelaire would write in 'The Salon of 1859', at the end of the section on 'Landscape':

> I would rather go back to the diorama, whose brutal and enormous magic has the power to impose a genuine illusion upon me! I would rather go to the theatre and feast my eyes on the scenery, in which I find my dearest dreams artistically expressed, and tragically concentrated! These things, because they are false, are infinitely closer to the truth; whereas the majority of our landscape-painters are liars, precisely because they have neglected to lie.

For the *daguerréotypistes*, taking a picture from the top of a building was one of the most common practices: portraits and interior views were difficult for reasons of lighting, and the cameras, heavy and fragile, were awkward to take out into the street. Hence the images of streets seen from above, which painting would take up thirty years later (Monet's *Boulevard des Capucines* series, Pissarro's *Place du Theâtre-Français*, Caillebotte's perspectives towards Boulevard Malesherbes from his apartment on Rue de Miromesnil). On the Pont-Neuf, in the top floor of the house on the corner with the Quai de l'Horloge, the optician Lerebours, a specialist in the manufacture of lenses and plates, established a glass pavilion from which his customers could take views, including panoramic ones, in the

---

1 The barracks which now houses the Garde Républicaine was built on this site at the same time as the Place de République was cleared. Some authors maintain that Daguerre took this picture from the top floor of his house, which was just behind the diorama on Rue des Marais-du-Temple (now Yves-Toudic). The American Samuel Morse, in a letter to his brother dated 7 March 1839, described the picture as follows: 'The boulevard, generally filled with a chaos of walkers and vehicles, was perfectly empty, except from one man having his boots shined. His feet, of course, could not move, one being on the polisher's box and the other on the ground. This is why his boots and his legs are so clear, while he lacks a head and a body, which moved' (Cited in Françoise Raynaud, ed. *Paris et le Daguerréotype*, exhibition catalogue [Paris-Musées, 1989]).

direction of the Pont des Arts, the Louvre colonnade and the Institut de France.

It was doubtless inevitable that a procedure of such novelty should be misunderstood, considered as a means of automatically and exactly restoring the 'real' – an opinion upheld by Daguerre himself, for whom 'the daguerreotype is not an instrument to be used for drawing nature, but a chemical and physical procedure which gives nature the ability to *reproduce itself*'.[2] But viewed in this way, photography had the result of hastening the demise of an aesthetic – already rather outworn – based on imitation as the essence of art. The existence of a machine able to satisfy mechanically the demands of the reproduction of reality forced other purposes to be found for artistic activity. This idea found its way into the public domain with amazing speed. You could read in *Le Charivari* for 10 September 1839:

> When you have the Tuileries pavilions, the Montmartre hills or the Montfaucon plain before you with an infinitesimal fidelity, not drawn but automatically traced, do you really believe that this will be art? Do you believe that this is how genuine artists proceed? There will be those who take such pictures on commission, but not artists. The artist selects, arranges, idealizes. The daguerreotype brutally copies nature – or rather, plagiarizes it.[3]

As soon as it arrived, photography thus found itself pushed outside the borders of art and forbidden to encroach on its territory. On the door of Atget's studio, at the end of the century, a plaque informed the visitor that his trade was to supply 'documents for artists'. This was not simply a sign of modesty (as certainly was, around the same time, Douanier Rousseau's sign, in Rue Perrel at Plaisance: 'Drawing, painting, music. Lessons at home, moderate prices'). Atget probably wanted to show that he had not lost sight of Baudelaire's injunction, in 'The Salon of 1859' and repeated in many other texts, that:

---

2 Advertisement for the invention, in 1838 (my emphasis). Fox Talbot, whom some people see as the true inventor of photography (and it was his friend the astronomer John Herschel who coined the word in 1844), titled his first album presenting the marvels of the process, *The Pencil of Nature*.

3 Some eighty years later, André Breton wrote in his preface to the catalogue for a Max Ernst exhibition: 'Now that a blind instrument allowed them to reach with utter certainty the goal that they had hitherto set themselves, artists rashly claimed to be breaking with the imitation of appearances' ('Max Ernst', in *The Lost Steps* [Lincoln: University of Nebraska Press, 1996], p. 60).

It is time, then, for [photography] to return to its true duty, which is to
be the servant of the sciences and arts – but the very humble servant, like
printing or shorthand, which neither created nor supplemented literature
... let it be the secretary and clerk of whoever needs an absolute exacti-
tude in his profession – up to that point nothing could be better ... But
if it be allowed to encroach upon the domain of the impalpable and the
imaginary, upon anything whose value depends solely upon the addition
of something of a man's soul, then it will be so much the worse for us!

In the unending controversies as to the respective territory and role of
painting and the new medium, Parisian photography occupies a special
place, privileged by virtue of having no competition. In the era of the
invention's first flight, from 1840 to 1870, there was not really any painting
of Paris as such. This was certainly a major period for engraving: Granville,
Daumier, Meryon, Nanteuil, Potémont and Bracquemond continue a lineage of illustrators and engravers of Paris that goes back to the sixteenth
century. Nor was there a shortage of good artists, such as Eugène Lami
or Constantin Guys, who 'captured' – with techniques such as watercol-
our, tinted drawing or gouache, generally held to be minor – lively and
colourful street scenes. But in the reports of the Salons of this period when
Paris photographers were creating so many masterpieces, there was not to
my knowledge a single canvas whose subject was a Parisian townscape.
This absence was nothing new. In the work of the great painters who had
worked in Paris since the seventeenth century, from Le Sueur to Géricault,
from Philippe de Champaigne and Simon Vouet to Ingres and Delacroix,
you can count the paintings with Paris as their subject on the fingers of one
hand.[4] When Watteau painted *The Sign* for his dealer and friend Gersaint,
who had his premises on the Pont-Neuf, all he showed of the city were
four sets of paving-stones parallel to the threshold of the shop, which a
woman dressed in pink is crossing with great elegance. Chardin, who spent
almost his whole life on Rue de Seine, and only left it to cross the river
and settle in the Louvre quarter, never made the slightest sketch of these
places so familiar to him. And it was only in exceptional circumstances that
David, expecting the guillotine after Thermidor, painted from his cell a
view of the Luxembourg gardens as fine as *The Gardens of the Villa Medici*
by Velasquez – who had advised his pupils to go out into the landscape and
draw on the motif.

4   In 'grand' painting, the only exceptions I know are the fine canvases of
Hubert Robert such as *The Demolition of Houses on the Pont-Neuf* (1786) or *The
Removal of the Pont de Neuilly* (1772), and a superb *Quai des Orfèvres* by Corot that
dates from 1833.

So Paris was until then a city without images – as distinct from Amsterdam and Delft, Venice or Rome. There were certainly Parisian *vedute*, often quite charming, but these were designed for the tourists and were not considered works of art.[5] The 'view of Paris' did not fit into any of the styles that the Salon recognized: neither history, not landscape, nor 'genre' – the outdoor scenes of the latter being located in conventional frameworks. The only city whose representation was accepted in the category of landscape was precisely Rome, since it was considered the cradle of painting, and French artists, most commonly scholars at the Villa Medici, showed only picturesque ruins, timeless gardens, and an idealized countryside.

Yet though photography had no competition in Paris, it started in a documentary mode. The very nature of daguerreotype certainly contributed to this: its extreme definition and its lack of depth were somewhat like engraving. It was perhaps this fineness – in the dual sense of the term, precision of detail and sensation of a thin layer – that explains Balzac's superstitious fear, as reported by Nadar: convinced that 'each body in nature is made up of a series of spectres, in endlessly superimposed layers', he thought that 'every operation of the daguerreotype would surprise, detach and retain one of the layers of the depicted individual'.[6] The most frequent subjects also belonged to the documentary genre – the Louvre, the Tuileries, the Madeleine, the Hôtel de Ville, the Invalides, Notre-Dame in all its aspects, the Panthéon: the daguerreotypists worked around monuments whose unencumbered situation made for good lighting, rather than in the alleyways. Perhaps, too, these pioneers, who were for the most part former painters trained in the major studios, experienced a more or less conscious desire to recompose the hierarchy of genres, the monument being a more noble subject than the muddy backstreets of 'gloomy Paris'.

In the years 1845–50, the photographic image underwent a complete change of nature, with the negative-positive system. A photograph was now 'taken' on a paper negative, followed by 'printing', likewise on paper,

5   In the sixteenth and early seventeenth century, *vedute* of this kind were painted by Flemish artists (Abraham de Verwer, Pieter Bout, Theodor Matham and Hendrik Mommers, well represented in the Carnavelet museum). The French only appeared later in this field. In the second half of the seventeenth century, they included excellent artists such as Raguenet and Pierre-Antoine Demachy, who might have been members of the Académie and exhibited at the Salon, but not their views of Paris.

6   Félix Nadar, *Quand j'étais photographe*. Nadar had photographically copied an extraordinary daguerreotype of Balzac, which he had bought from Gavarni. He remarked that, given Balzac's corpulance, a couple of layers less would have done him no harm.

which delivered the positive image. Not only could the picture be printed in several copies (whereas the copper plate of the daguerreotype was necessarily unique), but the result was very different.[7] The resolution was less fine, the image often even a little vague; the grain of the paper was visible, and above all, by playing with contrast in the course of printing, the photographer could accentuate the opposition between dark masses and lighter zones, characteristic of the narrow streets in which the light falls in geometrically regular patches. Parallel with this, the exposure time was shorter and the moving human figure now made an appearance. In 1851, Charles Nègre – who had come from Delaroche's studio, like his friend Le Gray, and Le Secq who introduced him to Meryon[8] – lived on the Île Saint-Louis. From his courtyard at 21 Quai de Bourbon, which he used as an outdoor studio, he took a photograph titled *Chimney Sweepers Under Way*, a frieze of three individuals walking east towards the rising sun. The only clear element in this photo is the dark grey stone of the island's parapet. In the distance, the Quai des Célestins on the other side of the river offers an irregular line of roofs and a tight rhythm of dark windows in the bright aureole of the houses. In the foreground, the almost white pavement is a little burned by the printing. Of the three individuals, the one who walks ahead is scarcely taller than the top of the parapet; this is a child, needed in the team to climb up the chimneys. He wears a cap and looks towards the river, so that his features cannot be seen. Behind him, the two other figures are men, each carrying a bag on his shoulder, their faces blackened by soot and darkened even more by the visors of their caps. From a technical point of view, the characters are too dark, not very clear, and the printing is too contrasted. But it is precisely this vagueness and the violent opposition of values that give this image a mysterious novelty. Nothing like it had ever been seen before, neither in engraving nor in painting, whose subtlest *sfumato* was never as disturbing as the vibration of photography in this brief and marvellous period of innocence.

The writers and artists of the time were fascinated, despite a certain reticence on principle. The great Nadar – the only person to have photographed, over a span of thirty years, the four members of that relay team of genius: Delacroix, Baudelaire, Manet and Mallarmé – recalls that people toured photographers' studios as they nowadays do galleries of contemporary

---

7   Fox Talbot, inventor of this system, which he called 'calotype' (from *kalos*: beautiful), considered that this was the true invention of photography. Disputes over paternity are very prominent in the history of these early years. Despite being fed up with the French, Fox Talbot nevertheless visited Paris in the 1840s and took some wonderful photographs.

8   Charles Nègre had exhibited an *Embarkation for Cythera* in the Salon of 1845.

art. These were grouped on the boulevards between Rue de la Paix and
the Madeleine: Nadar at 35 Boulevard des Capucines (a façade of glass and
metal that was heavy with history, and destroyed by Crédit Foncier in the
early 1990s to install a shoe shop), the Bisson brothers and Le Gray a little
further up towards the Madeleine:

> The Bissons' shop raised great excitement. It was not simply the extraor-
> dinary luxury and good taste of the establishment, nor the novelty and
> perfection of its products, that halted the passerby; there was a no less
> lively interest in contemplating through the plate-glass windows the
> illustrious visitors who followed one another on the velvet covers of the
> great circular divan, passing the proofs of the day from hand to hand.
> It was really like a meeting place of the Paris intellectual elite: Gautier,
> Cormenin Louis, Saint-Victor, Janin, Gozlan, Méry, Préault, Delacroix,
> Chassériau, Nanteuil, Baudelaire, Penguilly, the Leleux brothers – every-
> one! I twice saw there another amateur who was equally essential in his
> way, M. Rothschild – Baron James, as people called him – who was very
> affable but by this time could no longer manage to appear young. And
> these leading figures of Paris society, when they left the Bissons', finished
> their tour by going on to the portraitist Le Gray.[9]

Although place was slowly made for the new invention among other artistic practices – from 1859, photography was exhibited in the same building
as the Salon – the major work of Paris photographers in the nineteenth
century was the result of a technical and documentary commission. In
1865, the municipal administration decided to have photographed the
old roads that were going to be demolished, and entrusted this work
to Charles Marville. With a reputation as an illustrator (he had been
involved with Huet and Meissonier in a famous romantic edition of
Paul et Virginie), his beginnings in photography dated from the 1850s,
in particular with studies of clouds at sunset in the sky above Paris – and
it was certainly by choice that this cultivated man sought to rival the
colours of Constable and Delacroix on this subject, with his nuances of
grey. The task presented to him was unprecedented: to describe what
was going to be destroyed, with the aim of demonstrating that what was
about to disappear was not worth the trouble of being preserved. But
Marville showed the silent charm of what others liked to see as disturbing and unhealthy. Without any quest for the picturesque, without the

---

9 Nadar, *Quand j'étais photographe*. Baron James de Rothschild was Balzac's
major model for Nucingen in *La Comédie humaine*.

least resort to an aesthetic of poverty, he simply used the resources of photography in a way that much later would be described as 'objective' (Marville was to the streets of Old Paris what Sander would be to the people of Cologne in the 1930s). He placed his camera very low, almost at street level, so that the paving stones occupy a large surface, with a perspective effect that evokes the theoretical drawings of Renaissance Italy.[10] Often glistening with rain, the street reflects the light of early morning or evening, when beautiful shadows accentuate the reliefs and contrasts. And although there are no human beings in his pictures, he uses the writing that was omnipresent in Paris at this time – signs and advertisements painted on walls – to give an impression of the comic or melancholy. In Rue de la Monnaie, where the only sign of human presence is a cart with a cover like a Magritte head, there is a 'Librería española' with a sign of the siege of Sebastopol; on Rue de la Tonnellerie, above the old pillars of Les Halles, an advertisement advises the treatment of 'glazings on the breasts (and elsewhere)' with 'Cosmétique Liébert' (remember Birotteau!), while the other wall of the same corner building has a 'keeper of horse- and hand-carts'. There are the 'Russian baths' on the Place Saint-André-des-Arts, the 'Dunkirk oysters warehouse' on Rue Mondétour, the 'Demolition material for sale' on the Passage des Deux-Soeurs, and 'Henriat, tiler and stove-setter' on the Cour du Dragon – all activities that Marville catalogued on the eve of their disappearance without any detectable sentimentality, the effect being all the more striking.

The 425 photographs that Marville took between 1865 and 1868 are the only major visual souvenir that remains of a Paris that has completely disappeared. They are there in every detail, these streets of the Île de la Cité that existed already in the days of François Rabelais or even François Villon. They are the streets that Victor Hugo paced while writing *Notre-Dame de Paris*, those of Charles Nodier, Aloysius Bertrand, Gérard de Nerval: Rues de Perpignan, des Trois-Canettes, Cocatrix, des Deux-Ermites, des Marmousets, Saint-Landry, Haut-Moulin, Saint-Christophe – where, on the shop facing the foundlings hospital of Les Enfants-Trouvés, a notice-board indicates that 'on the coming 15 October the edge-tool workshop will be transferred to 20 Rue Zacarie'. The demolition was under way: the old corner posts, the little shops, the paving whose irregularity was fashioned over centuries, the bars, the cant walls with bay windows, the lampposts, the signboards, the courtyards – this whole world would disappear to make

---

10 Atget, on the contrary, tried to prevent the lower part of his images from being occupied by the pavement; with this object, he did not always pull the shutter fully open.

way for the Prefecture of Police and the Hôtel-Dieu, the most sinister of Paris hospitals, which is saying a great deal.

Marville's images are sometimes used to illustrate Baudelaire's Paris. This is acceptable, on condition that the possessive case simply denotes the era and nothing more. Baudelaire never expanded on the charm of old stones, and if you want Baudelairean images of Paris – a legitimate search with someone who wrote of 'glorifying the cult of images (my great, my sole, my original passion)' – it is not in Marville's photos that you should look, but rather in Manet. In France, however, the official history of nineteenth-century art is so compartmentalized that the relationship between Baudelaire and Manet is most often described in a very curious fashion.[11] You can often read that Baudelaire 'did not understand' Manet, that he preferred Constantin Guys. I suspect in this haste to trip Baudelaire up the reflex of museum curators against someone whom they well sense would not have been on their side. They forget, or pretend to forget, that when Baudelaire wrote Manet the letter that is so often cited, replying to the painter who complained of not being understood: 'What you demand is really crazy. People tease you; their jokes annoy you; no one knows your real worth. Do you think you're the only man in that position? Do you have more genius than Chateaubriand and Wagner? But they were jeered at, weren't they? It didn't kill them. And to avoid turning your head, I'll add that those men were models, each in his own way, and in a very rich world, whereas you, you're only the first in the decline of our art'[12] – that when he sent these murderous lines he had not seen *Olympia*. He had seen *Lola de Valence*, and wrote on the corner of a tablecloth the famous quatrain on the 'pink and black jewel'. He had seen *Le Déjeuner sur l'herbe* in the same year as he wrote *The Painter of Modern Life*, as well as *Music in the Tuileries*, that first image of Paris showing the city as a theatre for flâneurs.[13] But he was unable to see *Olympia*,

---

11   American art historians – the great Meyer Shapiro, T. J. Clark, Robert Herbert, Harry Rand, Michael Fried – have succeeded in thinking outside the frame of exhibition catalogues, crossing disciplines and bringing art out of its ghetto. Nineteenth-century French painting has thus become an American subject, whether we like it or not.

12   11 May 1865, *Selected Letters of Charles Baudelaire*, p. 175. Manet had written to him: 'I would indeed like to have you here, my dear Baudelaire, insults are raining down on me like hail … I would have liked to have your healthy judgement on my pictures, for all these shouts are disturbing me, and it is clear that someone is mistaken.'

13   As we know, Baudelaire himself figures among the characters represented, several of whom are recognizable: Manet and his brother Eugène, Aurélien Scholl, Offenbach, Théophile Gautier …

as for a year then he had taken himself off to Brussels, and his question in the same letter — 'is it really a cat?' — is a hiccup of astonishment that such a Baudelairean motif had made its appearance in the painting. Baudelaire was unable to 'understand' Manet because he did not have time to, because he was unable to see any of the masterpieces of Manet's maturity. When he was brought back to Paris, his mind was destroyed. Manet came to see him every day at Dr Duval's clinic, and the only moments that the sick man showed any signs of contentment were when Mme Manet played him extracts from *Tannhäuser* on the piano.

Olympia is a 'Paris painting'. The only person to have said this at the time was a certain Ravenel, in *L'Époque*, a newspaper of the republican opposition: 'A painting of the Baudelaire school, executed by someone who is largely a follower of Goya; the strangeness of the girl from the suburbs, one of Paul Niquet's daughters of night, of *The Mysteries of Paris* and the nightmares of Edgar Allan Poe. Her look has the bitterness of a premature creature, her face has the disturbing perfume of a *fleur du mal*.' It was perhaps this that explains the most violent 'rain of insults' that had ever been provoked by a painting — a body that recalls the horror of the morgue, a skeleton dressed in a layer of plaster, a courtesan with dirty hands and rough feet, a picture drawn with charcoal on the edges and pomade in the middle, and that toad-like hand placed over her sex. These metaphors of dirt and disease, the repeated references to plaster, sweat and charcoal, reveal a fear and hatred of the poor, especially those poor who do not know their place. We need to remind ourselves what the 'normal' nude was at that time. Two plates in a book by T. J. Clark show side by side the canvases bought by the state after the Salon of 1865 — Schutzenberger's *Europe enlevée par Jupiter*, *Le Sommeil de Vénus* by Girard, a pupil of Gleyre, *L'Enlèvement d'Anymoné* by Giacomotti, Prix de Rome for 1854, and *La Perle et la vague* by Baudry: soft white thighs, ecstatic pose, drapery flying in the sea breeze.[14] In the midst of these sad obscenities that mark the final decadence of a genre, just imagine the effect produced by Victorine Meurent, her velvet ribbon, her Black servant and her cat, and you will understand the fury of those whom Thoré was addressing in his 'Salon de 1865': 'Who encourages a mythological and mystic art, the Oedipuses and Venuses, or the madonnas and saints in ecstasy? Those whose interest it is that art should mean nothing, and have no bearing on modern aspirations. Who encourages the nymphs and erotic scenes à la Pompadour? The Jockey-Club and Boulevard des

---

14 T. J. Clark, *The Painting of Modern Life. Paris in the Art of Manet and His Followers* (Princeton University Press, 1984).

Italiens. And who buys these pictures? The traders and rich winners of the Bourse.'[15]

Théophile Gautier, despite being the dedicatee of *Les Fleurs du mal*, was among the most virulent critics: '*Olympia* cannot be explained from any point of view, even by taking her for what she is, a sickly model stretched out on a sheet. The tone of the chairs is dirty, the representation appalling. Shadows are indicated by stripes of polish of varying width. And what can we say of the Negress holding a bouquet wrapped in paper, or the black cat that has left the imprint of its dirty paws on the bed?' Gautier was close to the Goncourts, who were beginning their *Manette Salomon* – a novel of the devastating influence of a Jewish model on the painter Coriolis – at the very time of the scandal over *Olympia*. Coriolis's *The Turkish Bath* inspired by Boucher, the Black servant, the 'nudity that had suddenly cast into the studio the radiance of a masterpiece': all this is undoubtedly an indirect criticism of Manet's *Olympia*, which the Goncourts held as a provocation that, like Baudelaire, heralded disaster for the arts.[16]

After the events of 1870–71 – the siege of Paris, when he served with Degas in the artillery of the National Guard, then the Commune – Manet felt he could no longer paint as he had before. The massacres of Bloody Week shocked him so much that he even thought of stopping painting altogether. This is not a matter of Manet's political opinions, which are generally commented on with vague allusions to 'republican sympathies', referring for example to *The Rue Mosnier Decked with Flags*. It would be clearly absurd to see Manet as any kind of revolutionary. But three points are worth noting: Firstly, that it was not politically neutral to paint *The Execution of Maximilien* in 1868, when this event was less than a year old and the shameful end of the Mexican expedition had shaken the Empire. The engraving that Manet made for the reproduction of this picture was banned by the censors.

Secondly, during the 1860s Manet had his studio on Rue Guyot (now Médéric), on the edge of the wretched quarter of Petite-Pologne which Haussmann had already started demolishing to drive through Boulevard Malesherbes.[17] It was in these parts that Manet hobnobbed with the gypsy Jean Lagrène, who lived in a temporary encampment harassed by the police, earning his living by playing the barrel-organ, and whom Manet took as

---

15 Thoré, a republican exiled under the Second Empire, was famous under the name of Thoré-Bürger for having 'rediscovered' Vermeer during the years he spent in the Netherlands.
16 Gautier was a regular at the dinners organized by the Goncourts at Magny, along with Flaubert, Turgenev, Renan, Taine and Sainte-Beuve.
17 See above, p. 146.

his model for *The Old Musician*. Behind him, seated on the bank, is the ragpicker Collarder – a Baudelairean character par excellence – whom he also used as a model for *The Absinthe Drinker*, rejected by the Salon of 1859: 'Manet has chosen only themes congenial to him – not simply because they were at hand or because they furnished a particular colouring or light, but rather because they were his world in an overt or symbolic sense and related intimately to his personal outlook.'[18]

Manet's interest in those on the margins of society, the bohème of the street, is related by Antonin Proust (for whom, 'in Manet, the eye played so great a role that Paris had never known a flâneur the like of him, or one who put his flânerie to better use') in his *Souvenirs*: 'One day we walked together up to what has since become Boulevard Malesherbes, amid demolition interspersed with the gaping openings of land already cleared ... A woman came out of a sordid bar, holding up her dress and with a guitar in her hand. He went straight up to her and asked her to come and pose for him. She burst out laughing. "I will paint her," he said, "and if she doesn't come, I've got Victorine."'[19]

Thirdly, during the Commune, Manet left Paris to give his family the protection of the provinces. But his name still figured on the list of the Commission des Artistes, officially drawn up in his absence, which shows that he was considered as favourable to the movement. He was on the best of terms with Courbet, who chaired the Commission and whose name recurs on several occasions in connection with the insults that surrounded *Olympia*. Manet made two lithographs of Bloody Week, both dated 1871: *The Barricade*, in which, at the centre of a Paris crossroads that is hastily sketched, a squad of Versaillais soldiers – the same grouping and even the same attitudes as in *The Execution of Maximilien* – shoot at point-blank range an insurgent whose horrified face alone stands out in the smoke above the pavement; and *The Civil War*, in dark flat tints and thick lines, with the corpses of two insurgents at the foot of a dismantled barricade, a civilian and a National Guard of whom you see only the leg of his striped trousers.

When he went back to work, Manet's painting completely changed, and his new style was heralded by a manifesto-painting. For the first time, an

18 Meyer Shapiro, 'Review of Joseph C. Sloane's *French Painting Between the Past and the Present: Artists, Critics and Tradition from 1848 to 1870*', *Art Bulletin*, 36 (June 1954). Cited in Harry Rand, *Manet's Contemplation at the Gare Saint-Lazare* (Berkeley: University of California Press, 1987), p. 8. Shapiro continues by noting 'the intense contemporaneity of so many of Manet's themes and his positive interest in the refractory, the independent, the marginal, and the artistic in life itself'.
19 In *La Revue blanche*, vol. 44, 1 and 15 February 1897. *The Street Singer* was the first of the several canvases in which Victorine Meurent posed for Manet.

image of Paris was exhibited at the Salon: known either as *The Railway* or
La Gare Saint-Lazare, which is of little importance, since neither one or the
other is visible.[20] This work triggered a new outcry. A drawing by Cham,
for the cover of the special issue of *Le Charivari* devoted to the Salon of
1874, was titled *The Seal Lady*, and beneath it: 'These unhappy creatures
tried to escape being painted, but with great foresight he put up a fence that
cut off any retreat.' And another: 'Two madwomen, afflicted by incurable
Monomanétie, watch carriages pass outside the bars of their cell.' Burty and
Duret, generally supporters of Manet, were both disconcerted. Zola could
only find praise for 'the charming palette', repeating with scant conviction
that Manet was 'one of the rare original artists that our school can boast'.[21]

Nothing at all like this picture had previously been seen. It is set in the
Europe quarter, where Manet had just moved (his new studio was at 4
Rue de Saint-Pétersbourg).[22] But it was not just the novelty of the setting
and subject – the train, as symbolic of modern life as the Place de l'Europe
was of modern Paris – that made this painting a scandal. Its very technique
creates a feeling of strangeness, transgressing the rules, and this is because
the influence of photography makes itself felt. Not that Manet worked on
or after a photograph – as his neighbour, the engineer Caillebotte, indeed
did: the images on which he based the impeccable perspectives of *Rainy
Weather in Paris, at the Crossroads of the Rue de Turin and the Rue de Moscou,*
and *Le Pont de l'Europe*.[23] The foreground of *La Gare Saint-Lazare* is both
very close and very clear: Victorine Meurent, shown full face, wears around

---

20   When this picture was exhibited at the Salon of 1874, its title was *Le Chemin
de Fer*. It had already been purchased by the great baritone Jean-Baptiste Faure, a
regular buyer of Manet, who later portrayed him as Hamlet in Ambroise Thomas's
opera. When Durand-Ruel took the picture to the United States, he changed its
title to give it a 'French touch'.

21   *Le Sémaphore de Marseille*, 3–4 May 1874.

22   Juliet Wilson-Bareau has established after deep investigation, in *Manet,
Monet, la gare Saint-Lazare* (exhibition catalogue, Réunions des Musées nationaux
and Yale University Press), that the picture was painted, or at least largely sketched
out, at the studio of a painter friend of Manet's, Albert Hirsch, whose daughter
Suzanne posed for it. This studio was entered from 58 Rue de Rome, but on the
other side of the building there existed – and still does – a small garden wedged
between the building and the fences that border the railway cutting. This is the
space of the picture's foreground, flat by the choice of the painter, but also in reality. Wilson-Bareau has also shown that the door of the building, which can be seen
in the background above Victorine's hat, is that of Manet's own studio. Before the
construction of the Messageries (now the Garage de l'Europe), the buildings of
Rue de Rome could be seen from the bottom of Rue de Saint-Pétersbourg.

23   To keep a record of pictures he had sold, Manet generally made small water-
colour or gouache copies on a photograph print.

her neck the velvet ribbon that was *Olympia*'s only clothing, while little Suzanne is seen almost from behind, looking away towards the tracks. But beyond the railing, the background is not clear, as in a photograph with a weak depth of field. This is not just an effect of the smoke that is rising above the unseen railway: Manet has deliberately chosen to place a very shallow foreground against a vague background, a procedure contrary to all the rules that had governed open-air perspective since at least the time of Leonardo, but one that was quite current in photography. In other views of Paris made a short time earlier by painters close to Manet – Monet's paintings from the second floor of the Louvre in 1867, *Saint-Germain-l'Auxerrois*, *The Jardin de l'Infante*, *The Quai du Louvre*; or again Caillebotte's *Bare-Headed Man Seen from Behind at a Window*, painted from his apartment on Rue de Miromesnil, or Renoir's *The Pont-Neuf* – despite the 'impressionist' feeling of the brushwork, the distances are as clear as in Van Eyck. On top of this, *La Gare Saint-Lazare* is painted in almost a single colour: blue with white highlights for Victorine's dress; white with a large blue bow and blue embroidery for little Suzanne's; the blue-black railing; and bluish white for the cloud of smoke that is not just a sign of absence, but almost a third character in the painting. And as for Victorine herself, raising her eyes from the book in which she was absorbed – her fingers placed between its pages like bookmarks, suggesting that she is comparing passages or consulting notes – her character expressing nothing more than a vague surprise is archetypically photographic in the way it renders the sudden and accidental. It is a snapshot, there is no story attached (Duret was quite vexed: 'In fact, there is no subject at all'), no psychology either in the sense of the portraits of Rembrandt or even Goya. If Manet chose Victorine Meurent so many times as his model, from *The Street Singer* through to *La Gare Saint-Lazare*, it was because she had this unfathomable look, which, without expressing anything legible, creates an expectation, a disturbance. This look – dark, frontal and mysterious – which Victorine already had turning her head towards the viewer with an adorable shyness in *Mlle V in the . . . Costume of an Espada*, is what Manet gave to the many unforgettable women of his Paris, to Berthe Morisot in *The Balcony*, to Henriette Hauser in *Nana*, right through to the last, the blonde Suzon in *A Bar at the Folies-Bergère*. And when the gaze of his models was clear and oblique – the elegant bourgeoise of *In the Conservatory* or the poor girl alone in *La Prune* – only then does something like a trace of melancholy slip in.

Manet did indeed manage to wrong-foot his critics. By being handsome and warmhearted, rejecting the customary pictorial signs of emotion, not 'composing' his pictures in the usual sense of the term – while in Monet's *Gare Saint-Lazare* series, no matter how innovatory he was, each canvas is as structured as a landscape by Poussin – he was taken for an unfinished artist, a painter without ideas or culture, with the critics particularly maintaining that he had so well internalized the inheritance of Hals, Goya and Velasquez that he could no longer be distinguished. Even Zola reached the point of failing to understand anything. But for Mallarmé, who stopped off at his studio every evening on his way back from the Lycée Fontane (now Condorcet, on Rue du Havre in front of the Gare Saint-Lazare), Manet was 'the painter to whom no other can be compared',[24] and he describes him 'in his studio, a fury raging on the empty canvas, as if he had never painted before'.[25] Mallarmé was, it is true, better placed than Zola to understand Manet in his later years, the Manet who has his place in the lineage of enigmatic painters, 'difficult' as they are called, whose paintings can certainly be dated, described, X-rayed, followed from one collection to another, but whose intentions remain veiled, and with whom obscurity is in some sense a part of his meaning. Who can be sure of having really understood Urbino's *Flagellation*, even after Carlo Ginzburg has identified the three characters placed in the foreground by Piero della Francesca, in a confabulation that will remain forever mysterious?

In official historiography, the 1870s are presented as the time when modern parliamentary democracy was established in France, when secular education was developed, and a country shaken by defeat and civil war was rebuilt both materially and morally. The pretence is made of forgetting that this was a period of reaction such as always follows the defeat of revolution. The very nature of the regime was not settled until 1875, when the majority in parliament voted for a republic almost by a stroke of luck. It was in these years that Monet painted *Flags on the Rue Montorgueil on the 14th July*, and Manet *The Rue Mosnier Decked With Flags*, the tricolour flag reappearing after it had been almost absent from painting since Delacroix's *Liberty*, and at a time when it had a very particular meaning, opposed to the white flag of the Comte de Chambord whom his supporters sought to enthrone as Henri V. Tens of thousands of Communards were still exiled, imprisoned, deported or transported.[26]

---

24 Thadée Natanson, *Peints à leur tour* (Paris: Albin Michel, 1948).

25 Stéphane Mallarmé, *Quelques médaillons ou portraits en pied*. Manet and Mallarmé had become acquainted a year before *La Gare*. Mallarmé lived at that time on Rue de Moscou, a couple of steps away from Manet. He moved to 87 Rue de Rome in 1875. In 1885 he wrote to Verlaine: 'For ten years I saw Manet every day, and I find his absence today inconceivable.'

26 Those 'deported' were imprisoned in the territories to which they were sent: Guyana and New Caledonia, whereas those 'transported' – including Louise Michel, and Rochefort whose *Escape* Manet painted in 1880 – were free in their movements.

These years saw both the appearance of the expression 'moral order', and a phenomenon that can be taken as the revelation of its hidden face. It was the start of a brief period – thirty or forty years at the most – when Paris became what it had never been before, the principal subject of modern painting. Not by its famous sites, its old stones, the play of sunshine on its monuments, the elegant ladies of the Bois de Boulogne; what Degas and Manet chose instead – for initially it was more or less them alone – was rather the world of pleasure, of nighttime entertainment in which all strata of the city mingled, a world whose life continued without even the most vigilant police force managing to check it. A kind of dialogue, if certainly a silent one, now developed between these two painters: they observed one another with a greater interest than had Monet and Renoir at La Grenouillère, if without a common purpose and without working together.

They did however have a great deal in common. Both of them – and this is the essential thing – were true Parisians, the only ones among the major painters of the day. Degas, who was born on Rue Saint-Georges and died on Boulevard de Clichy, never moved far from Pigalle, just as Manet always remained between the Batignolles, the Quartier de l'Europe and the Place Clichy. But when Manet exhibited *A Bar at the Folies-Bergère* at the Salon of 1882, Degas wrote to Henri Rouart: 'Manet, stupid and refined, a playing card without strength, Spanish trompe l'oeil – a painter ... in the end, you'll see.' The connections between them were Berthe Morisot, a follower of both Degas and Manet, and Mallarmé, one of the few writers who impressed Degas, himself an amateur poet. The two painters each expressed a different aspect of Mallarmé's character: in Manet's portrait – his hand holding a cigar, its smoke against the white paper, his look again unfathomable, focused, lost in the distance – it is his genius; in Degas's photograph – where Mallarmé is standing in profile, smiling lightly as he turns towards a seated Renoir – his particular goodness.

Women on café terraces, customers and waitresses, musicians in the pit at the new Garnier opera, whom Degas catches against the light in an unprecedented framing, Manet's *Masked Ball at the Opera* – which could be an illustration for the start of Balzac's *Scenes from a Courtesan's Life* – music-hall singers, brothel scenes, the Cirque Fernando where Degas painted Mademoiselle Lala on her flying trapeze, and barefacedly claimed to be rivalling Tiepolo's ceilings: in more than ten years there are hundreds of sketches, pastels, canvases. But there is no joy in this world of pleasure. Degas's studies of the effects of electric light – which had now replaced gas for the illumination of stage performances – however subtle they are as an urban nocturnal counterpart to Monet's effects of sunlight on Rouen cathedral, accentuate the 'ugliness' of the café-concert singers. The dumpy waitresses of Manet's brasseries, the tired bar-girls, the customers in their suits or work clothes, all look elsewhere, ordinary and distant. Nothing like the orgies at Les Flamands or the lighthearted melancholy of *fêtes galantes*. Certainly neither Manet nor the reactionary, misogynist, and anti-Semitic Degas deliberately used the theme of pleasure in Paris to reveal the seamy side of society, but they were so striking in an elliptical sense, so strong in showing without describing, that the attitudes, looks, and groupings bring out the truth of the time. Without coal porters or famished beggars, they can tell the reign of money (Degas's masterpiece *La Bourse*). They show the loneliness of the city, a loneliness *à deux* in Degas's *Absinthe*, an unqualified loneliness in Manet's *La Prune*. They show the exploitation of women, the thin *gamines* of the Opéra's corps de ballet, the aging prostitutes waiting for custom on the boulevard terraces – and those poor little Olympias, those unripe Nanas whose confusion is scarcely indicated with a few pencil lines, in the shadow of the top hats.

It is by the theme of nocturnal entertainment, following *A Bar at the Folies-Bergère* and Manet's death soon after, that the connection is made with the following generation: the generation of Seurat, whose most disturbing drawings in Conté crayon were devoted to the café-concerts, and whose *Chahut* is a dissonant painting of a scandalous dance; of Lautrec, who spent his nights drawing in a brothel or music-hall; and of Bonnard, whose *France-Champagne*, the first lithograph poster, covered the Paris walls. All three painters were connected with *La Revue blanche*, and it was in the offices of the magazine, on Rue Lafitte, that Fénéon would put on the first Seurat retrospective a few months after the painter's death. Bonnard's *Place Clichy* series, and Vuillard's *Public Gardens*, were the last great moments of Paris painting, which came to an end at the same time as *La Revue blanche*, in the years 1900–05.

The transformation that took place then came out of symbolism, which had no place for either the aesthetics or the political poetics of the big city. At the turn of the century Paris ceased almost suddenly to be what it had been from the time of *La Comédie humaine*, *Les Misérables* and *Les Fleurs du mal*, from the beginnings of photography, from *Olympia* and *Women on a Café Terrace, Evening* – the great modern subject. The new paradigm that emerged and took its place was built around inventions that relegated the steam engine to archaeology, and which had in common the thing that would be the distinguishing mark of the new century, constantly redefined: speed. No other capital came to take the place of Paris, as it was the very imaginary of the city that changed. In Apollinaire's 'Zone', placed strategically at the start of *Alcools*, the city he describes ('You've had enough of living in Greek and Roman antiquity/Here even the cars appear to be old') is close to the projects drawn by Sant'Elia, El Lissitzky, Le Corbusier – imaginary cities, aerodromes hanging from the top of immense towers, power stations like cathedrals, great deserted avenues like those of De Chirico's Turin. At the same time a follower of Verlaine and a futurist, Apollinaire – the *'flâneur des deux rives'* – was well placed to theorize, from his own great gap between two worlds, and it was his friend Sonia Delaunay who marked what was perhaps the end point of Paris painting with *Le Bal Bullier*, where she herself so often went dancing and which she shows as a shower of multicoloured balls in the night, a magnificent painting between Degas's *Ambassadors* and the first Kandinsky.[27]

Nothing better shows this change of paradigm than *À la recherche du temps perdu*, which despite its great ancestry in Balzac, basically has very little to say about Paris. The countless passages in which the Narrator talks about painting deal mainly with landscapes, sometimes portraits, but never Paris. Very often, by the play of comparisons (which for some reason, I don't know why, critics call metaphors), Proust slips into other cities more colourful and propitious to the unfurling of his images: 'It is of the poorer quarters [of Venice] that certain poor quarters of Paris remind one, in the morning, with their tall, splayed chimneys to which the sun imparts the most vivid pinks, the brightest reds – like a garden flowering above the houses, and flowering in such a variety of tints as to suggest the garden of a tulip-fancier of Delft or Haarlem.'[28] Proust's temperament was not that of a flâneur. Perhaps his asthma was partly responsible for this, but in reality the very motive of the *Recherche* makes the streets of the big city unsuited to nourishing his story.[29] It was through his bedroom window that Proust heard the noises of Paris (the start of *The Captive* in which the awakening Narrator makes out what time it is from the first sounds, 'according to whether they came to my ears deadened and distorted by the moisture of the atmosphere or quivering like arrows in the resonant, empty expanses of

---

27 There was certainly later on Robert Delaunay's *Eiffel Tower* and Matisse's *Notre-Dame*, but these are rather formal investigations of the famous silhouettes. There would also be Utrillo, Chagall, Dufy, de Staël, etc., but this is no longer the same kind of painting.

28 Proust, *The Guermantes Way, Remembrance of Things Past*, vol. 2, p. 394.

29 With the exception of the Champs-Élysées gardens and the Bois de Boulogne, descriptions of which are among the most famous passages in the *Recherche*. These are cutoff parts of the city that rather represent the 'Lartigue's way' side of Proust, perhaps not his best side.

a spacious, frosty, pure morning' (p. 1), and observed its spectacle: 'if, on rising from my bed, I went to the window and drew the curtain aside for a moment, it was … also to catch a glimpse of some laundress carrying her linen-basket, a baker-woman in a blue apron, a dairymaid with a tucker and white linen sleeves, carrying the yoke from which her milk-churns are suspended, some haughty fair-haired girl escorted by her governess …' (p. 20). Only rarely does Proust cite the name of a Paris street, or precisely localize an encounter or an event. Even the Guermantes hôtel, the Narrator's domicile and the central location of the work, is not clearly situated: it often appears to be in the 7th arrondissement, whereas it is actually close to the Parc Monceau, so that the description of the duchess's salon as 'the first in the Faubourg Saint-Germain' really is metaphorical on this occasion. The temporal gaps in the *Recherche* – in comparison with which the gap Proust admired in *A Sentimental Education* would be a 'very shallow stream'[30] – make for an alternation between passages that are chronologically indeterminate and moments that are perfectly dated and characterized: the *Recherche* is unequalled on the Dreyfus affair as seen by the aristocracy and haute bourgeoisie, and on the atmosphere in Paris during the First World War nothing comes close to the passage in *Time Regained* that begins, in supreme irony, with a description of women's fashions: 'As if by the germination of a tiny quantity of yeast, apparently of spontaneous generation, young women now went about all day with tall cylindrical turbans on their heads, as a contemporary of Mme Tallien's might have done, and from a sense of patriotic duty wore Egyptian tunics, straight and dark and very "war", over very short skirts …' (p. 743). Proust's subtle manipulation of time might well have been impeded by too precise a localization of the characters and events in the city, and the topographical looseness backs up the chronological haze in which it is so delightful to wander.

Like Marville for Baudelaire, Atget is often called on to illustrate Proust's Paris. An odd idea, given that Atget's and Proust's locations do not match each other at all. Proust spent all his life in the new quarters of the Right Bank – Rue de Courcelles, Boulevard Malesherbes, Rue Hamelin. This is where he locates the Guermantes hôtel, as we have seen, and when his characters have an exact address, it is most often in the elegant quarters between the Opéra and the Étoile.[31] Atget almost never photographed

30   'A "blank", an enormous "blank", and without the shadow of a transition, suddenly the measure of time is no longer in quarters of an hour but in years and even decades …' (Marcel Proust, 'À propos du "style" de Flaubert', *Nouvelle Revue française*, 1 January 1920).
31   Swann was an exception, living on the Quai d'Orléans.

these districts, as he devoted his work to pre-Haussmann Paris, and the little tradespeople he shows in front of the church of Saint-Médard certainly have little in common with those of Boulevard Malesherbes, whose cries the Narrator hears from his bed in *The Captive*.[32]

A long career, an enormous and disparate work – over ten thousand photographs whose numbering and classification are a labyrinth within a labyrinth – a solitary life which has left only a few discordant traces, everything conspires to make Atget one of the 'artists of Paris' who is hardest to understand properly.[33] If there is a work of literature with which he should be associated, it would clearly be *La Comédie humaine*: Pons on Rue de la Perle, Rastignac and de Marsay on Rue Montorgueil at Le Rocher de Cancale, Birotteau at the corner of Rues Pirouette and Mondétour, Esther on Rue Sainte-Foy by Rue d'Alexandrie – one could almost find a photo for each episode, so true it is that the Paris of Atget, despite Haussmann, was closer to Balzac than to our own day. But even if neither Charlus, nor his cousin Oriane, nor M. de Norpois, would have been pillars of Atget's bars – whose names and addresses already bear the magic of Parisian toponomy: *À l'Homme Armé* on Rue des Blancs-Manteaux; *À la Biche* on Rue Geoffroy-Saint-Hilaire; *Au Réveil-Matin* on Rue Amelot; *Au Soleil d'Or* on Rue Saint-Sauveur – let alone familiar with the ragpickers' camps on Boulevard Masséna, there is a deep affinity between Atget and Proust in that both are advanced promontories – in every sense of the term – of the nineteenth century within the twentieth. It matters little that Proust appears today as the dazzling end to a literature born more than two centuries earlier with the favourite authors of the Narrator's grandmother,

32 'In the middle of the symphony an old-fashioned tune rang out; replacing the sweet-seller, who generally accompanied her song with a rattle, the toy-seller, to whose kazoo was attached a jumping-jack which he sent bobbing in all directions, paraded other puppets for sale, and, indifferent to the ritual declamation of Gregory the Great, the reformed declamation of Palestrina or the lyrical declamation of the moderns, warbled at the top of his voice, a belated adherent of pure melody: "Come along all you mammies and dads,/Here's toys for your lasses and lads!/I make them myself,/and I pocket the pelf./Tralala, tralala, tralalee./Come along youngsters ..."' (Proust, *The Captive*, *Remembrance of Things Past*, vol. 3, p. 133).

33 Thanks to Berenice Abbott, who bought nearly 2,000 negatives of Atget's that were left in his studio on his death and bequeathed them to the Museum of Modern Art in New York, the major works on Atget are American; among others, John Szarkowski and Maria Morris Hambourg, *The Work of Atget*, 4 vols (New York: The Museum of Modern Art, 1981–85); Molly Nesbit, *Atget's Seven Albums* (New Haven: Yale University Press, 1992). Several major American photographers, Walker Evans and Lee Friedlander among them, were very familiar with Atget's work.

Saint-Simon and Mme de Sévigné, whereas Atget on the other hand is viewed as a link between pictorial photography and Surrealism – a role that he did not actually play, and the invention of which derives from the need to manufacture a linear history, even one with discontinuities and unevenness. Atget's work and that of Proust are the last two great efforts in France to reach a totality, not in the sense of the 'total work of art', but that of the total exploration of a world.

Atget worked a good deal on commission, which may seem to contradict this ambition. But one of the features that you can be sure of with him is his independence of mind, his stubborn character: he interpreted the commissions in his own fashion, so that even what is apparently his most repetitive work – the series of door-knockers taken for maniacal decorators in search of '*grand siècle*' motifs, or the details of the buttresses and roofs of Saint-Séverin – do not form catalogues but genuine series, as one says of Monet's *Poplars on the Bank of the Epte* or Picasso's *Corridas*. It would be vain to seek a difference in quality between his personal work and his commissions.[34] His *Nudes*, photographed in the brothels of the La Chapelle quarter, on floral bedspreads against floral wallpaper, smooth and with no relief, taken in all positions without the faces ever being seen – these monumental and mysterious bodies that make the more celebrated nudes of Weston or Irving Penn seem superficial, were the result of a commission from Dignimont, a theatre painter and designer who was quite famous in the interwar years.

Atget's own classifications and the studies devoted to him present his work either in terms of its themes (for example the *Albums*),[35] or else by topography. The risk here is to fail to recognize the development of this work over time, to view it as homogeneous whereas it was spread over more than thirty years. During this whole period, it is true, Atget remained faithful to the material of his beginnings: the bellows camera, the heavy frames with 18 x 24 cm glass plates, the wooden tripod, the bag of lenses, this whole heavy bric-a-brac that he carried every morning from Rue Campagne-Première. And yet there is a whole world between his *Petits Métiers* photographed between 1898 and 1900 – baker's boy, woman bread-carrier, porcelain restorer, organ grinder, asphalters, teaselers, strong men from Les Halles, taken close up, frontally, and very posed – and the *Zoniers* of 1912–13, where he takes en masse, in the disorder of their trolleys, their wooden huts and their encampments, the ragpickers, their wives, their flocks of children, their gatherings, their dogs, their carts. In fifteen

34   As John Szarkowski tries to do in *The Work of Atget*, vol. 1.
35   These *Albums* are: *L'Art dans le vieux Paris*; *Intérieurs parisiens*; *La Voiture à Paris*; *Métiers, boutiques et étalages de Paris*; *Enseignes et vielles boutiques de Paris*; *Zoniers*; and *Fortifications de Paris*.

years, Atget had moved from the 'picturesque types' that are seen in nine-teenth-century engravings to the representation of poverty at the gates of the big city.[36]

On the Place de la Bastille, close to the Arsenal basin, along a cast-iron railing that no longer exists, some thirty or so individuals grouped around a lamppost are observing the sky, all in the same direction, through small rectangles that they hold in their hands. This photograph of Atget's appeared on the cover of no. 7 of *La Révolution surréaliste*. The image is titled 'Last-Minute Conversions'. The photographer's name is not mentioned, either because Atget did not appreciate this use of his picture (his own title was 'The Eclipse, April 1912'), or rather because he refused to personalize what he always held to be documents. Leafing through the collection of the same magazine, three other photos are to be found, likewise uncredited but certainly by him: in the same no. 7, the window of a corset shop illustrating a dream of Marcel Noll's, and a prostitute awaiting a customer for René Crevel's 'Le Pont de la mort'. In no. 8, a Louis XV stair-rail in wrought iron, undoubtedly reframed, was reproduced in Éluard's *Les Dessous d'une vie ou la pyramide humaine* ('At first there came to me a great desire for solemnity and pomp . . .'). Atget's contacts with the Surrealists certainly did not go beyond this. They were due, as we know, to a neighbourly connec-tion[37] with Man Ray, who circulated Atget's work in the Montparnasse studios, and with Ray's companion of the time, Berenice Abbott, who occasionally bought one of his photographs. In 1927, the year of Atget's death, she made a striking portrait of him (a single portrait, even though it has two views, one full-face and the other in profile like an identity photo), showing his bright eyes, undoubtedly blue, the tiredness of age, and the cumulative effect of everything he had watched with such affectionate concentration for thirty years.

Atget never had any direct contact with the Surrealist group: groups were not his forte, and he never took part in such things. Among the photos that Breton chose to illustrate some of his books, none was by Atget, and his name is nowhere mentioned in the group's publications. It is evident

36 On Atget's political opinions, the best indication is provided by his gift to the Bibliothèque historique de la Ville de Paris of issues of *La Guerre sociale*, Gustave Hervé's anarcho-syndicalist newspaper, and *La Bataille syndicaliste*, organ of the CGT that was then a fighting union (Molly Nesbit, 'La second nature d'Atget', in *Actes du colloque Atget*, special issue of *Photographies*, March 1986).
37 At 17 Rue Campagne-Première, which was not a building but rather an avenue between Rue Campagne-Première and Rue Boissonade, bordered by little houses.

enough that 'these Paris photos herald Surrealist photography, that advance detachment of the only important column that Surrealism succeeded in shaking'.[38] You can see what would have struck the Surrealists about these empty streets, like a dwelling without a tenant, in which the few human indications are the silhouettes of café waiters behind the windows, or the vague trace, during the exposure, of a passing individual or phantom. De Chirico also lived at 17 Rue Campagne-Première. With the shop windows that Atget photographed in his last years – the hairdresser on Boulevard de Strasbourg, the taxidermist on Rue de l'École-de-Médecine, the hatter on Avenue des Gobelins, the wigmaker at the Palais-Royal – with his extraordinary 'accumulations' of boots, vegetables, caps, Atget anticipated Aragon's *Paris Peasant*.[39] He crossed the early years of the century in his occult, stubborn and ungraspable fashion, a 'city artist' in the sense that Hamish Fulton or Richard Long would later be 'land artists', creating along the way, with amazing images, the inventory-installation – *Interior of M.C., Apartment Decorator, Rue du Montparnasse* or *Small Room of a Working Woman, Rue de Belleville*.

The period between the wars was a new golden age for Paris photography – indeed for French photography in general. It escaped the tendency that invaded painting, sculpture, literature, music and architecture around 1925: the return, after all those excesses of foreign origin, to well-polished craft, noble material, calm forms and fine language, the values of the French soil and culture. It was not only the followers of Charles Maurras who championed this neo-neoclassicism: the line Derain–Chardonne–Cocteau–Maillol–new-style De Chirico–Valéry (Trocadéro 1937 version) triumphed in Paris against a background of xenophobia and anti-Semitism. It was in no way surprising that a good number of virtuosos in bronze and the imperfect subjunctive found themselves in the Pétainist camp a few years later, if they were not open Nazis like Vlaminck or Brasillach.

If photography emerged unscathed from this pass, it was thanks to two interventions. There was first of all the violent antagonism of Dada, followed by Surrealism – co-substantial with photography – towards everything represented by Cocteau's 'return to order' (Breton called Cocteau 'the most hateful creature of his time'),[40] as well as towards the gener-

---

38   Benjamin, 'A Short History of Photography'.
39   Waldemar George, *Arts et Métiers graphiques*, special issue on photography, 1930. This is clearly an allusion to the description of the shop windows in the Passage de l'Opéra, and particularly the purveyor of canes.
40   André Breton, letter to Tzara, cited in *Oeuvres complètes*, vol. 1, p. 1294, note.

alized academicism into which various avant-gardes would collapse (e.g. 'Le Boeuf sur le Toit'), newly converted to the values and charms of the bourgeoisie ('the Valérys, Derains, Marinettis, tumbling into the ditch one by one').[41] The other protective element was the influx of foreign photographers to Paris. Man Ray brought from New York the Dada spirit he had contracted from Marcel Duchamp. His charm gathered round him a group of photographers and artists of great talent and beauty – Berenice Abbott, Lee Miller, Meret Oppenheim, Dora Maar, 'these women who expose their hair day and night to the terrible light of Man Ray's studio'.[42] He was only the most popular in a long British and American line of Paris photographers: after Fox Talbot there was Alfred Stieglitz, Edward Steichen, Alvin Langdon Coburn and Lewis Hine, and the series continued after 1945 with William Klein, Bill Brandt, Irving Penn and above all Robert Frank. (This natural openness of Anglo-American photographers contrasts with the little interest in Paris shown by English writers. Apart from Henry Miller's *Quiet Days in Clichy*, Hemingway's disturbing *Paris est un fête*, or Orwell's sympathetic but hardly convincing *Down and Out in Paris and London*, Henry James's *The Ambassadors*, a subtle work by a subtle author, fails in its object of depicting what is supposedly the motive of the book, the charm of Paris in summer. Even the addresses of his characters strike a false note, even their very names – so important a point that Balzac, as we saw, spent whole days roaming the city to hunt them out, whilst Proust, in his work on the *Recherche*, abandoned the symbolism of *Jean Santeuil* for surnames that are so extraordinarily pertinent – Swann, Charlus, Verdurin.)

Apart from Man Ray, almost all the photographers who settled in Paris between the two wars came from the East, that great East that has constantly fertilized Parisian life ever since the eighteenth century. Either Jews or political refugees (or both at once, like Robert Capa or Gisèle Freund), they had left Germany (Ilse Bing, Joseph Breitenbach, Raoul Hausmann, Germaine Krull, Wols), Poland (David Seymour, known as Chim, one of the founders of the Magnum agency), Lithuania (Izis, Moï Ver) or Hungary (Brassaï, André Kertész, François Kollar, Rogi André, Éli Lotar). They brought with them the German and Soviet photographic techniques of the years 1917–22. They also brought the faculty of astonishment, a new gaze on the metropolis. Tzara wrote in 1922 (and this passage that Walter Benjamin cites in his 'Short History of Photography' applies to them very well): 'When everything that goes under the name of art has

---

41   Breton, *The Lost Steps*, pp. 81–2.
42   André Breton, 'Le surréalisme et la peinture', *La Révolution surréaliste*, no. 9–10, 1 October 1927.

become paralysed, photography lights up its thousand-watt bulb, and sensitive paper absorbs the darkness of some everyday objects. It had discovered the importance of a tender and virgin flash of light, more important than all the constellations offered for the pleasure of our eyes.'

'The invention of photography dealt a mortal blow to the old modes of expression, both in painting and in poetry, in which the automatic writing that appeared in the late nineteenth century was a genuine photography of thought.' This is how Breton began his text for the catalogue of Max Ernst's 1921 exhibition at the Sans-Pareil – one of the great Dada demonstrations in Paris. It was also the start of the ambiguous relationship between photography and what would become Surrealism; even (or especially) with the most automatic camera, photography did not readily produce images dictated by an automatism, as defined by the First Surrealist Manifesto. The Surrealists invented all sorts of procedures to draw photography out of its 'realism': rayogram, solarization, multiple exposure (or 'over-impression'), sometimes photomontage (more of a Dadaist or German technique), or again brûlage, a technique which Raoul Ubac, its inventor, explained was 'an automatism of destruction, a complete dissolution of the image in the direction of the absolutely unformed'.[43] In Surrealist photography, there is a cleavage between the manipulated image and that 'naturally' obtained, a cleavage as deep as that separating the automatism of Miró or Masson from the magic illusionism of Magritte or Ernst. Aside from some few exceptions (Tabard's solarized *Place Vendôme*, or Dora Maar's distorted *22 Rue d'Astorg*), the Surrealist images of Paris are not manipulated photographs. Man Ray, a great inventor of various tricks, took very few photographs of Paris, and when Breton asked him to take some pictures to illustrate *Nadja*, he passed the job on to his assistant Jacques Boiffard, apart from the portraits of Éluard, Péret and Desnos.

In *Nadja* Breton obeyed his own injunction ('And when all valuable books are no longer illustrated with drawings, appearing only with photographs'[44]) with a very precise idea of what he wanted. In September 1927 he wrote to Lise Deharme:

I am going to publish the story that you know, accompanied with some fifty photographs relating to all the elements that it brings in: the Hôtel

43 Brûlage involved submerging the negative in hot water, which caused the emulsion to partially melt. Ubac's text is quoted in *Explosante Fixe, photographie et surréalisme*, exhibition catalogue (Paris: Centre George-Pomidou/Hazan, 1985), p. 42, note.
44 Breton, 'Le Surréalisme et la peinture', apropos Man Ray.

des Grands Hommes, the statue of Étienne Dolet and the one of Becque, a sign saying 'Bois-Charbons', a portrait of Paul Éluard, one of Desnos asleep, the Porte Saint-Denis, a scene from *Les Détraques*, the portrait of Blanche Derval, of Mme Sacco, a corner of the flea market, the white object in a casket, the *L'Humanité* bookshop, the wineshop on the Place Dauphine, the window of the Conciergerie, the Mazda advertisement, the portrait of Professor Claude, the woman at the Musée Grévin. I will also have to go and photograph the 'Maison Rouge' sign at Pourville, the Ango manor-house.[45]

In a short *Avant-dire* of 1962, he wrote that 'the purpose of the abundance of photographic illustration is to eliminate all description'. This was certainly not his only reason. The reinforcement of text by image produces the same gap as the double exposure of a photo, as *La Marquise Casati*'s two pairs of eyes in Man Ray's picture, and this disturbing effect is deliberately underlined by the repetition of the corresponding phrase in the text as the caption for the photo, a procedure used in the popular novels that the Surrealists so appreciated.

The only success here – the illustrations to Breton's *Mad Love* or *Communicating Vessels* are too heteroclite to have the same effect – was Boiffard's images for *Nadja*, often described as banal and equated with postcards,[46] but which are among the only Surrealist photographs in which the influence of Atget can be felt. Boiffard was indeed directly acquainted with Atget; as Man Ray's assistant, he worked at Rue Campagne-Première and lived there for a while. The locations are almost all empty of people, and the framing, as in Atget's late years, does not try to grasp an ensemble but rather to point out significant detail, such as the big arrow ('Sign up here') on the *L'Humanité* bookshop, the signboard of the Sphinx Hôtel, the cart and ladder under the enormous lightbulb of the 'illuminated Mazda advertisement on the Grands Boulevards'). Like Breton and Aragon, Naville and Fraenkel, Boiffard came to photography from medicine, and when Breton maintained that the tone he adopted for the narrative of *Nadja* was precisely copied from that of medical observation, Boiffard knew what he was talk-

---

45 Cited by Marguerite Bonnet in the notes to *Nadja* in *Oeuvres complètes*, vol. 1.
46 See for example Dawn Ades in *Explosante Fixe*, and R. Krauss, 'Photographie et surréalisme', in *Le Photographique, pour une théorie des écarts* (Paris: Macula, 1990). One need only compare Boiffard's photos with the views of Paris in *Nadja* that are not by him (the statue of Étienne Dole in the Place Maubert, for example), to see what really is a banal photograph.

ing about.[47] If anything is banal in this series of photos, it is the clinical style: in clinical examination, everything is banal except the result.

From the Cyrano on the Place Blanche to the Promenade de Vénus on Rue de Viarmes, the collective life of the Surrealist group was spent in a number of cafés. The Surrealists were the first to bring photography inside these places, which had so often been captured from outside by Atget. (This was a time of great advances in photographic film and materials: the Leica, the first 24 x 35 camera, was contemporary with *Nadja*.) With the greatest photographers – and for photos of cafés, this means Brassaï and Kertész, despite the possible objection that they were not formal members of the Surrealist group – there is the enormous and perceptible difference between an anecdotal image and a literary one. A young woman with lowered eyes is reading a newspaper in a café. Behind her through the window is the uniform grey of the empty street. In front of her, occupying the whole of the right half of the photo, is a cylindrical stove in punched metal, and on a small round table with a zinc border an empty cup of coffee. The young woman, wearing a black coat with a fur collar and a cloche hat with her hair escaping below it, is in the narrow space between the enormous stove and the windows on to the terrace – a position in which she seems threatened or at least fragile. This picture by André Kertész, which is like the start of a novel, is dated 1928 and carries the dreamy caption *A Winter Morning at the Café du Dôme*. In the corner of another café, this time on the Place d'Italie, a man and a woman look into each other's eyes, close enough to touch. Above the benches, the two walls that meet in a corner have large mirrors that almost come into contact at the centre of the picture, so that the woman's face is reflected in profile in the right-hand mirror and the man's in the left-hand one. The two mirrors are also reflected in each other. You see the abyss between these two individuals: the woman, mouth open, on the edge of ecstasy, and the man, who has his back to the photographer, but whose calculating look is detectable in the mirror. This is a photo of Brassaï's dated 1932, and titled with a certain cruelty *A Pair of Lovers in a Small Paris Café*.

The Surrealist photographers did indeed photograph love – whether tender as in Kertész's *Self-portrait with Élisabeth in a Montparnasse Café*, an exceptional image of amorous joy, or venal as in Brassaï's brothel scenes, in the tradition of Degas and Lautrec. They were the first to photograph the night (not *at night*, but night as a subject, as one photographs the sea),

---

47   Boiffard in fact returned to medicine around 1935, and practised as a radiologist at the Hôpital Saint-Louis until the late 1950s.

the particular Paris night, the milieu of Surrealist culture, from Max Ernst's *Rvolution by Night* to 'La Nuit du tournesol' in Breton's *Mad Love*, or the grating double of *Nadja* that is Philippe Soupault's *Last Nights in Paris*. Along with the painters and sculptors, they laid down the markers of a different tropism of movement, that of the object, and singularly of the found object, giving eternal life to such fetish objects as the metal mask ('a very developed descendant of the helm') that Breton and Giacometti discovered at the flea market and that was photographed by Man Ray for *Mad Love*, or *Nadja*'s bronze glove. And they extended the idea of the found object to fragments of Paris streets: Brassaï's graffiti, the details of gutters, railings around trees, paving stones and the torn posters photographed by Wols – twenty years before Hains and Villeglé tore these off walls to make them into 'paintings'.

In the 1960s, the old connection between Paris and photography began to unravel. Among the explanations for this would be the global asphyxiation of black-and-white photography, the end of a generation of photographers formed at the time of the Popular Front, the Spanish war and the great films of Jean Renoir. And above all the unsteadiness of Paris under the brutal blows dealt it in the era of de Gaulle and Pompidou – what use would there be in showing its gaping wounds, its ulcers, its formless bumps? At the close of this era, May 1968 gave rise to the last famous photos of Paris, those of Gilles Caron, Dityvon, and a newcomer, Raymond Depardon, who would go on to invent a new genre of documentary on the city, the last example of which, with the simple title *Paris*, can be seen as a homage to the Gare Saint-Lazare.

Like any rupture, this dénouement can lead to nostalgia. If it is true, as Michelet put it, that each epoch dreams the following one, it is even more clear that each epoch lives in nostalgia for its predecessor, above all in a period when this sentiment, promoted like a washing-powder, fits marvellously into an ideological scaffolding, the strategy of 'ends' – of history, of the book, of art, of utopias. Turbulent Paris is on this list of programmatic 'ends', which does not prevent the necessary measures being taken to conjure away those spectres that some people fear, not without reason, will return to haunt their streets.

'Each era does not just dream of its successor, but in dreaming it seeks to awaken', wrote Walter Benjamin in his 'Theses on the Concept of History'. And at the present time, after thirty years of torpor, thirty years in which its centre has been renovated-museumified and its periphery ravaged in silence, Paris is seeking to awaken. The tacit understanding with past generations is beginning to be renewed, and another 'new Paris' is taking shape and growing before our eyes, which are not always fully open. It is leaving the west of the city to advertising executives and oil tycoons, and pressing as always towards the north and east. Supported by the *ramblas*, the Boulevards of La Chapelle, La Villette, Belleville and Ménilmontant, it is spilling over the line of hills from Montmartre to Charonne, crossing the terrible barrier of Boulevard Périphérique – in the expectation that this will disappear like its predecessors, be demolished and buried, transformed into a tree-lined promenade – and stretching towards what is already de facto the twenty-first arrondissement, towards Pantin, Le Pré-Saint-Gervais, Bagnolet, Montreuil and what remains of its peach-lined walls. As is the general rule, going back to Philippe Auguste, this expansion, with the disastrous exception of the 'new towns', is not being effected by administrative measures or government decisions. What is precipitating it is the organism of a big city in perpetual growth, a youthfulness that once again feels itself confined in a Paris that might have seemed immutable and definitive, that of the twenty arrondissements within the concrete wall of Boulevard Périphérique.

One of the Paris walks that is most weighty with meaning and memory is the climb up the Montagne Saint-Geneviève from the Jardin de Plantes and the statue of Lamarck – can we imagine the genius needed to conceive the idea of evolution in the late eighteenth century? – or, if you like, from Cuvier's house, Jussieu's cedar tree, Verniquet's belvedere or Buffon's plane tree. The streets on this slope bear the names of naturalists and botanists, as they were called in this blessed age when science was still innocent. Linnaeus, the great Swede, Geoffroy Saint-Hilaire, the dedicatee of *Old Goriot*, as well as Cuvier, Jussier, Quatrefages, Thouin, Daubenton, Lacépède and Tournefort: certainly a magnificent bunch, whose names, celebrated or sometimes now rather obscure like those of the Latin authors cited by Montaigne, are flashes of light that shine here in the city – just as their counterparts shine in Montaigne's *Essays*. At the top, on a little square – once again shaped like a 'Y', where Rue de la Montagne-Saint-Geneviève forks to let Rue Descartes go off towards Rue Mouffetard, towards Italy – is the main entrance to the old École Polytechnique. Above its side gates are two great scrolls symbolizing the careers of the school's first students, trained to defend the Republic against threatening tyrants: the symbols of artillery on the left and of the navy on the right. The central gateway is surmounted by five medallions in the antique style, representing the founders of the school. Their features have been eroded by time, and the inscription identifying them is hardly visible. In the middle, the place of honour is given to Monge, the school's first organizer as well as the founder of descriptive geometry and the theory of surfaces. Beside him are Lagrange, professor at the Turin school of artillery at the age of nineteen, and the first to apply trigonometry to celestial mechanics; Berthollet, disciple and friend of Lavoisier; Fourcroy, whose chemistry lessons at the Jardin des Plantes recall what was noblest about antiquity: in Cuvier's words, 'it was as if we rediscovered those assemblies in which a whole people hung on the words of a speaker', and the great amphitheatre of the Jardin des Plantes had to be enlarged twice over to make room for the crowd who came to hear this peerless professor. The fifth figure is Laplace, who has his street just opposite. His main claim to fame is his hypothesis on the formation of planets, which he explained to Napoleon. But he was also a physicist, and we owe to him the law defining the relationship between the tension of the walls of a sphere, the pressure within it, and the radius. By extrapolation, Laplace's law applies also to the cylinder, and by further extrapolation, it could be applied to Paris itself. It indicates that, at constant pressure, the tension increases with the radius. Those who think that the game is over in Paris, those who maintain they have never seen an explosion in a museum, those working each day to tidy up the façade of the old republican barracks, should reflect on the variations in the bursting force of Paris, which so regularly surprised all their predecessors over the course of centuries.

Index

abandoned babies and children, 153, 318
abattoirs. *See* slaughterhouses
Abbott, Berenice, 359n33, 361, 363
acrobats, 85, 164
aeronautics industry, 186
African immigrants, xii, 135, 203, 217
Algeria and Algerians, xii, 87, 255, 51, 163, 217
Anne-Marie-Louise d'Orléans, 14
apartment buildings, 113–14, 206, 224
Apollinaire, Guillaume, 79, 168–69, 193, 197, 321, 356–57
Apponyi, Rodolphe, 258–64 passim, 271n97
Arab immigrants, xi, xii, xiii, 202
Arago, François, 174, 247, 258, 262n75, 278, 302
Aragon, Louis, 40, 79, 82, 170, 362, 365
Arc de Triomphe, 116, 118n17, 232
Arc de Triomphe du Carrousel, 31
arcades, 38–40, 52, 80, 134
arches, 17, 31, 54, 61n76, 100. *See also* gates
architects in the Marais, 64–65
aristocracy, 101, 113, 115
emigration from the Marais, 65–66, 104
arrondissements, 6, 15, 115, 172–75, 175
2nd, 238
3rd, 238
6th, 104, 163
7th, 102
9th, 139, 142, 146, 197, 238
10th, 214
11th, 67, 123, 214, 239
12th, 123, 153, 157, 221, 234, 274
13th, xi, 182, 188–89, 229, 238
14th, 161, 163, 182, 185, 187–88, 228
15h, 182, 183, 185
16h, 190, 192, 194
17h, 194
18h, 199, 236
19h, 213
20th, 174, 213
21st (de facto), 368
Art Déco, 193, 212
art galleries, 78–79, 124n34
Art Nouveau, 193, 209
artists, 164, 362. *See also* painters and painting
artists' models, 196, 350–53 passim
assassinations, 36, 50, 61–62, 132, 207, 211n76
attempted, 85–86, 211
Asselineau, Charles, 97, 328, 330n29, 334
Atget, Eugène, 6, 189, 205, 222, 342, 347n10, 358–62, 365
Aubervilliers, xiii, xiv
Auteuil, xi, 3, 181, 182, 190–94
automobiles, 194
Avenue de l'Opéra, 37, 38

Babou, Hippolyte, 299, 304n168, 316
Bailly, Jean-Christophe, 35
ballrooms, 120, 166–67
Baltard, Victor, 42
Balzac, Honoré de, 76, 145, 148
   The Atheist's Mass, 248
   Baudelaire on, 333
   on Cadran Bleu and Café Turc, 87
   at Café Tabourey, 97
   La Comédie humaine, 40, 77, 103, 192n30, 321–28 passim, 359
   La Cousine Bette, 29–30, 121n26, 147
   Evelina Hanska and, 121, 150, 192
   on executions, 161n98
   on Faubourg Saint-Antoine, 122
   Ferragus, 4, 29, 114, 151, 230, 321

flânerie and, 315, 321–28
The Girl with the Golden Eyes, 90
on *grisettes*, 126
'Histoire et physiologie des Boulevards de
    Paris', 40, 71, 76, 77, 80, 81, 84–85
house in Passy, 192–93
on Latin Quarter, 94
The Lesser Bourgeoisie, 17, 144
Lily of the Valley, 25
on *lorettes*, 144n70
on loss, 30
Lost Illusions, 22–23, 25, 48–49, 53, 71,
    93, 96
The Magic Skin, 24
Marais and, 66
on Montparnasse, 163
Old Goriot (*Le Père Goriot*), 5, 91, 208
on poor people, 153–54
Saint-Germain-des-Près and, 102
Scenes from a Courtesan's Life, 37, 100
A Woman of Thirty, 31n27
The Wrong Side of Paris, 89
bankers and banking, 35, 55, 72, 79, 140–41,
    262, 271n97, 322, 326
banlieue, xii–xiii, 176, 181, 182
Banque de France, 35–36, 37n36
Banque Nationale de Paris, 79
Banville, Théodore de, 94, 97, 328, 333
Barbès, Armand, x, 197, 256, 257, 264, 266, 268
Barbey d'Aurevilly, Jules-Amédée, 233
Barère, Bertrand, 32
barracks, 28, 131, 143, 251n50, 341
Barras, Paul François Jean Nicolas, vicomte
    de, 22, 32
Barrès, Maurice, 49, 97, 145, 168
barricades, 92, 160, 229, 232, 238–45 passim,
    249, 255, 257, 295, 299
    in art, 351
    coup of 1851 and, 303, 305, 306, 307
    June rebellion (1832), 253
    May 1968, 310
    revolution of 1848, 261, 274, 276, 281, 283,
        284, 291
barriers (*barrières*), 30–31, 47, 114, 128n43,
    129, 132, 152, 165. *See also* barricades;
    walls
Bastille, xi, 3, 11, 14, 15, 72, 261, 262
Batignolles, xi, 4, 182, 194–96
Baudelaire, Charles, 40, 74, 90, 126, 218,
    224, 265–66, 345, 346
    at cafés and taverns, 96, 97, 164
    on Balzac, 114n12
    on Daumier lithograph, 255

'Dawn', 114
L'Exposition universelle, 18
Les Fleurs du mal, 74, 102, 289, 335,
    338–39
on Goya, 78
'The Litany of Satan', 253n54
'Loss of a Halo', 39–40
Manet and, 348
on Meryon, 106
on modernity, 316n3
on Musset, 128n42
read on barricades by Michel, 236
'The Salon of 1859', 198, 341, 342–43
'The Swan', 19, 26–27, 289
Baudin, Alphonse, 124, 287, 303, 306,
    307n172
bazaars. *See* markets
Beaubourg centre. *See* Centre Beaubourg
Beaumarchais, Pierre, 72
'*beaux quartiers*', xi
Bedeau, Marie-Alphonse, 261, 279–82
    passim, 304
Bedford, Duke of. *See* Duke of Bedford
beggars and begging, 16, 154–55, 224,
    317–18
Belleville, xi–xiv passim, 10, 50, 178, 182,
    188, 210–17, 234, 278, 311
Benedictines, 101
Benjamin, Walter, 3, 5–6, 40, 69, 266, 315
    on Balzac, 322
    at Bibliothèque Nationale, 34–35
    on Baudelaire, 329, 338–39
    on 'city of mirrors', 340
    on eras and successors, 367
    on Faubourg Saint-Jacques, 161
    on Métro station names, 209
    on Seine, 87
    on Surrealist photography, 362
    on street names, 205
    on time, 16, 312
    on 'timeless squares', 171
Bercy, 221–22
Berlioz, Hector, 71, 85, 193
Bernheim, Alexandre, 78
Bernini, Gian Lorenzo, 45–46, 64
Bibliothèque Nationale, 34–35, 36, 39, 176,
    181
Bibliothèque Royale, 34
Bicêtre, 154–55, 161, 162
bicycle police, 16, 166
Bièvre, ix, 5, 159, 176, 182–83
Blanc, Louis, 237n23, 262n75, 264–65, 271,
    290, 291, 300

Blanche, Jacques-Émile, 192, 193
Blanchot, Maurice, 318n5
Blanqui, Louis Auguste, 94n146, 119, 234, 243, 256–57, 264–68 passim, 287, 294–96, 309
blind crusaders (legend), 28
blind orchestras, 24
Blondel, François, 14, 89, 101n166
Blondel, Jacques-François, 141n63
blood libel, 28
Bloody Week, 181, 208, 229, 351
Blücher, Gebhard von, 24
Bofill, Ricardo, 32–33, 186
Boiffard, Jacques, 364–66 passim
Bois de Boulogne, 121, 149, 182, 193, 223, 317, 355, 357n29
bombings, 30, 98
Bonaparte, Louis-Napoleon. See Napoleon III
Bonaparte, Napoleon. See Napoleon I
Bonaparte, Pierre, 162, 280
Bonnard, Pierre, 79, 356
Bonnier, Louis, 190
bookshops, 92, 95, 98–99, 170
Bouchot, Henri, 52n59
Boulevard Beaumarchais, 3, 55
Boulevard de Bonne-Nouvelle, 82
Boulevard de Clichy, x, 3, 5
Boulevard de la Madeleine, 72, 76
Boulevard de Rochechouart, x, 3, 5, 111
Boulevard des Italiens, 77, 79, 90
Boulevard du Temple, 37, 83–84, 341
Boulevard Haussmann, 79, 141
Boulevard Montmartre, 15, 38, 48, 49, 80, 305
Boulevard Périphérique, ix, xii, xiii, 7, 15, 16, 149, 201, 206, 224, 368
Boulevard Poissonière, 81
Boulevard Saint-Martin, 82–83
Boulevard Sérurier, xiii
boulevards, 15
    Left Bank, 87–91
    See also Grands Boulevards
boundaries, 3–16. See also walls
bourgeoisie, 31, 114
    Auteuil, 195
    Boulevard Saint-Martin, 82
    Breda, 144
    cholera and, 250
    Faubourg Saint-Jacques, 188
    gardening and, 156
    gentrification and, xi
    Hugo on, 307
    Marais, 67

Passy, 192
Plain-Monceau, 6
Prussians and, 234
revolution of 1848 and, 268–70 passim, 287
Saint-Germain-des-Près, 101
Vaugirard, 183, 184
    See also haute bourgeoisie
Bourse, 23, 33–38
Bousquet, René, 185
Brassaï, 170, 205, 363, 366, 367
Brasillach, Robert, 219
Bréa (general), 283, 284, 293n147
Breda, 142, 143–44
Breton, André, 82, 87, 145, 170, 203–4, 321, 361–67 passim
    on Place de Clichy mud, 139n59
    on Porte Saint-Denis, 54
    on photography, 342n3
Brice, Germain, 34, 36
Brongniart, Alexandre-Théodore, 33
Bruant, Libéral, 65, 69, 154, 169, 197
brûlage, 364
Brunet, Marguerite. See Montansier, Mme
Bugeaud, Maréchal, 294–95
Bullet, Pierre, 14, 89
Butte-aux-Cailles, 182, 188–89
Butte-aux-Gravois, 52–53
Butte des Moulins, 37, 38, 53n60
Buttes-Chaumont, 3, 202, 205–10

Cacoub, Olivier, 101n166
Café Certa, 82, 170
Café de Foy, 20, 21, 24, 77
Café de la Mairie, x
Café Voltaire, 97–98
cafés, 20, 24, 75, 77, 80, 129–30
    Batignolles, 196
    Belleville, 215
    Champs-Élysées, 119
    Latin Quarter, 92–98 passim
    Montmartre, 169, 170, 198–99
    music and, 120
Calet, Henri, 182, 187, 188
Canal de l'Ourcq, 182, 205
Canal Saint-Denis, 205
Canal Saint-Martin, xii, 5, 131–32
Capet, Louis. See Louis XVI
Capuchins, 160
Carco, Francis, 15, 18, 96, 97–98, 168–69, 198, 201
Carmelites, 152
Carmona, Michel, 106n179

Carnival, 126–29 passim
carnivals, 84
carpet manufacturers, 154n84, 159
Carrel, Armand, 256
Carrousel, 26–31
Cartier-Bresson, Henri, 148–49, 188
caryatids, 49
Castille, Hippolyte, 270, 288n133
Catacombes, 46, 207, 208
Catherine de Médicis, 45, 59, 90
Catherine de Vivonne, marquise de
    Rambouillet, 28–29
Cavaignac, Louis-Eugène, 275, 276, 280–88
    passim, 290, 294, 304, 308
Ceinture railway, 180, 194, 203, 205, 206,
    219, 220
Céline, Louis-Ferdinand, 40
cemeteries, 138n58, 152, 157–58, 164, 198,
    199, 211, 329. See also Clamart ceme-
    tery; Innocents cemetery; Père-Lachaise
    cemetery
censorship, 350
Centre Beaubourg, x, 48, 65
Centre Pompidou, x
Cézanne, Paul, 79
chain restaurants, xi
Champs-Élysées, 17, 116–20, 121, 231, 264
Charles Ferdinand, duc de Berry, 36
Charles V, 57
wall of, 10, 11–14, 37, 51, 55, 57
Charles VII, 58
Charles VIII, 58
Charles X, 141, 246, 247
Charlot, Claude, 68
Charonne, xiv, 180, 182, 217–20, 220
Château d'Eau, 84n126
Château des Tournelles, 36
Château du Bercy, 221
Château-Rouge, 202
Chateaubriand, Armand de, 184
Chateaubriand, François-René de, 167n111,
    170, 174
    Armand Carrel and, 256
    on barricades, 242
    on Champs-Élysées, 119
    on execution of his cousin, 184
    on Passage des Panoramas rotunda, 38–39
    on royalists, 248n41
    on suppression of press freedoms, 245n31
Chaumette, Pierre-Gaspard, 36
chemical industry, 183–84, 222
Chevalier, Louis, 5, 18, 46–48 passim, 105,
    196, 201, 206

Chevalier, Maurice, 210, 214–15
children, 39, 123, 233, 297–98, 317
    in photographs, 345
Chinese immigrants, xi, xii, 189, 204, 215
Chirac, Jacques, 101n166
cholera, 249–50, 296
Chopin, Frédéric, 145
Le Cid (Corneille), 62, 65
cinemas. See film theaters
circuses, 132
Cirque d'Hiver, 86, 231, 234
Cité Doré, 156
Cité du Wauxhall, 133
Citroën, André, 187
Clamart cemetery, 157–58
Clarette, Jules, 40
Clébert, Jean-Paul, 19
Clichy, 194–96
Clignancourt, 199–200
Cloître Saint-Merri, 48
clubs, 32, 265, 268
Cocteau, Jean, 362
collaborators and collaboration, 228–30
    passim, 233, 234
Commission des Artistes, 89, 101, 351
Committee of Public Safety, 142
Commune (Revolution), 122, 158
Commune (1871), 231–41, 291
Communist party, 310, 311
Compagnie des Indes, 51
Constant, Benjamin, 247–48
Constituent Assembly, 114, 264–72 passim,
    281, 282, 301, 302
Convention, 32, 120
Corneille, Pierre, 62, 65
coup of 1851, 299–308 passim
Courbet, Gustave, 78, 96, 165, 198n45,
    232–33, 351
Courtille, 126–29 passim, 143, 212–13, 215
Crédit Lyonnais, 79

Dabit, Eugène, 181, 202–3, 215
Dada, 362–64 passim
Daguerre, Louis, 38, 131, 341–42
daguerreotype, 341–42, 344–45
dance halls, 118, 125, 135, 167–68, 198, 202,
    213
d'Angennes, Julie, 29n25
Daudet, Léon, 49, 90, 91, 96, 98
Daudet, Lucien, 216
Daumier, Honoré, 78, 255n59, 299, 343
d'Aussy, Legrand, 129
David, Jacques-Louis, 24, 133, 141, 142, 343

Davioud, Gabriel, 84n126
De Chirico, 362
de Kock, Paul, 83n124, 86
de Paul, Vincent, 134
Debord, Guy, 204, 210
Degas, Edgar, 78, 196, 197, 350, 355–56
Delacroix, Eugène, 78, 192, 244, 297, 345, 346
   Baudelaire and, 126, 336
   Balzac dedication to, 90
   monument to, 91
   Plain-Monceau and, 150
   Saint-Georges and, 145
Delaunay, Sonia, 357
Delescluze, Charles, 237, 239–40, 248, 275,
   287, 292, 293n147
Delorme, Marion, 63
Delvau, Alfred, 90–97 passim
   on Carrousel, 27
   on Champs-Élysées promenaders, 121
   on Comte de Charolais, 143
   on Barrière de la Chopinette, 132
   on Boulevards nightlife, 75
   on Faubourg Saint-Honoré, 122
   on houses like 'rabbit holes', 156
   on learning to hate oppression, 195–96
   on Montmartre 'temples to beer', 197
   on plaster, 209
   on Ramponeau, 128–29
   on Rue de Richelieu, 37
demolition of buildings. See razing of buildings
demonstrations and demonstrators, 245, 247,
   259–60, 266, 268, 311
Denfert-Rochereau, 187–88
Depardon, Raymond, 367
deportation, 143, 354n26
Desargues, Gérard, 63
Descartes, René, 29n25, 63
'descent de la Courtille', 126–29
Desgranges, Henri, 185n 20
Desmoulins, Camille, 21–22
Diderot, Denis, 20, 94, 100
dioramas, 131, 341
docks, 203
Doisneau, Robert, 48, 205, 341
domes, 5, 69
Du Camp, Maxime, 147n75, 152, 154, 162,
   232, 233
Duchamp, Marcel, 124, 329, 363
dueling, 24, 61n75, 256
Duke of Bedford, 58
Dumas, Alexandre (pére), 45, 86n132, 89,
   95, 160
   The Three Musketeers, 99

dumps, 6, 146, 205
Dupin, Charles, 296–97
Durand-Ruel, Paul, 78, 352n20
dyers, 159

Eco, Umberto, 99
École des Beaux-Arts, 69n90, 102
École Polytechnique, 91, 368–69
'Egyptomania', 51–52
elections, 264, 265
electric lights, 16, 355
elevated streets, 188
Enfants-Rouge, 61, 67
Enfants-Trouvés, 152n81
engraving and engravings, 61, 343, 344
epidemics, 249–50, 296
Ernst, Max, 342n3, 364, 367
Espaces Verts department. See Service des
   Espaces Verts
executions and executioners, 133n51,
   156, 161–63, 184, 200n51, 205, 231,
   289n137, 293n147, 305
   Place de Grève, 94n146, 161, 247
   See also guillotine

façadisation, 72, 79
fairs and fairgrounds, 101, 135
Fargue, Léon-Paul, 98, 180, 181, 195
Farmers-General wall, 15, 109–16, 136–39
   passim, 222
   Bercy, 220
   building of, 16, 109–11 passim
   curve of wall today, x, 5
   demolition of, 109, 138, 175
   Faubourg Saint-Marcel, 154, 155
   Montparnasse, 163
   Plaine Monceau, 149
   train stations and, 176
   wine duties and, 129
fashion trade, 125
fast-food outlets, xi, 79
Faubourg du Temple, 125–33, 241, 274, 284,
   302–3, 311, 326n15
Faubourg Montmartre. See Montmartre
Faubourg Poissonière, 5, 284
Faubourg Saint-Antoine, 116, 121–23, 131,
   132, 241, 242, 259, 274, 275, 284–87
   passim, 302–3, 311, 326n15
Faubourg Saint-Denis, xii–xiv passim,
   133–39, 284
Faubourg Saint-Germain, 65–66, 102–5, 153
Faubourg Saint-Honoré, xi, 65, 103, 116–17,
   120–21, 151, 230

Faubourg Saint-Jacques, 153, 160–63, 188
Faubourg Saint-Marcel, 151–60, 50, 147, 259, 283, 325
Faubourg Saint-Martin, 4, 132, 133–39
faubourgs, 10, 109
   Baudelaire and, 336–37
   Left Bank, 116–50
   Right Bank, 151–71
Favre, Jules, 233–34
Fénéon, Félix, 98n160, 356
Ferme-Général, 110. See also Farmers-General wall
Fieschi, Giuseppe Marco, 85, 211
film theatres, 121, 170, 215, 231
flags. See red flag; tricolour flag
flânerie and flâneurs, 62, 76, 80, 117, 121, 164, 315–39, 351
Flaubert, Gustave, 4, 83, 154, 162, 222, 234, 289–90, 350n16
flea markets, 138, 188, 200
Flicoteaux, 95–96
floods, 182–84
Folies-Bergère, 142
Folies de Chartres, 149
follies, 143
Fontaine, Pierre François Léonard, 31, 138, 147
footbridges, xi
Fort, Paul, 97, 168
fortifications. See walls
Foucault, Michel, 134n53, 155
foundlings. See abandoned babies and children
fountains, ix, 36, 45, 60, 84, 221n94
   clogged and trash-laden, 47, 108
   Faubourg Saint-Antoine, 123
   Faubourg Saint-Germain, 104
   Montmartre, 198
   Saint-Sulpice, 99
Fournel, Victor, 106, 119–20
Fox Talbot, William, 342n2, 345n7, 363
France, Anatole, 87
François I, 57–59 passim, 61n77, 92
Frank, Robert, 223, 363
freedom: laws constraining, 245, 254–56 passim
Frochot, Nicolas, 39

Galerie Dorèe, 35, 36
Galerie d'Orléans, 22, 23
Galerie Véro-Dodat, 38
Galeries de Bois, 22–24
galleries, 38, 104n173. See also art galleries
gambling, 22, 24, 77

garbage dumps. See dumps
gardens, ix, xi, 57, 58, 72, 88, 125, 185, 221
   Champs-Élysées, 118n17, 119
   Charterhouse, 89
   as disguise for roundabout, 70
   Faubourg Saint-Germain, 103
   Faubourg Saint-Honoré, 120
   Latin Quarter, 93
   Montmartre, 170
   Passy, 191
   Plain Monceau, 149
   Quartier de l'Europe, 146, 148
   revolution of 1848 and, 287
   so-called, 47, 181–82
   See also Luxembourg Palace and gardens; Tuileries Palace and gardens
Gare d'Austerlitz, 156, 176–80 passim
Gare de Bercy, 179
Gare de l'Est, 5, 133–34, 176, 179
Gare de Lyon, 4, 176, 220
Gare des Batignolles, 195
Gare du Nord, 133–34, 136–37, 176, 179
Gare Montparnasse, 152n82, 180, 185–86
Gare Saint-Lazare, 146–49 passim, 176, 194, 367
garment trade, 50
gas lights, 74–75, 120, 167, 171, 355
Gastineau, Benjamin, 127
gates, 61n76, 82. See also Porte de Buci; Porte de Clignancourt; Porte de la Muette; Porte de Pantin; Porte d'Orléans; Porte Saint-Denis; Porte Saint-Honoré
Gauguin, Paul, 78, 164
Gautier, Théophile, 183, 232, 323–24, 346, 350
Geffroy, Gustave, 213–14, 215n85
Genet, Jean, 216
gentrification, xi–xii
Giacometti, Alberto, 170, 187, 216, 349, 367
Ginsberg, Jean, 193
Girault de Saint-Fargeau, Eusèbe, 133, 149
Glacière quarter, 5, 187
Gobelins, 5, 154, 159, 160, 183n16
Goncourt brothers, 15, 137, 145, 162, 179–80, 193, 199–200, 232, 350
   on Baudelaire, 331
Goujon, Jean, 46
Goutte d'Or, xii, 3, 200–2
Goya, Francisco, 78, 349
Gozlan, Léon, 324
Grand-Chaumière, 166–67, 169
Grand-Hôtel, 73, 76
Grands Boulevards, 14, 15, 26, 71–87, 139

grave robbing, 158
Greater Paris, xiii–xiv
Grenelle, 182–85
Grimod de La Reynière, Laurent, 119, 140, 149
grisettes, 126, 174
guillotine, 94n146, 119, 133n51, 162, 163, 234–35
guingettes, 164–65, 218–19
Guizot, François, 258, 259, 260n69, 265
gunpowder factories, 184, 256, 271

Halévy, Daniel, 124
Halles. *See* Les Halles
Halperin, Joan, 98n160
Hanska, Evelina, 121, 150, 191
Haussmann, Georges-Eugène, xi, 17–19 passim, 34, 40, 116, 105–8, 131, 174, 181
  Belleville and, 213
  Boulevards and, 85, 86
  Champs-Élysées, 121
  Les Halles and, 48
  Marais and, 67, 70, 71
  Mémoires, 84n126
  Petite-Pologne and, 350
  Sentier and, 53
Haute-Borne, 212
haute bourgeoisie, 62, 148
Heine, Heinrich, 33, 83, 102, 247n39, 248n40, 250–58 passim, 315, 321n9
Henri II, 14, 36, 59
Henri III, 146n74, 242
Henri IV, 59–60, 61, 102, 103, 132, 200, 230
Herzen, Alexander, 258n64, 262n75, 264
Hippodrome, 195
Hittorff, Jacques Ignace 83, 86, 136
'Horloge quarter', 48
horses, 157, 165, 205–6, 209
hospitals, 28, 134, 137, 151–54 passim, 160
Hôpital Général, xiii, 90, 154, 155
Hôtel Carnavelet, 59, 64
Hôtel de La Vrillière, 35
Hôtel de Montmort, 63
Hôtel de Nantes, 31
Hôtel de Rambouillet, 28–29, 30
Hôtel de Soissons, 45
Hôtel de Ville, 280, 281, 294, 299
Hôtel des Menus-Plaisirs, 141, 142
Hôtel des Tournelles, 56–58 passim
Hôtel Dieu, 157, 348
Hôtel Saint-Pol, 56–58 passim

hotels, 28, 31, 72, 73, 140, 141
Marais, 58, 59, 64–67 passim
  Faubourg Saint-Germain, 104
  Faubourg Saint-Honoré, 120
Houssaye, Arsène, 184, 232–33
Hugo, Victor, 18, 70–71, 145, 257, 292, 297, 300–308 passim
  on architecture, 33
  Baudelaire on, 332
  on Blanqui, 268
  Commune (1871) and, 235–36
  coup of 1851 and, 300, 303–8 passim
  on executions, 161–62
  The History of a Crime, 131n46, 300–8 passim
  Les Misérables, 4n2, 40, 146–47, 153–56 passim, 160, 161, 207, 241, 249–52 passim, 302
  Montparnasse home, 164
  on National Workshops, 272
  Notre-Dame de Paris, xiv, 33
  on Palais-Royal, 21
  revolution of 1848 and, 282, 283, 286
  Things Seen, 18, 253n52
  on young women at the barricades, 277
Humboldt, Alexander von, 25
hunger riots, 122
Hurtaut, Pierre-Thomas-Nicolas, 118n17, 140, 143, 154–55, 163
Huysmans, Joris-Karl, 97, 142, 165, 178, 179, 186, 217, 220, 321

Île de Cygnes, 184, 185
Île de la Cité, 106–8, 167, 250
immigrants, xi–xiii passim, 19, 51, 52, 130, 136, 189, 215, 224
  artists, 363
  in the Resistance, 227–29 passim
  See also African immigrants, Arab immigrants; Chinese immigrants
Imprimerie Nationale, 35
Innocents cemetery, 16, 45, 46, 208
Institut de France, 47
insurrections, 244, 249, 255–57 passim, 309.
  See also May revolution (1968); June rebellion (1832); revolution of 1830; revolution of 1848; youth revolts of 2005
Internationale situationniste, 309–10
Italie quarter, 47

Jacobins, 32, 184, 237n23
James, Henry: *The Ambassadors*, 363
Janin, Jules, 23n16

Jardin des Plantes, ix, 53n60, 154, 222, 368, 369
Jarry, Alfred, 79, 168
Jaurès, Jean, 50, 291
Jesuits, 112
Jewish quarter, x, 69–70
Jews, 52, 62, 69, 215, 216
  in Vichy France, 185, 215, 227–31 passim
Joan of Arc: statues of, 203
July revolution. See revolution of 1830
June rebellion (1832), 250–54
June revolution. See revolution of 1848
Jünger, Ernst, 230–31

Kafka, Franz, 340
Kertész, André, 170, 218, 363, 366–67
knacker's yards, 205–6
Knights Templar, 56–57
Kreefelt, Marin, 115–16

La Bédollière, Émile de
  on 'Amérique' quarry, 206n63
  on an aptly named avenue, 221
  on Auvergnats, 296
  on Boulevards, 76, 80–81, 84n126
  on Ceinture railway, 180
  on Charonne, 218
  on Clignancourt, 199
  on last vestiges of countryside, 176
  on life outside the Farmers-General wall, 137–38
  on lorettes, 144
  on Place de l'Europe, 148
  on taverns of Courtille, 212–13
La Chapelle, 6, 181, 202–5, 216, 278
La Goutte d'Or. See Goutte d'Or
La Grange-aux-Belles, 5
La Hyre, Laurent de, 62, 64
La Rochefoucauld, François de, 29n25, 63
La Villette, 3, 182, 202–5, 278
Labrouste, Henri, 35
labyrinths, 53n60, 58
Laclos, Choderlos de, 115
Lagrène, Jean, 350–51
Lamarque, Maximilien, 250–51
Lamartine, Alphonse de, 174, 244, 262–63, 269, 271n97, 280–82 passim, 302
Lamennais, Hugues Felicité Robert de, 286, 291, 299
Lamoricière, Christophe Léon Louis Juchault de, 276, 277, 281, 285, 287, 304, 310
Lariboisière (hospital), 137

Laroque, Benjamin, 287
Latin Quarter, 3–5 passim, 11, 18, 91–98
  Baudelaire in, 329
  May 1968, 311
  publishers in, 104
Vichy France, 229
Laugier, Abbé, 111–12
Lautrec. See Toulouse-Lautrec, Henri de
Lavoisier, Antoine, 110
Le Camus de Mézières, Nicolas, 118–19
Le Corbusier, 180, 190, 193, 357
Le Marais. See Marais
Le Peletier de Saint-Fargeau, Louis-Michel, 22
Le Vau, Louis, 65, 154, 221n96
leather trade, 135
Léautaud, Paul, 39, 90, 92, 98, 142, 145
Leconte de Lisle, 97, 233
Ledoux, Claude Nicolas, 72, 109, 111–12, 136, 140, 141, 197
Ledru-Rollin, Alexandre Auguste, 265, 290, 300
Left Bank, x, xi, 10, 87–108, 324
  medieval layout of, 11
  walls, 14n13–14
Leleux, Adolphe, 297–98
Lemaire, Madeleine, 78–79
Lemaître, Frédérick, 71, 126
Lemer, Julien, 74, 75, 86
Lenclos, Ninon de, 63
leper colonies, 134
Léri, Jean-Marc, 28n23
Leroux, Pierre, 269, 304n168
Les Buttes-Chaumont. See Buttes-Chaumont
Les Enfants-Rouge. See Enfants-Rouge
Les Halles, xi, 19, 40–48, 181, 196, 319, 320, 347
Les Tuileries. See Tuileries
Lescaut, Manon, 71, 116, 219
Levallois, xiii
Le Libérateur, 256
libraries, 34–35, 63, 170
Lion of Denfert-Rochereau, 3, 182, 187, 188
Lissagaray, Prosper-Olivier, 231, 239–40
lithography, 52
locomotive works, 184–85, 194
l'Orme, Philibert de, 45
Louis-Philippe I, 86, 150, 211, 247, 259
Louis-Philippe II. See Philippe-Egalité
Louis IX, 28
Louis XI, 18, 58
Louis XII, 58

Louis XIII, 61, 66, 103, 117
Louis XIV, 14–16 passim, 18, 19n7, 64, 66,
    122, 192
  monuments to, 53–54
  wall of, 154
Louis XV, 146
Louis XVI, 21–24 passim, 57, 72, 88, 123,
    147
Louis XVIII, 76, 88, 138, 147, 184
Louis, Victor, 20, 26, 36
Louvre, x, 11, 17, 26, 31, 35, 113
Lully, Jean-Baptiste, 37, 63
'lumpenproletariat', 270
Luxembourg Palace and gardens, 4, 90–91,
    188, 289
Lyon, 51, 249, 255, 272

Madeleine (church), 14, 15
Madeleine cemetery, 138n58
Maison Dubois, 136
Maison Dorée, 79
Malesherbes, Guillaume-Chrétien de
    Lamoignon de, 63, 147
Malibran, Maria, 145, 199
Mallarmé, Stephane, 79, 97, 194, 345, 354,
    355
Malraux, André, 19, 67, 83n124, 114, 310
Man Ray, 169, 361–67 passim
Manet, Éduard, 77, 78, 148–50 passim,
    195, 197n45, 329n25, 345, 348–56
    passim
Mansart, François, 35, 36, 62, 64, 65, 69
Marais, x, 4, 19, 55–71, 298, 319, 325. See
    also Jewish quarter
Marat, Jean-Paul, 35, 68
Marguerite de Valois, 103
Marie-Antoinette, 119, 138
Marie de Médicis, 90, 117, 154n84
Marigny, Marquis de, 118
markets, xii, 6, 32, 42–48 passim, 61, 101,
    134, 138, 214, 320
  flowers, 84
  horses, 157, 209
  old clothes, 67–68
  See also flea markets
Marmont, Auguste de, 211, 246
Marouk, Victor, 110, 270, 284, 289n136,
    290n139, 291, 292–93
Marrast, Armand, 255
Martin, Alexis, 136, 137, 159
Marville, Charles, 38, 70, 346–48
Marx, Karl, 174, 228n3, 234n18, 256, 268,
    270, 275, 292, 300, 307

Masonic lodges, 102
massacres, 255, 279, 288–89, 305
Maupassant, Guy de, 75, 194–95
Montausier, Charles de Saint-Maure, duc de,
    29n25
May revolution (1968), 309–11, 367
Ménard, Louis, 261–62, 269, 270, 275,
    287–88, 289n136, 290
Ménilmontant, xiv, 176, 182, 210–17
Mercier, Sébastien, 21, 39, 55n63, 140, 174,
    208
  on boundaries of Paris, 7n8
  on Champs-Élysées, 118
  on Charterhouse gardens, 89
  on cemeteries and the Catacombes, 46,
    157–58
  on dangerous streets, 112–13
  on Farmers-General wall, 109
  on Faubourg Saint-Antoine, 123
  on Faubourg Saint-Marcel, 50, 151
  on first publications of poets, 92–93
  on Left Bank–Right Bank contrast, 88
  on Marais, 66
  on Montreuil, 122
  on pavement, 88n139
  on refuse dumps, 6
  on Rue Vivienne, 35
  on street lighting, 16
  on street numbering, 115–16
  on tax fraud, 110
Le Mercure de France, 98
Mersenne, Marin, 62–63
Meryon, Charles, 106, 328, 343, 345
metal trade, 68
Métro, xiv, 111, 136, 179, 203, 208, 214
  no. 2 line, 5
  no. 3 bis line, 212
Meurent, Victorine, 148, 351–53 passim
Michel, Louise, 196, 229, 231, 235, 236–37,
    240–41, 354n26
Middle Ages: alive in nineteenth century,
    18–19, 39, 93, 94, 105
Millière, Jean-Baptiste, 306
mimes, 85
moats, 51, 55, 117
Mobile Guard, 265–69 passim, 276–81
    passim, 288
Molière, 29, 63, 191
Molinos, Jacques, 32, 45
Moncey, Bon-Adrien Jeannot de, 195, 196
Monet, Claude, 148, 353, 354, 360
'Mont-Saint-Hilaire', 18
Montagne party, 300

Montagne Sainte-Geneviève, 5, 10, 11, 325, 368
Montansier, Mme, 36
Montfaucon, 205, 206n62
Montgomery, Gabriel, comte de, 59
Montmartre, xiv, 3, 4, 50, 139–44, 178, 182, 196–202 passim, 320
  boundaries, 5–6
  Commune (1871) and, 235–36
  Montparnasse and, 169
  Surrealists and, 82
Montparnasse, 4, 82, 89, 153, 163–71
  cemetery, 329
  publishers in, 104
Montreuil, xiv, 122
monuments, 3, 31, 36, 45, 53–54, 91, 196. *See also* gates; statues
Moore, George, 197
Moréas, Jean, 97
Morisot, Berthe, 353, 355
mud, 39, 52, 66, 88, 93, 163, 207, 298, 302, 336
Murger, Henri, 145, 164, 237
museums, 38, 69
music, 86, 120, 139, 141–42, 214. *See also* dance halls
Musset, Alfred de, 127–28, 145

Nadar, Félix, 78, 207, 330, 344, 345–46
Napoleon I, 2, 30–32 passim
Napoleon III, x, 19, 34, 36, 106, 131, 176, 219, 300. *See also* coup of 1851
National Guard, 249, 253–59 passim, 265–72 passim, 276–83 passim, 288, 297, 301
National Workshops, 271–74 passim, 299, 301, 307n172
naumachias, 119
Nazi occupation. *See* Vichy France
Nègre, Charles, 345
Nerval, Gérard de, 24, 30, 40, 136, 137, 192, 199, 319–21
newspapers, 49
Notre-Dame-de-Bonne-Nouvelle, 53
Notre-Dame-de-Lorette, 5, 143
Notre-Dame-des-Vistoires, 36
Nouvelle-Athénes, 3, 144–45
Nouvelle-France, 142, 143
nude in art, 349–50
nuns, 64n81

octroi system, 110
Odéon, 98–99

Oehler, Dolf, 108, 290n138
old-clothes dealers, 67–68, 113, 138
Olympia (Manet), 148, 348–51 passim
Opéra de la Bastille, xi
Opéra Garnier, 36, 73, 141
Opéra Nationale, 36–37
Opéra (Théâtre de l'Académie Royale de Musique), 78
orchestras of the blind. *See* blind orchestras
Ourcq canal, 187

painters and painting, 38, 64, 78–79, 168, 197, 297–98, 341, 348–56
Palais des Congrès, 47
Palais-Égalité, 22
Palais-Royal, 19–26, 36, 71, 73, 150
Panthéon, 5, 222, 278, 280, 283, 299
parading. *See* flânerie
Parc de la Villette, 205
Parc des Buttes-Chaumont, 205
Parc Monceau, 149–50
Parc Montsouris, 182, 188
Pardigon, François, 273, 275, 287, 288, 289, 292n144
Paris Opéra. *See* Opéra (Théâtre de l'Académie Royale de Musique)
Parnassians, 38
Pascal, Blaise, 63
Passage Choiseul, 38, 40
Passage Colbert, 38
Passage de l'Opéra, 75, 78, 79, 82, 170
Passage des Panoramas, 38–39
Passage du Caire, 52
Passage du Prado, 134
Passage Reilhac, 135
Passy, xi, 10, 182, 190–94
pavement, 88n139, 90
Pei, I. M., x, 28
Pension Laveur, 96
Percier, Charles, 31, 138, 147
Père-Lachaise cemetery, 112, 125, 217–20, 229
Perec, Georges, x, 19, 99
Pereire brothers, 6, 150
Pereire, Émile, 147
Perier, Casimir, 248n40, 249, 250
Périphérique. *See* Boulevard Périphérique
Le Peuple constituant, 291, 299
Philippe Auguste, 42
  expulsion of Jews, 69
  wall of, xii, 7, 10–11, 57, 59, 88
Philippe-Égalité, 20, 86, 120, 149
Philippe le Bel, 15, 208

photographs, 38, 70, 148–49, 191, 222–23, 358–67 passim
of Baudelaire, 330
of Benjamin, 34
of Giacometti, 187
photography, 48, 205, 207, 340–48 passim, 358–67. *See also* brûlage
Piaf, Edith, 185, 198, 210
Picasso, Pablo, 102, 170, 196, 360
Piganiol de La Force, Jean-Aymar, 58, 67, 120, 122
pillories, 42, 44
Place de Clichy, x, 139, 196
Place de Grève, 94n146, 161, 171, 247, 263
Place de la Contrescarpe, 19
Place de la Commune-de-Paris, 189
Place de la République, 73, 131, 214, 311
Place de l'Europe, 148
Place d'Italie, 152n81, 153
Place du Caire, 52
Place du Châtelet, 70
Place du Marché-Saint-Honoré, 31, 32
Place Maubert, 93
Place Pigalle, x, 144, 197–98, 355
Place Robespierre, 31
Place Royale, 60–64 passim, 71, 73
Place Saint-Sulpice, x, 99
Place Vendôme, 32–33, 34, 171, 246
Plaine Monceau, xi, 6, 149–50, 194
Plaisance, 185–87
plaques, 50, 102, 210, 227, 229, 291, 342
street numbers on, 116
plaster, 209
Poe, Edgar Allan, 329–30, 338
poets in Montparnasse, 168
Poland, 228n3, 247, 249, 266–68 passim
Poles in the Resistance, 227–29 passim
police, xi, xiv, 16, 115, 274, 293
arrest Democrats, 304
crack down on presses, 245, 255
deal with revolutionaries and insurgents, 243–44, 289
expel hunger strikers, xii
murder Algerians, 87
patrol underground caverns, 206
round up Jews, 185, 214
supervise dance halls, 167
See also bicycle police
Pompadour, Marquise de, 51, 118, 146
Pompidou, Georges, x, xii, 19, 47, 163, 181
Pont-Neuf, 42, 60, 71, 88, 101, 102, 242, 246, 341, 343, 353
poor people, 147, 154–55, 161, 274

cholera and, 249
executions and, 162
in literature, 325
vertical mingling with rich people, 113–14
See also beggars and begging; ragpickers
Popincourt, 111, 125–33, 158, 234, 274, 278, 287
Porcherons, 142–43, 144
Porte de Buci, 101
Porte de Clignancourt, 200, 224
Porte de la Muette, xiii
Porte de Pantin, xiii
Porte d'Orléans, 182
Porte Saint-Denis, xii, 3, 14, 17, 51, 52, 134, 259, 261, 276
'very fine and very useless' (Breton), 54
Porte Saint-Honoré, 37, 203n58
ports, 203–5, 221
Portzamparc, Christian de, 181
Potlach, 181n13
Poulet-Malassis, Auguste, 40, 97, 102, 328, 330
Prarond, Ernest, 330, 334
printing and presses, 35, 48–49, 92, 102, 168, 245, 318–19
prisons, 57, 134, 146, 162, 269, 291
Privat d'Anglemont, Alexandre, 18, 97, 126–27, 130, 136, 157, 167, 176
promenading. *See* flânerie
prostitutes and prostitution, 22, 24, 37–38, 52n57, 60–61, 71, 129, 164, 214, 277n109
in art, 38, 355, 356, 366
protesters and protests. *See* demonstrations and demonstrators
Proudhon, Pierre-Joseph, 265, 290
Proust, Antonin, 351
Proust, Marcel, 103, 148–50 passim, 191n28, 328, 330, 335, 336, 357–60 passim, 363
Prouvé, Jean, x
Pruskovski, Christof, 190
Prussian occupation, 231–41 passim
public health, 6, 46, 113
public housing, 211
public transportation, 74. *See also* Métro
publishers, 23, 38, 40, 92–93, 99, 100n164, 104–5, 255, 256

quarries, 198, 206, 207
quarters, 6, 15, 19n7
Left Bank, 87–108
Right Bank, 19–87

Quartier de l'Europe, 146–49, 327
Queneau, Raymond, 187, 210, 218
Quinze-Vingts (hospital), 28

Racine, Jean, 63, 88, 102, 190
ragpickers, 156–57, 164, 222, 351, 360
railways, 179–80, 185–86, 194–95, 202–4
    passim, 220–21. *See also* Ceinture
    railway
Rambouillet, Catherine de Vivonne,
    marquise de. *See* Catherine de Vivonne,
    marquise de Rambouillet
Rambuteau, Claude-Philibert Barthelot,
    comte de, 83, 246n35, 298
Ramponeau, 128, 140
Ramuz, Charles-Ferdinand, 168
Raspail, François, 247, 266, 268
Rat-Mort, 197
rats, 206
Ravaillac, François, 61
razing of buildings, etc., 17, 31n28, 32, 36,
    37, 40, 72, 79, 83n124
Les Halles, 42, 45, 48
Marais, 59, 70
Sentier, 53
'red belt,' xiii
red flag, 251, 254, 263
religious orders, 88, 120, 160. *See also*
    Benedictines; Capuchins; Carmelites;
    Jesuits
rendering yards. *See* knacker's yards
repressive laws, 245, 254–56 passim
Resistance, 227–31
restaurants, 20–25 passim, 77, 129–30
    Auteuil, 191
    Champs-Élysées, 119
    South Asian, 135, 126
    Latin Quarter, 93, 95–96
    Montparnasse, 165
    Saint-Germain-des-Prés, 102
    See also cafés; chain restaurants
Restif, Nicolas-Edme, 318–20
Revolution, 21–23 passim, 32, 35, 102, 136,
    150, 158–59
    Faubourg Saint-Antoine and, 122, 123
    See also Commission des Artistes
revolution of 1830, 161, 184, 211n73, 247,
    248
revolution of 1848, 72n97, 91, 95, 106–11
    passim, 258–94, 299, 305, 307
La Revue blanche, 79, 356
Rey-Dussueil, M., 253, 254, 294, 297
rich and poor: vertical mingling. *See* poor

people: vertical mingling with rich
    people
Richelieu, Cardinal, 20, 21n10, 36
Richelieu, Maréchal (duc de), 64, 72, 146,
    191
Rigault, Raoul, 95
Right Bank, xi, 19–89 passim, 104, 151, 230
    faubourgs, 116–50
Rimbaud, Arthur, 128n42
riots, 248, 249, 252, 272. *See also* hunger riots
River Bièvre. *See* Bièvre
River Seine. *See* Seine
roads, underground. *See* underground roads
Robespierre, Maximilien, 22, 31, 32, 35, 36
Rome, 61, 344
Rosny, J.-H., 166
Rostopchin, Fyodor, 25
rotundas, 38–39, 72, 119
roundabouts, ix, 31, 70, 73, 117, 200
Rousseau, Henri, 78, 164, 169, 341
Rousseau, Jean-Jacques, 40, 42, 176, 212,
    316–18
royalists, 32, 248n41, 282, 301
Rue Amelot, 3, 72n97, 85
Rue Dauphine, 102
Rue de Clichy, 146
Rue de Fossés-du-Temple, 55, 72n97, 85
Rue de la Chaussé-d'Antin, 140
Rue de Richelieu, 30, 34, 37, 49
Rue des Archives, 68–69
Rue des Rosiers, x
Rue du Croissant, 49–50
Rue du Doyenné, 29, 30
Rue du Temple, 57, 63, 65, 67, 68, 69, 84,
    208, 261
Rue Fromenteau, 29
Rue Montmartre, 48, 49
Rue Montorgueil, 48
Rue Mouffetard, ix
Rue Oberkampf, xii, 216
Rue Saint-Antoine, 68–69, 71
Rue Saint-Denis, 44, 51, 53, 54, 80, 105,
    134, 238, 243, 246, 272
Rue Saint-Honoré, 20, 26, 32, 38
Rue Saint-Jacques, 92–93, 280
Rue Saint-Martin, 53, 55
Rue Saint-Maur, xii, 125, 128, 129, 130,
    240–1, 287, 299
Rue Saint-Nicaise, 30, 31
Rue Sufflot, 91, 92
Rue Transnonain, 106, 255, 257, 260, 287,
    293
Rue Transnonain massacre, 255

ruins, 30, 47
Russians, 20, 25

Sacré-Coeur, 136, 196, 200n51
Saint Bartholomew's Night, 71, 87
Saint-Bernard, xii, 201
Saint-Eustache, 42–44 passim, 47, 196, 209
Saint-Georges, 144–45
Saint-Germain-des-Prés, xi, 3, 6, 11, 98,
    100–102
Saint-Germain-l'Auxerrois, 70–71
Saint-Jacques-de-la-Boucherie, 45
Saint-Lazare, 134, 136, 139
Saint-Médard, ix, 158, 359
Saint-Sulpice, 99–100
Saint-Vincent-de-Paul, 137, 152n81
Salle du Manège, 32
Salle des Machines, 32
Salle Favart, 37, 77
Salmon, André, 165–66, 168, 169, 196
Salon de Paris, 344–55 passim
salons, 29, 63, 145, 194
Salpêtrière, 4n2, 16, 69, 109, 132, 154, 155,
    179
Sand, George, 145, 234, 249
sanitary conditions, 6, 46, 113
Sarcey, Francisque, 234
Sartre, Jean-Paul, 90, 170, 181
Sauvage, Henri, 193
Sauval, Henri, 28–29, 36, 44, 46, 52, 54, 58,
    59, 60, 61, 68, 69, 117n16, 159
    on Jewish quarter, 69
    on promenading, 117
savant animals, 84, 85, 138
Scarron, Paul, 62, 64, 101
Scudéry, Mlle de, 63
sculptures, 4, 37, 150, 170
Seine, xi, 5, 87–88, 90, 140n62, 221
    Charles V wall and, 14
    Philippe Auguste wall and, 11
    squalor of quarters bordering, 18–19
    Tour Nesle beacon on, 16
Sentier, 4, 19, 48–55
Serpollet, Léon, 194n37
Servandoni, Giovanni Niccolo, 99, 100
Service des Espaces Verts, ix, x
Seurat, Georges, 356
Seveste brothers, 138
Sévigné, Mme de, 63–64
sewers, 140, 207
sex shops, 54, 139
shop windows in photography, 362
sidewalks, first, 39

slaughterhouses, 111, 113, 205
slumming, 86
Societé des Amis du Peuple, 247
Societé des Droits de l'Homme, 255, 297
Societé des Familles, 256
Societé des Gens de Lettres, 160
Societé des Saisons, 256
Societé Républicaine Centrale, 265
Society of 10 December, 34
Society of the Friends of Liberty and Equality,
    32
Sorbonne, 93, 276
Soufflot, Jacques Germain, 32
spinning works, 123
squalor, 18–19, 22–23, 46, 154n85, 296, 302
squares, 60–61, 67, 70, 84, 131, 136, 170,
    210
stairs, 26, 55, 63, 189, 198, 201
statues, 72, 99, 109, 126, 137, 139n59
    of Henri IV, 17, 246–47
    of Joan of Arc, 203
    of Ledru-Rollin, 290n139
    of Louis XIII, 61n75
    of Louis XV, 119
    of Marshal Ney, 4,167n112
    of Serpollet, 194n37
Stendhal, 26, 149, 199, 218, 323
Stern, Daniel (Comtesse d'Agoult), 259–60,
    265, 269, 277n109, 278–79, 290, 292
streams, 217
street fighting: Blanqui and Bugeaud on,
    294–96
street lights, 15, 74–75, 192, 316
street names and naming, 181, 196, 204, 205,
    218, 219
street numbering, 115–16, 123
streets, elevated. See elevated streets
strolling. See flânerie
students, 95, 96, 167, 246, 247, 251, 258,
    259, 278, 287, 311
suburbs. See banlieue
Sue, Eugène, 40, 68n88, 89, 106, 121–22
Sully, Maximilien de Béthune, duc de, 61,
    102
Surrealists and Surrealism, 82, 360–67 passim
symbolists, 97

tanners and tanneries, 159, 206
tapestry, 159
taverns, 126n39, 127–29 passim, 138–43
    passim, 152, 165, 197–98, 212–14
    passim, 221, 222

taxation, 109, 129, 268
tennis courts, 65
Texier, Edmond, 167
textile industry, 51, 215
Théâtre de l'Académie Royale de Musique.
    See Opéra (Théâtre de l'Académie
    Royale de Musique)
Théâtre de l'Ambigu-Comique, 83
Théâtre de l'Odéon, 88
Théâtre des Variétés, 39
Théâtre Déjazet, 86
Théâtre Moderne, 82
theatres, 36, 65, 77, 81–88 passim, 133–39
    passim. See also film theatres
Thélusson, Mme, 140
Thiers, Adolphe, 228n3, 232, 233, 254–55
    wall of, 15, 16, 174–75, 221, 222
Thoré-Bürger, Théophile, 349–50
Tivoli gardens, 146
Tocqueville, Alexis de, 154, 258, 259n67,
    261, 262, 266–74 passim, 279–86
    passim, 298
    on attacking unarmed men, women, and
    children, 276n106,
    on men of war, 246n34
Tokyo, 7
Tortoni, 77–78
Toulouse-Lautrec, Henri de, 38, 144, 195,
    196, 356
traffic, 70, 90
trains. See railways
trees, 118, 122, 170, 171, 195, 199n48
Trélat, Ulysse, 247, 248
tricolour flag, 244, 264, 354
Tuileries Palace and gardens, xi, 17, 30, 31,
    90, 104, 117, 118, 262, 289, 301, 305
Tuileries-Saint-Honoré, 31–33
tunnels, 31, 147, 179, 180, 194–95, 206
Turgenev, Ivan, 162, 261, 350n16
Tzara, Tristan, 363–64

Ubac, Raoul, 364
underground Paris, 206–8 passim
underground roads, 70, 125
uniforms, 269–70, 288n133
universal suffrage, 308
uprisings. See insurrections

Val-de-Grâce, 4, 5, 151, 160n96
Valance, Georges, 106n180
Vallès, Jules, 90, 94, 95, 98, 165, 197n45,
    214, 234, 239, 292
Varin, Quentin, 64

Vaugirard, 182–85
'végétalisation,' x
velodromes, 185
Verlaine, Paul, 49, 90, 92
Vers et Prose, 168
Veuillot, Louis, 131
Viardot, Pauline, 145
Vichy France, 227–31
Vidoqc, E., 129
Vignon, Claude, 64
villages, 122, 174–81
    Left Bank, 181–89
    Right Bank, 189–223
Villiers de l'Isle-Adam, Auguste, 75, 145,
    218, 321
vineyards, 53n61, 199, 202
Violet, Léonard, 184
Visitation (church), 69
Vollard, Ambroise, 79
Voltaire, 17, 72
Voltaire (café). See Café Voltaire

walks and walking, 39, 75, 317. See also
    flânerie
walls, 7–15 passim, 83, 123, 151, 163. See
    also Charles V: wall of; Farmers-General
    wall; Philippe Auguste: wall of; Thiers,
    Adolphe: wall of
warehouses, 203, 221
Wars of Religion, 59, 62
Wauxhall d'Été, 133, 135
Wilde, Oscar, 91, 102, 239
Wilson-Bareau, Juliet, 352n22
windmills, 53, 146
Wolff, Albert, 78
women
    Commune (1871) and, 232–41 passim
    in paintings, 148, 349–56 passim
    in photographs, 360, 361, 366
    lorettes, 144
    revolution of 1848 and, 277
    See also grisettes
wood industry, 122–23
Wooden Galleries. See Galeries de Bois
working class, xi, xii, xiv, 125–31 passim,
    168, 205, 209, 296–99
    revolution of 1848, 270

youth revolts of 2005, xii

Zola, Emile, 111, 150, 201, 333, 352, 354
    Nana, 39, 73–74